NORTH-WEST HIGHLANDS

For northern area see Rear Endpapers

NORTH-WEST HIGHLANDS

Dave Broadhead
Alec Keith
Ted Maden

Series Editor: Rob Milne

SCOTTISH MOUNTAINEERING CLUB
HILLWALKERS' GUIDE

Published in Great Britain by the Scottish Mountaineering Trust, 2004

ISBN 0 907521 81 9
A catalogue record for this book is available from the British Library

Front Cover: Sail Liath and Corrag Bhuidhe from Sgurr Fiona, An Teallach (photo Jim Teesdale)

Title Page: Leaving Mullach an Rathain, Liathach (photo Dave Broadhead)

Back Cover Top Left: Ladhar Bheinn and Loch Hourn from Buidhe Bheinn (photo Jim Teesdale). Top Right: Sgurr Dhomhnuill from Sgurr Craobh a' Chaorainn (photo Tom Prentice). Bottom: Heading towards Creag a' Mhaim on the South Glen Shiel Ridge (photo Alec Keith)

Production: Scottish Mountaineering Trust (Publications) Ltd
Design: Tom Prentice, Ken Crocket
Typesetting: Ken Crocket
Maps: Tom Prentice
Colour separations: Core Image, East Kilbride
Printed and bound in Spain by Elkar mccgraphics, Bilbao

Distributed by Cordee, 3a DeMonfort Street, Leicester. LE1 7HD
(t) 0116 254 3579, (f) 0116 247 1176, (e) sales@cordee.co.uk

Contents

Introduction

North-west Highlands

Derek Sime

Arkle and Lone cottage by Loch Stack, North-west Sutherland

The North-west Highlands is the largest and most varied mountain area in the British Isles, covering all of mainland Scotland north and west of the Great Glen. Far from the main centres of population, and with some of the finest scenery and most challenging routes, these hills have always had a special place in the hearts of generations of hill lovers.

This guide has been written for the benefit of walkers, climbers, ski tourers and anyone interested in the hills, aiming to provide:

- an outline of routes on the principal hills,
- background information on a variety of topics such as access, accommodation, geology, and the natural and human history of the hills and their immediate surroundings,
- a starting point for finding out more about topics of particular interest.

Land, Sea and Mountains

Gleann mor na-h Albin (*the great glen of Scotland*), usually known simply as the Great Glen, is the line of a remarkable geological fault which cuts neatly across the Scottish Highlands. With the highest mountains and the main tourist attractions to the south and east, few casual visitors travel further than the bustling town of Fort William or the fledgling city of Inverness.

Situated on opposite coasts, these two centres are connected by a busy road, the A82, and by the Caledonian Canal, a historic waterway linking the chain of natural lochs along the Great Glen, including world famous Loch Ness. They also serve as gateways to the North-west Highlands, which lie to the west and north, including some of the most rugged and remote parts of Europe. Apart from much of Caithness and a narrow coastal strip of Easter Ross, the entire district is mountainous, with enough variety and interest to occupy a lifetime of visits by hill-goers.

The North-west Highlands extend some 290km from Rubha an Ridire at the southern tip of Morvern to Duncansby Head at the north-eastern corner of Caithness. The former lies almost as far south as the city of Dundee, while the latter is at approximately the same latitude as Stavanger in Norway. For much of this distance the watershed runs close to the west coast, tending to form short glens falling away steeply to the west and long straths opening gently eastwards. The district is further divided by the line of the Inverness to Kyle of Lochalsh railway, the traditional boundary between the Western Highlands and the Northern Highlands, which runs through Strath Bran and Glen Carron. One feature of the Western Highlands is a series of parallel glens running west from the Great Glen, which form natural divisions between groups of hills. In contrast, the main straths and glens of the Northern Highlands radiate outwards from the Cromarty and Dornoch Firths.

Around the tortuous West Highland coastline a number of long narrow sea lochs reach deep inland. Loch Linnhe, Loch Sunart, Loch Ailort, Loch Nevis, Loch Hourn, Loch Duich and Loch Carron all enclose rugged peninsulas, and narrow freshwater lochs further separate the ranges of hills. Loch Shiel, Loch Morar, Loch Arkaig, Loch Quoich and Loch Cluanie all add character to the mountains which rise up steeply from their shores.

Morvern, Sunart, Ardnamurchan and Ardgour form the south-western corner of the district. Usually reached by a short ferry across Loch Linnhe at the Corran Narrows, these areas

The Access Code

Approach to the hills

- Make use of public transport and share cars where possible to minimise congestion and protect the environment.
- If going by car, park safely off-road and do not block tracks or gateways.
- When passing through enclosed land and woodland, walk along tracks, paths or field edges.
- Use gates and styles, leaving gates as you find them.
- Avoid damage to any fences or dykes that have to be crossed.
- Respect the needs and privacy of those who live and work in the countryside.

Care for the mountain environment

- Avoid disturbance or damage to animals, birds, trees and plants.
- Minimise erosion. Avoid widening paths, cutting corners on zigzags and running downhill.
- Remove all litter and food scraps.
- Refrain from building new cairns or leaving waymarks.
- Bury excrement well away from paths or watercourses and do not pollute streams or lochs.

Land management

- Avoid disturbing farm animals.
- Keep dogs on a lead when crossing enclosed land or on the hill during breeding season. Avoid taking dogs into fields with livestock.
- Avoid sheep just before and during the lambing season (March to May).
- If you come across deer calves, leave them alone.
- Before setting out for the hills during the stalking and shooting season (critical period mid-August to mid-October) make local enquiries.

Consider others on the hill

- Avoid making unnecessary noise.
- Keep groups small and act unobtrusively.
- If you come across equipment, leave it. Others may depend on it for work or safety
- Make sure you are properly equipped and have the skills and fitness necessary for what you mean to do in the hills.

Looking west from The Saddle, South Glen Shiel

have a distinctly insular feel. The lighthouse at Point of Ardnamurchan marks the westernmost point on the British mainland, on the same longitude as Dublin. The modest altitude and isolation which may limit the appeal of their hills to some will be attractive to others and similar considerations apply to Moidart, Morar and Loch Eil. It is not until Glenfinnan that the steep-sided summits start to reach Munro height. These are the hills of a walker's dreams, with peak after peak joined by high ridges, narrow enough to be interesting without being technically difficult, giving spectacular views on clear days. Unfortunately, this is also one of the wettest parts of Scotland, so dreams do not always come true.

From Loch Arkaig to Glen Garry, Loch Quoich to Glen Shiel, and then Kintail, range follows range. The isolated Knoydart peninsula, remote from any road access, remains one of the wildest parts of the British Isles, with Ladhar Bheinn the most westerly mainland Munro. In Strath Cluanie and Glen Affric the landscape opens out as the hills become higher and more massive, culminating in Carn Eighe, at 1183m the highest point north of the Great Glen. Glens Cannich, Strathfarrar and Strathconon all drain eastwards into the head of the Moray Firth, enclosing extensive ranges of hills which continue west to Glen Carron, Killilan and West Monar.

The Applecross peninsula forms the south-west corner of the Northern Highlands, where the appearance of sandstone hills marks a sudden change in the landscape. With their characteristic bands of crags and terraces, often capped with quartzite, these hills continue through Coulin and most famously through Torridon. Between the Loch Maree to Loch Broom area and the Fannaichs lies a great wilderness of hills and lochs, not crossed by any roads.

Less spectacular but almost as remote, the many and varied hills of Beinn Dearg and Easter Ross extend from coast to coast. Close to the western seaboard, the Coigach and Assynt hills have been eroded into distinctive shapes which give this area its unique and spectacular scenery. Rugged hills continue through North-west Sutherland almost to Cape Wrath and across North-east Sutherland, including Ben Hope, the most northerly Munro. Caithness has the most extensive area of flat, low lying ground in the district, including the remarkable Flow Country, and this county also has some interesting lower hills and extensive coastal cliffs and sea-stacks.

Principal Hills

Within the North-west Highlands district stand 102 of the 284 Munros, 102 of the 219 Corbetts and 84 of the 224 Grahams. For this new edition of the guidebook, the authors have endeavoured to describe all of these hills, as detailed in *Munro's Tables* ®, revised and edited by Derek Bearhop. A number of other notable hills have also been included. The chapters are set out working from south to north and within each chapter the hills are arranged in the order that seems most logical in the context of the chapter.

Each hill is identified by name, height and six-figure grid reference, along with the OS Sheet number of the relevant 1:50,000 Landranger map. A translation of the Gaelic name is also given. Cumulatively, the authors have almost one hundred years of experience of climbing these hills, but none claim any expertise in the Gaelic and have avoided giving advice on Gaelic pronunciation.

The distinctive characteristics of each hill or group of hills is described, along with any other interesting background information, but most of the text outlines routes by which each may be climbed. Part of the appeal of hillwalking in Scotland is that every hill can be climbed by more than one route and can be linked with others in longer traverses. Many suggestions are given but these are only a start to the possibilities, and readers are encouraged to use their own imaginations in planning outings.

Descriptions of walking routes are not intended to be detailed or comprehensive, since that level of information is available in other guidebooks. (See Further Reading.) To avoid confusion, the authors have followed the usual convention of giving distances as 'metres' and abbreviating heights to 'm'.

Maps

The sketch maps in this guidebook are intended to supplement the text, to help the reader envisage the land and appreciate the position of the hills and the routes described relative to each other. They have been drawn from half inch survey maps that are more than 50 years old, with added data from the authors, Scottish Mountaineering Club members, and many

Munros, Corbetts and Grahams

The publication of Sir Hugh Munro's *Tables of Heights over 3000 feet* in the 1891 Scottish Mountaineering Club Journal set a challenge that has inspired hill-goers ever since. First to climb all the Munros was the Reverend Archibald Eneas Robertson in 1901, and since then over 3000 people have had the pleasure of repeating this feat. Munro did not specify strict criteria to distinguish separate mountains from Tops (subsidiary elevations above the 3000ft contour) which has added interest over the years as altitude revisions resulting from new Ordnance Survey data have led to promotions and demotions around the critical 914.4m level.

John Rooke Corbett became only the second person to complete all the Munros and Tops in 1930 and went on to list and climb all Scotland's 2500ft mountains, including all those of height between 2500ft (762m) and 3000ft (914m) with a drop of at least 500ft (152m) between each listed hill and any adjacent higher one. This latter category of hill now bears his name.

The Grahams were named in memory of the late Fiona Graham who published a list of Scottish hills between 2000ft (610m) and 2499ft (761m) in 1992. This was amended by Alan Dawson to include all such hills with a drop of at least 150m all round.

Cul Mor from Stac Pollaidh, Coigach

other members of the hillwalking public. Symbols are used on these maps to indicate different categories of summit: Munro – black triangle; Munro Top – white triangle; Corbett – black circle; Corbett Top – white circle; Graham – black diamond; Other – crossed circle. These are sketch maps and they should not be used for navigation.

For a more detailed picture and before attempting to climb any hills it is essential to look at the appropriate Ordnance Survey 1:50,000 Landranger maps. These give excellent topographical detail plus visitor information such as picnic areas, viewpoints etc.

Excellent though they are, the OS maps may contain occasional mis-spellings, and there may be unmarked bridges and paths, marked but non-existent bridges, new forest plantings etc. The maps are regularly reprinted with some revisions and the newer editions tend to have more hill features named.

The Ordnance Survey 1:25,000 Pathfinder maps are being replaced by larger format Explorer maps. Much extra detail is given on these new maps, and this will be of use to some. However most hill-goers are likely to find the Landranger maps sufficient for all but the most complex areas, so the text has been written on the assumption that the reader is utilising the Landranger series. The excellent Ordnance Survey 1:25,000 Outdoor Leisure map of Torridon with the Cuillin of Skye on the reverse side has long been the favourite map for these areas. Harvey's produce waterproof 1:25,000 Superwalker maps of Torridon and Kintail & Glen Shiel with a visitors' guide on the reverse.

The Ordnance Survey 1:250,000 Road Map 1 of Northern Scotland, Orkney & Shetland covers almost the whole of the North-west Highlands district in a single sheet and is particularly useful for route planning, motoring and identifying distant hills. All heights on this map are in feet, with a reminder to multiply by 0.3048 to convert to metres.

Transport and Accommodation

The railways which brought the first Victorian mountaineers still serve extensive areas of the North-west Highlands, despite occasional threats of closure. Services run from Fort William to Mallaig and Inverness to Kyle of Lochalsh on the west coast and from Inverness to Wick and Thurso in the far north.

Buses operate between the larger towns, connecting with cities further south, and post buses link smaller villages and the more remote communities. Each chapter contains a brief outline of current bus services. Highland Council publishes a Public Transport map and comprehensive timetable books. Public transport details can also be obtained from local Tourist Information Centres listed in each chapter.

Most hill-goers now travel by car, and major improvements in the road system in recent years have made the North-west Highlands much more accessible. Beyond the main roads there are still many single-track roads which should be driven with care. In summer, nervous tourists, caravans and sheep are common hazards, while in winter the gritting of icy roads may be infrequent and deer wander down to graze roadside verges, particularly at night. Each chapter has a brief outline of road access. Do not drive along private roads without permission, and when parking please show consideration for other road users and avoid blocking access to gates, etc.

A wide range of accommodation is available to suit all tastes and budgets. Each chapter

Highland Roads – Some History

The remote and rugged nature of the Highland landscape has always made travel difficult and the first long distance routes were the drove roads. 'The wealth of the mountains is cattle', declared Dr Johnson in 1773, and for centuries these and latterly sheep were the main cash crop of the Highlands and Islands. Lack of winter fodder meant that every autumn large droves of animals were taken to the markets or trysts. For many years the largest and most important of these was the Michaelmas Tryst at Crieff, which transferred to Falkirk by 1770. Moving across the grain of the mountains, the drovers and their cattle preferred the open hill with its free grazing, converging on the obvious passes. The long journey south followed two main routes: through Drumochter and Atholl from northern and eastern Ross and Inverness-shire, and through Glencoe and the Blackmount from Wester Ross and the Western Isles.

A more sombre function was served by the kirk and coffin roads which lead to places of worship and traditional burial grounds. Osgood Mackenzie, writing in *A Hundred Years in the Highlands,* recorded that when Lady Mackenzie died in Gairloch in 1830 five hundred men took turns to carry her coffin the sixty miles east to Beauly Priory.

Following the Jacobite Risings of 1689 and 1715, King George I sent Major-General George Wade 'to inspect the present situation of the Highlanders'. Wade's suggestion to establish 'roads of communication' was quickly followed up and is still remembered in the old ditty:

If you'd seen these roads before they were made,
You'd lift up your hands and bless General Wade.

Two such roads in the North-west Highlands were from Fort Augustus to Glenelg and from Contin to Poolewe, though these were subsequently abandoned because of maintenance difficulties.

A second phase of road building started at the beginning of the 19th century, supervised by Thomas Telford. Half the expense of these 'parliamentary roads' was met by the government and much of the North-west Highlands benefited with new roads; from Fort William to Arisaig; Loch Oich to Kinloch Hourn; Corran Ferry to Loch Moidart; Dingwall to Loch Carron and Kyle of Lochalsh, and also to Wick, Thurso and Tongue.

The Scottish Parliament had made Justices of the Peace responsible for 'mending all highways' in 1617, but this had little effect. A scheme of statute labour introduced in 1669 was no better, and was gradually superseded by the turnpike system involving collection of tolls from 1713. Maintenance of roads was finally taken over by local authorities in 1878.

Coire Fionnaraich bothy and Sgorr Ruadh, Coulin hills

contains a brief outline of what may be available, with more detailed and up-to-date information readily available from The Highlands of Scotland Tourist Board and the appropriate local Tourist Information Centres.

A number of comfortable hotels still cater for shooting and fishing parties but tend to be busy in summer and may be closed out of season. Traditional bed and breakfast establishments are the mainstay of the vital tourist industry and a local enquiry will usually turn up something even at the last minute. Self-catering cottages and caravans are always in demand at holiday times, so it is worth booking well ahead. There are some useful Scottish Youth Hostel Association hostels in the area, plus a rapidly growing number of independently run 'backpackers' hostels and bunkhouses. Mountaineering clubs operate a number of huts, and current details of booking arrangements can be obtained from the Mountaineering Council of Scotland (MCofS).

Camping

Official campsites are thinly spread over the area and details are given in chapters. Opportunities for roadside camping are limited, and campers should try to be unobtrusive and remember the maxim 'pitch late and leave early'. Away from the road, wild camping can be a memorable experience which adds an extra dimension to enjoyment and appreciation of the hills. Please make every effort to minimise the impact of your visit and leave no trace of your stay.

Bothies

Scattered in remote situations, bothies were once the homes of shepherds, stalkers and their families, but have long since been abandoned. Now they offer basic shelter for passing walkers. Many are maintained, with the permission of the owners, by the Mountain Bothies Association (MBA), while others are still looked after by the estates. The MBA is a private company limited by guarantee and is a recognised charity. Its object is 'to maintain simple shelters in remote country for the use and benefit of all who love wild and lonely places'.

Sadly, the increasing popularity of bothies has also seen an increase in problems of overcrowding, vandalism and misuse so that some are now locked and no longer available and others have been completely destroyed. To avoid further strain on these buildings and their surroundings, this guidebook makes only passing reference to those bothies which are of most use to visitors to the hills covered and does not give specific details as to their locations. Please contact the MBA for further information. People using bothies are requested to act responsibly, to respect the buildings and other users, to have regard to any restrictions on use, and to give serious consideration to joining the MBA and helping to maintain these unique shelters.

Rock and Ice Climbing

Towards the end of the 19th century, the earliest members of the newly formed Scottish Mountaineering Club (SMC) discovered the potential for technical climbing in the North-west Highlands. Due to the district's remoteness, development has always tended to be sporadic, but each generation of climbers has been able to discover new routes to rank with Scotland's finest. Most recently there has been considerable rock climbing activity on lower crags, particularly along the coast, as these tend to dry out more quickly and catch the better weather.

The coasts also have some of the most spectacular cliffs and sea stacks to be found around mainland Britain, presenting unique and serious challenges to climbers, particularly where access can only be gained by boat. Despite the relatively low altitude and proximity to the coast of many of the hills (as well as growing evidence of global warming) winter continues to produce enough challenging icefalls and mixed routes to justify the effort of long and arduous approaches.

The authors of this guide have sought to mention briefly what they consider to be significant crags, climbs and climbers in the hope that this will be of interest to all hill-goers. Comprehensive route details can be found in the three volumes of Northern Highlands Rock and Ice Climbs compiled by Andy Nisbet and published by the SMC. *Northern Highlands North* covers climbing north of the Inverness to Ullapool road (published 2004). *Northern Highlands Central* will cover the area between the Ullapool road and Loch Maree including Strathconon, the Fannaichs, An Teallach and Fisherfield, while *Northern Highlands South* will cover Torridon, Applecross, Glen Carron, Glen Shiel and Knoydart (due to be published in 2005 or 2006). These areas are currently covered by *Northern Highlands Volume 1* (published 1993). Full details of new routes are published annually in the *Scottish Mountaineering Club Journal*, and on the club's web site www.smc.org.uk

Scotways

The Scottish Rights of Way and Access Society has as its objects the preservation, defence, restoration and acquisition for the public benefit of rights of access over land in Scotland, including public rights of way. Its work involves:

- signposting and bridge building
- maintaining the national catalogue of rights of way and other routes
- advice and mediation
- working with others
- educating and raising awareness
- walking and discovering.

Contact details can be found at the end of this introduction.

Slioch above Loch Maree

Skiing

Ski mountaineering is something of an opportunist activity in the North-west Highlands, but those lucky enough to catch that rare combination of good snow conditions and fine weather will enjoy a truly memorable ski tour. The definitive *Ski Mountaineering in Scotland*, edited by Donald Bennet and Bill Wallace, describes a number of tours in this district.

Safety

'Climbing and mountaineering are activities with a danger of personal injury or death. Participants in these activities should be aware and accept these risks and be responsible for their own actions and involvement.' (UIAA participation statement.)

Equipment and Planning

Anyone venturing into the Scottish hills should be aware of the possible hazards involved. Sadly each year brings its toll of injuries and fatalities. Many of the hills in the North-west Highlands can be serious undertakings, especially in winter, and the key to enjoying them safely lies in experience, good equipment and knowledge as to how to use it. By far the largest number of accidents and fatalities on the hills involve hillwalkers, with simple slips and stumbles the commonest cause of death. Poor equipment, not using axes and crampons, tiredness because the route is too long, or becoming lost, are often contributory factors.

Route planning should take into account weather and conditions underfoot, as well as the fitness, ability and experience of the party. Consultants at Raigmore Hospital in Inverness, who treat many mountain casualties, cite 'Plan-A Syndrome' as a common cause of accidents, arising from failure to have alternative plans for bad conditions. Planning ahead from the comfort of home should not assume good weather and favourable conditions on the hill.

Fortunately there are plenty of excellent low level alternative outings in the North-west

Highlands, particularly along the coast. Weather can improve just as quickly as it can deteriorate, and the western peninsulas can give excellent and unusual views of the inland hills as the clouds clear. Many of the lower hills can be climbed in an afternoon or a summer's evening.

Always take the appropriate map and a compass, and practise the skills required to use them effectively. Mountain rescue teams have identified poor navigation as a major cause of accidents. Do not rely exclusively on GPS as batteries and electronics can fail or easily be damaged. Leave word with someone as to where you are going and when you will be back.

Mountain Rescue

In the event of an emergency the police should be contacted in the first instance (telephone 999). Bear in mind that mobile phone reception is still patchy and unreliable over much of the Highlands. Give concise information about the location and injuries of the victim and any assistance available at the accident site. It is often better to stay with the victim, but in a party of two, one may have to leave to summon help. Leave the casualty warm and comfortable in a sheltered, well marked place.

Weather Forecasts

When planning any outing in the hills it is prudent to obtain some sort of weather forecast. Local weather tends to divide between east and west. The 'Cluanie curtain' phenomenon will be familiar to anyone who has driven west into thickening cloud and heavy rain. Less commonly, the east can be dismal under grey cloud and sea mist (haar) while the west basks in brilliant sunshine. Many forecasts are vague when using the term 'north', and there can be an element of luck in ending up on the right side of the line between the best weather and the worst.

Following the forecasts over a period of several days can also help build up a picture of possible conditions on the hills if travelling from further afield. Forecasts can be obtained from the following sources

Radio: Radio Scotland gives an excellent outdoor conditions forecast for walkers and climbers. At the time of writing this is broadcast each evening at 18.58 Monday to Friday, 06.58 and 18.58 on Saturday and 06.58 and 19.58 on Sunday. Radio 4 gives detailed national

Stalking and Estate Management

Much of the land covered by this guidebook is managed as sporting estates or hill farms, and climbers and walkers should take into account the seasonal activities involved. It is in everyone's interest to maintain good relations between hill-goers, landowners and farmers.

The stag stalking season is from 1st July to 20th October, although many estates do not start at the beginning of the season. Hinds continue to be culled until 15th February. The grouse shooting season is from 12th August until 10th December, although the end of the season is less used. These sporting activities can be important to the economy of Highland estates and it would be a responsible approach to keep disturbance to a minimum during these seasons by following advice from the MCofS and any reasonable local advice about alternative routes.

It is also important to avoid disturbance to sheep, particularly during the lambing season between March and May. Dogs should not be taken onto the hills at this time, and should be kept under close control at all times. The MCofS and Scottish Natural Heritage also operate a Hillphones service giving daily recorded information of the location of stalking on some estates in the popular hillwalking areas.

Climbers and hill walkers are recommended to consult *Heading For The Scottish Hills*, published by the Scottish Mountaineering Trust on behalf of the MCofS, which gives the names and addresses of factors and keepers who may be contacted for information regarding access to the hills. Please also remember that respect for personal privacy near people's homes is good manners.

Baosbheinn and Creag an Fhithich, Torridon

forecasts, usefully combined with the shipping forecast at 17.50 – listen for Hebrides (north-west) and Cromarty (north-east). The BBC web site provides a facility to 'listen again' to these broadcasts at any time.

Television: The forecast at the end of *Reporting Scotland* on BBC1 at about 18.55 is probably best. Teletext forecasts are always available on BBC Ceefax (400) and, even better, Grampian Oracle (154).

Newspapers: The broad-sheets publish synoptic charts, with more local detail in *The Scotsman* and *The Herald*. The Saturday editions of these papers incorporate specific outdoor activities forecasts for the weekend.

Telephone: There are a number of recorded messages and fax sources. These tend to be expensive, especially if using a public phone, but are regularly updated and can give highly specific forecasts. The Met. Office offers Mountaincall West 09068-500441 with a 10-day outlook on 09068-500443.

Internet: The current Radio Scotland outdoor conditions forecast is always available at www.bbc.co.uk More general weather information and an outlook is available at www.metoffice.gov.uk The avalanche and condition reports from the Scottish Avalanche Information Service are only produced in winter and do not cover the area of this guide. However, www.sais.gov.uk has useful links with other sites all year round, including www.onlineweather.com which has a 10-day forecast. There are an ever increasing number of web cams available allowing one to check the snow cover on the hills.

Avalanches

Avalanche forecasts from the Scottish Avalanche Information Service do not at present cover any of the areas of this guide (phone 01479-861264) www.sais.gov.uk. However, avalanches do occur and have caused several fatalities in these hills. A prudent rule of thumb is to avoid snow slopes and gullies for at least 48 hours following a heavy snowfall, and to be wary of windslab on lee slopes.

Liability

Individuals are responsible for their own actions and should not hold landowners liable for an accident, even if it happens while climbing over a fence or dyke.

Environment

The North-west Highlands district shows a wide diversity of land use. Change continues as it has for hundreds of years, with tourism and outdoor recreation now playing a major role in the local economy, especially the increasing numbers of hillwalkers and climbers. The pattern of land ownership is also changing. A number of communities have taken the opportunity to buy the land they live and work on, for example the Knoydart Foundation and the Assynt Crofters Trust. Conservation charities now own significant areas such as the National Trust for Scotland's Torridon estate and the John Muir Trust's Sandwood estate.

With ever larger numbers of walkers and climbers going to the Scottish hills, countryside and coasts, it is important that all who do so recognise their responsibilities to those who live and work in these environments, to our fellow climbers and to the environment in which we find our pleasure and recreation. The Scottish Mountaineering Club and Scottish Mountaineering Trust (SMT), who jointly produce this and other guidebooks, wish to point out that it is in everybody's interests that good relations are maintained between visitors and landowners. The right of access to a climbing, walking or skiing route in any of these publications is based on the individual abiding by responsible Access Codes.

Avalanche Awareness

Walkers and climbers venturing on to the hills in winter should be familiar with the principles of snow structure and avalanche prediction. To minimise the risk of exposure to avalanche it is sensible to avoid gullies during periods of thaw and immediately following a heavy snowfall. All gullies and most slopes between 30 and 60 degrees should be considered suspect. The greater the amount of fresh snow, the higher the risk. Fresh snow can include wind-blown deposits, so that stormy weather can maintain an avalanche risk for prolonged spells. Past and present weather conditions are very important.

Walkers preparing for a winter trip should familiarise themselves with basic avalanche theory. In the field, much can be learned by digging a pit and examining the snow profile, looking especially for different layers of snow with different degrees of bonding. Slab avalanches, for example, will be caused when a weakly cohesive layer of snow collapses underfoot. Such a weak layer may be hidden under a firmer layer, hence its great potential as a killer. The top layer will often break into slabby fragments, the first warning.

If avalanched, try either to jump free, or to anchor yourself for as long as possible, depending on circumstances. If swept down, protect your access to oxygen by 'swimming' to stay on the surface, by closing your mouth, and by preserving a space in front of your face if buried. Wet snow avalanches harden rapidly on settling, so try and break free if possible at this point. If trapped try to stay calm, which will reduce oxygen demand.

If you witness an avalanche it is vital to start a search immediately, given it is safe to do so. Victims will often be alive at first, but their chances of survival lessen rapidly if buried. Unless severely injured, some 80% may live if found immediately, but only 10% after a three-hour delay. Mark the burial sight if known, listen for any sound, look for any visual clue, search until help arrives if possible. A working knowledge of first aid may save a life, as many victims stop breathing.

Bob Barton and Blyth Wright's *A Chance in a Million?* is essential reading for anyone venturing onto the hills in winter.

Coire na Poite, Beinn Bhan, Applecross

Rights of Way and Hill Paths

Historical rights of way do exist in Scotland, though the fight to maintain these goes back as far as 1845 with the formation of what became the Scottish Rights of Way Society. Their publication *Scottish Hill Tracks*, edited by D.J.Bennet and C.Stone, describes many of these rights of way and is an excellent source of information on low level walks.

Footpath Erosion

The number of walkers and climbers on the hills is leading to increased, and in some cases, very unsightly, footpath erosion. Part of the revenue from the sale of this and other Scottish Mountaineering Club books is granted by the Scottish Mountaineering Trust as financial assistance towards the repair and maintenance of hill paths in Scotland.

However, it is important for all of us to recognise our responsibility to minimise our erosive effect, so that the enjoyment of future climbers shall not be spoiled by our damage of the landscape.

As a general rule, if a path exists then try to stay on it. If the path is wet and muddy avoid walking along its edges as this only extends the erosion sideways. Do not take short-cuts at the corners of zigzag paths. The worst effects of erosion are likely to be caused during or soon after prolonged wet weather when the ground is soft and waterlogged. At such times a route on stony or rocky hillside is likely to cause less erosion than one on bare soil or grass. Always try to follow a path or track through cultivated land and forests, and avoid causing damage to fences, dykes and gates by climbing over them carelessly.

The proliferation of navigation cairns detracts from the feeling of wildness, and may be confusing rather than helpful as regards route-finding. The indiscriminate building of cairns on the hills is discouraged.

Mountain Bikes

Private estate roads and tracks penetrate many glens, but with the increasing popularity of the hills their gates now tend to be securely locked. Mountain bikes can cut out the tedium of long walks along such roads and make some of the remoter hills more accessible. Unfortunately a small proportion of estate owners do not share this enthusiasm for 'the poor man's horse', and signs have appeared requesting that bikes should not be used.

The authors of this guide have deliberately avoided recommending when bikes should be used or not but have instead tried to distinguish in the text between estate roads and vehicle tracks, which are suitable for wheeled transport, and stalkers paths and footpaths, which are not. Cyclists are urged to act responsibly, to use discretion, and to ride their bikes on vehicle tracks only. Cycling on footpaths and open terrain does cause damage and erosion, particularly on soft ground.

Bird Life

When walking or climbing, do not cause direct disturbance to nesting birds, particularly the rarer species, which are often found on crags. Nesting usually occurs between early February and late July, but on coasts it may be later. Intentional disturbance of nesting birds is a criminal offence with the penalty, if convicted, of a fine up to £5000 and confiscation of equipment. It is the individual's responsibility to find out from the MCofS about voluntary restrictions at any particular location and to obtain advice as to whether their presence might disturb any nesting birds.

Vegetation

When cleaning routes in summer, climbers should take care what they remove, as some of the flora may be rare. Many crags are designated as Sites of Special Scientific Interest (SSSI). This does not mean climbing is not allowed, but it may mean there are restrictions on activity. When winter climbing, minimise damage to underlying vegetation by only climbing when it is fully frozen. Crag and winter climbing codes are available from the MCofS.

Litter and Pollution

Do not leave litter of any sort anywhere. Please take it down from the hill or crag in your rucksack. Do not cause pollution, and bury human waste carefully out of sight far away from any habitation or water supply. Avoid burying rubbish as this may also pollute the environment.

Mountaineering Council of Scotland

The MCofS represents the interests of Scotland's mountaineering and hillwalking clubs and a significant number of individual mountaineers. The aims of the MCofS are:

- to act as the representative body for mountaineers (including mountaineers on ski) climbers and hillwalkers in Scotland
- to protect the ethos of mountaineering in Scotland
- to safeguard and secure access to hill and crag
- to protect the mountain environment
- to initiate and encourage safe practice in the mountains
- to promote the views and interests of its members
- to co-operate with other organisations with common interests.

Contact details can be found at the end of this introduction.

Hamish Brown

4000 year old cup and ring markings beside Lochan Hakel, North-east Sutherland

Useful Contacts

Caledonian MacBrayne Ltd (ferries) Tel: 01475-650100 www.calmac.co.uk

Citylink (long distance coaches) Tel: 0870-550-5050 www.citylink.co.uk

The Forestry Commission 231 Corstorphine Road, Edinburgh EH12 7AT www.forestry.gov.uk

GNER (trains) Tel: 0845-722-5225 www.gner.co.uk

Harvey Maps 12-16 Main Street, Doune FK16 6BJ Tel: 01786-841202 Fax: 01786-841098 E-mail: sales@harveymaps.co.uk www.harveymaps.co.uk

Highland Council Roads and Transport Glenurquhart Road, Inverness IV3 5NX Tel: 01463-702695 Fax: 01463-702606 E-mail: public.transport@highland.gov.uk

Highland Hostels, c/o 1 Achluachrach, by Roybridge PH31 4AW Tel/Fax: 01397-712900 E-mail: info@highland-hostels.co.uk www.highland-hostels.co.uk

The Highlands of Scotland Tourist Board Peffery House, Strathpeffer IV14 9HA Tel: 01997-421160 Fax: 01997-421168 E-mail: admin@host.co.uk www.visithighlands.com

Independent Backpackers Hostels – Scotland Tel/Fax: 01479-831331 E-mail: IBHS@scotmountain.co.uk www.hostel-scotland.co.uk

John Muir Trust 41 Commercial Street, Edinburgh EH6 6JD Tel: 0131-554-0114 or 0131-554-1324 E-mail: admin@jmt.org www.jmt.org

Mountain Bothies Association Information Officer, Ted Butcher, 26 Rycroft Avenue, Deeping St James, Peterborough PE6 8NT Tel: 01778-345062 www.mountainbothies.org.uk

Mountaineering Council of Scotland The Old Granary, West Mill Street, Perth, PH1 5QP Tel: 01738-638227 Fax: 01738-442095 E-mail: info@mountaineering-scotland.org.uk www.mountaineering-scotland.org.uk

National Express (long distance coaches) Tel: 0870-580-8080 www.nationalexpress.co.uk

National Rail Enquiries Tel: 0845-748-4950 Online rail ticket purchases www.thetrainline.com

National Trust for Scotland Wemyss House, 28 Charlotte Square, Edinburgh EH2 4ET Tel: 0131-243-9555 Fax: 0131-243-9589 www.nts.org.uk

Ordnance Survey Romsey Road, Southampton, SO16 4GU Tel: 0845-050505 E-mail: enquiries@ordsvy.gov.uk www.ordnancesurvey.co.uk

Post Buses Tel: 08457-740740 www.royalmail.com

Scottish Landowners' Federation 25 Maritime Street, Edinburgh EH6 5PW

Scottish Natural Heritage www.snh.org.uk

ScotRail Services Tel: 0845-755-00339 (Telesales) www.scotrail.co.uk

Scottish Rights of Way Society Limited 24 Annandale Street, Edinburgh EH7 4A Tel/Fax: 0131-558-1222 E-mail: info@scotways.com www.scotways.com

Scottish Tourist Board www.visitscotland.com

Scottish Youth Hostels Association 7 Glebe Crescent, Stirling FK8 2JA Tel: 01786-891400 0870-155-3255 (Bookings) Fax: 01786-891333 E-mail: syha@org.uk www.syha.org.uk

Walking Wild www.walkingwild.com

Specific useful contact details are also given in the information box of the relevant chapter.

Acknowledgements

The individual sections were authored as follows: Noel Williams, Geology; Ro Scott, Flora and Fauna; Alex Keith, chapters 1-5; Ted Maden, chapters 6-10, Dave Broadhead, chapters 11-18. Writing in 1932, W.N.Ling finished his introduction to the first edition of *The Northern Highlands* with the simple declaration 'On with the work'. The present authors, in doing just that, acknowledge their gratitude to their predecessors. Thanks also go to Derek Bearhop, Donald Bennet, Ken Crocket, Dave Hewitt, Angus MacKinnon, Sybil Maden, Andy Nisbet, Tom Prentice and John Watt.

The National Trust for Scotland

The NTS is a charity supported by a membership of a quarter of a million people. With more than 100 properties in its care, including some 75,000 hectares (185,000 acres) of countryside, the Trust looks after some of Scotland's finest mountain areas. Properties in the North-west Highlands include:

- Balmacara Estate & Lochalsh Woodland Garden
- Corrieshalloch Gorge
- Falls of Glomach
- Glenfinnan Monument
- Hugh Miller's Cottage, Cromarty
- Inverewe Garden
- Kintail & Morvich Estate
- Shieldaig Island
- Strome Castle
- Torridon Estate
- West Affric Estate

Access is assured throughout the year and, to counter erosion, footpath repair and maintenance has a high priority. To support this work, the Trust has set up its Sole Trading upland footpath appeal. Contact details can be found above.

Geology

Cambrian quartzite overlying Torridonian sandstone in Coire Mhic Fhearchair, Torridon

The North-west Highlands lie north and west of the Great Glen, a major trough-like depression which cuts right across the Scottish mainland from Fort William to Inverness. This remarkable physical feature has been formed by erosion along the line of the Great Glen fault, a fundamental dislocation in the earth's crust which has been active intermittently over hundreds of millions of years.

The Great Glen fault has a very complex history, and movement took place along it in different directions at different times. It was particularly active about 410-370 million years ago, during which time it is thought to have behaved as a tear fault, with sideways movement of the rocks on either side. Numerous comparatively small displacements over time resulted in the North-west Highlands slipping sideways many tens of kilometres relative to the rest of the country.

The balance of evidence suggests that the most significant episode of movement along the Great Glen fault was the rocks on the north-western side sliding in a south-westerly direction. The huge forces associated with this fault activity pulverized the rocks along the plane of the fault, and shattered the rocks for a kilometre on either side. As a consequence the rocks along the fault have eroded preferentially to produce the Great Glen.

The Great Glen fault is the most important member of a set of south-west to north-east trending faults which fracture the rocks of the Highlands. Other members of this set which lie within the North-west Highlands area include the Strathconon and Strath Glass faults. A lesser set of north-west to south-east trending faults includes one which passes through Kinloch Hourn and another which marks the hollow of Loch Maree.

Moine Thrust

One of the fascinating aspects of the geology of the North-west Highlands is the extraordinary contrast in the character of the mountains in the far north-west with those in the remainder of the area. The boundary between these two regions is marked by another major geological structure, the Moine Thrust, which extends in a south-south-westerly direction (i.e. roughly parallel to the western seaboard) from Whiten Head on the north coast, through Kinlochewe down to Loch Alsh on the west coast. From there it leaves the mainland and continues onto the Sleat peninsula of Skye.

A thrust is a fault which is orientated at a low angle to the horizontal. The Moine Thrust itself is the highest and possibly oldest of a series of parallel thrusts which lie within a narrow belt of dislocated rocks known as the Moine Thrust zone. The plane of the Moine Thrust slopes up gently towards the west-north-west. During the Caledonian mountain building episode about 430 million years ago, Moine metamorphic rocks were pushed several tens of kilometres west-north-westwards up onto the rocks forming the north-west 'foreland'. The three distinctive rock groups which make up this foreland area are as follows.

Lewisian

Rocks belonging to the Lewisian Complex form the foundation or 'basement' of the foreland area. The complex consists mainly of extremely old, metamorphic rocks generally referred to as banded gneisses. These are permeated by countless basic dykes, granite sheets and pegmatite veins which themselves have been metamorphosed to varying degrees. Two ancient metamorphic episodes can be recognised in these gneisses (Scourian 2900-2300 and Laxfordian 2300-1700 million years ago). The Outer Isles, which formed part of the foreland area, are themselves built almost entirely from Lewisian rocks – hence the name.

Lewisian gneiss is widely distributed throughout the far North-west Highlands. Being crystalline and impervious it tends to form rugged, lochan-peppered moorland. It seldom forms much of the high ground, although Ben More Assynt and Ben Stack in Sutherland, and the hills around Carnmore by Fionn Loch, are notable exceptions. The rocks of the Lewisian complex were deeply eroded before the next sequence of rocks was deposited.

Torridonian

At least seven kilometres of sandstones and conglomerates, with lesser amounts of mudstone, were subsequently deposited on the very irregular land surface of Lewisian gneiss. Hills and valleys cut into the original land surface are still preserved where the mantle of Torridonian sandstone has remained intact. This buried relief (or 'fossil' land surface) is well revealed on the slopes of Slioch above Loch Maree.

The sedimentary deposits belonging to the Torridonian sandstone group were laid down some 1000-800 million years ago, probably under semi-arid conditions as extensive alluvial fans. Exotic pebbles found within these deposits suggest that some of the material was derived from south-eastern Greenland, which at that time lay close to the Scottish area and formed part of an upland region. Torridonian rocks are too old to contain recognisable fossils, but microscopic fossils of primitive life forms have been extracted from some beds. Despite its great age, Torridonian sandstone has survived without being metamorphosed, so it must have remained outwith any mountain building areas.

The extensive outcrops of Torridonian sandstone which occur throughout the foreland area are largely responsible for its unique character. The Torridonian sequence is the best exposed sedimentary formation in Britain, and being red in colour and evenly stratified it contrasts starkly with the contorted crystalline gneiss on which it rests. The extraordinary difference in character between these two rock types has been emphasised by erosion, and has produced some of the most dramatic mountain scenery in the country.

The Torridonian rock strata are mainly gently inclined or horizontal, and are cut by numerous vertical joints. They weather to produce terraced cliffs with steep chimneys and gullies, as well as rounded bastions and pinnacled ridges.

Suilven, though by no means the highest, is perhaps the best known and certainly one

Noel Williams

Vertical section through Pipe Rock in Cambrian quartzite near Inchnadamph, Assynt

of the most spectacular of the peaks in the foreland area. It consists of an isolated remnant of flat-lying Torridonian sandstone resting on a platform of Lewisian gneiss. The normal access route to the bealach on the summit ridge follows the line of a vertical fault. The main summit lies on the downthrown side of this fault. Several distinctive porphyritic intrusions occur within the sandstone strata forming the eastern top. Among the other peaks of Torridonian sandstone situated north of Ullapool are Cul Beag, Stac Pollaidh and Ben Mor Coigach. Several other peaks in that area (notably Quinag, Canisp and Cul Mor), consist chiefly of Torridonian strata but have a capping of Cambrian quartzite.

Further south mighty An Teallach is built largely of Torridonian sandstone. Beinn Alligin is one of many peaks built entirely from this rock, whilst Liathach and Beinn Eighe have minor and major caps of quartzite respectively. The Applecross hills are also carved from rocks of Torridonian age.

The Torridonian rocks suffered considerable erosion and gentle folding prior to the deposition of the next group of rocks.

Cambrian and Ordovician

About 570 million years ago the sea began to transgress across the land, and some 1500m of marine sandstones and limestones were laid down on an almost level platform of Lewisian and Torridonian rocks. The earliest deposits consist mainly of siliceous sandstones called quartzites, including a distinctive type known as Pipe Rock. This is characterised by numerous vertical tubes or pipes up to a metre in length. The pipes are thought to represent the sand-filled burrows of organisms.

As time went by the sandy sediments gave way to limestones and dolomites of the Durness Group. Fossils found in these rocks lead geologists to believe that the foreland area, which lies north-west of the Moine Thrust, must once have formed part of the large North American 'plate'. The collision between this plate and the European plate, of which the rest of Britain formed a part, resulted in the formation of the Caledonian Mountain Chain about 450 million years ago.

The base of the Cambrian strata dips to the south-east, so the present horizontal orientation of the Torridonian sandstone is fortuitous. The whole sequence must have been tilted south-eastwards after the Ordovician rocks were deposited.

Only in a few cases is the greater part of a mountain composed of Cambrian quartzite, Foinaven and Arkle in the north of Sutherland being the best examples. There the quartzite rests directly on Lewisian gneiss. However, for the most part the quartzite forms a cap or top tier to what are largely Torridonian sandstone mountains.

Towards the end of the Caledonian mountain building episode about 430 million years ago, Moinian metamorphic rocks were pushed onto the more stable north-western foreland. This resulted in older Moine schists being superimposed on younger Cambro-ordovician quartzites and limestones. The thrust zone is very complex and numerous slices of the foreland rocks are present within it.

The discovery of the Moine Thrust in 1883 had a profound influence on geological thinking. The geological memoir to the region, published in 1907, is regarded as one of the most important by the British Geological Survey. A nature trail at Knochan Cliff near Elphin visits a fine exposure of the Moine Thrust.

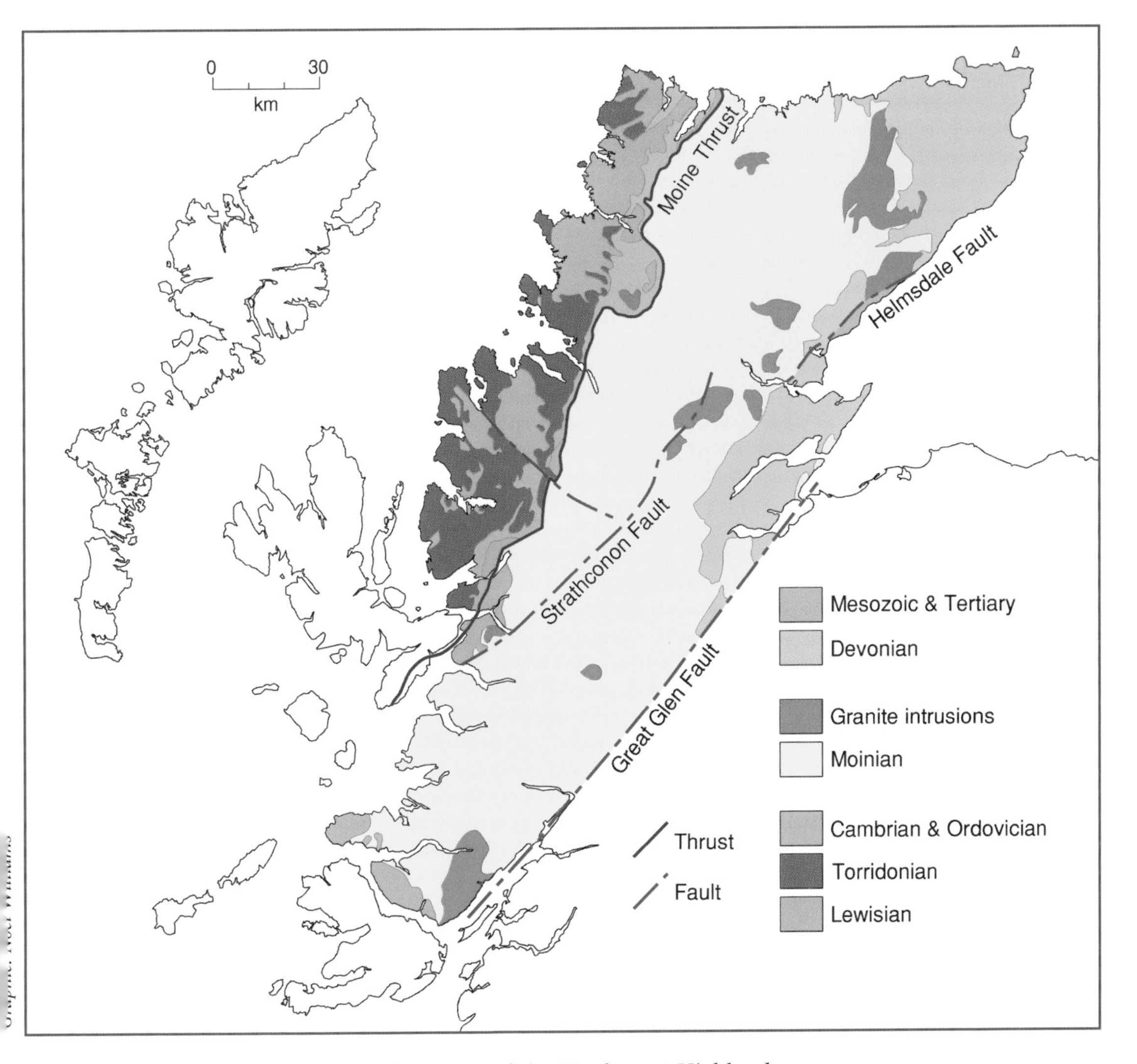

Geology map of the North-west Highlands

Striped schist – tightly folded Moine psammite and pelite

Moinian

The greater part of the North-west Highlands, which lies south-east of the Moine Thrust, consists of a broad belt of metamorphic rocks belonging to the Moine succession. These rocks originally accumulated as water laid sediments about 1200 – 1000 million years ago, but they were subsequently changed and deformed by more than one period of metamorphism. The final phase of metamorphism took place some 520 – 440 million years ago during the formation of the Caledonian mountains.

Prior to being eroded and fragmented, the Caledonian mountain chain ran from the eastern side of North America, across Ireland and Scotland, and up the western side of Scandinavia to Spitsbergen. The Moine rocks that we see today represent the exposed root of part of this enormous mountain chain.

The Moine rocks are structurally very complex, and it is difficult to unravel the various episodes of deformation they have suffered. However, it is clear that they have been overturned into gigantic flat-lying folds called 'nappes', and dislocated by major thrusts and slides. In places this intense squeezing has also exposed the underlying Lewisian basement.

Two main types of metamorphic rocks can be recognised. The first type, known as 'quartz-granulites' (or psammites), were originally sandy sediments, whilst the second type, called 'mica schists' (or pelites), were originally shales. Where the two types alternate rapidly they are described as 'striped schists'.

In many places where the mica schists are permeated by granite-like material they have produced a rock known as 'gneiss'. Also intruded into the mica schists are broad, white and pink veins of coarsely crystalline pegmatite. Sizeable plates of flaky mica are sometimes conspicuous within these veins. Countless dykes and sheets, composed of various igneous rocks, have been injected throughout the area.

Larger igneous masses are also present within the Moine rocks, and although there are fewer of these than in the rocks of the Central Highlands and Cairngorms, they are more varied in character. Some of the older intrusions appear to predate, and hence were metamorphosed by, the Caledonian orogeny (e.g. the Carn Chuinneag granite), whilst others were formed after the main period of metamorphism had waned (e.g. the Strontian and Cluanie granites). Of particular interest is the Ben Loyal syenite, a more alkaline igneous rock than granite, which has weathered in the form of slabby buttresses and tors.

Devonian

Of the deposits which were laid down following the Caledonian orogeny, the only ones well represented in the area are the conglomerates and flagstones of Devonian age, which outcrop in the north and east. These rocks are only of minor mountaineering interest, since on the whole they form fairly featureless lowland – Morven in Caithness being the most significant summit. However, the northern coastline is very scenic, and fossils of freshwater fish are found at many localities from John o' Groats to the Black Isle.

Mesozoic

A narrow strip of much younger sedimentary rocks (of Jurassic age) outcrops south of the Helmsdale Fault between Brora and Helmsdale. A metre-thick seam of coal was worked at Brora for many years. Much further south around Lochaline, Jurassic rocks are overlain by an unusually pure sandstone (99.7 per cent silica) of Cretaceous age, which has been worked as a source of glass sand.

Tertiary (Palaeogene)

A spectacular episode of volcanic activity broke out along the west coast of Scotland in Tertiary times about 60 million years ago, when Greenland began to drift away from Britain. Much of this activity took place in the Inner Hebrides, rather than the North-west Highlands, but basalt lavas from an enormous volcano on Mull extended as far as Morvern. A great volcanic centre also developed on the Ardnamurchan peninsula. Although the centre has since been deeply eroded, its outline can readily be picked out from aerial photographs. It is built mainly of gabbro.

Quaternary

The final moulding of the North-west Highlands was brought about mainly by the action of the huge ice sheets and glaciers which built up and melted down many times during the Ice Ages of the last two million years. Large quantities of rock were scooped out of the corries and glens. At times of maximum glaciation most of the country was covered by ice, but at other times the ice built up principally where precipitation was greatest i.e. over western hills. Then large glaciers flowed eastwards towards the hollow of the Great Glen. Glacial moraines generally increase in thickness in an eastwards direction as a consequence. Shorter glaciers spilled westwards to the coast, and gouged out deep fjords, including the deepest sea-loch in Europe – Loch Nevis. Loch Morar, just to the south of Loch Nevis, is the deepest freshwater loch in Britain, although its floor is more than 300m below sea level at its deepest point. Only glacial debris blocks off its previous link with the sea at its south-west corner.

Strong freeze-thaw action occurred on summits exposed above the ice, and on ground surrounding glacial areas. Such periglacial conditions produced various features, which hillwalkers can observe on the ground today. These include shattered bedrock, scree, stone stripes and polygons, as well as debris showing signs of downslope movement or solifluction.

The last remnants of glacial ice disappeared from the Highlands only 6000 years ago. It would seem that the cycle of ice ages and interglacials is likely to continue for quite some time, unless our output of greenhouse gases upsets the workings of nature.

Flora and Fauna

Stags below Sgurr na Lapaich, Strathfarrar

Whilst the underlying geology provides the form and framework of the landscape, many factors combine to determine what type of vegetation covers the land surface. The chemical composition of the underlying rock and rate of weathering determine the availability of minerals in the soil to feed plant life. The combination of latitude, altitude, aspect and prevailing climate influences the intensity and duration of sunlight, rainfall and freeze-thaw action, which affect both the rates of weathering and of plant growth.

The species composition of the present-day vegetation of the North-West Highlands is the result of ten thousand years of history, spanning the period since the last glaciation. Variations in climate since the Ice-Age, and the activities of human beings since their arrival about 5,000 years ago have brought about the extinction of some species and the introduction of others. Today's vegetation and the animal life which it supports are the result of this continuing interplay between natural forces and human activity.

Under present climatic conditions, oceanic (westerly) and boreal (northerly) influences struggle for dominance of the North-west Highlands. The presence of high ground close to the west coast increases the climatic differential, producing a rain shadow to the east. Across this great sweep of land, from Cape Wrath and Duncansby Head in the north to Rubha an Ridire and Ardnamurchan point in the south, there is a tremendous gradient in rainfall, seasonal temperature differential and windiness from west to east and, to a lesser extent, from south to north. Plants which are found at high altitudes to the south and east, for example, the yellow saxifrage (*Saxifraga aizoides)* and mountain avens (*Dryas octopetala*), descend to sea level in North-west Sutherland. The tree-line similarly descends towards the north and west.

Most tree-lines are now artificially low because of the long history of grazing and the practice of burning vegetation (muirburn) to provide fresh young shoots for domestic stock, deer or red grouse. These human influences have tilted the balance in favour of the more grazing tolerant plants, the grasses, at the expense of woody shrubs such as heather, and trees. The more adaptable animals such as the fox and hooded crow have also benefited, being better able to survive in this modified landscape than species with narrower tolerances.

Some knowledge of wildlife can add greatly to the enjoyment of any day on the hill, but to appreciate the full range of plant and animal life which the North-west Highlands has to offer, one must take some detours from the most direct routes. Identification of any species is best carried out in situ using an appropriate field guide. Photographs and notes can help to avoid the need to collect specimens. The remainder of this chapter explores the major habitat types to be found in the North-west Highlands, and outlines their characteristic species.

Woodlands

Before *Homo sapiens* arrived on the scene, more of the North-west Highlands would have been wooded than it is today. The maximum extent of woodland vegetation is thought to have existed about 4,000 years ago, when the climate was at its most benign, following the end of the glaciation. Many of the pine stumps found in peat bogs date from that time. The onset of peat formation marked the beginning of climatic deterioration, which is thought to have coincided with the spread of human colonisation in the Highlands. It is impossible to disentangle the effects of these two factors on the subsequent loss of woodland cover. In recent decades the remaining fragments of native woodland have been augmented by forestry plantations, mainly of non-native conifers. These usually consist of evenly and densely spaced trees offering, in wildlife terms, a poor imitation of native woodlands developed over thousands of years. Their dense cover, as at Loch Shin, provides a refuge for the introduced Japanese sika deer, which are able to interbreed with red deer.

In areas of deeper and more fertile soils, usually on warmer south-facing slopes, woodlands of oak (*Quercus robur* and *Q. petraea*) survive. Whilst their ground floras may be dominated by heather (*Calluna vulgaris*) and blaeberry (*Vaccinium myrtillus*), the western oakwoods are remarkable for their profusion of lichens, mosses, liverworts and filmy ferns. Typical birds of these woods are the redstart and wood warbler. A butterfly speciality is the Chequered skipper (*Carterocephalus palaemon*), which occurs only within a 30-mile radius of Fort William. More typical butterflies of the woodland and woodland edge are the speckled wood, green hairstreak, pearl-bordered, small pearl-bordered and dark green fritillaries.

On more calcareous soils, for example the Tertiary basalts of Morvern, oak gives way to ash (*Fraxinus excelsior*), wych elm (*Ulmus glabra*) and hazel (*Corylus avellana*). Here the ground flora also tends to be richer, with bluebell (*Hyacinthoides non-scripta*), dogs' mercury (*Mercurialis perennis*) and sanicle (*Sanicula europaea*). The richest ash woods are to be found on the Durness limestone at Kishorn. Where the ground is permanently damp, as on the inland side of the Mound embankment in Strathfleet, alder and willow woodlands have developed. On poorer soils and further north, the hardier birch can survive where oak and ash cannot, and forms woodlands such as those at Lochinver, Drumbeg and Loch Stack.

The most extensive native pinewood remnants north of the Great Glen are those of Glen Affric and Glen Strathfarrar. These support all of the characteristic pinewood plants; juniper (*Juniperus communis*) as an undershrub, with one-flowered and intermediate wintergreens (*Moneses uniflora* and *Pyrola media*), twinflower (*Linnaea borealis*), creeping lady's tresses orchid (*Goodyera repens*) on the forest floor. The more northerly pinewoods of Beinn Eighe,

Deer fencing ensures the regeneration of Caledonian pine forest in Glen Affric

Sheildaig, Coulin, Amat and Alladale lack some of these species, but still convey the pinewood atmosphere. Among the birds, crossbills are specialist feeders on conifer seeds, whilst goldcrests and crested tits seek out small insects among the foliage. Capercaillie are now extremely scarce north of the Great Glen. The black grouse, a woodland edge species, has undergone a similar decline.

The pine beauty moth, which coexists with native pine, caused severe damage in some of the early plantations of Lodgepole pine in the north. Wood ants make their characteristic nest mounds of pine needles. Whilst roe deer remain largely confined to their woodland habitats, red deer have also taken to life on the open hill. Woodlands provided a stronghold for the pine marten, wildcat, badger, and red squirrel which managed to survive intense persecution during the late 19th and early 20th Century. Less fortunate were the wolf, brown bear, beaver, lynx and reindeer which were hunted to extinction in earlier centuries and whose only physical remains are found in archaeological deposits, such as the bone caves of Inchnadamph.

Bogs

Peat is able to form only where high rainfall allows the survival of bog mosses (*Sphagnum* species). Each moss plant consists of a single stem with its growing point at the top. As growth proceeds and the surface rises higher, the lower parts die. Sphagnum plants hold a lot of water, and the low oxygen and high acidity levels in it preserve the dead moss, forming peat. Also preserved in the peat are the remains of other plants growing with the Sphagnum, including pollen grains. Many pollen grains can be identified to species and the examination of ancient pollen preserved at different depths in peat, combined with radiocarbon dating to determine its age, has given new insights into the history of Highland vegetation. So, as well as being the first fossil fuel known to man, peat constitutes an irreplaceable historical archive.

The peatlands of the North-west Highlands consist of two major types. In areas of low relief such as the Flow Country of Caithness and Sutherland, peat is able to cover the whole surface, forming blanket bogs. Blanket bogs can also form on broad hilltops and ridges. Where extremely high rainfall combines with suitable topography, the peat surface builds up higher than the surrounding water table, forming raised bog. Various intermediate forms can also occur. The great Claish and Kentra Mosses at the southern end of Loch Shiel contain elements of both types.

The wide skies of the Flow Country, filled with the haunting cries of greenshank, curlew, dunlin, golden plover and skylark, present a formidable landscape experience. However the lie of the land can only truly be appreciated by viewing the broad brown sweep of the peatlands, with their constellations of dubh-lochans, from a suitable summit – Morven, Scaraben or the Ben Griams for example. In closer proximity, the peat surface has its own array of plants, well adapted to the nutrient-poor, acidic and wet conditions: common and hare's-tail cottongrasses, (*Eriophorum angustifolium* and *E. vaginatum*); bog asphodel (*Narthecium ossifragum*); carnivorous sundews (*Drosera* species) and common butterworts (*Pinguicula vulgaris*); bog blaeberry (*Vaccinium uliginosum*); cranberries (*Vaccinium microcarpum* and *V. oxycoccos*); deergrass (*Trichophorum cespitosum*); cross-leaved heath (*Erica tetralix*); dwarf birch (*Betula nana*); lousewort and marsh lousewort (*Pedicularis sylvatica* and *P. palustris*).

The western bogs have their own specialities including the diminutive bog orchid (*Hammarbya paludosa*), pale butterwort (*Pinguicula lusitanica*) and brown beak-sedge (*Rhynchospora fusca*), whose British strongholds are in western Scotland and the New Forest. Bog myrtle (*Myrica gale*) prefers to grow where there is lateral water movement through the peat. In such places, swathes of purple moor-grass (*Molinia caerulea*), unpalatable to deer and sheep, support caterpillars of the Scotch argus butterfly, which flies in July and August. This grass is deciduous and its dead leaves, picked up by the wind, give its alternative name of 'blow grass'.

In bog pools, bog bean (*Menyanthes trifoliata*), and bladderworts (*Utricularia* species) are found. These pools provide important breeding grounds for dragonflies. Plentiful craneflies and spiders supply the high-protein food required by wader chicks, and enable the peatlands to support large breeding populations of these birds. Along the north coast, the boglands host an indigenous population of greylag geese, which do not migrate north to breed, but are resident all year round.

Heaths and Moorlands

With increasing slope, or decreasing rainfall, there is a subtle transition from bog into wet heath and then to dry heath. Many of the same plant species are present, but their proportions in the vegetation change. Wet heaths cover extensive areas in the west. Sphagnum mosses are still present, but cover a smaller proportion of the surface. Heather and cross-leaved heath are the dominant dwarf shrubs, accompanied by deergrass, purple moor-grass, common cottongrass, lousewort, tormentil (*Potentilla erecta*) and heath milkwort (*Polygala serpyllifolia*). Towards the east of the country, the drier climate allows heather to dominate extensive areas. Depending on the management history, where muirburn has not been intense, a greater variety of dwarf shrubs including blaeberry (bilberry) (*Vaccinium myrtillus*), crowberry (*Empetrum nigrum*), cowberry (*Vaccinium vitis-idaea*), bearberry (*Arctostaphylos uva-ursi*), cloudberry (*Rubus chamaemorus*), dwarf cornel (*Cornus suecica*) and dwarf juniper (*Juniperus communis* ssp. *nana*) can occur. Under leggy heather, the tiny lesser twayblade orchid (*Listera cordata*), with its paired leaves, may be found.

In the west, tall heather can also shelter a particular community of liverworts known as the North Atlantic hepatic mat. These delicate plants depend on the extremely sheltered microclimate found under the heather and would quickly be eliminated by muirburn. In

Common lizard – shy moorland dweller

drier unburned areas, grey *Cladonia* lichens can be noticeable. Alpine bearberry (*Arctostaphylos alpinus*) and mountain everlasting (*Antennaria dioica*) are characteristic of exposed knolls. Where there is water seepage, a different community of plants will be found. If the water is alkaline, these may include the Scottish asphodel (*Tofieldia pusilla*), black bog-rush (*Schoenus nigricans*), and broad-leaved cottongrass (*Eriophorum latifolium*).

Dry heath is the typical habitat of the red grouse, but grouse moor management in the North-west Highlands is nowhere near as intense as in the Grampians. The patchwork of different-aged burned patches may be seen wherever drier heathlands occur, but the highest density of red grouse is found in East Sutherland. Mountain hares too prefer the drier side of the country. Red deer range over most of the moorlands and deer stalking is an important industry. Among the smaller animals, common lizard, adder, and slow worm can be found on the moors, along with a variety of moths and butterflies. The hairy caterpillars and papery pupal cases of the Northern eggar moth can be more conspicuous than the adult insects. Emperor moth caterpillars resemble heather shoots, with small pink dots imitating the flowers. Of particular concern to land managers is the heather beetle, which can devastate sizeable areas in 'outbreak' years, leaving characteristic rust-coloured patches. Ticks too cause problems, being carriers of disease for both grouse, sheep and hillwalkers. The ubiquitous midges are merely an irritation!

In some places, notably Kintail and An Teallach, the deer and sheep are augmented by populations of feral goats. Characteristic birds of the moors are the meadow pipit, (whose nest is often targeted by the cuckoo), stonechat, whinchat and wheatear, all of which provide food for merlins and hen harriers. Populations of field voles, although at lower densities than in grassland habitats, support mammal-eating predators such as the short-eared owl.

Grasslands and Glens

The predominantly brown landscape of the North-west Highlands is punctuated by islands of green, where the efforts of previous human generations and the grazing of their livestock, have created and maintained grassy swards. In some places, as on the Dalradian limestones of Durness, Kishorn and Assynt, and the base-rich Tertiary igneous rocks of Morvern and Ardnamurchan, the greater initial soil fertility gave a head start. All of these calcareous grasslands are extremely species-rich and present a colourful spectacle in early summer, with a proliferation of orchids, common birds-foot-trefoil (*Lotus corniculatus*), eyebrights (*Euphrasia* species), mountain avens, wild thyme (*Thymus polytrichus*) and fairy flax (*Linum catharticum*). Grassland flowers provide nectar for a variety of butterflies including the Meadow brown, Green-veined white, and Orange tip.

At Kishorn, Inchndamph and Durness small areas of limestone pavement occur, where grazing-sensitive plants are able to survive in the shelter of deep cracks, or grykes, where water has dissolved the bare rock. Limestone streams in Assynt provide an atypical habitat for the water vole, now endangered in many places by the spread of the predatory American mink. Burrowing animals such as moles and rabbits are restricted to the drier grassland areas. In the cultivated glens, lapwing, curlew, oystercatcher, snipe and redshank nest in pastures and arable fields.

On less calcareous soils, grasslands of bents and fescues may be poorer in numbers of flowering species, but provide favoured grazings for red deer and domestic stock far up onto the hill. At high altitudes a viviparous fescue (*Festuca vivpara*), in which the seeds germinate whilst still attached to the parent plant, shows adaptation to the harsher conditions. Under heavy grazing the unpalatable mat-grass is able to colonise, diminishing the feeding value of the sward.

Crags and Corries

At higher altitudes the effects of grazing on the vegetation are less obvious. In summer, the concentrated growing season allows the vegetation a limited chance to grow faster than it can be consumed. The richest plant communities are found on the more friable and easily-weathered rocks, which also tend to be those with a higher calcium or magnesium content (and the least popular for climbing!)

Scotland's highest altitude flora includes two main elements – Arctic or boreal species reaching the southern limit of their range and Alpine species, otherwise found in the much higher mountains of southern Europe. Some species, the Arctic-Alpines, are common to both areas. These include some of Scotland's rarest plants, found only on the highest hills, usually in north-facing corries, growing on ledges or in rock-crevices, free of competition from more vigorous species. The Arctic species found in the North-west Highlands include tufted saxifrage (*Saxifraga cespitosa*), Highland saxifrage (*Saxifraga rivularis*), rock whitlowgrass (*Draba norvegica*) and Arctic mouse-ear (*Cerastium arcticum*). Cyphel (*Minuartia sedoides*) represents the Alpine element. Among the Arctic-Alpines are Alpine mouse-ear (*Cerastium alpinum*), Highland cudweed (*Gnaphalium norvegicum*), northern rock-cress (*Arabis petraea*) and Alpine saxifrage (*Saxifraga nivalis*).

The Lewisian and Torridonian hills to the west of the Moine thrust tend to have the least varied floras, but even here, an occasional treasure such as the extremely rare tufted saxifrage may be found. Along the Dalradian limestone outcrops which follow the Moine thrust from Assynt to Durness, montane species such as mountain avens, whortle-leaved willow (*Salix myrsinites*), and alpine cinquefoil (*Potentilla crantzii*) may be seen at relatively low altitudes, most notably at Inchnadamph.

To the east of the Moine thrust, the predominantly hard and acidic rocks of the Moine series contain occasional richer outcrops of mica schists and psammites. Where combined with high altitude, as on Seana Bhraigh, Beinn Dearg, Sgurr na Lapaich and the Fannaichs these give rise to the richest montane floras north of the Great Glen. The alkaline granite of Ben Loyal and narrow band of epidiorite & hornblende schists on Ben Hope make these hills the northern outposts of floristic richness.

Steep and unstable cliffs protect vegetation from grazing and allow the survival on ledges of plant communities which would be more widespread if grazing pressure was less. At lower altitudes these usually consist of common species, but growing and flowering with a luxuriance unequalled in grazed situations. Wood crane's-bill (*Geranium sylvaticum*), globeflower (*Trollius europaeaus*), wild angelica (*Angelica sylvestris*), great wood-rush (*Luzula sylvatica*), water avens (*Geum rivale*), melancholy thistle (*Cirsium helenioides*), roseroot (*Sedum rosea*), northern bedstraw (*Galium boreale*), thrift (*Armeria maritima*), alpine saw-wort (*Saussurea alpina*), alpine lady's mantle (*Alchemilla alpina*) and stone bramble (*Rubus saxatilis*) are typical of such situations. In a few places, such as Sgurr na Lapaich, Ben Wyvis and Ben Hope the last remnants of montane willow scrub (including downy willow (*Salix lapponum*), woolly willow (*S. lanata*) and net-leaved willow (*S. reticulata*)) cling to inaccessible ledges. Burnsides are enlivened by hanging curtains of purple saxifrage and mountain sorrel (*Oxyria digyna*). In damp grasslands alpine bistort (*Persicaria vivipara*) and alpine meadow-rue (*Thalictrum alpinum*) are found, whilst more open stony flushes have russet sedge *Carex saxatilis*, yellow saxifrage, some of the more unusual rushes (three-flowered rush (*Juncus triglumis*), two-flowered rush (*J. biglumis*), chestnut rush (*J. castaneus*)) and the chunky worm-like moss *Scorpidium scorpioides*.

Where snow lies late into the summer, a distinctive vegetation develops, with mat-grass, the clover-like Sibbaldia (*Sibbaldia procumbens*) and dwarf cudweed (*Gnaphalium supinum*). The high corries provide secure nesting sites for golden eagles and ravens and secluded pastures for calving red deer hinds. In summer, the migratory ring ouzel arrives to breed and its fluting song epitomises the high places.

Ridges and Summits

Out on the exposed ridges and summit plateaux, only the toughest mountain plants survive. Wind and weather are the dominant influences and a small suite of species tend to occur, regardless of the geology. On the more fractured and angular rock types, for example the Torridonian sandstones and Cambrian quartzites, the summits and ridges may appear practically bare of vegetation. But a closer look reveals the intricate crazy paving of tiny lichens on the rock surface.

Many plants of the exposed tops form dense cushions of leaves anchored by long tap roots – the trailing azalea (*Loiseleuria procumbens*), moss campion (*Silene acaulis*) and cyphel are examples. Other typical species are the spiked wood-rush (*Luzula spicata*), dwarf willow (*Salix herbacea*), stiff sedge (*Carex bigelowii*), alpine clubmoss (*Diphasiastrum alpinum*), Icelandic reindeer-moss (*Cetraria islandica*) (a lichen despite its name) and three-leaved rush (*Juncus trifidus*). On broader ridges and plateaux, as on Ben Wyvis, the woolly fringe-moss (*Racomitrium lanuginosum*) forms extensive grey carpets. On the most calcareous hills of Inchnadamph and Morvern the Norwegian sandwort (*Arenaria norvegica* ssp. *norvegica*) clings to open stony ground.

Of the birds whose breeding is restricted to the high tops, ptarmigan are widespread. They remain all year round, relying on their changeable plumage for camouflage. Snow bunting and dotterel have a more limited breeding distribution, using only the highest rocky summits and mossy plateaux respectively.

Lochs and Rivers

The main watershed of the North-west Highlands lies close to the west coast, delimited by the high massifs of Ben More Assynt, Beinn Dearg, the Fannaichs, Sgurr a Chaorachain, An

Thrift high on An Riabhachan, Glen Cannich

Socach (Mullardoch), Sgurr nan Ceathramhnan and Beinn Fhada. To the west of it, short steep rivers flow into the Atlantic, and the topography is deeply dissected by sea-lochs. The vagaries of sea-level change mean that some of these glacial troughs now hold freshwater lochs, including Loch Morar and Loch Shiel. The larger eastward-flowing river systems (Shin; Oykel; Carron; Conon; Beauly) make their way to the North Sea by gentler gradients. Fluctuating levels on the dammed lochs cause problems for shore-nesting black-throated divers. The westward-flowing river systems are generally low in nutrients and support species, such as the freshwater pearl mussel and dipper, which depend on clear sediment-free water for their food supply.

Smaller hill lochs are the preferred nesting haunt of red-throated divers. The piping call of the common sandpiper, along with the first frog spawn, announces the arrival of spring at the hill lochans. Brown trout populations, isolated since the ice-age, have developed loch-specific characteristics. In other undisturbed lochs, populations of Arctic charr survive. The water of most hill lochs is acidic and nutrient-poor and supports a limited but characteristic range of plants, including shoreweed (*Littorella uniflora*), water lobelia (*Lobelia dortmanna*), water horsetail (*Equisetum fluviatile*), bottle sedge (*Carex rostrata*), white water-lily (*Nymphaea alba*) and, in the most acidic waters, awlwort (*Subularia aquatica*). The water of the limestone lochs of Assynt and Durness, and the Caithness lochs underlain by Old Red Sandstone, is alkaline. Species such as mare's-tail (*Hippuris vulgaris*), blue water-speedwell (*Veronica anagallis-aquatica*) and the stoneworts, which are characteristic of richer conditions, occur here.

A well-chosen day's excursion, from shore to summit, in the North-west Highlands offers the opportunity to encounter a good selection of the habitats and species described here.

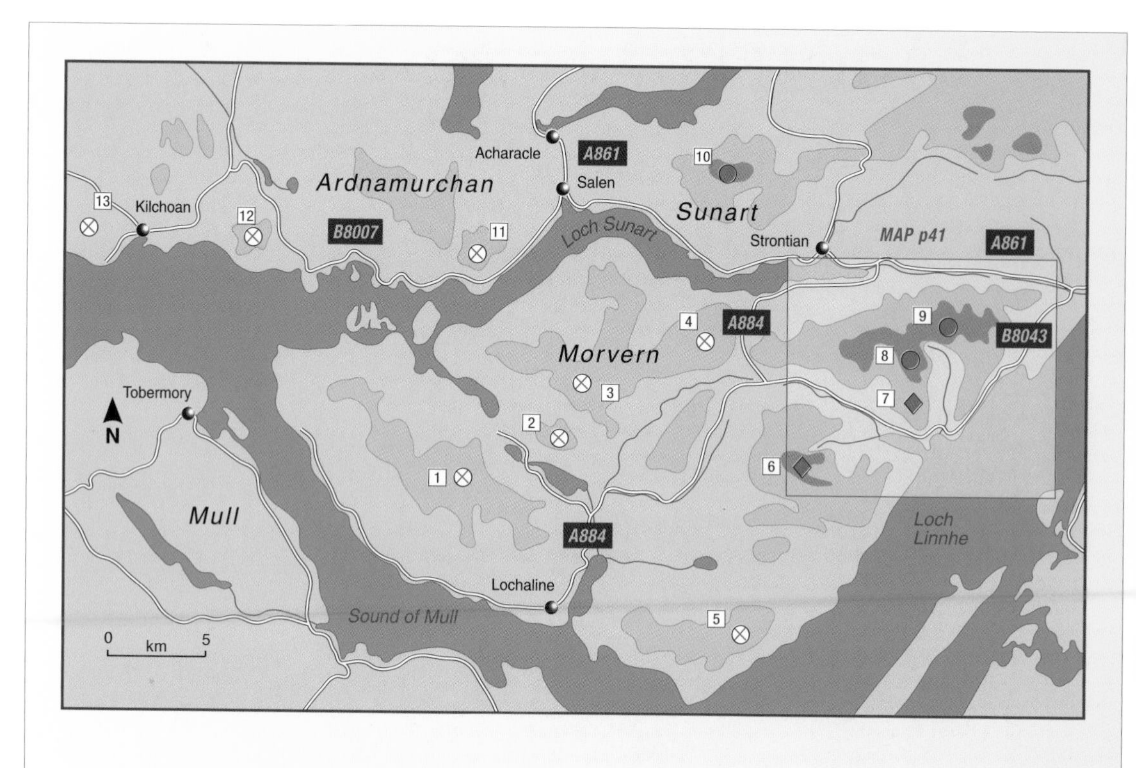

1.	Sidhean na Raplaich	551m	O	p39
2.	Beinn na h-Uamha	465m	O	p39
3.	Beinn Iadain	571m	O	p40
4.	Beinn nam Beathrach	582m	O	p40
5.	An Sleaghach	513m	O	p41
6.	Beinn Mheadhoin	739m	G	p42
7.	Beinn na Cille	652m	G	p43
8.	Fuar Bheinn	766m	C	p43
9.	Creach Bheinn	853m	C	p43
10.	Beinn Resipol	845m	C	p45
11.	Ben Laga	512m	O	p46
12.	Ben Hiant	528m	O	p46
13.	Beinn na Seilg	342m	O	p47

Morvern, Sunart and Ardnamurchan

Gill Nisbet

Loch Sunart from Beinn Resipol

If the mountains of the Northern and Western Highlands are to be compared to a symphony then the hills of Morvern, Sunart and Ardnamurchan make for a varied and gentle overture before the more stirring movements which lie ahead. These areas form the southern part of the mainland Highlands west of the Great Glen, and are made up of mainly low-lying ground and grassy rolling moorland dominated by the coastal scenery. To the mountaineer they represent something of a backwater, but the summits provide a sense of remoteness and tranquillity no longer offered by the country's higher and more famous peaks.

The name Morvern comes from A' Mhorbhairn (*the sea-gap*), and refers to the Sound of Mull which lies to the south. It is a large and diamond-shaped thrust of land, almost entirely surrounded by the sea, being bounded on the east by Loch Linnhe and on the north by Loch Sunart. At the close of the last Ice Age, Morvern and Ardgour formed one of the largest of the Scottish islands. Now the areas are linked only by a brief neck of land at the extreme north-east corner of Morvern, which is the part of most interest to hillwalkers. Much of the remaining land comprises rounded hills covered by extensive forestry, some of which has matured, and partial felling is taking place with second rotation planting following on.

The main accesses to Morvern are the A884 from Ardgour and Glen Tarbert, and the ferry from Fishnish, on Mull, to Lochaline. The road climbs from the head of Loch Sunart, reaching a height of over 200m. It then runs down Gleann Geal (*the white glen*, the colour referring to the river and its waterfalls) to the bottle-shaped sea loch of Loch Aline (*the beautiful loch*) from which the village takes its name. Lochaline is the main settlement in Morvern. It offers a variety of facilities for the visitor. However the setting is rather more beautiful than the village itself. The main sources of employment are forestry and mining. From Lochaline,

Beinn na Cille, Fuar Bheinn, Creach Bheinn and Castle Stalker from Loch Laich

a minor road follows the coast westwards past a number of interesting antiquities as far as Drimnin. A track continues round above Auliston Point, past the remains of the old village of Auliston, to Loch na Droma Buidhe and Oronsay, a tidal island of interest and beauty and a breeding ground for seals.

A few kilometres north of Lochaline, a quiet road leads from Claggan near Larachbeg over to Kinloch at the head of Loch Teacuis, passing Loch Arienas and the escarpment of Sidhean na Raplaich on the way. It was at Claggan that the former inhabitants of St Kilda were re-settled in 1930 after leaving their native island. This road takes the line of a geological fault that splits Morvern, and it gives access to a number of the area's western hills. A further 3km on from Kinloch, there is a dun or vitrified fort at Rahoy on a wooded knoll overlooking the entrance to Loch Teacuis. The dun was excavated by Professor Childe in 1936-7, and is still quite recognisable albeit rather overgrown. A model 'Gaelic wall' was built here from the same materials as the fort and deliberately fired to test the theories of vitrification, although it is still not clear if this mysterious process was the result of defensive or hostile actions. From Rahoy a footpath heads eastwards to Glencripesdale and then follows the shore of Loch Sunart to Liddesdale on the A884.

A single-track road leaves the A884 near its summit, descending eastwards to Loch Linnhe at Kingairloch, then leading dramatically north along the shores of Loch Linnhe to rejoin the A861 at Inversanda. It passes the finest hills in the area, which are the Creach Bheinn group and Beinn Mheadhoin. A good coastal walk takes the path from Kingairloch south to Glen Sanda, below the super-quarry, where there is an old castle by the shore of Loch Linnhe. Continue up by the Glensanda River then drop down to Loch Tearnalt and follow a track to the public road at Achranich near the head of Loch Aline.

Morvern was of considerable strategic value in years gone by, and its past is probably of greater interest than its present. Ardtornish Castle, situated on a peninsula south-east of Loch Aline, was the stronghold of the Lords of the Isles in the 14th and 15th centuries, and later of the MacLeans of Duart. Now a ruined fortress, it is a fine viewpoint, and its setting was used by Sir Walter Scott in his book 'Lord of the Isles'. Kinlochaline Castle is on a crag at the head of the loch, a square keep once the seat of the Chiefs of the Clan MacInnes, but stormed and burned in the 17th century by Cromwell's troops. It was restored in 1890 and is worth a look inside. Morvern fared very badly in the Clearances, and the signs of depopulation are still obvious. The evictions are particularly associated with Patrick Sellar, who was a leader of earlier clearances in Sutherland. He moved to Ardtornish House in Morvern, where he repeated his atrocities, and many townships especially in the north-west of the area were wiped out altogether.

Sunart is no more than the south-west extension of Ardgour, and is dominated by its one hill of note, Beinn Resipol, a landmark made all the more conspicuous by its relative isolation. The A861 runs westwards for 16km along the beautifully wooded north shore of Loch Sunart from Strontian near the head of the loch to the village of Salen. To the north lies fresh-water Loch Shiel, and a single-track road goes from Strontian over a pass to it and the isolated forestry village of Polloch, reaching 342m then dropping down past Loch Doilet into heavily forested Glen Hurich. The western boundary of Sunart is the road from Salen to the village of Acharacle at the foot of Loch Shiel. Strontian (*ridge of the fairies*) is the biggest settlement hereabouts. In the 1960s the Highlands & Islands Development Board was involved in creating a new infrastructure for Strontian and that, coupled with the village green, makes it atypical by Highland standards. Strontian is famous for the mining works in

Access and Transport

By road: the main route of access is by the Corran Ferry across Loch Linnhe, and from there along the A861 to Strontian, Salen and Acharacle. These villages can also be reached from the north, using the A830 from Fort William to Lochailort then the A861 south from there to Acharacle. From the head of Loch Sunart, the A884 leads to Lochaline in Morvern. From Salen the B8007 goes to Portuairk at the western tip of Ardnamurchan.

By bus: Lochaline to Fort William; Kilchoan to Fort William (both via the Corran Ferry) (Shiel Buses, tel: 01967-431272).

By ferry: the Corran Ferry (vehicles & foot passengers. Highland Council, tel: 01855-841243); Lochaline to Fishnish; Kilchoan to Tobermory (Caledonian MacBrayne Ltd, tel: Tobermory office 01688-302017; general enquiries 01475-650100).

By rail: the nearest stations are at Fort William and Lochailort.

Accommodation and Information

Hotels and guesthouses: Lochaline, Strontian, Salen, Acharacle, Glenborrodale and Kilchoan.
Campsites: Resipole Farm (tel: 01967-431235); Strontian; Balmeanach Park, Fishnish (tel: 01680-300342)

Tourist Information Centres: Strontian (tel: 01967-402381) (Easter - October); Fort William (tel: 01397-703781); Kilchoan (tel: 01972-510222) (Easter - October); www.ardnamurchan.com is a comprehensive site for visitors.

Maps

Ordnance Survey: 1:50,000 Landranger sheets 40 (Mallaig and Glenfinnan), 47 (Tobermory and North Mull) and 49 (Oban and East Mull); 1:25,000 Explorer sheets 383 (Morvern and Lochaline) and 390 (Ardnamurchan).

the hills to the north, and it makes a good base for exploring the surrounding area. Indeed, a former editor of this guide was moved to describe the village as 'a pleasant place for car-ferrying, non-climbing wives to spend the day'. It is to be hoped that editorial attitudes have advanced, like Strontian, into the 21st century!

Ardnamurchan (*the great point of the ocean*) lies immediately west of Sunart. The peninsula extends for 28km to the Point of Ardnamurchan, the westernmost tip of mainland Britain. The Point's famous lighthouse stands some 35m high, and can be seen for 30km. It is open to visitors and gives a great view of the nearby islands. Ardnamurchan is of great historical significance, occupying a tactically important location, and it was peacefully inhabited from the Stone Age until the arrival of the Vikings. The eastern part is composed of metamorphic rock and rough moors. West of Loch Mudle the rock is mainly glacially scoured gabbro, and the scenery is most unusual. The hills may be low but they are rugged and offer splendid viewpoints, and there are many short rock climbs to be enjoyed on the outcrops scattered on their slopes. Ardnamurchan is also a major breeding ground for birds and home to a surprising variety of plant-life.

Access is by the 'main' road, the B8007, a narrow and twisting route along the north shore of Loch Sunart. Progress along it can be slow and laborious, deteriorating towards arterial thrombosis at times in the summer months, but it is a contender for the most beautiful road in Argyll and one of the area's principal scenic assets. It passes through Glenborrodale then divides at Kilchoan, with three prongs terminating at Sanna, Portuairk and the Point itself, where the wonderful sandy beaches and wild rocky seascape are justifiably popular visitor attractions. The lighthouse has an exhibition, a cafe and other visitor facilities and is worth a visit. (www.ardnamurchan.u-net.com, tel: 01972-510210.) The north side of the peninsula is less frequented, and there is little by way of habitation. It does, however, offer a series of paths and tracks, and these can be linked to give a memorable coastal outing. One can walk from near Sanna via Kilmory and Ockle to Arivegaig at the head of Kentra Bay 2km west of Acharacle. There are great views to Moidart and across the Sound of Arisaig. At one time the local authority planned to create a public road along this route, an idea that has now hopefully been quietly shelved.

Also of interest in Ardnamurchan are the ruins of Mingary Castle, a hexagonal-shaped keep of obscure origins just east of the pier at Kilchoan. It was built in the 13th century and occupies a strategic position overlooking the Sound of Mull. The castle has a bloody history, having changed hands violently on a number of occasions between the feuding Campbells

Sand, Musket Balls and Fireworks

One of the main industries in Morvern is mining. There is a sand mine at Lochaline where unusually pure white sandstone (99.7% silica) is worked, to be crushed to make fine optical glass. Some 60,000 to 70,000 tons have been mined since 1939, and there are almost 30 miles of tunnels. There is also the vast open Glensanda super-quarry on the east side of Beinn Mheadhoin in Morvern. Granite is shipped out in large bulk carriers down Loch Linnhe, access being available only by sea. It has provided the material for lining the Channel Tunnel amongst other projects.

There is also a long history of mining on the hillsides east of Beinn Resipol at the back of Strontian. Workings date from 1722, an early shareholder having been General Wade of road-building fame. French prisoners-of-war worked them for lead, which was made into bullets for the Napoleonic wars. 60 tons of Strontian lead was used in 1753 for the re-roofing of Inveraray Castle. In 1764 the mineral strontianite was discovered, taking its name from the village. This led to the isolation of the element strontium. A yellow metal once isolated, it burns with a brilliant red flame and is used in fireworks. Production ceased in 1904. The largest of these mines was re-opened in 1963, and again briefly in 1980 for barytes, used in the oil-drilling industry.

and MacDonalds. The initial occupants were the MacIains of Ardnamurchan, close relatives of the Lords of the Isles. In the late 15th century, when the Lordship of the Isles was forfeited, King James IV visited Mingary twice to receive the allegiance of the island chiefs, and a century later Spanish troops laid siege to it (hence the name of the bay below – Port nam Spainteach). In 1644 Colkitto MacDonald, supporting Montrose and Charles I, took the castle from the Campbells and then withstood a siege by Argyll's army. The Campbells later regained possession, and were occupying Mingary in 1745 when they sent the first warning to London of Prince Charlie's landing near Arisaig. In the early part of the following century Ardnamurchan was sold by the clan chiefs, money and social positions having become more important to them than land, and an unfortunate cycle was established. Evictions followed and ownership changed hands many times. The story is a sad one of the destruction of the old ways of life, just as in other parts of the Highlands. The main economic activities now are agriculture, forestry, tourism and fish farming.

Principal Hills

Sidhean na Raplaich; 551m; (OS Sheet 49; NM635517); *fairy hill of the screes*

An extensive hill lying some 8km north-west of Lochaline, Sidhean na Raplaich forms the highest point of the Fiunary forest. The terrain is principally high moorland and forestry, and is proof, if such is needed, that circumforestation can be an art form! Some areas of trees have been felled and are being replanted, so the best route of ascent may vary from time to time. The presence of numerous tracks in the forest means that it should never be particularly difficult to reach the open hillside above. The finest aspect of the hill is the north-east one, a volcanic escarpment running for several kilometres above Loch Arienas and Loch Doire nam Mart. This, combined with the relatively flat skyline above and the forestry below, gives the hill an unusually regular appearance, and access is taken from this side with more interest and speed than from elsewhere.

There are two recommended approaches at the time of writing. Firstly, one can start from a lay-by (NM682505) about 2km along the Loch Teacuis road from the A884 turn off, just where the road reaches the shore of Loch Arienas. Above rises Sidhean an Aoinidh Bhig, also known as the Little Bonnet of Lorne due to the knoll's distinctive craggy outline. Take the track south from here for a couple of hundred metres before making a brief incursion into light forestry to emerge relatively unscathed onto the ridge of An t-Sreang. Follow this for some 5km over gently undulating grassy hillsides to the summit.

Secondly, starting from the car park at the west end of Loch Arienas (NM667518), take a marked path past the ruins of the old township by the Allt an Aoinidh Mhoir. This path leads to a forest track. From here there are a couple of options. Either scramble steeply over brashings to emerge at the col just below the mast 1.5km south-east of the top. Alternatively take the track northwards to below a spur at about NM647523, and then follow a fence through forest rides to emerge on the open hillside 1.5km north-east of the summit. The area round the summit slopes only gradually, to the point of obscuring much of the more immediate scenery, but magnificent views can be enjoyed on a good day to Mull and Ardnamurchan.

Beinn na h-Uamha; 465m; (OS Sheet 49; NM682534); *hill of the cave*

The unusual table-like summit area of Beinn na h-Uamha makes it well worth climbing. Its top is surrounded on most sides by horizontal basalt strata, most pronounced and

The hills of Morvern seen from Lismore

dank on the north. The name comes from a shallow cave located in the south flank of the escarpment, about 1km west of the summit. The ascent is best made from the forestry car park at the west end of Loch Arienas, described above for Sidhean na Raplaich, starting along the track towards Durinemast before heading up a broad shoulder. This merges into steeper upper slopes, and the scrappy rock above should be avoided to arrive at the west end of the plateau. A grass ridge leads to the summit, from where there are fine views down Loch Teacuis and across to the escarpments of Sidhean na Raplaich.

Beinn Iadain; 571m; (OS Sheet 49; NM692561); possibly *hill of pain, or hill of ivy*

Lying to the north of Beinn na h-Uamha, Beinn Iadain is set back from the road and is quite remote. It can be reached from the road-end at the head of Loch Teacuis. Access has been considerably simplified by the closure of the old experimental deer farm at Kinloch, from where a good track heads high into Coire an Tuim. Continue from the end of this track to the head of the corrie, at the foot of the north-west ridge of Beinn Iadain. This is the most interesting side of the hill, particularly so to geologists who will notice a 35cm layer of chalk intervening between the flat bands of lava and metamorphic rock. The ridge itself is relatively narrow but leads without difficulty to the grassy summit, marked by a trig point. For variety the descent can be made by the southern slopes, avoiding the steeper crags to the west, and going down the pathless Coire Beinn na h-Uamha back to Kinloch. The outing can be significantly extended by combining Beinn Iadain with Beinn na h-Uamha as a circuit from Kinloch.

Beinn nam Beathrach; 582m; (OS Sheet 49; NM752572)

The loftiest hill in the part of Morvern west of the A884 is Beinn nam Beathrach. It is conveniently located immediately above the high point of the road, which is also the logical starting place, and the summit can be reached very quickly from here.

There are two prominent gullies on the south-east flank, and one should follow the more northerly until it peters out near the gentle upper slopes. The summit itself lies 1km further on, beyond a confusing area of knolls and undulations. There is a trig point and a good view down Gleann Dubh, the west branch of Gleann Geal.

Beinn nam Beathrach throws out a lengthy west ridge over a number of lesser tops, and this can be followed as far as Beinn Iadain if desired.

An Sleaghach; 513m; (OS Sheet 49; NM764434); *the spear*

The south-east corner of Morvern is a little-known area. No roads penetrate it and human habitation is scarce. The less interesting inner moorland is, however, cradled by a rim of higher ground, which contains a number of summits perched above the coastline. This rim drops steeply to Loch Linnhe and the Sound of Mull beyond. Indeed it is from the Oban to Craignure ferry that this part of Morvern is seen to best advantage, rising as it does straight from the sea. While An Sleaghach is the

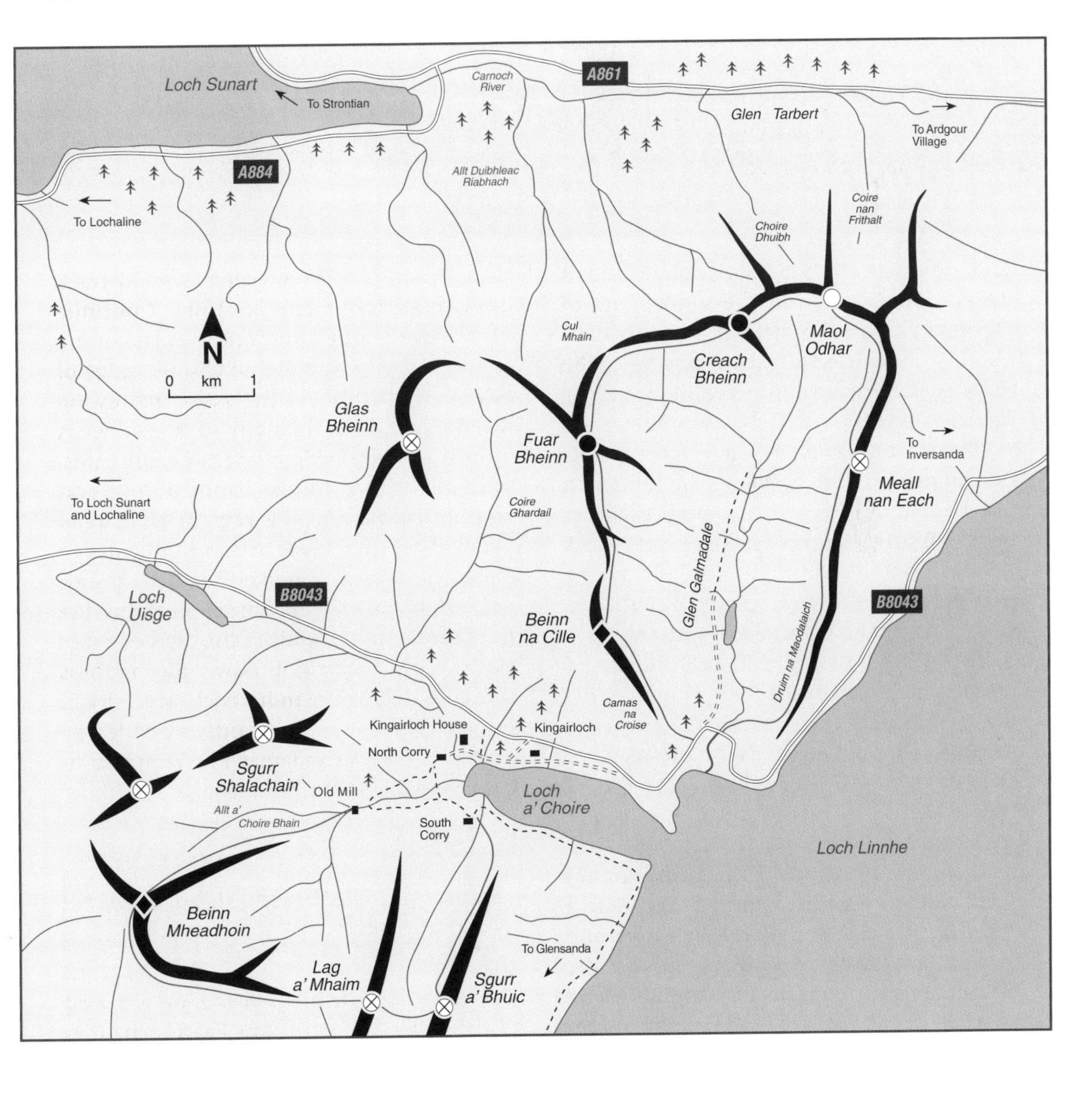

Approaching Beinn Mheadhoin from Kingairloch

highest of the hills, it is recommended a number of the neighbouring tops be taken in as well in order fully to appreciate the surroundings.

The starting point is the road-end near the sprawling farm buildings of Achranich near the head of Loch Aline. A track follows the winding Rannoch River to Loch Tearnalt and its crannog (a fortified island, partly natural and partly artificial). Continue across featureless ground by a path which leads to the top of the pass to Eignaig, then bear off to the south, either skirting or including Meal a' Chaorainn (481m). The final ascent to An Sleaghach is steep and craggy. The summit is perfectly situated on the bend of the ridge to give splendid views over an amazing amount of sea up both Loch Linnhe and the Sound of Mull, and across to the islands of Lismore and Mull. Head west, either over or round Mam a' Chullaich (462m) by traversing it on the south past a beautifully perched fold which holds the loch of the same name.

There is a sudden change in rock scenery from granite and rough ground to basalt and smoother slopes as one reaches and ascends the rocky plug of An Dunan. Also known as the Table of Lorne, this is an unusual feature formed from a flat-lying layer of basaltic lava, and is prominent in views from the south, such as that from Oban. Continue to Glais Bheinn (479m), gentle and grassy on all sides except the north-east where there is an escarpment above Coire Slabhaig, then descend directly to Achranich over Ghoirtean Dearg.

Beinn Mheadhoin; 739m; (OS Sheet 49; NM799514); *middle hill*

A miniature mountain range, Beinn Mheadhoin lies just opposite the north tip of the island of Lismore. Its north-eastern side comprises a series of deep albeit mainly grassy corries which lie above Loch Linnhe's Loch a' Choire bay. Separating the corries are ridges offering straightforward walking which can be combined as desired to give shorter or longer excursions offering better entertainment than is suggested by a distant view of this rather flat-topped hill. Rather dull slopes fall away south-west to the Lochaline road in Gleann Geal, whilst the south side of the hill (or what is left of it) houses the colossal Glensanda super-quarry, a scene of devastation generally only visible from Loch Linnhe or the mainland around Oban. As the hill has a number of subsidiary tops, several route choices are possible.

The best line of ascent is the ridge leading directly to the summit from behind the ruined Old Mill beside the Abhainn na Fearna, south-west of Kingairloch House. There is limited parking on the nearby public road, and the road leading to Kingairloch House is private, so it is better to approach by either the path or the track which lead down into Kingairloch House's policies from the woods above.

Sign-posted paths lead through the grounds, past some estate cottages, then through fields towards the Old Mill and an area of decaying forestry beyond. The ridge is quite steep in its lower reaches, but its few rocky outcrops are easily turned. It soon levels off and gives a fine situation, gullies falling off to either side. Follow the ridge (with one short step high up) without difficulty to the summit. There is a great panorama over Loch Linnhe and across to the mainland.

It is well worth continuing south-east along the ridge above Coire nan Each and Coire Riabhach to the Lag a' Mhaim col as this gives an amazing aerial perspective of the Glensanda super-quarry. This enormous excavation is simultaneously awful in its ugliness and fascinating in its vastness. From the col, descend to South Corry either down the Meall an Doire Dhuibh ridge or (better) over the top of Sgurr a' Bhuic (569m). Follow the path back to the public road.

The hill can also be climbed by ascending either Sgurr Shalachain (531m) or Meall na Greine (604m), leaving the road between Loch Uisge and Tigh Ghardail, where there is a footbridge over the Abhainn Coinnich. If one starts from higher up the burn, then there is no bridge, but no trees to overcome either: correspondingly it will be further to walk to complete the circuit. This gives a pleasant and undulating way to the summit by the Bealach a' Choire Bhain. The return should then be made by one of the other routes already described.

Beinn na Cille; 652m; (OS Sheet 49; NM854542); *hill of the church*

Fuar Bheinn; 766m; (OS Sheet 49; NM853564); *cold hill*

Creach Bheinn; 853m; (OS Sheet 49; NM871577); *plunder hill*

Located in the extreme north-east corner of Morvern, these high peaks have more in common with their rugged Ardgour neighbours than the undulating moorland of the area's other hills. They are bounded on the north by Glen Tarbert and the A861, on the south by Loch a' Choire and the B8043 from Kingairloch to Lochaline, and on the east by Loch Linnhe. The western sides are not of interest, being generally featureless and grassy. To the north, Coire nam Frithalt and Choire Dhuibh are quite rough and have craggy flanks that offer a little less by way of good rock than may appear from below.

It is in the south and south-east that the most interesting features are to be found, and the horseshoe round of the hills from the foot of Glen Galmadale (to the north-east of Loch a' Choire) gives what is certainly the best excursion Morvern has to offer. Indeed, the approach to Glen Galmadale along the road by the shore of Loch Linnhe from Inversanda is spectacular in its own right.

There is barely room for the single-track road to squeeze in between the sea on one side and the line of plunging red granite rocks of the Druim na Maodalaich on the other. These crags are rather broken by

Looking west from Beinn Resipol over Claish Moss and Loch Shiel to Rum

basalt dykes forming tree-lined gullies and chimneys, providing a better habitat for the resident goats than for climbers.

The round of these hills is best started just a little south of Camas na Croise, whose name (and that of the hill above) is one of the few obvious remnants of what was an ancient Christian settlement. Beinn na Cille's south slopes provide a straightforward line of ascent, easing off just before the summit. The east sides of this hill and Fuar Bheinn contain a number of steep little corries, but the rock is discontinuous and vegetated, and grassy spurs give direct access to the hills above. The crags and corries of Beinn na Cille look quite spectacular when the sky is gloomy or the high tops are obscured, however it is easy to pick a line through the difficulties either to Beinn na Cille or to its col (the Bealach Coire Mhic Gugain) with Fuar Bheinn. This route is better avoided in low mist when such an approach would be a bit of a lottery. Beinn na Cille enjoys very fine views down Loch Linnhe and across to Lismore and to the mainland. In particular, Ben Cruachan is well seen from here on a good day.

Gain Fuar Bheinn by its broad south ridge from the Bealach Coire Mhic Gugain. It is worth staying on the east side to appreciate the drop into Glen Galmadale. From a little north of its summit, one can turn and drop west to take in the outlying Glas Bheinn (623m) as an optional extra, or even as a circuit in its own right from Tigh Ghardail. It is better however to continue to Creach Bheinn by descending to the featureless Cul Mhaim, then climbing the stony ridge to the top. Creach Bheinn has a better view than Fuar Bheinn, being in a position to see both up and down Loch Linnhe. A curiosity hereabouts is what the OS map calls a 'camp' just north of the summit. It is in fact a substantial dry-stone walled enclosure, reputed to have been a lookout post from the time of the

Napoleonic wars, but more likely to have been built by the OS itself in the course of survey work. The descent is marvellous, a narrow section of ridge leading to the col with Maol Odhar (794m). Pass over that hill's rounded top and head south over Meall nan Each (591m) and down the Druim na Maodalaich, enjoying the ridge's superb position above Loch Linnhe. The ridge can be followed back to the foot of Glen Galmadale and the starting point.

Creach Bheinn can be most swiftly ascended from Glen Tarbert. Fuar Bheinn may also be included in this excursion with a little less logic and a less aesthetically pleasing result than the route just described, as its northern side offers far less excitement than does Glen Galmadale. The Carnoch River can be a serious obstacle after rain, particularly in its lower reaches. The ridges either side of Choire Dhuibh provide good approaches above the short and steep broken buttresses on their eastern sides. To ascend both hills, tackle the western ridge from a point 2km up Glen Tarbert from the head of Loch Sunart by ascending roughly through a native birch wood. Easy slopes and ridges then lead to Creach Bheinn. A quick return can be made from Fuar Bheinn to the Glen Tarbert road by making a descending traverse from the Cul Mhaim to pick up the Allt Duibhleac Riabhach. Follow this back down to the Carnoch River.

Beinn Resipol; 845m; (OS Sheet 40; NM766654); *hill of the horse farm* or *hill of the homestead*

Beinn Resipol is a fine prominent peak, the area's only Corbett, and the only hill of consequence in Sunart. It will certainly be a high priority for visitors. Best seen from the west shore of Loch Shiel, from the waters of which it rises as a graceful cone, the hill lies equidistant between Loch Sunart and Loch Shiel, and only marginally closer to Strontian than to Salen. Just as Sunart is the south-west appendage of Ardgour, so Beinn Resipol is linked to Sgurr Dhomhnuill by a long and undulating moorland ridge which never falls below 300m. It is in this area that both the older and the more recent mine workings are located.

The west side of Beinn Resipol falls away quickly to lower ground, which is boggy in places and is presently heavily forested. Part of it comprises the Claish Moss Nature Reserve on the south shore of Loch Shiel, the moss being a raised mire with intriguing growth patterns. The hill's isolated location makes it a splendid viewpoint, and the ascent should be saved for a good day. The upper slopes are quite rocky in places, but on closer acquaintance prove to be lacking in difficulty, although some scrambling can be enjoyed on the way to the summit. If transport can be arranged, the traverse of the hill makes an excellent outing.

The preferred starting points are either the Resipole campsite, or Ariundle just north of Strontian. Resipole lies on the shores of Loch Sunart 5km west-south-west of the summit, and from here a track starts up the east bank of the Allt Mhic Chiarain. This soon becomes a path that follows the burn through pretty oak and birch trees before becoming indistinct once open ground is reached. Either follow the burn to Lochan Bac an Lochain and climb directly to the summit, or ascend the slightly easier upper section of the west ridge.

The 'traditional' route is rather longer and follows the old miners path which leads to the disused shafts in Coire an t-Suidhe. This path starts near Ariundle at NM813633, and can be reached either on foot from Strontian or by parking near the road junction around the 100m contour. A cairn marks the high point of the path after 3km. An old coffin route comes over here from Loch Sunart and drops to Loch Doilet and Loch Shiel. It was formerly used by funeral processions to reach Loch Shiel's ancient burial site on Eilean Fhianain. Just beyond the cairn, leave the path and head west over Meall an t-Slugain, climb the jaw-breaking slopes of Leac Chlann Domhnuill Mhic Dhughaill and follow Beinn Resipol's east ridge to the summit. The wonderful view extends from Ben Nevis to Ben More on Mull and on along the western coastline all the way to the jagged outline of the Skye Cuillin, as well as to the wild tangle of the closer peaks of Ardgour and Moidart either side of the trench of Loch Shiel. A further approach can be made from almost due south of Beinn Resipol, starting up the access track to the isolated house at Ardery. Pass over Beinn an Albannaich (572m), reach Lochan Bac an Lochain and climb to the top as previously described. There is also potential for seekers of adventure to approach from the north by canoe across Loch Shiel providing they are prepared to take on the extensive forestry on this side of the hill.

Ben Laga; 512m; (OS Sheet 40; NM645621); *hill of the hollow*

This rugged little hill rises steeply above Loch Sunart some 5km west of Salen, and is the highest point in the eastern part of Ardnamurchan. It is easiest to climb it from the south-west, starting from Laga on the shore of Loch Sunart, 2km east of Glenborrodale. A rough track leads steeply up from Laga to join the Glenborrodale to Acharacle path. Take this track for approximately 1km before heading east directly to the summit. The upper part of Ben Laga is covered in deep heather and numerous large boulders, generally making for very tough and slow going. The summit gives a bird's eye view up and down Loch Sunart.

Ben Hiant; 528m; (OS Sheet 47; NM537632); *holy mountain*

An old volcano, Ben Hiant is the highest hill in Ardnamurchan, and is both shapely to look at and a delight to climb. It is located on the south side of the peninsula, 8km west of Glenborrodale and 5km east of Kilchoan. Its southern flanks rise steeply from the Sound of Mull, the lower slopes forming a very precipitous and bold headland called MacLean's Nose. The northern aspects are mainly grassy, the higher corries dropping towards flatter tree-planted moorland. The name may well come from associations with the Cladh Chiarain (*graveyard of Ciarain*), located at Camus nan Geall south-east of the hill. St Ciarain died and was buried in Ireland in 584 AD. This site was dedicated to him, possibly by St Columba of Iona, and a tall pillar of reddish stone marks the spot.

The quickest and most pleasant ascent of Ben Hiant is from the north-east, starting just before the high point of the road from Glenborrodale to Kilchoan, a short track on the east side of the road providing parking space. The old Kilchoan footpath leads up on to the grassy north-east ridge, along the east flank of which is a basalt escarpment. Bearing out the popularity of Ben Hiant, a path has formed above this escarpment, giving an enjoyable and undulating ridge walk to the top. There is short pull to the summit itself, avoiding a steep north-facing basalt buttress on its south-east.

The summit view is excellent, particularly to the south and east up Loch Sunart, across to Mull and into the lonely recesses of Loch Teacuis backed by the hills of Morvern. To the west there is the fine sight of the Inner Hebrides and on a good day you will see some of the outer isles as well. The hill can also be climbed from the west, starting 2.5km before Kilchoan. A track leads across grazing land and a path heads to the foot of Beinn na h-Urchrach, which is really the north-west shoulder of Ben Hiant. Pick a line over this (avoiding some small crags on the lower slopes) and climb steadily to the summit.

Beinn na h-Urchrach (376m) (*the hill of the throw*) takes its name from an incident in 1266 AD, when Muchdragon, the feared Viking leader of the time, was seeking to foist his unwanted attentions on the wife of a local man. Knowing that this could only mean death for him, the husband fled with Muchdragon in hot pursuit. It was on

Ben Hiant from Cladh Chiarain to the south-east

the slopes of Beinn na h-Urchrach that the desperate husband flung his axe at Muchdragon, with fatal consequences for the fast-closing Viking.

Beinn na Seilg; 342m; (OS Sheet 47; NM456642); *hill of hunting*

Despite its lack of height, the ascent of Beinn na Seilg is essential for the visitor to Ardnamurchan. Its location just 5km from the Point of Ardnamurchan gives it an absolutely stunning view to be lingered over, there being no hill of greater height between it and the shores of the Atlantic, and it is undoubtedly the most interesting peak in this area. On a good day you will look out to Eigg and Muck and the Cuillin of Rum and Skye, as well as south to Mull and even as far as the Western Isles. An added benefit is the comparative lack of effort required to reach the summit.

The hill itself is shapely, rising above rough moors 3km west of Kilchoan, and there is a lot of bare gabbro on it. The prehistoric remains of Greadal Fhinn (*Fingal's griddle*) are located on the lower eastern slopes. Artefacts have been found here, and there is a chambered cairn, the sepulchre of which has been dated to 2000 BC.

The simplest route is to ascend the hillside from the shore at Ormsaigmore to Lochain Ghleann Locha, and then to climb easy slopes to the summit. A slightly shorter but generally boggier and duller approach can be made over the moorland from the east by Lag a' Choire.

There are a number of crags in a superb location high on the western side of the small peak to the north of the main summit. These give some enjoyable rock climbs on excellent gabbro. The older climbs are in the lower grades, whilst there are now some more modern and harder routes as well.

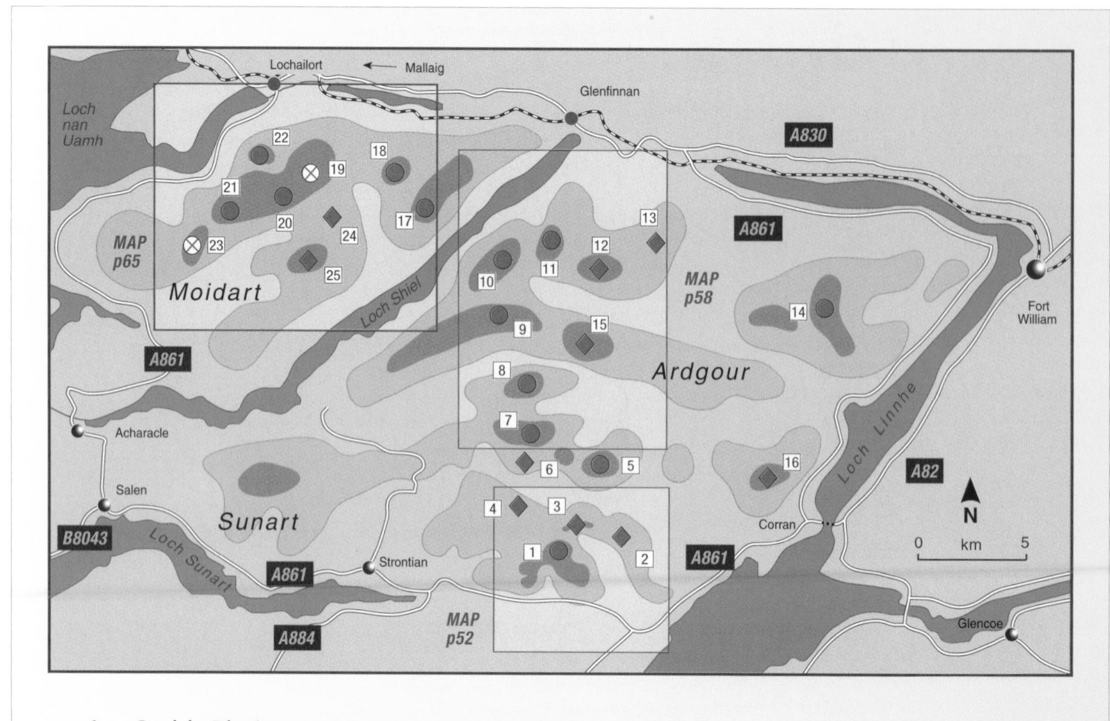

1.	Garbh Bheinn	885m	C	p52
2.	Sgorr Mhic Eacharna	650m	G	p54
3.	Beinn Bheag	736m	G	p54
4.	Sgurr nan Cnamh	701m	G	p55
5.	Beinn na h-Uamha	762m	C	p56
6.	Sgurr a' Chaorainn	761m	G	p56
7.	Sgurr Dhomhnuill	888m	C	p57
8.	Carn na Nathrach	786m	C	p59
9.	Stob a' Bhealach an Sgriodain	770m	C	p61
10.	Sgurr Ghiubhsachain	849m	C	p62
11.	Sgorr Craobh a' Chaorainn	775m	C	p62
12.	Meall nan Damh	723m	G	p63
13.	Glas Bheinn	636m	G	p63
14.	Stob Coire a' Chearcaill	771m	C	p63
15.	Stob Mhic Bheathain	721m	G	p65
16.	Druim na Sgriodain	734m	G	p65
17.	Beinn Odhar Bheag	882m	C	p66
18.	Beinn Mhic Cedidh	783m	C	p66
19.	Druim Fiaclach	869m	O	p68
20.	Sgurr na Ba Glaise	874m	C	p68
21.	Rois-Bheinn	882m	C	p68
22.	An Stac	814m	C	p68
23.	Sgurr Dhomhuill Mor	713m	O	p70
24.	Croit Bheinn	663m	G	p71
25.	Beinn Gaire	666m	G	p71

Chapter 2

Ardgour and Moidart

Jim Teesdale

Garbh Bheinn from Coire an Iubhair

Many hillwalkers think that the West has no mountains of note south of the Mallaig road. Such a mistaken belief should be quickly dispelled by the sight of the jagged outline of Ardgour (*the point of the goats*) which dominates the view across Loch Linnhe from the Ballachulish Bridge. The peaks of both Ardgour and Moidart are of the grassy, craggy nature so characteristic of this region of Scotland, and they are much more impressive than one would think from their comparatively low altitude, being both rugged and shapely. These areas give some superb walking in remote glens and on rough ridges where spectacular lochs and extensive views are constant companions. The tussocky and boggy nature of the lower slopes makes the terrain amongst the toughest and most challenging in Scotland.

Along with Sunart, Ardgour is surrounded by four major lochs, Linnhe, Eil, Shiel and Sunart, and the low-lying glens between them. Given that the watershed between Loch Eil and Loch Shiel is less than 20m above sea level, it would not take much to return Ardgour to being part of a large and highly complex island as indeed it was until the close of the last Ice Age. The interior is deserted, being mainly mountainous deer forest in the hands of sporting proprietors. The only roads are round the perimeter, much of which is given over to forestry, besides which there is some crofting and farming. Such habitation as exists is found along the sparsely populated shores of the sea lochs. Strontian is Ardgour's largest village, and is a good base from which to tackle the southern hills. The most convenient access for the bulk of visitors is by the Corran Ferry across the fast-moving tidal narrows of Loch Linnhe 13km south of Fort William. Arriving at Ardgour village gives one the uplifting feeling of visiting an island, although the penalty of missing the last ferry is a slow drive of some 70km round by Fort William and the head of Loch Eil.

Ardgour's fine glens display the east-west pattern typical of the Western Highlands. They represent the beheaded parts of Scotland's original drainage system, cut off by the over-deepening along the Great Glen fault. On the area's southern boundary, the dramatic and steep-sided Glen Tarbert carries the A861 from Ardgour village to Strontian and Loch Sunart. At its watershed is the Allt a' Chothruim (*the burn of the balance*), which runs off Garbh Bheinn. In the past, it would sometimes flow east to Loch Linnhe and at other times west to Loch Sunart, depending on the state of the gravel accumulation at its delta. Construction of the road has tamed this vagary, but the name 'corrom' is preserved as the scientific term for a delta watershed.

From Inversanda low down Glen Tarbert, Coire an Iubhair leads to the foot of Garbh Bheinn, the area's outstanding peak and one of the finest mountain rock climbing venues on the mainland. The next glen north is Glen Gour, which rises from Sallachan just south of Ardgour village. At its top is a narrow pass, from where one can descend west towards Strontian through the beautiful natural woodlands of the Ariundle Nature Reserve. The Reserve occupies some 70 hectares, and is a remnant of the oak forest that once stretched along Britain's west coast from Sutherland to Devon. Oak grows on south-facing slopes, and pine and birch on north-facing ones. There are also ash, wych-elm, alder and willow, as well as some 250 species of lichens, mosses and liverworts.

Between Glen Gour and Ardgour village, the main road runs round a flat area made up of a great accumulation of gravel washed out of a glacier which formerly ran down Loch Linnhe. The lochans just west of the village are probably the sites of large masses of ice which were engulfed in the gravel, subsequently melting away to leave pits or 'kettle holes' which are now filled with water. Further north of Ardgour village, the Cona Glen and Glen Scaddle converge near Loch Linnhe's Inverscaddle Bay. These glens are attractively wooded, particularly in their lower reaches, and after their initial parting they run almost parallel to one another for many kilometres above their confluence.

One can continue from the watershed of Glen Scaddle past Lochan Dubh and through the superb scenery of Mam Beathaig into forested Glen Hurich and down to Polloch, an isolated forestry village close to Loch Shiel. From the upper Cona Glen a path heads north to Callop on the Mallaig road just east of Glenfinnan, or alternatively one can reach Glen Hurich by climbing south over the Bealach an Sgriodain. These glens culminate in the high and very fine peaks of Sgurr Dhomhnuill and Sgurr Ghiubhsachain amongst others. Some ascents in Ardgour require lengthy approaches as a number of the hills are quite remote, with plenty of scope for through walks or back-packing trips.

Moidart (*heights of the sea spray*) lies to the west of Ardgour, between it and the Atlantic coast. The two areas are separated by the glacially formed trench of Loch Shiel, at 28km one of the longest and narrowest lochs in the country. The view of the loch from Glenfinnan is justly famous, the sheet of water and its pine-tree clad island being symmetrically framed by the slopes of Sgurr Ghiubhsachain and Beinn Odhar Mhor. At the loch's narrows near its foot is Eilean Fhianain. It was once home to St Finnan, who came from Ireland to spread Christianity in its infancy. He died in 575 AD, but his chapel was rebuilt in the 16th century, and his bronze Celtic hand-bell is said to rest still on the altar. After his death the island became a destination for pilgrims and a sacred burial ground.

West of Moidart one finds Ardnamurchan, the Sound of Arisaig and the sea lochs of Loch Moidart and Loch Ailort (from the Norse, meaning *deep fjord* or *eel fjord*). Moidart's northern edge is the narrow and delightful Loch Eilt (*loch of the hinds*). The 'road to the Isles' (known to non-romantics as the A830) follows the north shore, and the railway the south one. It is an area of great contrasts and considerable historical resonance. The south-west corner is beautifully wooded and cultivated near the River Shiel which flows from Loch Shiel for a few brief kilometres down to Loch Moidart.

Acharacle makes a good centre for exploration, a straggling village spread out along the open shore at the foot of Loch Shiel. It is *Torquil's ford*, named after the Viking who came to plunder Moidart, and whom Somerled, the first Lord of the Isles, eventually drove from Scotland. The rest of the area is wild and mountainous, what little habitation exists being scattered along the roadside between Acharacle and Lochailort. Moidart's highest peaks have a wild feel to them, but most of them are easily reached from the road. They form a lengthy barrier south of Loch Eilt, with Rois-Bheinn overlooking Loch Ailort, and Beinn Odhar Bheag standing above the head of Loch Shiel. South of the mountains lies the surprisingly fertile Glen Moidart, the river of the same name flowing west through woods of lime, beech and chestnut into the sea. One can drive up this glen for a few kilometres, and a path extends into its now deserted upper reaches.

As with the Glenfinnan area, Moidart is closely associated with Prince Charles Edward Stuart. After landing at Loch nan Uamh the Prince came south to stay at Kinlochmoidart House for several days before MacDonald clansmen rowed him from Dalilea up Loch Shiel to Glenfinnan, where he raised his standard. A line of beech trees stands in the meadow on the north side of Loch Moidart, commemorating the Seven Men of Moidart, who were the original followers to accompany the Prince from France. One tree has never flourished, and it and another have been replaced after suffering storm damage in 1988. In the heart of the region is the seldom visited and extremely remote Glen Aladale, which descends from the back of Croit Bheinn and Beinn Mhic Cedidh to about half way along the west shore of Loch Shiel. Once this glen was an important base of the MacDonalds, but those days are long gone. Reputedly treasure is buried there. The instructions are to dig where seven rounded peaks can be seen, so take a shovel when you visit!

Access and Transport

By road: for Ardgour, drive to Nether Lochaber on the A82 and take the Corran Ferry across Loch Linnhe to Ardgour village. Alternatively, continue to Fort William and follow the A830 towards Mallaig, turning off at the head of Loch Eil on to the A861. This leads to Ardgour village, then follows the coasts of Ardgour and Moidart to rejoin the A830 at Lochailort. For Moidart, stay on the A830 to Glenfinnan and Lochailort.

By bus: Acharacle to Fort William via Lochailort; Lochaline to Fort William via Carnoch Bridge and the Corran Ferry; Fort William to Mallaig; Acharacle to Mallaig; Kilchoan to Fort William via Strontian and the Corran Ferry (Shiel Buses, tel: 01967-431272). Fort William to Stronchreggan via Banavie (Highland Country Buses, tel: 01397-702373). Fort William circular route by Kinlocheil, Ardgour village and the Corran Ferry (Royal Mail, tel: 08457-740740).

By rail: the nearest stations are at Fort William, Glenfinnan and Lochailort.

By ferry: the Corran Ferry (vehicles and foot passengers) between Nether Lochaber and Ardgour village (the Highland Council, tel: 01855-841243). The Council also runs a passenger ferry between Camasnagaul and Fort William (tel: 01397-772483). Boat cruises on Loch Shiel from April to October (Loch Shiel Cruises, tel: 01687-470322).

Accommodation and Information

Hotels and guesthouses: Onich, Ardgour village, Strontian, Salen, Acharacle, Glenuig, Lochailort and Glenfinnan.

Independent hostel: Glenfinnan Sleeping Car (tel: 01397-722295)

Campsites: Resipole Farm (tel: 01967-431235); Strontian

Tourist Information Centres: Strontian (tel: 01967-402381) (Easter - October); Fort William (tel: 01397-703781).

Maps

Ordnance Survey: 1:50,000 Landranger sheets 40 (Mallaig and Glenfinnan) and 41 (Ben Nevis); 1:25,000 Explorer sheets 390 (Ardnamurchan) and 391 (Ardgour and Strontian).

Principal Hills

Garbh Bheinn; 885m; (OS Sheet 40; NM904621); *rough hill*

Situated in the south-east corner of Ardgour, Garbh Bheinn instantly strikes a chord with all who enjoy Scotland's more mountainous peaks. Its crenellations are obvious when looking across Loch Linnhe from near Onich, and even from this distance it excites interest and invites exploration of its bold ridges. The tremendous east face is the main attraction for rock climbers, and at close range this side of the peak provides a magnificent array of buttresses, gullies, towers and slabs.

Garbh Bheinn certainly is a rough hill, with much bare rock on its flanks. It rises relentlessly from the Glen Tarbert road, and its east face lies up Coire an Iubhair, reached from Inversanda. The corrie approach gives a fine appreciation of the peak, although one has to walk up the path for 3km before the face itself is revealed. Rising directly to the summit is the 300m high Great Ridge, left of which is the sheer South Wall which holds the bulk of the harder rock climbs. Right of Great Ridge is the dark gash of Great Gully, and right again are the towers of Pinnacle Ridge.

The flat summit is perched on top of the South Wall, with a subsidiary top (862m) a few hundred metres west. North of the summit a broad rocky ridge passes over Pinnacle Ridge and the slabby North-East Buttress (which is marked by a small

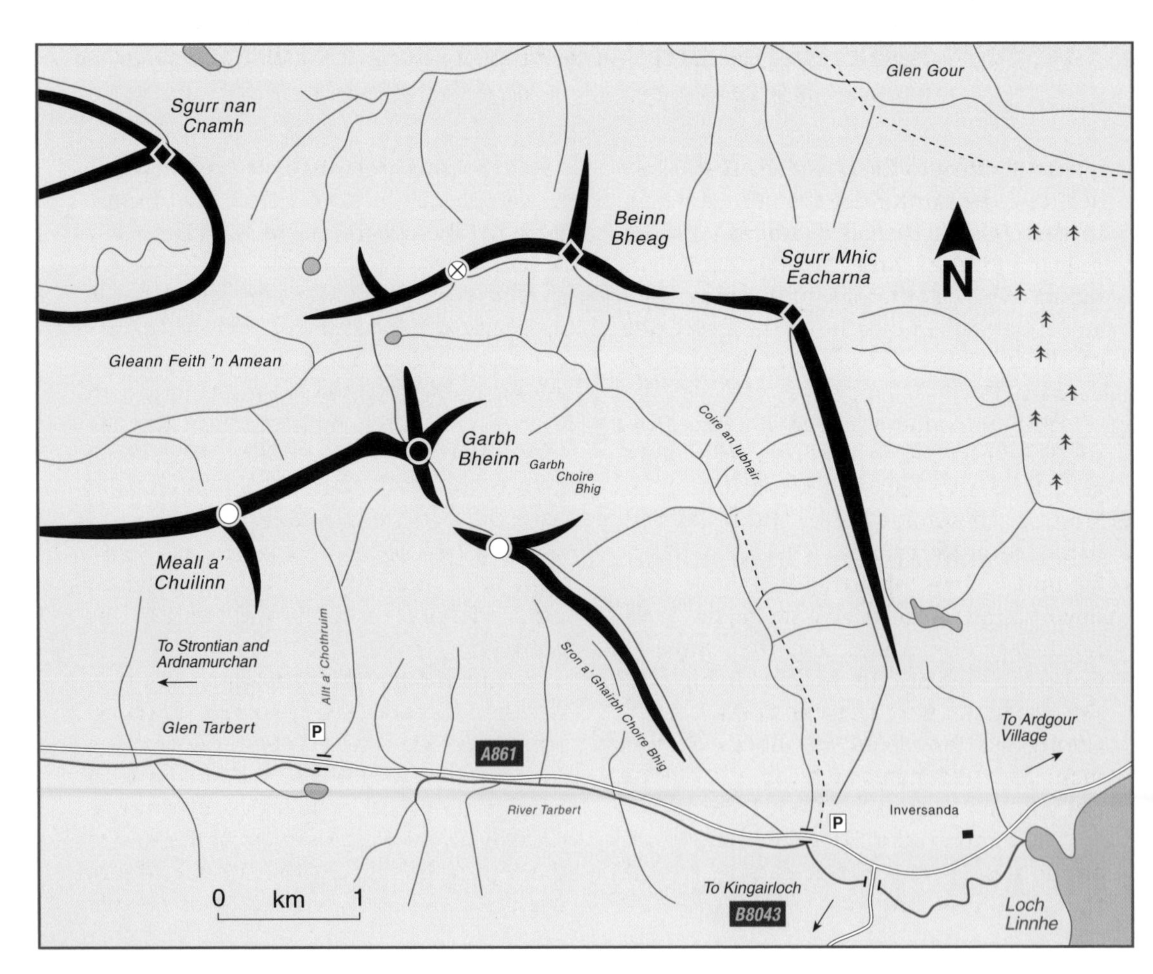

The remote north side of Garbh Bheinn seen from Loch nan Dearcag

quartzite cairn) to the top of the North Face buttress. The north ridge then drops steeply to the classical U-shaped Bealach Feith 'n Amean (536m) and Lochan Coire an Iubhair. On the other side of this pass, Coire an Iubhair is hemmed in by the lower hills of Beinn Bheag (736m) and Sgorr Mhic Eacharna (650m).

From its summit Garbh Bheinn drops south by easy rocky steps to a col (748m), and then rises again south-eastwards to Sron a' Ghairbh Choire Mhoir (823m), named after the extremely craggy corrie on its north. This top extends a long ridge down to the bridge at Inversanda, its slabby north-east face completing the cirque of Coire an Iubhair. On Garbh Bheinn's far side, its south-west ridge encloses Coire a' Chothruim (unnamed on the Landranger map) and terminates at Meall a' Chuilinn (687m) 2km away above Glen Tarbert.

Three routes start from the foot of Coire an Iubhair. There is a large parking area off the road near the old bridge over the Abhainn Coire an Iubhair, with some popular camping spots nearby. The obvious way is up the corrie path on the east side of the stream. While the path has been improved in its lower reaches, it is muddy and boggy in places still. It leads to the foot of the great east face, which teases as it gradually reveals itself the further one gets up Garbh Choire Mor. From the junction of the two main streams at the foot of the face, climb up the side of the southern burn by a faint path through huge boulders. This gives a first rate view of Great Ridge and the South Wall as one nears the 748m col, at which turn right and make the final pull to the summit.

Scenic though the corrie approach is, it is somewhat enclosed, and the ridges on either side give more interesting walking with better views of the surrounding hills. A faint path follows the ridge of Sron a' Gharbh Choire Bhig for most of the way to the top of Sron a' Ghairbh Choire Mhoir, starting about 100 metres west of the old bridge. It gains height gradually up broken rocky outcrops. From the top there is a grand view across the intervening corrie to the South Wall. Descend to the 748m col, and climb to the summit as before. The excellent Druim an Iubhair approach is partly described in relation to Beinn Bheag and Sgorr Mhic Eacharna.

The full circuit of the corrie is the best outing that Ardgour has to offer, although it is recommended to go in an anti-clockwise direction as the line on the north side of Garbh Bheinn can be difficult to find in descent. The north ridge rises very steeply from the Bealach Feith 'n Amean, with the rocky North Face buttress on the left and a straight gully on the right. In between is a steep slope of mixed rock and grass. This is an easy scramble in summer, although under snow (when Garbh Bheinn should be treated with some care) the gully can be straightforward and may be easier. Above this, clamber up rough but easy-angled rock to the little cairn on top of North-East Buttress, then continue over the top of Pinnacle Ridge to the summit.

A fourth approach is that from the south, climbing directly and unaesthetically up Coire a' Chothruim. Start from the bridge near the high point of the Glen Tarbert road and follow an occasional path up the east bank of the burn. Bear north-east from the burn to reach the 748m col, and climb to the summit. Although the shortest way, this route is a noted flog, but one often used by climbers approaching the South Wall.

The beautifully striped quartzo-felspathic gneiss of Garbh Bheinn's east face gives superb rock climbing. The rock is wonderfully rough, often contorted to form pockets and flakes, making excellent holds. The classic route is *Great Ridge* (300m Difficult 1897), the striking feature which rises from Coire an Iubhair and tapers as it nears the summit. First climbed by J.H.Bell and W.Brown, it gives good solid climbing in a tremendous situation. In winter it is grade III, but this is perhaps an under estimate for typical conditions. Left of *Great Ridge*, and separated from it by *South-East Chimney*, is the popular South Wall, a two-tiered crag holding the finest climbs, with routes to suit all tastes.

The Upper Tier contains the hardest routes, of particular note being *Kelpie* (45m E6 1986), and *White Hope* (55m E4 1984) which ascends the very steep lightly coloured central wall. Just to the right is *Excalibur* (75m Hard Very Severe 1972) with its unlikely leftward traverse on the lip of a roof. Like *Scimitar* (105m Very Severe 1952), *Butterknife* (105m Very Severe 1956) climbs both tiers on 'the best rock in the world', following an obvious and continuous fracture line from the right end of the lower tier. Right of *Great Ridge*, *Great Gully* is another classic of a previous era which is climbed, albeit rarely, in both summer (270m Very Difficult 1946) and winter at grade IV (1969).

Pinnacle Ridge appears spectacular from below, but is in fact no more than an easy scramble. North again, beyond a slanting gully, the broad mass of North-East Buttress is broken into four tiers. The best climb on it is *Route II* (330m Very Difficult or Severe 1939). The grade depends on which variations are taken. It ascends the Leac Mhor, the great smooth slab at the centre of the buttress. There are a number of other less significant crags and climbs on the hillsides around Coire an Iubhair.

Sgorr Mhic Eacharna; 650m; (OS Sheet 40; NM928630)

Beinn Bheag; 736m; (OS Sheet 40; NM914635); *little hill*

The ridge of Sgorr Mhic Eacharna and Beinn Bheag forms the north-eastern retaining wall of Coire an Iubhair. The hills give an excellent walk either on their own or as a means of approach to Garbh Bheinn. Their main attribute is the constantly changing but always excellent view of Garbh Bheinn's east face. Start at the car park at the foot of Coire an Iubhair, from where Beinn Bheag is seen as an obvious and pointed peak at

Beinn na h-Uamha from Sgurr Dhomhuill

the head of the glen.

This is a sight that may be familiar to filmgoers who recognise the setting of some of the scenes in the 1990s blockbuster '*Rob Roy*'. Follow the corrie footpath for a short way, then climb steeply to gain the gentle Druim an Iubhair. This is followed north to the summit of Sgorr Mhic Eacharna with a rough section just below the top. As well as being a fine vantage point for Garbh Bheinn there are good views north to other parts of Ardgour, Sgurr Dhomhnuill in particular, and to the back of Ben Nevis. Descend westwards to a col, the Bealach nan Airigh, (c480m) and climb Beinn Bheag. Continue west for 1km along the narrow ridge, passing over Beinn Bheag's prominent and finely formed lower summit (696m), which projects from the ridge rather like a chimney from the roof of a house.

Descend a gully of steep grass and scree some 400 metres west of this top, and drop to the beautiful Lochan Coire an Iubhair in the Bealach Feith 'n Amean. Either climb Garbh Bheinn's north ridge as already described, or return to the road down Coire an Iubhair. It is also possible to carry on westwards over Sgurr nan Cnamh (701m) and thus to complete a fine traverse through to Strontian.

Sgurr nan Cnamh; 701m; (OS Sheet 40; NM886643); *peak of the bone*

Sgurr nan Cnamh is the western outlier of Beinn Bheag, from which it is some 3.5km distant. Other than this link, the hill stands by itself in a great sweep of rough moorland between Sgurr Dhomhnuill and the Carnoch River in Glen Tarbert. The north flanks above Lochan a' Chothruim are craggy and steep, while its other sides are easier-angled but still quite complex.

The most straightforward route of ascent follows the track described for Sgurr Dhomhnuill up the Strontian Glen from

Sgurr a' Chaorainn and Beinn na h-Uamha

Ariundle through the beautiful oak forest of the Nature Reserve. Take the right-hand branch where the track forks, emerging at an attractive meadow. Pass the ruined farm at Ceann a' Chreagain, cross the Strontian River, and climb the hill's north-west ridge over Sgurr a' Bhuic (461m). After passing over a reasonably level section of ground, climb steadily to the summit. The return will usually be by the same route. Sgurr nan Cnamh can also be taken in as a continuation of the traverse of the Beinn Bheag ridge. The ground between the two hills is very wild, particularly near the scenic Lochan nan Dearcag, from where one gets an unusual view of Garbh Bheinn.

Beinn na h-Uamha; 762m; (OS Sheet 40; NM917664); *hill of the cave*

Sgurr a' Chaorainn; 761m; (OS Sheet 40; NM895662); *peak of the rowan*

These hills form an attractive and lofty twin-topped ridge lying south-east of Sgurr Dhomhnuill and north of the watershed between Glen Gour and the Strontian Glen. Although their heights are almost identical, Beinn na h-Uamha's extra metre gives it the kudos of Corbett status and as such it is more frequently climbed. Lying 7km up Glen Gour, it is seen from Sallachan as a prominent peak with much bare rock on its eastern flanks. Take a rough track (not marked on the Landranger map) up the south side of the glen. This passes Loch nan Gabhar, an interesting and marshy spot, the level of which was once raised by an ill-founded dam whose ruins can still be seen a little upstream from the old road bridge.

The loch is a good place for ornithology, and there are traces of an ancient fort on its north shore. Cross the River Gour above its confluence with the Allt an t-Sluichd, and ascend Beinn na h-Uamha's long and rocky south-east ridge, passing the obvious knoll of Stob an Uillt Dharaich at mid-height. On the south side of this ridge are some gneiss crags, such as the interestingly-named Wooden Gazelle Crag, on which a few short climbs are to be found. The summit gives a good view of Sgurr Dhomhnuill.

The broad summit ridge falls to a col (556m), then rises steeply to Sgurr a' Chaorainn some 2.5km further west. This makes a logical continuation, but at the same time takes one further from Sallachan. The descent from Sgurr a' Chaorainn should therefore be either south-east into Coire na Laire (unnamed on the Landranger map) and so back to Glen Gour, or, if transport has been arranged, by continuing the traverse to Ariundle. Drop to the Bealach Mam a' Bhearna (493m) (the col with Sgurr na h-Ighinn) and into the Strontian Glen, to pick up the path and track through the woods of the Ariundle Nature Reserve to the public road 2km north of Strontian. One can return to Ardgour village by bus if necessary.

For those intent on climbing Sgurr Dhomhnuill as well, Sgurr a' Chaorainn should be included; however height can be saved by bypassing it on its north side on the way from Beinn na h-Uamha. Traverse initially from the 600m contour on Sgurr a' Chaorainn, then slant downwards to the top of the obvious gorge high up Gleann Mhic Phail. A further cunning line in ascent can be used north-westwards to largely avoid Sgurr na h-Ighinn. Beinn na h-Uamha can also be climbed by its north-east ridge from upper Glen Scaddle, giving a good circuit if combined with Sgurr Dhomhnuill's north-east ridge.

Sgurr Dhomhnuill; 888m; (OS Sheet 40; NM889678); *Donald's peak*

The highest mountain in Ardgour, Sgurr Dhomhnuill is a graceful and pointed peak and a conspicuous landmark, its southern spur giving it a slightly lopsided appearance from some angles. The north face is steep and rocky and the hill is very remote, centrally situated above the head of the Strontian Glen and Glens Gour, Scaddle and Hurich, so an ascent will involve a long day from any direction. Sgurr Dhomhnuill is clearly visible from many surrounding points, although it is from Strontian that one gets the closest view of the peak, 10km distant at the head of the Strontian River.

Sgurr Dhomhnuill has three principal ridges. The north-east one drops into upper Glen Scaddle. The south one links it to the outlying Sgurr na h-Ighinn (766m) and then descends to the Bealach Mam a' Bhearna, the col with Sgurr a' Chaorainn. The north-west ridge descends to the Glas Bhealach, rises to the former Corbett Druim Garbh (803m), and then continues west as a broad and featureless shoulder for 5km to the top of the road from Strontian to Loch Doilet. Druim Garbh also connects with Carn na Nathrach (786m) to its north.

The best starting point is 2km north of Strontian, from the car park just inside the Ariundle Nature Reserve. The walk up the glen through the Reserve's beautiful pine and oak woods is an excellent start to the day. The forest track climbs gradually, rising high above the Strontian River, and gives fine views of Sgurr Dhomhnuill ahead. Take the track's left fork, then follow a path to the abandoned mines by the Feith Dhomhnuill. Cross the stream and climb easily onto Druim Leac a' Sgiathain, Sgurr na h-Ighinn's narrow west spur. Climb this, including Sgurr na h-Ighinn or bypassing it by a rising traverse along a broad terrace on its north-west face. From the 682m col reach Sgurr Dhomhnuill's summit trig point up the south ridge in two steps.

An alternative route from the Strontian side starts at the top of the Loch Doilet road. This gives a shorter walk and saves on ascent, although it lacks the delightful approach up the Strontian Glen. Instead, traverse a lochan-studded ridge to Druim Garbh, then descend to the Glas Bhealach. Scramble up Sgurr Dhomhnuill's rocky north-west ridge to the summit. It is more interesting to make a circuit of this by leaving the road at around c280m and traversing east, past Bellsgrove Loch. Descend to

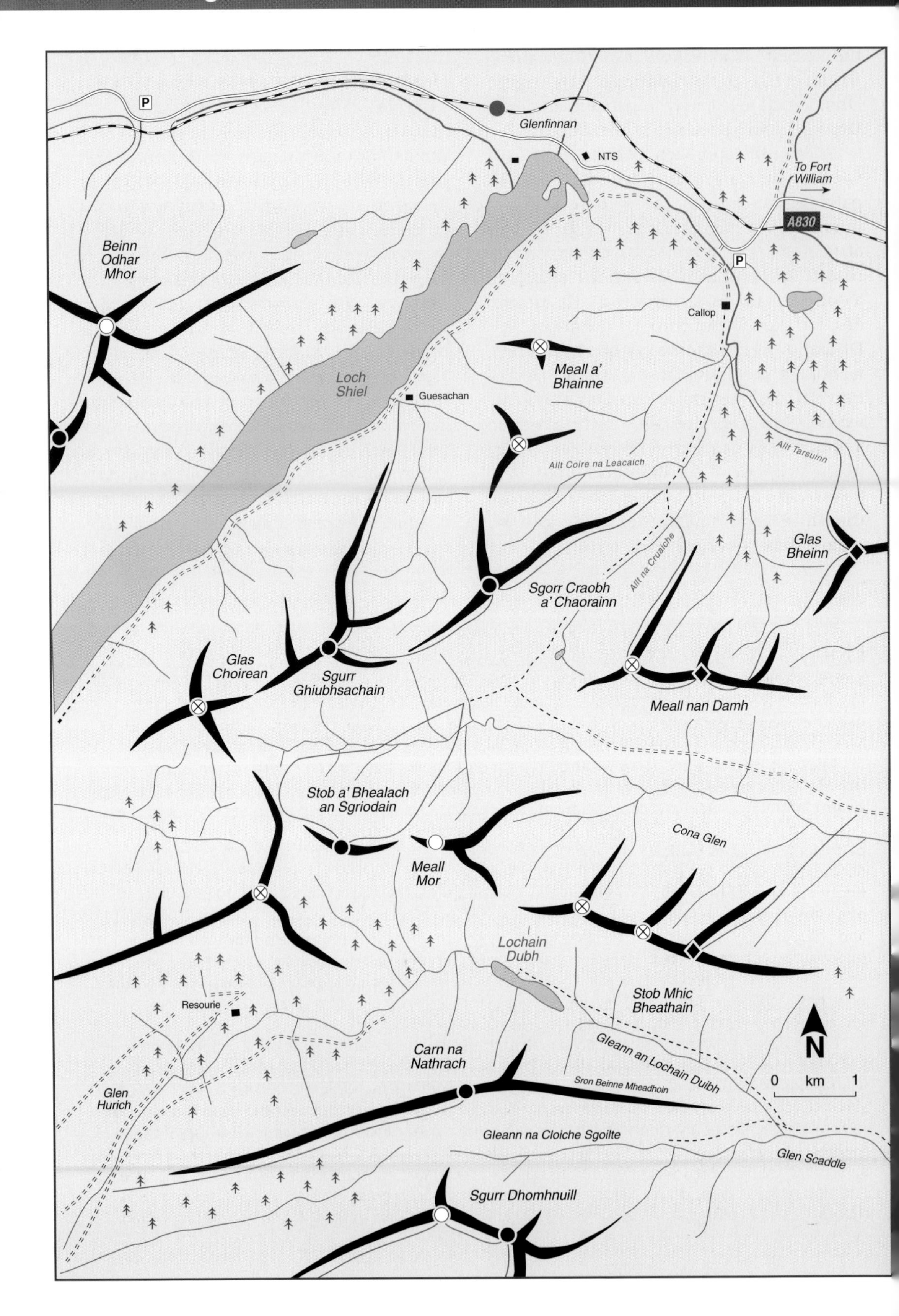

P
Glenfinnan
NTS
To Fort William
A830
P
Callop
Beinn Odhar Mhor
Loch Shiel
Guesachan
Meall a' Bhainne
Allt Coire na Leacaich
Allt Tarsuinn
Allt na Cruaiche
Glas Bheinn
Sgorr Craobh a' Chaorainn
Glas Choirean
Sgurr Ghiubhsachain
Meall nan Damh
Stob a' Bhealach an Sgriodain
Meall Mor
Cona Glen
Lochain Dubh
Stob Mhic Bheathain
Resourie
N
0 km 1
Carn na Nathrach
Gleann an Lochain Duibh
Sron Beinne Mheadhoin
Glen Hurich
Gleann na Cloiche Sgoilte
Glen Scaddle
Sgurr Dhomhnuill

the old Feith Dhomhnuill lead mines, climb Druim Leac a' Sgiathain to Sgurr Dhomhnuill as before, and return down Druim Garbh to the top of the road.

A lengthy approach can be made up Glen Scaddle, involving 11km of tracks and paths to the foot of Sail a' Bhuiridh, the mountain's north-east ridge. The glen offers attractive camp spots in its upper reaches near to where it trifurcates. The ridge gives a direct and pleasing line of ascent. For those continuing from Sgurr Dhomhnuill to Carn na Nathrach, the link is not entirely obvious as Druim Garbh's north ridge, Sron Doire nan Cabar, is awkwardly blind in descent and is better avoided. Instead, drop north-east then north from the Glas Bhealach, and slant below Druim Garbh's craggy face to cross the Allt Gleann na Cloiche Sgoilte as high up as can be managed.

Carn na Nathrach; 786m; (OS Sheet 40; NM887699); *peak of the adder*

Situated in the remote heart of Ardgour and just north of Sgurr Dhomhnuill, Carn na Nathrach is awkward of access and somewhat overshadowed by neighbouring hills, so it sees relatively few ascents. Although known as Carn na Nathrach, this name may relate to the summit area only. Beinn Mheadhoin is the name given to the lengthy ridge which stretches from lower Glen Hurich to the upper reaches of Glen Scaddle, and the peak does indeed appear as the 'middle hill' when viewed from either end. The western arm rises to a minor top (602m), above the craggy northern shoulder of Creag Bheag.

The shortest approach is from Kinlochan, just east of Loch Doilet on the

Culicoides impunctatus - The Highland Midge

For the summer visitor to the Scottish Highlands, the most significant 'fly in the ointment' is likely to be the presence of the Highland midge (*Culicoides impunctatus*; to the Gael, *meanbh-chuileag*, or *tiny fly*). Rather like drops of mist, midges are seldom experienced in small numbers, but will tend to gather cloud-like round their prey. The effects of biting vary between mild irritation to mental torture. Most people experience annoyance and some mild swelling, but some suffer more than others.

Midges thrive on a mixture of warmth and moisture; like tourists, their peak season is between late May and mid-September, when countless thousands will rise from the vegetation to nibble and swarm around the wary and the unwary alike. This undoubtedly takes a significant bite out of the income generated by tourism in the Highlands. The northern and western hills and glens form a particularly favoured habitat, with a measure of respite being available in some parts of the drier north-east. Peak midge times are in the morning and in the evening during calm, humid weather. Bright conditions, heavy rain, wind and altitude (midges are less prevalent above about 600m) all offer some protection, although biting may occur at any time in daylight hours when it is overcast and still. Those of an academic persuasion may care to note that they are being bitten by female midges, blood being an essential part of the reproduction diet after the laying of the initial batch of eggs, to provide protein to form yolk for further batches. Humans and other large animals are thus eagerly sought after during the breeding season. For further information see George Hendry's succinct and accessible *Midges in Scotland* (Mercat Press 1996).

Certain preventative measures can be taken; despite past government research, eradication is sadly not an option. Not visiting at all would be an overly radical choice. Repellents are available from outdoor suppliers, of greater or lesser chemical strength and effect. Citronella candles, wood smoke and smoke coils can work well in confined spaces. Midge netting over the head is useful but claustrophobic. Some try cigarette smoke, seeing the risk of cancer as a small price to pay if the midges are kept at bay. Dark clothing is more attractive to midges. Many home made remedies exist, some of them may even work. To limit the damage naturally, camp in places exposed to any breeze, and not next to water; do not linger in bogs, heather or long grass; keep your head down on still mornings and evenings; and keep moving or go indoors (as appropriate) if you are getting bitten.

Sgurr na h-Eanchainne and the Corran Ferry

road from Strontian to Polloch. Glen Hurich is heavily forested, so the route of access to the hillside will depend on the state of felling and replanting at the time. Take the forest track up the glen, crossing the bridge over the river after 2km, and continue up the track on the north side of the Allt an Dubh Choirein. 1km after the bridge, use forest rides to gain the finely situated nose of Beinn Mheadhoin, and follow this steadily for the next 4km over a few knolls and along a final narrow and rocky section of ridge to the summit.

Descend either by re-tracing your steps, or alternatively by returning to Point 602m and heading north down the rough ridge on the west flank of the deep gully below. The Glen Hurich forest track leads back to the start. Ascents from the east are rare, due to the 11km approach that is required up Glen Scaddle. Nonetheless, the shapely ridge of Sron Beinne Mheadhoin gives a direct and worthwhile route to the summit from that side, and a bicycle would make access easier.

Combining Carn na Nathrach with its neighbours is not without brutality. From the south there is a steep and strenuous grassy plod from upper Gleann na Cloiche Sgoilte to the top. The north side is very craggy, so it is best to head west from the summit for just under 500 metres, then to descend directly and roughly by the side of a burn (the Uillt Choire Ghlais-mhoir) to just below the west end of Lochan Dubh in upper Glen Hurich. The scenery around the loch and in the upper part of the glen is spectacular, the River Hurich twisting between the steeply craggy hillsides that enclose it, although the blanket forestry has disguised some of the finer features for the time being.

Stob a' Bhealach an Sgriodain;
770m; (OS Sheet 40; NM874727);
peak of the pass of screes

This hill has suffered an identity crisis in recent years, having formerly been known as Druim Tarsuinn (*transverse ridge*), a name that in fact applies to the north-west spur only. The present name has been adopted, the Bealach an Sgriodain being the pass between the summit and Druim Tarsuinn over which an old route goes from the upper Cona Glen to Glen Hurich. It is a remote peak, forming the culminating point of the long and undulating ridge between Glen Scaddle and Cona Glen, and it can be approached from a number of directions. The shortest route is from the Callop turn-off, 2.5km east of the Glenfinnan Visitor Centre, and this allows the hill to be combined with its northern neighbour Sgurr Ghiubhsachain.

Follow the well-made Allt na Cruaiche path past Callop cottage, taking care after rain when the Allt Coire na Leacaich can be difficult to cross. Pass over the col (the Feith nan Con) above the upper Cona Glen, and descend to cross the Cona River at a prominent loop. Climb by the west bank of a stream to the Eag a' Mhadaidh Ruaidh, the col west of Meall Mor (759m), from where a rough ridge leads west over knolls to the summit of Stob a' Bhealach an Sgriodain. Sgurr Ghiubhsachain dominates the peak but there is a fine sense of space looking down the length of Glen Scaddle to the back of Ben Nevis. Descend to the Bealach an Sgriodain, easily identified by an incongruously solitary iron gate, the surrounding fencing having long since rusted and disintegrated. Drop north-east to pick up a poor path in the upper Cona Glen which leads indistinctly back to the Feith nan Con. If the Cona River is high then it will be necessary to use this route in ascent as well.

Glen Hurich is not so obvious a starting point, so this approach is used less often. Leave the Strontian to Loch Doilet road at Kinlochan, and follow the forest track to above Resourie bothy, itself a useful base in this remote corner. A bicycle will ease access considerably. Gain the edge of the forest from the track, then climb steeply north-east below Teanga Chorrach and cross upper Coire an t-Searraich to the Bealach an Sgriodain 500 metres north-west of the summit.

The approach to the hill by Glen Scaddle or the Cona Glen is a lengthy 14km and is better combined with a camping trip. If ascending from the west end of Lochan Dubh, follow the forest fence up and westwards, then gain the Eag a' Mhadaidh Ruaidh, the col west of Meall Mor, and continue to the summit as before. The south-east ridge of Meall Daimh (575m) is another option which can give some decent scrambling from near Resourie. The link to Sgurr Ghiubhsachain is simpler. Continue north-west over Druim Tarsuinn to the Bealach Scamodale, then avoid Meall nan Creag Leac (755m) by a traverse into the corrie on its south-east side. Climb to the col west-south-west of Sgurr Ghiubhsachain, a gentle ridge then leading over some outcrops to the pointed summit.

Maclean's Towel

There is a striking set of waterfalls to be seen at the back of Ardgour village on the slopes of Druim na Sgriodain. MacLean's Towel, as it is known, cascades down water-worn slabs for a considerable distance, and is clearly visible from the A82 to Fort William as it passes Nether Lochaber. Although never steep, these falls make a fine sight, especially after rain, and it is reputed that the MacLeans, lairds of Ardgour since the 15th century, will continue their tenure until such time as the falls run dry. As with the Towel, this old prophecy still 'holds water', although the MacLeans' land-holding is much reduced these days. Note that the policies of Ardgour House lie beneath the Towel, so one should obtain prior permission if intending to enter the grounds.

Sgurr Dhomhnuill from Sgurr Craobh a' Chaorainn

Sgurr Ghiubhsachain; 849m; (OS Sheet 40; NM875751); *peak of the little pinewood*

Sgorr Craobh a' Chaorainn; 775m; (OS Sheet 40; NM895758); *peak of the rowan tree*

Dominating north-west Ardgour, Sgurr Ghiubhsachain is a shapely and conical peak which is well-known as the leftmost of the pair of picturesque mountains seen in the superb view down Loch Shiel from Glen Finnan. Its western flanks and the slabby faces of its lower north-east tops drop steeply into the waters of the loch. The hill stands at the head of the lonely Cona Glen, but is very accessible from the north, from which direction most ascents are made. A good traverse can be made by its north and east ridges to include Sgorr Craobh a' Chaorainn, its north-eastern outlier. Sgurr Ghiubhsachain is quite a rocky mountain, and deserves respect in winter conditions.

Start from the Callop turn-off 2km east of the Glenfinnan Visitor Centre, and cross the bridge over the Callop River. It is not possible to cross the river any nearer to its outflow, as it is deep and sluggish. Walk along the forest track for 5km by the shore of Loch Shiel to Guesachan cottage, which was home in the 19th century to Margaret Cameron, a staunch member of the Free Church. She would walk each Sunday to worship at the floating church near Strontian, a round trip of some 56km.

Gain Druim an Sgriodain, Sgurr Ghiubhsachain's sharp and alluring north ridge, by following the Allt Coire Ghiubhsachain until one can traverse north-west above the craggy lower spur. The ridge is delightfully located and can give some scrambling as one climbs over the knoll of Meall a' Choire Chruinn (634m). It ends abruptly, a brief horizontal section leading to the large summit cairn and an excellent view down the length of Loch Shiel and to Ardgour's wild interior.

Descend south-east by steep slabs and grass to gain the broad and rounded shoulder which trends round the head of Coire Ghiubhsachain. Sgorr Craobh a' Chaorainn's south-west ridge is easy-angled until the final section. A steep face lies west of the rocky summit which can give a good scramble if tackled direct, while any difficulties can be avoided on the east side. The quickest return is made by continuing north-east over the plug of Meall na Cuartaige (566m) to pick up the Allt na Cruaiche path which leads back to Callop. Alternatively, a worthwhile extension can be made by heading north from Sgurr Craobh a' Chaorainn and continuing over Meall Doire na Mnatha and Sgorr nan Cearc (668m). Descend by the Allt Coire na Leacaich and follow the Allt na Cruaiche path to Callop. One can include Meall a' Bhainne (559m) as well, although some care is required to circumnavigate the slabby crags hereabouts.

Return to the road down the Allt na h-Airigh. These northern tops are attractive hills with much bare rock, and some short climbs have been recorded on a long crag just west of Meall Doire na Mnatha. A good circuit can also be made by climbing Sgorr Craobh a' Chaorainn, then continuing over Sgurr Ghiubhsachain to Stob a' Bhealach an Sgriodain. Return from the upper Cona Glen as described for that hill.

Meall nan Damh; 723m; (OS Sheet 40; NM919745); *hill of the stag*

Glas Bheinn; 636m; (OS Sheet 40; NM938758); *grey green hill*

These two hills lie south-west of the head of Loch Eil. Although much lower than their neighbours, Meall nan Damh has a finely shaped twin-topped summit ridge, whilst Glas Bheinn is altogether more rounded and looms large in any view westwards from the shore of the loch. They can be linked in an enjoyable round from Callop, from where they can also be combined with Sgorr Craobh a' Chaorainn. Meall nan Damh's best feature is the rough north-east ridge leading to its slightly lower west top (722m).

Approach from Callop and the Allt na Cruaiche path, taking this through a beautiful mix of old woods to just after the crossing of the Allt Coire na Leacaich. Ford the burn, now known as the Allt Feith nan Con, although this may be difficult after heavy rain. Climb the undulating north-east ridge over some brief steeper sections to the west top. A pleasant 1km walk eastwards leads to the true summit. There are good views of the surrounding peaks at the head of the lonely Cona Glen.

Continue east from the summit for just over 500 metres until it is possible to trend north-east down a grassy spur which drops to the Glas Bhealach, the col (c480m) with Glas Bheinn, and climb that hill by its easy south-west side. Glas Bheinn's summit lies a short distance north-west of the trig point, and from here one can enjoy a fine prospect down the length of Loch Eil. Descend north-west to the densely planted lower slopes. Fortunately the forest rides are reasonably helpful, and at the time of writing the upper one accessed down the side of the Allt Tarsuinn can be followed quite directly to the Allt na Cruaiche about 500m south of Callop. It may be hard to cross the river here, but if necessary the east bank can be followed back to the bridge just before the turn-off from the public road.

Stob Coire a' Chearcaill; 771m; (OS Sheet 41; NN017727); *peak of the circular corrie*

Many walkers and climbers on Ben Nevis will have admired this generally cetaceous hill due to its prominent summit crag. Stob Coire a' Chearcaill lies within the angle created by Loch Eil and Loch Linnhe, and is the highest and most interesting point in the range of rounded tops north of the Cona Glen. The attractive Coire a' Chearcaill lies on its east side, and there is a good view of it up Gleann Sron a'

Chreagain from the southern outskirts of Fort William. The A861 from Kinlocheil to Ardgour follows the edge of the hill on its north and south-east aspects, and access can be taken from a number of points.

The shortest route starts on the north side, 1.5km east of Duisky. From just east of the forestry (NN024769), find a way through open woodland before following the line of an old fence up bland slopes to the stony upper part of the Braigh Bhlaich ridge. This leads over one minor undulation to the summit, set back a few metres from the trig point. The view is panoramic, although the foreground is a little lacking in interest. From close range the summit crag is less appealing than it appears from a distance. An obvious rough track also allows access from Blaich, a few kilometres east of Duisky. It makes for easier going up the lower slopes, but lengthens the excursion as it reaches the Braigh Bhlaich ridge some 3.5km from the summit.

The Gleann Sron a' Chreagain approach gives a more enjoyable outing, albeit a longer one. From Fort William, one can use the passenger ferry to Camusnagaul, and walk along the road for 3.5km to Stronchreggan. If driving round, take care not to block the passing places hereabouts as they often double as local accesses. Follow the path on the north side of the Abhainn Sron a' Chreagain through fields for just under 2km. There is a gate slightly above the path and shortly before the last fence. Go through this to gain the open hillside. Climb this northwards to reach the Braigh Bhlaich ridge and follow this to the summit as before. Another relatively short approach leaves the road at its high point 500 metres north-east of the Conaglen House entrance. Climb north to near

Castle Tioram

Castle Tioram (*dry land*) is situated on the shore of Loch Moidart. It is in a delightful setting of islands, crags, woods and water, and is well worth a detour. It is reached from Shiel Bridge, a narrow road going north for 4km along the east bank of the river to end at Doirlinn. The castle stands on a rocky knoll, which at high tide becomes a little island, but which at low tide can be reached across the sandy isthmus. Behind it are the wooded shores of the beautiful Eilean Shona straddling the mouth of Loch Moidart. The castle was built in 1353 by Amie, the divorced wife of the first Lord of the Isles, and became the stronghold of the MacDonalds of Clanranald.

Many are the dark stories and colourful tales about Castle Tioram. An oozing brownish stain near the door of the dungeon is locally attributed to blood from a murder of unusual atrocity rumoured to have been committed there. It may not actually be blood, but it looks like it, and the stain will not go away. Cromwell's men occupied the castle in the 17th century, but it was never taken by siege despite a few attempts. It met its end at the hands of its owner in 1715. Allan Mor, the then clan chief, was to join the Jacobite rising under the Earl of Mar. However he doubted the Earl's wisdom and ability and believed that he would not return from the campaign. Not wishing the castle to fall into the hands of the Campbells, he had it burnt. His fears were well founded as he died at the Battle of Sheriffmuir. What presently remains is a roofless and deteriorating pentangular structure with high curtain walls and a turreted keep.

In the 1990s it acquired a new owner, millionaire businessman Lex Brown, whose company, Anta Estates, has plans to restore and convert it 'sympathetically' for habitation again. At the time of writing, those proposals are lodged in the mire of the planning process. A public enquiry was held in June 2001, and upheld Historic Scotland's objections. Revised applications have been submitted, but the outcome is unknown at the time of publication, and the whole matter could well end up before the Scottish courts. Clearly there is a major decision to make. Should our heritage, once ruined, simply be left to decay until all that is left is a pile of boulders, albeit romantic ones, or should we encourage preservation and progress when the price will be a complete transformation of so historic a site? Can these very different agendas be addressed simultaneously? An emotive question, and no doubt the reader will shortly be able to contemplate the answer, whatever it is, by the quiet Atlantic waters of Loch Moidart.

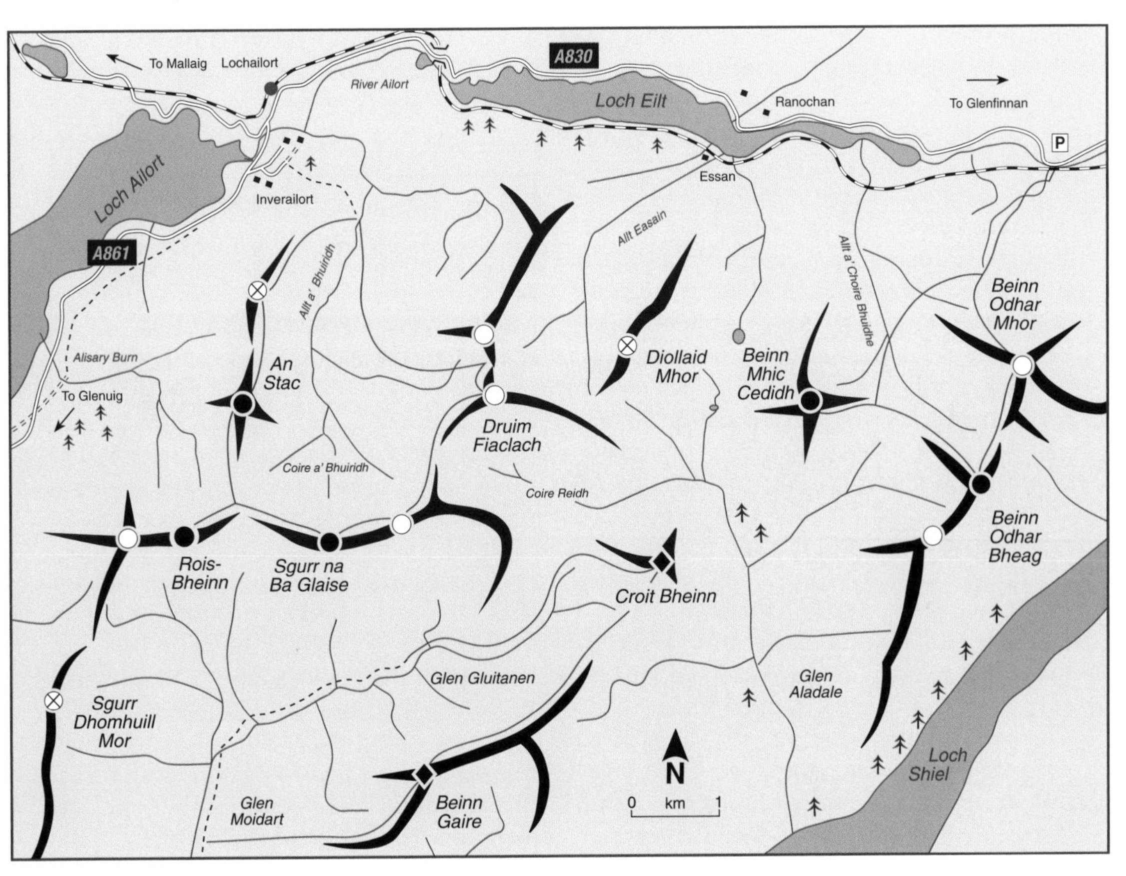

Lochan na Cruaich and follow the south-east ridge to the summit, on terrain similar to the Braigh Bhlaich ridge. It gives a pleasant circuit if combined with Sgurr an Iubhair (722m) to the south-west.

Stob Mhic Bheathain; 721m; (OS Sheet 40; NM914713)

With its central location, and being situated about as far away from any road as is possible, Stob Mhic Bheathain is the remotest hill in Ardgour. It is the most notable summit on the lengthy and interesting ridge of lower hills lying between the upper Cona Glen and Glen Scaddle, and can be reached by the track up either glen with an approach of about 10km. Both glens are quiet places and worth exploring, but Cona Glen is preferred for this hill as it brings its fine northern features into play. Stob Mhic Bheathain has three summits, the south-east one being marginally the highest, and well-defined ridges fall north-eastwards from each into the Cona Glen.

The lower section of the glen is very pretty, with a variety of natural woodlands. The main obstacle is likely to be crossing the Cona River, which is difficult after heavy rain. The ridge leading directly to the summit is enjoyable, and any craggy sections can easily be avoided. The central ridge, the Sron a' Choire Leith Mhoir, is the finest and still perfectly straightforward. Stob Mhic Beathain gives a good view of the higher Ardgour peaks further inland. One can continue along the undulating ridge over Meall Mor (759m) to Stob a' Bhealach an Sgriodain 5.5km further west.

Druim na Sgriodain; 734m; (OS Sheets 40 and 41 NM978656); *ridge of the screes*

Rising to the west of Ardgour village, Druim na Sgriodain forms a beautiful backdrop to the prospect across Loch Linnhe from Nether Lochaber and the 'mainland'. Due to its comparatively low altitude, however, it receives fewer ascents than it does admiring glances from waiting ferry passengers. Druim na Sgriodain is the rounded top west of Coire Dubh. Rising to the east is the pointed Sgurr na h-Eanchainne (730m) (*peak of the brains*), often given the name Beinn na Keil, which is certainly more pronounceable but refers in fact to the less significant north top of the hill. Sgurr na h-Eanchainne is very prominent in views up and down Loch Linnhe anywhere between Lismore and Fort William. It is slightly lower but a better viewpoint than Druim na Sgriodain and a more attractive objective, so it is best to traverse Coire Dubh in order to take in both summits.

Start just beyond the Clan MacLean burial ground 2km north of Ardgour village at NN014658 and climb Sgurr na h-Eanchainne's obvious south-east ridge. This rises steeply at first, and there are some minor outcrops to avoid. The ridge relents briefly at c470m, where one crosses the head of a gully before making the final pull to the summit. There is a trig point and a superb view up the Great Glen, across to Glen Coe and Ben Nevis, and down to the waters of Loch Linnhe far below.

Druim na Sgriodain lies 2km further west, and is reached by a broad and gently undulating grassy ridge. Pass Lochan a' Choire Dhuibh and climb easily to the flat summit which is tucked beyond two lochans. The prospect is less fine, although there are interesting views up Glen Gour and Glen Scaddle to Ardgour's higher hills. In descent, follow Druim na Sgriodain's south-east ridge to c600m. Drop south to 500 metres west of Sallachan to avoid the crags of Creag Shallachain, and walk 4km along the road back to Ardgour village. Alternatively, continue down the ridge, trending east into lower Coire Dubh, and come down the side of MacLean's Towel above Ardgour House. Providing the burns are not too high, one can cross Coire Dubh to descend by the north-east side of the Towel to a mast. Return directly across undulating ground to the road just over 1km north of the village.

Beinn Odhar Bheag; 882m; (OS Sheet 40 NM846778); *little dun-coloured hill*

Beinn Mhic Cedidh; 783m; (OS Sheet 40 NM828788); possibly *hill of the son of Katie* or *Kitty*

Along with its subsidiary Beinn Odhar Mhor (870m), Beinn Odhar Bheag dominates the horizon beyond the west end of Loch Eil, and it can look much higher than it really is when its slopes and gullies are flecked with spring snow. In keeping with its name, Beinn Odhar Bheag is the less bulky of the two, although it is the higher. Its principal features are the craggy hillsides sweeping continuously down to Loch Shiel, capped by great rock faces on its south-east flanks at the head of Coire nan Clach. The lower buttresses dominate the view of the hill from Glenfinnan, with its top just visible above. Beinn Mhic Cedidh is a rounded and relatively reclusive peak lying about 2km west of and separated from Beinn Odhar Bheag by the deep Bealach a' Choire Bhuidhe. It has a narrow and rocky north ridge, which gives the hill a steep and rugged appearance when seen from the Mallaig road on the north shore of Loch Eilt.

These hills are frequently climbed together from the north, starting about 2km east of Loch Eilt. One used to be able to take access by stepping stones some 200 metres above the mouth of the Allt Lon a' Mhuidhe. However, a small dam at the west end of the loch has slightly raised the water level, such that the burn is now deep and sluggish and the surrounding ground tends to be water-logged, so the stepping stones are no longer advised. Instead, leave the A830 from a lay-by at NM857813. Cross the Allt Lon a' Mhuidhe by a bridge, then cross the railway line with care.

Jim Teesdale

The west ridge of Sgurr na Ba Glaise

Climb west-south-west up fairly easy ground to a skyline notch (NM845807) (c400m) on the lower slopes of the north-north-west ridge of Beinn Odhar Mhor. This ridge is better defined in its upper reaches and gives a straightforward route to the summit. Beinn Odhar Bheag is 1.5km further south, reached by a pleasant and initially broad ridge, which drops to c750m and then becomes narrower and quite rocky. There are no difficulties, and one soon reaches the pointed summit and its appropriately small cairn. It is a magnificent viewpoint above the narrow waters of Loch Shiel. Its more rounded subsidiary, Beinn a' Chaorainn (773m), lies 1km to the south.

Beinn Odhar Mhor can also be approached from Glenfinnan village by crossing the potentially awkward Abhainn Shlatach. Beyond this one follows the Allt na h-Aire to Lochan nan Sleubhaich, passing over Point 529m to gain the top by Sgurr Boinaid. Another possibility is from 3km further west of the village, by crossing the Allt a' Ghiubhais. Both routes are quite rough and require good judgement in assessing the best line up complicated hillsides. Avoid the shore of Loch Shiel as it gives heavy going and is compromised by forestry.

To reach Beinn Mhic Cedidh, descend Beinn Odhar Bheag's grassy north-west ridge to the Bealach a' Choire Bhuidhe (c480m) and grind steadily uphill. The summit is an excellent place from which to admire the east end of the Rois-Bheinn ridge. It is quite possible for fit and experienced walkers to continue west to climb the Rois-Bheinn hills as well in a long day. This involves another big drop to an unnamed col (c350m) followed by a rising line to about the 570m contour on the south slopes of Diollaid Mhor (751m), itself worth including if energy levels allow. Traverse south across a flat corrie floor to gain the narrow east ridge of Druim Fiaclach above a craggy nose. Follow the ridge for 1.5km to the summit of Druim Fiaclach, where one picks up the route described later for Rois-Bheinn.

The best line back to the road from Beinn Mhic Cedidh is not obvious. One can drop down the attractive north ridge to reach a bridge (unmarked on the Landranger map) over the Allt a' Choire Bhuidhe 500m south of the railway line. A rough all-terrain vehicle track goes under the railway at NM840814, and the Allt Lon a' Mhuidhe can be crossed after 1km of boggy and tussocky ground. Follow the road back to the start. An invitingly direct return lies along the railway line, and through two tunnels, but this is illegal and this guide cannot endorse such a risky act of trespass.

The most economical option is to return from Beinn Mhic Cedidh to the Bealach a' Choire Bhuidhe, then to drop into Coire Buidhe. Cross the burn at around c320m, and make a gradual rising traverse north-eastwards across grassy slopes. Pass over a little spur, then continue the traverse to the skyline notch on the north-north-west ridge of Beinn Odhar Mhor mentioned earlier, and return to the starting point.

The only recorded climbing on these hills is found on Beinn Odhar Mhor's south-east slopes, located at about 400m on the spur called Sgurr an Iubhair. Shiel Buttress gives a number of rock climbs, the best of which is the eponymous *Eyrie* (130m Hard Very Severe 1973). Access to the crag is difficult due to the remote location and rough terrain, so the best option may well be to approach by canoe.

Druim Fiaclach; 869m; (OS Sheet 40; NM792792); *toothed ridge*

Sgurr na Ba Glaise; 874m; (OS Sheet 40; NM770777); *peak of the grey cow*

Rois-Bheinn; 882m; (OS Sheet 40; NM756778); *horse hill*

An Stac; 814m; (OS Sheet 40; NM763793); *the stack*

The Rois-Bheinn hills form an imposing group of rough peaks located on the northern edge of Moidart near the head of Loch Ailort. They are linked by a rocky, twisting and constantly interesting ridge. Climbed together these four hills and their intervening tops give one of the best mountain traverses in this part of the country. Rois-Bheinn is a particularly outstanding mountain, rising directly from the western seaboard and commanding a stunning view across the Sound of Arisaig and out to the islands of Rum and Eigg in particular.

The prominent and isolated cone of An Stac lies due south of the head of Loch Ailort. South of An Stac is a col (559m), beyond which a short slope rises to the wide and grassy Bealach an Fhiona (701m) separating Rois-Bheinn from Sgurr na Ba Glaise. This pass is the line of an old path, perhaps a coffin route, between Lochailort and Loch Moidart. Rois-Bheinn's western appearance is as a sharp peak falling steeply towards the narrow mouth of Loch Ailort. A contorted ridge runs east from its summit, then north-east for several kilometres over Sgurr na Ba Glaise and its shoulder, An t-Slat-bheinn (c820m), to the former Corbett Druim Fiaclach.

The north side of these tops encloses the large and grassy Coire a' Bhuiridh which drains towards Lochailort. Uniform slopes of grass drop south from Rois-Bheinn and Sgurr na Ba Glaise into upper Glen Moidart. The ridge turns south-east again beyond the splendid Druim Fiaclach. Spurs project north from it to the outlying tops of Beinn Coire nan Gall (787m) and Diollaid Mhor (751m) which cradle remote Coire nan Gall above Loch Eilt.

The most challenging outing is the complete traverse of the Rois-Bheinn hills, starting with Beinn Odhar Mhor and finishing on An Stac. Use of a bicycle or the train between Glenfinnan and Lochailort can help solve logistical conundrums. A more manageable day climbs the north ridge of Beinn Mhic Cedidh from the east end of Loch Eilt, and continues west from there. The Coire a' Bhuiridh horse-shoe gives a

Eigg and Rum from An Stac

shorter but equally fine and still quite full day, traversing the ridge from Druim Fiaclach westwards, allowing one to enjoy the seaward views ahead. For this, start from Inverailort 1km south of the Lochailort road junction.

A track leads past the salmon hatchery properties and some old brick buildings (relics of the Second World War) towards the wooded Tom Odhar. Take a pretty path through the little pass on the south side of this knoll. This is a better approach than the route which leads past Glenshean Lodge and up and into. Coire a' Bhuiridh as this degenerates into a boggy all-terrain vehicle track. Walk up the corrie, cross the Allt a' Bhuiridh and climb easily up the side of a burn to a lochan at the col between Druim Fiaclach and Beinn Coire nan Gall. There is a steep rocky pull from the col to Druim Fiaclach's summit. If approaching from Beinn Mhic Cedidh, one climbs up the narrow east ridge of Druim Fiaclach, passing over some rocky little towers on its crest, these being the teeth from which the peak takes its name.

The traverse west from Druim Fiaclach is excellent, the hill's south-west ridge having a precipitous face above Coire Reidh, the highest recess of Glen Aladale. There is a brief southward twist and an abrupt drop to Bealach an Fhalaisg Dhuibh, then the ridge broadens and turns west again along the undulating crest of An t-Slat-bheinn, above the long plunge into upper Glen Moidart. Sgurr na Ba Glaise rises ahead, distinguished by its steep north face cleft by a long gully. An easy descent leads to the Bealach an Fhiona, and from there one follows the remnants of an old wall to Rois-Bheinn's summit and trig point. It is worth visiting the lower west top (878m) 750 metres further on, as it has a better view with a wonderful panorama out to the west from Ardnamurchan to Knoydart and the Inner Hebrides.

Looking east from Sgurr na Ba Glaise towards Beinn Odhar Bheag and Croit Bheinn

The best return to Inverailort is over An Stac 2.5km to the north-east. Return to the west end of the Bealach an Fhiona and drop north (still following the broken wall) to the lower col at the foot of An Stac's steep south ridge. Climb this directly to the summit with some brief rocky sections. Continue northwards in descent to the col with Seann Chruach (521m), drop east to the Allt a' Bhuiridh, and return to the road by the Tom Odhar path. Be careful in the descent from An Stac in mist or under snow and ice as its north side has numerous rocky bluffs which are not obvious from above.

There are two other accesses to Rois-Bheinn and An Stac to mention, both from the shore of Loch Ailort. Firstly, Rois-Bheinn's long west ridge can be climbed from Roshven Farm. It is easy-angled but a little lacking in interest and is therefore recommended only as a descent route for its excellent westward views. Secondly, from Alisary some 4km south of the Lochailort junction, one can follow a narrow and in places rather overgrown path high on the south bank of the Alisary Burn to the top of the forestry. An Stac can then be climbed by its steep but relatively straightforward north-west slopes. Alternatively, gain Rois-Bheinn by continuing up a tributary of the Alisary Burn into Coire na Cnamha, where a dry-stone dyke leads to the head of the corrie and so to the ridge north-east of the summit.

Sgurr Dhomhuill Mor; 713m; (OS Sheet 40; NM740758); *big Donald's peak*

Lying south-west of Rois-Bheinn, Sgurr Dhomhuill Mor is somewhat eclipsed by its neighbour, to which it is connected by an interesting ridge. As such it makes a worthwhile diversion or descent route from Rois-Bheinn. The hill looks out west over an extensive tract of moorland stretching towards Glen Uig and the tip of Moidart. It can easily be climbed from Roshven Farm by its north-west ridge on the south side of Gleann Dubh. More unusually it can be approached from Glen Moidart, and indeed the circuit of the glen (up Sgurr Dhomhuill Mor and along the Rois-Bheinn ridge, returning by Croit Bheinn and Beinn Gaire) makes an excellent jaunt.

Sgurr Dhomhuill Mor can also be reached by a path leading to Loch nam Paitean from near the junction of the Glen Moidart road and the A861, giving a pleasant walk to the summit by the undulating south-west ridge over Brunery Hill (472m). The approach can be shortened by starting from the car park at the Glen Moidart road-end (NM741723). Cross the river after 1km by a footbridge above Loch nan Lochan and gain the south ridge up the slopes west of Coire Fearna.

Croit Bheinn; 663m; (OS Sheet 40; NM810773); *croft hill*

An ascent of the reticent Croit Bheinn demands a high degree of single-mindedness. It is a conical peak located in the very heart of Moidart, three sides falling steeply into isolated Glen Aladale. It has a rocky north side facing across the glen to the back of Beinn Mhic Cedidh, from which aspect it takes on a brooding and slightly sinister appearance. Croit Bheinn's north-west ridge links it by a col to the east end of Sgurr na Ba Glaise.

The big drop in between means that the connection is not often made and simply adds to the hill's aura of inaccessibility. Indeed, the higher peaks to the north rather dominate Croit Bheinn, but it is a worthy objective nonetheless. Ascents are rare, but there are rewards in looking down the seldom-visited Glen Aladale to the waters of Loch Shiel far below.

The most straightforward approach is up Glen Moidart, starting from the end of the public road. Take the track on the east side of the glen, cross the river by the footbridge just above Loch nan Lochan, and follow the path until it runs out just before the ruin of Assary. Stay on the boggy north side of the river, taking care at the gorge named on the map as Bealach na Lice. This can be negotiated with some scrambling, but if the river is high then avoid it by the hillside above.

Continue into rough Glen Gluitanen beyond, following the burn to the watershed north-west of Croit Bheinn (the Bealach a' Choire Dhuibh), from which climb to the summit. Either descend the same way, or drop south to the Bealach a' Choire Mhoir, then climb broad and gradual slopes to Beinn Gaire and return to the road as described for the ascent of that hill.

Beinn Gaire; 666m; (OS Sheet 40; NM781748); *hill of proximity*

A rolling and extensive hill, Beinn Gaire lies on the east side of upper Glen Moidart, between the glen and Loch Shiel. By no means spectacular, it is a pleasant walk in itself, or it can be combined with Croit Bheinn. From the end of the public road in Glen Moidart, walk up the track on the east side of the glen, taking the right branch (unmarked on the Landranger map) just before the sizeable waterfall above Glenforslan cottage (the Eas Briadha).

Climb to the unnamed loch in Glen Forslan, cross this by a dam, and ascend Sron Dubh an Eilich, Beinn Gaire's initially steep south-west ridge. The angle soon eases and there is a further 2km of gentle and grassy ground to the summit.

Finding the cairn in poor conditions is a test of navigational skills – despite the translation of its name, Beinn Gaire's summit may be further away than you think! The hill gives an excellent view of the grassy south wall of the Rois-Bheinn ridge flanking upper Glen Moidart.

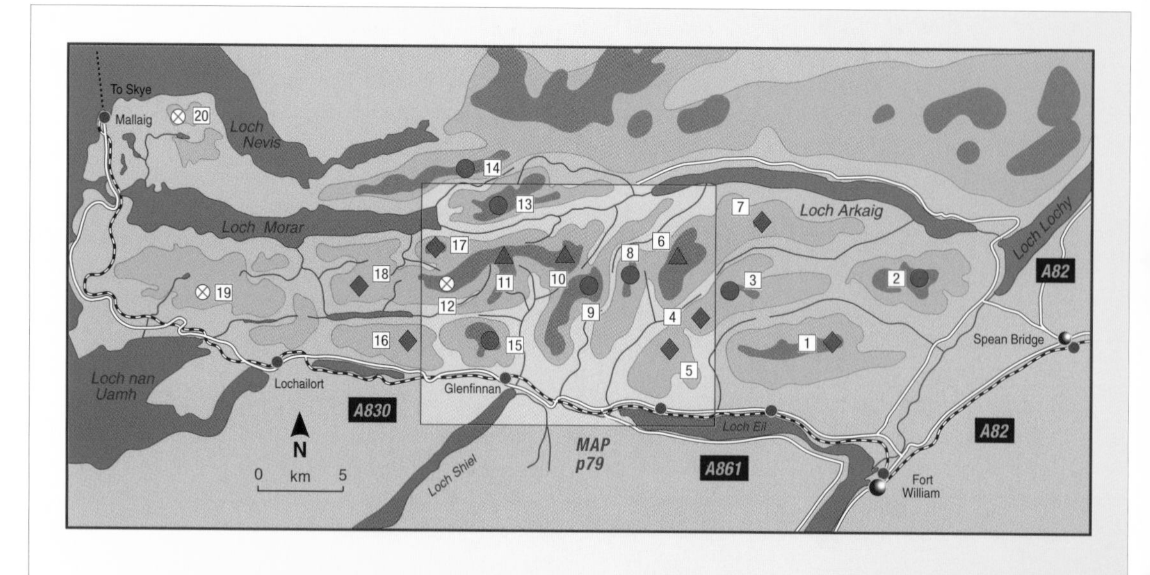

1.	Druim Fada	744m	G	p77
2.	Beinn Bhan	796m	C	p78
3.	Meall a' Phubuill	774m	C	p78
4.	Meall Onfhaidh	681m	G	p79
5.	Aodann Chleireig	663m	G	p79
6.	Gulvain	987m	M	p80
7.	Mullach Coire nan Geur-oirean	727m	G	p80
8.	Braigh nan Uamhachan	765m	C	p81
9.	Streap	909m	C	p82
10.	Sgurr Thuilm	963m	M	p84
11.	Sgurr nan Coireachan	956m	M	p84
12.	Beinn Gharbh	896m	O	p84
13.	Carn Mor	829m	C	p86
14.	Bidean a' Chabair	867m	C	p87
15.	Sgurr an Utha	796m	C	p88
16.	Glas-charn	633m	G	p89
17.	An Stac	718m	G	p89
18.	Meith Bheinn	710m	G	p90
19.	Sidhean Mor	601m	O	p90
20.	Sgurr Eireagoraidh	548m	O	p90

Locheil, Glen Finnan and Morar

Jim Teesdale

North-east towards the summit of Braigh nan Uamhachan

Lochiel, Glen Finnan and Morar are places forever linked with bloody tales from clan histories, glorious albeit futile rebellion, and sun-kissed silvery beaches. With the exception of the beaches, however, these associations owe more to romantic interpretations of the past than to the prosaic reality. This is an area of contrasts, with three quite distinct types of scenery running together. The smooth-sided peaks of west Lochaber rise gently from the Great Glen, giving way to higher and more dramatic mountains that crowd the landscape round the village of Glenfinnan. The small but rugged heather clad hills of Morar then fall to the Arisaig coastal strip. The topography is dominated by dramatic sea lochs indenting the coastline and parallel fresh-water lochs lying inland. The natural fault running from sea to sea between Loch Eil and Loch Ailort is the area's southern boundary, a line followed by both the A830 from Fort William to Mallaig and the West Highland railway line. The northern divide stretches from Loch Arkaig over by Glen Dessarry and the Finiskaig River to Loch Nevis.

The eastern section of this area comprises the pleasant and rounded Locheil tops, the meat in the Loch Arkaig and Loch Eil sandwich. Freshwater Loch Arkaig is one of the country's lesser known scenic resources, despite a number of rather unsightly caravan berths along its north shore, being unspoilt by hydro-electric schemes, lacking in through traffic, and with numerous secluded bays and much native woodland along its edges. Achnacarry House lies near its east end, the home of the chief of the Clan Cameron since the 1660s. It houses the Clan Cameron museum at Achnacarry, open between April and October, and the curator can be contacted on tel: 01397-712480. In 1746 it was laid to waste by the Duke of Cumberland in revenge for the support given by the Camerons to Bonnie Prince Charlie's uprising.

More recently it was the headquarters for commando training in the Second World War. The bravery of those men is recognised by the Commando Memorial which was unveiled by the Queen in 1952, and is located not at the rather secluded Achnacarry, but in a superb position above Spean Bridge looking over to Ben Nevis and the Grey Corries. Loch Arkaig is reached from Gairlochy and the west shore of Loch Lochy, and then from Clunes through the aptly named Mile Dorcha, or Dark Mile, so called due to its old close-set beech trees. Even though many of the original trees have been blown down, this remains an atmospheric and gloomy little pass notable for its thick mossy growth by the roadside. Another item of interest for days of poor weather is Neptune's Staircase on the Caledonian Canal, where eight locks bridge the 19.5 metre difference between loch and sea over just 457 metres. Thomas Telford supervised construction, which was completed in 1822. The Great Glen Way follows the canal towpath up to Loch Lochy on its way from Fort William to Inverness.

Heavily forested glens cut into these hills from Loch Eil and the south. From Fassfern a track then footpath follows Gleann Suileag north then east to a watershed with Glen Loy (*calf glen*), which descends to the Caledonian Canal just south-west of Gairlochy. From the head of Loch Eil, Gleann Fionnlighe leads over to Glen Mallie, which descends to the shores of Loch Arkaig at Inver Mallie 4km from that loch's east end, the top of the pass being almost pathless for several kilometres. A good track runs along the south shore of Loch Arkaig to Inver Mallie from the forestry car park at Eas Chia-aig, a recessed and sometimes voluminous waterfall close to the loch's east end.

The central part of the area contains the best known and most interesting peaks for the hillwalker, in particular the Munros of Sgurr Thuilm and Sgurr nan Coireachan, and the superb but slightly lower Streap. These hills are rough and pointed, the glens deep and steep-sided. From the south, access is either by the forested and relatively unfrequented Gleann Dubh Lighe, equidistant between Glen Finnan and Gleann Fionnlighe, or by Glen Finnan itself. Although these southern glens are quicker and easier to reach, the Loch Arkaig approach is very worthwhile as it tends to provide a wilder and more exploratory hill experience, and indeed that is the normal approach for the Glen Dessarry hills.

Glenfinnan village is little more than a hamlet, but it does lie adjacent to two of the country's most photographed visitor attractions. Just east of the village is the gently curving railway viaduct, while the famous monument to the raising of Bonnie Prince Charlie's Standard in 1745 stands at the head of Loch Shiel. The National Trust for Scotland maintains the monument, and has provided a visitor centre and coffee shop. Glen Finnan reaches far into the hills to the north, leading to the Bealach a' Chaorainn, the name given to the glacially worn and eye-catching symmetrical pass between Streap and Sgurr Thuilm. On the other side of the pass, an intermittent path descends Gleann a' Chaorainn, and crosses the River Pean about 2km west of the head of Loch Arkaig. This provides useful access for backpackers heading for the Glen Dessarry hills and Knoydart.

Glen Finnan Viaduct

This spectacular railway viaduct was constructed by Robert McAlpine between 1897 and 1900, and was one of the earliest to be built from reinforced poured concrete. It cost £18,904, and consists of 21 spans, each of which is 15.24 metres in width. A story has it that during construction a horse and cart toppled backwards into one of the hollow piers. A survey in 2001 detected that these unfortunate articles indeed remain vertically embedded in a pier, but in the nearby Loch nan Uamh viaduct instead. A lasting concern is, however, the possibility that the rail link from Fort William to Mallaig may be closed for economic reasons. The line clearly has huge importance for this remote area where there is so little by way of infrastructure, and the scenic value of the line is essential for the tourism industry, so any move towards closure should be vigorously opposed.

The northern access to these central hills is by the narrow and twisting roller coaster of a single-track road along the north shore of Loch Arkaig. The road terminates at the west end of the loch 1km east of Strathan (NM987916), and parking can be awkward here at busier times. The river bifurcates at Strathan, with the splendid Glen Dessarry and Glen Pean continuing west. A forest track goes up Glen Pean for 3.5km, then a deteriorating path leads past Pean bothy and through spectacular scenery before virtually disappearing near Loch Leum an t-Sagairt (*the loch of the priest's jump*) which is best passed on its south side. The origin of the loch's name is unknown but it clearly testifies to a tremendous feat, a leap of faith perhaps!

In places the glen is so narrow there is no room for flat ground at the bottom, and steep craggy hillsides fall directly to the riverbed. Beyond the top of the pass, Glen an Obain Bhig soon descends to the remote east end of the shores of Loch Morar. In 1746, 35,000 Louis d' Or were brought up from the loch through Glen Pean to support Bonnie Prince Charlie's campaign, but arrived too late. Reputedly the treasure is buried near Murlaggan beside Loch Arkaig, but other reasons suggest themselves for its disappearance.

Glen Dessarry is a popular access route to Loch Nevis and other places further west. Broader than Glen Pean, it too has been heavily planted with forestry, and as a result it is

Access and Transport

By road: on the south side of the area, the A830 goes from Fort William by the north shore of Loch Eil to Glenfinnan, Lochailort, Arisaig, Morar and Mallaig. On the north side, the B8004 leads from Banavie to Gairlochy and on to the Commando Memorial junction 2km north-west of Spean Bridge, and the B8005 continues from Gairlochy by the north shore of Loch Arkaig to the west end of the loch 1km east of Strathan.

By bus: Acharacle to Fort William via Lochailort; Mallaig to Fort William; Acharacle to Mallaig (Shiel Buses, tel: 01967-431272). Fort William to Ardgour village via Kinlocheil (Royal Mail, tel: 08457-740740). Fort William to Stronchreggan by Kinlocheil; Fort William to Mucomir via Achnacarry and Clunes (Highland Country Buses, tel: 01397-702373).

By rail: stations along the Fort William to Mallaig line, also stopping at Banavie, Corpach, Loch Eil, Locheilside, Glenfinnan, Lochailort, Glen Beasdale, Arisaig and Morar.

By ferry: Mallaig to Tarbet (Fridays); Mallaig to Inverie (Mondays, Wednesdays and Fridays) (Bruce Watt Sea Cruises, tel: 01687-462320). It may be possible to make an arrangement to be put ashore at the head of the loch.

Accommodation and Information

Hotels and guesthouses: Fort William, Corpach, Glenfinnan, Lochailort, Arisaig, Morar and Mallaig.

Independent hostels: Farr Cottage Hostel, Corpach (tel: 01397-772315); Smiddy Bunkhouse, Corpach (tel: 01397-772467); Sheena's Backpackers Lodge, Mallaig (tel: 01687-462764); Glenfinnan Sleeping Car (tel: 01397-722295)

Campsites: two on the northern outskirts of Fort William - Lochy Caravan Park (tel: 01397-703446) and Linnhe Lochside (tel: 01397-772376); Mucomir; the Arisaig area has a number of campsites, including Camusdarach (01687-450221) and Gorten Sands (01687-4502830)

Tourist information Centres: Fort William (tel: 01397-703781); Mallaig (tel: 01687-462170). (Easter - October); Spean Bridge (tel: 01397-712576). (Easter - October)

Maps

Ordnance Survey: 1:50,000 Landranger sheets 33 (Loch Alsh, Glen Shiel and Loch Hourn), 34 (Fort Augustus and Glen Albyn), 40 (Mallaig and Glenfinnan) and 41 (Ben Nevis); 1:25,000 Explorer sheets 398 (Loch Morar and Mallaig) and 399 (Loch Arkaig).

now served by two tracks. The original estate track is on the north side and leads past Glendessarry Lodge to Upper Glendessarry. A path continues above the tree line, crossing the Allt Coire nan Uth by an inconspicuous but sometimes indispensable footbridge (unmarked on the Landranger map) down by the forest fence. A forestry track on the south side leads past A' Chuil bothy to end at a footbridge (also unrecognised on the Landranger map) at NM930934, from where a path finds its way through the trees to join up with the north path just west of the forest edge. The south track will be quicker if a bicycle is used, while the north route is boggier but a little shorter overall for the pedestrian.

Beyond the junction a variable path leads over the Bealach an Lagain Duibh (310m) and on through huge fallen boulders to the Mam na Cloich' Airde and Lochan a' Mhaim. The scenery is wild and grand, the pass hemmed in on its north side by the vast wall of Garbh Chioch Mhor and the rugged crags of Druim nan Uadhag. On reaching the Finiskaig River, a rather better constructed path drops to the head of Loch Nevis. A footbridge (again unmarked on the Landranger map) crosses the potentially hazardous Allt Coire na Ciche. Care may be needed elsewhere, as there are a number of other seemingly innocuous streams along the way that in heavy rain can be all but impassable. The first Munroist, the Reverend A.E.Robertson, suggested that this path might date from the days of herring fishing in Loch Nevis, it having been made to carry the fish to southern markets. However it seems more likely to have been part of General Wade's road building programme. The path continues past Sourlies bothy and over the Mam Meadail to Inverie.

A third pass, the very fine Gleann an Lochain Eanaiche, leads from the upper reaches of Glen Dessarry to Kinlochmorar. There is no path at the top, although a good one exists on the Loch Morar side, and it is used less than the neighbouring routes. Combined with Glen Pean it gives a superb low level circuit of Carn Mor from Strathan.

The landscape of Morar is made up of an expanse of rough undulating moorland with craggy summits rising to some 500m or 600m interspersed by some deep faults cradling fine lochs, of which Loch Beoraid is a spectacular albeit little known example. The hills then give way to the wonderful coastline of Arisaig with its machair and sandy beaches, its stunning views of Rum, Eigg and Skye, and a rash of caravan sites. At the north-west extremity is the busy fishing port of Mallaig, the main centre of habitation in the area and the starting point for ferry access to Loch Nevis and the nearby islands. It has perhaps unfairly been described by one jaundiced commentator as 'little more than an industrial fishing station built to feed Glasgow with kippers'! Visitors will make up their own minds. The villages of Arisaig and Morar are justifiably popular holiday destinations. This part of the country is well worth exploring despite the lack of mountains, and both the Ardnish and Rhue peninsulas give enjoyable coastal walking. Ardnish offers a number of low-level crags which give short but pleasant climbing in an attractive setting.

Of particular interest is Loch Morar (from Mor Dobhar, meaning *big water*). At over 300m it is the deepest inshore loch in Britain. The great depth is the product of glacial forces, but it is an even more remarkable statistic as the nearest point where the sea reaches a similar depth is 270km away, between St. Kilda and Rockall. Loch Morar is some 19km long, hemmed in by hills and almost untouched by civilisation. But for the brief area of land at Mointeach Mhor and Morar, this would be a sea-loch and would make a double peninsula of North and South Morar. As it is, the River Morar flows for just 300 metres before reaching the sea. A circumnavigation of the loch itself would give a tough but rewarding walk, as well as a chance to try to spot Loch Morar's own beastie, Morag, a rival to Nessie for the attentions of monster hunters, who appears only before the death of a MacDonald of Clanranald.

The area is somewhat disappointing for the climber. There are a number of small crags on the western hills, but elsewhere, despite some large areas of rock, few routes have been recorded, probably due to a combination of vegetation, weather and remoteness.

North-west across Loch Arkaig towards Glen Dessarry from Mullach Coire nan Geur-oirean

Principal Hills

Druim Fada; 744m; (OS Sheet 41 NN087824); *long ridge*

Despite its lowly altitude, Druim Fada should not be overlooked as it gives one of the finest views of Ben Nevis and its neighbours rising far above the unlikely urban sprawl of Fort William. The hill occupies an extensive tract of ground, bounded on the south by Loch Eil and on the north and west by Glen Loy and Gleann Suileag respectively. The southern slopes are heavily forested and rather unexciting albeit obvious and direct, with the benefit of the scenery behind. If they must be tackled then use the Annat track starting just west of the Corpach paper-mill entrance. Leave the track after about 3.5km, follow a break in the forestry and head straight for the summit.

From the east, Druim Fada is seen as a more interesting conical hill, somewhat overshadowed by Beinn Bhan to its north and it is from that side that the most entertaining ascent is made, starting from Puiteachan at the head of the Glen Loy road. Climb through an area of fine old Scots pines and aim for the ridge between Coire Dubh and Coire Odhar, which passes a prominent cairn on the skyline and leads directly to the summit, which comprises an old volcanic neck. The fine outlook extends from the Glen Finnan hills in the west to the Mamores, Ben Nevis and the Grampians in the east. The descent can be by the west flank of Coire Dubh back into Glen Loy, although, if transport can be arranged, it is better to enjoy the ridge walk westwards to Coille Mhor and descend to Fassfern beside Loch Eil. Either skirt Gleann Suileag forest on the north to gain the main track, or pick a line through the trees down the Allt na Coille Moire by seeking out felled areas.

Beinn Bhan; 796m; (OS Sheets 34 and 41 NN140857); *white hill*

A rounded hill with an extensive summit area, Beinn Bhan rises above the Caledonian Canal just west of Gairlochy, with Glen Loy to its south and Loch Arkaig and Glen Mallie generally to the north-west. Its curving summit ridge encloses the south-facing Coire Mhuilinn and gives a fine elevated walk with great views over to the Ben and the Grey Corries and up the Great Glen. This ridge makes an excellent par twenty-something for those with an inclination to carry a five-iron around on the hills! The best outing is the circuit of Coire Mhuilinn from the deserted farm-house at Inverskilavulin in Glen Loy. Ascend either directly to the summit on the east bank of the stream, or up the west flank of the corrie passing an obvious cairn at the south-west end of the summit ridge. Old fence posts form a convenient navigational aid round the top of the corrie. The summit itself is quite flat and the trig point (situated by the edge above the northern cliffs) may be difficult to locate in poor conditions.

A lengthy but unusual approach can be made from Inver Mallie starting from the Eas Chia-aig car park at the east end of Loch Arkaig. Cross the River Mallie by a suspen-sion bridge (NN113879), then ascend to the west of the depths of Coire Bhotrais through old Scots pines – hard going initially through deep heather. The corrie contains some crags but these are unlikely to repay exploration. A less interesting but quite direct approach can be made up Monadh Uisge Mhuilinn just south of where the B8004 crosses the Allt Coire Chraoibhe. The upper slopes can give a good ski descent into Coire Chnamh when snow cover is thick.

Meall a' Phubuill; 774m; (OS Sheet 41 NN029854); *hill of the tent*

A grassy dome-shaped hill, Meall a' Phubuill is centrally located above the Glen Loy-Gleann Suileag and Glen Mallie-Gleann Fionnlighe watersheds, and it affords a good perspective of the surround-ing hill scenery. The usual and quickest line of ascent is from Fassfern, following a good track up the east side of Gleann Suileag to cross the An t-Suileag river by a bridge lying a few hundred metres west of the privately maintained Glensulaig bothy. Meall a' Phubuill rises directly behind. Take a rough track uphill, which ends at a footbridge over the Allt Fionn Doire. Strike up uniform slopes to the summit.

Meall a' Phubuill can be linked with Gulvain, although there is a big drop between the hills. The best start is from Gleann Fionnlighe as for Gulvain. Atten-tion can be given to the unusual loch at the col between the two, an Ordnance Survey oddity as the map suggests that it dis-charges into both the River Mallie and the Fionn Lighe!

The hill can be climbed from Glen Loy, a longer approach but with more character, taking the reasonable track that extends beyond the scattered trees of Brian Choille. After the trees climb up north-west to gain the Druim Gleann Laoigh some way west of its lowest point, then continue to the sum-mit. The descent can be made from the col 1km east of the summit, following the burn. This allows one to take in a long water slide of fragmented dark rock: the agglomerate of a volcanic vent, rare in this area. A lengthy day combines Meall a' Phubuill with its eastern neighbour Beinn Bhan. A pleasing horseshoe can also be made from the ruined Glenmallie cottage, sharing the approach described for Gulvain from the north. Cross the River Mallie by a footbridge about 500m upstream of the ruin, and a fine if remote circuit follows the shoulders of Monadh Beag (528m) and Druim Gleann Laoigh (698m).

Meall Onfhaidh; 681m; (OS Sheet 41 NN010840); *hill of fury*

Aodann Chleireig; 663m; (OS Sheets 40 and 41 NM994825); *the face of the clergyman*

Lying between Gleann Suileag and Gleann Fionnlighe, these lower hills form the western end of the broad and rounded ridge of grassy summits continuing as far as Beinn Bhan. They can be climbed with one or other of their loftier neighbours to give a more varied circuit. From Gulvain or Meall a' Phubuill, however, it is still a fair pull to the summit of Meall Onfhaidh, and the bealach between it and Aodann Chleireig is also quite low at c350 m. These hills, like Druim Fada, are compensated for what they lack in height with the quality of their vista. In particular, the view across Loch Eil to Ben Nevis is very fine.

If ascending Meall Onfhaidh without such a combination then it is best approached from Gleann Suileag and the track to the Allt Fionn Doire mentioned for Meall a' Phubuill. Aodann Chleireig can be reached either from Fassfern or from Gleann Fionnlighe. From the former, tracks and forest breaks are followed north-west on to Druim Beag which leads to the summit. Beware of new plantings, ditches and other forestry obstacles on the lower reaches. If approaching from Gleann Fionnlighe, take the track as far as the

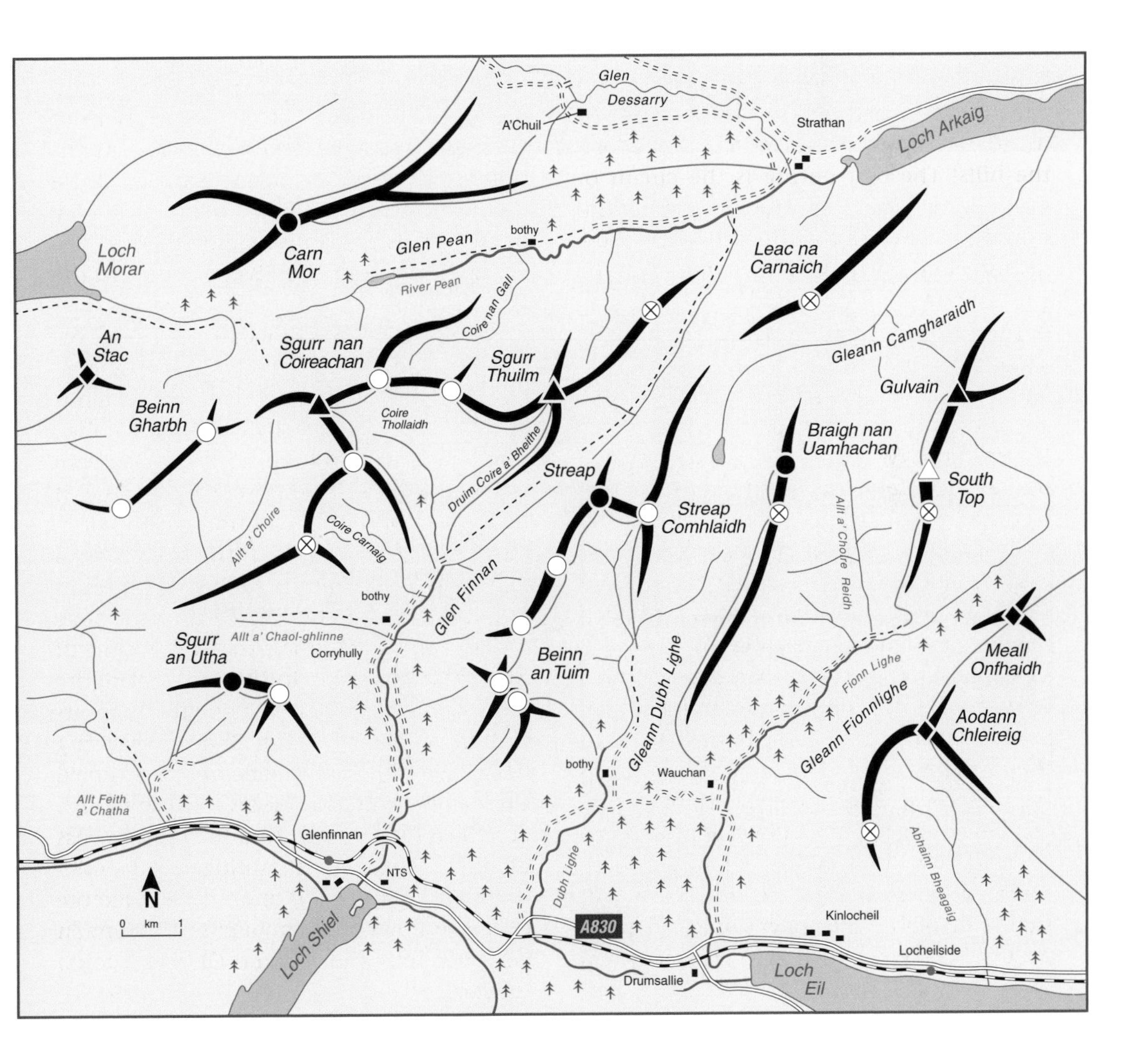

The west flanks of Gulvain from Braigh nan Uamhachan

bridge before Wauchan. Gain the outlying shoulder of Beinn an t-Sneachda (649m) which can be included or skirted according to inclination, although this is quite featureless ground and navigational attention will be needed in the mist.

Gulvain; 987m; (OS Sheets 33, 34, 40 and 41 NN500287); *filthy hill or noisy hill*

Mullach Coire nan Geur-oirean; 727m; (OS Sheets 33 and 41 NN049892); *hill of the corrie of the sharp edge*

Gulvain (or Gaor Bheinn) is the highest hill in the eastern section of the hills covered in this chapter. It rises far above its neighbours, its bulk and its height combining with its location to make it seem quite isolated. Lying between Gleann Fionnlighe and Glen Mallie, Gulvain takes the form of a steep-sided grassy ridge with twin summits, giving the hill a distinctive saddle-like appearance from either side. From the south Gulvain appears rather more monolithic. What little rock that is exposed is granite gneiss but it does not offer any climbing.

The western flanks are steep and slabby, and should be treated carefully – stags shot on these slopes are rumoured to 'fall right down the mountain'. Hillwalkers take note! The OS has done Gulvain few favours, having located the hill on a logistically taxing four Landranger sheets. Even the north and south summits are on different maps, and many ascents will no doubt have suffered premature termination at the trig point on the lower South Top (962m).

The normal approach is the southern one from Gleann Fionnlighe, and is quite straightforward. Follow the rough private track on the east bank of the Fionn Lighe, starting from the A830 almost opposite the junction to Ardgour. Pass the ruin of

Wauchan, where remnants of anti-midge candles can be found, the candles having ultimately destroyed more than just the insects they were designed to counteract. Continue through a mixture of forestry for a further 4km to a footbridge over the Allt a' Choire Reidh. Old shielings here are reputed to be the site of a former inn from the days of the drove roads. This point can usefully be reached by bicycle. Gulvain rises massively ahead, and indeed the ascent from here is a sair trachle. A stalkers path gives an initial leg-up before an unavoidable slog with over 600m of climb to the South Top, passing a craggy knoll at 855m. The true summit lies 1km further north of the South Top, reached by an airy ridge that dips then narrows briefly during the final pull to the cairn. The views are excellent.

Alternative routes can be followed from the north and the east. From Strathan an ascent can be made by Gleann a' Chaorainn (note that the bridge shown on the map at NM977909 no longer exists and that the footbridge 1km west will have to be used instead) and the low col between Leac na Carnaich (569m) and Streap Comhlaidh (898m). Descend to the Allt Camgharaidh, make a rising traverse to Gualann nan Osna (*panting pass*) between Gulvain and Braigh nan Uamhachan, then climb the steep western slopes to the col between Gulvain's twin summits. A good excursion for the aquatically equipped is to approach Gleann Camgharaidh by canoe and make an ascent of Gulvain's remote and rarely explored north ridge.

From the east a long approach can be made starting at the Eas Chia-aig car park at the end of Loch Arkaig, and taking the good track to Inver Mallie. Beyond the bothy, the track deteriorates for a while as it follows the attractive River Mallie's west bank past areas of old Caledonian pines, then it improves for the final section to the ruined Glenmallie cottage where alders line the river. Continue by a rough footpath past the sparse trees of Coille an Ruighe Mhoir, then climb up grassy slopes to the col between Gulvain and Mullach Coire nan Geur-oirean. This way takes one through remote and attractive scenery but it is rather lengthy and is likely to appeal only to those staying at Inver Mallie or using mountain bikes.

Mullach Coire nan Geur-oirean can also be included in this itinerary, although the name is somewhat longer than is justified by the glories of the hill. A remote peak, it is the highest point of the 15km ridge thrown out by Gulvain north-east towards Loch Arkaig. The shortest approach is by Inver Mallie. One can climb directly to the summit from just before Coille an Ruighe Mhoir. Alternatively, leave the track just before Glenmallie cottage to gain the easy angled but rather featureless Druim na Giubhsaich and climb up broad slopes to its summit. A pleasant ridge joins it to Gulvain, affording fine views of the glacially formed Coire Sgreamhach.

Braigh nan Uamhachan; 765m; (OS Sheet 40 NM975866); *brae of the caves*

Less a peak than a long and undulating ridge, Braigh nan Uamhachan separates Gleann Dubh Lighe from Gleann Fionnlighe. It is more interesting than its appearance on the map might suggest, giving a fine outing particularly if combined with Streap or Gulvain – or both. It can be reached by either of the southern glens. From Gleann Fionnlighe, follow the Gulvain approach as far as the bridge over the Allt a' Choire Reidh. From there climb grassy slopes to gain the ridge either on or just north of Sron Liath (c710m) from which a sturdy dry-stone dyke runs along the crest towards the summit. More varied, however, is the route up the less frequented Gleann Dubh Lighe. Due to heavy forestation it is best to use the track on the west of the river rather than the footpath on the east. Cross the river by a bridge at NM944816. A track (unmarked on the Landranger map) crosses from the privately maintained Dubh Lighe bothy over to

Streap and Sgurr Thuilm from Strathan

Wauchan in Gleann Fionnlighe. Climb to the highest point on this then head north by broad slopes over the knolls of Na h-Uamhachan to Sron Liath and so on to the top. (This track can also be accessed from Gleann Fionnlighe from which glen one can also climb the hill from 2km north of Wauchan, making a rising traverse across the east face of Sron Liath to gain the ridge 500m south of the summit.) Alternatively one can gain Na-Uamhachan from the track 1km north of the bothy.

Braigh nan Uamhachan is less often climbed from the north, but this can certainly be done from Strathan. Cross the River Pean by the bridge at NM968906, passing over the col south-west of Leac na Carnaich (569m), and drop into Gleann Camgharaidh before the final ascent. This route is quite straightforward and fairly direct.

Streap; 909m (OS Sheet 40 NM946863); *climbing hill*

Lying between Glen Finnan and Gleann Dubh Lighe, Streap is a sharp-edged twisting ridge of many summits, and it is certainly one of the most dramatic and worthwhile peaks in the area. The former Corbett Beinn an Tuim (810m) lies at the south end, rising on the east side of the River Finnan above the railway viaduct. From it the ridge runs north-east over a number of tops, including Meall an Uillt Chaoil (844m) and Stob Coire nan Cearc (887m), to the main summit. To the east of Streap is the outlying Streap Comhlaidh (898m). The ridge then drops steadily downwards to the west end of Loch Arkaig. There are a number of fine corries on the flanks of the hill which, despite being rugged, are not of interest to climbers. To the north-west an extremely steep and grassy face rears up above the Bealach a' Chaorainn (471m). A similar slope lies on Sgurr Thuilm opposite and the symmetry of the two is both pleasing and an obvious feature of views of these hills.

Streap can be approached from Glen Finnan or Gleann Dubh Lighe. More unusually it can also be climbed from the north. A full traverse from Glen Finnan through to Loch Arkaig is rewarding if transport is available or if a trip of several days' duration is planned. It can also be combined either with Braigh nan Uamhachan, or, more adventurously, with the Munros to the west, although the north-west face is of an unrelentingly high angle and cannot be recommended either in descent or in the wet, and great caution must be exercised here.

Gleann Dubh Lighe is the best starting point to enjoy the full ridge traverse. Take the track on the west of the glen to emerge from the forestry after 3km, just opposite the Dubh Lighe bothy. Now head over Beinn Tuim's South Top (795m) to Beinn an Tuim itself (which gives a great view along the whole Streap ridge and right down the length of Loch Shiel) and follow the ridge with much undulation to the pointed summit. The final section is sharp and exposed and the steep slopes on either side

Bonnie Prince Charlie

Much of the area is inescapably associated with Prince Charles Edward Stuart, or the Young Pretender, heir to the Jacobite claim to the British throne. The Prince arrived from France on the brig *Du Teillay* on 25th July 1745, landing on the shores of Loch nan Uamh at the bay west of Rubh Aird Ghamhsgail near Glen Borrodale. After converting the initially sceptical clan chiefs to his cause, he was rowed up Loch Shiel to Glenfinnan where the Bratach Bhan, the Stuart banner, was raised on 19th August 1745. By evening on that day a total of some 5,000 men had joined him. Each man marching for the Prince placed a stone on a cairn. On returning, each man removed a stone. Many cairns were left altogether undisturbed in the wake of the Prince's defeat, and their stones were partly used to construct the site's famous monument, built by Alexander MacDonald of Glenaladale in 1815. The figure on top of the monument is not in fact the Prince, but a bearded Highlander, in tribute to the loyal clansmen who fought and died for him.

The Prince took his men up Gleann Suileag and down Glen Loy to Invergarry. Sir John Cope retreated before them and the Prince led his rebel army over the Corrieyairack Pass to success at Prestonpans, doubt at Derby and calamity at Culloden on 16th April 1746. In the immediate aftermath of his defeat the Prince fled by the Dark Mile and Loch Arkaig to Loch Morar and back to Glen Borrodale. He made his way to the Outer Hebrides in the hope of gaining a French ship. With the Hanoverians closing in, he returned to the mainland across Skye, landing at Mallaig Bheag. He then faced a grim and deadly game of hill-walking hide-and-seek for ten weeks, pursued over Sgurr Thuilm and over to Loch Quoich, skulking for many days above the Dark Mile. Word was brought to him at Cluny's Cage on Ben Alder that a French ship, *L' Heureux*, was waiting at Loch nan Uamh, from which he left the country forever on 20th September 1746. The route of the Prince's flight is well worth tracing and pondering, as it remains a considerable feat of survival and endurance.

The modern version of the Bonnie Prince Charlie story, particularly as told for the benefit of visitors, generally comes with a whole heap of sanitised tartan tack for baggage. Our national recollection still tends to over-romanticise the Prince's lofty ambitions and the tragedy that was Culloden, but fails to take full account of the folly of the leader and the terrible social engineering that followed once he had fled. The grim reality was brutal repression, destruction of property, mass slaughter, wholesale clearances of people from the glens to make way for sheep, lasting disruption of the clan system and a ban on the wearing of tartan. It has profoundly shaped the modern landscape. The Prince was less a brave dreamer, and more a misguided waster. There were no romantic upsides at the time - in a modern context it would be called genocide. But our country needs to re-assess its view of the historical horizon, and to do away with the mawkish sentimentality for the past that still seems to overshadow our present.

give a great sense of space. On the south, Coire Chuirn contains the remnants of a large land-slip, and signs of recent rock-fall hereabouts testify to some continuing instability. From Streap be sure to continue south-east to the outlying Streap Comhlaidh, whose steep but grassy south ridge descends to the upper reaches of Gleann Dubh Lighe. A path on the east side of the burn leads to the forest track, past the bothy, and so back to the road.

The Glen Finnan approach, with its good private road, gives a quicker route to the top, although the full traverse is less likely to be achieved due to the topography of the mountain. Cross the river 1km beyond the viaduct, then use forest tracks to gain the open hillside and climb Beinn an Tuim by its south-west ridge. The Allt an Tuim forms an enclosed but mainly grassy gully to the east of this which can give an unusual line of ascent though care should be taken to avoid some minor crags high up. The easiest return from the summit of Streap is by retracing one's steps for 1km to just before the col with Stob Coire nan Cearc and making a descending traverse by a grassy rake into the upper reaches of Glen Finnan. Cross the burn below Druim Coire a' Bheithe and return down the Glen Finnan track to Corryhully. The speediest route uses this rake in both ascent and descent.

The twin peaks of Streap and Streap Comhlaidh are quite distinctive from the north, as is the huge gash of the Bealach a' Chaorainn, which is the pass leading to Glen Finnan. From Strathan cross the footbridge over the River Pean just below the Allt a' Chaorainn (the bridge marked on the map at NM977909 no longer exists). Continue up Gleann a' Chaorainn (or Gleann Cuirnean according to the Explorer map), then strike up on to the Streap Comhlaidh ridge south-west of Leac na Carnaich. Follow this to Streap Comhlaidh, and continue to the summit of Streap. The same route should be used in descent as well, as the north ridge of Streap is not particularly distinct but is steep and craggy in places and could be awkward in poor conditions. That ridge does, however, give an unusual and direct if rather brutal line of ascent from the head of Gleann a' Chaorainn.

Sgurr Thuilm; 963m; (OS Sheet 40 NM939879); *peak of the rounded hillock*

Sgurr nan Coireachan; 956m; (OS Sheet 40 NM902880); *peak of the corries*

Beinn Gharbh; 896m; (OS Sheet 40 NM882877); *rough hill*

Dominating the upper part of Glen Finnan, Sgurr Thuilm and the aptly named Sgurr nan Coireachan form a huge and grassy amphitheatre round deep Coire Thollaidh and Coire a' Bheithe. From the north they are seen as a high and impressive barrier, their wild corries and rough slopes rendering Glen Pean a strikingly gloomy place which sees less than its fair share of sunshine. Some of these corries are quite craggy, and a steep but not particularly continuous area of rock lies just north of the summit of Sgurr Thuilm. A well-defined ridge links the summits, narrow and steep in places, and the traverse of these peaks is justifiably one of the most popular outings in the area.

The usual line of ascent starts near Glenfinnan village, using the private road as far as Corryhully bothy. There is parking just off the A830, some 200 metres north-west of the nearby National Trust for Scotland Visitors Centre. The tarmac road extends as far as Glenfinnan Lodge, the large and modern estate house seen at the head of the glen. This building seems somewhat out of context, having the air of a property that has made a successful escape from the confines of suburbia. Use of a bicycle on this road will save time and effort. Above Corryhully bothy, the arms of Sgurr a' Choire Riabhaich and Druim Coire a' Bheithe extend down from the summits, and the horseshoe which they present can be tackled either way. A clockwise circuit has the advantage of dealing with the bulk of the scrambling in ascent, whilst an anti-clockwise one allows aesthetes to walk towards the finer views of the west.

If climbing Sgurr nan Coireachan first, take the stalkers path which branches off the main track 1km north of Corryhully. The path leads up on to Sgurr a' Choire Riabhaich (852m). Easy scrambling takes one along a narrow ridge to this subsidiary summit which is in a grand situation with deep corries on either side. Thereafter the ridge broadens and terminates without difficulty on the summit of Sgurr nan Coireachan itself, giving excellent views of Knoydart and Morar.

Strathan

Strathan lies 1km west of the road-end at the west end of Loch Arkaig, and is at the hub of a number of fine passes radiating through the surrounding mountains. It is little more than a handful of estate and farm buildings now, but it is the central starting point for hillwalkers visiting the area. In years gone by Strathan was an important strategic point and also sustained a fair size of population. After the 1745 rebellion, the government built a small barracks at Strathan to patrol the surrounding area. A century later, the glens were cleared, probably of somewhere around 1,000 people, to make way for 20,000 sheep and their shepherds from the south. The small and extremely dilapidated corrugated iron building, still standing by the track, was the local school. A lady, later resident in Spean Bridge, used to attend it, and recollects how, as a teenager, she and her family would regularly walk to Glenfinnan in the summer. They would catch the train to Fort William to do the shopping, returning the same evening. The father required a special pass as their route led through the commandos' training ground.

Heading east towards Sgurr Thuilm, follow a line of old fence posts along the well-defined ridge over Meall an Tarmachain (826m) which provides one awkward step in descent, and Beinn Gharbh (825m). Straightforward slopes then lead to a final steep pull up to the summit of Sgurr Thuilm. Again, the views are very fine over the corries to the neighbouring hills. Descent is by the attractive Druim Coire a' Bheithe passing between low-lying forestry plantations to cross the bridge over the river at NM921855.

These hills are less often climbed from the north, and the approaches from there are not so obvious. However the corries on this side are wild, remote and well worth a visit. The start is from the road-end east of Strathan. Treat the River Pean with respect, particularly after rain. Even up at Pean bothy it can be wide and potentially uncrossable, despite the presence of stepping stones. Above the bothy, the flanks of the hills are rough and it is best to pick a line over Point 406m by the ridge rising south-westwards from the bothy, aiming to gain the summit ridge at the col just east of Meall an Tarmachain.

The north-east ridge of Sgurr Thuilm gives straightforward walking in descent over Meall an Fhir-eoin (581m), although again care must be taken with the Allt a' Chaorainn after rain as it will have to be forded prior to re-crossing the River Pean by the footbridge just below its junction with the Allt a' Chaorainn.

Beinn Gharbh is the remote outlying western shoulder of Sgurr nan Coireachan. It throws out a blunt and rough-sided ridge for a number of kilometres west to abut into Meith Bheinn between Loch Morar and Loch Beoraid. The hill's lack of listing (presently evading either Munro or Corbett status by just a few metres) coupled with its general inaccessibility mean that it is rarely ascended. A trip to the surrounds of Beinn Gharbh will provide a genuine sense of exploration no longer afforded by the more glamorous 'wilderness' areas of the country. The easiest route is a simple out-and-back

Oban Bay and Carn Mor, Loch Morar

detour from Sgurr nan Coireachan. Otherwise ascents will require a degree of calculation by anyone other than the backpacker who happens to be at its foot. From the north side a helpful stalkers path leads high up the hillside from the Glen Pean–Glen an Obain Bhig watershed. The slopes of Coire a' Bheithe just to the east of this path provide rough access as well. From Oban bothy, the western shoulder of Beinn Gharbh can be reached just east of Cruach Bhuidhe (598m) from the Gleann Taodhail path. There are no particularly obvious approaches from the south, although the most direct one is to use the path west of Sgurr an Utha up the Allt Feith a' Chatha followed by a drop to pick up the path on the north side of the potentially difficult Allt a' Choire. From here, one can approach the hill over the outlying Sgurr an Ursainn (817m).

Carn Mor; 829m; (OS Sheets 33 and 40 NM903909); *big peak*

A considerable hill lying between Glen Pean, Glen Dessarry and its offshoot Gleann an Lochain Eanaiche, Carn Mor throws a major ridge east to just above Strathan. This end of the hill is mainly grassy and gives pleasant walking. The summit lies far to the west, and beyond it the ground turns rockier, two shoulders enclosing the remote Ile Coire and ending in buttresses which drop vertiginously to the dark waters of Loch Morar. Bonnie Prince Charlie passed northwards over the hill in the night during his flight after Culloden.

The ascent is usually made from the Loch Arkaig road-end, and a number of approaches suggest themselves. The easiest one is to follow the south Glen Dessarry track to the forest edge just west of A' Chuil bothy. Leave the track, and either make a rising traverse to climb steep grassy slopes over Meall nan Spardan to the summit, or follow the eastern retaining spur of Coire an Eich instead. Another route is to follow the track to its end, and take the path towards Gleann an Lochain Eanaiche as far as the forest edge. The Druim a' Choire Odhair then gives a rough but direct route to the summit. An unusual option is to ascend either of the western shoulders of Druim Ile Coire and Meall nan Each (589m) which are seldom climbed but give brilliant views down the length of Loch Morar.

The return can be made by following the full 7km east ridge to Monadh Gorm (478m) which provides a rough descent to Strathan with a brief tussle through the trees before the forest track is regained. A circuit is recommended, as this ridge is a little monotonous in ascent. The rocks at the east end of the hill are reputed to have an effect on the reliability of the compass. A huge land-slip has taken place south-east of the summit, between it and Lochan Leum an t-Sagairt, and these flanks are in any event uniformly steep and unrelenting, so this part of the hill is best avoided, particularly under snow when the land-slip area could prove quite treacherous.

Bidean a' Chabair; 867m; (OS Sheets 33 or 40 NM889931); *pinnacle of the hawk*

This very striking mountain is formed by a long and undulating ridge located between the spectacular passes of Mam na Cloich' Airde and Gleann an Lochain Eanaiche. The ridge itself stretches for many kilometres west from the head of Glen Dessarry, eventually forming the spine of land lying between the upper reaches of Loch Nevis and Loch Morar. The flanks to the north and south are precipitous, and should be approached with some caution. The summit itself is a sharp and distinctive spire, well seen from Loch Arkaig, from where it is easily mistaken for its loftier neighbour, Sgurr na Ciche.

For those making the ascent in the course of a single day, the usual route is from Glen Dessarry, starting at the road-end east of Strathan. Bidean a' Chabair is an uplifting sight on a fine day rising with graceful symmetry at the head of the glen. The best route is to gain the main ridge by ascending Meall na Sroine (674m). This point is reached by taking the track on either the north or south side of Glen Dessarry to the western edge of the forest. Make a rising traverse generally south-west to avoid slabby ground, reaching easier slopes which lead to the top of Meall na Sroine. The ridge undulates gently ahead for some 3km over rocky knolls to the main summit, passing two lochans on the crest of Druim Coire nan Laogh. The summit gives an easy if exposed final scramble, avoidable on the south. The views down to Loch Morar and over to Knoydart are superlative, and if you are lucky you may see an eagle soaring above the ridge.

A quicker variant is to take the track on the south side of Glen Dessarry, past A' Chuil bothy, then follow the path which leads towards Gleann an Lochain Eanaiche. This path runs out shortly beyond the forest edge and is rather overgrown, but the Bidean a' Chabair ridge can be gained west of Meall na Sroine, thus avoiding some unnecessary ascent. The south-east flanks of the hill are, however, brutal and unrelenting, and this is less satisfying than following the crest of the ridge itself.

The sides of the mountain are steep and quite slabby. From the north a good and direct ascent can be made with much interesting scrambling from the upper part of the Finiskaig River. The hill is also an obvious excursion from Sourlies bothy, from which the best route is by grassy Coire Dubh; the tricky bit may be the crossing of the River Finiskaig. From Coire Dubh climb on to Sgurr na h-Aide (859m), the slightly lower west top of Bidean a' Chabair. The main summit lies another 750m along the ridge. To the south there is a plunge of

Loch Beoraid and east to Sgurr an Utha

700m at an average angle of 45 degrees to Gleann an Lochain Eanaiche. Whilst much of this is grass, areas of crag make this an area in which to exercise caution, particularly in descent. When combining this hill with Carn Mor it is best to climb Carn Mor first. If descending Bidean a' Chabair on its south side, the safest route is to follow the burn which starts about 500m east of the summit (the Allt Reidh na Cluaise) and continues in that direction for a similar distance before dropping south-east to upper Gleann an Lochain Eanaiche. This section of the pass is rather unusual in that the floor of the glen is remarkably level and the stream is correspondingly lazy and sluggish and may be surprisingly difficult to cross dry-shod.

An unusual excursion is the grand traverse of Bidean a' Chabair, taking the passenger ferry from Mallaig to Tarbet on Loch Nevis and following the length of its ridge over the subsidiary tops of Sgurr Mor (612m), Sgurr Breac (728m) and Sgurr Meirleach (747m) to the summit some 11km away. With Loch Morar to the south and Loch Nevis to the north this will provide a pleasingly peninsular feel to the day.

Sgurr an Utha; 796m; (OS Sheet 40 NM885839); *peak of the udder*

Rising at the back of Glenfinnan village and to the west of Glen Finnan itself, gnarly Sgurr an Utha is a surprisingly retiring peak. To vary the cliché about wood and trees, sometimes it is hard to see the hill for the mountains. With Sgurr an Utha, the eye is drawn instead to its more photogenic neighbours. Also the hill is so steep and so close to the road that it is difficult to appreciate its top due to its lower slopes. Nonetheless its central location makes this an exceptional viewpoint for the surrounding hills and lochs, particularly over to the Loch Shiel peaks and to Sgurr Thuilm and Sgurr nan Coireachan. Unless combined with another hill, Sgurr an Utha will occupy little more than a half day.

It can be climbed from Glenfinnan railway station, the slopes of Tom na h-Aire giving an interesting ridge approach to Fraoch-bheinn (790m), a lower top which lies a little over 1km east of Sgurr an Utha's sharp summit. From the south-west an approach can be made by the forest track up the Allt Feith a' Chatha, starting some 3km west of Glenfinnan village on the Mallaig road. A track (unmarked on the Landranger map) ascends to NM881827 on the Druim na Brein-choille, from which Fraoch-bheinn can either be included or bypassed on the way to the main summit. A more direct line can be taken by crossing the Allt an Utha by a wooden footbridge on the Allt Feith a' Chatha path and climbing steeply up the slopes of Sidhean Mor (582m). If descending this way care should be taken as Sidhean Mor sports a number of short but steep crags which need to be avoided. Sgurr an Utha can conveniently be combined with its eastern neighbour Glas-charn. Alternatively it can be used to vary the approach to or return from Sgurr nan Coireachan over Sgurr an Fhuarain Duibh. Again one must be careful if descending Sgurr an Utha's north side as it is craggy, and the best line uses a gully system starting some 250m west of the summit.

Glas-charn; 633m; (OS Sheet 40 NM846837); *grey-green peak*

An unsurprisingly seldom-noticed hill, Glas-charn rises between Loch Eilt and Loch Beoraid, to the north of the Mallaig road. Whilst its western and southern slopes comprise extensive areas of undulating hummocks and lochans, its northern aspect takes the form of a spectacular plunge into the narrow confines of Loch Beoraid far below, and its summit gives fine views south to the Rois-bheinn ridge. A direct ascent can be made from several places along the shore of Loch Eilt, the best starting point being just east of Ranochan, following the broad ridge to the east of the Allt Raineachan. It is easier to use the same approach described for the south-west aspects of Sgurr an Utha, crossing the Allt an Utha by a wooden footbridge and continuing up the path beside the Allt Feith a' Chatha. The path becomes vague, but take it to the col with Sidhean Mor then follow the burn west to its source 1km east of the summit. Locating the cairn in mist is likely to prove troublesome because of the number of false tops. This route can conveniently be combined with an ascent of Sgurr an Utha and a pleasant circuit made by including Sgurr a' Mhuidhe and returning over Point 562m.

An Stac; 718m; (OS Sheet 40 NM866889); *the stack*

A hill with a location of superb remoteness, An Stac lies to the south-east of Loch Morar, protected on the south by Meith Bheinn and Beinn Gharbh, and it enjoys wonderful views down the loch to the west and east through to Glen Pean and beyond. Compact and generally conical in shape, it has a particularly craggy and rough aspect above Glen an Obain Bhig.

An Stac receives fewer ascents than it deserves, due to its isolation and lack of height. As the east end of Loch Morar is not a particularly obvious place to visit on a day trip, the bulk of visitors will be back-packers and bothy-goers. From Oban bothy, there are two recommended lines. Firstly, follow a path round into the wooded lower reaches of Gleann Taodhail, to the foot of the west-south-west ridge of An Stac. This gives some pleasant but avoidable scrambling, terminating on a false top on the flattish summit area. Alternatively, head east from Oban by the path towards Glen Pean, but leave the main glen and follow the path southwards from just before the watershed. Follow the western tributary of the burn to gain Cnoc Gorm (527m) and then ascend by broken ground to the summit. These approaches will most easily be made from the east. With a bit of determination upper Gleann Taodhail can also be reached from Arieniskill at the west end of Loch Eilt. The route to Loch Beoraid is as described for Meith Bheinn. Rise slightly from the bridge at the west end of Loch Beoraid, following the path along the north shore of the loch, and then take a line up the west side of the outflow from Lochan Tain Mhic Dhughaill (the Allt na Plaide) to the loch itself. Head north to Lochan a' Bhrodainn, following its outflow (the Allt Reidh an Fraoich) in turn down to the foot of An Stac's west-south-west ridge. The scenery on this route is magnificent.

Meith Bheinn; 710m; (OS Sheet 40 NM821872); *sappy hill*

Sprawling between Loch Morar and Loch Beoraid, this hill has a complex and sometimes confusing summit area. A trip to Meith Bheinn involves a visit to tremendous and rarely frequented countryside. If one has access to a boat or a canoe then a fascinating approach would be by Loch Morar and Camas Luinge north of Meoble Lodge. Meoble's meaning is rich soil.

For the landlubber, Meith Bheinn is best ascended from Arieniskill at the west end of Loch Eilt. A path leaves the road, goes under the railway and follows the Allt na Criche. Take the east branch when the path divides, past one of the area's many caves reputed to have been slept in by Bonnie Prince Charlie, located amongst several large blocks that have fallen from a nearby crag. The west branch of the path gives better views but is lengthier. Descend through trees to the footbridge at the south end of Lochan Lon a' Ghairt, savouring the prospect of the narrow and inky Loch Beoraid. This track continues to Meoble Lodge and Loch Morar. After crossing the footbridge, however, head up the initially steep slopes of Meith Bheinn and so to the more undulating and navigationally challenging summit area. A number of lochans lie south of the summit, which is marked by a trig point and bears the name Sgurr na Maothaith.

A worthwhile approach can also be made from the east by taking the path from Oban round to Gleann Taodhail, as for An Stac. Providing the river can be crossed where the glen turns to the south-east, climb steeply to gain the rough north-east ridge of Meith Bheinn. This is probably the hill's finest feature and it leads steadily to the summit.

Sidhean Mor; 601m; (OS Sheet 40 NM727866); *big fairy hill*

There is an extensive area of rolling hills within the corner of South Morar lying west of the River Meoble, and bounded by the Lochailort-Morar road and Loch Morar. There are numerous summits which give brief but enjoyable outings, from which Sidhean Mor is distinguished only as the loftiest. The quickest line of ascent is from the path up Glen Beasdale, but more pleasing is a circuit of the rough ground lying above Loch a' Choire Riabhaich. Best of all is to sample the varied scenery of a traverse of this area with the assistance of the hill track leading from Kinloid (just north of Arisaig village) to Scamadale at the south-west corner of Loch Morar, following this path towards the Borrodale Burn. A sweep of the hills can be made from just east of Carn a' Mhadaidh-ruaidh (503m) round by Druim Comhnard (556m) to Sidhean Mor, descending by Coire an Eas Bhain to the path by the Borrodale Burn. The train can be used as an obvious means of connecting the loose ends. The summit of Sidhean Mor lies a little to the south-west of the trig point and gives an extensive panorama of peaks, islands and peninsulas, particularly to the south and south-west. A crag just below the summit gives a number of pleasant but short climbs, and there are other routes in Gleann Mama (2km south of Sidhean Mor) with plenty of scope for further one-pitch climbs on the numerous outcrops hereabouts.

Sgurr Eireagoraidh; 548m; (OS Sheets 33 or 40 NM716964); *peak of the goats*

Anyone arriving by ferry at Mallaig can scarcely fail to be impressed (unless the cloud is down) by the group of low but craggy hills which rise from the back of the village. Situated above the north-west corner of Loch Morar these peaks are quite

Brocken Spectre from Sgurr an Eilein Ghiubhais

isolated and are a superb viewpoint down the loch itself and also for Skye, the Small Isles, the Arisaig coast and the length of Loch Nevis. The circuit of the three main Loch Eireagoraidh hills makes an excellent short day. The logical starting point is Glasnacardoch, 1km south of Mallaig. A path heads inland from the hotel here, and two further parallel paths start just to the north. These are boggy and easily lost, but a reasonable line can be found by following old sections of water piping, which is visible in places. Loch an Nostarie is a beautiful expanse of water, and, higher up, the An Leth-allt turns into a fine gorge just below the outflow from Loch Eireagoraidh. A jumble of boulders on the south side of the stream houses a serviceable but draughty howff below the crags of Carn Mhic a' Ghille-chaim.

Carn a' Ghobhair is the shoulder rising steeply on the north of the gorge, and the ground up to its summit is broken and craggy. The angle eases off before the final steepening of Sgurr Eireagoraidh. Sgurr an Eilein Ghiubhais (522m) should also be visited to consider its excellent view of Inverie and the spectacular drop to Loch Nevis below – 500m of vertical fall-off occurs over a horizontal distance of just 750m. Tussocky moorland leads back to craggier ground on the final hill of the circuit, Sgurr Bhuidhe.

An alternative route starts from Mallaig Bheag, just beyond and east of Mallaig, taking the Mallaigmore footpath. From here follow heathery slopes either directly over Aonach Beag to Sgurr Eireagoraidh or go inland to the An Leth-allt and Loch Eireagoraidh as above.

Most of the recorded climbing of note in the area covered by this chapter is found on these hills. The crags of Carn Mhic a' Ghille-chaim have a couple of good quality two pitch rock routes on its Central Pillar, and there are a number of shorter lines. Sgurr Bhuidhe offers a high, prominent and potentially sun-kissed south-facing crag, home to three short but spectacularly located climbs. Creag Mhor Bhrinicoire is reached from Bracorina at the road-end on the north-west shore of Loch Morar, and this is a more extensive cliff with areas of quartz studs and some steep juggy climbing.

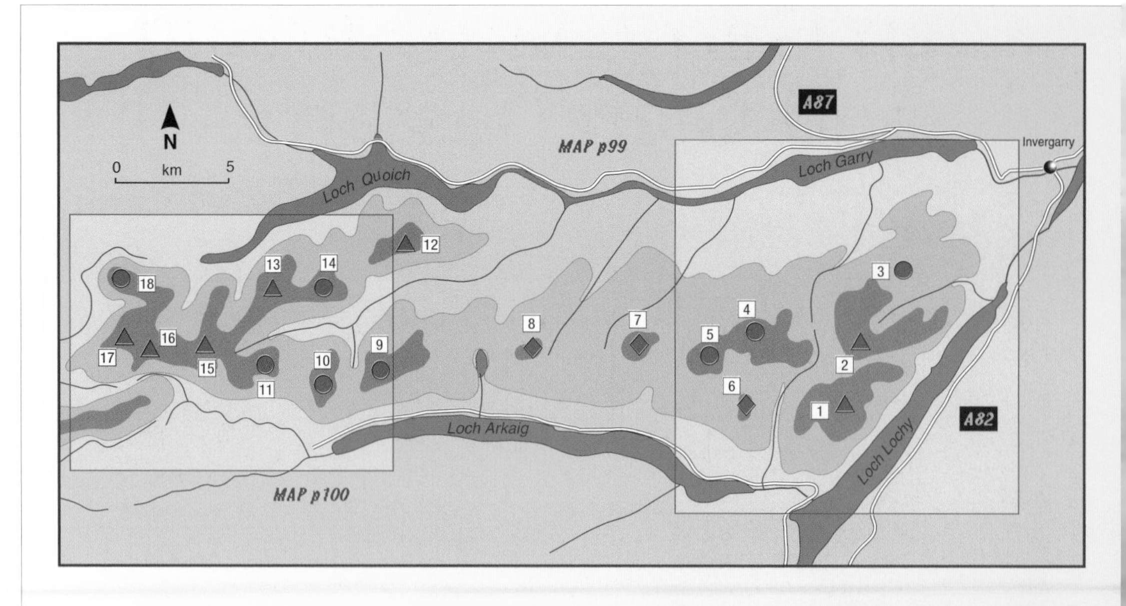

1.	Meall na Teanga	918m	M	p96
2.	Sron a' Choire Ghairbh	937m	M	p96
3.	Ben Tee	904m	C	p98
4.	Meall na h-Eilde	838m	C	p98
5.	Geal Charn	804m	C	p98
6.	Glas Bheinn	732m	G	p99
7.	Sgurr Choinich	749m	G	p100
8.	Meall Blair	656m	G	p100
9.	Sgurr Mhurlagain	880m	C	p101
10.	Fraoch Bheinn	858m	C	p101
11.	Sgurr Cos na Breachd-laoigh	835m	C	p102
12.	Gairich	919m	M	p103
13.	Sgurr Mor	1003m	M	p103
14.	Sgurr an Fhuarain	901m	C	p103
15.	Sgurr nan Coireachan	953m	M	p104
16.	Garbh Chioch Mhor	1013m	M	p105
17.	Sgurr na Ciche	1040m	M	p105
18.	Ben Aden	887m	C	p107

Glen Garry, Loch Arkaig and Glen Dessarry

Hamish Brown

Sgurr Mor from Feadan na Ciche

As with so much of the Western Highlands, the scenery described in this chapter is clearly demarcated by long east-west glens and lochs. It covers the remote countryside north of the Loch Arkaig–Glen Dessarry-Loch Nevis fault, and south of Glen Garry and its western continuation, Loch Quoich. On the east side lies Loch Lochy, one of the long and narrow lochs of the Great Glen, whilst the west boundary is the narrow glen leading from the head of Loch Quoich down the River Carnach to Loch Nevis. In between is a microcosm of the Scottish hills, from low-lying moorland to the rough and rugged peaks above Glen Dessarry, the undoubted highlight being the inspiring and craggy landmark of Sgurr na Ciche looking out over the Atlantic coastline. These mountains are very isolated, with little by way of habitation or infrastructure, and visitors need to be self-sufficient.

In the east of the area, Meall na Teanga and Sron a' Choire Ghairbh rise steeply from Loch Lochy, as does the lower but symmetrical and distinctive Ben Tee. West of here lies an extensive tract of land between Loch Arkaig and Glen Garry that is rolling and rather featureless by comparison. It contains some rounded tops and a fair amount of forestry and bog, and hillwalkers will generally pass it by in preference for the higher and more mountainous peaks beyond. When these central hills are climbed, it is usually from the road along the side of Loch Arkaig. Access can be taken from the north, although this approach is less often used, as the distances are somewhat greater.

Glen Garry is part of a huge depression stretching for some 40km west from Invergarry to Loch Quoich and ultimately over the watershed and down to Loch Nevis. Lower Glen Garry is wooded and beautiful, soon giving way to Loch Garry itself, a loch greatly enlarged by hydro-electric damming and almost surrounded by forestry, but it is generally a peaceful and attractive place. A very fine view of the loch and also of Gairich and the other hills around Kingie can be obtained from a lay-by on the A87 about 3km west of the Kinloch Hourn junction. The River Garry meanders down from Tomdoun to the west end of Loch

Sgurr an Fhuarain from the River Kingie

Garry through a succession of wide pools and small lochs. The road emerges from the forestry at Loch Poulary as one heads west, and thereafter the landscape becomes increasingly wild. At Kingie 6km west of Tomdoun you will find the confluence of the Gearr Garry (the outflow of Loch Quoich) and the River Kingie, which issues from Glen Kingie to the west-south-west. Kingie is little more than a handful of forestry cottages. Beyond it there are only hills, lochs and emptiness.

Glen Kingie lies parallel to and between Loch Arkaig and Loch Quoich. It is hemmed in by a cirque of wild hills, the highest of which is Sgurr Mor. The glen extends for 17km from Kingie and is desolate and uninhabited, the only spartan shelter being Kinbreack bothy. The River Kingie is generally sluggish, and it tends to be wide and deep. After rainfall, its tributaries rise rapidly and crossing it becomes a serious or impossible undertaking, there being no bridge other than the one 2km upstream from Kingie. Access up the glen is on foot, there being an initial section of forest track west of Kingie, which soon gives way to paths of variable quality.

Glen Kingie can also be reached from the dam at the east end of Loch Quoich or from Strathan, the latter in most cases being the more convenient approach to the glen's hills other than Gairich. A major ridge continues west from Sgurr Mor and the head of Glen Kingie, turning more rugged and the peaks ever finer, its contorted backbone culminating in the splendid Sgurr na Ciche far above remote Loch Nevis. Whilst geographically these mountains lie to the east of the Rough Bounds of Knoydart, they share many of the characteristics of that area and give hard and rewarding hill days.

The west end of Loch Arkaig gives access to upper Glen Kingie by two separate passes. The Dearg Allt path crosses over from Strathan by the Feith a' Bhrolaich, and the Feith a' Chicheanais path sets off a little further west from Glendessarry Lodge. Both descend into the glen near Kinbreack bothy, a useful base for climbing the peaks around Sgurr Mor. Mention has been made in Chapter 3 *(p72)* of Glen Dessarry and also the magnificent Mam na Cloich' Airde pass which can be followed to Loch Nevis and on over the Mam Meadail into Knoydart if desired. This route will be the usual access to Sgurr na Ciche and its neighbours.

To continue on to Glen Carnach from Sourlies bothy, one must pass above the rocky headland at the foot of Druim a' Ghoirtein (unless the tide is out when the sandy shore can be followed instead). A faint path then continues on over the saltings by Loch Nevis to the ruined keeper's house at Carnoch. There is a suspension footbridge here (rather rickety at the time of publication), beyond which a variable path follows the west bank of the River Carnach and peters out after 4km or so under the neck-craning brows of Ben Aden. The glen then gives very rough going round to the stunning Lochan nam Breac (surely one of the country's top ten wilderness camp spots), near which the Mam Unndalain path can be picked up and followed to the west end of Loch Quoich.

Loch Quoich lies north of the extensive Gairich-Sgurr na Ciche ridge, its surroundings also isolated and devoid of habitation. The single-track Kingie to Kinloch Hourn road passes along its north shore before descending to the sea. The loch has been dammed at both ends and its level substantially raised, again as a hydro-electricity scheme. These operations flooded the old shooting lodge, and have rendered access to the hills south of the loch far

Access and Transport

By road: from the south, the single-track B8005 leads from Gairlochy along the north shore of Loch Arkaig. This can be followed to the west end of the loch 1km east of Strathan, as described in Chapter 3 *(p72)*. From 8km west of Invergarry, a single-track branch of the A87 leads past Tomdoun to Kinloch Hourn, giving access to the area from the north. Generally Loch Quoich forms a major barrier, so the south approach is more convenient for the bulk of the hills.

By bus: Invergarry Post Office to Kingie (daily except Sundays); Invergarry Post Office to Kinloch Hourn (Mondays, Wednesdays and Fridays) (Royal Mail four-seater post bus, tel: 01809-501401 and 08457-740740). Inverness to Fort William (Scottish Citylink Coaches, tel: 08705-505050, and Highland Country Buses, tel: 01463-222244). Uig to Glasgow/Edinburgh via Fort William (Scottish Citylink Coaches).

By ferry: Mallaig to Inverie (Mondays, Wednesdays and Fridays); Mallaig to Tarbet (Fridays) (Bruce Watt Sea Cruises, tel: 01687-462320). It may be possible to make an arrangement to be put ashore near the head of the loch. Alternatively, walk from Inverie over the Mam Meadail.

By train: the nearest stations are Spean Bridge, Fort William, Glenfinnan and Mallaig.

Accommodation and Information

Hotels and guesthouses: Spean Bridge, Fort Augustus, Invergarry and Tomdoun.

SYHA hostel: Loch Lochy (tel: 01809-501239)

Independent hostel: Invergarry Lodge (tel: 01809-501412)

Campsites: two near Invergarry - Faichem Park (tel: 01809-501226), and Faichemard Farm (tel: 01809-501314); Fort Augustus (tel: 01320-366618); Mucomir; Spean Bridge (tel: 01397-712711)

Tourist Information Centres: Fort William (tel: 01397-703781); Fort Augustus (tel: 01320-366367); Spean Bridge (tel: 01397-712576) (Easter - October)

Maps

Ordnance Survey: 1:50,000 Landranger sheets 33 (Loch Alsh, Glen Shiel & Loch Hourn), 34 (Fort Augustus and Glen Albyn) and 40 (Mallaig and Glenfinnan); 1:25,000 Explorer sheets 398 (Loch Morar & Mallaig), 399 (Loch Arkaig) and 400 (Loch Lochy & Glen Roy).

more difficult. The water level is often very low, revealing an ugly tidemark. The loss of the natural shoreline has also given the waters a sense of lifelessness, despite the grandeur of the setting. At the west end of the loch there are two cut-off dams, but for which the raised Loch Quoich would instead flow westwards into the Atlantic. The extraordinary asymmetry of the Western Highlands is well illustrated here, as water flows west to Loch Nevis in the space of just 10km whilst to the east water does not reach the sea until Inverness, some 95km away.

Loch Quoich is surrounded by high hills, the more spectacular of which lie above its west end, and the road gives a grandstand view of Gairich and the distinctive shapes of Sgurr Mor and Sgurr na Ciche. One way of reaching the more westerly of these hills and the head of Loch Nevis is to start from the Kinloch Hourn road near NG986037, where it finally leaves the loch. Follow the rough and pathless shore as far as the Abhainn Cosaidh. There is no bridge over this river, which must be given considerable respect during or after rain as it can be completely unfordable for many kilometres upstream, and being on the wrong side of it in such conditions is extremely committing. Beyond the Abhainn Cosaidh a track (built to aid the reservoir construction works) runs to the head of the loch. It is also possible to take access from the road along or across Loch Quoich by dingy or canoe.

Generally the Glen Dessarry access is easier than the Loch Quoich route, the paths being better, the ground less rough and there being bridges over the larger burns. The hills around Sgurr na Ciche provide many permutations, particularly excellent being the full traverse of the ridge from Gairich over Sgurr Mor and Sgurr na Ciche all the way to Ben Aden. This is most easily achieved as a backpacking trip from the north and gives an unforgettable expedition if one is favoured with good weather.

There is very little recorded climbing on the hills covered in this chapter. This is no surprise in relation to the eastern peaks, which are not craggy. Elsewhere, there is no shortage of rock, but it is just not arranged in a particularly climber-friendly manner, in that the cliffs are remote and rather discontinuous with a fair amount of vegetation. Nonetheless, exploratory climbing will surely prove possible in the corries of some of the western mountains.

Principal Hills

Meall na Teanga; 918m; (OS Sheet 34; NN220924); *hill of the tongue*

Sron a' Choire Ghairbh; 937m; (OS Sheet 34; NN222945); *jutting peak,* literally *nose, of the rough corrie*

Rising boldly from the west shore of Loch Lochy, these peaks dominate the loch for almost its full length. Together with Ben Tee to the north, Meall na Teanga and Sron a' Choire Ghairbh are known as the Loch Lochy hills and are prominent features from many parts of the Great Glen. The eastern slopes are continuously steep, finely sculpted corries falling away at a somewhat unlikely angle to lower forested areas. From other aspects the hillsides are rather less dramatic and the summits are generally rounded. The two Munros are usually climbed together, making a fine outing which can be enjoyed either from the north or the south, or, even better, as a traverse from one end to the other, possibly to include Ben Tee as well.

Meall na Teanga is really the middle of a line of three high level tops, the other two being Meall Dubh (837m) to its north and Meall Coire Lochain (906m) to its south. Sron a' Choire Ghairbh, however, takes the form of an enormous horseshoe above the huge but mainly grassy Coire Glas, in which a small lochan nestles. Between the hills lies a glacially formed pass, the Cam Bhealach, which is crossed by a path leading from Loch Lochy over to the south shore of Loch Garry. This pass reaches c615m and is the normal route of access. The recommended starting point is the north-east end of Loch

A Remarkable Feat

Reference to the Loch Lochy hills would be incomplete without making mention of the extraordinary efforts of Richard Wood, for twenty years a resident of Invergarry. In 1998 he made his 1000th ascent of Ben Tee, at which point he had also ascended a quite awesome 6278 Munros. He achieved his 1000th ascent of Sron a' Choire Ghairbh in February 2000, and has also been up Meall na Teanga over 800 times. He then moved to Cannich, where he has turned his prodigious attentions to Sgurr na Diollaid.

Lochy as that allows an appreciation of the juxtaposition of the hills and the loch. Cars can be left just before the bridge at Kilfinnan on the west bank of the Caledonian Canal, near the end of the minor road from North Laggan, (for which the farmer may ask for money). The Cam Bhealach path certainly saves a bit of effort, and is reached by following the upper forest track along the loch side for about 3.5km before the path breaks off west. Forestry operations hereabouts to fell and replant have left some areas looking ugly and bare, however the path soon enters a steep-sided glen and then reaches the pass.

Climbing south from the col, Meall Dubh can be bypassed on its west side, and a bouldery slope leads to Meall na Teanga, whose cairn is towards the south end of its summit ridge. Return to the col, then take a stalkers path north up the grassy hillside. This path gains more height than the Landranger map shows. A short mossy walk leads to Sron a' Choire Ghairbh's summit. The views from these hills are very fine, both up and down the Great Glen, and their central location allows many distant peaks to be identified on a clear day. The descent can be made by the rough and undulating ridge over Sean Mheall (887m) and Meall nan Dearcag (689m) and so down to Kilfinnan. Care is necessary, as there are some scrappy crags to avoid if coming off the nose of the ridge. This route may be used in ascent, but the ground gives quite slow going. One can also return by the Cam Bhealach path.

The north ridge of Sron a' Choire Ghairbh is called Meall a' Choire Ghlais (900m), a strikingly flat projection for some 3km, after which it plunges roughly to the col with Ben Tee. This slope is best avoided on a spur to its north. The area south of the col is less boggy than the Landranger map suggests. This part of the hill can also be reached mainly by forest tracks from Greenfield and the bridge over the narrows at Torr na Carraidh near the west end of Loch Garry, then by the path up the bank of the Allt Bealach Easain.

The south approach is from the Eas Chia-aig car park between the Mile Dorcha and the east end of Loch Arkaig. In August 1745 Prince Charles spent two weeks lurking in 'sundry fast places' round here, one of his hideouts being a cave in Gleann Cia-aig, another being a big tree. Take the footpath from the car park up past the waterfalls to gain a forest track on the east of the Abhainn Chia-aig, following this and then a path past the edge of the forest and across the footbridge at NN187928. The path leading below Meall an Tagraidh to Fedden is very sketchy, but gives the right line. Fedden was a much frequented drovers' stance a couple of centuries ago, but all that remains now is a ruin. Just before it, cut across haggy ground to reach the Cam Bhealach path as it leads east round to the col. Climb Sron a' Choire Ghairbh as already described, then traverse to Meall na Teanga and continue south-west to Meall Coire Lochain. Follow the ridge above the crags of Meall Odhar (871m) and drop west down to Gleann Cia-aig again.

A narrower section of ridge lies just north-east of the summit of Meall Coire Lochain which will need some care in winter. An alternative descent from Meall Coire Lochain, if transport can be arranged, is to head south-west past the knoll of Leac Chorrach (588m) to pick up the forest track at NN200890 and follow this down to the public road at Clunes. Meall Coire Lochain also boasts the only recorded climb on these hills, *Central Gully* (120m III 1986), located on the crags of Coire Lochain south of the summit.

Ben Tee; 904m; (OS Sheet 34; NN240971); *hill of the fairy hill*

Given the predictable nature of the Gael when it came to naming his mountains, it is perhaps surprising that Ben Tee was not called Sgurr na Ciche or similar, although there is an inevitability to there being a Ben Tee Room at its foot. An attractive cone, and so regular in its appearance that it is sometimes referred to as the Schiehallion of the north, Ben Tee is very prominent from the Great Glen and is also well seen from further west around Glen Garry and Loch Quoich. Lying just north of Sron a' Choire Ghairbh, it can easily be combined with its neighbour or climbed on its own.

The obvious way is from Kilfinnan at the north-east end of Loch Lochy. Avoid the path by the Kilfinnan Burn as this leads only to the waterfall. Instead, climb directly up the hillside to the north-east, using a stile over a fence near NN271968. Beyond this, a tract of tussocky moorland leads to the steep and bouldery summit slopes. There is an extensive view, particularly to the north-east, and west to Gairich. Another approach can be made from Torr na Carraidh near the west end of Loch Garry, using the forest tracks past Greenfield to the foot of the Allt Bealach Easain, and following a path up the side of that stream. This is the line of an old coffin route and right of way to Laggan. Climb the steep south-west slopes above the col. Another good route is from the forestry car park at White Bridge near the east end of Loch Garry, from where forest tracks and then a path can be used to gain and follow the Allt na Cailliche to the foot of the upper slopes.

Ben Tee is steep and rough in places, particularly west and north-west of the summit, so care must be taken in descent if continuing to Sron a' Choire Ghairbh.

Meall na h-Eilde; 838m; (OS Sheet 34; NN185946); *hill of the hinds*

Geal Charn; 804m; (OS Sheet 34; NN156942); *white peak*

Although almost 4km apart, Meall na h-Eilde and Geal Charn are joined by a broad and easy ridge and are usually ascended together. These hills form the unspectacular principal summits in the area of rolling ground of middle height lying immediately west of the Loch Lochy hills, from which they are separated by the wide and symmetrical pass running from Gleann Cia-aig to Loch Garry. The usual starting points are either the Eas Chia-aig car park, or Achnasaul 2.5km further west along Loch Arkaig. By the former approach, take the route described for Meall na Teanga, crossing the footbridge beyond the forestry. Leave the path and ascend due north up grassy slopes to the summit of Meall na h-Eilde. On the way up the glen from the road the most prominent feature is Meall na h-Eilde's conical subsidiary top, Meall an Tagraidh (761m), which can easily be included as well. It was on this hill that the fleeing Bonnie Prince Charlie hid for several days, Cameron of Clunes reportedly taking him bread, cheese and whisky and keeping him company, lying in their plaids together near the top in the rain. The modern hill-walker will sympathise as nothing much has changed since then, other than the introduction of Gore-Tex, Thermos flasks, Kendal mint cake and GPS.

A rough track leaves the road from the bridge west of Achnasaul, and leads up the east bank of the Allt Dubh to the foot of Geal Charn. This is climbed by its heathery south-east slopes. This hill is more open to the west and so has the better view. There are some ups and downs on the way to Meall na h-Eilde, but the route is straightforward and passes over Meall Coire nan Saobhaidh (826m). The circuit may equally well be made in either direction, and the round trip is recommended with a short

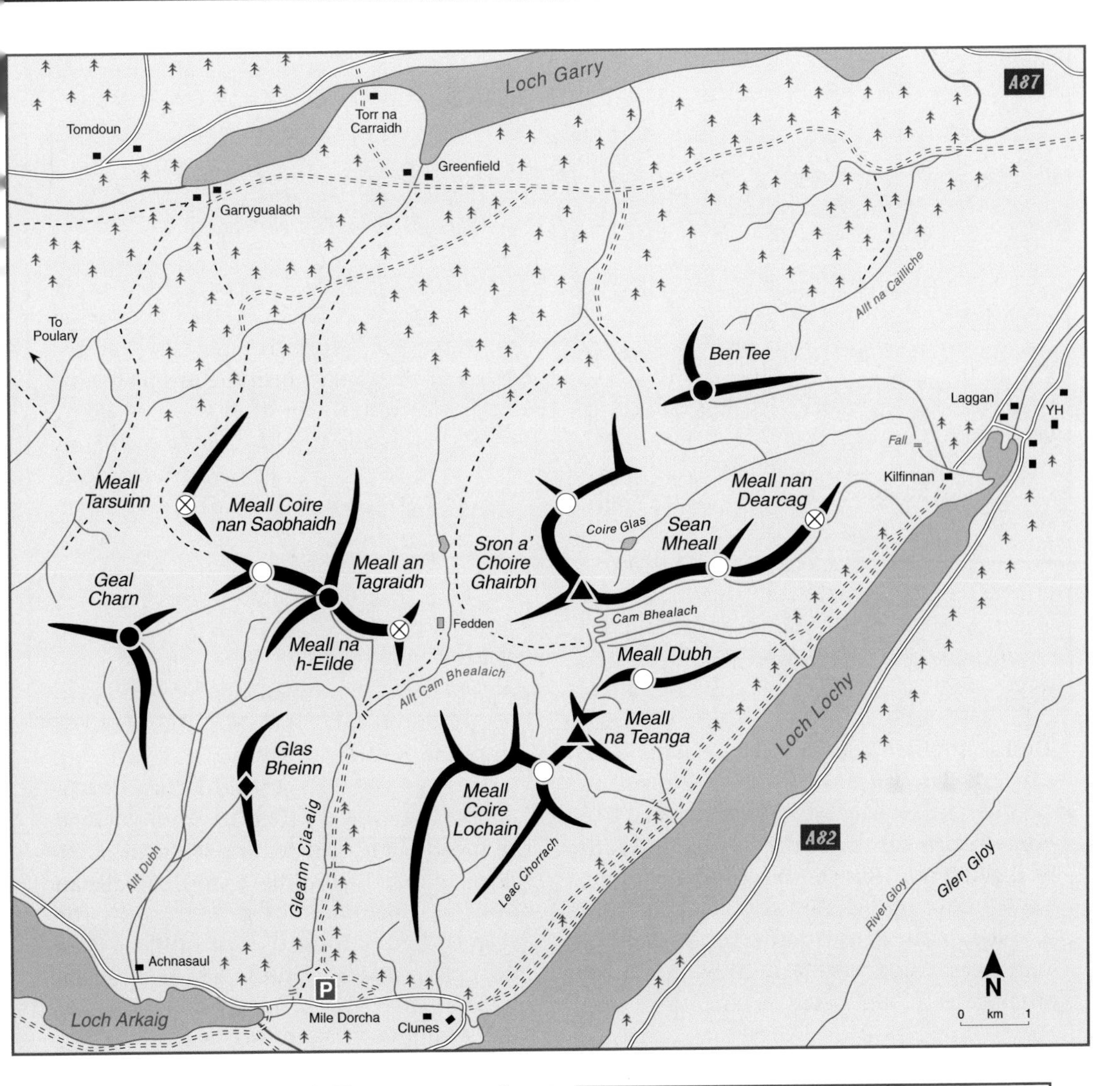

walk back along the road. If you want to the avoid the road then Achnasaul is the better starting point.

These hills are seen to advantage from Loch Garry and there is a network of paths and tracks accessible from Greenfield and the bridge over the narrows of the loch at Torr na Carraidh. This approach is less often used as it is rather longer than that from the south and Geal Charn is slightly out on a limb. A good circuit can be made round Coire nan Saobhaidh, initially using the stalkers path which climbs over Meall Tarsuinn (660m) to the col with Meall Coire nan Saobhaidh. The paths pass through areas now planted with forestry and care must be taken not to lose them.

Glas Bheinn; 732m; (OS Sheet 34; NN171919); *grey-green hill*

Glas Bheinn is the outlying hill situated between Loch Arkaig and the Geal Charn-Meall na h-Eilde ridge. As such it can easily be included either as an hors d' oeuvre or as a dessert to the circuit of its neighbours. For this the approach is best made from Achnasaul, following the path for 2km before trending steeply north-east on to the hill. There is an excellent view from the summit up the length of Loch Arkaig to the peaks that rise beyond.

Glas Bheinn connects by its broad north slopes to the watershed between the Allt

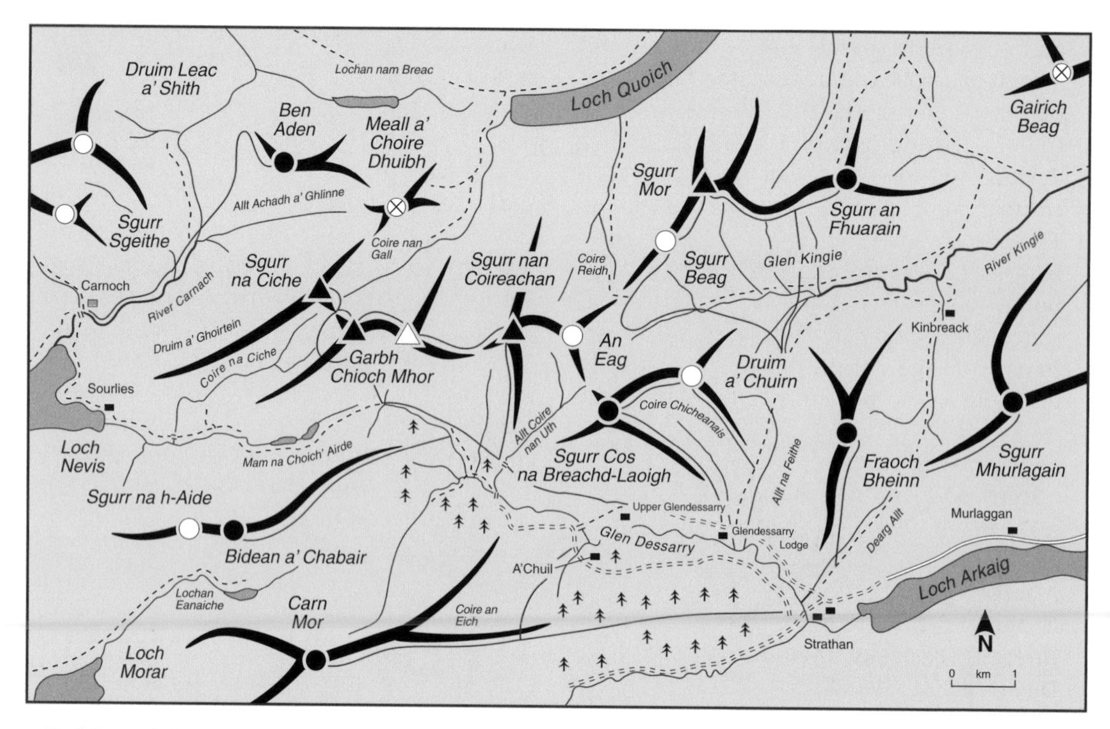

Dubh and the Allt Tarsuinn from which it is easy to gain either Geal Charn or Meall na h-Eilde. An alternative is the approach by Gleann Cia-aig described for Meall na Teanga. Take the track and path to the footbridge beyond the forestry, cross the Allt Tarsuinn and climb to the gently curving north-east ridge, which is followed to the summit.

Sgurr Choinich; 749m; (OS Sheet 34; NN127949); *mossy peak*

This retiring hill is in the middle of the unfrequented and low-lying ground between the Loch Lochy hills and the rugged peaks of Glen Dessarry. Its finest features are reserved for those who ascend from the north, from which side a narrow ridge and craggy face can be appreciated. From Poulary, cross the bridge over the River Garry, leave the track and follow a path through forestry. This emerges from the plantations on to the shoulder of Teanga gun Urrainn from where there is a moorland flog of some length to the north-east ridge. The upper section of this gives enjoyable walking.

The summit of Sgurr Choinich cannot be seen from the easier Loch Arkaig approach. This is more straightforward but less inspiring. Start just west of the bridge over the Allt Mhuic, from where a narrow band of native forestry soon gives way to the open hillside. Climb for 4km to the summit. The view is a fair reward for the relative tedium of the uniform slopes scaled.

Meall Blair; 656m; (OS Sheet 33; NN077950); *hill of the clearing*

Lying about half way along the north shore of Loch Arkaig, Meall Blair is the undemanding western neighbour of Sgurr Choinich. It gives a pleasant outing with a good view. Its north side has elements of interest with a few broken crags and a defined ridge, and these can be seen distantly from Kingie in Glen Garry. The southern flanks, gentle and grassy, give the more obvious route due to the proximity of the Loch Arkaig road.

One can follow the Allt Caonich from the back of the house of the same name, and this leads to just below the summit area. It is better to start from the high point of the road about 500 metres west of Caonich, using a poor track that takes a devious line to Loch Blair. From the loch continue up the broad south-west slopes. There are a number of tops, the summit being the eastmost one, where there is a trig point. It gives a grand view across the waters of Loch Arkaig and over to the east flanks of Sgurr Mhurlagain, which rise impressively immediately to the west.

Sgurr Mhurlagain; 880m; (OS Sheet 33; NN012944); *peak of the sea-inlet*

A somewhat solitary hill, Sgurr Mhurlagain is the most easterly of the increasingly interesting peaks that rise above Glen Dessarry and Glen Kingie. Its higher rocks are made of attractive pale granite gneiss and it lies on the boundary between the smooth eastern granulite hills and the rugged schist mountains of the west. Its triple north-east ridges dominate the south side of middle Glen Kingie, but due to their remoteness they are seldom visited. This aspect is however more stimulating scenically than the continuously steep hill-sides above Loch Arkaig.

If one is feeling strong but brainless then the quickest approach is to start at Murlaggan a little before the west end of Loch Arkaig, from which just climb the hill direct. Better and more aesthetic routes of ascent can be followed. From the road-end east of Strathan, follow the Dearg Allt path to the col (the Feith a' Bhrolaich) between Fraoch Bheinn and Sgurr Mhurlagain. The south-west ridge then provides an easy-angled and stony route to the summit. The hill can also be conveniently climbed with Fraoch Bheinn or taken in on the way either to or from Kinbreack bothy in upper Glen Kingie.

Rain

This area is renowned for its rainfall, in the eyes of both the statistician and the mountaineer. A rain gauge at the west end of Loch Quoich (prior to the raising of the loch's level) used to give an average annual reading of about 400cm. In 1961 it was a staggering 520cm! This compares unfavourably with nearby Ardnamurchan's average of perhaps 100cm a year. The greatest reading over a 24-hour period was 20.5cm on 11 October 1916. Do not despair, as the sun does shine at times. However careful attention should be paid to weather forecasts, and one must be prepared to be flexible in route-planning, particularly in view of the potentially dangerous nature of many of the burns which can rise rapidly and alarming after just a few hours' rainfall.

Fraoch Bheinn; 858m; (OS Sheets 33 & 40; NM986940); *heather hill*

Fraoch Bheinn is the sharp and compact peak sandwiched between Sgurr Mhurlagain and Druim a' Chuirn. Steep flanks fall on either side of the hill to cols with the Dearg Allt and Feith a' Chicheanais paths which climb from Strathan and Glendessarry Lodge and drop north into Glen Kingie. A ridge runs south from the summit to Strathan, whilst twin ridges are thrown out generally northwards, both steep and rocky. In particular, Fraoch Bheinn's narrow north-east ridge is well worth visiting, as it gives some enjoyable scrambling with interesting rock scenery, and it is a fine feature viewed from Kinbreack bothy. The summit is at the south end of a short level ridge, which leads in about 500 metres to the north top (854m). Coire na Cloiche Moire lies to the east, at the head of which there is a huge fissured rock-slip.

If climbing the hill from Strathan one should follow the Dearg Allt path, trending west at c350m onto the south ridge. The slopes above the col at the head of the Dearg Allt are steeper but quite manageable, and they can be used to combine this hill with Sgurr Mhurlagain. The north-east ridge should be included in the itinerary if

Garbh Chioch Mhor from Sgurr na Ciche

possible, and is most conveniently climbed from Kinbreack bothy. The north-north-west ridge meantime can be used to descend to the top of the Feith a' Chicheanais path and so back to Glen Dessarry. The ridge should be followed to just north of the col to avoid a band of crags below.

Sgurr Cos na Breachd-laoigh; 835m; (OS Sheets 33 & 40; NM948947); *peak of the hollow of the speckled fawns*

Located just behind Glendessarry Lodge, this horseshoe-shaped ridge gives a pleasant albeit short circuit by itself, and can also be used as a convenient approach to or return from An Eag and the Sgurr Mor-Sgurr na Ciche ridge. The complex name may, it has been suggested, properly be Sgurr Cois Breacaich (*stony-footed peak*). The summit is at the west end of the hill, while at the east end is the lower Druim a' Chuirn (822m). In between is a ridge, narrow and precipitous on the north side, with a flaky little pinnacle, A' Chioch, on the crest. This pinnacle gives some scrambling and is a prominent skyline feature when viewed from Glen Dessarry.

The normal approach is from Glendessarry Lodge. Either follow the Feith a' Chicheanais path north for 1km to the foot of Druim a' Chuirn's south-east ridge, climb this and traverse A' Chioch on the way to the summit, or head north-west from the lodge to gain the south-east retaining spur of Coire Chicheanais. This leads to the flatter upper corrie then more steeply to the summit itself. Alternatively, if one follows the Feith a' Chicheanais path to the col with Fraoch Bheinn, some discontinuous but easy scrambling can be enjoyed on the fine rough slabs on Druim a' Chuirn's east slopes.

To continue to An Eag, make a steep descent north-west with a drop of some 200m to the col at the head of Glen Kingie.

Gairich; 919m; (OS Sheet 33; NN025995); *roaring*

This fine mountain stands as a proud and isolated sentinel of the stunning range of peaks extending to its west. The north and east flanks overlooking Loch Quoich are craggy, and steep slopes fall south into Glen Kingie. It is a striking feature from the Glen Garry road, and makes an easier outing than most of the other peaks in this part of the area.

The ascent is usually made from the east end of Loch Quoich. Start along a path (boggy in places) from the south end of the dam, the first few hundred metres of which are now submerged in the raised waters of the loch. There is a junction above the forest in Glen Kingie, from which a good stalkers path climbs up on to Druim na Geid Salaich, petering out somewhat where the ridge levels off. A faint path traverses easy ground south of Bac nam Foid (584m) to the foot of the final steepening, south of the crags of Coire Thollaidh. Take an obvious path for a while, abandoning it when it heads off across the south side of the hill. The route (now well worn by hillwalkers) then picks its way through some rocky steps to end abruptly on the mossy summit dome. Care is required under snow or ice.

Gairich is usually climbed on its own, but one can continue west along the chain of hills towards Sgurr na Ciche by passing over the shoulder of Gairich Beag (730m) and dropping steeply down a zigzag stalkers path into the top of the A' Mhaingir glen. This connection is not often made as the top of this pass is at a relatively low c360m. This pass is the approach to use from Kinbreack bothy (the level of the River Kingie permitting), from where one follows the path to the upper part of the Allt a' Choire Ghlais and so to the head of A' Mhaingir.

Sgurr Mor; 1003m; (OS Sheets 33 & 40; NM965980); *big peak*

Sgurr an Fhuarain; 901m; (OS Sheets 33 & 40; NM987979); *peak of the spring*

The highest peak above Glen Kingie, Sgurr Mor is a huge saddle-shaped hill which dominates the upper part of the glen as well as the views from the north shore of Loch Quoich. It is quite a remote hill, as Loch Quoich bars access from that side, whilst on the south the closest road is the Loch Arkaig one. While the ascent can be made from the Loch Quoich dam with a long walk up Glen Kingie, the more normal starting point will be the west end of Loch Arkaig. Sgurr Mor's eastern subsidiary is the pyramid of Sgurr an Fhuarain, to which it is connected by a graceful curving ridge. On the Glen Kingie side are somewhat monotonous grass slopes riven by numerous shallow gullies. To the north the hills are less craggy than the map

Trouble In The Trees?

The lower slopes of many of the hills featured in this book have been heavily planted with commercial forestry, and Glen Dessarry is a good example of this. Whilst forestry brings with it welcome local employment and income, it is also accompanied by massive changes to the landscape. The trees are not indigenous, and bear no relation to the ancient forests which once covered so much of the west of Scotland. Forest tracks can be helpful to hillwalkers and to mountain-bikers, particularly compared to boggy paths, and they have eased the way for countless pairs of weary legs. But the Glen Dessarry of today is very different from that of the 1970s, before planting took place, and the wild land here, as with many areas of Scotland, is now partly obscured under a choking green blanket. And it's not just the aesthetics that suffer; straying from the beaten path can be a laborious experience, and a short cut may well turn out to be a laceration rather than a saving of time!

Sgurr na Ciche from near Beinn Bhuidhe

suggests, and an old stalkers path ascends the north ridge of Sgurr an Fhuarain from Loch Quoich. This path, however, dates from the days of the old Glenquoich Lodge, now submerged beneath the enlarged waters of the loch, so it will only be of use to those approaching by canoe.

From the road-end east of Strathan, follow the track to Glendessarry Lodge and take the Feith a' Chicheanais path between Druim a' Chuirn and Fraoch Bheinn. Leave this shortly after the col, then make a descending traverse west to pick up the stalkers path in upper Glen Kingie, following it to the col north-east of An Eag. This is one of the country's more dramatic man-made paths, at one point taking the form of a carefully crafted stone staircase. It can be followed along a splendid section of ridge over the fine subsidiary peak of Sgurr Beag (890m) to Sgurr Mor and, if desired, as far as Sgurr an Fhuarain. One can descend the slopes of Doire nan Cluainean south into Glen Kingie from the low point on the ridge between Sgurr Mor and Sgurr an Fhuarain and so back over the Feith a' Chicheanais path. For those with rather more time available, Kinbreack bothy makes a good base for exploring upper Glen Kingie. The direct ascent of Sgurr Mor from the bothy is a grind, however, and it is preferable to climb the hill either by the Sgurr Beag path or by Sgurr an Fhuarain's east-south-east ridge. The latter is a good option, and is reached by the paths leading across to the Allt a' Choire Ghlais.

Sgurr nan Coireachan; 953m; (OS Sheets 33 & 40; NM933958); *peak of the corries*

Rising on the north side of upper Glen Dessarry, Sgurr nan Coireachan is quite a shy peak which is not easily seen other than from its near neighbours. It is centrally located on the Gairich-Sgurr na Ciche ridge and throws out additional ridges to the north-east and south. On the west there is a steep drop to the Bealach Coire nan Gall (733m) and the adjoining Garbh Chioch ridge. Its slopes are steep and the upper parts of its corries are very rocky in places.

The hill can be climbed by a number of routes, although its Munro status means it is frequently combined with Garbh Chioch Mhor and Sgurr na Ciche. The usual starting point is the Loch Arkaig road-end, from where the track then path on the north side of Glen Dessarry should be taken as far as the Allt Coire nan Uth. There is a footbridge (not shown on the Landranger map) down by the forest edge over the burn, essential if the water is high. From here climb the rather uncompromising south ridge of Sgurr nan Coireachan. It leads directly to the summit, the ridge narrowing and edged with crags in its upper stages.

If continuing to Garbh Chioch Mhor, head west initially then steeply south-west down to the Bealach Coire nan Gall. If desired one can continue the descent south into Glen Dessarry as a means of returning to Strathan. Another possibility from the top of Sgurr nan Coireachan is to follow the scrambly crest over its eastern outlier An Eag (873m), the 'Eag' or notch being a curious joint-face lying across the ridge just east of the top. An Eag occupies a pivotal position above Loch Quoich and Glen Kingie, with ridges radiating in three directions, giving a number of options. It is also a good point from which to admire the beautifully smooth ice-moulded schist slabs of Coire nan Uth.

The best route back to Strathan from An Eag is over Sgurr Cos na Breachd-laoigh and its south-east ridge. One can also descend into Glen Dessarry by following the Allt Coire nan Uth from the col between these hills, but the topography of the corrie is unhelpful, always pushing one towards the steep-sided burn. Another possibility is to continue east to pick up the Sgurr Beag-Sgurr Mor path and return to Strathan by upper Glen Kingie.

Sgurr nan Coireachan extends a major ridge north, the Druim Buidhe, which drops over An t-Sail (695m) to near the cut-off dams at the west end of Loch Quoich, and a stalkers path climbs up it for some way. While the dams are not a logical starting point unless you already happen to be there, this ridge does facilitate an excellent round from Sgurr nan Coireachan to Ben Aden.

Garbh Chioch Mhor; 1013m; (OS Sheets 33 & 40; NM909961); *big rough place of the breast*

Sgurr na Ciche; 1040m; (OS Sheets 33 & 40; NM902966); *peak of the breast*

These remote and exciting hills are located in the middle of the huge wild area between upper Glen Dessarry, the head of Loch Nevis, and the far south-west corner of Loch Quoich. There is no habitation, and the nearest road is several hours' walk away. The knobbly cone of Sgurr na Ciche is one of the most distinctive sights in the Western Highlands and is the culmination of the superb twisting ridge which stretches from Gairich. It is a steep and craggy peak, its south-west ridge dropping to the waters of Loch Nevis over a distance of 5km, whilst its rocky north ridge descends to the head of Loch Quoich, connecting also with Ben Aden. Garbh Chioch Mhor, only a little lower, is far less prominent, being a rough east-west ridge running from Sgurr na Ciche towards Sgurr nan Coireachan.

Although these hills lie beyond Knoydart's true boundaries, they remain closely associated with the name 'the Rough Bounds', and one wonders if Garbh Chioch Mhor has its roots instead in the name 'Garbh-chriochan', which translates as *'rough bounds'*. Semantics aside, the day spent traversing these summits makes one of the classic outings in the Scottish hills. The isolated setting is stunning, the views can be excellent, and the hills are as rugged as any others on the mainland. Indeed, there is a lot of rock, particularly on Garbh

Loch Quoich, Gleouraich, Spidean Mialach, Gairich and Sgurr Morast from Ben Aden

Chioch Mhor, and some scrambling experience is necessary. On a good day the traverse will be exhilarating but straightforward, while in poor conditions frequent potentially confusing detours are required to avoid obstacles. Generally, route finding should not be too complicated as there is a robust wall running along the crest of Garbh Chioch Mhor. It serves both as a navigational aid and also as a folly to the harshness and excess of the feudal system of land ownership that decreed such a construction to be necessary at all.

Ascents usually start either from Glen Dessarry or Sourlies bothy, and parties will often either camp or base themselves in bothies due to the remoteness of the hills. Day trips are feasible but quite lengthy, even in summer. From Strathan, Garbh Chioch Mhor is best gained either over Sgurr nan Coireachan by its south ridge as described, or by ascending to the Bealach Coire nan Gall from just west of the Allt Coire nan Uth. From the bealach simply follow the dyke along the rugged ridge of rocky outcrops over Garbh Chioch Bheag (968m) to the main summit. Coire nan Gall lies to the north and is very rough. It overlooks Loch Quoich and contains large and impressive sweeps of slabby rock that may reward the exploratory climber. The southern flanks above the Mam na Cloich' Airde form an imposing wall, but are less continuously rocky.

An alternative approach from Strathan, which can be used to climb either peak, is to take the path to just west of the Bealach an Lagain Duibh (310m) (the name given to the top of the pass between the Mam na Cloich' Airde and Glen Dessarry). Follow a burn to reach the level grassy terrace on the south-west shoulder of Garbh Chioch Mhor at c620m. The Explorer map indicates that a path follows the burn, which would be helpful if it could be located.

Traverse north-west at this level on a grassy terrace into a steep-sided bouldery gully up which there is a faint path to the col on the ridge above. This gully is known as the Feadan na Ciche (*chanter of the breast*), an apt name if you pass by on a breezy day with the wind whistling through the gap. Turn right for Garbh Chioch Mhor or left for Sgurr na Ciche. The way to either summit is rough and involves some easy scrambling. A vague path to the latter leads left initially, then back right through a maze of boulders and outcrops. The view of Loch Nevis from both summits is superb, and there is a tremendous sense of space looking down from Sgurr na Ciche to the River Carnach over 1000m below.

These hills are often climbed from Sourlies bothy, which makes a scenic but rather small and potentially busy base. The Druim a' Ghoirtein rises from the waters of Loch Nevis and leads in a series of steps to a final rocky rise before the summit. While this ridge looks very aesthetic on the map, it gives a prolonged route of ascent. From Sourlies it is quicker to go up the Mam na Cloich' Airde path for 2km to a junction and take the north branch into Coire na Ciche. The Allt Coire na Ciche is then followed to the foot of the Feadan na Ciche, and the summit is reached as above.

Sgurr na Ciche is sometimes climbed from the west end of Loch Quoich, but the walk-in along the loch-side is quite arduous albeit only a little longer, and the river crossings are more committing. The round of Coire nan Gall from the north makes a very fine circuit which justifies the additional effort.

Gain the north-east ridge of Sgurr na Ciche over Meall a' Choire Dhuibh (740m), using a stalkers path that leaves the main Coire nan Gall path about 500 metres south of Loch Quoich. This north-east ridge is the rockiest feature of Sgurr na Ciche. It rises in a series of awkward slabs and rough outcrops, which in descent are rather blind and care will be needed. Meall a' Choire Dhuibh can be bypassed by climbing directly to Bealach na h-Eangair (taken to be at NM913976) from high up Coire nan Gall.

Ben Aden; 887m; (OS Sheets 33 & 40; NM898986); *hill of the face*

Somewhat overlooked in the general Munro stampede, Ben Aden is a shapely mountain and a worthy coda to Sgurr na Ciche. It is as fine as any peak to be found in Knoydart and encapsulates the main attributes of the area. Ben Aden's location is both wild and beautiful, remotely situated at the west end of Loch Quoich, and it looms like a tombstone when viewed from Carnoch at the head of Loch Nevis. All sides of the hill are rough, falling into deep glens far below, and it provides a tremendous view of the surrounding peaks.

The north side is very craggy, rising steeply through a scattering of trees for some 600m above the stunning and enclosed Lochan nam Breac, and there are large areas of rock shot through with white seams of granite pegmatite around and just below the summit. The rather more open south face is also rocky, and can give some scrambling in a fine situation.

From any side Ben Aden will test your route-finding skills, particularly in the mist when the numerous knolls and crags can be quite confusing. The hill is equally capable of being approached from Barrisdale, Strathan, Inverie or the Loch Quoich road. Other than a tent, however, the only obvious nearby base is Sourlies bothy.

The usual line of ascent from Loch Nevis is by the rough path up Glen Carnach to the junction of the River Carnach and the Allt Achadh a' Ghlinne. From here climb the south-west face, with a northwards traverse high up to avoid the steep rocks below the summit, to gain the north-west ridge, which is followed over a couple of false tops to the summit.

The Allt Achadh a' Ghlinne can alternatively be followed for 1.5km into a wild corrie, taking a tributary up to the Bealach a' Chairn Deirg (NM906985), and then scrambling up the east ridge to the summit.

If approaching from the west end of Loch Quoich, either follow the Allt Coire na Cruaiche easily to the Bealach a' Chairn Deirg, or gain then follow the sporting east-north-east ridge all the way to the summit. Ben Aden can also be combined with Sgurr na Ciche over the slabs and knobbly crags of Meall a' Choire Dhuibh, giving a superb circuit from Glen Carnach.

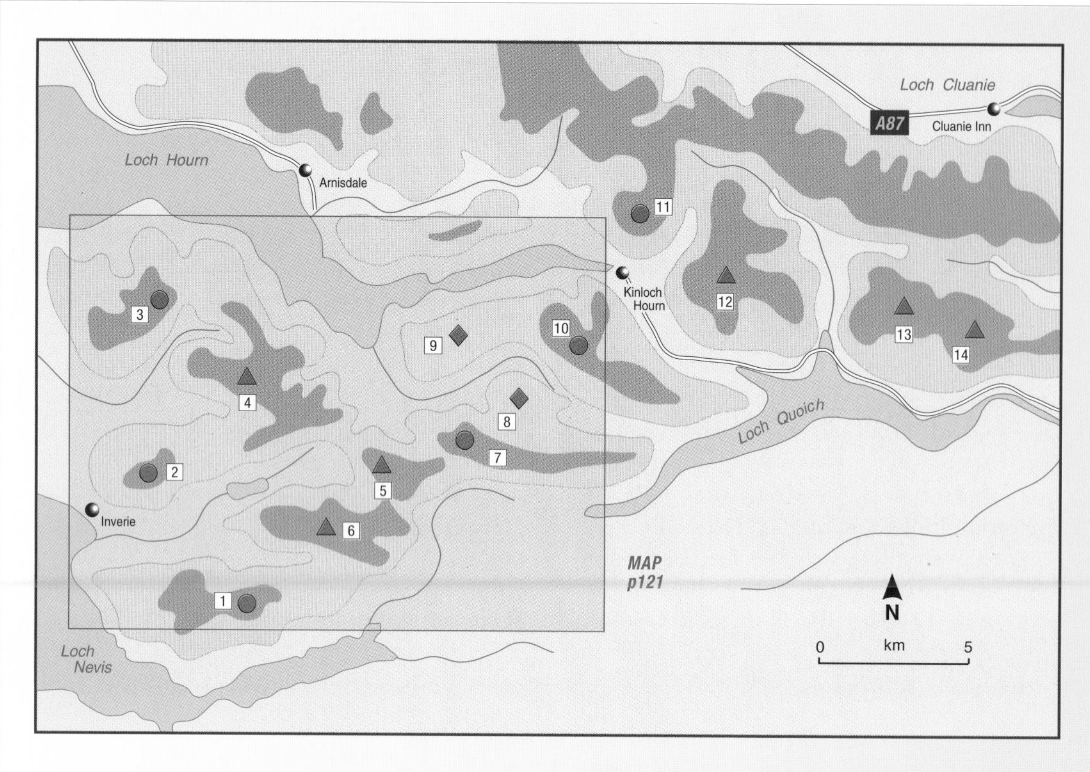

1.	Beinn Bhuidhe	855m	C	p113
2.	Sgurr Coire Choinnichean	796m	C	p113
3.	Beinn na Caillich	785m	C	p114
4.	Ladhar Bheinn	1020m	M	p115
5.	Luinne Bheinn	939m	M	p118
6.	Meall Buidhe	946m	M	p118
7.	Sgurr a' Choire-bheithe	913m	C	p120
8.	Slat Bheinn	700m	G	p121
9.	Meall nan Eun	667m	G	p122
10.	Sgurr nan Eugallt	898m	C	p122
11.	Buidhe Bheinn	885m	C	p124
12.	Sgurr a' Mhaoraich	1027m	M	p125
13.	Gleouraich	1035m	M	p126
14.	Spidean Mialach	996m	M	p126

Chapter 5

Knoydart and Loch Quoich

Stuart Rae

Ladhar Bheinn seen across a temperature inversion

Although part of mainland Scotland, no roads penetrate the fastness of Knoydart. Its remoteness combined with its peninsular nature mean that the area shares many of the attributes of an island. Coupled with the untamed nature of the land and the splendid mountain scenery, it is a unique venue for all who seek wilderness, solitude and adventure, whether by climbing the hills, back-packing through the glens, canoeing along the coastline, or just mellowing in the splendour. Bounded on three sides by dramatic sea lochs and the sea itself, Knoydart is hemmed in on the fourth side by wild and mountainous ground forming a very effective barrier around the west end of Loch Quoich. This chapter also describes the hills of this barrier and those situated above Loch Quoich's north shore.

Much of Knoydart's atmosphere and sense of character come from its superb sea lochs. Particularly impressive is Loch Hourn (*loch of hell*) and its wooded and steep-walled narrow upper reach, Loch Beag, which has much in common with a Norwegian fjord. 20km long, Loch Hourn forms Knoydart's northern coastline. Enclosed by high peaks, in poor conditions it can be a gloomy and sombre spot. On the south side is Loch Nevis (by way of contrast, *loch of heaven*), also narrow and about 20km long. Loch Nevis is crowned by the graceful Sgurr na Ciche at its head and has a generally more gentle nature than Loch Hourn, as the lower hills of Morar rise from its south shore and give it an open feeling.

In between the lochs lies the almost uninhabited interior, a tangle of rough and high peaks, well deserving of the moniker 'the Rough Bounds of Knoydart'. The most famous summits are Ladhar Bheinn and the excellent combination of Luinne Bheinn and Meall Buidhe. Ladhar Bheinn is one of the more compelling mountains in the country and is a suitable crowning peak for so fine an area. In particular the wild and spectacular Coire Dhorrcail is a tremendous arena, dominated by the considerable and patently challenging cliffs which make so tremendous sight from Arnisdale on the north shore of Loch Hourn.

South and west of Ladhar Bheinn, lower and more rounded countryside gives way to the coastline looking across the Sound of Sleat, and it is in this part of the peninsula that one finds such little infrastructure as there is. The main habitation is the small village of Inverie situated beside the pleasant crescent-shaped bay of the same name, facing south-west across Loch Nevis towards the Inner Hebrides. The one public road on the peninsula runs from Inverie to Airor, a tiny settlement about 10km away on the west coast, along which there are a few isolated dwellings. At the time of writing the population stands at about 70. The main land uses in Knoydart are sheep farming, deer-stalking, crofting and forestry.

The only means of reaching the hills in Knoydart is on foot or by boat. There are a number of significant paths and passes for getting around within the area. For many, these are the preferred way of getting to the area as well, as the only scheduled transport to Knoydart is the ferry service from Mallaig to Inverie. The four principal walking access routes from the east are more fully detailed later. If the ferry is not used, then the approach to Knoydart is likely to be lengthy, but the paths are well made and give generally good going.

The Mam Barrisdale path is an important one as it gives access to the highest hills and provides a convenient link between the two main bases for walkers and climbers on the north and south sides of the peninsula.

Knoydart's history is a sorry one. Originally owned by Clan Donald, territorial rights were assumed by the MacDonells of Glengarry in the 1500s. Emigration took its toll after the 1745 rebellion, partly 'encouraged' by the MacDonells, who did not serve the area well, and the population fell from around 1000 to some 600 by the early 19th century. Then in 1846 a potato blight and the failure of the herring to arrive in Loch Nevis combined to cause famine. Aeneas, the 16th clan chief, had left for Australia in 1840, but returned to Inverie to die in 1852. In an act which was notably callous even by the standards of the time, his widow Josephine then drove 400 people from Airor, Doune, Inverie and Sandaig, to be taken away on a government transport ship to America. The remaining handful of desperate souls clung on to what little they had left, but died that winter. The purpose of this dreadful episode was simply to clear the land of people so as to enhance its value for grazing before

Access and Transport

By road: the public roads end some distance to the east. The B8005 from Gairlochy reaches the west end of Loch Arkaig 1km east of Strathan. From 8km west of Invergarry, a single-track branch of the A87 runs along Loch Quoich to Kinloch Hourn, where a small charge is made for using the private parking facilities. In really bad conditions the small lochs between Loch Quoich and Kinloch Hourn may swell so as to render the road impassable to vehicles.

By bus: Invergarry Post Office to Kingie (daily except Sundays); Invergarry Post Office to Kinloch Hourn (Mondays, Wednesdays and Fridays) (Royal Mail four-seater post bus, tel: 01809-501401). Kyle of Lochalsh to Arnisdale post bus service for those who have arranged boat access across Loch Hourn (daily except Sundays) tel: 01599-522233. For further post bus information contact the Royal Mail, tel: 08457-740740. Mallaig to Fort William (Shiel Buses, tel: 01967-431272). Inverness to Fort William (Scottish Citylink Coaches, tel: 08705-505050, and Highland Country Buses, tel: 01463-222244); Uig to Glasgow/Edinburgh via Fort William (Scottish Citylink Coaches).

By rail: the nearest station is Mallaig on the Fort William to Mallaig line.

By ferry: Mallaig to Inverie (Mondays, Wednesdays and Fridays) (Bruce Watt Sea Cruises, tel: 01687-462320). Arrangements can sometimes be made for boat hire either at Arnisdale (contact Len Morrison, Croftfoot, Arnisdale, tel: 01599-522352, email: croftfoot@btopenworld.com) or Corran on the north shore of Loch Hourn, and also with the Inverie locals who regularly make the journey to and from Mallaig in their own boats. At the time of writing, consideration is being given to upgrading the Inverie jetty, which may result in Caledonian MacBrayne providing a service from Mallaig in the future.

By canoe or dingy: Arnisdale makes a good starting point, it being a short crossing to Barrisdale. One can also set out from Kinloch Hourn and enjoy the interesting upper part of the loch. It has additional it was sold to a Lowland sheep farmer. If that is the source of our 'wilderness', then perhaps we would have been better off without it.

The land has changed hands many times since. In the 1930s it was owned by Lord Brocket, who was a Tory MP, Nazi sympathiser and infamous absentee landlord. He built the monument on Torr a' Bhalbhain, 3km east of Inverie, in memory of his father. Lord Brocket made life generally intolerable for the locals, his behaviour leading to a famous land raid in 1948 when the Seven Men of Knoydart (who were ex-servicemen) seized land in an attempt to create a new lifestyle for themselves independent from the feudal system. Lord Brocket raised a court action for interdict, and the raid failed, having received no support from the Labour government. Lord Brocket sold the estate soon afterwards, and better management practices followed for a while. The situation deteriorated again in the early 1980s, and that story is outlined in the panel on 'The Knoydart Foundation'.

As one heads east, Knoydart merges into the Barrisdale Forest (deer not trees), which lies between Loch Hourn and Loch Quoich. The Barrisdale hills march with the area described in Chapter 4 *(p92)* by Lochan nam Breac and down the River Carnach to Loch Nevis. The peaks north of this boundary are less famous than those of Knoydart proper, being a little lower, but they are equally rugged and just as deserving of attention as their neighbours. The lengthy ridges of Sgurr nan Eugallt and Sgurr a' Choire-bheithe dominate this part of the area, rising from Loch Quoich and falling again towards Barrisdale Bay. Gleann Cosaidh separates them, and their flanks demarcate three of the main pedestrian routes of access to Knoydart. To the north-east of Sgurr nan Eugallt is the one road which gives comparatively straightforward public access to some of the hills described, running as it does down to the small collection of buildings at Kinloch Hourn.

The fertile ground and toweringly enclosed location of Kinloch Hourn contrast markedly with the savagely empty landscape through which the road passes as it travels along the north shore of Loch Quoich. The defile between Loch Quoich and Loch Hourn is a very wild

attractions with seals often being seen, and there is a heronry on Eilean Mhogh-sgeir. However at low water both Barrisdale Bay and Loch Beag dry out in places, and the tide races through Caolas Mor, so it will be necessary to allow for the tides before starting.

By foot: see Paths in the Knoydart and Loch Quoich area, *p112*.

Accommodation and Information

Knoydart facilities: Inverie has a shop, an estate hostel, B&B accommodation and some cottages for let. It is home to the Old Forge Inn, the remotest pub in mainland Britain. Camping is available near the village. At Barrisdale there is a small estate bothy, but this is frequently crowded. Again, there is camping close by. A small charge is payable. Accommodation may sometimes be available at Kinloch Hourn, about which enquiries should be made locally. There are a few bothies but these are small and may be crowded at times. The tent is the alternative.

Independent hostel: Sheena's Backpackers Lodge, Mallaig (tel: 01397-462764); Knoydart Hostel (enquiries to the Knoydart Foundation office)

General Information: the Knoydart Foundation office (tel: 01687-462242)

Tourist Information Centre: Mallaig (tel: 01687 462170) (Easter - October).

Maps

Ordnance Survey: 1:50,000 Landranger sheets 33 (Loch Alsh, Glen Shiel and Loch Hourn) and 40 (Mallaig and Glenfinnan); 1:25,000 Explorer sheets 398 (Loch Morar and Mallaig), 413 (Knoydart, Loch Hourn & Loch Duich) and 414 (Glen Shiel and Kintail Forest).
Harvey:1:25,000 Superwalker, Kintail and Glen Shiel.

and beautiful place, and was an inspiration to the Victorian artist Landseer who painted and sketched in this area. It is also the line of the old drove road by which cattle were driven from Skye to the southern markets. The rock outcrops hereabouts provide a fine example of glacial action.

This pass was also the setting for an unusual 19th century wager between a Mr Green, tutor to the family of the Glengarry clan chief, and his employer. The chief boasted one day that he had driven the 27 miles from Kinloch Hourn to Invergarry in just 4 hours, leading Mr Green to suggest he could manage the journey as fast on foot. The chief bet him £20 that he could not, and one of his men was also backed to beat the tutor in a straight race. The laird of Glenquoich entered a wager that 'an old wife' off his farm could beat the pair of them.

The race started, and the Glengarry man soon ground to a halt on the steep climb from Kinloch Hourn with a nosebleed, whereupon the tutor took the lead. The Glengarry man did recover sufficiently to reach Invergarry first. The tutor still won his wager with the chief, having completed the distance within the 4 hour deadline. The old wife is reported to have managed the first 7 miles from Loch Hourn, but then to have fallen by the wayside!

Also covered are the fine hills that lie above and north of Kinloch Hourn and Loch Quoich, three of which reach Munro height. These peaks look across the glens to the back of the South Glen Shiel ridge, and are smoother and more grassy than their Knoydart neighbours. They are relatively easy of access, lying close to the public road and give shorter and less serious hill days. Information on Loch Quoich is given in Chapter 4 *(p92)*.

Paths in the Knoydart and Loch Quoich area

One of Knoydart's charms is that it cannot be reached by car. This is both a defining characteristic and a logistical challenge. For most it is a long walk from the nearest road. The main pedestrian accesses to Knoydart are as follows:

1) The footpath from the road-end at Kinloch Hourn to Barrisdale (10km). This is a beautiful walk but with a fair amount of ascent built in. From Barrisdale a path continues over the Mam Barrisdale (c450m) to join an estate track which leads down Gleann an Dubh-Lochain to Inverie (14km, 24km in total).

2) The footpath from the road-end at the west end of Loch Arkaig up Glen Dessarry, then over the Mam na Cloich' Airde and down to Carnoch at the head of Loch Nevis (15km). Continue over the Mam Meadail path (c550m) to Inverie (12km, 27km in total).

3) The right of way (pathless in places) along the north shore of Loch Quoich to the cut-off dams at the loch's west end, then past Lochan nam Breac and down the variable path on the west bank of the River Carnach to the head of Loch Nevis (20km). Continue over the Mam Meadail path to Inverie (12km, 32km in total). Alternatively, follow the path over the Mam Unndalain (c550m) from Lochan nam Breac, and descend to Barrisdale (19km in total). These routes involve crossing the notoriously difficult Abhainn Chosaidh.

4) The right of way along the initially pathless north shore of Loch Quoich, then by Gleann Cosaidh and the north side of Slat Bheinn to Barrisdale (16km). This route does not involve any major river crossings, only a number of relatively minor ones, and is the sensible option after heavy rain.

A number of these paths were constructed many years ago by James Watt. He was an engineer who returned from Rhodesia under a cloud and sought discrete employment. Contracted to link the Knoydart glens, he did this to continuing effect with the help of just two men. Where paths are shown on the map, they exist and are well made. Off the paths the ground can be extremely rough and will give slow going. The area has a high rainfall, and this will greatly increase the size of the burns. Care must be taken in route planning at such times, even on these comparatively major paths. The Abhainn Chosaidh rapidly becomes completely unfordable, and many other seemingly innocuous streams can also rise extremely quickly to pose difficult or insuperable obstacles.

Principal Hills

Beinn Bhuidhe; (855m; (OS Sheets 33 & 40; NM821967); *yellow hill*

In terms of acreage, Beinn Bhuidhe is the most extensive of Knoydart's hills. It takes the form of a lengthy high-level ridge of many summits which runs west from Meall Bhasiter (718m) above the head of Loch Nevis, and falls to the sea again beyond Sgurr Coire nan Gobhar (787m) at the mouth of the Inverie River some 14km away.

Its grassy southern slopes form a lengthy rampart along Loch Nevis, while to its north-east side it is connected to Meall Buidhe by the Mam Meadail (c590m), with a succession of rugged corries overlooking the south side of Gleann Meadail. The lower slopes and corries on the west and north contain attractive areas of native woodland. The west end of the hill is complex, its slopes broadening and falling over a mix of crags and gentler ground down to the crescent-shaped Loch Bhraomisaig. For all Beinn Bhuidhe's bulk and roughness, Creag Mhor on Meall Bhasiter is the hill's only real crag. Although rather low, it might give interesting mixed winter climbing in the right conditions.

If approaching from Inverie, then it is quickest to take the Mam Meadail path to the bridge over the Allt Gleann Meadail (NM813988), and then to ascend into the corrie (Coir' an Fhir-eoin) to the south-east. Either follow a burn generally south-west to the col 500m west of the summit, or, more entertainingly, scramble up the spur due south of the triple stream junction at c250m directly to the summit. The summit and east end of Beinn Bhuidhe give a magnificent prospect of the knobbly cone of Sgurr na Ciche at its sharpest. In descent one can enjoy the beautiful west ridge as far as Sgurr nam Feadan, and all along here there are superb views of the waters of Loch Nevis. Drop down to the east shore of Loch Bhraomisaig and so to the bridge over the Inverie River just south-west of the Brocket Memorial on Torr a' Bhalbhain. Take care to avoid a number of outcrops on the way by staying to the east of the Allt Dubh.

From Carnoch on the east side of the hill, climb the path to the Mam Meadail so as to gain height as easily as possible. Follow the ridge over Meall Bhasiter to the Mam Uchd, and so to the summit, which is named Sgurr Coir' an Fhir-eoin after the corrie to its north. There is a false top (Sgurr an t-Sagairt) 500m east of the trig point. The full traverse of Beinn Bhuidhe gives a highly recommended outing in a tremendous setting, and is most easily accomplished from Inverie, using the Mam Meadail path for access either to or from the top of the pass.

Sgurr Coire Choinnichean; 796m; (OS Sheet 33; NG790010); *peak of the mossy corrie*

A fine cone rising at the back of Inverie, Sgurr Coire Choinnichean dominates the view when one approaches the village by boat from Mallaig. Correspondingly, the summit outlook over Inverie Bay towards North Morar and the Inner Hebrides is quite superb, and it is also a good spot from which to see the extensive corries on the north side of Beinn Bhuidhe. A well-defined ridge extends north-east to the Mam Suidheig (c490m), connecting to Aonach Sgoilte (849m) some 6km away. In some ways Sgurr Coire Choinnichean is a harbinger for Ladhar Bheinn, and indeed it makes a worthy and logical extension to any ascent of that hill from Inverie. Its flanks are steep and craggy in places, and at first sight it looks as if the logical route from Inverie will be directly up the rather brutal nose of the hill above Inverie House. While the slopes to the east of the Allt Slochd a' Mhogha give the quickest line, slightly longer but more amenable approaches are recommended instead and an ascent should still take no great length of time.

From Inverie one can leave the Mam Uidhe track where it emerges from the trees just before the top of the pass (135m). Ascend the Leac nan Caiseachan to the remarkably level lower ground of Coire Choinnichean, which is probably the flattest area of ground on the whole peninsula. Above is a steep and rocky face. Either gain the sharp south-west ridge by skirting the top of the deep Slochd a' Mhogha gorge, or cross the corrie and climb the curving north ridge above the Garsley Burn. If the former, note that there is a lower top (779m) lying a few hundred metres south-west of the true summit.

If approaching from the south-east, climb steeply to the Mam Suidheig from Loch an Dubh-Lochain and follow the narrow ridge westwards over Stob an Uillt-fhearna (661m). Alternatively climb up the grassy Coire Dubh by the side of the Allt nan Gleannan from the estate track by the Inverie River. The Mam Suidheig can also be reached from its gentler northern side if one takes the long approach by the Mam Uidhe track and the path up Gleann na Guiserein. On a fine day the views make the summit a place to linger.

The lower part of the north side of Sgurr Coire Choinnichean above Folach is quite craggy. The Garsley Burn enters an unusual recessed slot on these slopes, and is well worth a detour to see.

Beinn na Caillich; 785m; (OS Sheet 33; NG795067); *hill of the old woman*

Taking into account the logistical efforts required to reach it, Beinn na Caillich is the most remote and inaccessible of all the mainland Corbetts. It lies in the north-west corner of the Knoydart peninsula some 7km north of Inverie, and, whilst adjacent to Ladhar Bheinn, will usually be climbed on its own rather than with its neighbour. The hill is not particularly shapely, being a rounded peak fronted on its seaward sides by a number of lumpy foothills. These northerly aspects are rocky and interesting, but are extremely difficult to reach for all but the canoeist. To the east is the Mam Li (c460m), beyond which a complicated and undulating ridge merges obliquely into Ladhar Bheinn's northern slopes. Beinn na Caillich's south side, from which ascents are commonly made, is out of character with the rest of the hill and with Knoydart generally, being relatively smooth and bland by comparison.

The normal starting point is Inverie, from where one takes the forest track over the Mam Uidhe into Gleann na Guiserein. At the end of the track either ford the Allt Coire Torr an Asgaill or cross the bridge further upstream just before Folach. Continue up the footpath towards the Mam Li, admiring the Eas a' Chaorainn pools on the Abhainn Bheag. The path crosses the river by stepping stones shortly before the foot of Coire Each. One can leave the path and climb north-west up heathery slopes, or take a more scrambly line up some discontinuous crags slightly further east where the rock is a bit loose but does give some sport.

The more usual alternative is to continue on up the path to c350m and scramble easily up the rough rib of Carn Dubh to the summit. There is an unusual perspective of Ladhar Bheinn, and an excellent panorama of the Sleat peninsula, the Skye Cuillin and Beinn Sgritheall. In descent, head south-west over Meall Coire an t-Searraich (686m) and drop down to the Abhainn Bheag.

Beinn na Caillich can be reached by a long approach from Barrisdale. Follow the coastline past the John Muir Trust base at Li, avoiding the impressive Creag Dhubh above on its south side by the line of the Allt Li. The return can be made over Ladhar Bheinn if desired. A remote and unusual ascent can be made by those prepared to follow the coastal path north-east from Inverguseran to Croulin close to the northmost point of the peninsula. The best route from here is over Meall Breac, passing by the high and scenic Coire na Caillich.

Looking across Loch Hourn to Coire Dhorrcail and Ladhar Bheinn

Ladhar Bheinn; 1020m; (OS Sheet 33; NG823039); *hoof hill*

Ladhar Bheinn (pronounced 'Larven') is a mountain range, not a hill, and a magnificent and complex one at that. It is the most westerly mainland Munro, and is certainly the outstanding peak in the area as well as being high on most Scottish mountaineers' list of favourite summits. This level of esteem is due less to any one specific attribute as to a combination of features which exemplify all that is excellent about Knoydart.

Ladhar Bheinn is in a tremendous location, rising above the dark waters of narrow Loch Hourn. Its northern ridges and corries are narrow and rocky and draw the exploratory eye, particularly the stunning Coire Dhorrcail, which lies at Ladhar Bheinn's heart. And its remoteness and reputation for poor weather mean that a fine day on it provides a goal to strive for as well as a memory to cherish once attained. Happily, the John Muir Trust and the Knoydart Foundation now own the bulk of Ladhar Bheinn. It is only the ground overlooking the Mam Barrisdale that remains in private hands, so access to the hill is now assured all year round.

Ladhar Bheinn is better envisaged as two distinct mountain masses that link together above Coire Dhorrcail. The higher part has a vaguely tent-like shape to it. Its north side is very remote, the main corries being Coire Odhair and Coire Each, located on either side of contorted terrain stretching to Beinn na Caillich some 6km away. Parties have reported anomalies in the use of the magnetic compass hereabouts, although occurrences of temporary personal disorientation must not be ruled out either!

The narrow north-east ridge drops from the summit and rises over the minor outlying top of Stob a' Choire Odhair (960m), enclosing Coire Dhorrcail's west slopes. The summit ridge is level, running in a generally south-east to north-westerly direction for about 1km, and less interesting grassy flanks fall away south-west into Gleann na Guiserein. From near its summit Ladhar Bheinn extends a third ridge south-east to the Bealach Coire Dhorrcail (c710m). This ridge passes over Ladhar Bheinn's south top (858m), and forms the headwall of Coire Dhorrcail.

A further broad ridge rises beyond this bealach to the equally interesting subsidiary part of Ladhar Bheinn. Although unnamed on the Landranger map, it seems likely that this summit is in fact called Aonach Sgoilte (849m) (*the ridge of the split,* the 'split' being an obvious gully on the south side). Aonach Sgoilte runs at right angles to the slope rising from the Bealach Coire Dhorrcail. It stretches south-west for 3km to the Mam Suidheig (c490m) by which it connects to Sgurr Coire Choinnichean, while it continues for 750m north-east to end abruptly in the steep nose of Stob a' Chearcaill (840m). This is a splendid viewpoint and a shapely outlier, particularly when viewed from Barrisdale from where it appears as a graceful spire. Its north-east ridge falls sharply at first and then sweeps more easily down the Creag Bheithe ridge to Barrisdale Bay.

On the north side, the combination of Ladhar Bheinn and Aonach Sgoilte encloses Coire Dhorrcail, one of the most spectacular corries in the Western Highlands. This name, the derivation of which is uncertain, is generally applied to the entire arena, although the higher section is really divided into two. Upper Coire Dhorrcail is on the north-east slopes of Ladhar Bheinn, and its headwall is composed of great cliffs and deep clefts. The smaller Coire na Cabaig is part of the north side of Aonach Sgoilte, and is separated from Coire Dhorrcail by the prominent spur of Stob Dhorrcail. Although the lesser of the corries, it is no less dramatic, with towering slabby crags that bear more than a passing likeness to a miniature North Face of the Grandes Jorasses in the Mont Blanc range. Both corries are of considerable fascination to winter climbers, although this interest tends to be largely cerebral and seldom results in physical activity.

The classic Ladhar Bheinn outing is the circuit of Coire Dhorrcail, best undertaken from Barrisdale, although reaching this particular starting point involves a fair degree of effort in itself. The finest approach to Ladhar Bheinn is over Stob a' Chearcaill and Aonach Sgoilte. These are best reached by climbing the Creag Bheithe ridge, gained from the Coire Dhorrcail stalkers path. The lower ridge is grassy and gentle until it abuts into the upper part of Stob a' Chearcaill, and there are superb views across Coire Dhorrcail. The last section is slabby and involves some scrambling and traversing on exposed ledges to find the best route. It is not recommended in descent or in mist, and in winter it will be an outing for experienced climbers only. These upper difficulties can be skirted on their east side, and can be avoided by climbing Stob a' Chearcaill from the top of the Mam Barrisdale up the slopes of Coire a' Phuill.

From Aonach Sgoilte descend north-west to the Bealach Coire Dhorrcail (it is easy to drop down into Coire Dhorrcail from the bealach if desired) and climb the ridge beyond over rocky knolls, admiring the impressive scale of the cliffs and gully exits of Coire Dhorrcail on the right. A steep pull up the final slopes leads to the summit, located a little beyond the junction of the north-east and south-east ridges and 500 metres before the trig point. It enjoys a superb panorama of the surrounding area, as befits so fine a mountain.

The best route of return is down the north-east ridge and over Stob a' Choire Odhair, steep at first, and narrow and exposed in places, giving fine views across Barrisdale Bay and up to the head of Loch Hourn. Follow the Druim a' Choire Odhair until the ridge broadens and levels out, then drop south-east into Coire Dhorrcail and cross the Allt Coire Dhorrcail. This can be a serious obstacle in poor conditions. The lower part of the corrie is a great place from which to appreciate the almost

Himalayan ambience of this wonderful amphitheatre. A stalkers path on the east side of the burn climbs initially before contouring the lower nose of the Creag Bheithe ridge and dropping to cross flat ground on the way back to the bridge at Barrisdale.

The ascent from Inverie is less fine, but gives an easier and probably more convenient approach for the bulk of visitors to Knoydart. The circuit of upper Gleann na Guiserein is recommended, ascending Sgurr Coire Choinnichean as described earlier and continuing down to the Mam Suidheig. This pass can also be reached by a stiff climb north from Loch an Dubh-Lochain. Proceed with interest up and along the narrow ridge to the summit of Aonach Sgoilte. The ridge at one point parts into two parallel crests. Continue to the summit of Ladhar Bheinn as already described.

In descent, take the west-north-west ridge from the summit for 2km to the shoulder of An Diollaid and drop south-west down the grassy slopes of Coire Garbh to the ruin of Folach in Gleann na Guiserein. Note that continuing too far west down the nose of An Diollaid leads to much rougher ground. Inverie is a further 6km on along the Mam Uidhe track. It would be possible to make a strenuous extension to this outing to include Beinn na Caillich, by passing over the remote Mullach Li (668m), but this is time-consuming ground with much ascent and descent. The quickest and easiest route to Ladhar Bheinn from Inverie is the Coire Garbh line in both ascent and descent, but this does not do justice to the mountain's secrets.

Ladhar Bheinn is also a sought-after winter climbing venue. The main attractions are Coire Dhorrcail and Coire na Cabaig, the routes being from 200m to 350m in length. The profusely vegetated micaceous granulite and unfriendly strata make the crags unsuitable for rock climbing, but can provide great rewards under snow and ice. The possibilities were first recognised as long ago as the celebrated Scottish Mountaineering Club Yachting Meet of 1897, when Harold Raeburn made the first ascent of the prominent gully in Coire Dhorrcail which now bears his name, 240m III. In 1962 Tom Patey climbed two

'Do Something For Wildness And Make The Mountains Glad'

The John Muir Trust is a registered charity established in Scotland in 1983. It is guided by the vision of the late John Muir. Muir was born in Dunbar in 1838, his family emigrated to the USA while he was still a child, and he became the founding father of the world's modern conservation movements.

His basic beliefs were that wild areas should be cherished for their own sake and that man should not dominate but should live in harmony with nature. He has received far more recognition away from his home country for his philosophies and inspiration, but the formation of the John Muir Trust is finally allowing his message to be put into practice in the UK as well. The Trust now owns a number of high profile areas of huge scenic importance, including interests in Schiehallion, Sandwood Bay, Skye (Sconser, Strathaird and Torrin), and parts of Ben Nevis, the Aonachs and Glen Nevis. The first purchase was in Knoydart. The Trust is also a partner in the North Harris Trust.

The JMT's aim is to repair the damage inflicted on the land over the centuries, to conserve it on a sustainable basis, to maintain it in its natural state without development, and to preserve it as a legacy for the generations to come. It works closely with the people who live on Trust property, and recognises that visitors have the freedom to roam on its land. The Trust owns some 3,100 acres of the north side of Ladhar Bheinn, from the summit down to the sea and from the Mam Li to Coire Dhorrcail. The land was bought in 1987 with a major contribution to the purchase price coming from the Scottish Mountaineering Trust. The John Muir Trust has carried out much work to restore the native woodlands on the lower slopes of the hill and to repair the effects of erosion on the footpaths.

The John Muir Trust can be contacted at 41 Commercial Street, Leith, Edinburgh EH6 6JD (tel: 0131-554-0114). Alternatively visit the Trust web site at www.jmt.org

fine gully lines, *Viking Gully* 360m IV in Coire Dhorrcail, and *Gaberlunzie* 280m IV in Coire na Cabaig, reviving interest in the mountain's potential.

The 1970s saw much development, the great face of Spider Buttress at the left end of the Coire Dhorrcail cliffs now holding a number of climbs. The best is *Tir na Og* 350m V (1978), which takes a direct line to the obvious central snowfield (named 'The Spider', after a resemblance to the White Spider on the Eiger). There are routes up several of the corners further right. The main gully lines in Coire na Cabaig have been climbed at around grades III and IV. However the remote location coupled with the fickle conditions which are typical of hills so close to the Atlantic mean that climbers are comparatively rare visitors here.

Luinne Bheinn; 939m; (OS Sheet 33; NG869007); *swelling hill*

Meall Buidhe; 946m; (OS Sheets 33 & 40; NM849989); *yellow hill*

Dominating the central part of the mountainous Knoydart peninsula, Luinne Bheinn and Meall Buidhe lie inland from and between the head of Loch Nevis and Barrisdale Bay on Loch Hourn. They are very rough peaks, conveniently linked by the lengthy and rugged twisting edge of the spectacular Coire Odhair, and their traverse is amongst the best outings that the area has to offer. Luinne Bheinn is the more distinctive hill, an east-west wedge with steep slopes on either side. It is seen as a fine cone from some angles, whilst from others its twin-topped summit ridge is more obvious. A fine feature of the hill is Coire Glas, a shallow corrie facing north to Loch Hourn. The Luinne Bheinn ridge runs from the Mam Unndalain in the east to the Mam Barrisdale north-west from the summit.

It is usually ascended in an excellent circuit with its southern neighbour Meall Buidhe, thus allowing a full appreciation of the wildness of Coire Odhair. This great corrie faces north-west towards Ladhar Bheinn, remote twin lochans feeding down from it to Loch an Dubh-Lochain far below. It is an impressive example of the effects of the last Ice Age, containing much bare, glacially scoured rock, and is well worth a detour to explore or to camp in.

Meall Buidhe is a bulkier and subtly more interesting mountain, another twin-topped peak with a long and broad west ridge projecting from its summit towards Inverie. The main summit is mossy, whilst the South-east Top (942m) is a rather bolder feature above fine north-facing precipices, sending out well-defined ridges south-east to Sgurr Sgeithe (793m) and north-east to the Bealach Ile Coire. The north side comprises a number of craggy upper corries and steep and contorted slopes, dropping into Coire Odhair. Meall Buidhe's southern slopes are also steep, but are generally grassy, and fall away into Gleann Meadail, the Mam Meadail lying just 1km south of the South-east Top.

Of particular interest on the eastern slopes of Meall Buidhe is Ile Coire. Situated far above the River Carnach, this corrie is a little known place of solitude with slabs descending into a beautiful lochan in its upper reaches. It lies beneath the South-east Top and is enclosed by the arms of Meall Buidhe's outliers, Sgurr Sgeithe and Druim Leac a' Shith (839m), the latter being the further south of twin hummocks lying on the ridge joining the two Munros.

The most logical starting point for the traverse is Inverie, from where a superb horseshoe round can be made. Approach by the estate track up Gleann an Dubh-Lochain, following the path as far as the Mam Barrisdale, and then climb steeply to a brief levelling at Bachd Mhic an Tosaich (665m). Above, Luinne Bheinn's well-defined north-west ridge leads to the summit which is marked by a small cairn. Note that a larger one lies a little lower down this ridge. Being very much the pivotal point of the Knoydart peaks, Luinne Bheinn gives a brilliant view in all directions. About 500m further on lies the East

Ladhar Bheinn and Loch Hourn from Buidhe Bheinn

Top (937m), which should be traversed before dropping south-east initially, then south-west, to the Bealach a' Choire Odhair (684m). Proceed round the undulating rim of the corrie, passing over the twin tops of Meall Coire na Gaoithe 'n Ear and Druim Leac a' Shith, to the Bealach Ile Coire. These tops can be avoided and height saved by traversing them on their north-west side by grassy terraces and ledges.

The navigation can be complicated here and the ground is rocky, so this is only recommended in good visibility. Meall Buidhe's north-east ridge rises above the bealach and becomes steeper and rockier as one nears the South-east Top. The main summit lies 500m further on across a grassy dip. Descend the pleasant west ridge for 4km, passing over An t-Uiriollach (826m). Either drop into the lower reaches of Gleann Meadail east of the Allt Gleann Meadail footbridge, or follow the Druim Righeanaich (paying attention to its lower outcrops) to the junction of the Inverie River and the Allt Gleann Meadail. There are footbridges over both rivers near the junction, although only one is marked on the Landranger map.

Barrisdale is frequently used as a base from which to ascend these hills, giving an excellent but less logical circuit. Luinne Bheinn can be climbed either from the Mam Barrisdale as before, or by taking the attractive Gleann Unndalain path to the pass at its head, then following the slabby and complex but easy-angled east ridge to the top. The route to Meall Buidhe is as already described, but the return to Barrisdale is not particularly obvious, and there are a few choices available. The most efficient in terms of minimising height loss is to descend carefully into Coire Odhair, either from the col between Meall Buidhe's summit and its South-east Top or from the Bealach Ile Coire, aiming for the twin lochans below. Pass just west of them and make a gradually descending traverse north on grassy terraces across Luinne Bheinn to the Mam Barrisdale. Note that the corrie is very rough and the going will be slow.

Easier ground can be gained either by taking the same initial descent line, but dropping lower down Coire Odhair, or by descending into Torc-choire and passing east of Cnuic nan Eildean (243m) to pick up the Mam Barrisdale path. The latter route involves much more effort to regain the pass.

The traverse of these hills is also a recommended outing from Sourlies bothy. It is easier to ascend Meall Buidhe first by climbing the path to the Mam Meadail and heading north to the col on the Sgurr Sgeithe ridge directly above. Follow the Coire Odhair rim round to Luinne Bheinn. One can then descend to the Mam Unndalain by Luinne Bheinn's east ridge and then head down rough ground to the upper waters of the River Carnach. However it is in fact quicker to return to the river by backtracking from Luinne Bheinn to the Bealach a' Choire Odhair and dropping down Coire na Gaoithe 'n Ear instead.

Combining these hills gives a reasonably full excursion for the average hillwalker, but it is quite possible to extend the traverse to include either Ladhar Bheinn, Sgurr a' Choire-bheithe or Beinn Bhuidhe, depending on one's starting point. Any of these are worthy additions to an already memorable day.

Sgurr a' Choire-bheithe; 913m; (OS Sheet 33; NG895015); *peak of the birch corrie*

Sgurr a' Choire-bheithe is a very remote peak which demands considerable commitment in the approach. Its summit is the highest point of the rugged Druim Chosaidh ridge which stretches from the confluence of the Allt Gleann Unndalain and the River Barrisdale in the west, and drops to the waters of Loch Quoich 9km further east. The ridge is very well defined throughout, falling away steeply on the south down rough slopes to Lochan nam Breac and the upper reaches of the River Carnach. The Mam Unndalain (c520m) lies just south-west of the summit, on the other side of which rises Luinne Bheinn. The River Barrisdale and the Abhainn Chosaidh hem in the north sides of both Slat Bheinn and Sgurr a' Choire-bheithe. Coire Beithe itself is on the north-west face of the hill, the lower slopes being wooded and falling to lower Glen Barrisdale. The mountain did enjoy a brief period in the limelight when it appeared that the summit might exceed the 914.4m Plimsoll line that determines what is and isn't a Munro, but this proved to be a false alarm and a state of tranquil obscurity has been restored.

The best feature of the hill is the undulating Druim Chosaidh east of the summit, Sgurr a' Choire-bheithe's spine giving a spectacular perch with great views on either side and some easy scrambling on the crest over a number of small towers near the top. If possible the full length of the ridge should be traversed by the succession of hills and tops from Meall an Spardain over Sgurr Airigh na Beinne (776m) to the conical summit itself which lies at the ridge's west end. This will however necessitate a lengthy approach along the north shores of Loch Quoich from the Kinloch Hourn road, including a crossing of the potentially difficult Abhainn Chosaidh. The return offers a couple of variations. One can descend to the Mam Unndalain path (dropping steeply from just east of a knoll 1km west of the summit) and follow it past Lochan nam Breac to the west end of Loch Quoich. Alternatively go down a rough corrie to the Gleann Cosaidh path from the col west of Sgurr Airigh na Beinne. Use of these paths permits a number of permutations, depending on one's starting point and accommodation (if any).

As the summit is at the west end of the hill, the ascent from Barrisdale is relatively straightforward. Gain the narrow west-north-west ridge from the Gleann Unndalain path just beyond Ambraigh and follow this steadily to the summit. The descent can be made down the path from

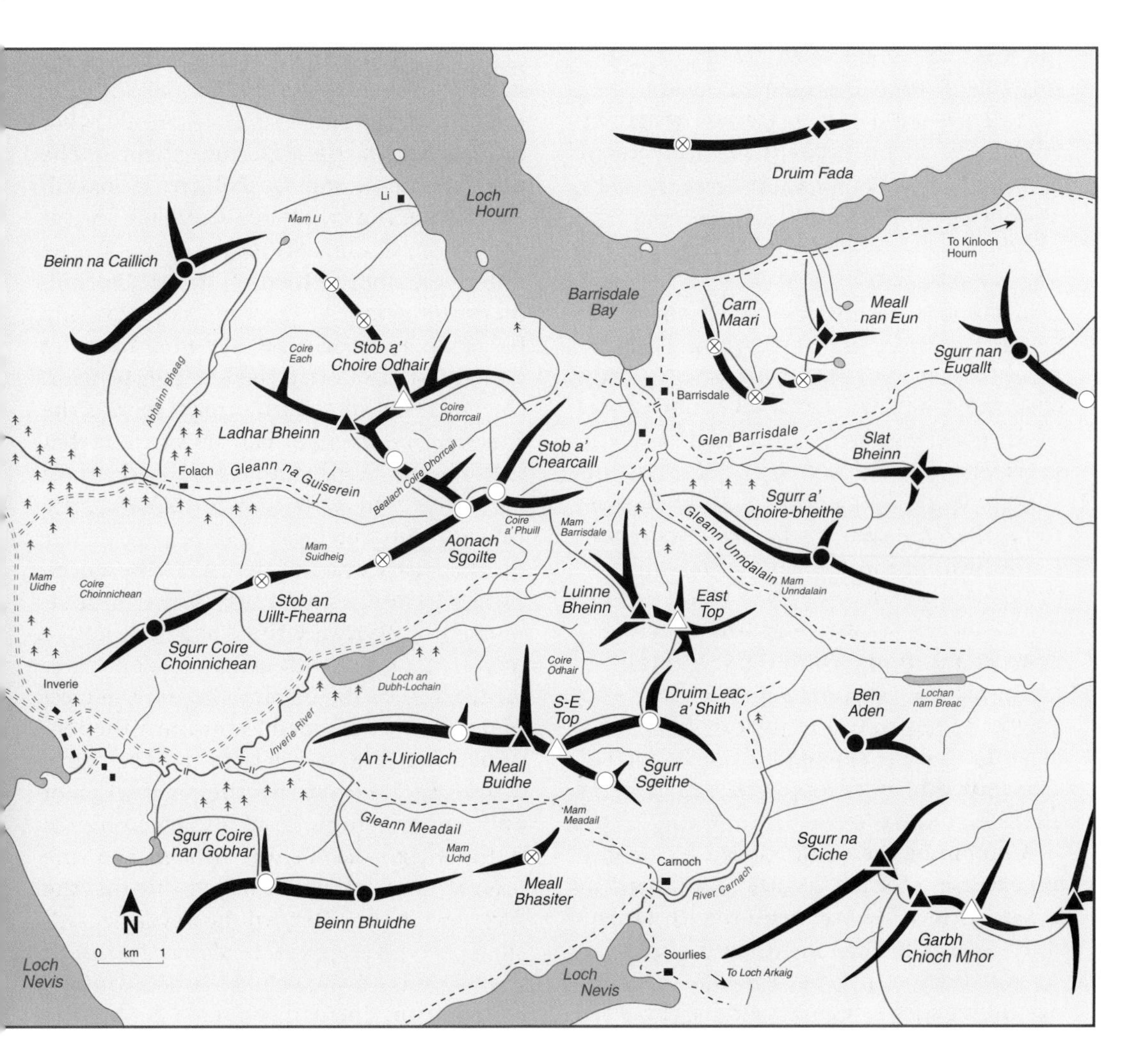

the Mam Unndalain as described. In addition, Sgurr a' Choire-bheithe has a fine north-east ridge which rises from just west of the tiny Loch Coire nan Cadha, allowing the hill to be combined with Slat Bheinn. This ridge gives some pleasant but avoidable scrambling. Care should be taken if descending this way, as the best route may not be obvious from above.

Slat Bheinn; 700m; (OS Sheet 33; NG910027); *rod hill*

Slat Bheinn is unusual in that it is shaped like a squat fortress in an area where jagged peaks are the norm. The location is relatively inaccessible, Sgurr nan Eugallt and Sgurr a' Choire-bheithe rising on either side of the hill and retaining it, almost as a pair of hands clasp a cup. Somewhat hemmed in, Slat Bheinn is thus a hill of glimpses rather than panoramas, with good views down the glens to Ladhar Bheinn in one direction and to Loch Quoich in the other. Gleann Cosaidh and Glen Barrisdale are the only means of low-level access so any ascent will involve a lengthy approach.

This is best diluted by climbing Slat Bheinn either in the course of a back-packing trip, or whilst based at Barrisdale. It is possible to use Slat Bheinn as a link between Sgurr nan Eugallt and Sgurr a' Choire-bhethe in a tough but excellent day from Barrisdale. If using one of the glens for access to Slat Bheinn instead, climb either the north-east ridge or the west-north-west ridge, depending on which glen is used. If a strenuous approach is made over Sgurr nan Eugallt, the logical route is the north ridge, reasonably well defined in its lower reaches. These ridges all give pleasant ascents over rough ground with outcrops broken by grassy faults.

The south-west ridge connects the hill to Sgurr a' Choire-bheithe, whose summit cone is well seen from Slat Bheinn. This ridge is principally slabby rock and gives a sporting ascent. In descent it is easier to locate a burn some 300 metres south of the summit and to follow this south-west down to Lochan Coire nan Cadha which is tucked in just west of the col between the hills.

Meall nan Eun; 667m; (OS Sheet 33; NG903052); *hill of the birds*

A hill to prove that height is not everything – what Meall nan Eun lacks in status it more than makes up for with stunning views down Loch Hourn and across to Ladhar Bheinn's fascinating corries and ridges. Its northern boundary is Loch Hourn, and it falls away steeply west and south to Barrisdale Bay and Glen Barrisdale. On the east it is joined to Sgurr nan Eugallt by the Bealach Mhinniceig (493m), and combining these hills by Sgurr nan Eugallt's west ridge is most rewarding.

The hollows of the hill hold some fine lochans both north and south of the summit, whilst the points of greatest interest lie to the west, the north-facing Coire Chaolis Bhig being very wild with four fine little tops enclosing it. There is some good gneiss, and the corrie contains a number of climbs, the best of which are on the north side of An Caisteal (622m). Here, three routes of around 200m in length at VS standard find their way up a narrow and clean central sweep of pleasant Etive-like slabs. Easier and shorter climbs are found on the various minor crags on the west flank of Meall nan Eun. The bulk of the climbing was done in the late 1960s and early 1970s, and there are unlikely to have been many repeat ascents. The remote and scenic location of the corrie is likely to be the main attraction rather than the quality of the climbs themselves.

Few will ascend Meall nan Eun specifically from Kinloch Hourn (in which case one would approach up the Allt a' Chamuis Bhain), but there is an excellent circuit to be made from Barrisdale round the tops which enclose Coire Chaolis Bhig. It is best to climb directly on to Carn Mairi (502m), then to continue over Beinn Bhuidhe (569m) and An Caisteal. In some places the ground is a mix of bog and tussocks, in others it can be craggy, and respect should be paid to this terrain which is very rough, notwithstanding the relatively low altitude of the hill. Lochan Coire Chaolais Bhig is a wonderful spot to savour before the final steep climb to the west top (666m) of Meall nan Eun, which gives an uninterrupted vista down Loch Hourn. The true summit is 500 metres further east, but is a less fine viewpoint. Return to Barrisdale either by dropping down rough ground to the Loch Hourn path, or by trending steeply south to pick up the path in Glen Barrisdale.

Sgurr nan Eugallt; 898m; (OS Sheet 33; NG927048); *peak of the furrowed rocks*

Compared to most of the nearby Knoydart hills, Sgurr nan Eugallt's summit is perhaps too accessible for its own good, the remainder of this fine hill being somewhat underappreciated and overlooked as a result. It is an extensive, interesting and scenic mountain, comprising a rough and lengthy ridge of many tops running south-west of and parallel to the Loch Quoich to Kinloch Hourn road, and north of Gleann Cosaidh and upper Glen Barrisdale. With waters like these on either side, an earlier translation of the hill's name as *peak of the death streams* is less fanciful than it may sound!

The ascent is usually made from the ruin at Coireshubh (*corrie of the raspberries*), just

Inverie village – accessible only by foot or by boat

before the road begins its final descent to Kinloch Hourn. Beside the loch is a rather surprising but well-established monkey-puzzle tree. Parking is available some 200 metres north of the start of the obvious stalkers path. This makes for fast progress up Sgurr Dubh's east ridge. The path runs out, then some gentle and avoidable scrambling leads easily up the crest to the trig point (894m). The true summit lies some 600 metres north-west along a pleasant ridge, a fact long suspected, but only acknowledged by the OS in 2001. The summit may be difficult to locate in the mist, as the Landranger map is quite inaccurate in its depiction of the summit contours, seeming to place a small loch at the point where the summit is to be found. There are superb views down Loch Quoich one way and Loch Hourn the other.

There is more to Sgurr nan Eugallt than this, however, and the hill gives a highly satisfying traverse. Its western outlier is Meall nan Eun, described above, which can be reached by passing over the western outlier Sgurr Sgiath Airigh (881m). The return should be made down the Allt a' Chamuis Bhain to Loch Hourn. From the summit the ridge stretches south-east for some 7km over the tops of Sgurr a' Chlaidheimh (841m) and (838m) before dropping down Sron Lice na Fearna to Loch Quoich, and this makes an excellent extension too.

The little corries on the north side of the ridge are extremely tussocky with numerous awkward rocky bluffs, and extra time should be allowed if descending this way.

It was by one of these corries, Coire Beithe, that Bonnie Prince Charlie and his five companions broke through a cordon of Hanoverian troops in darkness in July 1746, slipping past the sentries near Loch Coire Shubh before heading north by Coire Sgoireadail to Glen Shiel and Glen Affric.

Buidhe Bheinn; 885m; (OS Sheet 33; NG963090); *yellow hill*

Seen from Kinloch Hourn, Buidhe Bheinn's steep hillsides form part of the northern side of the looming green barrier which hems in the glen, helping to create the illusion (on a fair day) of a Caledonian Shangri-La. Buidhe Bheinn is a more isolated mountain than it may appear, connected only on the north by a high level knobbly ridge to Sgurr a' Bhac Chaolais and the South Glen Shiel ridge. On all other sides there are huge drops to the glens or to Loch Hourn far below. It has a narrow summit ridge, and is in a perfect position to give a spectacular view right down the narrows of the loch to Ladhar Bheinn and the north shores of Knoydart.

Buidhe Bheinn was a Corbett until the 1981 revision of the Tables, when Sgurr a' Bhac Chaolais was declared to be higher and received the accolade instead. The 1997 revision found both hills to be of equal height and therefore the status is presently shared. However, the fact is that the re-ascent between the two, 122m, is insufficient to justify this equivalence, and no doubt the balance will eventually tilt again. Never mind the lists, this is a great hill and should be climbed for that reason alone. Users of the OS Explorer map will find that the 2002 edition shows the west top as the summit, giving it a spot height of 897m. Be warned that this is an OS error caused by a transposition of figures, and the true summit is as described here and in the SMC guide *The Corbetts & Other Scottish Hills.*

The ascent is usually made either from Kinloch Hourn or as a foray from Glen Shiel. If the latter is preferred, then follow the route of ascent from the Glen Shiel road, described for Sgurr a' Bhac Chaolais in Chapter 6 *(p128)*. The rugged and undulating ridge south to Buidhe Bheinn gives a fine outing, passing over Cadha nam Bo Ruadha (815m) and Beinn Bhuidhe's north

The Knoydart Foundation

In the early 1980s the future of Knoydart entered a period of great uncertainty. There was talk for a while of it being bought by the Ministry of Defence as a military training ground. Philip Rhodes, a Surrey businessman, acquired it in 1983, having first set up a holding company, Knoydart Peninsula Limited, and proceeded to sell off various parcels of land, reducing the estate from 58,000 acres to just 18,000 acres.

In 1993 Knoydart Peninsula Limited was sold to the troubled Titaghur Limited, along with the rump of the estate. Titaghur had plans for an activity and outdoor leisure centre, but these never came to fruition. Titaghur's difficulties mounted, and its problems transmitted to Knoydart too. In 1998 estate workers went unpaid, and control of the company passed to a businessman, Graham Avery, and then to his associate, Stephen Hinchcliffe, the latter described by a High Court judge as 'unfit to be involved with the management of a company'. By October of that year the receivers stepped in, and, after much negotiation, the estate was purchased in early 1999 for £750,000 by the community-based Knoydart Foundation.

The Foundation is a company with charitable status limited by guarantee. One of its objectives is to allow access and opportunities for recreation all year round whilst at the same time implementing the required conservation and management measures. Its membership is drawn from the local Community Association, the Highland Council, the Chris Brasher Trust, Highlands & Islands Enterprise, and the owners of the neighbouring John Muir Trust Estate and Kilchoan Estate. The Foundation quickly established a number of initiatives to help pursue its objectives, upgrading the community's hydro-electric scheme and commencing a substantial woodland regeneration project. It is sincerely hoped that it will flourish and bring Knoydart the stability and self-determination which have been absent for so long.

The Foundation office is at Inverie (tel: 01687-462242). Its web-site address is www.knoydart-foundation.com, where more information is available.

top (828m). The return is by retracing one's steps. The Kinloch Hourn approach is tougher but geographically more appropriate to the location of the hill. Start from the car park by Loch Beag at the end of the public road, cross the bridge and take the track past the lodge. Slog up the Arnisdale footpath by the electricity pylons for 1.5km to the Cadha Mor, then turn off and head generally north up the second of two zigzag stalkers paths. This path ends at about c670m and from here gain the north-west ridge and follow this over the west top, the point given a spot height of 879m on the Landranger map and an exaggerated height on the Explorer map. It also gives the finest view. The true summit lies a further 750 metres or so along the ridge and is 6m higher. The descent can be made the same way, or by continuing 500 metres north-north-east to a col and dropping to the Coire Sgoireadail path. For those with strong knees, a steep return is also possible down the rough south-east ridge from the west top. This leads directly back to the bridge and the road.

A very fine horseshoe circuit can be made by continuing from Buidhe Bheinn over Sgurr a' Bhac Chaolais to Sgurr na Sgine. Descend Sgurr na Sgine's south-west ridge, Sron Glac na Gaoithe, to pick up a stalkers path which connects with the Arnisdale path and follow this back to Kinloch Hourn.

Sgurr a' Mhaoraich; 1027m; (OS Sheet 33; NG983065); *peak of the shellfish*

If a mountain rotation machine is ever invented, then Sgurr a' Mhaoraich is a prime candidate for being turned through 135 degrees and its fine north-eastern features put on more public display. Its local name, Sgurr a' Mhorair, or *peak of the landowner*, says much about the feudal history of the countryside round here. A solitary peak, it is in fact quite bulky, and has a number of significant ridges, corries and tops. It is bounded on the south by Loch Quoich, and on the east by the loch's narrow and steeply enclosed northern arm outstretched towards Alltbeithe. The hill lies north-east of the low pass which leads down by Coireshubh to Loch Hourn, and indeed from the head of the loch Sgurr a' Mhaoraich towers overhead, its lush walls seeming to completely block any land exit from the glen.

The Allt Coire Sgoireadail descends the deep glen on the hill's north-west side, whilst at the head of this burn Sgurr a' Mhaoraich's north top, Sgurr Thionail (906m), connects by the Bealach Coire Sgoireadail (526m) to the Buidhe Bheinn-Sgurr a' Bhac Chaolais ridge outlying the South Glen Shiel hills. Wester Glen Quoich lies below the northern flanks. Shaped rather like a £ sign, ridges radiate in several directions from the summit, the more important ones being the east ridge connecting the summit to Sgurr Coire nan Eiricheallach (891m) and the north-eastern spur of Am Bathaich (892m). These ridges retain the impressive east-facing Coire a' Chaorainn.

This corrie and many of the other northern aspects are steep-sided and craggy. By contrast, the south slopes are grassy and lacking in features, spurs falling from Sgurr Coire nan Eiricheallach and the main summit to Loch Quoich. These enclose Coire nan Eiricheallach and provide the most accessible (although not the most interesting) walking routes. With a good covering of snow these southern hillsides will give an enjoyable tour for the ski mountaineer.

The recommended outing on foot (which can be done in either direction) is the circuit of Coire a' Chaorainn, starting 1km south-west of the road bridge over the north arm of Loch Quoich. There is limited parking. Take a stalkers path northwards up Bac nan Canaichean and follow this ridge to Sgurr Coire nan Eiricheallach. Descend to a col (823m) and climb the east ridge above. In places this is steep and a little contorted and gives some easy scrambling. Iron spikes have been driven into the rock in places, and are relics of old fencing. The ridge ends just south of the summit. There is a tremendous view down on the narrow trench of upper Loch Hourn, although even this can be bettered by visiting the subsidiary Top of Sgurr a' Mhaoraich Beag (948m) 1km further west.

Head north from the main summit, past a slender pinnacle situated just to the east, and descend to the Bealach Coire a' Chaorainn (784m). Climb north-east over rough ground to the projecting spur of Am Bathaich, which gives a fine perspective on the corries on either side. Continue east down Am Bathaich's grassy crest, picking up a stalkers path which leads to the Alltbeithe track just south of the bridge over the River Quoich. Follow the track back to the road and the starting point.

Another stalkers path starts at the west edge of the Coire nan Eiricheallach forestry, and climbs into the corrie to c470m. Although at the time of writing an estate deer management sign asks walkers to not to enter this corrie, the path does still allow quick access to the top if one diverts from it early on (thus avoiding the corrie) to climb the knobbly south ridge, Leac nan Gaidhseich. This ridge also provides a rapid alternative descent after reaching the summit by the Sgurr Coire nan Eiricheallach route. The circuit of Sgurr a' Mhaoraich's lower slopes by the Wester Glen Quoich and Allt Coire Sgoireadail paths is an interesting low-level walk or wet weather alternative, provided one can organise transport or face the 9km tarmac thole (*plod*) between the glens.

Gleouraich; 1035m; (OS Sheet 33; NH039053); *roaring noise*

Spidean Mialach; 996m; (OS Sheet 33; NH066043); *peak of deer*

Rising massively above the eastern end of the north shore of Loch Quoich, Gleouraich and Spidean Mialach provide a pleasant and accessible high-level outing with fine views all round, in particular across the loch to Gairich, Sgurr Mor and Sgurr na Ciche. The hills take the shape of a long and undulating ridge parallel to Loch Quoich, the ground above the loch being mainly grassy slopes with a few crags and gentle corries. Gleouraich is the more westerly of the two, enjoying a splendid position above the corner formed by the loch's narrow northward extension. Its north side looks across Easter Glen Quoich to the back of the South Glen Shiel ridge, and is made up of a number of rough corries (the finest of which is found beneath the summit) and little known rocky spurs.

Spidean Mialach is slightly lower, but with the same contrast between its north and south flanks, the former falling to the upper waters of the River Loyne, and the latter holding Loch Fearna above its lower craggy hillsides. Its extensive east ridge runs for 9km, becoming less defined as it merges into the broad and boggy area between Loch Loyne and Loch Garry. Both hills are conveniently situated above the Loch Quoich road, whilst the summits themselves lie just 3km apart with relatively straightforward ground in between, so their traverse is not particularly demanding. Under a good covering of snow these hills give an excellent and technically demanding ski traverse, it being recommended to ascend Gleouraich first.

Two stalkers paths lead to the hills from a point some 5km west of the dam at the east end of the loch, leaving the road just 400 metres apart. An old but now irrelevant estate sign requests walkers to avoid the Coire Mheil approach to reduce disturbance to deer. Scenically it would be preferable to climb Spidean Mialach first, as the descent south-west from Gleouraich gives the best outlook across the loch, however it is more efficient to make use of the Gleouraich path in ascent, so this is the route described.

Take the western stalkers path, which follows the Allt Coire Peitireach through woods and rhododendrons, the last signs of the former grounds of the now flooded Glenquoich Lodge. The well-constructed

Spidean Mialach from Loch Loyne

path trends west to gain Sron a' Chuilinn, and this leads to Druim Seileach, Gleouraich's south-west ridge. The path is in a spectacular location high up above Loch Quoich, a dramatic drop on the west down into the loch's waters far below giving a sense of slight exposure. The path ends at c850m, and a final section of ridge leads eastwards to the summit.

Continue east for 1km over Craig Coire na Fiar Bhealaich (1006m), and make a significant descent to the Fiar Bhealach (742m) by a steep zigzag stalkers path. Climb steadily, then simply follow the ridge round the finely scalloped edge of three corries to reach the summit of Spidean Mialach. In winter these hold gently arcing cornices of great beauty. The best line of descent from Spidean Mialach is to head south-west down slopes of scree and grass into the shallow Coire Glas. Pick up the western retaining spur of Loch na Fearna, and follow this broadening ridge down to the road some 1.75km east of the start. The stalkers path is even more accommodating. The route can be reversed, although the pathless section to Loch na Fearna requires some extra effort in ascent.

The rarely visited north side of Gleouraich can be reached from the bridge over the narrow northern arm of Loch Quoich, taking the track to Alltbeithe and continuing up the Easter Glen Quoich footpath. While the rock may give some scrambling, it does not appear to be sufficiently continuous to repay climbing exploration.

Walkers may find it helpful to use the path that climbs to c700m on the Sron na Breun Leitir (845m), Gleouraich's north-west ridge. For those wishing to explore the northern aspect of Spidean Mialach, it is best to take access by the path from above Loch Poulary. It follows the east bank of the Allt a' Ghobhainn, crosses the east ridge of Spidean Mialach, and then drops down to the River Loyne. Various paths lead into the hill's remote northern corries above.

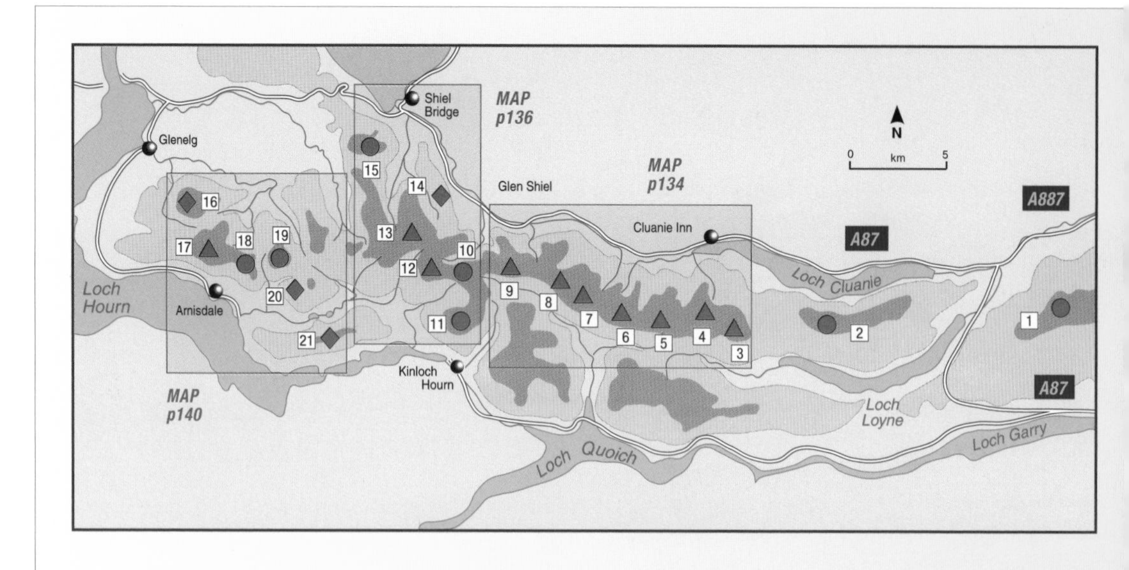

1.	Meall Dubh	788m	C	p131
2.	Beinn Loinne (West Peak), Druim nan Cnamh	790m	C	p131
3.	Creag a' Mhaim	947m	M	p132
4.	Druim Shionnach	987m	M	p132
5.	Aonach air Chrith	1021m	M	p132
6.	Maol Chinn-dearg	981m	M	p132
7.	Sgurr an Doire Leathain	1010m	M	p132
8.	Sgurr an Lochain	1004m	M	p132
9.	Creag nan Damh	918m	M	p132
10.	Sgurr a' Bhac Chaolais	885m	C	p134
11.	Buidhe Bheinn	885m	C	p134
12.	Sgurr na Sgine	946m	M	p135
13.	The Saddle	1010m	M	p135
14.	Biod an Fhithich	644m	G	p135
15.	Sgurr Mhic Bharraich	779m	C	p137
16.	Beinn a' Chapuill	759m	G	p138
17.	Beinn Sgritheall	974m	M	p139
18.	Beinn na h-Eaglaise	805m	C	p139
19.	Beinn nan Caorach	774m	C	p139
20.	Beinn Clachach	643m	G	p139
21.	Druim Fada	713m	G	p141

South Glen Shiel, Glenelg and Arnisdale

Derek Sime

The shapely profile and airy ridges of The Saddle

The line of glens comprising Glen Moriston, Strath Cluanie and Glen Shiel is one of the major east-west features of the Western Highlands. The region that extends westwards from Strath Cluanie is renowned for its mountainous scenery and high concentration of Munros. Most of the mountains described in this chapter form the southern boundary of the Cluanie-Shiel glen system. Also included is the distinct group of hills of the Glenelg peninsula, some of which overlook the northern shore of Loch Hourn.

The majority of travelers will approach Cluanie and Glen Shiel via the A87 trunk road from Invergarry in the Great Glen. One of the great west Highland panoramas can be viewed from a roadside parking place above Glen Garry, with many of the mountains that were described in the last two chapters arrayed on the south-western horizon. Then the road swings to the north-east, past Loch Loyne and its dam, to the junction with the A887 at the bridge over the River Moriston. From here the A87 ascends westwards to the Cluanie dam, continuing by Loch Cluanie, whose attractiveness varies with the water level, like many other lochs that are harnessed for hydro-electricity. Whatever the level of the loch, one cannot fail to be thrilled by the first glimpse of the high mountains that rise beyond, especially when they are seen in silhouette against the evening sky.

Prominent among these mountains are the eastern peaks of the celebrated South Glen Shiel Ridge. From the Cluanie Inn and past the almost imperceptible rise of the watershed between Strath Cluanie and Glen Shiel this ridge dominates the southern skyline, extending for fourteen kilometers and containing seven Munros. Beyond their western end, and part of the same chain of mountains, are Sgurr na Sgine and The Saddle. The latter, with its commanding position and sharp ridges, is one of the finest peaks in the area.

Just beyond the Shiel Bridge petrol station the road to Glenelg branches off to the left from the main A87 trunk road. Soon afterwards a second branch goes along the shore of Loch Duich to Ratagan and the communities beyond. Meanwhile, the Glenelg road climbs steeply to Bealach Ratagain (345m), giving spectacular views back across the head of Loch Duich to the Five Sisters of Kintail, which are described in Chapter 7 *(p142)*.

Beyond Bealach Ratagain, nestling by Glenelg Bay, the village of Glenelg is a focal point for the surrounding farming and forestry communities in Glen More and Gleann Beag. These glens are well worth exploring, especially Gleann Beag for the ancient Brochs of Dun Telve and Dun Troddan. The heads of the two glens are linked by a track and path passing Torr Beag (217m) and Suardalan. A recommendable low-level circular walk of about 25km, starting and finishing at Glenelg, crosses between the heads of the two glens.

There are further pleasant walks in the coastal area and forestry plantations to the north of Glenelg. The car park that overlooks the Kylerhea ferry to the Isle of Skye is a good starting point for exploring this area. Also, a longer walk starts from Totaig (NG877253) and goes west via a right of way through the forest above the coast to Ardintoul, continuing near to the shore by Loch Alsh and Kyle Rhea to the car park. Before setting out on this walk it is advisable to enquire at Ratagan as to the condition of the forest path to Ardintoul, and whether forestry operations are in progress. The walk can be facilitated by transport arrangements, with a drop-off at Totaig (which lacks convenient parking) and a rendezvous in the vicinity of Glenelg. Alternatively, a forest track from Bernera to Ardintoul can be taken to vary the return, giving a round trip from Totaig of about 28km.

The Bernera Barracks at Glenelg (NG815197) were a garrison for Royalist troops during the period of the Jacobite Uprisings. However, only the walls now remain, and these are wired off and behind private dwellings.

Further along towards Arnisdale the road passes the house of Upper Sandaig. Some 500 metres before the house is a gate by the north end of a lochan. Here, Gavin Maxwell enthusiasts can park and walk down through the forest to Sandaig Bay, site of the former Camusfearna of 'Ring of Bright Water' fame. In the forest it is important to cross the bridge at NG777148, so as to arrive at the bay on the correct (south) side of the Allt Mor Shantaig, which is a considerable torrent when in flood.

Just south of Upper Sandaig there is a roadside viewpoint with a splendid view of the

Access and Transport

By road: The area is easily accessed from the South by the A87 trunk road from Invergarry. This road continues from Shiel Bridge to Kyle of Lochalsh and the Skye bridge. From Inverness take the A887 from Invermoriston, joining the A87 3km east of the Cluanie dam. From Torridon the A896 via Lochcarron and then the A890 southwards give access to the A87 west of Dornie.

By bus: Scottish Citylink Coaches (tel: 08705 50 50 50) provide daily services from Glasgow and from Inverness via Glen Shiel to Kyle of Lochalsh. A four-seater postbus links Arnisdale, Glenelg, Shiel Bridge and Kyle of Lochalsh on Mondays to Saturdays.

Accommodation and Information

Hotels and guesthouses: Cluanie, the head of Loch Duich and Glenelg. Bed and breakfast accommodation is available at Ratagan, Glenelg and (at the time of writing) Corran.

SYHA hostel: Ratagan (tel: 0870 004 1147) is popular with hillgoers, and advanced booking is strongly recommended.

Further accommodation: See Chapter 7 *(p142)*, Kintail and Inverinate.

Maps

Ordnance Survey 1:50,000 sheets 33 (Loch Alsh, Glen Shiel & Loch Hourn) and 34 (Fort Augustus and Glen Albyn); Harvey 1:25,000 Superwalker series, Kintail and Glen Shiel.

Sound of Sleat and the Small Isles. Soon Beinn Sgritheall, the dominating mountain of the Glenelg peninsula, comes into sight and towers over the village of Arnisdale. Radiating to the north and east from Beinn Sgritheall are some fine smaller hills. Just beyond the village the road passes the foot of Glen Arnisdale before it terminates at Corran. Glen Arnisdale, with pastures at its lower end and enclosed and rugged further up, affords a passage by footpaths to Kinloch Hourn. The glen is partitioned from Upper Loch Hourn, as if by a curtain, by the long, steep-sided ridge of Druim Fada.

All of the mountains described in this chapter are readily accessible, none being more than about four kilometres from the nearest road. While lacking the sense of remoteness of the peaks of Knoydart, they form part of an impressive array of high hills. Hillwalkers are well rewarded by panoramas of surrounding peaks and, from the more westerly hills, vistas of sea and islands. Remoteness again takes over in the great tract of mountain ranges that extends northwards from Glen Shiel to Glen Carron, described in later chapters.

Principal Hills

Meall Dubh; 788m; (OS Sheet 34; NH245078); *black hill*

Meall Dubh is the highest point of a large tract of elevated moorland east of the A87 Invergarry to Cluanie road. Isolated from other mountains in the area, it is an excellent viewpoint. From the west or north it gives a pleasant half-day. There is a parking area by the entrance to a forestry track at Garbh Dhoire (NH207081). The gate to the forestry track may be locked and there is no stile. If one is installed, follow the track for just over 1km and then take the right fork to where it emerges from the forest. Continue up the rough heathery hillside to the summit, where there is a small cairn with a bigger one nearby.

Instead of descending the same way, an attractive alternative is to take the ridge westwards to Clach Criche (674m), passing several small lochans, and with fine views to the west. Then descend to the west-northwest to a track leading back into the forest near the starting point at Garbh Dhoire.

Another potential way up Meall Dubh is via a hill track that starts from the A887 at a locked gate 1.6km east of Mackenzie's cairn. The track ascends through pasture and a conifer forest, terminating above the forest. The summit is to the south-west up rough hillside, and the satellite Beinn an' Eoin (660m) can easily be included.

A third and much longer route, currently without access difficulty, is from Invergarry. Start at NH297012 and follow a path and track by the Aldernaig Burn. The attractive Loch Lundie is soon reached, and the track and a path are followed round the east and north sides of the loch to the Allt Lundie. Climb beside this burn, past several waterfalls, to high, open moorland. Meall Dubh is gained by way of the intermediate top, Mam a' Chroisg. This route ascends interesting, unfrequented terrain.

Beinn Loinne (West Peak), Druim nan Cnamh; 790m; (OS Sheets 33 & 34; NH131077); *ridge of the bones*

This is the highest point of the long ridge that extends along much of the southern shore of Loch Cluanie. The whole ridge is also called Beinn Loinne. The easiest ascent is up the old road from Cluanie to Tomdoun. From the highest point on the road, strike east across rough moorland, boggy at first, and continue to the summit, where there is a trig point. The top is about midway between the starting point and the Cluanie dam. Therefore with suitable transport a more interesting route would be to traverse the hill from east to west, starting from the dam.

The north side of the hill has several

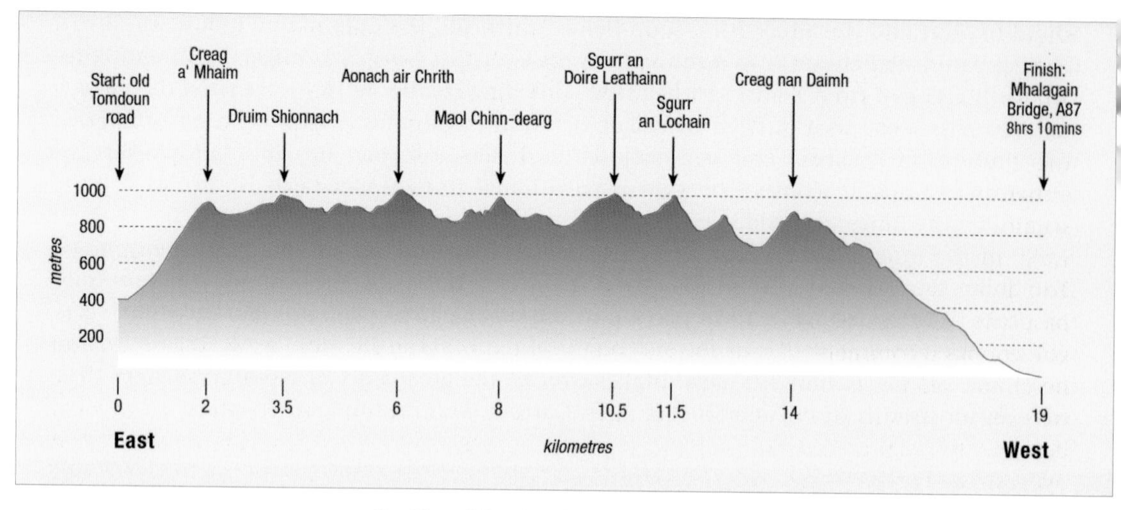

Profile of the South Glen Shiel Ridge

exposures of rock. Most of these are rather inaccessible due to the intervening Loch Cluanie (unless access by boat is considered). However, the compact and clean Cluanie Dam Slabs (NH177094) are only 20 minutes' walk from the dam. A climb on these slabs is *Persistent Reward*, (55m VS 4c 1996).

Creag a' Mhaim; 947m; (OS Sheet 33; NH087078); *rock of the large rounded hill*

Druim Shionnach; 987m; (OS Sheet 33; NH074085); *ridge of foxes*

Aonach air Chrith; 1021m; (OS Sheet 33; NH051083); *ridge of trembling*

Maol Chinn-dearg; 981m; (OS Sheet 33; NH032088); *bald red hill*

Sgurr an Doire Leathain; 1010m; (OS Sheet 33; NH015099); *peak of the broad oak grove*

Sgurr an Lochain; 1004m; (OS Sheet 33; NH005104); *peak of the little loch*

Creag nan Damh; 918m; (OS Sheet 33; NG983112); *rock of the stags*

The peaks to the south of the head of Strath Cluanie and extending along the length of Glen Shiel comprise a continuous high-level skyline, with a succession of corries sculpted by former ice-age glaciers. The section from Creag a' Mhaim to Creag nan Damh affords one of the great classic ridge-walks of the Western Highlands, the South Glen Shiel Ridge. The ridge comprises seven Munros and two lesser peaks.

The distance from Creag a' Mhaim to Creag nan Damh is 11km; from the old Tomdoun road to Bealach Duibh Leac (NG968112) is 14km. The drops between the peaks are not big, and in good conditions the traverse of the seven Munros is straightforward, airy and extremely enjoyable. Steep grass slopes disappear into the fastnesses of Glen Loyne to the south, and craggy corries flank the ridge to the north. It is possible for a fit party to extend the traverse to The Saddle and indeed to Sgurr Mhic Bharraich. However, this is not recommended for a first visit to the area, as the grain of the land becomes less favourable after Bealach Duibh Leac, and The Saddle in any case merits a separate day.

It is also possible, for a more leisurely approach or when conditions are unfavourable, to do the ridge from Creag a' Mhaim to Creag nan Damh in two or more stages, making use of stalkers paths that can be accessed from the A87 at NH044114, or of other northerly spurs.

For the full traverse, arrangements

should preferably be made to avoid the hazards of walking back along the busy A87 afterwards. Use of two cars, or of a local bus service can enable prior parking of a car at the finish. The traverse can be done in either direction, east to west being perhaps scenically the more attractive. To do the walk in this direction, start up the old Tomdoun Road from Cluanie. Continue past the Allt Giubhais bridge. (Previous guidebooks recommended quitting the road here, but fencing is now in place to allow tree regeneration.) Soon after rounding a bend to the right there are three bridges over streams that come down from the right.

If the north flank of Creag a' Mhaim is free of snow, or if winter equipment is carried, a fairly direct way to the top is to head west up rough hillside from the second of the three bridges to a broad shoulder (NH088083). An ascent via the north spur exits about 200 metres west of the summit. It is as well to be aware that a snow band may linger below this exit until late May, presenting an obstacle if frozen. A sure but slightly longer alternative from the three bridges is to continue on the road for about 1km beyond its highest point, to where a stalkers path goes up the south-east ridge of Creag a' Mhaim for most of the way to the summit.

Once on the main ridge there are no obstacles. A path has formed and is becoming eroded in places. Narrow sections occur before the summit of Druim Shionnich and on the descent from Aonach air Chrith. The latter has an impressive outlier, A' Chioch, which can be reached by scrambling if desired. The summit of Sgurr an Doire Leathain is about 100 metres north of the main line of the ridge.

Early in the season, water is obtainable from the foot of a snow patch before the summit slope of Aonach air Chrith. Further on, beyond Sgurr an Lochain, water can be had from a spring on the south slope of Sgurr Beag, a secondary top which is often bypassed for this reason and due to its lack of status. From Creag nan Damh there are

Heading towards Creag a' Mhaim on the South Glen Shiel Ridge

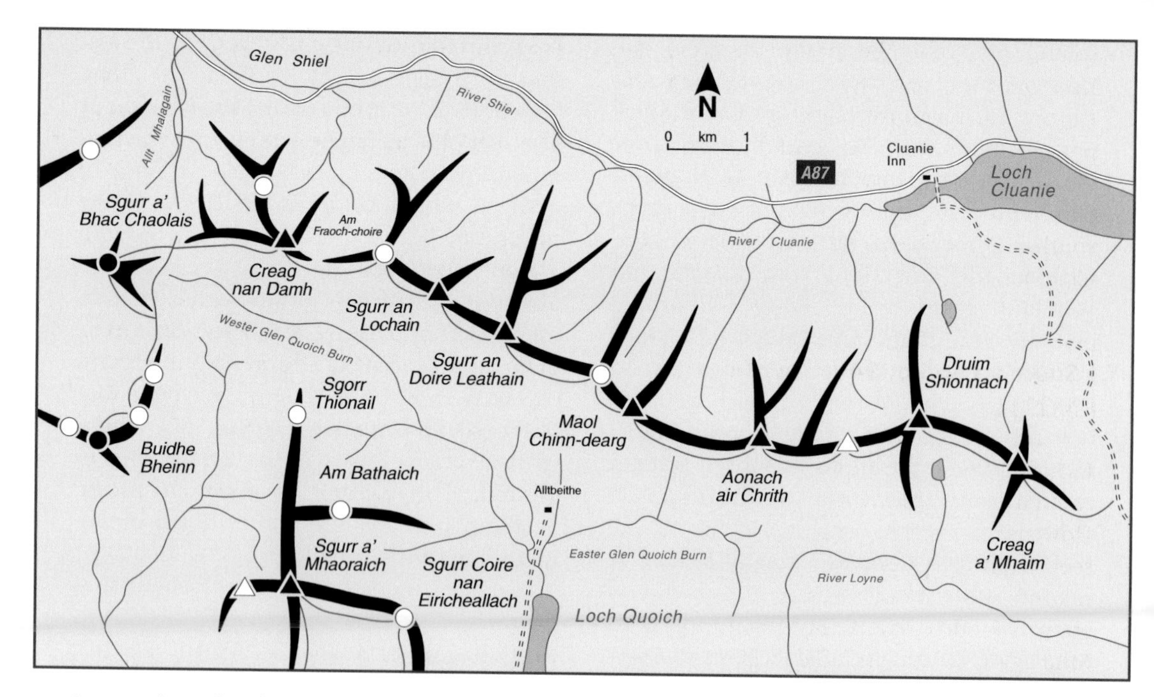

two options for descent. The first is to continue west along the ridge, with some scrambling at first, to Bealach Duibh Leac. From there a path, which is initially difficult to find, zigzags down to the Allt Mhalagain, and so to Glen Shiel at Mhalagain Bridge. The crossing of the Allt Mhalagain normally presents no difficulty but may be problematical when it is in spate. Alternatively, Creag nan Damh can be descended by its north-east ridge, which is narrow and rocky in places. A stalkers path is joined in Am Fraoch-Choire and this descends to the road-bridge in Glen Shiel at NG991132, near to a notice commemorating the Battle of Glen Shiel (1719).

Sgurr a' Bhac Chaolais; 885m; (OS Sheet 33; NG958110); *peak of the sandbank of the narrows*

Buidhe Bheinn; 885m; (OS Sheet 33; NG963090); *yellow hill*

Sgurr a' Bhac Chaolais is one of the less frequented points on the South Glen Shiel skyline, tucked away between the 'classic' South Glen Shiel Ridge just described and the north-western continuation to Sgurr na Sgine and The Saddle. Bare exposures of rock near the top give the peak a somewhat wild aura comparable to the Rough Bounds of Knoydart. The hill is connected by a high-level ridge to Buidhe Bheinn to the south, and both hills can be climbed together from Kinloch Hourn as described in Chapter 5 *(p108)*.

However, if Sgurr a' Bhac Chaolais is the day's primary objective, or if transport to Kinloch Hourn is unavailable, the ascent can be started in Glen Shiel from the bridge over the Allt a' Mhalagain. The stalkers path is taken to the Bealach Duibh Leac, and the east ridge of Sgurr a' Bhac Chaolais is followed to the summit. The descent can be made either by the route of ascent or to the west. The latter involves some scrambling down a rocky barrier, and leads to a broad col with a rather secluded atmosphere, beneath the imposing south-east face of Sgurr na Sgine. From the col, descend north into Coire Toteil, eventually rejoining the ascent path.

Sgurr a' Bhac Chaolais is a sister Corbett with Buidhe Bheinn. Both have the same official height, but the drop between them is not sufficient to qualify them as two Corbetts. From the summit of Sgurr a' Bhac Chaolais, the undulating but fine ridge south to Buidhe Bheinn can be traversed. Return by the same way, making a traverse to the Bealach-Duibh Leac and the descent path. Other routes to Buidhe Bheinn are described in the previous chapter. Some climbs have been done on a cliff below and south-west of the summit of Sgurr a' Bhac Chaolais.

Sgurr na Sgine; 946m; (OS Sheet 33 NG946113); *peak of the knife*

From Glen Shiel, Sgurr na Sgine is partly hidden by its prominent satellite Faochag. However, its striking south-east face is well seen from the peaks just described. A natural line of approach is up the north-east spur of Faochag, starting from the Mhalagain Bridge in Glen Shiel. From the summit of Faochag an airy ridge leads west before dropping south to a col. Sgurr na Sgine is directly ahead. Climb to the subsidiary North-west Top, and continue south-east to the main summit, which is unmistakable, as the cairn directly overlooks the precipitous south-east face. After returning to the col, the descent can be varied by dropping down to Bealach Coire Mhalagain and thence to Meallan Odhar (see for The Saddle, below).

The mountain can also be approached from Sgurr a' Bhac Chaolais. In this case it is recommended that the south-east face of Sgurr na Sgine, with its steep ribs and unstable gullies, be avoided. The face can be bypassed by a flanking movement to the south, traversing above a stone wall until a grassy slope leads up to the broad south-west ridge. From here the summit is about 100m above.

Sgurr na Sgine is often climbed after an ascent of The Saddle (see below). Unfortunately the descent from Faochaig is becoming eroded as a result of this combination. Lastly, Sgurr na Sgine can be climbed from Kinloch Hourn, either on its own or in combination with Buidhe Bheinn and Sgurr a' Bhac Chaolais as described in Chapter 5 *(p108)*, or with The Saddle (see below).

The Saddle; 1010m; (OS Sheet 33; NG936131)

Biod an Fhithich; 644m; (OS Sheet 33; NG950147); *point of the raven*

The Saddle is perhaps the finest and certainly the most individual of the South Glen Shiel peaks. Shapely to look at, with airy ridges, and affording panoramic views from its summit, it is one of Scotland's classic mountains. Its distinctive profile is well seen from the A87 in Glen Shiel.

In plan the mountain resembles a letter

Climbing in Glen Shiel

The climbing potential of the northern corries of the South Glen Shiel Ridge remained largely unfulfilled for many years. *Silver Slab* (100m Severe 1938), on the west face of Druim Shionnach, was the only climb to be mentioned in the 1993 edition of the Northern Highlands Climbing Guide Volume I. This climb is of historical interest because the leader of the first ascent, J W Haggas, also put up two well-known Lakeland classics: *Hangover*, Very Severe, on Dove Crag (1939), and *Gordian Knot*, Very Severe, on White Ghyll (1940). Since 1993 the situation has been totally transformed, with numerous winter routes reported in the Scottish Mountaineering Club Journal from 1994 onwards. The climbs range in height from 70m to 270m, and in difficulty from Grade I to Grade VI. On the west face of Druim Shionnach the prominent central gully is *Cave Gully* (110m IV,4 1994), and *Silver Slab* has given a hard winter climb, (100m VI,7 1996). Creag Coire an t-Slugain has yielded several climbs of various grades including *Pioneer Gully* (110m II 1993), *Flakey Ridge* (110m III,4 1995) and *Rowaling* (135m V,6 1997). On Aonach air Chrith, *Mica Schist Special* (180m III 1994) is quite a long middle grade route. The east face of Sgurr an Lochan offers the centrally located *Flying Gully* (200m, Grade I), described as 'high in its grade, often steep low down and at the cornice'.

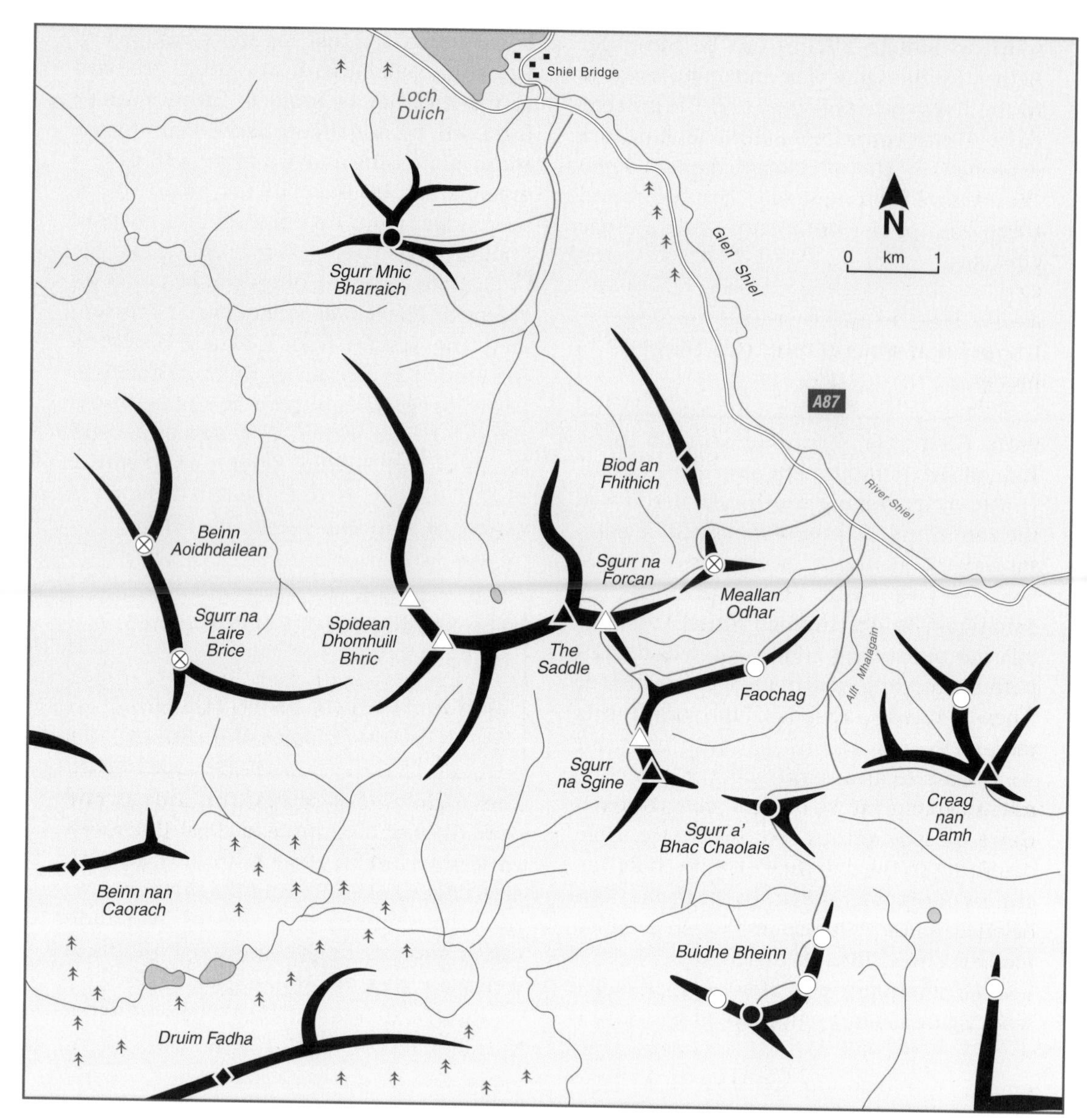

E with arms encompassing two deep northern corries, Coire Chaoil to the east and Coire Uaine to the west. The streams from these corries unite to form the Allt Undalain, which joins the River Shiel at Shiel Bridge. The most popular route of ascent is by the Forcan Ridge, which descends to the east-northeast from Sgurr na Forcan, the east top on the summit ridge. This ascent affords an exposed and rocky scramble, and is described first. A way that avoids the exposed ridge is also described.

Start in Glen Shiel at NG968143, about 1km up the road from Achnagart. Cars can be parked in a layby 200 metres down the road. Follow a good stalkers path to the col between Meallan Odhar and Biod an Fhithich. The latter can be climbed from here and is an impressive viewpoint steeply overlooking Glen Shiel. Allow about an hour for this diversion. From the col, continue up south then south-west to where the rocks of the Forcan Ridge spring upwards. The ridge is well trodden, simplifying route-finding.

After an initial rise, a horizontal knife-edge is encountered at mid-height, spectacular but straightforward. Above this, any difficulties on the crest are avoidable on the right. Shortly beyond the summit of Sgurr na Forcan there is a short but steep rocky descent with good holds. This pitch can be avoided by descending an obvious gully to the left and then rejoining the crest of the ridge below the step. Continue along the crest, or just below to the left, climb to the east top of The Saddle, and continue along a level ridge to the summit cairn. The OS trig point is not on the summit, but 100 metres to the west and about 1m lower.

In winter the Forcan Ridge is a classic grade II climb with considerable exposure, and parties should be equipped accordingly.

An alternative way to the summit from the foot of the Forcan Ridge is to contour south-west above a stone wall towards Bealach Coire Mhalagain, then make a rising traverse north-west towards the summit, keeping below the rocks. An eroded path emerges onto a broad shoulder, whence the trig point is readily gained up to the right.

There are various options from the summit. A descent can be made towards Bealach Coire Mhalagain by reversing the way described in the previous paragraph. Then either contour to rejoin the ascent path just below the foot of the Forcan Ridge, or alternatively climb Sgurr na Sgine from the bealach. A descent can then be made to the road after traversing Faochag. This otherwise attractive round is suffering from increasing erosion on the descents of both The Saddle and Faochag.

A more direct descent from the summit of The Saddle, which is only to be recommended in good visibility and relatively snow-free conditions, is initially north towards Sgurr na Creige, then east-north-east into the top of Coire Chaoil. Continue down the corrie for 1.5km in the direction of the col between Meallan Odhar and Biod an Fhithich. A short climb leads to the col, where the stalkers path is joined for the return to the road.

A third possibility is to visit the western Tops, Spidean Dhomhuill and Sgurr nan Each. These Tops are fine viewpoints, but are somewhat out on a limb in relation to the start from near Achnagart. Alternative access can be made via a circuit starting from Shiel Bridge. (See Sgurr Mhic Bharraich, below, for the initial approach.) Given the 'E' plan of The Saddle, various horseshoe routes are possible.

It may be mentioned for the connoisseur that The Saddle can be climbed from Kinloch Hourn. The right of way towards Arnisdale is followed for about 5km to a ruined cottage in Gleann Dubh Lochain, from where the Mullach Gorm Ridge leads to the west peak of The Saddle, about 500 metres from the summit.

Sgurr Mhic Bharraich; 779m; (OS Sheet 33; NG917173); *peak of the son of Maurice*

On a clear day, Sgurr Mhic Bharraich affords excellent views of Loch Duich and out to Skye. The hill can be ascended and descended in a few hours in good conditions. The most straightforward ascent starts from the campsite at Shiel Bridge by the path along the Allt Undalain, initially by the east bank until a footbridge is crossed after about 700 metres. The path continues south along the floor of the glen, and then climbs west to Loch Coire nan Crogachan. (Avoid a left fork of the path on the way up to the loch.) Turn north across the outlet of the loch and climb to the broad summit ridge, continuing north-west to the summit. It is easiest to descend by the same route.

A more direct descent, for the strong-kneed, goes eastwards from NG922172 down a slope of continuously steep grass to the path by the Allt Undalain about 1km south of the footbridge.

A direct ascent of the hill can be made by going steeply uphill to follow a fence line shortly after the footbridge. The deep heather low down makes for hard going, but the walking is fine in the upper corrie.

The Allt Undalain also gives access to the horseshoe walk routes on The Saddle,

Sgurr na Forcan from The Saddle, with The Forcan Ridge in silhouette on the left

mentioned above.

An alternative way to Sgurr Mhic Bharraich is from Bealach Ratagan, but this entails rough going for 2km on a hilly ridge followed by steep ground on the north-west flank of Sgurr Mhic Bharraich.

Beinn a' Chapuill; 759m; (OS Sheet 33; NG835148); *hill of the horse*

Beinn a' Chapuill is a substantial outlier of Beinn Sgritheall. It is a fine Graham, and misses Corbett status by only a few metres. The hill possesses a sizable and secluded summit plateau, studded with lochans and flanked on three sides by crags. Only the east ridge affords an easily accessible and crag-free line of ascent. The actual summit overlooks the south-east end of the eastern-most lochan, and is not at the more north-westerly point 742m named Beinn a' Chapuill on the OS 1:50,000 map.

Drive up Gleann Beag to Balvraid, passing two brochs mentioned in the introduction to the chapter. Continue by foot on the track for about 2.5km, passing the remains of another broch, Dun Brugaig, to a suspension footbridge at Strath a' Chomair (NG866158). Cross the bridge and ascend to a low col, from which the east ridge of Beinn a' Chapuill rises to the right.

After a short climb, a section with level stretches and gentle rises gives superb views of Beinn Sgritheall to the south and into Gleann Beag and across to Skye in the north-west. After about 2km, the mainly grassy ridge rises more steeply to the summit plateau. Then continue for another 500 metres to the actual summit, where there is a small cairn. On a clear day there are excellent views to the Inner Isles and to the many peaks nearer at hand, especially Beinn Sgritheall,

It is easiest to descend by the same route. It is also possible to continue to Beinn Sgritheall, making for a much longer day. The initial descent of about 250m to Bealach na h-Oidhche should be commenced well to the west of the summit of Beinn a' Chapuill so as to avoid the cliffs to the north of the summit. For the continuation of the circuit, see the description of the northern approach to Beinn Sgritheall, below.

Beinn Sgritheall; 974m; (OS Sheet 33; NG836127); *probably scree hill*

Beinn Sgritheall rises steeply from the north shore of Loch Hourn just west of Arnisdale. Its profile is well seen from across the Sound of Sleat at Isle Oronsay in Skye. The mountain provides a particularly fine prospect to the islands of Skye, Rum and Eigg, as well as the grand Knoydart peaks of Ladhar Bheinn and its neighbours a short distance across Loch Hourn.

There are three main routes of ascent. The shortest starts from the roadside about 3km north-west of Arnisdale, near a crag called Creag Ruadh. Leave the road at about NG825116. There are several enlarged passing places where a car can be parked. Climb steeply up the hillside, aiming to reach the west shoulder of Beinn Sgritheall a few hundred metres west of the main summit. Continue to the summit, or first make a diversion to visit the North-west Top (928m). The ascent is rewarded by a rapidly expanding panorama across Loch Hourn and to the Inner Isles.

The second route starts immediately before the village of Arnisdale, where a sign points to the correct way. Occasional white-painted stones indicate the way up and then rightwards across a stream, well above the houses of Arnisdale and their gardens. Continue up a rough path to Bealach Arnasdail, then climb the fairly steep slope to the east top of Beinn Sgritheall (906m). Go along the delightful east ridge to the main summit. This route is somewhat enclosed until Bealach Arnasdail is reached, and it is becoming eroded. However, it affords a useful route of ascent if it is planned to climb Beinn na h-Eaglaise and Beinn nan Caorach afterwards (see below).

The third route is from the north. This side of the mountain is quite remote, and its multiple corries make for some degree of topographical complexity. Therefore the northern approach is only recommended for reasonably good weather, when it gives an excellent outing with an exploratory feeling.

Drive up Gleann Beag to Balvraid and continue by foot for 2.5km to the suspension bridge at Strath a' Chomair, as described above for Beinn a' Chapuill. Cross a low col by the conifer plantation on the left to join a stalkers path at NG866156. This rises gradually to the south-west for 1.5km by the Allt Srath a' Chomair.

The northern corries then present several possibilities. The most attractive is to follow the Allt Bealach na h-Oidhche to the Bealach, then ascend south-east to the entrance of a high corrie. The North-west Top of Beinn Sgritheall then can be gained by its north-east ridge, which gives fine situations and some scrambling.

From the North-west Top the mountain can be traversed by the main summit and east top to Bealach Arnasdail, before descending north-east to Rosdail and the Allt Strath a' Chomair. More extensive circuits are also possible, taking in Beinn a' Chapuill (see above) and/or Beinn na h-Eaglaise and Beinn nan Caorach in addition to Beinn Sgritheall.

The North Buttress climb of Beinn Sgritheall ascends to the North-west Top via crags to the right of the north-east ridge. It has been climbed in both summer (Difficult) and winter (III).

Beinn na h-Eaglaise; 805m; (OS Sheet 33; NG853119); *hill of the church*

Beinn nan Caorach; 774m; (OS Sheet 33; NG871121); *hill of the sheep*

Beinn Clachach; 643m; (OS Sheet 33; NG885109); *stony hill*

Beinn nan Caorach and Beinn na h-Eaglaise give a pleasant circuit, which can be

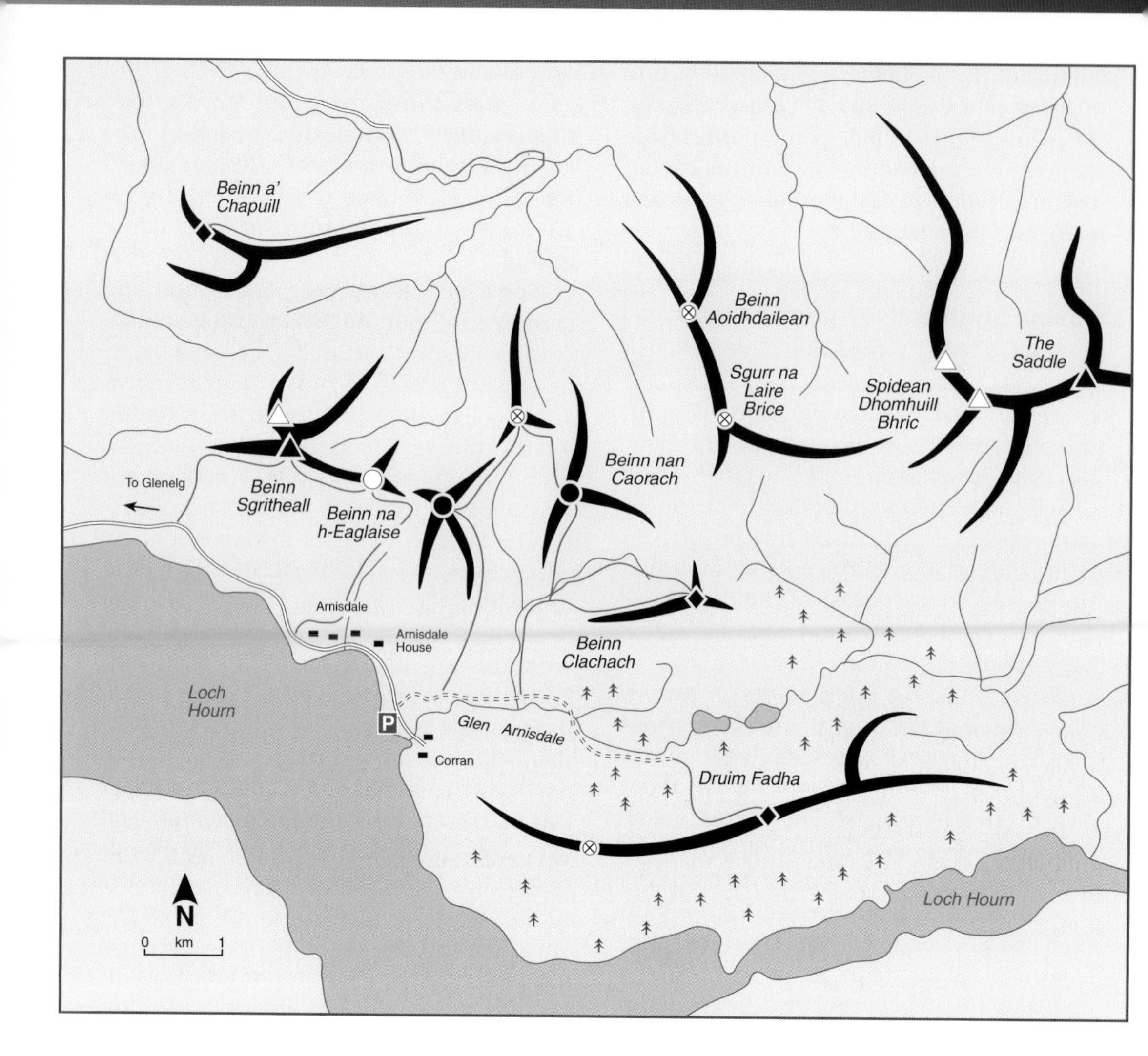

extended by including Beinn Clachach. The anti-clockwise direction is scenically the more attractive, and also utilizes good tracks for the start. Park at the car park at Corran. Walk back 400 metres to the Glen Arnisdale track and take this for 1.5km to a bridge. Do not cross this, but turn north across a field, pass a ruined cottage and climb a stalkers track for about 1km (300m of ascent). To the left, an impressive waterfall plunges over cliffs into a ravine.

If Beinn Clachach is not to be included, quit the track soon after entering Coire Chorsalain, cross the stream and climb Beinn nan Caorach by its steep south flank. (Alternatively, if the water level in the stream is high, continue up the Coire Chorsalain path to the bealach at the head of the corrie and ascend the east ridge of Beinn nan Caorach.) From the top, descend north-west to the col near point 605m, and south-west to the foot of the north-east ridge of Beinn na h-Eaglaise. The ridge is climbed past old fence posts to the summit. There are fine views across Loch Hourn and to Beinn Sgritheall nearer at hand. The best descent from Beinn na h-Eaglaise is initially south-southeast over the shoulder of Beinn Bhuidhe, then south-southwest fairly steeply to near the start of the track in Glen Arnisdale.

It is possible, but not easy, to continue from Beinn na h-Eaglaise to Beinn Sgritheall. The direct descent from the top of Beinn na h-Eaglaise to Bealach Arnasdail is dangerously steep with exposed crags and gullies. To avoid these, go south along the ridge for about 5 minutes from the summit, where a steep grassy gully without rock outcrops can be descended. From its base, contour rightwards to the bealach. It is also possible to outflank the steepest ground by descending from slightly north-east of the summit and then contouring leftwards to the bealach. But the best option for combining Beinn Sgritheall with Beinn na h-Eaglaise is to commence with Beinn Sgritheall, as the difficulties on the steep flank of Beinn na h-Eaglaise are then visible from below and therefore more easily avoided.

For Beinn Clachach, start from Glen Arnisdale as for Beinn nan Caorach. The easiest route is to go up into Coire Chorsalain and then ascend south-east into Coire Luachrach. This leads up to a broad col, whence the summit is gained about 400 metres to the north-east. There are several knolls. The highest one has a small cairn and overlooks a tiny lochan. (Note that this highest point, 643m, is about 1km east-northeast of the point marked Beinn Clachach, 618m, on the OS map.) An interesting variation, involving some scrambling, can be made by leaving the stalkers track at the region overlooking the waterfall before the entry into Coire Chorsalain, and climbing directly to point 618m.

Then continue via the col to the summit. If the hill is being climbed on its own, the most straightforward descent is via Coire Luachrach as described above for the easy ascent route. If it is planned to continue to Beinn nan Caorach, descend the north ridge of Beinn Clachach, avoiding a band of crags to the west, to the bealach at the head of Coire Chorsalain. Then climb the east ridge of Beinn nan Caorach. The south flank of Beinn Clachach above Dubh Lochain is very steep in places, and is not recommended, especially as an unseen route of descent.

Druim Fada; 713m; (OS Sheet 33; NG894083); *long ridge*

Druim Fada is the long, rough ridge that separates Glen Arnisdale and Glen Dubh Lochain from inner Loch Hourn. The summit area gives dramatic views across the latter into Knoydart and the Barrisdale Forest peaks.

The most direct route to the top is from upper Glen Arnisdale. However, this route is on steep ground; therefore alternatives are given below. For the direct route, take the track up the glen for 1.5km, cross the bridge, and continue for 2.5km to where a stream that descends from a ravine high on Druim Fada crosses the track at NG884091. The glen is now a steep sided gorge reminiscent of the Glen Nevis gorge. (A short distance beyond, the track crosses by a bridge over the River Arnisdale below its exit from Dubh Lochain.)

From the east bank of the stream just mentioned, go up to the crest of a steep spur, aiming to reach this at a small saddle above the lowermost rocks. A view of Dubh Lochain unfolds here. Ascend the spur by the line of least resistance, to emerge on the summit ridge about 500 metres west of the summit. The actual summit is the eastern of two knolls about 50 metres apart, both with small cairns.

In descent this route is steep enough to be potentially dangerous, especially in bad conditions. Care should be taken to keep to the general line of the crest of the spur, with only minor diversions to avoid small rock bands, and keeping clear of the flanking slopes, for these, especially that of the ravine on the west, are very steep indeed.

Alternative routes for ascent or descent avoid the steep north face by making much more use of the undulating summit ridge. One way is to ascend directly from near the bridge in Glen Arnisdale (NG861097) and then traverse the ridge eastwards to the summit, returning the same way for the descent. Another route is from Kinloch Hourn by a good stalkers path onto Carn nan Caorach. If transport can be arranged, the complete traverse from Kinloch Hourn to Corran via Carn nan Caorach and the bridge in Glen Arnisdale makes a fine expedition on which to savour this spectacular arena of mountains and sea.

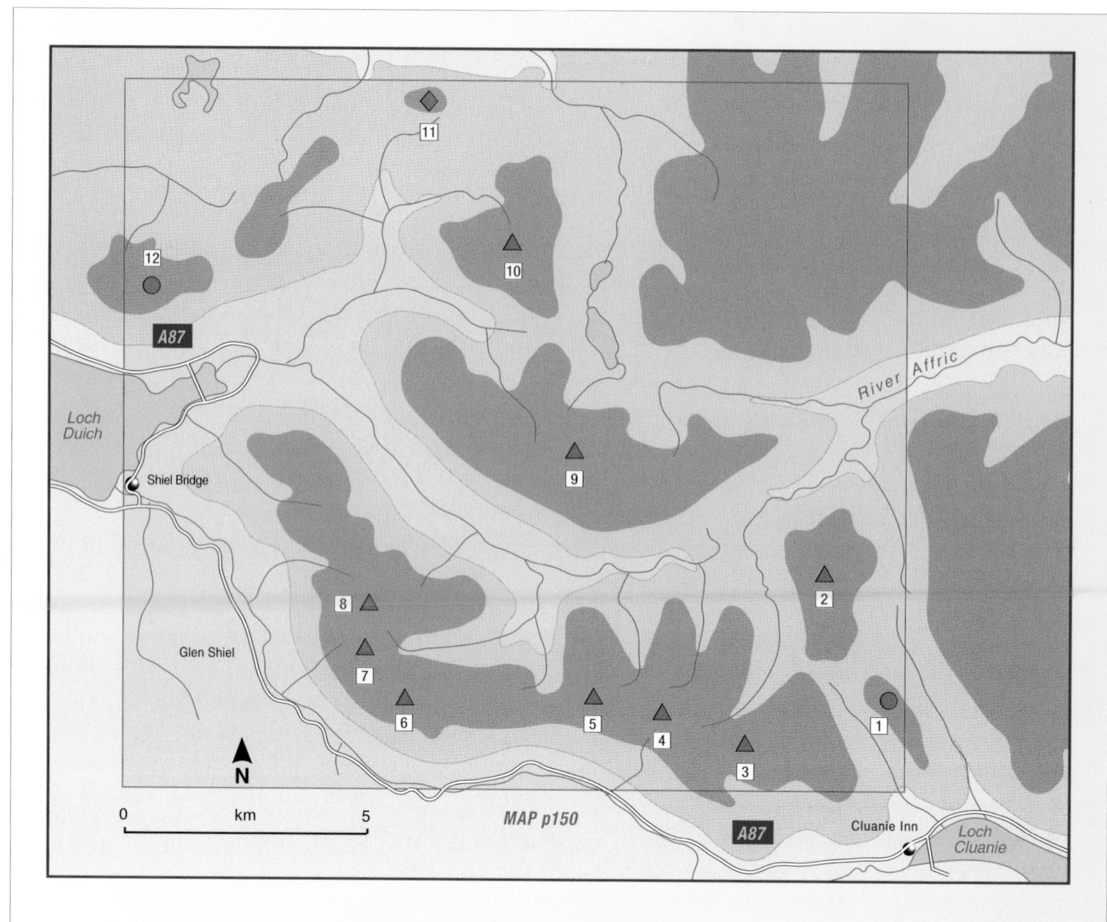

1.	Am Bathach	798m	C	p145
2.	Ciste Dhubh	979m	M	p145
3.	Aonach Meadhoin	1001m	M	p147
4.	Sgurr a' Bhealaich Dheirg	1036m	M	p147
5.	Saileag	956m	M	p147
6.	Sgurr na Ciste Duibhe	1027m	M	p148
7.	Sgurr na Carnach	1002m	M	p148
8.	Sgurr Fhuaran	1067m	M	p148
9.	Beinn Fhada	1032m	M	p151
10.	A' Ghlas-bheinn	918m	M	p151
11.	Carnan Cruithneachd	729m	G	p154
12.	Sgurr an Airgid	841m	C	p155

Kintail and Inverinate

Richard Wood

The Five Sisters from the east

Kintail and Inverinate are relatively compact adjacent regions to the north of Glen Shiel and Loch Duich. The Five Sisters of Kintail rank among the most famous and recognizable of all Highland peaks, dominating the skyline when seen from the south shore of Loch Duich. Images of this spectacular group adorn postcards and all manner of souvenirs, yet on a fine, clear day the reality of the view transcends expectations, especially in spring when snow sparkles on the summits.

The area is bounded on the south and south-west by the A87 from Cluanie through Glen Shiel to Shiel Bridge, and then along the north shore of Loch Duich to Dornie. Shortly after Shiel Bridge the main road passes the wide entrance to the U-shaped Strath Croe, where a secondary loop road gives access to the hamlet of Morvich. From Dornie the narrow Loch Long penetrates deeply inland to Glen Elchaig, and this loch and glen together form the northern boundary of the area. The eastern boundary is defined by the irregular line of glens from An Caorann Mor near the head of Loch Cluanie to the Falls of Glomach above Glen Elchaig.

The area is divided into two parts of different character by a natural line that extends from Strath Croe north-east over the Bealach na Sroine to the Falls of Glomach. To the south and east of this dividing line is Kintail. The Five Sisters comprise the north-western end of a long ridge system between Glen Shiel and Gleann Lichd, a deep glen carrying the River Croe. This ridge system complements the South Glen Shiel Ridge described in the previous chapter, and is accordingly called the North Glen Shiel Ridge. The eastern peaks on the ridge are often referred to as the Brothers, by analogy with the Five Sisters at the western end. Ciste Dhubh and Am Bathach are to the north and east of the Brothers, across the fairly deep Bealach a' Choinich.

Across Gleann Lichd rises the massive Beinn Fhada, and to the north again is A' Ghlas-bheinn. The North Glen Shiel Ridge and Beinn Fhada are characterized by long, very steep grass slopes on their south-west flanks and by fine corries on their northern and eastern aspects. By contrast Ciste Dhubh has a cliff to the south-east and steep grass to the north

The descent from Sgurr na Moraich towards Loch Duich

and west. The steep grass slopes on all of these peaks are subject to avalanche danger during and after substantial snowfalls, and should be avoided under such conditions.

To the north-west of the dividing line is the Inverinate Forest, less mountainous but wilder than Kintail. The two main peaks here are Sgurr an Airgid and Carnan Cruithneachd. Behind Sgurr an Airgid is an elevated hinterland, rough and secluded, with rocky hills and remote lochans.

Habitations abound along both shores of Loch Duich and in Morvich, and many people live and work in Kintail, in contrast with depopulated regions elsewhere in the North-west Highlands. For visitors, features of interest in and near Kintail include Eilean Donan Castle, the Kirk Cemetery at the entrance to Strath Croe, and the Balmacara Estate and Lochalsh Woodland Garden. Eilean Donan was probably named after the Irish saint, Donan, who came to Scotland in about 580AD. A castle was built here in the 13th century for defence against the Vikings. During the following centuries the castle was occupied by the Mackenzies and Macraes. In 1715 it was garrisoned by government troops and then retaken by the Jacobites. It was bombarded by government war-ships in 1719, and remained in ruins for almost 200 years. It was bought in 1911 by John Macrae-Gilstrap, and the castle was rebuilt under his direction between 1912 and 1932. In 1983 the Macrae family formed the Conchra Trust to care for the castle. A visit is highly recommended. An official guidebook, published by the Trust and for sale at the castle shop, gives information on the history and restoration.

Much of Kintail, including the Five Sisters and some of the neighbouring mountains, was purchased for the National Trust for Scotland with funds given by Percy Unna, a past president of the Scottish Mountaineering Club. The normal restrictions that affect much of the Highlands in the stalking season do not apply to NTS land and those Kintail mountains in Trust territory are accessible during the stalking season. The boundary of the National Trust for Scotland property is shown on the Ordnance Survey map.

Principal Hills

Am Bathach; 798m; (OS Sheet 33; NH073143); *the byre*

Ciste Dhubh; 979m; (OS Sheet 33; NH062166); *black chest*

These two peaks stand one behind the other to the north of the Cluanie Inn, Am Bathach rising as a whalebone ridge, Ciste Dhubh as a narrow spine overlooking the remote Fionngleann. The two peaks can be climbed together as a moderate day's outing in good conditions. Alternatively, Am Bathach can be climbed on its own following an afternoon arrival (or a wet morning!). Ciste Dhubh can be ascended on its own en route to or from the Alltbeithe youth hostel, or it can be included with part or all of the North Glen Shiel Ridge (see below).

As noted above, Ciste Dhubh has steep slopes, which can be avalanche-prone in winter conditions, especially to the north and east. The following description is for

Access and Transport

By road: The mountains of Kintail are readily accessible, the main A87 from the south to Kyle of Lochalsh and Skye passing close to most of them. On the south side of Strath Croe there is a car park at Morvich, access to which is signposted. On the north side of the strath a narrow road leads to a Forestry Commission car park at the roadhead near Dorusduain (NG978222). This road has recently been gated at the forest boundary, but the car park, which is about 750 metres beyond the gate, is accessible at the time of writing. There is a public road up the west side of Loch Long as far as the hamlet of Camas-luinie. The road on the north side of Glen Elchaig is private and cars are not permitted beyond a car park at NG940303 shortly before Killilan.

By bus: From Glasgow or Inverness by Scottish Citylink Coaches. A post-bus serves Dornie, Killilan and Kyle of Lochalsh. Some bed and breakfast proprietors will transport hillwalkers to starting points for ridge walks or other point-to-point walks, usually for a small fee. Inquiries can be made in advance by phone.

Accommodation and Information

Hotels and guesthouses: Cluanie, and at the head of Loch Duich, and at Dornie and Ardelve on opposite sides of the mouth of Loch Long. Bed and breakfast accommodation and houses and caravans to rent abound, particularly at Ratagan and Inverinate where there are communities of Forestry Commission workers.

SYHA hostels: Ratagan (tel: 0870-004-1147) near the head of Loch Duich and Alltbeithe in the remote upper part of Glen Affric.

Club Hut: Glenlicht House, Gleann Lichd is leased by the National Trust for Scotland to the Edinburgh University Mountaineering Club.

Outdoor Centre: At Morvich the Morvich Outdoor Centre is run by a trust for visiting parties of climbers and others.

Bothies: Just to the north-east of the watershed at the head of Gleann Lichd is the remote bothy of Camban, renovated by the Mountain Bothies Association in memory of the late Philip Tranter.

Campsites: Shiel Bridge, Morvich, Ardelve, and Balmacara.

Maps

Ordnance Survey 1:50,000 Sheet 33 (Loch Alsh, Glen Shiel and Loch Hourn) and Sheet 25 (Glen Carron and Glen Affric). (Sheet 33 covers the entire area except part of the north shore of Loch Long and Killilan, which are on Sheet 25.) Also, Harvey 1:25,000 Superwalker series, Kintail and Glen Shiel.

The Five Sisters from from Sgurr a' Bhealaich Dheirg

both peaks together.

Leave the A87 at a gate beyond the eastern end of a conifer plantation about 1.5km east of the Cluanie Inn and just before the road bridge over the Allt a' Chaorainn Mhoir. (There is a parking area by the conifers.) A stalkers path leads for a short distance onto the south-east ridge, whence the upper slopes are easily gained. Am Bathach's summit ridge is an airy highway, flanked by the deep glens of An Caorann Beag and An Caorann Mor. The summit is a particularly fine viewpoint. It is at the hub of a semicircle of Munros, and its modest height accentuates the massive scale of A' Chralaig and Mullach Fraoch-choire across An Caorann Mor to the east.

Continue north-westwards, descending to the boggy Bealach a' Choinich (567m). Thence the steep south slope of Ciste Dhubh rises ahead. There is an emerging path towards the left hand side, or the grass slope can be ascended anywhere, amidst a profusion of wild flowers in early summer. Higher up, the slopes converge to a narrow ridge, which is followed over a forepeak to the airy summit. The top overlooks cliffs to the south-east and the wilds of Fionngleann to the north.

For the descent, either return to Bealach a' Choinich and continue down a rough path on the east side of the Allt a' Chaorainn Bhig, or alternatively descend steep grass slopes to the north-east, swinging east to join the path and track on the east side of the Allt a' Chaorainn Mhoir.

The steep south-east face of Ciste Dhubh has some winter climbing. The central gully between the two cliff faces gives a grade I route. The right hand face has afforded *Kissed Ye Quick* (70m II 1995), *The Mantelshelf* (70m V,6 1996) and, for collectors of climbs with macabre names, *The Undertaker* (70m III,4 1995).

Aonach Meadhoin; 1001m; (OS Sheet 33; NH049137); *middle ridge*

Sgurr a' Bhealaich Dheirg; 1036m; (OS Sheet 33; NH035143); *peak of the red pass*

Saileag; 956m; (OS Sheet 33; NH017148); *little hill;* literally, *little heel*

These three Munros, together with Sgurr an Fhuarail (*peak of the cold hollow*, 987m), the eastern top of Aonach Meadhoin, comprise the eastern half of the North Glen Shiel Ridge, and are sometimes known as The Brothers. Their traverse in either direction is an enjoyable ridge walk with fine views. Ciste Dhubh can also be included, giving an appreciably more strenuous day. The traverse is described from east to west. In this direction the descent leads to a car park at NH009136, and the end of the day may be more enjoyable if arrangements can be made for transport to be waiting here, for it is about 7km back up the busy road to the starting point at Cluanie.

Sgurr an Fhuarail can be climbed either by its south-east ridge from Cluanie, crossing a small knoll at 864m on the way, or by the broad grassy slope from the Bealach a' Choinich if coming from Ciste Dhubh. From Sgurr an Fhuarail a pleasant ridge leads to Aonach Meadhoin, whose top is a small level plateau, an excellent lunch balcony on a fine day. The descent westwards from Aonach Meadhoin contains a short narrow section, which may become corniced in winter.

Continue up to Sgurr a' Bhealaich Dheirg, the highest point on the eastern half of the ridge. The actual summit is about 100 metres along a narrow lateral ridge to the north-east. This short ridge is adorned with a remarkable dry stone dyke, a relic of yesteryear. The summit bears a fine cairn and is another magnificent viewpoint, the wild north-eastern aspect of the Five Sisters dominating the horizon to the west.

The continuation to Saileag is straightforward, and this summit yields fine views down Gleann Lichd. A descent of about 250m leads to the Bealach an Lapain. From here a path that is becoming eroded in places leads steeply down to Glen Shiel, with a short rightwards section half-way down to avoid conifer plantations. The A87 is reached close to the parking area at NH009136.

A very different way up Sgurr a' Bhealaich Dheirg is by its fine north-north-east ridge. A bicycle facilitates the approach from Morvich to Glenlicht House. From the top of Sgurr a' Bhealaich Dheirg a pleasant horseshoe can be completed by way of Saileag's north ridge and back to Glenlicht

Right Versus Might: Crofter Overcomes Capitalist In Kintail

A crucial legal decision on trespass in Scotland dates back to the late 19th century, when American railroad baron Walter Winans leased 200,000 acres of deer forest in Wester Ross, including Strathfarrar, Glen Affric and Kintail. Grazing rights were curtailed in Kintail to provide winter grazing for deer. A crofter, Murdoch Macrae, grazed a pet lamb locally. Winans raised an action of interdict to prevent this trespass on his land. Macrae challenged the interdict. A legal battle ensued, in which Macrae finally triumphed, the Court of Session ruling in 1885 in favour of the crofter and against the capitalist, on the basis that the trespass was so trivial and with so little ensuing damage that the court was not prepared to give Winans the remedy he sought.

The same year, the first Crofters Act became law, giving security of tenure and various compensations to such as Murdoch and his fellow crofters in Kintail and elsewhere in the Highlands. Murdoch Macrae lies buried in the old graveyard at the entrance to Strath Croe. Further details of the Winans story are to be found in Ian Mitchell's *Scotland's Mountains before the Mountaineers* and (for archive enthusiasts) in *The Ross-Shire Journal*, 15 October, 1999, in an article also by Mitchell. A photograph of 'the scourge of the crofters Walter Winans', looking uncompromising with gun, accompanies the newspaper article.

Sgurr an Fhuarail and Aonach Meadhoin

House. A longer option is to continue along the main ridge to Sgurr Fhuaran and then down the east ridge of the latter (see below).

Sgurr na Ciste Duibhe; 1027m; (OS Sheet 33; NG984149); *peak of the black chest*

Sgurr na Carnach; 1002m; (OS Sheet 33; NG977158); *rocky peak*

Sgurr Fhuaran; 1067m; (OS Sheet 33; NG978166); *peak of the wolf*

These three Munros, together with Sgurr nan Saighead (929m) (*peak of the arrows*) and Sgurr na Moraich (876m) (*peak of the sea-plain*) comprise the celebrated Five Sisters of Kintail. Just to the east of the Five Sisters proper, another top, Sgurr nan Spainteach (990m) (*peak of the Spaniards*) is on the approach ridge from the Bealach an Lapain.

The latter peak takes its name from the Battle of Glenshiel (1719). A small force of Jacobites were supported by about 250 Spanish soldiers who had landed at Eilean Donan castle. The Hanoverian army defeated the forces, and the Spaniards took flight up the slopes of the peak. A plaque describing the battle and its historical background is located at NG992133 on the north side of the A87.

On both sides the slopes of the Five Sisters ridge drop very steeply into the glens below. The south-west face of Sgurr na Ciste Duibhe falls 1000m in a horizontal distance of just over one kilometre, one of the longest and steepest continuous slopes in Scotland. Sgurr na Carnach and Sgurr Fhuaran present long grassy spurs separated by deep gullies on the Glen Shiel side. The Gleann Lichd aspect is much wilder, with fine, remote corries.

Because of its steep slopes, the Five Sisters Ridge is not easy to escape from in bad conditions, especially during or after snowfall when there may be danger of avalanches. Therefore the Five Sisters are best done in good conditions. The classic expedition is the complete traverse. This is described from east to west, for in this direction the best views are ahead. It is recommended to make transport arrangements so as to eliminate the need to walk back along the busy A87 after the traverse.

Start at the gap in the forest plantations on the north side of the glen, where there is parking at NH009136 (also reached after descending from the eastern half of the North Glen Shiel Ridge, described above). Climb steeply to the Bealach an Lapain. A path has been worn by many climbers, and eighty minutes or less should suffice. At the bealach a grand panorama unfolds to the north. Turn left along the grassy ridge, which gradually rises over an intermediate top to Sgurr nan Spainteach. The ridge then drops more abruptly, with one short rocky pitch, which requires care, to the col below Sgurr na Ciste Duibhe.

At this col there is a curious hollow in the ridge, which one bypasses on the right or left before climbing steeply to the summit of Sgurr na Ciste Duibhe. (This hollow can be confusing in mist, particularly if one is traversing from west to east.) On the summit of Sgurr na Ciste Duibhe a massive cairn stands on a rock plinth.

The main ridge now swings northwards, and a well-worn path is followed down a bouldery slope to Bealach na Gaoibhe (850m, unnamed on the OS 1:50,000 map) and over Sgurr na Carnach. From the next col, Bealach na Carnach (868m, also unnamed on the 1:50,000 map) a steep pull of 200m leads up to the summit of Sgurr na Fhuaran, the highest of the Sisters and a magnificent viewpoint.

On its north side Sgurr na Fhuaran is very steep, so descend west-north-west for a short distance down a spur which drops all the way to Glen Shiel. At a short level section of the spur, turn right and make a slightly descending traverse north-east to regain the main ridge below the steep summit slopes. The ridge to Sgurr na Saighead gives an impressive view of the steep slabby east face of this peak, which appears as a pyramid from the south.

From Sgurr an Fhuarail towards Loch Cluanie

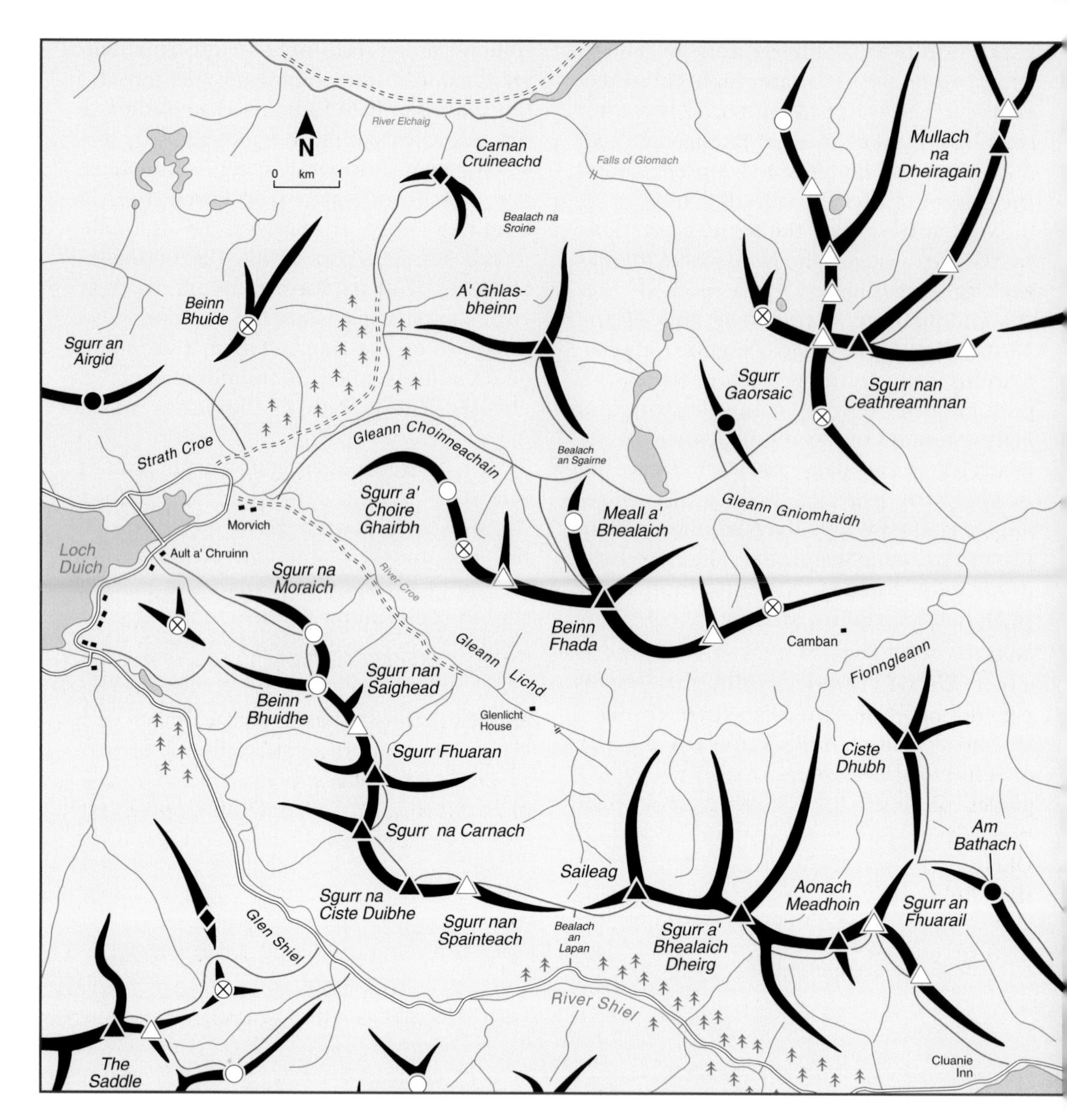

Beyond the summit of Sgurr na Saighead the ridge turns west then north-west, and is narrow for a short distance to the lower north-west peak, called Beinn Bhuidhe (869m). This point commands a fine view, both westwards towards Loch Duich and Skye, and south-east back along the main ridge. The true finish of the traverse continues over the last of the Five Sisters, Sgurr na Moraich, which has a broad summit ridge and a fine maritime view.

This hill has steep heathery slopes above Loch Duich and Morvich. These are avoided on the descent by heading due westwards from the summit to the Allt a' Chruinn. A path is joined above this burn, shortly before the burn starts to descend steeply. The path descends less steeply, well to the right of the burn, to the Morvich road at the cottages of Ault a' Chruinn, near to the junction with the main A87. (The north-west ridge of Sgurr na Moraich rises from Carn-gorm, NG953206. However, this is quite steep, and is more suitable for ascent than descent.)

If Sgurr na Moraich is to be omitted, either of the following descents can be taken from Beinn Bhuidhe.

1. Down the north-west ridge to the 443m col before Sgurr an t-Searraich, then down the steep hillside to Loch Shiel, and by its north shore to Shiel Bridge. Sgurr an t-Searraich can be visited if desired. (Note, there are no bridges over the River Shiel between the bridge to Achnagart farm, NG962150, and Shiel Bridge. A bridge marked on the map near the entry to Loch Shiel, NG947182, no longer exists.)

2. Down by the north bank of the Allt a' Chruinn from the col between Beinn Bhuidhe and Sgurr na Moraich, joining the path mentioned above that descends to the road at Ault a' chruinn.

Sgurr Fhuaran can also be climbed or descended by its long east ridge, which rises from Glenlicht House. A circuit of the north-northeast ridge of Sgurr a' Bhealaich Dheirg, the main ridge to Sgurr Fhuaran and the east ridge of the latter, done in either direction, gives a fine outing encompassing some spectacular northern corries.

The northern corries contain a number of winter climbs in the easier to middle grades, of which the following are a selection. Ghlas Choire of Sgurr a' Bhealaich Dheirg has yielded *Resolution Gully* (150m III 1986) (or IV,3 by the *Direct Finish*,1999), and *Solution Gully* (200m II 1997). These hold snow well after a thaw. In Coire Druim na Staidhre, the eastern corrie of Sgurr nan Saighead, the deep gully in the centre of the face is *Forked Gully* 140m. This gives a grade II with a steep ice finish by its left fork, or a grade I by its right fork (1957). The sharp arête on the right of *Forked Gully* is *Edge of Reason* (210m IV,4 1986). The summit crag on the north face of Sgurr Fhuaran is split by *Trident Gully* (220m II/III 1957).

Circuit of Beinn Fhada

An excellent circular walk around Beinn Fhada can be done from Morvich, by way of the Bealach an Sgairne, the south end of Loch a' Bhealaich and through the 'Gates of Affric' into Gleann Gniomhaidh, returning by way of Fionngleann and Gleann Lichd. In upper Gleann Lichd the route passes through the dramatic gorge of the Allt Grannda waterfalls before going down to the footbridges above Glenlicht House. From there a track leads down to Morvich. The walk can be done either way round. In the direction described, the highest pass, the Bealach an Sgairne, is crossed early on. The distance is 26km, and much of this is in superbly wild country.

Beinn Fhada; 1032m; (OS Sheet 33; NH018192); *long hill*

A' Ghlas-bheinn; 918m; (OS Sheets 25 & 33; NH008230); *the grey-green hill*

To the north of the Five Sisters rises the great bulk of Beinn Fhada, which stretches for eight kilometers from Morvich to Glen Affric. Its anglicised name, Ben Attow, appears in many atlases. On the south-west side it has very steep slopes dropping into Gleann Lichd, offering no attractive routes of ascent from that glen. On the north-east there are several fine corries.

The summit of Beinn Fhada is not visible from the road, being hidden behind outlying tops. From the road causeway at the head of Loch Duich the western peak, Sgurr a' Choire Ghairbh, appears as a fairly rounded ridge with several knolls, the Faradh Nighean Fhearchair. These knolls are the crests of a series of slabby buttresses dropping on the other side of the ridge into Choire Chaoil, the finest of Beinn Fhada's corries, where there are several climbs.

To the east the spine of the mountain widens and merges into a great plateau, the Plaide Mhor, at whose furthest point is the summit. Beyond there the main crest continues for some distance further east to the East Top (962m) before dropping into Glen Affric. A northward ridge from the Plaide Mhor leads to the rocky top of Meall a' Bhealaich, which overlooks the Bealach an Sgairne, an important pass through which goes one of the two rights of way from Loch Duich to Glen Affric.

The summit cliffs and the Plaide Mhor of Beinn Fhada

To the north of the Bealach an Sgairne rises A' Ghlas-bheinn, whose skyline is prominent from Strath Croe. The Bealach is a fairly deep defile between the two mountains, conferring on A' Ghlas-bheinn a relatively isolated character. Its summit affords fine prospects in all directions, especially over the wild country to the north and east.

In late spring or early summer the ascent of both mountains gives an excellent day. In limited daylight or under snowy conditions the two are better climbed separately. The following description is for both mountains together, but is adaptable for separate ascents.

The normal starting point is the Morvich car park. Walk eastwards for 750 metres along the public road to near its end and cross a bridge over the River Croe (signposted to the Falls of Glomach). Follow the path round the base of Beinn Bhuidhe, a grassy spur of Sgurr a' Choire Ghairbh, and beneath its steepening northern slope.

The path can also be joined here from the Forestry Commission car park at Dorusduain (this shortens the day by 3km). A few minutes walk east of this car park a small path drops down through trees to cross a footbridge over the Abhainn Chonaig, whence the path from Morvich is joined.

The path continues east up Gleann Choinneachan below the steep craggy face of Sgurr a' Choire Ghairbh. Further up, cross the Allt Coire an Sgairne. (This crossing can be difficult in spate conditions.) Ascend zigzags, then at a bifurcation take the right (stalkers) path up the corrie and onto the ridge connecting Meall a' Bhealaich with Beinn Fhada at NH011206. Continue south up this ridge, which merges into the Plaide Mhor, and thence to the summit cairn and shelter wall. The summit is a magnificent viewpoint, ringed by high mountains of Kintail and Affric near at hand, and with glimpses of Loch Alsh and Skye on the western horizon.

To continue to A' Ghlas-bheinn, return to the head of the stalkers path. There are now two options. The surer route is to descend the stalkers path to the junction with the main path. The latter leads up the narrowing defile to the Bealach an Sgairne. Alternatively, the bealach can be reached from Meall a' Bhealaich. The hillside that drops directly from this peak to the bealach is prohibitively steep and craggy. Avoid it by descending east then north-east until it is possible to traverse horizontally north to the bealach. This route is only to be recommended in good visibility and snow-free conditions.

A' Ghlas-bheinn was formerly notorious for its several false tops on the ascent from the Bealach an Sgairne. Now, however, a path has formed for much of the way and route-finding is easy. The little Loch a' Chleirich is passed on the way, and excellent views open out over Loch Gaorsaic towards Sgurr nan Ceathreamhnan.

From the summit, a pleasant descent can be made down the west ridge in conditions of good visibility. For most of the way the ridge is broad and easy-angled, but it is trackless and somewhat lacking in features. Towards the bottom, where it steepens, aim for the point where the path from Strath Croe to the Bealach na Sroine emerges from the forest.

Continue down southwards through the forest, the path soon becoming a track, to a clearing where the house of Dorusduain once stood. Cross the Abhainn Chonaig by a footbridge (mentioned above) and return along the path to Morvich.

A number of alternatives to the above itinerary can be considered.

1. A spectacular way onto Beinn Fhada is to ascend via the grassy west slope of Beinn Bhuidhe and thence up to and along the crest of Sgurr a' Choire Ghairbh. This knobbly ridge gives fine views, but near its end there is a descent of 20m down a groove of slabby rocks. These call for some skill in scrambling and may require protection with a rope in bad conditions. The obstacle is not easily avoided, although a somewhat exposed way can be found by backtracking for a few minutes to a small col, then turning east (right) and slanting down to the south on steep grass. The first part of this bypass is above cliffs, but one emerges onto easy ground below more crags. After passing under these, the col below the original slabby step is gained.

The way then continues airily but without difficulty over the subsidiary top of Meall an Fhuarain Mhoir and onto the Plaide Mhor. In summary, this is a fine route up the mountain, but it is not recommended to walkers who are uncomfortable scrambling.

2. A' Ghlas-bheinn can be descended by its north ridge to the Bealach na Sroine so as to join the path to the Falls of Glomach (see below).

3. The complete circuit can be done in reverse, starting with A' Ghlas-bheinn. In this direction it is easy to see the steep north slope of Meall a' Bhealaich and to outflank it on its left. Moreover, an attractive option is to drop down from the Bealach an Sgairne by the path to the head of Loch a' Bhealaich, and then to climb south-eastwards up Coire an t-Siosalaich to the East Top of Beinn Fhada before continuing to the main summit. If the traverse is then continued to Sgurr a' Choire Ghairbh the rock step is reached from below, where it is more easily inspected and tackled, or avoided, than when approached from above.

4. Beinn Fhada can be climbed by its east ridge from the Alltbeithe youth hostel or Camban bothy.

Most of the climbing on Beinn Fhada is on the east face of Sgurr a' Choire Ghairbh, which is characterized by a series of slabby buttresses that rise from Choire Chaoil. Though the cliffs appear spectacular from a distance, the climbing is of variable quality.

The right hand buttress, *Summit Buttress* (200m), rises to the summit of Sgurr a' Choire Ghairbh and gives a somewhat disappointing climb in both summer (Difficult, 1961) and winter (III, 1984). *Left-Hand Gully* (135m III 1983) is the left hand of two gullies that start at the base of this buttress. The gully contains numerous short steps, which can bank out, reducing

Looking east up Glen Elchaig from Carnan Cruithneachd

the grade to II.

To the left of Summit Buttress is *Needle's Eye Buttress* (150m), named after a square projection half way up the buttress that is pierced by a hole. The crest of the buttress gives a summer climb of Difficult standard (1949). The winter route climbs a central turfy trough (II, 1994). To the left again is another buttress with *Guide's Rib* 100m, on its crest. This has been climbed in summer at Very Difficult (1955) and in winter at IV,6 (1996); an exciting winter climb.

Furthest up the corrie are two slabby buttresses, beneath which goes the sketchy path that bypasses the awkward rock step on the ridge of Sgurr a' Choire Ghairbh, mentioned above. *The Needle* (110m Severe 1952) is on the left hand of these two buttresses.

Lastly, on the approach to Coire an Sgairne from the stalkers path, the first buttress encountered is twin-tiered and provides *The Kintail Blanket* (185m, Very Severe).

Carnan Cruithneachd; 729m; (OS Sheets 25 & 33; NG994258); *wheat cairn*

The isolated Carnan Cruithneachd rises fairly gently from the moorland about 3km to the north-north-west of A' Ghlas-bheinn. Its northern slope plunges precipitously into Glen Elchaig, for which its summit is a splendid viewpoint.

Start from Morvich or from the Dorusduain forest car park. Follow the forest track initially as for the route to the Falls of Glomach. At a fork (NG984230) just before a bridge, keep on the track on the left side of the river, and eventually ascend by zigzags through the forest to a gate at NG983241.

The track continues, becoming a path. After about a kilometre the hill can be climbed directly up slopes of grass and heather, or one can continue a little further north and then scramble up the rocky west ridge. The summit affords a dramatic view to the north and east, down into Glen Elchaig and to the hills beyond. One can return by the same route, or explore some of the surrounding country or continue to the Falls of Glomach (see below).

Sgurr an Airgid; 841m; (OS Sheets 25 & 33; NG940227); *peak of silver*

This hill rises steeply above Inverinate village and Strath Croe. It can easily be climbed in a half day. It is best to park at the A87 layby below the churchyard. Walk along the Strath Croe road and start uphill from a point just west of Ruarach. Low on the steep hillside ahead a stalkers path rises from right to left. Join this and follow it via zigzags to the skyline at NG957230. Turn west here. After about 500 metres a faint walkers path appears and is followed via a rocky ridge to the summit. This is a splendid viewpoint, both to Loch Duich and Skye to the west, and to the expanse of moorland and lochans of the Inverinate Forest to the north. Biod an Fhithich lies about 5km north of Sgurr an Airgid's summit and offers several schist rock climbs. *The Hump* (120m 1971), was graded Very Difficult in *Northern Highlands* Rock and Ice Climbs Vol 1, now re-graded to Hard Severe, and is recommended. Recent developments are in the higher grades, and feature *Biosynthesis* (110m Hard Very Severe 1998) and *Bionic* (30m E3 2000).

The Falls Of Glomach

These famous Falls drain the considerable catchment area of Gleann Gaorsaic with its lochs and surrounding mountainsides. The Abhainn Gaorsaic flows quietly along the upper glen and then plunges spectacularly into a deep gorge whose outflow, the Allt a' Ghlomaich, enters Glen Elchaig. The fanciful visitor might be reminded of Kubla Khan's Alph, the sacred river, which, after 'meandering with a mazy motion...sank in tumult to a lifeless ocean'.

There are three main approaches: from Strath Croe, from Glen Elchaig, or via Carnan Cruithneachd. The latter two ways give a better appreciation of the gorge below the Falls, but involve crossing the Allt a' Ghlomaich or its tributary the Allt na Laoidhre, which may be impassable in spate conditions. Therefore the way from Strath Croe is described first.

From the Morvich car park follow the signs to the Falls of Glomach, crossing the Abhainn Chonaig by the footbridge (NG982223), or alternatively start from the Dorusduain forestry car park. Follow the forest track, taking the right fork at NG984230 and crossing a bridge. Upon emerging from the forest the track becomes a path, which leads over the Bealach na Sroine and down to the Abhainn Gaorsaic at the Falls. These plunge 100m in two leaps, and due care should be taken in the vicinity. To really get the most from the visit, continue on the path overlooking the deep ravine and descend to the Allt na Laoidhre, before returning by the same route.

For the Glen Elchaig route the nearest parking is at Camas-luinie. Follow a footpath on the south side of the River Elchaig for 2km, then cross and walk up the private road to Loch na Leitreach. (This point can also be reached by bicycle from Killilan.) Cross the River Elchaig by the A.E.Robertson Memorial Bridge, and then cross the Allt a' Ghlomaich. (As noted above, this may be impassable in spate.) Continue into the gorge, cross the Allt na Laoidhre which comes in from the right, and climb the path overlooking the gorge to the Falls. The traverse from Glen Elchaig by way of the Falls to Strath Croe is an excellent walk (15km starting from Camas-luinie) provided transport can be arranged to the start or from the finish.

The Carnan Cruithneachd route is only recommended in good visibility and when the Allt na Laoidhre is not likely to be in spate, as this stream must be crossed. From the summit, descend initially south and then go along the east ridge overlooking Glen Elchaig for 2km until a steep descent is made to the gorge just north of the confluence with the Allt na Laoidhre. There is a good view of the falls from near the top of the descent, and the slope is in bloom with bluebells in spring. The main path from Glen Elchaig to the falls is joined in the gorge. Cross the Allt na Laoidhre and continue up the path overlooking the ravine to the Falls. Return over the Bealach na Sroine to Strath Croe.

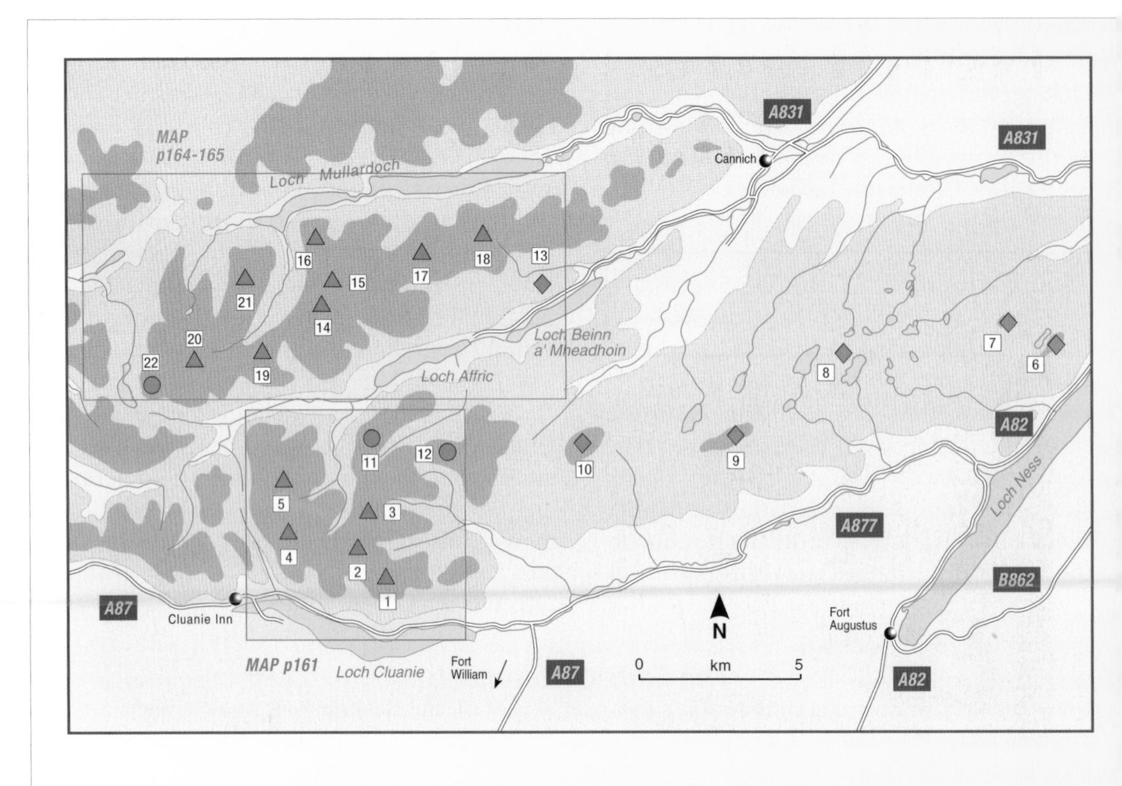

1.	Carn Ghluasaid	957m	M	p160
2.	Sgurr nan Conbhairean	1109m	M	p160
3.	Sail Chaorainn	1002m	M	p160
4.	A' Chralaig	1120m	M	p160
5.	Mullach Fraoch-choire	1102m	M	p160
6.	Meall Fuar-mhonaidh	699m	G	p163
7.	Glas-bheinn Mhor	651m	G	p163
8.	Meall a' Chrathaich	679m	G	p165
9.	Carn Mhic an Toisich	678m	G	p165
10.	Carn a' Chaochain	706m	G	p167
11.	Carn a' Choire Ghairbh	865m	C	p167
12.	Aonach Shasuinn	888m	C	p167
13.	Beinn a' Mheadhoin	610m	G	p170
14.	Mam Sodhail	1181m	M	p170
15.	Carn Eighe	1183m	M	p170
16.	Beinn Fhionnlaidh	1005m	M	p170
17.	Tom a' Choinich	1112m	M	p170
18.	Toll Creagach	1053m	M	p170
19.	An Socach	921m	M	p173
20.	Sgurr nan Ceathreamhnan	1151m	M	p173
21.	Mullach na Dheiragain	982m	M	p173
22.	Sgurr Gaorsaic	839m	C	p175

Chapter 8

North Strath Cluanie and Glen Affric

Tom Prentice

Looking west up Glen Affric to Beinn Fhada

The area described in this chapter extends eastwards from the boundary with neighbouring Kintail and Inverinate. In comparison with that relatively compact region, the present domain is much larger and more varied. The western boundary is the system of wild glens comprising Gleann Gaorsaic, Gleann Gniomhaidh and An Caorann Mor. The southern boundary consists of Strath Cluanie and its continuation, Glen Moriston. To the east is the shoreline of Loch Ness from Invermoriston to Drumnadrochit, and to the north are Glen Urquhart, Glen Cannich, Loch Mullardoch and the upper reaches of Glen Elchaig.

The area contains several of the highest mountains to the north of the Great Glen. The most famous of these are the big Munros to the north of Glen Affric: Mam Sodhail, Carn Eighe, Sgurr nan Ceathreamhnan and their companion peaks. To the south of Glen Affric are the five Munros of the Cluanie Horseshoe. To the east of these is a tract of moorland with lesser hills that offer their own quiet charm.

Most of the area is drained by three river systems, two of which are extensively harnessed for hydro-electricity. The Cluanie Dam and Loch Cluanie are familiar to all users of the A87 from Invergarry to Kyle of Lochalsh. The piped waters from Loch Cluanie and Loch Loyne drive a power station near Ceannacroc Bridge (NH227106). Thereafter the River Moriston flows with stately splendour through the pastures and coniferous woodlands of Glen Moriston. At another power station the glen narrows and is mainly wooded to Invermoriston, where the river flows into Loch Ness. A major tributary of the River Moriston, the River Doe, joins from the north just below Ceannacroc Bridge. The Doe drains a wild basin headed by Sgurr nan Conbhairean, one of the big peaks of the Cluanie Horseshoe. The distant headwall forms an impressive sight to travellers driving up Glen Moriston.

The second major river is the Enrick, which rises in a large area of moorland and

Heading north to Sgurr nan Conbhairean from Carn Ghlusaid

lochans to the north of Glen Moriston. The river drains the northern flank of the moor and continues eastwards through the scenic Glen Urquhart to its outlet at Urquhart Bay in Loch Ness. The jewel in the crown of the area is Glen Affric. The upper part of the glen is wild and bare, but where the River Affric flows into Loch Affric the character of the glen changes completely. The loch is one of the most beautiful in Scotland, flanked by Scots pines and surrounded by shapely peaks. The river then descends in scenic rapids into Loch Beinn a' Mheadhoin (pronounced 'Benevain'). Here the public road from Cannich ends at a car park just to the west of the head of the loch. The shores of Loch Beinn a' Mheadhoin are richly forested. Although the loch provides water for a power station lower down the glen, the water level is kept constant by controlled inflow through an underground pipe from Loch Mullardoch.

Lower down the glen the River Affric is joined by two major tributaries. The Abhainn Deabhag flows in from the south-west shortly before the power station. Just to the east of the village of Cannich the River Cannich joins from the north. The road bridge in the village affords an attractive view of the Cannich gorge. Downstream from Cannich the river takes on the new name of the River Glass, which continues through the mainly agricultural Strath Glass. After Struy the river changes its name yet again to become the River Beauly, which flows into the Beauly Firth.

Although most of the drainage of the area is to the east, the north-western flanks of Sgurr nam Ceathreamhnan drain into Glen Elchaig, some of the waters by way of the Abhainn Gaorsaic and the spectacular Falls of Glomach, described in the previous chapter.

The eastern glens offer several walks and attractions. The Dog Falls in Glen Affric and the Plodda Falls of the Abhainn Deabhag are spectacular, especially when in flood, and both sites are starting points for forest walks of various lengths. At the Affric roadhead car park there is a short loop walk where the River Affric flows past Scots pines into the head of Loch Beinn a' Mheadhoin. The circuit of Loch Affric reveals superb, changing scenery from the Caledonian forest at the eastern end to the bare, western upper reaches of the glen, and is about 16km. With suitable transport arrangements at either end one can enjoy a superb crossing of about 28km from the Affric roadhead to Morvich. After the remote youth hostel at Alltbeithe the walk can be completed either by Gleann Gniomhaidh and the Bealach an Sgairne, one of the major passes of the Highlands, or by Fionngleann and Gleann Lichd, with fine waterfalls in the upper reaches of the latter. (See the box, Circuit of Beinn Fhada, in Chapter 7 *(p151)* for further information on these glens.)

Connoisseurs of prehistory can visit the well-preserved chambered cairn at Corrimony. Urquhart Castle by Loch Ness is a historical site on the tourist trail through the Great Glen. Car parking has been augmented, the strategic outlook from the Castle over the Loch being a major attraction for visitors who hope to glimpse the fabled monster, Nessie.

Access and Transport

By road: From the south, the shortest approach to Strath Cluanie is by way of the A87 from Invergarry, as described for Glen Shiel and Kintail. A slightly longer approach, via Fort Augustus and up the A887 through Glen Moriston, is rewarded by the imposing prospect of the Sgurr nan Conbhairean massif to the west. The Great Glen also gives access to Glen Affric from the south. At Drumnadrochit, turn west on the A831 through Glen Urquhart and continue over a wooded pass to Cannich.

Alternatively, the A9 from Perth to Inverness can be taken for Glen Affric. Shortly before the descent into Inverness a magnificent panorama unfolds, from the Moray Firth in the north-east to the multitude of mountains in the north and west. From Inverness itself, Cannich is easily reached by way of Drumnadrochit and the A831. If one does not plan to visit Inverness en route, then a scenic way to Cannich is over the Kessock Bridge to Tore, and then via Muir of Ord, Beauly and Strathglass. For visitors travelling from England, the approach via Fort William and the Great Glen is the shorter in distance, but the A9 route is on faster roads.

By bus: Scottish Citylink Coaches run daily between Glasgow and Kyle of Lochalsh, passing through Strath Cluanie, and also between Inverness and Kyle of Lochalsh, passing through Glen Moriston and Strath Cluanie. Highland Scottish Omnibuses run on Mondays to Saturdays between Inverness and Cannich via Drumnadrochit. W.Macdonald operates a service between Beauly and Cannich via Strathglass on Tuesdays and Fridays.

Accommodation and Information

Hotels and guesthouses: Strath Cluanie is served by the Cluanie Inn, and also, within a fairly short driving distance, by the accommodation near Loch Duich (Chapters 6 and 7, *pp 128, 142*). There is limited B&B accommodation in Glen Moriston. Cannich contains a hotel, a youth hostel and some B&B accommodation.

SYHA hostel: Alltbeithe in upper Glen Affric is only accessible on foot or mountain bicycle. It is open from early April to late October; the precise dates and further particulars can be obtained from the SYHA.

The two commonly used routes of access are as follows. From near Cluanie, start via the track up An Caorann Mor and continue by the boggy path over into Glen Affric, crossing the River Affric by a footbridge opposite the hostel (about 9km). The other route is from the roadhead car park at Loch Beinn a' Mheadhoin in Glen Affric. Follow the forest road and track along the south side of Loch Affric, and cross the River Affric by the bridge at Athnamulloch (NH133206) before continuing on the track on the north side of the river to the hostel. The latter route is longer (13km) but is suitable for mountain bicycles.

Maps

Ordnance Survey 1:50,000 Sheet 25 (Glen Carron and Glen Affric), Sheet 26 (Inverness and Strathglass area), Sheet 33 (Loch Alsh, Glen Shiel and Loch Hourn) and Sheet 34 (Fort Augustus Glen Albyn and Glen Roy)

Principal Hills

Carn Ghluasaid; 957m; (OS Sheet 34; NH145125); *peak of movement*

Sgurr nan Conbhairean; 1109m; (OS Sheet 34; NH129138); *peak of the houndkeepers*

Sail Chaorainn; 1002m; (OS Sheet 34; NH133154); *hill* [literally, *heel*] *of the rowan tree*

A' Chralaig; 1120m; (OS Sheet 33; NH094148); *the basket*

Mullach Fraoch-choire; 1102m; (OS Sheet 33; NH095171); *summit of the heathery corrie*

These are the five Munros of the Cluanie Horseshoe. From its outside the curve of the horseshoe overlooks Loch Cluanie. The inside opens via Gleann na Ciche into Glen Affric. Carn Ghluasaid is an outlier to the south-east of Sgurr nan Conbhairean. Because of this configuration, traversing the five Munros usually involves a dogleg. Nevertheless, the complete traverse is an excellent and not too demanding an outing in summer. In winter the mountains are more serious, especially A' Chralaig and Mullach Fraoch-choire, which are flanked by steep slopes.

A complete traverse starting from the Cluanie side and suitable for summer conditions is described. Under less favourable conditions, or if otherwise preferred, the horseshoe can be split into two separate outings. These and other variations are mentioned later.

The starting point is at Lundie (NH145104), where there is a parking area, and the usual finish is at the junction of the An Caorann Mor track with the A87. There are various options for eliminating or shortening the return walk along the busy road to the starting point. A party with two cars can park one of them at the finish, where there is parking by the plantation just to the west of the Allt Chaorainn Mhoir bridge. It is also possible to park at Cluanie and take a bus to the start at Lundie. A third option is to use a somewhat restricted parking space about 2km west of Lundie; this reduces the final walk back along the road to 4km.

Starting from Lundie or from this more restricted parking place, gain the Old Military Road marked on the OS map and follow it (west from Lundie, east from the smaller car park) to where a stalkers path branches northwards (NH136103). The path zigzags up Carn Ghluasaid to the summit plateau. The plateau is fairly small and the summit cairn is on the northern edge. It may be somewhat difficult to locate in mist. On a clear day it affords fine views overlooking the wilds of Coire Dho and towards the east face of Sgurr nan Conbhairean. The latter, the highest peak of the eastern half of the horseshoe, is reached without difficulty after passing over an intermediate top (Creag a' Chaorainn, 998m).

From Sgurr nan Conbhairean, descend northwards for 200m to a col, from which Sail Chaorainn is gained. This hill has two summits of almost equal height. The first (1002m) has a fairly small cairn; the second and more northerly one (Carn na Coire Mheadhoin, 1001m) has a larger cairn and is the better viewpoint. The upper reaches of Coire Dho are spread out to the east, while to the west are the depths of Gleann na Ciche and the backdrop of A' Chralaig and Mullach Fraoch-choire.

Some 250m down to the east from the top of Sail Chaorainn is Prince Charlie's Cave, which is marked on the OS map, and which enthusiasts may wish to visit. The cave is a kind of Shelter Stone formed by several large boulders. Bonnie Prince Charlie was in hiding there for a week during his escape from the Hanoverian troops following his defeat at Culloden. (See Chapter 3, *p72*, for coverage of the Pretender's fugitive wanderings in the Western Highlands.)

The next objective is the Bealach Choire

a' Chait. To reach it, either return to the summit of Sgurr nan Conbhairean or skirt about 100m below the summit on the north-west flank, in either case so as to gain a col (NH125135) on this mountain's south-west ridge. Continue over the subsidiary top, Drochaid an Tuill Easaich (1001m), and descend the ridge of the Cluanie-Affric watershed to the Bealach Choire a' Chait.

Continue west then north-west up to A' Chralaig, the highest peak of the horseshoe. There is a tall, solidly built cairn here. The way to Mullach Fraoch-choire is along a delightful high-level ridge. After an intermediate Top, Stob Coire na Cralaig (1008m), descend about 60m to the north-east to a col. A rocky ridge with pinnacles rises to Mullach Fraoch-choire. The ridge can be climbed direct, with exposed scrambling, or the first part can be bypassed to the east, where a path has formed. The bypass is itself on steep ground, and care should be taken.

From the summit, return either to the col before the rise to Stob Coire na Cralaig, and then down Coire Odhar, or continue over Stob Coire an Cralaig and down Coire a' Ghlas-thuill. The latter is more direct but involves descending quite steep grass. Either way leads to the An Caorann Mor path,

A' Chralaig towering above the Cluanie pass into Alltbeithe

which soon becomes a track. A further alternative is to return to A' Chralaig and to go down initially to the south-east (the route of ascent), then continue down the southern spur and veer south-west, aiming for the An Caorann Mor track shortly before it reaches the A87.

If time permits, it is also well worth visiting A' Chioch (947m), a rewarding viewpoint at the focus of the horseshoe, before descending. This requires significant extra effort, and the most logical descent is then down Coire a' Chait and by the stream of that name to the A87, involving some rough going.

There are several other options for climbing the peaks of the Cluanie Horseshoe. For example, the need for a dog-leg can be eliminated by doing an 'inverted' horseshoe, crossing from Sail Chaorainn (or from Tigh-mor na Seilge, 929m) to Mullach Fraoch-choire by descending deeply into the upper reaches of Gleann na Ciche.

If the two arms of the horseshoe are to be done separately, then the easiest way for the eastern arm is to start from Lundie as described above and to return from Sail Chaorainn by the same route. Alternatively, one can vary the return by continuing to Drochaid an Tuill Easaich and down its south ridge to join the Old Military Road 2km west of Lundie.

The best starting point for the western arm is the foot of the An Caorann Mor track. Leave the track almost immediately and head up long, moderately steep grass slopes, with a profusion of wild flowers in early summer. Join the southern spur of A' Chralaig, continue to the summit, and then to Mullach Fraoch-choire as described for the complete traverse.

In winter the rocky south ridge of the latter or its bypass on the eastern flank may require crampons and possibly a rope, depending on the conditions. Moreover the steep western flanks of A' Chralaig and Mullach Fraoch-choire may be avalanche-prone, in which case the safest descent is to return to the summit of A' Chralaig and go down to the south-east and south as described above.

It is aesthetically attractive to do the circuit from the north, the direction in which the horseshoe opens. The north-west ridge of Mullach Fraoch-choire is a good line of ascent from Glen Affric, and Sail Chaorainn can be descended to Gleann na Ciche, where a track leads through the forested lower glen. However, the northern approach involves several kilometres of walking or cycling from the roadhead at Loch Beinn a' Mheadhoin, unless one is based at Alltbeithe or is planning to include the horseshoe as part of a longer expedition. Finally, the eastern peaks of the group can be approached from the vicinity of Ceannacroc Lodge, where a car may be parked. This involves a long but rewarding approach up the wild Coire Dho.

Several winter climbs are located on the eastern flanks of Sgurr nan Conbhairean. The base of the mountain is reached from Ceannacroc Lodge and Coire Dho by the way just mentioned, or by descending north-eastwards from the Glas Bhealach, NH130134. The East Buttress consists of two ridges separated by a prominent gully that springs from the head of a snow bay. *Ceannacroc Couloir* (300m II 1992) ascends this deep and narrow gully, trending left at the top to finish up a fine snow arete to the summit. *East Ridge* (300m II 1996) starts from the same snow bay as Ceannacroc Couloir but takes a shallow gully in the left hand ridge. The final snow crest is the same as that joined by Ceannacroc Couloir, and leads to the summit cairn.

Further climbs have been done on the north-east face, and some of these are described in The Scottish Mountaineering Club Journal, 1996. (A collected description will appear in the Scottish Mountaineering Club Climbers' Guide *Northern Highlands South*, 2005 or 2006)

An excellent but fairly demanding ski traverse of Carn Ghluasaid, Sgurr nan Conbhairean and A' Chralaig is described in *Ski Mountaineering in Scotland*; (see Further Reading).

Meall Fuar-mhonaidh; 699m; (OS Sheet 26; NH457222); *hill of the cold slopes*

Glas-bheinn Mhor; 651m; (OS Sheet 26; NH436231); *big grey-green hill*

These two Grahams rise from near the eastern end of the extensive tract of moorland flanked on the south and east by Glen Moriston and Loch Ness. Meall Fuar-mhonaidh is easy of access and is a superb viewpoint, so its ascent is popular. The usual route is from a small car park at Balbeg. This is reached via a minor road starting just to the east of Borlum Bridge (NH513291) near Drumnadrochit.

From the car park a well signposted path leads initially up through woodland, passing by a picturesque miniature ravine. Upon emerging onto a heathery hillside, continue up the path so as to reach the deer fence at a stile. The main whaleback ridge of the hill is then ascended to the south-west past various cairns to the furthest cairn at the summit.

Below, the rift of the Great Glen is visible almost from end to end, while to the west and north-west, beyond the intervening moorland, are the arrayed Munros of Glens Affric, Cannich and Strathfarrar. Naming these Munros from this distant vantage point is an interesting topographical challenge.

Although the hill is usually descended the same way, the walk can be substantially extended to include Glas-bheinn Mhor, which is also a fine little hill, remoter in character than Meall Fuar-mhonaidh. The hillside that drops from Meall Fuar-mhonaidh directly to Loch nam Breac Dearga is steep and craggy. Avoid this by continuing down the south-west ridge until just above the loch, then head north-west,

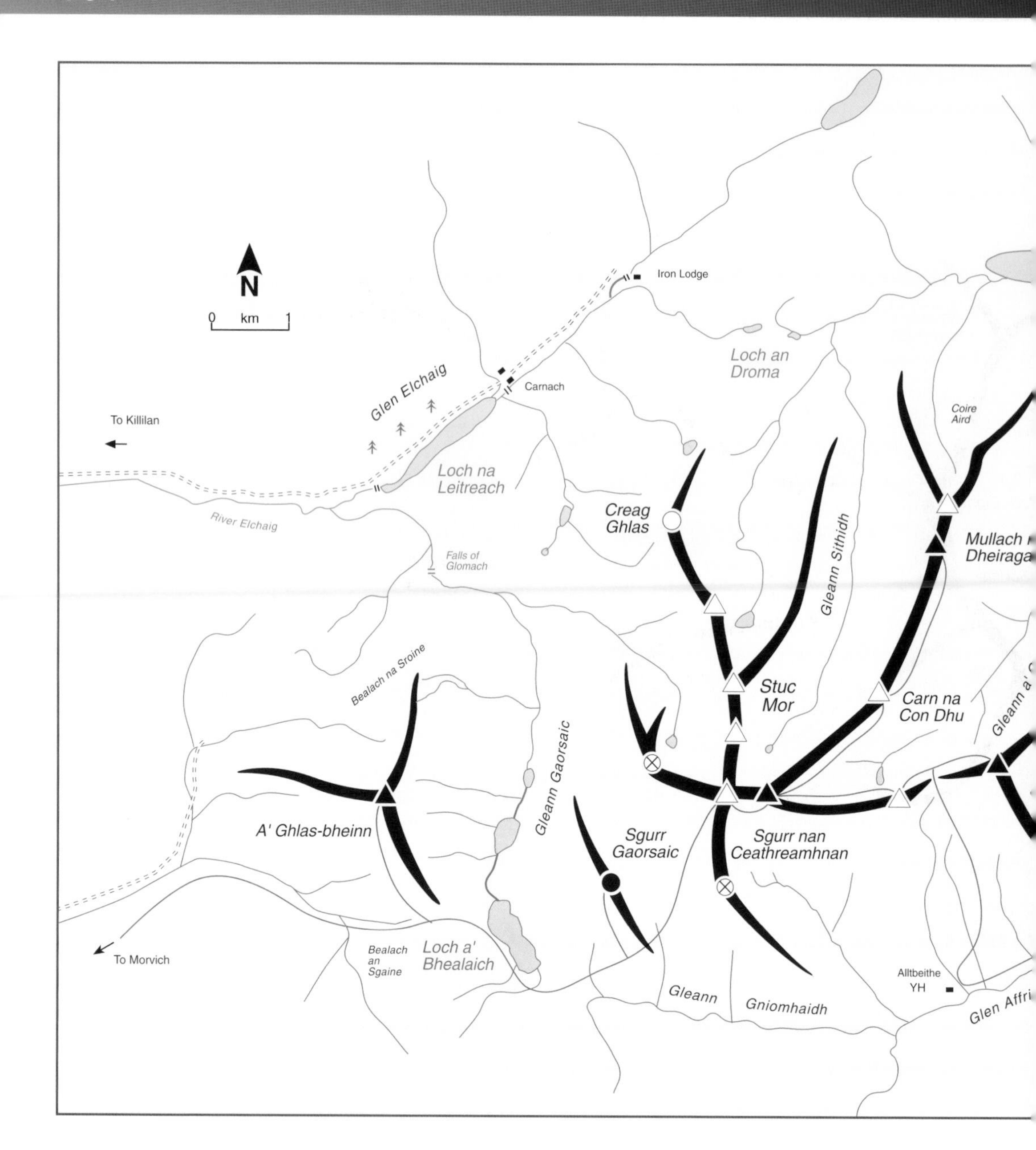

crossing the outlet of the loch, and climb Glas-bheinn Mhor by trackless but easy ground, passing a small lochan on the way up.

At the top there is a cairn and a trig point 50 metres beyond. The summit affords extensive views over the surrounding moorland, from the glens leading down to Drumnadrochit in the north-east to the Sgurr nan Conbhairean group on the western horizon. To return to the car park at Balbeg, head east past the northern end of the loch, and aim to rejoin the whaleback of Meall Fuar-mhonaidh about where the path descends from the ridge to Balbeg.

The two hills can also be approached by starting up a forest track from the Youth Hostel at Alltsigh. Above the forest, a system of moorland roads leads northwards to terminate at around NH439217. Both hills can be climbed from here, but the approach is perhaps most useful if it is intended to ascend Glas-bheinn Mhor without having to climb Meall Fuar-mhonaidh as well.

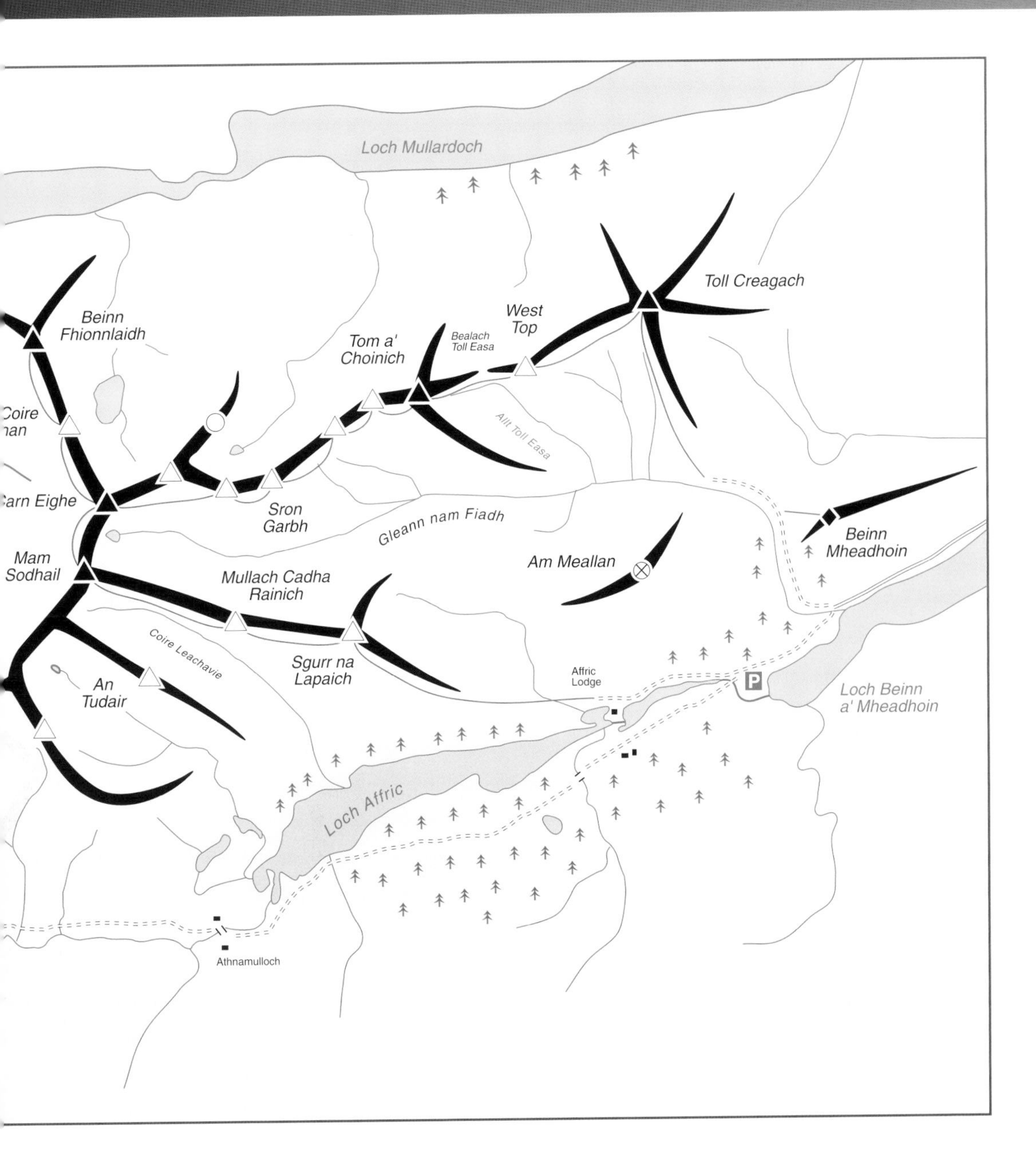

> **Meall a' Chrathaich**; 679m; (OS Sheets 26 & 34; NH360220); possibly *shaking hill*
>
> **Carn Mhic an Toisich**; 678m; (OS Sheet 34; NH310185); *Macintosh hill*

These two hills are at the centre of the great moorland region to the north of Glen Moriston. Their ascent gives a relatively long but rewarding day in this secluded hinterland. Start at Bhlaraidh in Glen Moriston. A forest track leaves the A887 immediately east of the road bridge (NH380165). After 1.5km, take the left fork. Leave the track where it divides shortly before Loch Liath. To reach Carn Mhic an Toisich, either traverse the intermediate hill, Carn na Caorach (610m), or bypass this by rough moorland to the north, where there is an indistinct path that leads eventually to the bealach between Carn na Caorach and Carn Mhic an Toisich.

Northwards along the ridge from A' Chralaig to Mullach Fraoch-choire

The latter is climbed by its pleasant east-north-east ridge, and the summit affords a pleasant lunch spot, though with electricity pylons in the middle distance to the west.

Return to the track just before the fork at Loch Liath and continue along the right branch to its end at Loch ma Stac. Meall a' Chrathaich is about 2km to the north-east, and is attained after crossing or bypassing a subsidiary south-east top (632m). Either way, the going is fairly rough and tussocky. Though only about 150m above the surrounding moors, Meall a' Chrathaich gives fine views of the lochan-studded moorland and of the great peaks of Affric to the west and north-west.

The most straightforward descent is back to the south end of Loch ma Stac and down the track of the ascent route. However, an interesting circuit can be made by descending north-east then east from the summit and continuing round the north and east sides of Loch a' Chrathaich. There is a sketchy and intermittent path to the dam and the start of another track. Follow this track mainly downhill, but with an uphill section to a fork at NH375193. Here take the right fork, rejoining the ascent route 1.5km from the start at Bhlaraidh.

Another alternative, if suitable transport arrangements can be made, is to descend to the north to Corrimony. A track which services a fishing lodge at the north end of Loch ma Stac is joined and followed down the course of the infant River Enrick. After 4km there is a ford across the Abhainn na Ruighe Duibhe, a major tributary of the Enrick, so this route should only be planned for fairly dry conditions.

Carn a' Chaochain; 706m; (OS Sheets 34 & 25; NH235177); *peak of the streamlet*

This rather remote Graham is well worth climbing for its fine prospect over the wild Coire Dho and the eastern aspect of Sgurr nan Conbhairean. The easiest access is from the Guisachan Forest to the north. From Cannich, drive up the glen of the Abhainn Deabhag through the attractive village of Tomich to the Plodda Falls, both of which are worth visiting in their own right. Continue up the forest track and park just before a fork where the main track swings north to Cougie. Take the left fork (to the south-west) and walk about 500 metres to where a stream comes down the hillside on the left. The stream is flanked by old Scots pines, which remain standing after the felling of the surrounding conifers, and are conspicuous as a landmark.

A path ascends by the stream, emerging from the forest at a stile over a deer fence at NH243200 (exactly at the junction of OS Sheets 34 and 25!). Continue to the Bealach Feith na Gamhna and then up the north-east ridge of Carn a' Chaochain. A trig point is reached at a false top at 704m. The true summit is 500 metres to the south along an almost level ridge. After enjoying the extensive panorama from the summit it is best to descend by the same route, for the northern and western flanks of the hill are girdled by a deer fence.

Carn a' Choire Ghairbh; 865m; (OS Sheets 34 & 25; NH136188); *peak of the rough corrie*

Aonach Shasuinn; 888m; (OS Sheets 34 & 25; NH173180); *height of the saxon* [sassenach]; *ridge of England*

These two Corbetts are in a relatively unfrequented area to the south of Glen Affric, and they are the first hills in this chapter for which Glen Affric is the usual starting point. Park at the roadhead car park west of the head of Loch Beinn a' Mheadhoin. Cross the bridge over the River Affric just west of the car park and continue along the forestry track through the native Caledonian pinewoods of the Pollan Buidhe forest. Much of the pinewood has been fenced off, allowing successful regeneration.

After 2km a cottage is passed, followed shortly by a bridge over the Allt Garbh. Take a muddy path, inconspicuous at first, up the west bank of the Allt Garbh, then a rightwards fork to ascend by the edge of the forest (now a conifer plantation) and onto

Who Was Fhionnlaidh?

The story of Fhionnlaidh has been researched and recounted by Ian Mitchell in *Scotland's Mountains before the Mountaineers*. Fhionnlaidh was a retainer of Mackenzie of Gairloch, a keeper of Affric, and a formidable archer. His exploits were passed down by word of mouth among Affric keepers. A chapter on oral traditions in *History of the Clan Macrae*, by A. Macrae, Dingwall, 1899, recorded that 'There was once a famous archer of the Clan Macrae called Fionnla Dubh nan Fiadh (Black Findlay of the Deer) a forester of Glen Cannich'. One day Fionnla encountered an intruder, a Macdonald, in a hunt on the top of a hill. He challenged the intruder, who resisted, so Fionnla shot him dead with an arrow. The hill was thence named after Fionnla. By tradition the event can be localised to this vicinity, although possibly not to itself, because the corpse was said to have been dumped in Lochan Uaine Gleannan nam Fiadh, which lies beneath Mam Sodhail and Carn Eighe (Loch Uaine on the OS map).

The murder led to a quarter century feud between the Mackenzies and the Macdonalds, ending with a charter on land rights in 1607. During the hostilities a dozen avengers were sent by Macdonald of Glengarry and eleven were poisoned by Fionnla's wife. Then in two separate incidents two further dozens were slain by Fionnla's arrows! Fionnla's illustrious career ended when an itinerant Macdonald, a medical man, thrust a needle into Fionnla's brain.

Mullach Fraoch Choire from the north-east

Na Cnapain, where the path peters out. There is a superb view across Loch Affric. Continue over Carn Glas Iochdarach (771m) to Carn a' Choire Ghairbh. The first (north) top is the higher.

Descend south-west and then south to a col, the Cadha Riabhach (664m, unamed on OS Sheet 34), which overlooks the steep slopes of Gleann na Ciche to the west. Then climb steeply south-east up the spur of Carn a' Choire Ghuirm and continue east past the little Loch a' Choinich. Tigh Mor na Seilge, the northernmost top of the east limb of the Cluanie Horseshoe, rises to the right. Bear north-east over point 862m, with the steep slope down to Allt Garbh on the left, to reach the Bealach an Amais (652m). (Failure to swing north-east will result in descent into the remote Gleann Fada at the head of Coire Dho.)

Bealach an Amais can also be reached by taking a more direct line from Carn a' Choire Ghairbh, flanking Carn a' Choire Ghuirm to the north. This option may be preferable in misty conditions, but omits the attractive Loch a' Choinich. From the bealach, climb steeply east to the whaleback summit ridge of Aonach Shasuinn. There are two tops, the eastern one (888m) being the higher.

There are two options for the descent. In conditions of high water it is advisable to return to the Bealach an Amais and then go down to the north so as to cross the Allt Garbh well above Loch an Sguid. A track is joined near the outlet of the loch. Quit the track before the ford of the Allt Garbh, and continue on rough ground to rejoin the ascent route near the tree line below Na Cnapain. Return by this route to the forest track. Alternatively, when water levels are low and crossing the Allt Garbh will not be problematical, one can continue north-east over Carn na Coireachan Cruaidh and then north over Cnap na Stri (724m). This way affords fine views over the Guisachan Forest to the north-east. Then descend to the north-west. The track from Loch an Sguid, mentioned above, swings east to Cougie. Do not be tempted to follow it, but continue down to ford the Allt Garbh. Soon rejoin the ascent route and return down it to the forest track. (Following the east bank of the Allt Garbh to the forest track involves climbing a deer fence, and should only be done in an emergency.)

These hills can also be climbed, together or separately, from various other starting points. From the west end of Loch Affric an excellent stalkers path climbs up to the north-east shoulder of Carn a' Choire Ghairbh. From Cougie the track that continues west gives access to Cnap na Stri and thence Aonach Shasuinn.

The latter can also be approached from Coire Dho, with the possibility of a ski traverse in favourable conditions, continuing over Carn a' Choire Bhuidhe (847m). The gentlest line of descent is then beside the Allt a' Choire Bhuidhe to the path southwards from the watershed down to Coire Dho.

Beinn Fhionnlaidh's Case (The Broxap Round)

At 9.20 am on the muggy Sunday morning of 26 June 1988, Jon Broxap and two pacers crossed their finish line at Cluanie. Starting at 10.00 the previous morning, Broxap had traversed 28 Munros entirely on foot, the record for a 24-hour circuit. The epic Round was described by Broxap in The Fell Runner, September 1988, under the title 'Beinn Fhionnlaidh's Case', and in an accompanying account by Graham Holden, one of the pacers. Broxap's account was reprinted in the October 2000 issue of The Fellrunner.

The Round was accomplished with six pacers, a relatively small number for such an undertaking, helping in relays over four sections. All of the Munros of the South Glen Shiel Ridge, including Sgurr na Sgine and The Saddle, and of the North Glen Shiel Ridge including Ciste Dhubh, were taken at a blistering pace, and Broxap arrived at his second support point at the Allt Cam-ban ahead of his pacers, having taken only nine hours from the start to this point. His supporters were not expecting him so soon, and he had difficulty in picking out their green tents. He recommends orange tents under these circumstances!

On the next section, to quote the original account, a 'spot on' descent from Beinn Fhada to Bealach an Sgairne avoided the crags, and the many false tops of A' Ghlas-bheinn were also avoided. Entering the wilderness, a direct line down to Loch Thuill Easaich, which had not been reconnoitred, went well, and the way up Sgurr nan Ceathreamhnan was picked up 'bang on'. Descending from Mullach na Dheiragain at 11.30 pm one of the pacers inadvertently did a double somersault, luckily without injury. Beinn Fhionnlaidh, Carn Eighe, Mam Sodhail and An Socach were traversed in twilight and some mist to the third support point in Glen Affric.

Six hours remained for the Cluanie Horseshoe. Two pacers, Mark Rigby and Pete Barron, were now on their second supporting sections. Most of the Horseshoe summits were above the early morning mist, but Carn Ghluasaid's summit had to be found in clag. The Round was completed with A' Chralaig, Mullach Fraoch-choire and a triumphal trot down An Caorann Mor to the finish at Cluanie.

Subsequently Sgurr na Carnach of the Five Sisters has been promoted to Munro status. Fortunately, Broxap went over rather than around that, so the tally for the Round now stands at twenty-nine Munros. Can this record be broken? The only regions with sufficient clusters of Munros are Lochaber and the Glen Shiel-Glen Affric region. In the latter, the nearest 'extra' Munro is Tom aí Choinich, a very big diversion from Carn Eighe. Meanwhile, at the time of writing, the Broxap Round has not been repeated in its entirety.

Last but not least, it may be mentioned that the Round is an aesthetically superb circuit. Several of the logistical problems of how best to link peaks together, mentioned in Chapters 6 to 8 *(pp128, 156)* are beautifully solved. The Round can be considered not only as a sub-24 hour challenge for elite fell runners, but also as a multi-day objective for experienced backpackers.

Beinn a' Mheadhoin; 610m; (OS Sheet 25; NH218255); *middle hill*

This hill of modest height is eminently suitable for an ascent on a fine afternoon or evening upon arriving in the Cannich and Glen Affric area. Detached from other mountains, it rises at least 250m above its surroundings in all directions, and affords excellent views, especially of the big Affric peaks to the west and north-west.

From the car park at the bridge near the western end of Loch Beinn a' Mheadhoin (NH216242), follow the track round the western boundary of the coniferous forestry plantation. At its end, either turn right up a vehicle track, or, more enjoyably, continue a few hundred metres along the main track and then strike north-east up the open heathery hillside. The summit is just beyond a tiny lochan and is quite distinctive, partly ringed by miniature rock outcrops and with a sharp drop-off to the east.

Mam Sodhail; 1181m; (OS Sheet 25; NH120253); *large rounded hill of the barns*

Carn Eighe; 1183m; (OS Sheet 25; NH123262); *file peak*

Beinn Fhionnlaidh; 1005m; (OS Sheet 25; NH115282); *Finlay's hill*

Tom a' Choinich; 1112m; (OS Sheet 25; NH164273); *hill of the moss*

Toll Creagach; 1053m; (OS Sheet 25; NH194282); *the rocky hollow*

Containing the two highest peaks north of the Great Glen, this mountain group occupies a magnificent setting, embracing Gleann nam Fiadh to the immediate north of Glen Affric, and overlooking the wilds of Loch Mullardoch beyond Carn Eighe. On a fine summer day the complete traverse makes a superb long outing. As with the Cluanie Horseshoe, the traverse involves a dogleg, in this case for Beinn Fhionnlaidh. For walkers who are less energetically inclined, or in less favourable climatic conditions, the mountains can be tackled in two or three separate excursions.

Park at the Affric roadhead car park just to the west of the head of Loch Beinn a' Mheadhoin. Walk westwards along the track past the entrance to Affric Lodge. The track soon becomes a path, which climbs to about 300m and continues immediately above the forest on the north shore of Loch Affric. Here there are two possibilities. Either climb steeply north-west up the slopes of Sgurr na Lapaich (1036m), joining the south-east ridge which is followed to the summit, or alternatively continue along the Glen Affric path to where a stalkers path forks right and up into Coire Leachavie.

The Sgurr na Lapaich route is initially the more strenuous, but then gives an excellent ridge walk from this Top to Mam Sodhail. The Coire Leachavie path climbs to a bealach 500 metres south-west of the summit of Mam Sodhail, whence the summit is easily gained. The massive summit cairn dates from a three-day visit by the Ordnance Survey in 1848, when it was constructed to a height of 23 feet and a circumference at the base of 60 feet! (See *Scotland's Mountains before the Mountaineers*, Further Reading.) There are superb views in all directions, especially of Sgurr nan Ceathreamhnan to the west.

Descend northwards to the col (1050m) between Mam Sodhail and Carn Eighe. If Beinn Fhionnlaidh is to be included, some ascent can be avoided by contouring around the stony western flank of Carn Eighe for 750 metres to join that peak's north-west ridge. Alternatively, climb Carn Eighe and then descend the north-west ridge. The ridge swings down to the north over the small Top of Stob Coire Lochan (917m) and drops to the Bealach Beag (882m). From here, a distinct track has formed up Beinn Fhionnlaidh.

A short distance above the bealach and about 50 metres to the right of the track a spring provides the only easily accessible

The sharp ridge from Stob Coire Dhomhnuill to Sron Garbh, Carn Eighe group

water on these peaks. The prospect from Beinn Fhionnlaidh amply justifies the diversion. The summit cairn is poised above steep slopes that fall to the west, north and east. The big hills across Loch Mullardoch fill the northern skyline, while nearer at hand the dark waters of Coire Lochan brood beneath Carn Eighe. Return to Carn Eighe, where a circular shelter wall offers repose on this, the highest summit north of the Great Glen.

The ridge from Carn Eighe to Toll Creagach gives an excellent high-level traverse. It also affords a Top collectors' field day, with six Tops as well as the three Munros. The Tops are not named on the OS 1:50,000 map, but are identifiable on the map from their heights (or, in one case, the grid reference given below). Stob a' Choire Dhomhain (1147m), is soon reached. There then follows a narrow section with pinnacles that can be bypassed on the south flank, leading to Stob Coire Dhomhnuill (1137m, NH138262). Here there are wild views down to Loch Mullardoch to the north. The ridge continues to Sron Garbh (1131m) and then drops sharply to the north-east to the Garbh Bealach (1010m, spelt Garth on the map). This section is on rough quartzite. Traces of a once well-constructed stalkers path remain near the top of the descent to the bealach, but most of the way down is now suffering from wear and tear.

If time is running short, one can descend south-east from the bealach into

Sgurr nan Ceathreamhnan from the pass between Cluanie and Alltbeithe

Gleann nam Fiadh, where a path down the glen is joined. Otherwise, for the complete traverse, the continuation over An Leth-chreag (1051m) and Tom a' Choinich Beag (1032m) to Tom a' Choinich is straightforward. From this spacious summit, a spur descends slightly north of east, fairly steeply at first. A path has formed on the south flank of the spur, winding down to the Bealach Toll Easa. The direction of the descent should be carefully checked in mist. From the bealach, a short climb brings one to the West Top of Toll Creagach (951m). Then a broad level ridge leads in 1.5km to the final ascent of the conical Toll Creagach, where there is a fine prospect over the broad expanse of lesser heights to the east.

To descend from Toll Creagach, either return to the Bealach Toll Easa and then go down the path to the south into Gleann nam Fiadh, or else go directly down to the south from the summit, joining the Gleann nam Fiadh path shortly before it swings south above the Abhainn Gleann nam Fiadh. In mist, use of a compass is strongly advised for the descent from Toll Creagach, for the summit is peculiarly symmetrical, and a westerly line leads beguilingly down into remote and appallingly rough and heathery terrain above Loch Mullardoch.

In Gleann nam Fiadh the path eventually becomes a track and emerges at Loch Beinn a' Mheadhoin at the car park by the bridge over the burn, about 2km east of the starting point at the roadhead car park.

If tackling the hills in smaller bites, Toll Creagach and Tom a' Choinich form a natural pair. Start from the car park at the bridge at the start of the Gleann nam Fiadh track (NH216242). The traverse can be done either way round, anticlockwise being perhaps more attractive scenically. Toll Creagach is climbed from the south up the initially steep hillside, or alternatively from the south-east up Coire an t-Sneachda. Tom a' Choinich can be descended either by its rocky south-east ridge, or by the west ridge over Tom a' Choinich Beag and then down Coire Mhic Fhearchair, in either case joining the Gleann nam Fiadh path.

There is good ski mountaineering on these two mountains, see *Ski Mountaineering in Scotland*, Further Reading. Ascent or descent of the two mountains from Loch Mullardoch is not normally recommended, due to extremely deep heather on the lower slopes. However, see the box in Chapter 9 *(p186)* on the Mullardoch Round.

Mam Sodhail, Carn Eighe and Beinn Fhionnlaidh can be done either as an out-and-back expedition, or with a continuation from Carn Eighe to the Bealach Garbh as described above and descent into Gleann nam Fiadh. In the latter instance, one can return to the start either down the full length of the Gleann nam Fiadh path to Loch Beinn a' Mheadhoin, or else by a track that goes south over the moor from NH181258. The latter involves a re-ascent of 100m, but gives a more direct route back to the roadhead car park.

Another possibility is to combine Mam Sodhail and perhaps Carn Eighe with An Socach to the south-west. Lastly, to facilitate access to Beinn Fhionnlaidh, it may be possible to arrange transport by motor launch from the Mullardoch dam. Enquiries should be made locally at the cottage by the dam.

An Socach; 921m; (OS Sheets 25 & 33; NH088230); *the snout*

Sgurr nan Ceathreamhnan; 1151m; (OS Sheets 25 & 33; NH057228); *peak of the quarters*

Mullach na Dheiragain; 982m; (OS Sheets 25 & 33; NH080259); *summit of the kestrels*

Of the many fine mountains described in this chapter, Sgurr nan Ceathreamhnan (pronounced 'Kerranan') can justly claim pre-eminence. High, remote and complex, and flanked by superb corries to the north, this is a hillwalkers' prize. Its radiating ridges bear several Tops and also two separate Munros, An Socach and Mullach na Dheiragain. The three Munros form a horseshoe around the lengthy and deep Gleann a' Choilich, but due to its remoteness this glen is not often visited. Instead, three approaches are commonly used.

From Alltbeithe. The three Munros can be climbed in a convenient circuit from Alltbeithe. Either plan to stay at Alltbeithe Youth Hostel overnight, or camp nearby, or be prepared for a long day. Alltbeithe can be reached from Cluanie or from the Affric roadhead car park as described in the Accommodation section of this chapter. From the Youth Hostel, climb the stalkers path up Coire na Cloiche to the bealach. From here the circuit can be done either way round. It is described in the anticlockwise direction.

An Socach is 1km to the east and 100m higher than the bealach, and is climbed first. Return to the bealach and take the best line down initially steep ground to Loch Coire nan Dearcaig. Climb north-west to a bealach (NH065235) on the long north-east ridge of Sgurr nan Ceathreamhnan. Go over Carn na Con Dhu (967m) to Mullach na Dheiragain, one of the most distant Munros from any public road.

Return along the ridge and climb the narrow, rocky continuation to the summit of Sgurr nan Ceathreamhnan. In good weather the traverse of the airy summit ridge to the West Top should not be missed. The easiest descent to Alltbeithe is down from the main summit by the eastern ridge and over two subsidiary rises (970m and 941m) to join the stalkers path of the morning's ascent. Alternatively, one can descend from the West Top via Coire Allt an Tuirc or by the south ridge to point 910m and then south-east to Alltbeithe. The latter ways go down grass slopes that are fairly steep in places.

From Strath Croe. Strath Croe gives the shortest approach to Sgurr nan Ceathreamhnan from a public road. However, inclusion of Mullach na Dheiragain and/or An Socach would make for a long day, with substantial re-ascents on the return route. Therefore only the ascent of Sgurr nan

Heading up Gleann nam Fiadh towards Tom a' Choinich

Ceathreamhnan itself by this approach is described.

Park at Morvich or Dorisduan (see Chapter 7, *p142*). Follow the path up Gleann Choinneachain and over the Bealach an Sgairne. Continue past the southern end of Loch a' Bhealaich to the Gleann Gniomhaidh watershed. Strike diagonally uphill to the north-east, heading for a bealach just to the north of point 910m. Continue north to the West Top of Sgurr nan Ceathreamhnan and then east to the main summit. The return may be varied by including Sgurr Gaorsaic, which is described separately below.

From Glen Elchaig. The head of Glen Elchaig gives access to a superb round of Sgurr nan Ceathreamhnan by the remote northern ridges and corries of the mountain. It should be realised before setting out that this walk is not suitable for spate conditions. The walk can be shortened by use of a bicycle along the private road in Glen Elchaig. Cycles are best left near the outlet of Loch na Leitreach for the return at the end of the day. From Loch na Leitreach, continue on foot up the glen to Iron Lodge, and then take the track up to the east until 500 metres beyond Loch an Droma. Branch south along the path to Gleann Sithidh and cross the Abhainn Sithidh. This crossing may be difficult or impossible if the stream is high. Climb steeply up to Creag a' Choir' Aird and continue up the ridge over Mullach Sithidh (974m) to Mullach na Dheiragain.

The long, high-level ridge continues over Carn na Con Dhu to the summit of Sgurr nan Ceathreamhnan. Traverse the summit ridge to the West Top. Then either head north-west over Creag nan Clachan Geala (999m) or north over the Tops of Stuc Bheag (1075m), Stuc Mor (1041m) and Stuc Fraoch Choire (918m). (The latter two are un-named on the OS 1:50,000 map but their heights are marked.) If the river levels are low one can head down to cross the Abhainn Gaorsaic above the confluence with the Allt Coire Lochain and then continue down past the Falls of Glomach to the outflow of Loch na Leitreach. Alternatively, one can head north on a stalkers path that goes past Loch Lon Mhurchaidh and then down to the head of Loch na Leitreach.

Sgurr Gaorsaic; 839m; (OS Sheets 25 & 33; NH036219); Probably after *Abhainn Gaorsaic*, which means *thrusting stream*, or possibly *Peak of Horror*

Sgurr Gaorsaic is a rounded hill overlooking Loch a' Bhealaich. It is a satellite of Sgurr nan Ceathreamhnan, with which its ascent can be combined as mentioned above. However, the hill is sufficiently distinctive to be worthy of a separate outing, and is perhaps most often climbed on its own.

Start as for the Strath Croe approach to Sgurr nan Ceathreamhnan. Follow the path up Gleann Choinneachain, over the Bealach an Sgairne and past the southern end of Loch a' Bhealaich. Shortly before the Gleann Gniomhaidh watershed, a line of fence posts rises north-westwards up the slope of Sgurr Gaorsaic.

In due course a plateau with a small lochan is reached. The summit cairn is just beyond to the north-east. The hill affords a fine prospect down Gleann Gaorsaic and a close-up view of Sgurr nan Ceathreamhnan towering above.

West Affric from Alltnamullach

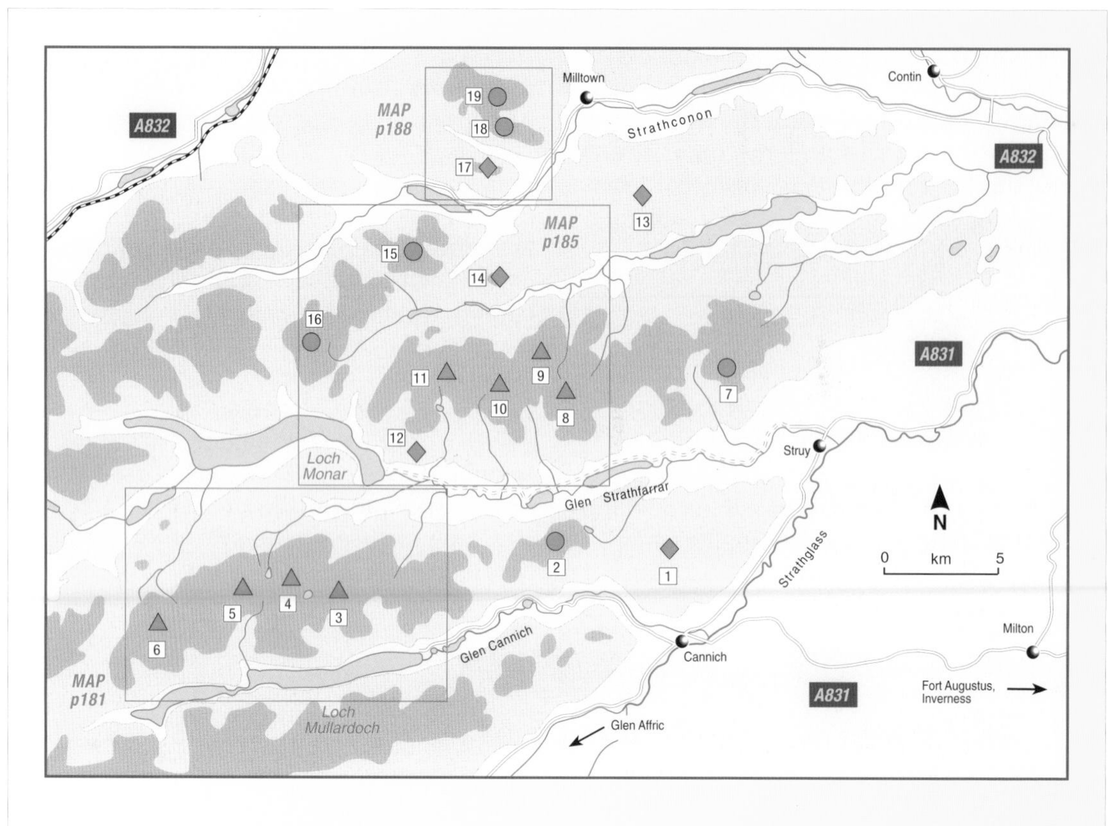

1.	Carn Gorm	677m	G	p180
2.	Sgorr na Diollaid	818m	C	p180
3.	Carn nan Gobhar	992m	M	p181
4.	Sgurr na Lapaich	1150m	M	p181
5.	An Riabhachan	1129m	M	p181
6.	An Socach	1069m	M	p181
7.	Beinn a' Bha'ach Ard	862m	C	p185
8.	Sgurr na Ruaidhe	993m	M	p186
9.	Carn nan Gobhar	992m	M	p186
10.	Sgurr a' Choire Ghlais	1083m	M	p186
11.	Sgurr Fhuar-thuill	1049m	M	p186
12.	Beinn na Muice	695m	G	p188
13.	Carn na Coinnich	673m	G	p188
14.	Beinn Mheadhoin	663m	G	p189
15.	Bac an Eich	849m	C	p189
16.	An Sidhean	814m	C	p189
17.	Meall na Faochaig	680m	G	p192
18.	Meallan nan Uan	838m	C	p193
19.	Sgurr a' Mhuilinn	879m	C	p193

Glen Cannich, Strathfarrar and Strathconon

Richard Wood

Loch Tuill Bhearnach and the east corrie of Sgurr na Lapaich from the summit

A glance at OS Sheet 25 reveals a great tract of wilderness centred on Loch Monar and extending throughout much of the area covered by the map. Many fine mountains form a ring around Loch Monar, and lateral ranges extend to the east, north and west. The dividing line between these mountains and those described in the preceding two chapters is the trough of Glen Cannich, Loch Mullardoch and Glen Elchaig. The present chapter describes the eastern part of the area, and Chapter 10 *(p194)* the western part.

Four major glens reach into the area from the east, separating the mountains into distinct groups. The glens are described first to provide an introduction to the topography and access.

Glen Cannich is attractively wooded in its lower section. Further up the glen the northern slopes are somewhat bare, but on the southern slopes, and extending along the south shore of Loch Mullardoch, native Caledonian pinewoods rise from very deep heather. The road terminates at Benula Lodge by the top of the gaunt dam of Loch Mullardoch. Photographs of the loch taken before the construction of the dam depict scenes of great beauty, with the loch then about 8km long and the Scots pines on the southern shore reaching down to the water's edge. Books published in that era are no longer readily accessible except in archival libraries. Some views may be found in *Escape To The Hills* by W.A.Poucher, Country Life, 1943. There is also an idyllic description in Chapter 4 of W.H.Murray's classic *Undiscovered Scotland.*

Following the building of the dam, the loch is now some 13km long, and because its waters are tapped in order to maintain Loch Beinn a' Mheadhoin at a constant level (see Chapter 8, *p156*), Loch Mullardoch is often ringed by a 'tidemark'. Nevertheless, with the great peaks of the Carn Eighe range to the south and the Sgurr na Lapaich ridge to the north,

Looking east to the Loch Monar peaks from the rocky summit of Sgurr na Diollaid

the loch occupies a dramatic setting, especially on a day of westerly winds when driving showers are interspersed with sunshine glistening upon dancing waves.

Northwards are Glen Strathfarrar, Glen Orrin and Strathconon, each of which has also been harnessed for hydro-electricity. For the most part the developments are fairly unobtrusive, but it is difficult to avoid noticing the disappearance of sparkling burns where they are swallowed into underground pipes for delivery to power stations.

The name Glen Strathfarrar is unusual in combining the words glen and strath. It has been suggested that the word glen refers to the narrower eastern section and strath to the broader central section. Farrar is believed to be derived from 'Varar', the name by which the whole Beauly River system was known in ancient maps and writings. The name River Beauly now designates the waters downstream from the confluence of the Rivers Glass and Farrar.

On the approach by the A831 from Beauly towards Strath Glass, a minor road branches right to Glen Strathfarrar. After 1km there is a locked gate at Inchmore. The road beyond is a right of way, so access on foot or by bicycle is unrestricted. An arrangement between Scottish National Heritage and the landowners allows access up the road by car. (See Access, below.) The gate is at the eastern boundary of the spectacularly beautiful Glen Strathfarrar National Nature Reserve, which was established by Scottish National Heritage in cooperation with the owners of the Culligran and Struy estates. The Reserve is designated a Site of Special Scientific Interest. Along the initial 8km of the road, through the Reserve, are fine stands of native Caledonian pinewood, especially to the south of the River Farrar. Sections are fenced off on a rotating basis to allow the regeneration by protecting young trees from browsing deer.

The Reserve ends soon after a small dam 1km before Loch Beannacharan. The road continues past this Loch and Loch a' Mhuillidh and then into the wider strath. Here deer are farmed and are often to be seen grazing in the fields. The high North Glen Strathfarrar Ridge is to the right of this section of the glen. Continuing up the road, access by car is allowed to the Loch Monar dam, across the dam and 3km further to the small power station in the subsidiary Gleann Innis an Loichel.

Loch Monar varies in level but the effect is softened by a tree plantation beyond the dam and by the pleasantly curved shape of the eastern part of the loch. Most of the water from the loch issues through the power station in Gleann Innis an Loichel, augmenting the Uisge Misgeach and thence the upper reaches of the River Farrar. Because of hydro-electric requirements the amount of water in the Uisge Misgeach and the upper River Farrar is liable to sudden changes, and walkers planning to visit this area should be aware of this. Beyond the power station Gleann Innis an Loichel becomes wild and remote, tucked beneath Sgurr na Lapaich and An Riabhachan, the great hills of the Cannich-Monar Divide.

An absorbing and exciting description of the hardships and rewards of life as a shepherd at the head of Loch Monar, before the construction of the dam and the rise in water level, is to be found in *Isolation Shepherd* (see Further Reading).

Glen Orrin is for the most part not easily accessible. The main feature of the lower part

Access and Transport

By road: Routes to Cannich from the Great Glen and from the A9 are described in Chapter 8 *(p156)*. The same approaches give access to Glen Strathfarrar via Struy Bridge.
Arrangements for access into Glen Strathfarrar by car beyond the gate at Inchmore are as follows. Between the last weekend in March and the end of October the gatekeeper, whose cottage is beside the gate, will unlock the gate daily, except for Tuesdays and Sunday mornings, during the hours 0900 to 1300 and 1330 to 1700, with last exit at 1800. Access on Sunday is between 1330 and 1700. During the rest of the year access may be permitted if the gatekeeper is at home; telephone 01463-761260 in advance. See the Mountaineering Council of Scotland's website for updated information: www.mountaineering-scotland.org.uk, or phone the MCofS on 01738 638 227
Strathconon can be reached from the Great Glen via Drumnadrochit, or from the A9. From Drumnadrochit, turn west along the A831 as for Cannich, then in 2km turn right (north) up a steep hill on the A833. This leads over delightful moorland, and then down through the farms and woodland of Glen Convinth, with views of the North Glen Strathfarrar Ridge to the west, to a junction with the A862 road from Inverness. Turn left, go through Beauly and Muir of Ord and then on the A832 to Marybank, where the road up Strathconon commences.
If coming via the A9, cross the Kessock Bridge at Inverness, continue to the Tore roundabout, take the A835 trunk road to Moy Bridge and turn south on the A832 to Marybank. Alternatively, continue on the A835 through Contin and then take the very narrow road past Loch Achilty, mentioned above, into Strathconon.

By bus: Highland Scottish Omnibuses run daily between Inverness and Cannich via Drumnadrochit. W.MacDonald, Beauly, runs a service between Inverness and Cannich via Beauly and Struy on Tuesdays and Fridays. Highland Scottish Omnibuses and Rapsons Coaches run between Inverness and Muir of Ord, Mondays to Saturdays. A post bus runs between Beauly via Muir of Ord and up Strathconon to Scardroy on Mondays to Saturdays.

Accommodation and Information

Hotels and guesthouses: Cannich has a hotel, limited B&B accommodation and a youth hostel. Serving the northern part of the area, Contin has hotel and B&B houses, and there is a youth hostel at Strathpeffer. Other hotels and B&B establishments are to be found in Beauly, Muir of Ord and Garve.

Maps

Ordnance Survey 1:50,000 Sheet 25 (Glen Carron & Glen Affric) and Sheet 26 (Inverness & Strathglass area).

of the glen is the Orrin Reservoir, which is well seen from some of the neighbouring hills. The reservoir waters are piped to Loch Achonachie in lower Strathconon, where there is a power station. The upper reaches of the glen are entered when visiting some of the adjacent hills by less frequented ways, as will be mentioned later.

The River Conon is one of the great rivers of the north of Scotland, and is an impressive sight when viewed from the vicinity of Moy Bridge (NH482548). From this vantage point the river appears to issue from the jaws of Strathconon. The traveller may well wonder why this glen should be bestowed with such a grand river. In fact Strathconon contributes only a minor proportion of the waters. The river is the final common outflow for a much larger area, including Glen Orrin, Loch Luichart and the Fannaichs, and the mountains to the north of Strath Garve extending as far north-west as Beinn Dearg. Most of these waters unite in the few kilometres west of Moy Bridge. There is a further inflow from Glen Orrin downstream from the bridge. Thus the hills between Glen Strathfarrar and Glen Orrin comprise a significant watershed separating the Beauly and Conon river systems, which drain respectively into the Moray and Cromarty Firths.

The narrow road up Strathconon starts at Marybank, passes Loch Achonachie and, entering a wooded area, continues to Loch Meig. This point can also be reached by an even narrower road that branches off the A835 just west of Contin to join the road from Marybank at the Loch Meig dam. This latter road passes Loch Achilty and then a power station on the big tributary of the River Conon that comes from Loch Luichart. After the dam the road continues past the wooded Loch Meig and crosses the river at Bridgend to the village of Milton (where there are currently no shops). It continues for several more kilometres, south-west towards Inverchoran and then west to Loch Beannacharain. The public road ends at a parking area near the west end of the loch 1km before Scardroy Lodge. The upper reaches of the glen give access to several fine hills.

Glen Strathfarrar and Strathconon are starting points for some long cross-country walks through wild terrain. From the car park to the east of Scardroy Lodge in Strathconon a walk of about 25km on paths and tracks leads up Gleann Fhiodhaig and through to Craig in Glen Carron. More possibilities for ambitious 'through' walks are mentioned in Chapter 10 *(p194)*.

Principal Hills

Carn Gorm; 677m; (OS Sheets 25 & 26; NH328355); *blue hill*

Sgorr na Diollaid; 818m; (OS Sheet 25; NH281362); *peak of the saddle*

Carn Gorm is the culminating point of an extensive tract of hilly moorland to the north-east of the lower reaches of Glen Cannich, and is something of a connoisseur's hill. The starting point for the ascent is behind the farm of Craskie, where a path goes up the hillside. However, as Craskie is private, the path should be reached from the bridge where the public road up the glen crosses the river (NH284335).

Walk east along the track past Muchrachd for 2km to the start of the path up the hill. Ascend this by the side of a wooded ravine with a burn and waterfalls. Higher up the angle eases and the moorland opens out. Cross the burn and aim for a conspicuous cairn on the skyline to the east. From the cairn, continue up a broad ridge to point 638m. Descend easily to Loch Coir' an Uillt Ghiubhais and ascend a gentle slope to the summit of Carn Gorm. A wide vista unfolds to the east and north-east, where the moors descend to the distant Beauly farmlands. The descent is by the same route unless a circuit via Sgorr na Diollaid is planned (see below).

The ascent of Sgorr na Diollaid also starts from the road bridge at NH284335. The most direct way is due north up the hill

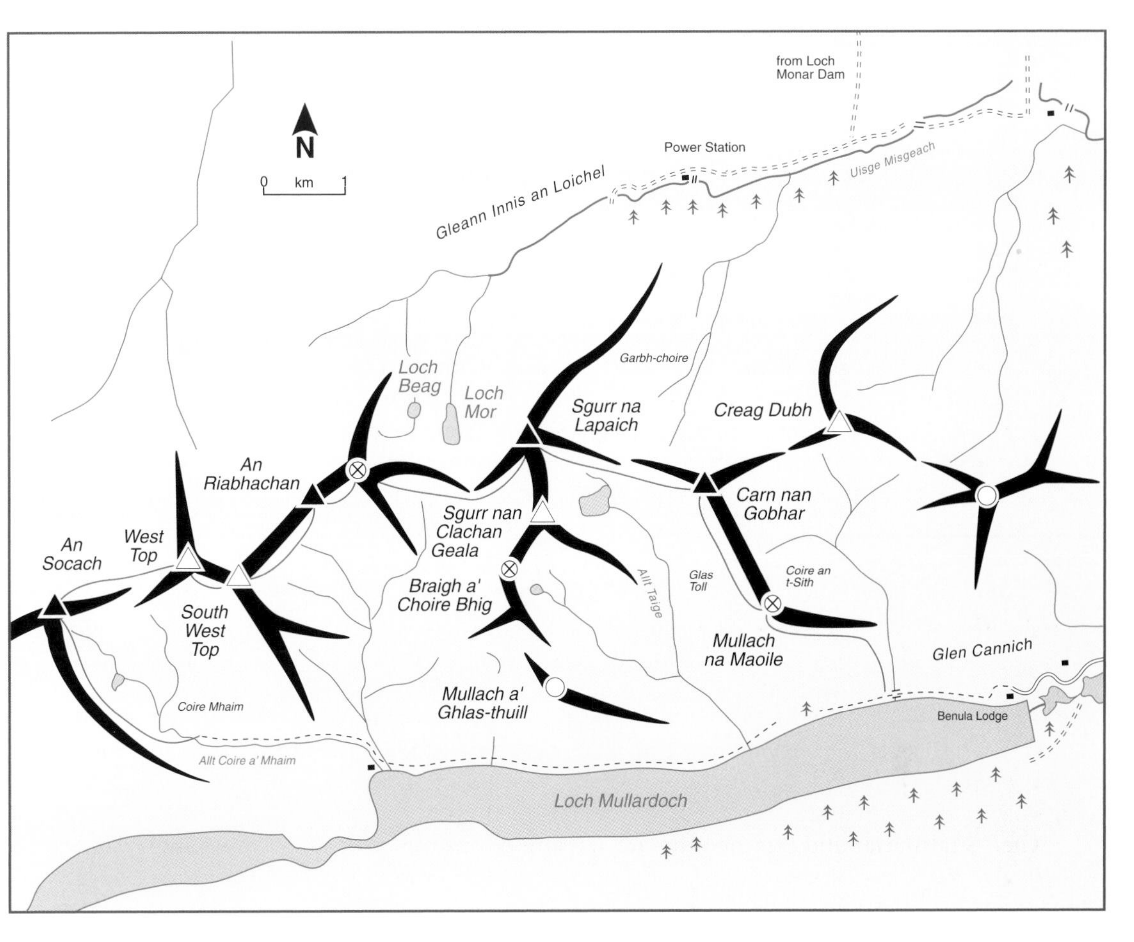

from the parking area, starting up a heathery spur. However, it makes for easier going to avoid the heather by first heading up west of north beside a stream, to emerge in a basin north of Mam Caraidh (328m). Then climb towards point 777m. At about 650m, turn east across a flat, somewhat boggy area to join a broad ridge with slabby rocks.

This ridge rises from the top of the heathery spur just mentioned, and leads via knolls to the pointed rocky top, which is a distinctive landmark at the north end of a line of rocky knobs. From the small summit area there is a dramatic view to the north, down a steep hillside into Glen Strathfarrar and to the mountains beyond. The return can be varied by walking round to point 777m before descending.

Sgorr na Diollaid and Carn Gorm can be combined in a circular walk. The two hills are separated by 5km as the crow flies. The intervening moorland is trackless and somewhat complex, and so this is definitely a walk for a clear day!

Carn nan Gobhar; 992m; (OS Sheet 25; NH181343); *peak of the goats*

Sgurr na Lapaich; 1150m; (OS Sheet 25; NH160351); *peak of the bogland*

An Riabhachan; 1129m; (OS Sheet 25; NH133344); *the grey or streaked one*

An Socach; 1069m; (OS Sheet 25; NH100332); *the snout*

These four mountains comprise a superb high-level ridge between Loch Mullardoch and Loch Monar. The complete traverse is a long but rewarding day and is suitable for reasonably fit walkers during good summer

Sgurr na Lapaich and Carn nan Gobhar from the Mullach na Maoile col (photo Tom Prentice)

conditions. It should be borne in mind that the western part of the traverse is in remote terrain. Conditions or circumstances may therefore dictate shorter outings on one or two of the mountains at a time, for which suggestions are made below.

The traverse can be done in either direction, and the respective merits are finely balanced. The views are more dramatic the east-to-west way, but a rather long walk out along Loch Mullardoch then remains at the end of the day. In the opposite direction the loch-side walk is disposed of early, or, alternatively, it may be possible to arrange for transport by motor launch from Benula Lodge by the Mullardoch dam to the foot of Allt Coire a' Mhaim (where there is a private chalet) and to start walking from there. Enquiries as to the possibility of transport by launch should be made locally (tel: 01456-415347). The east-to-west traverse is described here.

From the Mullardoch dam, take the loch-side path for 1.5km, cross the bridge over the Allt Mullardoch and climb the ridge of Mullach na Maoile. Continue up the broad ridge that ascends north-north-west to Carn nan Gobhar. A large cairn is reached shortly before the summit. The actual summit is at a smaller cairn 200 metres to the north-north-west. Descend by the ridge that goes slightly north of west to the Bealach na Cloiche Duibhe (796m), with an impressive view to Loch Tuill

Bhearnach and the cliffs of Sgurr nan Clachan Geala (1095m). These cliffs have difficult summer and winter climbs on them. Sgurr na Lapaich is climbed by its rocky east ridge or by easier ground to the left.

This is the highest peak of the day and is Scotland's highest mountain north of Carn Eighe. From its summit, descend the south-west ridge to the Bealach Toll an Lochain. In mist it is important to check the direction by compass so as to avoid the steep west face of Sgurr na Lapaich. The bealach is not named on the OS 1:50,000 map, but the adjacent Creagan Toll an Lochain, the precipitous north flank of the east ridge of An Riabhachan, is named.

Climb the east ridge of An Riabhachan, with spectacular views on the right down to Lochs Mor and Beag and Loch Monar beyond. There are some remote winter climbs in this northern corrie of An Riabhachan. The summit ridge of the mountain is well defined and comprises three main tops. The highest, 1129m, is 2km west of Bealach Toll an Lochain. The South-west and West Tops follow, 1086m and 1040m respectively. This is a wonderful high-level traverse, with continually changing views of the Carn Eighe group to the south and across the Loch Monar basin with its surrounding peaks to the north.

From the West Top, descend the fairly sharp and exposed south-west ridge (not a

Beinn a' Bhach Ard from the lead mine above Struy

place to miscalculate) to the Bealach Bholla (860m). Continue up the inviting east ridge of An Socach, where the prospect to the west unfolds into the depths of Glen Elchaig and its surrounding peaks. From the summit, swing round on the ridge to the south and south-east, descend into Coire Mhaim and join a path on the north bank of the Allt Coire a' Mhaim. This leads in 1.5km to the chalet by Loch Mullardoch. Eight tough kilometres lead along the loch-side, partly on paths and partly on rough ground, to the starting point at the dam. Any weariness may be compensated by glimpses into the shadowy northern corries of the Carn Eighe massif across the loch.

Among the shorter (but still substantial) outings on these mountains are the following. A circuit can be made of Carn nan Gobhar and Sgurr na Lapaich from the Mullardoch dam. This can be done in either direction, taking in the respective Tops Creag Dubh (945m) and Sgurr nan Clachan Geala. On the north side of the range a circuit can be made of Sgurr na Lapaich and An Riabhachan, starting and finishing at the power station in Gleann Innis an Loichel. The ascent of Sgurr na Lapaich starts from a bridge over the Uisge Misgeach 1km west of the power station and goes by way of Rubha na Spreidhe (1057m). The descent from An Riabhachan is via Meall Garbh to the west of Creagan Toll an Lochain. An excellent ski mountaineering route based on this circuit is described in *Ski Mountaineering in Scotland*. Also described in that book is a ski traverse of Creag Dubh and Carn nan Gobhar from the Mullardoch dam, with choices of ascent and descent routes to suit the conditions

An alternative route up An Socach is from Iron Lodge in Glen Elchaig. The walk can be shortened considerably by using a bicycle on the private road up the glen to the Lodge. From here, take the path that climbs to the north-east by the Allt na Dhoire Garbh. From the south-west end of Loch Mhoicean climb east to the almost level ridge overlooking Coire Lungard and continue north-east to the summit of An

Socach. The descent can be varied by passing over Meall Shuas (732m) and then going down to the path that links the head of Loch Mullardoch with Glen Elchaig, which is followed so as to regain the latter. As another option, Carn na Breabaig (see Chapter 10, *p194*) can easily be included in the walk.

Beinn a' Bha'ach Ard; 862m; (OS Sheet 26; NH360434); *hill of the high byre*

Beinn a' Bha'ach Ard is the sentinel that guards the entrance to Glen Strathfarrar. Rising well to the east of the Strathfarrar Munros, and separated by a drop of 250m from the hills to the immediate west and north-west, it is a conspicuous landmark from the eastern lowlands, and is well seen from the parking area overlooking the Beauly Firth to the north of the Kessock Bridge. The ascent is suitable for a short day. The circuit described includes Sgurr a' Phollain (855m), which overlooks the Orrin reservoir.

The starting point is Inchmore, where cars should be parked with care so they do not obstruct local residents or workers. Walk 2km along the glen to the power station. Follow a track south-west then west through woodland to a small dam on the

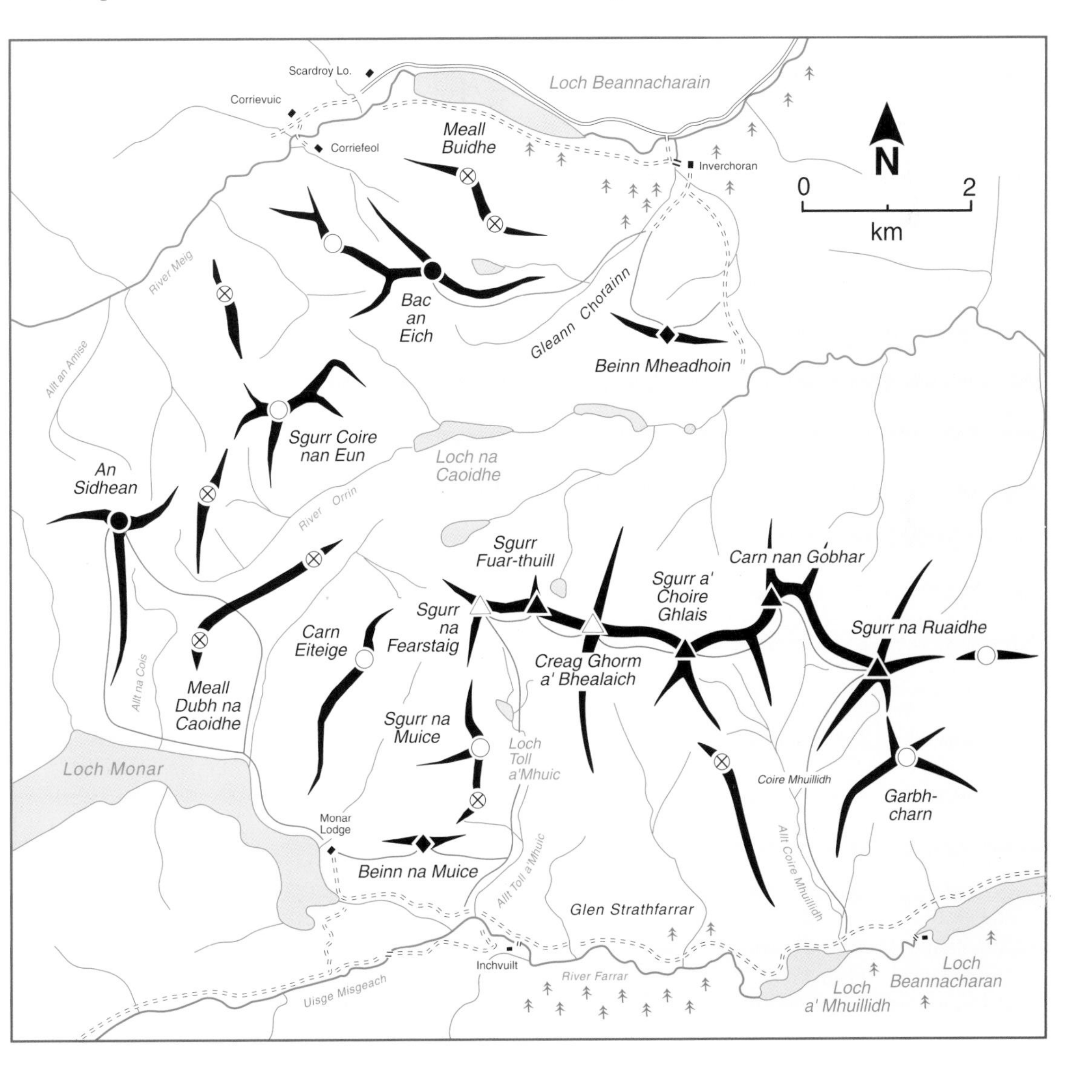

Neaty burn. Continue north-north-west up a path with vehicle tracks to a subsidiary burn (NH350421). Bear north-east up this and head for the skyline ridge. The summit is a short way north above a slight notch on this ridge. The trig point is an excellent lunch spot with a magnificent view to the Beauly Firth.

Continue north-east over a subsidiary top, 835m, to Sgurr a' Phollain and then another minor top, 713m, with views of lower Glen Orrin and its reservoir to the north. A path is marked on the map for the descent from Point 713m to Inchmore, but this is not easily discernible on the heathery hillside. After Loch na Beiste, farm tracks are joined for the final part of the descent. A slightly shorter variation of this circuit is described in *Ski Mountaineering in Scotland*.

Sgurr na Ruaidhe; 993m; (OS Sheet 25; NH288426); *peak of the redness*

Carn nan Gobhar; 992m; (OS Sheet 25; NH273439); *peak of the goats*

Sgurr a' Choire Ghlais; 1083m; (OS Sheet 25; NH259430); *peak of the grey-green corrie*

Sgurr Fhuar-thuill; 1049m; (OS Sheet 25; NH235437); *peak of the cold hollow*

These four peaks are the principal summits of the North Glen Strathfarrar Ridge. Visible from afar, the ridge beckons. On a clear day it affords an outstanding and memorable hill walk, with spectacular views into the flanking corries, and beyond to range upon range of mountains, from the Cairngorms on the south-eastern horizon, round the sweep of the Loch Monar hills, and to the Fannaichs in the north.

The traverse is usually done from Glen Strathfarrar. The start and finish are separated by 6km of road. Therefore, given the nine-hour access restriction to the glen by car, either a reasonably brisk pace is required or a strategy involving two cars (or the caching of a bicycle) should be considered.

The ridge can be traversed in either direction; east to west is scenically more attractive and is described here. Between Lochs Beannacharan and a' Mhuillidh a track leaves the Glen Strathfarrar road at a field on the north side and then heads uphill. Go up this for about 2km by the Allt Coire Mhuillidh to where a subsidiary burn joins from the north-east. Cross the subsidiary burn and continue up by it to the summit of Sgurr na Ruaidhe. Sadly, this route has become worn into a boggy track. This ceases at the summit, and in mist the use of a compass is advised to strike the correct north-westerly line off this symmetrical hill.

Descend to the bealach, designated Shabhach on the map, and continue up Carn nan Gobhar. The top is at the north-west corner of the stony summit plateau. By

The Mullardoch Round

It will not have escaped the attention of hillwalkers with a taste for strenuous 'rounds' that the mountains surrounding Loch Mullardoch afford an opportunity for a big circuit. This can be done either as a backpacking trip or as a sub-24 hour challenge. Various options are possible; a demanding one takes in all of the twelve Munros including the Sgurr nan Ceathreamhnan group and Beinn Fhionnlaidh. An occasion should be chosen when conditions are good and rivers that are to be crossed in the remote terrain to the west of Loch Mullardoch are not in flood. Moreover the party should have sufficient experience for the undertaking.

If the anti-clockwise direction is taken, the Sgurr na Lapaich ridge system is traversed first and in the aesthetically superior east-to-west direction, but the end of the round has 'a sting in the tail' in the descent of deep and trying heather towards the Mullardoch dam. The amount of heathery ground can be lessened by continuing eastwards along the ridge from Toll Creagach for 3km to point 878m before descending to the dam.

Sgurr na Muice from Sgurr na Fearstaig

a curious coincidence, it is the same height (992m) as its namesake on the Sgurr na Lapaich range.

From here onwards the ridge becomes well-defined, with steep corries to the north and an airy prospect out across upper Glen Orrin. Go south-west and then west down to a bealach and climb fairly steeply to the top of Sgurr a' Choire Ghlais, the highest peak of the ridge. There is a choice between two cairns and a trig point for a lunch-spot. The switchback ridge continues to Creag Ghorm a' Bhealaich (1030m) and then to Sgurr Fhuar-thuill. It is possible to descend to the south from here. However, it is easier and worthwhile continuing to Sgurr na Fearstaig (1015m) for a superb view of the peaks to the west of Loch Monar.

A stalkers path descends from just to the east of Sgurr na Fearstaig to Loch Toll a' Mhuic beneath the massive cliffs of Sgurr na Muice. There is extensive winter climbing on these cliffs. The path crosses to the west bank of the Allt Toll a' Mhuic and continues down to Glen Strathfarrar, becoming a track for the last kilometre.

A variation, which takes slightly longer than the descent just described, is to continue over Sgurr na Muice (891m). This prolongs the excellent view towards Loch Monar and the western mountains. The descent is slightly west of south towards Carn an Daimh Bhain, 625m, until well clear of the precipitous east face of Sgurr na Muice, and then east to join the path by the Allt Toll a' Mhuic.

It is also possible to access the main section of the North Glen Strathfarrar Ridge from the north. This way is useful when Glen Strathfarrar is not open to cars, but Sgurr na Ruidhe is not easily included. Drive up Strathconon to where a short private road goes south to the farm at Inverchoran. Walk past the farm, boulder-stepping or fording the burn, and take the track that goes initially south-east and then south, over and down into Glen Orrin.

Cross a bridge over the River Orrin (NH267468) and climb at first up a path and then the open hillside to Carn nan Gobhar. Once this peak is attained, the ridge can be traversed as far as Sgurr na Fearstaig. The descent is to the west-north-west for about 500 metres until it is possible to swing north-east below the steep upper slopes of Sgurr na Fearstaig. Most of the way back to the bridge over the River Orrin is on fairly rough ground.

A highly recommended ski mountaineering traverse of the ridge is described in *Ski Mountaineering in Scotland*. The route is essentially as in the main description from Glen Strathfarrar, but is in the west-to-east direction, which is more suitable for descents by ski.

Beinn na Muice; 695m; (OS Sheet 25; NH218402); *hill of the pigs*

This easily accessible and rewarding hill is suitable for a half-day or for when the higher peaks are out of condition. Like its bigger neighbour, Sgurr na Muice, mentioned above, it affords an excellent view of Loch Monar and the mountains to the west. It has a delightful east-west summit ridge of about 1km in length with a very steep flanking slope to the south, where there are some cliffs. The hill is best traversed from east to west.

From the parking area at NH224392, go up the track to the north-east for about 1km to the waterfall on the Allt Toll a' Mhuic, marked on the OS 1:50,000 map. Then climb the hill directly up fairly steep rough ground. Traverse the summit ridge, taking time to savour the spectacular view.

Carn na Coinnich; 673m; (OS Sheet 26; NH324510); *peak of the moss*

Carn na Coinnich is just the highest point of a large area of moorland between the middle section of Strathconon and Glen Orrin. It can easily be climbed in half a day. Park where the public road swings right over the River Meig at Bridgend. Go through the gate ahead and walk west along the private road past a plantation. Before the house, turn sharp left up a track. Beyond the woodland another track comes in from the right (west). Continue on the track to the south-east. It eventually becomes a stalkers path. Climb the path to the col. The summit of Carn na Coinnich is now visible about 750 metres ahead. Quit the path and go right and up a short slope. Continue on almost level ground, with the downhill slope on the left and moorland on the right, to a final short rise to the trig point.

There is an extensive view of the wild hills and moors surrounding the head of the Orrin reservoir. If desired, the return can be varied by heading west for 1.5km to another stalkers path, which is descended to Balnacraig. A valley track then leads past Dalbreac Lodge and back to the starting point.

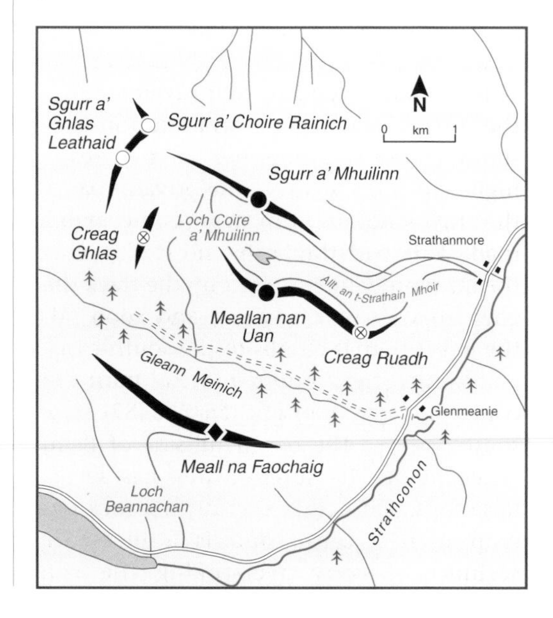

Sgurr a' Choire Ghlais from the north-west

Beinn Mheadhoin; 663m; (OS Sheet 25; NH258477); *middle hill*

This is easily ascended from Inverchoran in the upper reaches of Strathconon. The summit affords a fine view of the nearby higher hills. Park where the private road to the Inverchoran farm leaves the public road. Walk past the farm, and ford or cross the burn on boulders. Start up the track that goes up Gleann Chorainn, and soon take the left fork that climbs to the south-east.

Shortly after fording a lateral burn that comes in from the right (NH268487) strike south-west up the rough hillside of Beinn Mheadhoin. The summit area has several false tops. The actual summit is a rock outcrop with a cairn, and is a pleasantly secluded balcony overlooking the wild upper reaches of Glen Orrin, with the imposing skyline of the North Glen Strathfarrar Ridge beyond. The descent can be varied by going down to the north to a small lochan that nestles beneath Creagan a' Chaorainn (552m), and then down steep grass into Gleann Chorainn to join the track that leads back to Inverchoran.

The crag of Creag a' Ghlastail, to the south-east of Beinn Mheadhoin, has some winter climbing.

Bac an Eich; 849m; (OS Sheet 25; NH222489); *hollow of the horse*

An Sidhean; 814m; (OS Sheet 25; NH170453); *the fairy hill*

These two hills are at opposite ends of a

Meallan nan Uan

broad ridge system that rises from Inverchoran and is flanked on the north-west side by Gleann Fhiodhaig. Both peaks are excellent viewpoints. They can be climbed separately, but the traverse of the two gives a rewarding full day, taking the walker into wild and unfrequented country. The ascent of Bac an Eich on its own is described first, then the traverse of the two hills, and lastly the ascent of An Sidhean on its own.

The summit of Bac an Eich has very steep slopes overlooking Loch Toll Lochain. The usual ascent is from Inverchoran. Park where the private road to Inverchoran leaves the public road, as described above for Beinn Mheadhoin. Walk to Inverchoran farm, cross the burn behind the farm and go up the Gleann Chorainn track. After 2km this becomes a path that crosses the burn at the end of a woodland of Scots pines beyond the opposite bank.

Ascend diagonally west to a stream that exits from Loch Toll Lochain, then climb steeply up grass between small rock out-crops to the shoulder of Sgurr Toll Lochain (NH231485). The angle now eases and a gentle ridge curves west and north-west to the summit of Bac an Eich. A variety of descents are available, some utilising the ring of stalkers paths that surround the mountain. One descent is north-west to Corriefeol, returning to the starting point by the path along the south bank of Loch Beannacharain. Another is to drop down to the south to the Torran Ceann Liath bealach at the head of Gleann Chorainn. (Beinn Mheadhoin can be climbed by its east ridge from here.)

The shortest way to traverse Bac an Eich and An Sidhean is from the road-head at Loch Beannacharain. Walk past Scardroy to

Corriefeol and climb Bac an Eich either directly or by way of the stalkers path that ascends to the bealach at Drochaid Coire Mhadaidh (NH206481). From Bac an Eich descend to this bealach, where a branch path from the main stalkers path zigzags a short distance up the far (west) side towards a broad ridge. The ridge gives easy walking on grass and gravel, with the North Glen Strathfarrar Ridge ever-present to the left.

The way ahead is over Sgurr Coire nan Eun (789m) and point 768m to An Sidhean. On a clear day An Sidhean is a superb viewpoint, with the massive Maoile Lunndaidh straight ahead, and the furthest reaches of the Monar basin with its gleaming lochans and surrounding mountains far to the south-west. Descend north-west to join a stalkers path down the Allt an Amise. This leads down to the River Meig and, on the opposite bank, the path back to Scardroy.

A longer but attractive traverse of the two hills can be done by starting from Inverchoran and returning by the glens to the south of the ridge. Bac an Eich is climbed via Sgurr Toll Lochain as described above. From An Sidhean the magical mystery tour continues via Clach a' Chomharraidh (NH183441) and the source of the River Orrin into the wild and trackless uppermost reaches of Glen Orrin. A path appears by Loch na Caoidhe, where there are some old ruins. The uphill branch of the path is taken for the last ascent of the day to Torran Ceann Liath. Here the stalkers path from Drochaid Coire Mhadaidh is

Meallan nan Uan from the south

The horseshoe from Creag Ruadh to Sgurr a' Mhuilinn, from above Strathanmore

joined and is followed down Gleann Chorainn to Inverchoran.

If An Sidhean is to be climbed on its own it is easiest to start from the Loch Monar dam in Glen Strathfarrar, and this way gives an interesting and varied route. Walk up the road to Monar Lodge and continue on the right of way for 3.5km to Glen Dubh. Take the right fork up the hill to about 500m and then head directly north up the shoulder of Mullach a' Gharbh-leathaid.

After an initially steep climb this levels out into a plateau, which leads in 2km to the summit of An Sidhean and its panoramic view. Either return by the same route or, alternatively, go south-east to the Orrin-Monar watershed at Clach a' Chomharraidh. From here, cross the low ridge of Druim Dubh and drop down to a stalkers path which leads south by the Allt a' Choire Dhomhain to Loch Monar about 2km from Monar Lodge.

Meall na Faochaig; 680m; (OS Sheet 25; NH257525); *hill of the whelk*

Meall na Faochaig overlooks the bend in Strathconon at Inverchoran, although from the road it is concealed by the smaller eminence of Creag Iucharaidh. The ascent is suitable and pleasant for a half-day or evening. Park directly south of Creag Iucharaidh, opposite the track to Inverchoran farm. Walk 500 metres along the public road to the west to where a track branches off to the north-west up the hillside. After 1km this swings round to the east to a col between Creag Iucharaidh and Meall na Faochaig.

Shortly before the col, quit the track and climb the spur to the north of the shallow corrie that forms the southern aspect of Meall na Faochaig. The spur joins the almost level summit ridge about 500 metres west of the summit. The summit area gives a fine panoramic view, with Meallan nan Uan and the cliffs of Creag Ghlas across the forested Gleann Meinich, the Glen Strathfarrar Ridge beyond Beinn Mheadhoin to the south, and, on a clear day, the Torridon peaks in the distance to the west.

It is easily feasible to climb Beinn Mheadhoin and Meall na Faochaig in a day. In that case it is preferable to do Beinn Mheadhoin first, leaving Meall na Faochaig with its fine views to be further enhanced by the late afternoon or evening sunlight.

Meallan nan Uan; 838m; (OS Sheet 25; NH263544); *little hill of the lambs*

Sgurr a' Mhuilinn; 879m; (OS Sheet 25; NH264557); *peak of the mill*

The view up the glen from Bridgend in Strathconon is dominated by these two Corbetts, which are the principal summits of an attractive horseshoe. The horseshoe comprises six tops in all: Creag Ruadh (734m), Meallan nan Uan, Creag Ghlas (686m), Sgurr a' Ghlas Leathaid (844m), Sgurr a' Choire Rainich (848m) and Sgurr a' Mhuilinn. The two north-western peaks, Sgurr a' Ghlas Leathaid and Sgurr a' Choire Rainich, overlook the moors of Strath Bran to the north and are prominent from the A832 Garve to Achnasheen road. Creag Ghlas, by contrast, is tucked away above the forested Gleann Meinich.

The horseshoe is the most northerly group of hills in the Western Highlands, affording an extensive vista, especially across Strath Bran to the Northern Highlands. The circuit is justly popular. It can be done in either direction; clockwise has the advantage that Sgurr a' Mhuilinn, the highest peak, is saved till last.

Park by the unfenced road just south of Strathanmore. Climb by the south bank of the Allt an t-Srathain Mhoir until above the initial steep slope, then turn south-west to Creag Ruadh. Continue to the conical Meallan nan Uan, the first of two Corbetts on the round. About 1km further on is the small rise of Carnan Fuar (NH257551). There are now two options, long or short. For the former, go across rough moorland to Sgurr a' Ghlas Leathaid and Sgurr a' Choire Rainich.

The extensive view across Strath Bran can be assimilated to the full from these hills. (Creag Ghlas, being lower than the other hills and off the direct line of the horseshoe, is usually omitted from the circuit.) From Sgurr a' Choire Rainich, continue to Sgurr a' Mhuilinn. For the short option, cross directly from Carnan Fuar to Sgurr a' Mhuilinn, with Loch Coire a' Mhuilinn to the right.

Sgurr a' Mhuilinn, the highest peak of the horseshoe, affords superb views. To the north, across Strath Bran, are the serried ranks of the Northern Highlands, from Ben Wyvis in the north-east and the Fannaichs in the north, to the Torridon peaks in the west. Nearer at hand are the other Strathconon hills and the ever-present North Glen Strathfarrar Ridge, while on a clear day the Cairngorm plateau is visible far away to the south-east, gleaming with snow in winter or spring.

After tearing oneself away from this prospect (assuming good weather!), descend the moderately steep south-east ridge of Sgurr a' Mhuilinn, continue down and across a peaty moor, cross the Allt an t-Srathain Mhoir to the south-west bank and go steeply down to the road at Strathanmore.

The cliffs of Creag Ghlas in Gleann Meinich offer several rock climbs. *Salamander* (160m HVS 1994), is a classic, taking a central line up the slabs of the West Buttress. There is also rock-climbing on several crags in the vicinity of the Meig dam: Scoop Crag, Hidden Crag, Aspen Crag and Meig Crag. Details of these as well as the climbs mentioned previously are published in the Scottish Mountaineering Club Climbers' Guide, *Northern Highlands Central* (2005 or 2006).

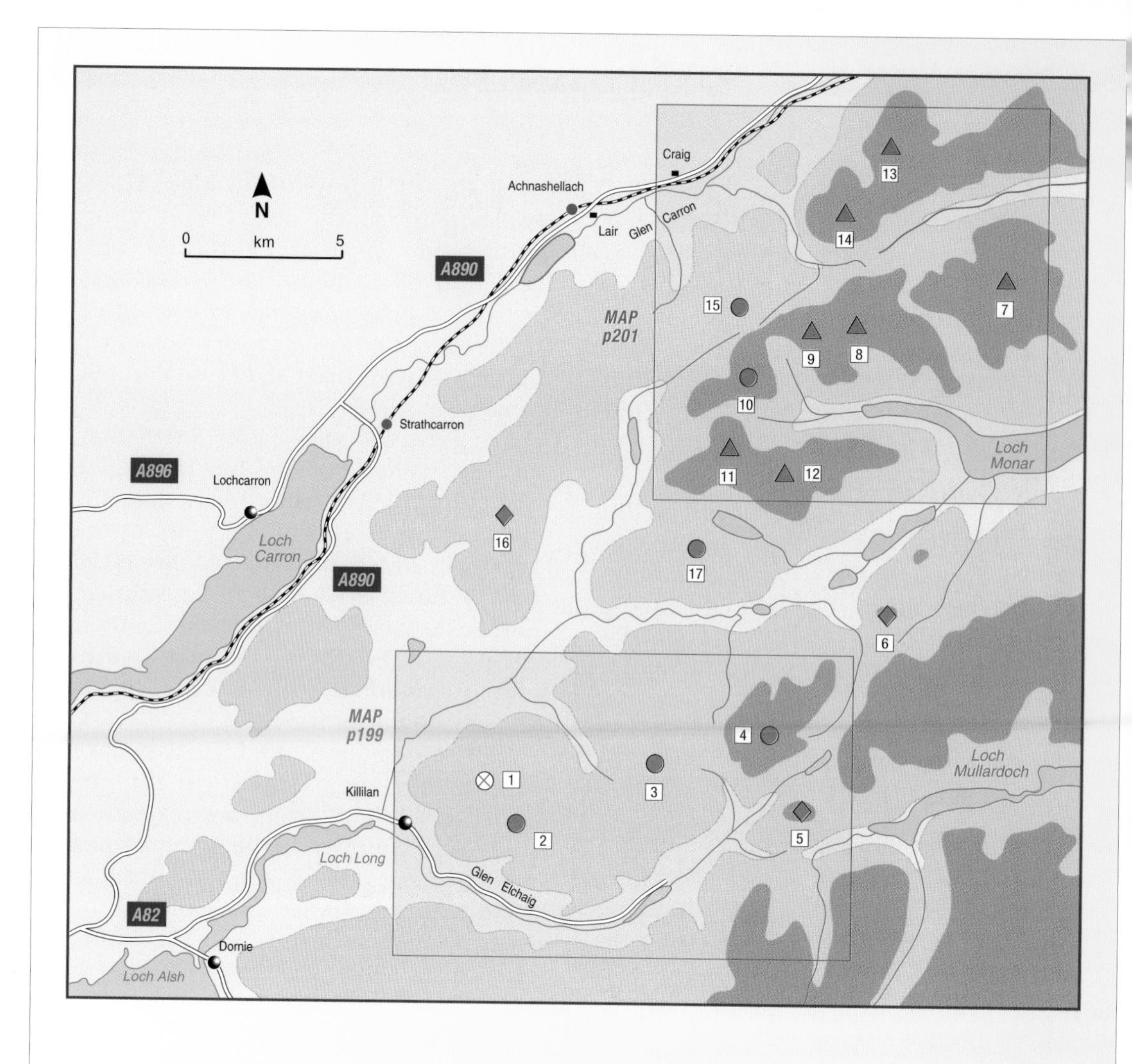

1.	Ben Killilan	754m	O	p197
2.	Sguman Coinntich	879m	C	p197
3.	Faochaig	868m	C	p197
4.	Aonach Buidhe	899m	C	p198
5.	Carn na Breabaig	678m	G	p199
6.	An Cruachan	706m	G	p199
7.	Maoile Lunndaidh	1007m	M	p200
8.	Sgurr a' Chaorachain	1053m	M	p200
9.	Sgurr Choinnich	999m	M	p200
10.	Beinn Tharsuinn	863m	C	p203
11.	Bidein a' Choire Sheasgaich	945m	M	p203
12.	Lurg Mhor	986m	M	p203
13.	Moruisg	928m	M	p206
14.	Sgurr nan Ceannaichean	915m	M	p206
15.	Sgurr na Feartaig	862m	C	p206
16.	Creag Dhubh Mhor	612m	G	p207
17.	Beinn Dronaig	797m	C	p209

Chapter 10

Killilan, West Monar and Glen Carron

Ted Maden

West over Loch Morar from Beinn na Muice to Lurg Mhor and Maoile Lunndaidh

The western part of the area centred on Loch Monar possesses a distinctive aura of remoteness. No public roads even enter, and long approaches are required to gain access to its innermost fastnesses. The area is bounded to the south and south-west by Glen Elchaig and Loch Long. The northern and western boundaries are defined for the most part by the A890 from Achnasheen to its junction with the A87 4km west of Dornie. From Achnasheen to Stromeferry the road runs parallel to the Kyle of Lochalsh railway. The Highland Watershed provides a rough basis for demarcating the eastern boundary. Several mountains are located on this section of the Watershed, and most of them are described in this chapter.

The finest of the mountains comprise a great arc around the head of Loch Monar, from Maoile Lunndaidh at the north-eastern end to the remote Lurg Mhor at the south-east. These peaks give wonderful walks on long summer days, and are justly prized among hill-walkers. An abundance of other hills are distributed in an irregular array around the inner arc, differing widely between each other in character, some of them also being quite remote. The rivers that drain the region to the west are relatively short, and they have not been harnessed for hydro-electricity, a noticeable difference from the areas described in the previous two chapters. The three main western rivers are the Elchaig, the Ling and the Carron. The Ling is formed in the heart of a large, wild basin from the confluence of two main tributaries. The southern stream, the Allt Coire nan Each, issues from hillside springs just north of Loch Mhoicean. First cascading down a narrow glen, it swings to the west beneath the remote An Cruachan, to flow through a lochan-studded moor, now with the name Allt an Loin-fhiodha, past Maol-bhuidhe bothy and for another 5km to the confluence. The northern tributary, the Uisge Dubh or Black Water, comes from Loch an Laoigh, of which the Abhainn Bhearnais is the principal feeder. The Uisge Dubh is a considerable watercourse, uncrossable

Access and Transport

By road: Killilan and Glen Elchaig give access to the most southerly of the hills described in this chapter.The usual approach to Glen Elchaig is from Kintail. At Ardelve a minor road branches off along the north-west side of Loch Long. As noted in earlier chapters, the road up Glen Elchaig is private and is closed to motor vehicles. However, it is a right of way, with access outside the stalking season. There is a car park just before Killilan and the start of the private road. It is also possible to park at Camas-luinie. The Killilan car park is suitable if it is planned to cycle along the road up the glen. Camas-luinie is an alternative starting point if it is intended to walk; a path to the south of the river leads in 2km to a bridge, which is crossed to join the glen road. The Camas-luinie starting point saves about 2km, but in darkness it is less easy to follow than the road.

Access points for the more northerly hills are from the A890 Achnasheen to Kyle road in Glen Carron and by Loch Carron. For travellers coming directly from the south to Glen Carron, the quickest route is by the A9 over the Kessock Bridge to the Tore roundabout and then the A835 Ullapool road as far as Garve, then the A832 to Achnasheen. For travellers who are already in the Kintail area, Glen Carron is most quickly reached via Dornie and then north-east on the A890.

By bus: Scottish Citylink Coaches run daily between Glasgow and Kyle of Lochalsh and between Inverness and Kyle of Lochalsh, passing through Dornie, and also between Inverness and Kyle of Lochalsh via Glen Carron. A four-seater post bus runs between Dornie, Killilan and Kyle of Lochalsh, Mondays to Saturdays.

By rail: The railway from Inverness to Kyle of Lochalsh is one of the most scenic in Scotland, and there are stations at Achnashellach and Strathcarron.

Accommodation and Information

Hotels and guesthouses: There are many hotels, B&Bs and cottages-to-let in the Kintail, Dornie and Ardelve areas, and at Lochcarron.

Campsites: Camp and caravan sites at Morvich (Loch Duich), Ardelve and Balmacara.
Independent Hostel: Craig in Glen Carron.

Bothies: There are three remote bothies in the area: Maol-bhuidhe, the Bendronaig Lodge bothy, and Bearnais bothy. The latter was refurbished at considerable effort in the 1980s (materials were carried over the rough terrain from Bendronaig Lodge) as a memorial to the late Eric Beard.

Maps

Ordnance Survey 1:50,000 Sheet 25 (Glen Carron and Glen Affric) covers all of the hills in this chapter. Sheet 24 (Raasey and Applecross) and Sheet 33 (Loch Alsh, Glen Shiel and Loch Hourn) are useful for some of the access roads and accommodation.

in spate except by the bridge on the estate road from Attadale to Bendronaig Lodge.

It was mentioned in the previous chapter that some long cross-country walks can be done through the Loch Monar area. In general, these follow rights of way and are fully described in *Scottish Hill Tracks*, published by the Scottish Rights of Way Society.

Walks that can be recommended for consideration include three for which brief notes are given here; the route numbers are those in *Scottish Hill Tracks*, in which fuller descriptions are given (see Further Reading).

Inchvuilt (Glen Strathfarrar) to Killilan by Pait Lodge and Glen Elchaig (route 262, 40km). The initial part of the walk is up Glen Strathfarrar. The track from the Monar dam to the power station in Gleann Innis an Loichel is then taken. Soon afterwards the route traverses trackless terrain to Pait Lodge. Here a path is joined that goes up by the Allt Coire nan Each to Loch Mhoicean and then down to Iron Lodge at the head of Glen Elchaig. From here it is 13km to Killilan. A variant of the walk is to take the path that crosses the Allt an Loin-fhiodha, continuing to Maol-bhuidhe where the night can be spent camping or in the bothy. The walk can then be completed in either of two ways. One way is by a path that climbs south over the bealach between Aonach Buidhe and Faochaig and then descends to Iron Lodge. (The bealach, 460m, is unnamed on the OS 1:50,000 map.) The other way is by wild terrain following the south bank of the River Ling until an estate track is joined at Coire-domhain (NG980343) about 6km from Killilan. The River Ling route involves crossing some sizeable tributaries, and is only recommended in dry conditions.

Inchvuilt to Loch Long by Bendronaig Lodge (route 263, 38km). This walk is initially as for the previous one to Pait Lodge. Here a bridge is crossed to the west, to join a former path, now an estate track, which goes past Loch Calavie to Bendronaig Lodge and its bothy. The route continues on the estate road towards Attadale. At NG957366 a left fork is taken into a forestry plantation. On emerging from the forest just east of Carn Allt na Brath the track becomes a path, which is followed to the south to join the west bank of the River Ling and thence the public road at the head of Loch Long.

Struy or Inchvuilt to Strathcarron (route 261, 59km from Struy). The central part of this long walk is a traverse of the north shore of Loch Monar followed by crossing the Bealach an Sgoltaidh between Bidein a' Choire Sheasgaich and Beinn Tharsuinn to Bendronaig Lodge. The exit is either via the estate road to Attadale or by a path that leaves this estate road at NG995386 and crosses the moor to Achintee.

Principal Hills

Ben Killilan; 754m; (OS Sheet 25; NG975317); *hill of Killilan*

Sguman Coinntich; 879m; (OS Sheet 25; NG977303); *mossy, sack-shaped hill*

Faochaig; 868m; (OS Sheet 25; NH022317); either *the whelk*, or *little heathery hill*

Sguman Coinntich and Faochaig are the highest points on a ridge that extends for several kilometres along the north side of Glen Elchaig. Also part of this group is Ben Killilan. Appearing to be a distinct hill when seen from the shore of Loch Long, Ben Killilan is actually connected to Sguman Coinntich by the high ground of the Bealach Mhic Bheathain, and rises only slightly above this to the west. Hence it is not a separate mountain; however, it is a fine viewpoint for the River Ling basin, the hills to the north as far as Torridon, and Skye to the west. The walk described takes in all three hills and gives a fairly long day. As an alternative, Faochaig can be climbed separately if preferred.

From Killilan, ascend the stalkers path into Coire Mor. This is initially a footpath, but higher up it joins an estate track that continues for some distance. Where the upper corrie starts to open out, strike up the hillside to the left to gain the broad, almost level summit ridge of Ben Killilan. The best viewpoint of all is the western top, Sgurr na Cloiche (753m). The main top is 1.5km to the east of this and almost due north from Sguman Coinntich. Traverse round to the latter, with a short scramble up from Bealach Mhic Bheathain. Just north-east of the summit is a trig point that overlooks the Allt a' Choire Mhor and is conspicuous from the stalkers path.

Seen from Sguman Coinntich, Faochaig looks to be quite a long way away. However, the undulating broad ridge affords easy walking with superb views of the surrounding corries and mountains. A small stream can be found before the final pull up onto Faochaig. This hill has a sizeable summit plateau that is worth walking around for the varied views. To the east, the hillside plunges steeply into the defile through which the path from Iron Lodge to Maol-bhuidhe makes its way. Aonach Buidhe rises steeply opposite, while the cottage of Maol-bhuidhe appears tiny in the distance to the north-east. Around and beyond Loch Monar are the Munros of the Lurg Mhor

Sgurr Coinnich from Sgurr a' Chaorachain

and north Glen Strathfarrar groups.

The descent is due south from the summit into a corrie. About half way down, a path is joined that leads to Carnach. The walk back to Killilan is 11km, but the glen is full of variety and interest. Carnan Cruithneachd looms above Loch na Leitreach, while of potential interest to rock climbers are some cliffs on the north side of the glen, 1 – 2km west of the loch, on which there have been some developments.

If it is decided not to do the complete walk described above, an easy descent can be made from Sguman Coinntich, first to the south-east and then down a stalkers path to Faddoch in Glen Elchaig. Faochaig can be climbed on its own from Carnach, which can be reached by cycling up the glen. The ascent is made starting steeply via the path from Carnach, just mentioned. An alternative descent is to the north-east, where a stalkers path, marked on the OS 1:50,000 map, goes down to join the path from Maol-bhuidhe to Iron Lodge.

Aonach Buidhe; 899m; (OS Sheet 25; NH058324); *yellow ridge*

Aonach Buidhe is a fine and complex hill that dominates the wild country to the north of the head of Glen Elchaig. Its southern aspect comprises a broad ridge whose lower grass slopes drop fairly steeply to the Allt na Doire Gairbhe 1km to the north-east of Iron Lodge. There is a crag to the south-west of these slopes, not shown on the OS 1:50,000 map. The eastern and western flanks of the hill overlook the paths to Pait Lodge and Maol-bhuidhe respectively. The best features are on the hill's northern side, where high ridges and secluded corries overlook Maol-bhuidhe and the many lochans of that remote area.

The hill can be climbed from Killilan by walking or cycling the 13km to Iron Lodge and then ascending the south ridge. The summit is a superb viewpoint for the mountains surrounding Glen Elchaig and the

Monar basin. It is worth descending to the south-east to visit the lonely Loch Mhoicean. Or a longer but even better alternative is to continue over the subsidiary tops of An Creachal Beag (870m) and Aonach Cas and then to descend the north-east ridge, eventually swinging east on a path, shown on the map, which joins the path up the Allt Choire nan Each to Loch Mhoicean.

Aonach Buidhe can also be climbed together with Faochaig, or as part of a longer backpacking trip into the Maol-bhuidhe area. To ascend both hills in a day with a bicycle, either leave the bike where the track crosses a stream NH043311 or continue almost to the Aonach Buidhe – Faochaig col. The path shown on the OS map is now a good track, although rough in places.

Carn na Breabaig; 678m; (OS Sheet 25; NH066301); *hill of the small peak*

An Cruachan; 706m; (OS Sheet 25; NH093358); *the stack*

These two hills are satellites of An Socach (1069m). They are described in this chapter because access to them is easiest from Glen Elchaig, whereas, as indicated in Chapter 9, An Socach itself is often climbed from the Mullardoch dam along with the other north Cannich Munros.

An Cruachan's remote position and its commanding location overlooking the West Monar wilderness place it amongst the most prized of Grahams. Carn na Breabaig is not so remote, but it does provide a spectacular through-view of the Mullardoch-Elchaig glen system.

The round trip from Killilan to An Cruachan and back is 52km, but the walking distance can be halved by cycling to Iron Lodge. Only a small extra effort is needed to include Carn na Breabaig, in which case it is perhaps preferable to climb this hill first, leaving An Cruachan as the day's climax.

For this combination, take the path that zigzags up to the south-east from Iron Lodge. After about 1km, head north-east up grassy slopes to Carn na Breabaig's summit. Then descend northwards to where the Allt na Doire Gairbhe flows out of Loch

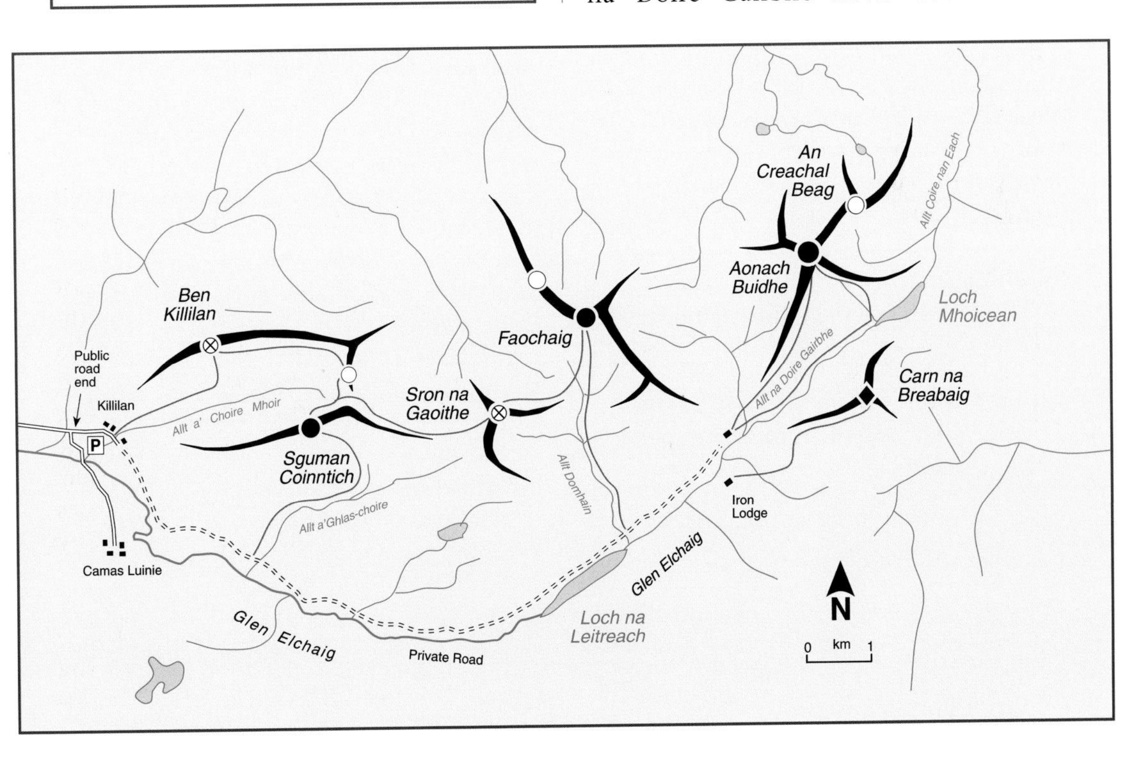

Mhoicean. Follow the path past the loch. An Cruachan comes into view soon afterwards, by a cairn overlooking the Allt Choire nan Each. (The OS 1:50,000 map indicates that the Allt na Doire Gairbhe and the Allt Choire nan Each both issue from Loch Mhoicean, from opposite ends. In fact the latter stream starts a short distance to the north-east of the loch, coming mainly from springs on the flank of An Socach.)

The path soon crosses the Allt Choire nan Each, leading ultimately to Pait Lodge. About 3km beyond Loch Mhoicean, quit the path and climb to the col between An Cruachan and the north-west slope of An Socach.

The summit of An Cruachan is gained after a moderately steep ascent of 200m. There is a well-constructed summit cairn, and this is a wonderful viewpoint, overlooking the wilds of Ling and Monar, and ringed by higher hills.

The eastern part of the track from Pait Lodge to Bendronaig Lodge is the only recent sign of human intervention; perhaps in time this will blend into the surroundings. Return by the same route to the south-east end of Loch Mhoicean, and continue down the path by the Allt na Doire Gairbhe to Iron Lodge.

As mentioned above for Aonach Buidhe, An Cruachan can readily be included as part of a backpacking trip, combining a number of hills in the Maol-bhuidhe area.

Maoile Lunndaidh; 1007m; (OS Sheet 25; NH135458); *bare hill of the wet place*

Sgurr a' Chaorachain; 1053m; (OS Sheet 25; NH087447); probably *peak of the torrent*

Sgurr Choinnich; 999m; (OS Sheet 25; NH076446); *mossy peak*

The head of Loch Monar is surrounded by a magnificent semi-circle of mountains. The northern section, from Maoile Lunndaidh to Sgurr Choinnich, is an east-west ridge with a deep col, the Drochaid Mhuilich, separating Maoile Lunndaidh from Sgurr a' Chaorachain's eastern Top, Bidean an Eoin Deirg (1046m).

Seen from the hills to the east of Loch Monar, the summit plateau of Maoile Lunndaidh and the conical Bidean an Eoin Deirg are conspicuous and contrasting features. Bidean an Eoin Deirg is a particularly fine viewpoint overlooking the head of the Loch. The traverse of these northern peaks affords an excellent and not unduly hard day, and is described here in the east-to-west direction. Options for separate ascents of Maoile Lunndaidh and the Chaorachain – Choinnich ridge are also mentioned. The best start is from Craig in Glen Carron, where there is a forestry car park just north of the road. Cross the railway by the level crossing and take the forest track up the glen of the Allt a' Chonais. Above the forest a grand prospect opens out, with the cliffs of Sgurr nan Ceannaichean to the left and the seemingly wall-like north faces of Sgurr Choinnich and Sgurr a' Chaorachain ahead. Some winter routes were climbed on Sgurr Choinnich in 2003. Continue easily on the estate track, rounding the corner leftwards at Pollan Buidhe and crossing the low watershed after another 2km.

Shortly after passing a small conifer plantation, quit the track and strike east across the peaty moor. After crossing the An Crom-allt there are two options. One of these is to climb south-east up a steep grassy spur between Fuar-tholl Beag and Fuar-tholl Mor. This leads up to Carn nam Fiaclan, from which the summit of Maoile Lunndaidh is gained 1.2km to the east along the plateau. The second option, which is recommended scenically, is to ascend in a more easterly direction towards the outlet of Fuar-tholl Mor.

A cascade plunges down a ravine to the left, and the prospect up into the crag-girt Fuar-tholl Mor on the right is impressive. Continue east to a col at 750m, where the view opens out over Loch a' Chlaidheimh with its little island, and Gleann Fhiodhaig and the upper reaches of Strathconon. The

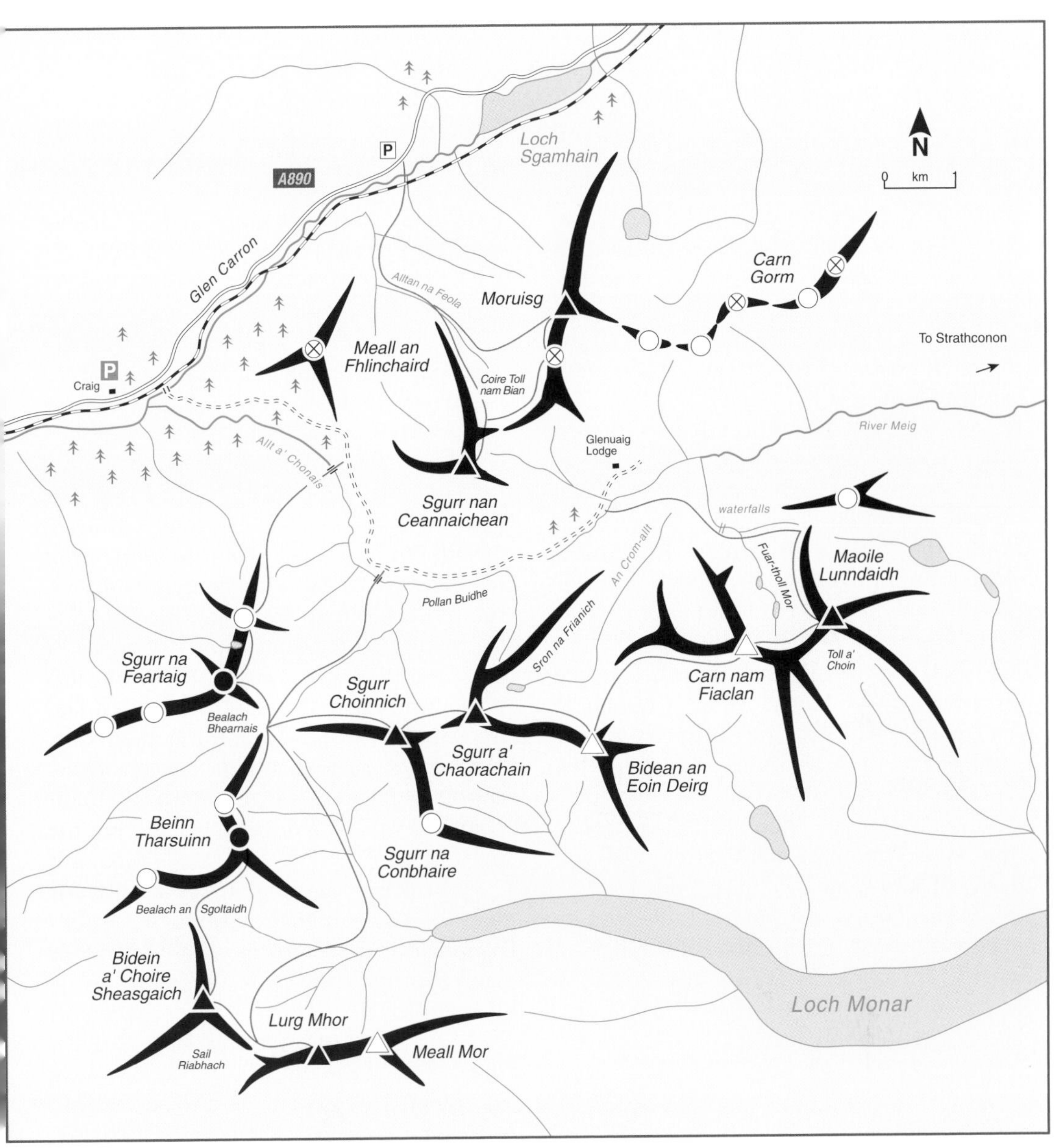

summit of Maoile Lunndaidh is gained after a steady ascent up its broad north ridge. The cairn is an excellent lunch spot.

The almost Cairngorm-like summit of Maoile Lunndaidh differs from the conical and ridge-shaped architecture of the surrounding West Highland peaks. The south-eastern corrie, Toll a' Choin, looks impressive when seen from the east, but somewhat less so from the summit plateau. It contains some recent winter climbs.

Continue along the almost level ridge to Carn nam Fiaclan, and then for another 1km west, where a steep descent west-southwest leads to the Drochaid Mhuilich. To climb Bidean an Eoin Deirg, either ascend a broad and mainly grassy gully to the summit ridge just west of the summit, or gain a spur to the left of the gully. The spur gives pleasant, easy scrambling in an open position, and leads directly to the very summit. With dramatic suddenness, Loch Monar and the array of encircling mountains are revealed in a superb panorama

The ridge continues easily to Sgurr a' Chaorachain and, after a col, Sgurr

Choinnich. There is the possibility of a detour to the satellite peak, Sgurr na Conbhaire (881m), a fine, isolated viewpoint. The notch in the ridge before Sgurr na Conbhaire can claim to be a historical site, for King James VI of Scotland traversed this feature when hunting with Lord Colin, First Earl of Seaforth, as recounted in *Isolation Shepherd*, p126, (see Further Reading). The hunters used bows and arrows and long spears, and the name of the notch, Bowman's Pass, commemorates their sport.

Sgurr Coinnich is descended by its west ridge, where a few rock steps must be negotiated. At the foot of the ridge is the Bealach Crudhain, which is near to, but distinct from, the Bealach Bhearnais. This somewhat complicated region could be confusing in mist, and it is important to swing right (north) and join the path that descends from the Bealach Bhearnais to the north-east down to the Allt a' Chonais at Pollan Buidhe. There was formerly a wire bridge for the river crossing at Pollan Buidhe, but it may no longer be intact. There is a footbridge about 200 metres to the west. The estate track is rejoined and leads back to Craig.

Maoile Lunndaidh can be climbed on its own essentially as described above, making either a clockwise or an anticlockwise circuit of Fuar-tholl Mor. For the clockwise circuit, the exit of Fuar-tholl Mor is crossed to gain the north ridge of the mountain as described above, and the descent is north-west from Carn nam Fiaclan to the An Crom-allt. For the anticlockwise circuit, Carn nam Fiaclan is climbed first. Maoile Lunndaidh can also be climbed from the Loch Monar dam or from the car park at the head of the public road in Strathconon. These approaches are somewhat longer than that from Craig, but they are rewarded by access to interesting terrain that the walker might not otherwise visit.

The route from the Monar dam goes past Monar Lodge and then via the loch-side path for 5km to where a stalkers path leads up into Toll a' Choin. From here the ridge on the right (north) leads directly to the summit. The route from Strathconon goes along Gleann Fhiodhaig and then up the path by the Allt an Amise. The stream that flows from Loch a' Chlaidheimh is crossed to gain the east ridge of the mountain. Alternatively, Creag Dhubh Bheag (627m) and Creag Dhubh Mhor (854m) can be climbed before gaining the mountain's north ridge.

To traverse Sgurr a' Chaorachain and Sgurr Choinnich without Maoile Lunndaidh, it is probably best to ascend Sgurr a' Chaorachain first, taking the north-

Carron To Cluanie With Dry Feet?

What do the following hills and mountains have in common: Moruisg, Sgurr nan Ceannaichean, Sgurr a' Chaorachain, Sgurr Choinnich, Beinn Tharsuinn, Bidein a' Choire Sheasgaich, Beinn Dronaig, An Cruachan, An Socach, Carn na Breabaig, Sgurr nan Ceathreamhnan, Sgurr Gaorsaic, Beinn Fhada, Sgurr a' Bhealaich Dheirg? Answer: they are all on the Highland Watershed. They comprise but a tiny fraction of the entire Scottish Watershed, which was walked throughout its length by Dave Hewitt and recounted in his epic book, *Walking The Watershed* (see Further Reading).

Nevertheless, walking even this section of the Watershed is a tough proposition, largely through remote terrain, and with several major descents from high mountains to relatively low-lying passes and boggy sections. Anyone contemplating undertaking such a walk needs to be competent and experienced in travel and backpacking in the wilds. For such walkers this would be an excellent way of experiencing the great roadless area between the head of Glen Carron (NH127542) and Cluanie (NH075117). By its nature, a watershed walk does not involve the fording of rivers. However, there are substantial sections on this itinerary that do not drain rapidly. If you expect to do the walk with dry feet, you probably should not be setting out on it!

east ridge, the Sron na Frianich, thereby avoiding the northern cliffs. If possible, time should be allowed to visit Bidean an Eoin Deirg for the view. Then return to Sgurr a' Chaorachain and continue over Sgurr Choinnich as described for the complete traverse.

Beinn Tharsuinn; 863m; (OS Sheet 25; NH055433); *transverse hill*

Bidein a' Choire Sheasgaich; 945m; (OS Sheet 25; NH049412); *pinnacle of the corrie of the fallow cattle*

Lurg Mhor; 986m; (OS Sheet 25; NH065404); *big shank*

The mountainous arc around the head of Loch Monar continues to the south and east with these three increasingly remote peaks. Lurg Mhor is famously inaccessible. It and two comparably remote Munros, A' Mhaighdean and Seana Bhraigh (see Chapters 13 and 15, *p248, 278*) were described by Hamish Brown in an evocative article, *Behind the Ranges* (Scottish Mountaineering Club Journal XXIX No. 162, 1971). Written a few years before his first continuous traverse of the Munros in 1974, the article was perhaps indicative of the genesis of the idea for his epic Mountain Walk. Bidein a' Choire Sheasgaich, irreverently dubbed 'cheesecake' by visiting Sassenachs, is Lurg Mhor's neighbour. Its characteristic pyramidal summit is visible for miles around, including, unexpectedly, the car park of the Loch Duich Hotel at Ardelve.

The most popular approach to these hills is from Craig. The walk is about an hour longer than the traverse of the Maoile Lunndaidh-Sgurr Choinnich ridge from Craig. It is not unusual for fit hillwalkers to do both walks on consecutive summer days, sometimes with the help of a bicycle on the initial track. Take the track up the glen of the Allt a' Chonais for 5km to where the main track swings left. Here a path branches right to the Allt a' Chonais. There was formerly a wire bridge here. If this is not intact, there is a footbridge 200 metres downstream. Continue up the stalkers path to the Bealach Bhearnais, which links Pollan Buidhe with the Bearnais area to the south-west. From the bealach, climb initially steep grass slopes onto the undulating ridge of Beinn Tharsuinn.

Traverse the subsidiary tops, or bypass them to the east, to gain the summit. Then a descent leads to a lochan, and a further considerable descent (starting with a small rock step) brings one to the Bealach an Sgoltaidh beneath Bidein a' Choire Sheasgaich. (On the OS 1:50,000 map the name of this bealach is misplaced down the stream to the east.)

An old stone wall at the bealach affords a pleasant lunch spot. The northern aspect of Bidein is ringed with cliffs and appears daunting. However, it is best to confront the obstacle directly, for the cliffs extend for a considerable distance in both directions, and the easiest passage is straight ahead. Ascend by the stone wall and some minor outcrops. Ahead, the main band of cliffs is split by a grassy gully that slants up to the right. This presents a fairly easy, enclosed scramble. Above, a tiny lochan is reached, followed by a larger one on the shoulder beneath the summit pyramid. (A few hundred metres to the right of the slanting gully, another gully presents a line of weakness that has been fairly well trodden. However, this line is more exposed than is apparent from below, and is not recommended.) The summit affords a wide panorama. By the laws of geometrical optics this should include, in the distance, the car park of the Loch Duich Hotel!

Descend south-east to the col between Bidein and Lurg Mhor, and walk up bouldery slopes of the latter to the summit cairn. High on the northern flank of Lurg Mhor is a fine quartzite crag, characterized by slabs and grooves. The crag is not visible from above, but can be seen from Bidein. It has several climbs on very good rock, including the aptly named *Munroist's Reward* (90m VS 1988) and *Monar Magic* (140m VS 1988). For the collector of Tops,

Sgurr a' Chaorachain and Sgurr Choinnich from Sgurr Feartaig (photo: Jim Teesdale)

Meall Mor (974m) awaits, about 800 metres to the east and separated from Lurg Mhor by a short but surprisingly sharp rock ridge that is not easily avoidable. The ridge makes a pleasant scramble, and the top affords a fine outlook over the length of Loch Monar.

Return to the col between Bidein and Lurg Mhor. From here, slant down to the left (north-west) for a few hundred metres on a path that has been formed by walkers. The path soon fades. There are now two possibilities. One of these is to traverse under Bidein to the Bealach an Sgoltaidh, and then to re-traverse Beinn Tharsuinn to the Bealach Bhearnais. The other is to swing round to the right and continue down the corrie. There is a profusion of wild flowers here in early summer. The rock-climbing crag just mentioned rears impressively above, and the head of Loch Monar is in view. (The floor of the corrie can also be reached directly from Meall Mor. However, this way is not recommended, for it involves descending very steep grass and

bypassing rock outcrops lower down.)

Cross the Allt an Sgoltaidh, and contour round the foot of Beinn Tharsuinn to the Allt Bealach Crudhain. Cross this and gain a path that ascends towards the Bealach Crudhain. After a while the path disappears but the ascent to the bealach is straightforward. Under most conditions the route via the corrie is probably less arduous than the return over Beinn Tharsuinn, but if the streams are high the latter may be safer. From the Bealach Crudhain, rejoin the path that goes down to the north-east from the Bealach Bhearnais to Pollan Buidhe, and thence the track to Craig.

It may be mentioned that either of the two bothies in the vicinity, at Bearnais and Bendronaig Lodge, afford alternative bases from which to explore these hills. In particular, the south-west ridge of Bidein via the spur of Sail Riabhaich affords a pleasant and relatively unfrequented way up the mountain. Paths that lead to these bothies are shown on the OS 1;50,000 map (Sheet 25);

see also the descriptions of Creag Dhubh Mhor and Beinn Dronaig, below.

Moruisg; 928m; (OS Sheet 25; NH101499); *big water*

Sgurr nan Ceannaichean; 915m; (OS Sheet 25; NH087480); *peak of the merchants or peddlers*

These two peaks are much more easily accessible than those that have just been described. They afford excellent views of the Maoile Lunndaidh-Sgurr Choinnich group to the south, and to the start of the Northern Highlands across Glen Carron. Moruisg has several subsidiary tops extending eastwards and enclosing a corrie with several rock climbs above Loch Cnoc na Mointeich. Sgurr nan Ceannaichean has an impressively craggy west face with only a few climbs so far recorded, possibly because the cliffs are somewhat broken up by vegetation.

The two hills are most readily climbed from the A890. Park in a parking area 1.5km west of the outlet of Loch Sgamhain. From here a bridge crosses the River Carron (NH082520), and another bridge under the railway leads out to open moorland. The most direct line of ascent to Moruisg is ahead to the south-east. However, it is easier underfoot to follow the stalkers path at first. This goes south-west and then south by the Alltan na Feola. After 2km turn left off the path and go east, well below a cliff, the Creag nan Calman.

To the left of the cliff grass slopes rise steeply at first and then more easily to the summit. From here it is about 2.5km to Sgurr nan Ceannaichean by way of a mainly grassy connecting ridge. The final section of the ridge is pleasantly steeper and narrower. The summit cairn is at the southern end of a small plateau. Retrace one's steps down the narrow section of the ridge, and continue moderately steeply down to the north on a broad spur to the Alltan na Feola. This is crossed to re-join the stalkers path that leads back to the starting point.

Sgurr nan Ceannaichean and Moruisg can also be climbed from Craig via the glen of the Allt a' Chonais. After 5.5km, from just beyond the bend in the glen at Pollan Buidhe, a stalkers path ascends northwards to about 750m on Sgurr nan Ceannaichean, whence grassy slopes lead to the summit. After reaching Moruisg another stalkers path can be used for much of the descent, commencing at the 750m contour (NH108488) and zigzagging down to the glen just east of Glenuaig Lodge. Alternatively, the traverse can be continued along the eastern tops to Carn Gorm (875m), with views of the northern corrie en route. From Carn Gorm, descent to the south brings one to the Gleann Fhiodhaig path about 3km east of Glenuaig Lodge. A longish but easy and pleasant walk leads back to Craig.

A ski traverse of the two mountains, starting and finishing to the west of Loch Sgamhain as indicated above, is described in *Ski Mountaineering in Scotland*. There are potentially tricky sections on both hills, and the description should be consulted for details.

Sgurr na Feartaig; 862m; (OS Sheet 25; NH054453); *peak of the sea-pinks* or *thrift*

In plan, Sgurr na Feartaig resembles a sickle with its blade at the east end and facing north. Its northern corries overlook Craig and Lair in Glen Carron; its grassy southern slopes fall steeply towards the Abhainn Bhearnais. The most rewarding way of climbing the hill is to traverse the summit ridge. From Craig, walk up the track that leads into the upper part of the glen of the Allt a' Chonais above the forest. Cross the burn by a footbridge at NH070481. A stalkers path goes up the hill, starting about 50m to the right of the bridge. High up and in misty conditions it is important to be aware that there is a false top (819m) on a transverse ridge. Continue directly over this

Bidein a' Choire Sheasgaich from Beinn Tharsuinn

ridge, heading south, and descend to Loch Sgurr na Feartaig. This is passed on its west side. The stalkers path skirts the summit to the right, so the final ascent is up stony ground. In clear weather a grand view of Beinn Tharsuinn and the Bearneas basin unfolds.

If the traverse is to be made, continue for about 3km to the west along the airy ridge with fine views, especially across Glen Carron to the peaks of Coire Lair and the Torridonian mountains to the north-west. At a junction with another path at Baobh-bhacan Dhuba (NH027449) go right (north) and descend to the River Carron opposite Lair. Formerly there was a wire bridge across the river, but at the time of writing the bridge is not in place. Therefore unless the river is low enough to be forded safely, follow the forest track eastwards to the junction with the outward route just east of Craig. This is in any case a pleasanter way of returning to the starting point than walking along the main road.

If a shorter walk than the traverse is desired, either return from the summit by the route of ascent, or descend steeply to the Bealach Bhearnais and return from there. The ascent can also be combined with Beinn Tharsuinn, although, as noted above, the latter hill is usually traversed on the way to Bidein a' Choire Sheasgaich and Lurg Mhor.

The northern corries of Sgurr na Feartaig contain impressive ice climbing in cold weather, including *The Stonker* (V,5) an ascent of the waterfall marked on the 1:50,000 map, and can be accessed either by a path starting up the east bank of the Allt Coire a' Bhainidh from the forest track or by a path up Coire Leiridh.

Creag Dhubh Mhor; 612m; (OS Sheet 25; NG982404); *big black cliff*

This outlying hill rises from the moors between Strathcarron and the Bearnais area.

North-east across Loch Monar from Lurg Mhor

Though of modest height, its isolated position makes it a fine viewpoint between mountains and sea. For this reason, and because the summit area could be confusing in mist, the ascent is best done in clear weather. A longish half-day should suffice.

The approach is by the path that goes from Achintee to Bearnais bothy. The start of the path is somewhat difficult to find. From the village centre, a signed path goes uphill past a transformer station. After 50 metres, turn left on an indistinct, slightly descending path by a fence and ditch. Cross a stream and ascend a heathery hillock. The path soon becomes more obvious, overlooking the gorge of the River Taodail, and then following a tributary of that river to below the steep northern aspect of the hill. It is best to continue slightly beyond this steep face to about NG990414. Leave the path here and turn south to gain the gentle north-east ridge. There are a number of subsidiary tops; the actual summit has a small cairn and overlooks a tiny lochan to the south-east.

An interesting circuit can be made by descending to the south and south-west. A group of lochans is passed, with the option of climbing Carn Geuradainn (594m) on the way. This latter hill has an even more isolated feel than Creag Dhubh Mhor. It affords at least an equally fine panorama, and is one of a minority of hills with a trig point constructed of stone rather than concrete.

About 1km south-west of the lochans a path from the Bendronaig Lodge estate road to Achintee is joined for the return to the starting point. (This path was mentioned earlier as one of the ways of finishing the cross-country walk from Struy or Inchvuilt to Strathcarron.)

Beinn Dronaig; 797m; (OS Sheet 25; NH037382); *hill of the little ridge or hump*

Last but not least, lonely Beinn Dronaig. This whaleback of a hill, set in the central wilds, is usually approached either from Attadale via the Bendronaig Lodge estate road, or from Achintee via the path, mentioned above, that joins the estate road. The Attadale route is slightly longer in distance, but is easier, and is described first. There is very limited space for parking at the railway station. Alternatively, it may be possible to obtain permission to park in the grounds of the Attadale Estate, particularly if the walk is preceded by a visit to the gardens.

Take the estate road past Strathan and then uphill by a conifer plantation. The track passes by the little Loch an Droighinn and then climbs further to a col between Aonach Dubh (461m) and Meall Ruadh (454m). Here the character of the country changes for the wilder as one descends gently in the direction of Bendronaig Lodge. The road crosses the impressive Uisge Dubh by a bridge about 1.5km before the lodge is reached. The bothy affords a lunch spot.

Climb directly up the steep but mainly grassy northern slope, and then head east along the broad summit ridge, which rises with undulations to the trig point. On a clear day there is a magnificent view of the Monar and Bearnais basins, with most of the mountains that have been described in this and the previous chapter encircling the horizon. The round trip by this route is 28km. Use of a bicycle between Attadale and Bendronaig Lodge greatly shortens the walking distance but the hilly and unsurfaced track does not make for leisurely cycling. The path from Achintee starts in the village as described for Creag Dhubh Mhor. Instead of turning left by the fence and ditch as in that description, continue uphill ahead. After some minor twists the path settles into a south-easterly direction and crosses wild moorland, joining the Attadale to Bendronaig Lodge estate road at NG995386. This is an attractive way by relatively unfrequented terrain, but it is less suitable than the Attadale estate road if daylight is likely to be limited for the return.

Beinn Dronaig, Bidein a' Choire Sheasgaich, Lurg Mhor and An Cruachan from An Socach

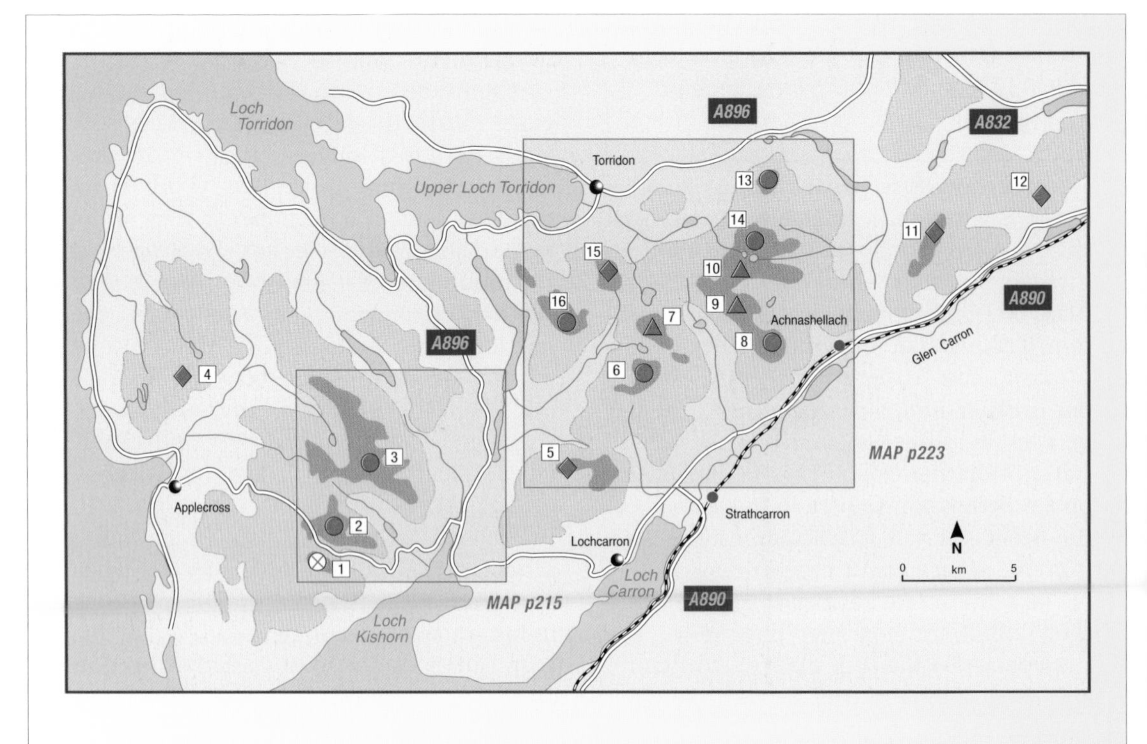

1.	Meall Gorm	710m	O	p214
2.	Sgurr a' Chaorachain	792m	C	p214
3.	Beinn Bhan	896m	C	p216
4.	Beinn a' Chlachain	626m	G	p218
5.	Sgurr a' Gharaidh	732m	G	p219
6.	An Ruadh-stac	892m	C	p220
7.	Maol Chean-dearg	933m	M	p220
8.	Fuar Tholl	907m	C	p221
9.	Sgorr Ruadh	962m	M	p221
10	Beinn Liath Mhor	926m	M	p224
11.	Carn Breac	678m	G	p224
12.	Beinn na Feusaige	625m	G	p224
13.	Sgurr Dubh	782m	C	p224
14.	Sgorr nan Lochan Uaine	871m	C	p224
15.	Beinn na h-Eaglaise	736m	G	p225
16.	Beinn Damh	903m	C	p226

Chapter 11

Applecross and Coulin

Jim Teesdale

West from Fuar Tholl to An Ruadh-stac and Maol Chean-dearg

Beyond the Inverness to Kyle of Lochalsh railway line, the character of the West Coast mountains suddenly changes, marking the start of the Northern Highlands. The long high ridges of the Western Highlands are left behind and the hills take on a more rugged individuality. Dark red Torridonian sandstone dominates the landscape, resting on a base of ancient grey Lewisian gneiss. Glaciation and subsequent weathering has sculpted monumental tops, skirted by terraced cliffs and great scooped out corries, enhanced by the occasional sprinkling of white Cambrian quartzite.

From the Applecross peninsula, a narrow range of rocky hills stretches east to Achnasheen. Bounded by Glen Carron to the south-east, Glen Docherty to the north-east and Glen Torridon to the north-west, these are hills of great character. Lacking perhaps the grandeur and reputation of their northern neighbours in Torridon, they offer challenging walking and superb climbing, easily reached by an excellent network of paths.

The name Applecross is a corruption of Aber Crossan (*estuary of the river Crossan*) and refers to the small bay, the village overlooking it and the entire peninsula. The latter is easily recognised on large scale maps and satellite photographs by its distinctive fish-tail shape, whose long straight western edge faces across the Inner Sound to the islands of Raasay and Rona, with the Trotternish hills of Skye beyond. On either side, long fingers of sea reach deep into the mainland hills, with Loch Torridon, Loch Shieldaig and Upper Loch Torridon to the north, and Loch Carron and Loch Kishorn to the south.

Archaeological excavations of a rock shelter on the coast at Sand, north of Applecross village, have revealed evidence of one of the earliest sites of human occupation in Scotland, dating from the Mesolithic period, 7500 BC. Inland, bleak and barren moorland, generously spotted with lochs and lochans, rises gently from the west to the tops of the hills which fall away much more steeply to the east. Until the present generation, this mountain barrier shut off the small communities dotted around the coast and kept them among the most remote and isolated in the Highlands, dependent on the sea for communication with the

The craggy north-east flanks of Sgorr Ruadh, facing Beinn Liath Mhor

outside world. Even well into the 20th century, MacBrayne's Stornoway mailboat from Kyle or Mallaig was the main carrier of passengers and goods.

Using a slight breach in the mountain barrier, the famous road across the Bealach na Ba (*pass of the cattle*) was one of the last of the Parliamentary roads, completed in 1822. One of the highest roads in Britain, it reaches 625m after climbing steeply up from sea level at Tornapress, at the head of Loch Kishorn. The notorious hairpin bends near the top have been improved over the years but winter snow can still block the road for long periods. Hill climbing visitors may not feel inclined to continue the long gradual descent to Applecross village, but the coastline is well worth exploring. From the head of Loch Shieldaig, the road around the north coast of the peninsula was finally completed in 1975 to service the Ministry of Defence development at Sand.

Applecross is separated from the hills to the east by Glen Shieldaig which runs roughly north-south and carries the A896 from Kishorn to Shieldaig. The continuation of this road along the south side of Upper Loch Torridon into Glen Torridon was only completed in the 1960s. Sections of the old pony track still wind through the woods between the bays of Loch Torridon below the new road.

On the north side of Glen Torridon, Liathach and Beinn Eighe dominate the road through to Kinlochewe. On the other side of the glen, the more open outlook to the less intimidating Coulin hills makes an appealing contrast. Coulin is the name of the largest of the sporting estates which make up the area and is also used to describe the whole range. Much of the history and culture of Coulin is tied in with Torridon, described in the next chapter, and part of the appeal of the Coulin hills is the spectacular view north to their magnificent neighbours.

Beyond Loch Clair, the northern corner of the area has little of interest to climbers and hillwalkers. From the village of Kinlochewe the A832 runs east, climbing steeply up through

Glen Docherty. As it starts the descent into Strath Bran, the outlook opens out again, giving fine views south-west across into the heart of the Coulin hills. Achnasheen has always been an important junction for road and rail travellers and in recent years the village has lost a hotel but gained a roundabout. The hotel bar was a popular watering hole for passing hill-goers which sadly burned to the ground, and the roundabout is part of an on-going program of road improvements, partly funded by the European Community, which is improving access to this whole corner of the North-west Highlands.

The Kyle of Lochalsh railway line and the A890 make the short climb south-west into Glen Carron before the long scenic descent to the sea at the head of Loch Carron. At this point the railway continues to its destination along the southern shores of the loch while the A896 leads into Lochcarron village, strung out along the north shore. A dead end road continues along the coast beyond Strome Castle, an interesting corner to explore when the hills are out of condition, while the main road turns north then west. After a short climb, the narrow glen of the Abhainn Cumhang a' Ghlinne leads down to the head of Loch Kishorn.

The North Sea oil boom of the 1970s saw the development of a platform fabrication yard on the northern shores of the loch. Apart from the deserted concrete wharf, little else remains of this incongruous project, the economic benefits of which were very short term. Much of the area remains as traditional sporting estates, with the usual mixture of crofting, fish farming, forestry and tourism sustaining the small communities around the periphery.

Access and Transport

By road: from Inverness the A9 continues north to the roundabout at Tore, where the A835 leads west to Ullapool. The A832 to Gairloch branches off just beyond Garve and passes through Achnasheen and Kinlochewe. From Achnasheen the A890 passes through Achnashellach and Strathcarron before leading south to join the A87 Glen Shiel to Kyle of Lochalsh road west of Dornie. Just north of Strathcarron, the A896 links Lochcarron, Shieldaig and Torridon, joining the A832 at Kinlochewe. Applecross is reached either by the famous climb over the Bealach na Ba which leaves the A896 just north of Kishorn or by the newer coast road from just south of Shieldaig.

By bus: Strathcarron to Shieldaig to Torridon; Applecross to Shieldaig to Torridon; Shieldaig to Achnasheen (Postbus, tel: 08457-740740 and Duncan Maclennan, tel: 01520-755239).

By rail: the line from Inverness to Kyle of Lochalsh runs south of the Coulin hills with stations at Achnasheen, Achnashellach and Strathcarron.

By foot: see Paths in Applecross and Coulin, *p216*.

Accommodation and Information

Hotels and guest houses: Achnasheen, Applecross, Kinlochewe, Kishorn, Lochcarron, Shieldaig, Strathcarron and Torridon.

SYHA hostel: Torridon (tel: 0870-004-1154)

Independent hostels: Craig (near Achnashellach) (tel: 01520-766232); Kinlochewe Hotel Bunkhouse (tel: 01445-760253)

Club huts: Ling Hut, Glen Torridon (Scottish Mountaineering Club); Inver Croft, Near Achnasheen (Jacobites Mountaineering Club)

Campsites: Applecross (tel: 01520-744268 & 744284); Torridon (tel: 01349-868486)

Tourist Information Centre: High Street, Lochcarron (tel: 01520-722357) (seasonal).

Maps

Ordnance Survey 1:50,000 Landranger sheets 19 (Gairloch & Ullapool), 24 (Raasay and Applecross), 25 (Glen Carron and Glen Affric).

Principal Hills

Meall Gorm; 710m; (OS Sheet 24; NG778409); *blue hill*

Meall Gorm lacks any designation and does not feature in any lists. However, the mountain dominates the view west across Loch Kishorn and its summit is uniquely accessible by a short, easy climb from the road as it crosses the Bealach na Ba. The top makes a magnificent viewpoint overlooking the extensive Applecross coastline to the islands of the Inner Sound and the hills of Skye beyond.

From the summit, a ridge extends south-east almost 2km towards Loch Kishorn. Unbroken slopes to the south offer little of interest but to the north and east a line of imposing cliffs enclose the Allt a' Chumhaing. Impressive from the road, these cliffs are too terraced and vegetated for good rock climbing but have a number of worthwhile and very accessible winter climbs. *Blue Pillar* (180m V,6 1958) climbs the conspicuous narrow pillar on the left of the massive *Cobalt Buttress* (170m IV,5 1970), which also has the sustained and varied *Rattlesnake (*200m V,7 1993).

Sgurr a' Chaorachain; 792m; (OS Sheet 24; NG796417); *peak of the torrent*

The southern cliffs of Sgurr a' Chaorachain tower above the road as it climbs up from the head of Loch Kishorn towards the Bealach na Ba. The summit of this dramatic mountain lies at the south-east end of a great crescent-shaped ridge which runs west then north some 4km to the Bealach nan Arr. On its eastern side a series of steep crags and terraces enclose the enormous Coire nan Arr (*giant's corrie*) which separates Sgurr a' Chaorachain from Beinn Bhan to the north-east. The easily accessible north top (773m) lies close to the Bealach na Ba but is marred by a large communications mast and access track. From this top, a rocky spur drops away to the east in a series of sandstone towers, terminating in the cliffs of A' Chioch (*the breast*) (Na Ciochan on the OS map). Well seen from the road as it crosses the Russell Burn, this forms the mountain's finest feature and encloses the north side of the rugged Coire a' Chaorachain.

The summit can easily be reached by a rising traverse from the road at the Bealach na Ba, but to appreciate the true character of the mountain a longer approach is recommended. Coire nan Arr is drained by the Russell Burn, which flows south-east beneath the road. There is space for parking on the east side of the bridge, the start of a rough path which follows the stream and then skirts the shore of Loch Coire nan Arr. However from the next bend up the road a rough track has been bulldozed to a dam at the outlet of the loch.

From the head of the loch a steep climb west leads below the towers of A' Chioch into Coire a' Chaorachain with its tiny lochan. The broken rocky headwall above is known as the Summit Buttress, south-east of which a steep climb up grass and boulders leads to a broad col at about 700m. The summit stands 1km further east along the ridge. A quicker route follows a small path up a narrow slope on the north side.

From the summit, the most direct route of return to the Russell Burn road bridge follows the crest of the south-east ridge and involves scrambling down a series of short easy walls linked by grassy ledges. For a longer round, head for the mast on the north top and continue north to the Bealach nan Arr, below the south-west shoulder of Beinn Bhan.

Sgurr a' Chaorachain offers a variety of climbing possibilities. The cliffs of A' Chioch were explored on several occasions early in the 20th century by Scottish Mountaineering Club stalwarts such as Collie, Slingsby, Ling and Glover but it was not until August 1960 that Tom Patey and Chris Bonington discovered what they

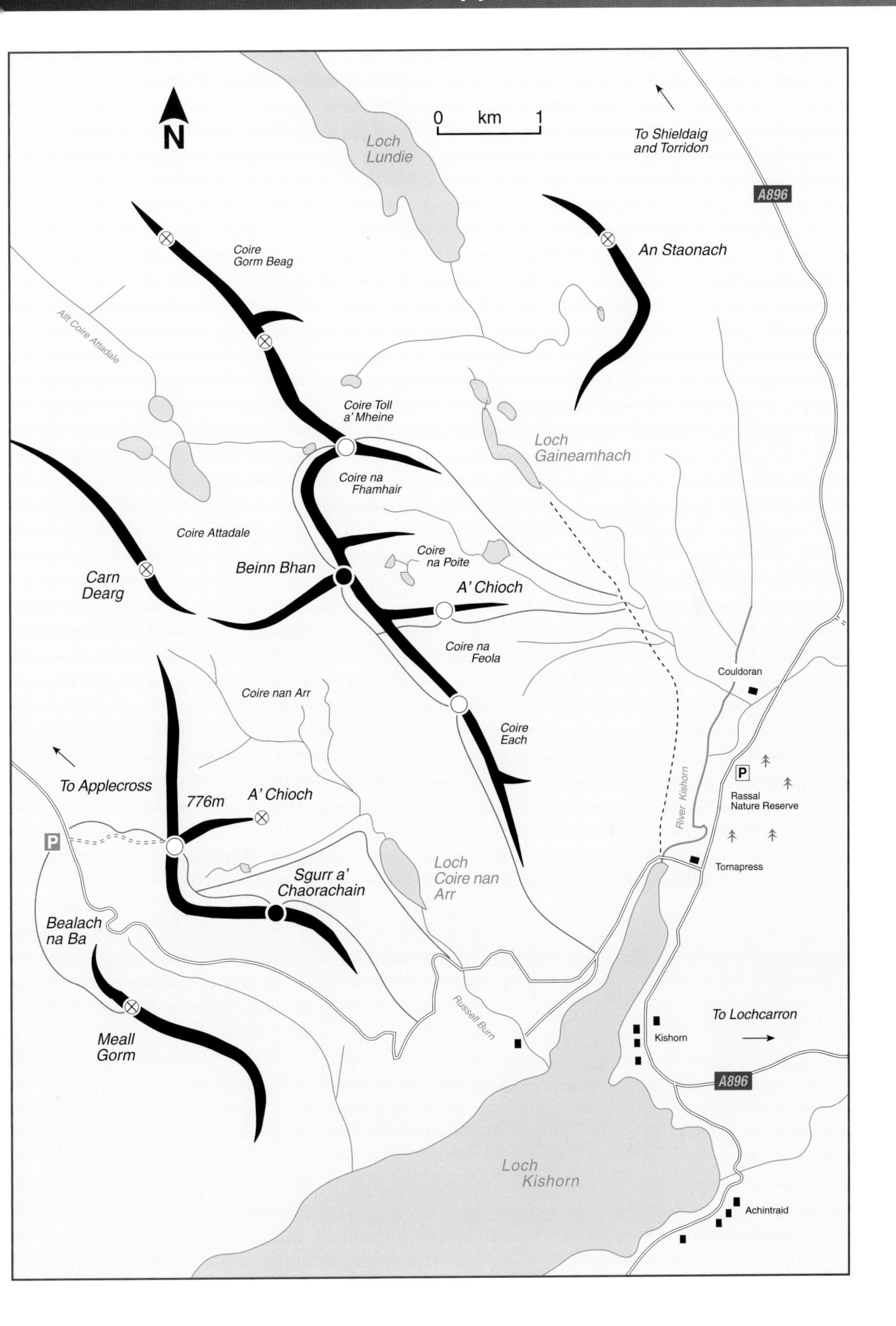

N
0 km 1
Loch Lundie
To Shieldaig and Torridon
A896
An Staonach
Coire Gorm Beag
Allt Coire Attadale
Coire Toll a' Mheine
Loch Gaineamhach
Coire na Fhamhair
Coire Attadale
Coire na Poite
Carn Dearg
Beinn Bhan
A' Chioch
Coire na Feola
Couldoran
Coire nan Arr
Coire Each
P
Rassal Nature Reserve
To Applecross
776m
A' Chioch
River Kishorn
P
Tornapress
Loch Coire nan Arr
Sgurr a' Chaorachain
Bealach na Ba
Russell Burn
To Lochcarron
Kishorn
A896
Meall Gorm
Loch Kishorn
Achintraid

described as 'the Diff. to end all Diffs!'. Climbed during their now famous 'holiday', which yielded a clutch of new routes in Torridon, Applecross and Skye, *Cioch Nose* (135m Severe 1960) has become a popular classic.

Starting from the Middle Ledge and climbing the south-east side of the buttress, the route finishes on the top of A' Chioch. Continuing over the series of towers which form the crest of this eastern spur gives a magnificent scramble, joining the summit ridge at the mast. Many climbing parties approach the climbs on A' Chioch from the Bealach na Ba, following the access track up to the mast. A broad grassy gully 100 metres to the east gives an easy descent into Coire a' Chaorachain.

The roadside South Face, Scotland's most accessible mountain crag, was also explored by Patey on subsequent visits and offers good clean rock climbs in the middle grades. *Sword of Gideon* (70m VS 1961) was the original route of the crag and is still considered a very enjoyable climb. The North Buttresses give some good winter climbs, as does the easily accessible Summit Buttress.

Beinn Bhan; 896m; (OS Sheet 24; NG804450); *white hill*

Beinn Bhan is the highest and finest of the hills on the Applecross peninsula. Its broad summit ridge rises gently from the head of Loch Kishorn and gradually curves north-west for some 8km before sloping down beyond an un-named top (712m) into the Applecross and Glenshieldaig Forests.

Like its neighbours, Beinn Bhan's finest features face east and comprise a dramatic row of six distinctive corries, lined by steep terraced cliffs and dark gullies separated by narrow towering sandstone spurs. This unique mountain wall can be seen from the A896 Kishorn to Shieldaig road and makes any approach to the hill from this side all the more interesting. From south to north these corries are:

Coire Each (*horse corrie*),
Coire na Feola (*corrie of the flesh*),
Coire na Poite (*corrie of the pot*),
Coire nan Fhamhair (*giant's corrie*),
Coire Toll a' Mheine (*corrie of the hole in the skin*),
Coire Gorm Beag (*little blue corrie*).

Paths in Applecross and Coulin

A network of excellent paths criss-crosses Applecross and Coulin. Originally built to facilitate stalking, some are also traditional rights of way. The following are particularly useful for approaching the Coulin hills from either Glen Carron or Glen Torridon:

1) Coulags (Glen Carron) to Annat (Loch Torridon) 15km. The A890 Glen Carron road crosses the Fionn-abhainn 3km north-east of the Strathcarron junction. From the bridge, the path follows the east side of the river, past the new Coulags Lodge. A wooden bridge crosses the river after 2km and further upstream, 1km beyond Coire Fionnaraich bothy, the path branches. The most direct route continues north-west, past Loch Coire Fionnaraich, crossing the Bealach na Lice (420m) then dropping down to Loch an Eion. The longer left branch climbs over the col between Maol Chean-dearg and Meall nan Ceapairean, then drops below the north face of An Ruadh-stac to Loch Coire an Ruadh-staic. After traversing the western flanks of Maol Chean-dearg, the path rejoins the other branch at Loch an Eion, then gently drops down to Annat at the head of Upper Loch Torridon.

2) Achnashellach (Glen Carron) to Annat (Loch Torridon) 16km. From the A890 Glen Carron road below Achnashellach railway station, follow the private road to the station. Cross the line and continue a short distance up the track opposite to a junction of forestry roads. Turn sharp left and follow the road for a few hundred metres until a new path branches off, sharp left again, leading to a gate in the deer fence, to join the Coire Lair path. (It is no longer possible to follow this path from its original junction with the railway west of Station Cottage.) The path follows the east side of the River Lair and its impressive gorge. Beyond the forest the gradient steepens. As it eases off again, magnificent Coire Lair opens out ahead. With the dark sandstone cliffs of Sgorr Ruadh to the left and the pale quartzite screes of Beinn Liath Mhor to the right, the path gradually continues to climb, trending west to reach the Bealach Coire Lair (650m) at the head of the corrie. (This pass is not named on the OS map but is distinguished by a small lochan on its south side). The path then drops north a short

Coire Each is somewhat open, but the next three corries are particularly fine. Coire na Feola and Coire na Poite each have an outer corrie leading to a higher inner corrie below a magnificent back wall. Coire na Poite is enclosed by two narrow sandstone spurs which form the prominent towering buttresses of A' Chioch to the south and A' Phoit to the north. Beyond A' Phoit, Coire nan Fhamhair is enclosed on its south side by one of the steepest cliffs on the Scottish mainland.

Coire Toll a' Mheine presents a steep north-east face towards Loch Lundie, which is overlooked in turn by Coire Gorm Beag. The unremarkable western flanks of the mountain fall away south-west into Coire nan Arr and west into Coire Attadale, two vast corries which meet at the Bealach nan Arr, north of Sgurr a' Chaorachain.

The approach to Beinn Bhan via the eastern corries starts from the road bridge over the River Kishorn near Tornapress and follows a good path which leads up towards Loch Gaineamhach. For a precipitous scramble, leave the path and follow the streams up to Lochan Coire na Poite. Climb south-west up the ridge to the top of A' Chioch then drop slightly to the foot of the final steep section which finishes south-east of the summit. In winter this becomes a much more serious undertaking and parties should be prepared for an excellent snow and ice climb at Grade II. A much less serious alternative route from Lochan Coire na Poite climbs the spur which forms the north side of Coire na Fhamhair.

From the summit, the quickest and most straightforward descent follows the main ridge south-east to reach the wide uniform slope which leads down to the road at the head of Loch Kishorn. Alternatively, an energetic party could continue south-west to the Bealach nan Arr and take in Sgurr a' Chaorachain. If suitable transport can be arranged, continuing north-west to descend into Srath Maol Chaluim and follow the Applecross River to Applecross Bay gives an enjoyable coast-to-coast traverse of the peninsula.

In winter, Beinn Bhan offers some of the finest climbing in the Northern Highlands, and good conditions are found here surprisingly often considering its low altitude and proximity to the sea. Patey and Bonington recorded the first major winter climb in

distance before contouring west again to the Bealach Ban (550m). Dropping south-west, the path joins the path from Coulags as it climbs up to the Bealach na Lice.

3) Ling Hut (Glen Torridon) connection. From the Coire Dubh Mor bridge on the A896 Glen Torridon road, a path around the east side of Lochan an Iasgair passes the Ling Hut and then climbs gradually south. The path continues further than indicated on the OS map, until it eventually peters out on the north-west slopes of Beinn Liath Mhor. A faint trail of cairns continues 1km south to meet the Achnashellach to Annat path midway between the Bealach Coire Lair and Bealach Ban.

4) Craig or Achnashellach (Glen Carron) to Glen Torridon – the Coulin Pass 14km. The historic Coulin Pass was described as early as 1803 by James Hogg, the Ettrick Shepherd. The Old Pony Track which he followed was obliterated by forestry for many years until its restoration in 1998 by Forest Enterprise and the Scottish Rights of Way Society and the start is now marked by a signpost and information board beside the A890 Glen Carron road between Craig and Achnashellach at NH029490. The path climbs the hillside above, which has been clear felled and partially replanted. Posts mark the line of the path until it joins the forestry track from Achnashellach, a few hundred metres below the pass. This track can also be joined lower down by continuing straight ahead at the junction above Achnashellach railway station.

From the pass, the track descends gradually northwards, crossing the River Coulin at the Easan Dorcha bridge. Another path climbs south-west up this beautiful glen, with its gnarled pines and sparkling waterfalls, crossing the south-east flanks of Beinn Liath Mhor to join the Coire Lair path. The Coulin track continues to a junction near some estate buildings. The right branch crosses the river again to Torran-cuillin, then a boggy path continues north-west past Loch Coulin to join the private road to Coulin Lodge. This road skirts the east side of Loch Clair with its classic views of Liathach and finally joins the A896 in Glen Torridon.

Loch Kishorn, Meall Gorm and Sgurr a' Chaorachain

1969 with the popular *March Hare's Gully* (300m IV,4) in Coire na Poite and there are now a variety of routes in all the eastern corries. The huge back wall of Coire na Poite often holds the biggest ice sheet in Scotland, climbed direct by *Silver Tear* (350m V,5 1977) which takes a line slightly left of the centre of the wall.

On the very steep face which forms the left side of Coire nan Fhamhair, *Gully of the Gods* (180m VI,6 1983) climbs the overhanging central gully, while *Die Riesenwand* (400m VII,6 1980) takes the line of least resistance up the face to its left. In 1989, local mountain guide Martin Moran made a bold continuous girdle traverse of the central triad of corries Feola, Poite and Fhamhair, following a line of natural ledges and terraces to give *Das Reingold* 2800m IV.

Beinn a' Chlachain; 626m; (OS Sheet 24; NG724490); *hill of the stepping stones*

Beinn a' Chlachain stands to the north-east of Applecross Bay and gives excellent views across to Raasay, Rona and Skye. Its south-eastern slopes drop steeply into Srath Maol Chaluim, which gives the most direct approach. Vehicles can only be taken a short distance up the glen. Follow the western edge of the plantation above the second bridge, continuing more steeply to gain the broad ridge above.

Continue climbing north-east past sandstone outcrops and several lochans to reach the summit. In descent it is easier to continue down the long gentle south-west ridge to meet the footpath from the road at Cruarg. This path crosses the shoulder known locally as 'the Gualainn' and predates the coast road.

Sgurr a' Gharaidh; 732m; (OS Sheet 24; NG884443); *peak of the dyke*

Sgurr a' Gharaidh stands between the hills of the Applecross peninsula to the west and the Coulin hills to the north-east and forms the highest point on the rugged and wild terrain immediately north of Lochcarron. More complex and craggy than the OS map suggests, it offers fine views of its more popular neighbours. The west ridge gives the most convenient approach, reached from the A896 Lochcarron to Shieldaig road at the south end of Loch an Loin. Follow the track north-east past a cottage, then head up towards the ridge, where a series of rocky walls offer plenty of scrambling.

A slightly longer but more interesting approach to the west ridge starts roughly 2km further south along the road, at the Rassal Ashwood Nature Reserve, where an outcrop of Durness limestone has produced a rich brown soil. A walk through the woodland here is a delight, particularly in early summer when primroses and orchids abound and the birds are in full song.

Above the reserve, a narrow strip of hillside has been fenced to prevent grazing. The resulting regeneration is striking evidence of the damage caused by sheep and deer. Continue climbing north-east along the narrow limestone ridge which runs above and to the west of the impressive wooded defile of the Allt Mor, with its spectacular waterfall. This ridge meets an all-terrain-vehicle track (not marked on the OS map) which leads into the broad corrie below the west ridge of the peak.

The final climb to the summit is not recommended in poor visibility as the terrain is so complex and rugged. On a fine day it is

Coire na Poite, Beinn Bhan

An Ruadh-stac from the Bealach a' Choire Ghairbh

worth continuing east past a series of lochans to Glas Bheinn (729m) (OS Sheet 25). This also has some impressive crags, particularly on the north side, where a number of summer and winter climbs have been recorded. A steep but straightforward descent south-east leads to Tullich at the head of Loch Carron, if arrangements have been made for transport. Otherwise a good stalkers path climbs around the north side of both hills, over the Bealach a' Ghlas Chnoic, back to Loch an Loin.

An Ruadh-stac; 892m; (OS Sheet 25; NG921480); *steep red hill*

Maol Chean-dearg; 933m; (OS Sheet 25; NG924499); *bald red head*

The grey quartzite cone of An Ruadh-stac is the most westerly of the major hills on the north side of Glen Carron, though its name does not seem appropriate. With its steep north face in profile, the mountain is well seen from the A896 Kishorn to Shieldaig road as it passes Loch Coultrie. In contrast, its taller northern neighbour, Maol Chean-dearg lives up to its name and its rugged sandstone dome can just be seen from Coulags on the A890 Achnasheen to Lochcarron road.

The hills are usually climbed together, using the excellent Coulags to Annat path. The southern approach tends to be more popular, with ample parking in the vicinity of the Fionn-abhainn (*fair burn*) road bridge. Beyond Coire Fionnaraich bothy, a distinctive boulder, Clach nan Con-fionn (*stone of Fingal's dogs*), is reputed to have been used by the legendary Fionn Mac Cumhail to tie up his dogs Bran and Luath while hunting in the glen. A short distance beyond, the path divides.

The left branch climbs below the craggy nose of Meall nan Ceapairean (655m) (*hill of the bannock*) to reach the Bealach a' Choire Ghairbh (c590m). Three ridges converge here and the path from Annat reaches this point by climbing around the east side of Beinn na h-Eaglaise to Loch an Eion, then skirting the west side of Maol Chean-dearg below the north face of An Ruadh-stac. A rough path continues north-west up quartzite screes to a level shoulder below the final dome of Maol Chean-dearg, a great pile of sandstone blocks. The small summit plateau has an enormous cairn near its north-west edge. Continue a few metres beyond this to enjoy the magnificent view to the north.

The northern and eastern flanks of Maol Chean-dearg have several bands of crags but ascent and descent via Loch an Eion is possible by the mountain's north-west spur. Descent to the Bealach na Lice to the north-east requires good visibility and good route finding skills, making a longer round possible, taking in Sgorr Ruadh and Beinn Liath Mhor. However most parties will prefer to leave these for another day, returning to the Bealach a' Choire Gairbh before continuing to An Ruadh-stac.

Four lochans sit below the north face of An Ruadh-stac, each one at a different level. A rocky ridge climbs south-west above the two highest lochans, giving a rough scramble over quartzite blocks to the summit. More challenging scrambling up long slabs of polished quartzite can be found on the south-east flank. The easiest descent is to reverse the climb, but on a clear day there are two more interesting possibilities.

Descend due south over the moors, picking a way between quartzite outcrops and tiny lochans, heading for Torr na h-Iolaire, then down easy slopes to the Glen Carron road. Alternatively, return to the Bealach a' Choire Ghairbh and make a short climb east to the top of Meall nan Ceapairean, which gives good views further east. Follow the south-east ridge until it is possible to descend back into the glen, heading for the Fionn-abhainn footbridge.

Some climbing has been recorded on the north face of An Ruadh-stac which comprises two tiers of blocky quartzite. The cliffs above Loch an Eion on Meall Chean-dearg and on the north side of Meall nan Ceapairean also have some climbs.

Fuar Tholl; 907m; (OS Sheet 25; NG975489); *cold hole*

Sgorr Ruadh; 962m; (OS Sheet 25; NG959505); *red peak*

Fuar Tholl and Sgorr Ruadh form a rugged 5km long ridge running north-west from Glen Carron. On their north-east side, a series of distinctive sandstone buttresses overlooking Coire Lair can be seen from as far away as the A832 Achnasheen to Kinlochewe road just before it crosses into Glen Docherty. The round of Coire Lair, taking in the two Munros Beinn Liath Mhor and Sgorr Ruadh and the fine Corbett Fuar Tholl, makes an excellent outing in either direction.

Seen from Lochcarron the gentle profile of Fuar Tholl has given rise to the local name 'Wellington's Nose' but from closer at hand, as one previous author noted, 'few mountains look so impressive from a railway station'. What catches the eye from Achnashellach is the impressive South-East Cliff which overlooks a small corrie just below the summit.

West of this line of crags, the southern slopes of the mountain are usually avoided. Steep heather interspersed with exposed sandstone slabs requires careful route finding, with easier ground further west. From the Coulags path the uniform south-west slopes are an uninspiring climb, but would give a safe descent route in bad weather. The south-east ridge of the mountain rises from a distinctive rocky nose on a lower band of crags. The upper part of this ridge forms a short narrow arete, reached by leaving the railway west of the River Lair, crossing the heather moor then scrambling up easy-angled slabs into the south-east corrie.

Fuar Tholl and Sgorr Ruadh are usually approached by the Coire Lair path from Achnashellach. Just inside the lip of the corrie a side path to the left crosses the river before climbing south-west towards the broad Bhealaich Mhoir (c.660m), which separates the two hills. This river crossing can be difficult in spate conditions, in

Fuar Tholl and Sgorr Ruadh from the east

which case a long detour around the head of Loch Coire Lair gives a safer alternative.

The most distinctive feature on this side of Fuar Tholl is the magnificent Mainreachan Buttress. Variously described as resembling 'the side of a pillar box (complete with overhang above)' and 'a great rock tombstone', few climbers will fail to be impressed by the sight of its 250m of vertical terraced sandstone towering above them. Leave the path and climb south towards the foot of the buttress, continuing up grass and scree to its left to emerge a short distance west of the summit of Fuar Tholl.

Extensive views complete what many consider to be one of Scotland's finest Corbetts. Continuing west along the summit ridge, Creag Mainnrichean (895m) forms the top of the Mainreachan Buttress, whose sheer profile is dramatically seen from the next top to the west. From here, a steep descent north-west down a rocky ridge leads to the lochans scattered across the broad Bhealaich Mhoir. This ridge needs care in mist and in winter as it may not be obvious to locate.

The summit of Sgorr Ruadh can be reached by a straightforward climb from here. Loch a' Bhealaich Mhoir, the largest of the cluster of lochans around the col, makes a useful landmark in descent. Parties approaching from Beinn Liath Mhor, doing the popular round of Coire Lair, will drop down to the Bealach Coire Lair (c.650m) on the north side of Sgorr Ruadh. This pass is not named on the OS map but is distinguished by a little lochan on its south side.

From here climb south-west to an even smaller lochan on the north-west ridge and follow this to the summit. Climbing Sgorr Ruadh and Maol Chean-dearg in the same outing faces the difficulty of avoiding the cliffs which skirt the un-named north-west top (785m) of Sgorr Ruadh and block direct access to the Bealach Ban. The winding path which links the Bealach Coire Lair with the Bealach na Lice via the Bealach Ban makes a safe but long and time-consuming detour.

The distinctive sandstone buttresses which make up the north-east face of Sgorr Ruadh dominate the upper reaches of Coire Lair, offering a number of middle grade winter climbs. Looking up the glen, Robertson's Buttress has *Robertson's Gully* (180m IV,4 1976), bounded on the right by *Academy Ridge* (350m II) with a fine direct finish at IV,5. *Raeburn's Buttress* forms the northern skyline climbed in summer at Difficult and in winter by the man himself in 1904, with *Direct Route* (300m IV 1967) bounded on the left by *Narrow Gully* (300m III 1978). Further on, the cliffs curve around to form a north face. Fuar Tholl has a much wider range of climbing possibilities. The so-called South-East Cliff actually faces north and holds a number of long and exacting winter routes. *Tholl Gate* (170m VI,6 1984) takes the magnificent icy line in the centre of the cliff, with *The Ayatollah* (190m VII,7 1989) further right. There is also some good rock climbing, particularly on the eastern section. Mainreachan Buttress was enthusiastically explored in the late 1960s but its popularity in summer has declined in favour of some steep and very serious winter climbs. *Sleuth/Enigma* (200m VII,7 1969) was probably the hardest route in Scotland when first climbed by Allan Fyffe, Hamish MacInnes and Kenny Spence.

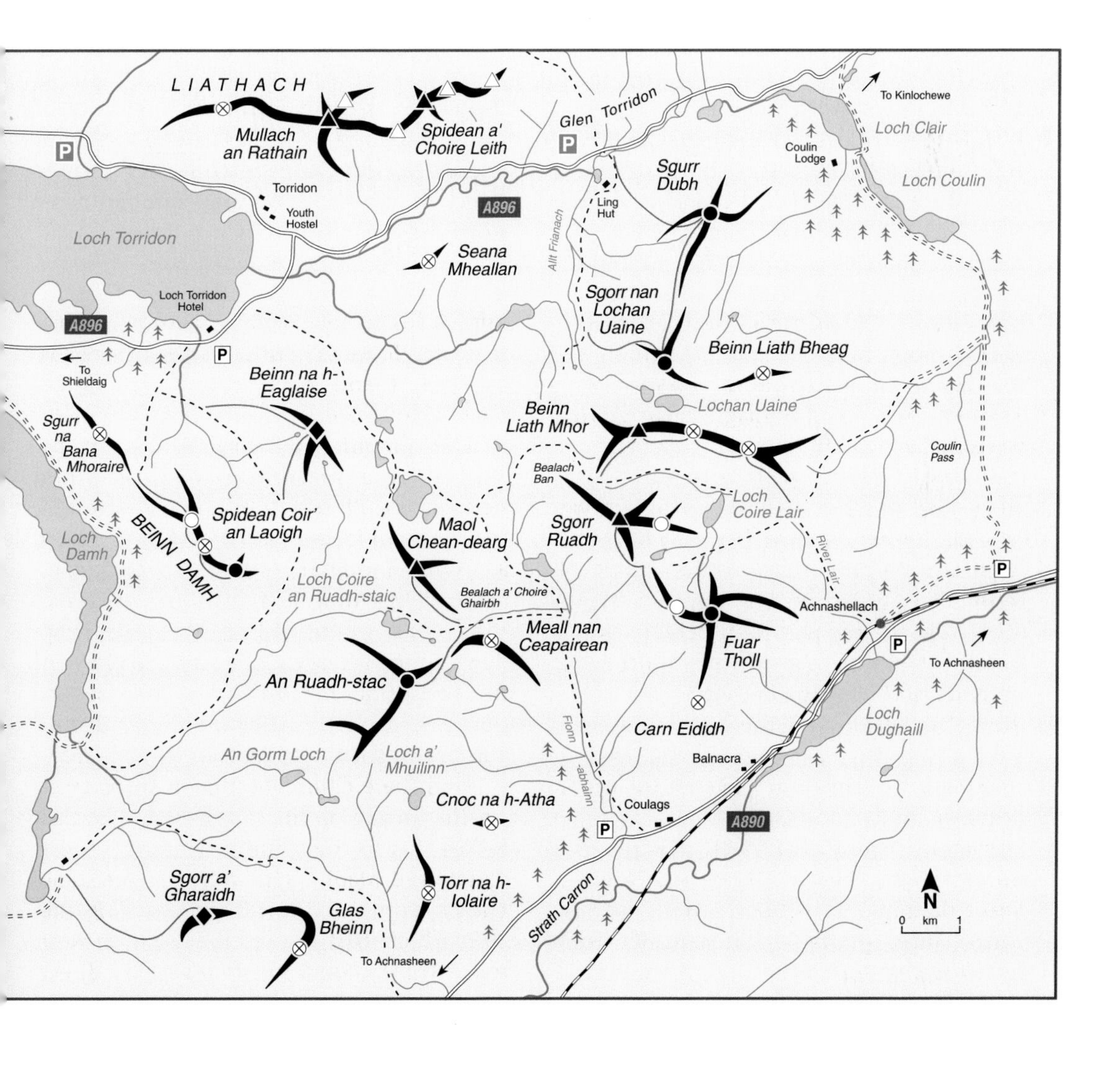

Beinn Liath Mhor; 926m (OS Sheet 25; NG964519); *big grey hill*

The three tops of Beinn Liath Mhor form a long ridge along the north side of Coire Lair, its white quartzite screes contrasting with the dark sandstone cliffs of Sgorr Ruadh and Fuar Tholl opposite. All three hills are often climbed together in a splendid round. If starting with Beinn Liath Mhor, follow the Coire Lair path from Achnashellach. Just beyond the Bhealaich Mhoir path junction another path branches off north-east, leading eventually to Loch Coulin. As this path crosses the south-east shoulder of Beinn Liath Mhor, head off to climb the broad ridge which leads to the eastern top (876m). Continue for 2km along the undulating ridge to the summit, enjoying spectacular views of the main Torridon ridges to the north.

The descent to the Bealach Coire Lair below Sgorr Ruadh is less straightforward. Follow the south-west ridge, picking a route through the line of crags where the quartzite changes to sandstone, aiming for a tiny lochan below a knoll which can be crossed to reach the bealach. Alternatively, descend west from the summit, aiming for another small lochan, then head south to meet the path climbing up to the bealach from the north-west.

Beinn Liath Mhor can also be climbed from Glen Torridon. Park at the Coire Dubh Mor car park then cross the road bridge to the start of a path on the other side of the road. This path trends south, skirting Lochan an Iasgair and passes the Ling Hut before climbing into Coire na Cheud Chnoic (*corrie of a hundred hills*).

As its name suggests, this shows a particularly fine example of hummocky moraines, formed from material deposited at the snout of the glacier which once filled the glen. The path eventually finishes on the lower slopes of Sgorr nan Lochan Uaine. Follow the stream up to Lochan Uaine, then make a straightforward climb to the summit.

Carn Breac; 678m; (OS Sheet 25; NH045530); *speckled peak*

Beinn na Feusaige; 625m; (OS Sheet 25; NH093542); *bearded hill*

Carn Breac and Beinn na Feusaige are an inconspicuous pair of rounded heathery hills which will probably interest only the most determined collectors of Grahams. However, they also make good viewpoints from which to admire their higher and more appealing neighbours. The view north-west from Carn Breac is particularly fine.

West of Loch Sgamhain, a section of the A890 Achnasheen to Lochcarron road has been straightened out as it crosses the Allt Coire Crubaidh. A loop of the old road remains, from which the path following the north side of the Allt Coire Crubaidh can be used to gain the broad north-east ridge of Carn Breac. The featureless upper section of this ridge could be very confusing in mist which would also spoil the wonderful view north-west across Lochs Coulin and Clair and the surrounding woodland, towards Beinn Eighe and Liathach just beyond. Return to the top of the path and continue east over Meallan Mhic Iamhair, past a lochan of the same name, to reach Beinn na Feusaige. This is also very tricky terrain in mist, with some peat hags to be avoided. The summit lies 200 metres east of a tiny lochan. Aircraft wreckage 500 metres to the west is the remains of a Martin B-26 Marauder which crashed in June 1943.

Sgurr Dubh; 782m; (OS Sheet 25; NG979558); *black peak*

Sgorr nan Lochan Uaine; 871m; (OS Sheet 25; NG969531); *peak of the little green lochs*

The rugged cone of Sgurr Dubh is the first of the Glen Torridon hills which comes briefly into view driving west along Strath Bran towards Achnasheen. It reappears again,

Ascending Fuar Tholl from Coire Mainnrichean

directly ahead, coming down Glen Torridon from Kinlochewe, but inevitably attention is drawn instead to Beinn Eighe and Liathach opposite. With Sgorr nan Lochan Uaine standing close behind Sgurr Dubh, this fine pair of hills forms a rugged ridge of terraced sandstone running almost due north at a right-angle to Beinn Liath Mhor. The traverse of the two peaks gives an opportunity to escape from well trodden trails and combine the challenge of route-finding with a bit of scrambling if desired.

The route to Lochan Uaine has already been described and Beinn Liath Mhor could easily be included in the outing. Lochan Uaine sits on the broad col between the Munro summit and Sgorr nan Lochan Uaine to the north, almost back to back with another slightly larger loch to the east (not named on the OS map). A steep but straightforward scramble leads from the lochs to the summit.

The broad contorted ridge which leads to Sgurr Dubh is dotted with smaller lochans. In good visibility it is easy to pick a way through, but this could be difficult in mist. This ridge can also be reached from the east, by following the private road along Loch Clair which crosses the river to Coulin Lodge. Behind the Lodge a narrow stalkers path follows the Allt na Luib up throught the Scots Pines into Coire an Leth-uillt, just below the ridge.

Sgurr Dubh can be climbed on its north-west side directly from the Glen Torridon road. From the Coire Dubh Mor car park, start by following the Ling Hut path, then leave it at the earliest opportunity and pick a way up the hillside above. Broken bands of sandstone give plenty of opportunities for scrambling.

Beinn na h-Eaglaise; 736m; (OS Sheet 25; NG908523); *hill of the church*

Most accessible of the Glen Torridon hills, Beinn na h-Eaglaise gives excellent views of the surrounding Coulin and Torridon hills.

Looking towards Maol Chean-dearg from Beinn na h-Eaglaise

Good stalkers paths pass each side to give a low level circuit of the mountain. Leave the A896 Torridon to Shieldaig road where it crosses the Allt Coire Roill, just beyond the Loch Torridon Hotel. A narrow path follows the gorge through a pine wood. Once above the tree line, be sure to look back at the magnificent views across Upper Loch Torridon to Beinn Alligin. Above the waterfall, at a fork in the path, bear left and cross the river.

The path makes a rising traverse across the hillside to the Drochaid Coire Roill, with massive Maol Chean-dearg directly ahead. A tiny lochan marks the col between Beinn Damh and Beinn na h-Eaglaise. Leave the path and turn north, climbing over a flat top to reach more lochans below the final climb to the summit. In descent, either follow the north-west ridge which curves towards the ascent route or alternatively descend south-east towards Loch an Eion to join the Coulags to Annat path. For the low-level circuit around the mountain, traverse eastwards from the Drochaid Coire Roill to meet this path on the broad bealach below Maol Chean-dearg.

Beinn Damh; 903m; (OS Sheet 24; NG892502); *hill of the stag*

Beinn Damh stands in splendid isolation, forming the western end of the dramatic skyline south of Glen Torridon. The craggy slopes of its northern outlier, Sgurr na Bana Mhoraire (687m) (*peak of the lady*) drop steeply down to the head of Upper Loch Torridon while the summit ridge curves gracefully south-east. More steep slopes drop westwards to Loch Damh and to the east a long line of broken buttresses and shallow corries overlook Coire Roill.

The most popular ascent route follows the Allt Coire Roill path which can also be used to reach Beinn na h-Eaglaise. At the fork above the waterfall, the right branch climbs south-west into the corrie of Toll Ban and joins the summit ridge at a broad bealach. It is worth considering a detour north-west from here to enjoy the view of Loch Torridon from Sgurr na Bana Mhoraire, even though the route to the summit continues in the opposite direction.

Enthusiasts may also wish to take in Creagan Dubh Toll nam Biast (868m) (not named on the OS map), but a more direct line avoids this to the west. Another lower top is linked by a narrow ridge to the summit, Spidean Coir an Laoigh. Perched on the edge of the steep eastern corrie, this has superb views of the other Coulin hills to the east, Applecross to the south-west and the Torridon giants to the north. Just south of the summit 'The Stirrup Mark' named on the OS map is a geological feature caused by an unusual rock slide which is best seen from the A896 Kishorn to Shieldaig road in the vicinity of Loch an Loin. If transport can be arranged it is a straightforward descent in this direction to the Srath a' Bhathaich path.

In poor weather, the circuit of Beinn Damh gives a long low level walk using the Doire Damh path along the east side of Loch Damh linked with the paths already mentioned. For a more challenging route to the summit, the north-east ridge gives a good scramble from the Drochaid Coire Roill while in descent the south-east ridge gives an easier way down to the same point. The walk up or down Coire Roill gives fine views of the eastern cliffs where a number of climbs have been recorded, mostly in winter.

North from Beinn Damh over Sgurr na Mhoraire to Loch Torridon

1.	Beinn Alligin (Tom na Gruagaich)	922m	M	p230
2.	Beinn Alligin (Sgurr Mhor)	986m	M	p230
3.	An Ruadh-mheallan	672m	G	p232
4.	Beinn Bhreac	624m	O	p232
5.	Beinn Dearg	914m	C	p235
6.	Liathach (Mullach an Rathain)	1023m	M	p236
7.	Liathach (Spidean a' Choire Leith)	1055m	M	p236
8.	Beinn Eighe (Ruadh-stac Mor)	1010m	M	p240
9.	Beinn Eighe (Spidean Coire nan Clach)	993m	M	p240
10.	Beinn Eighe (Ruadh-stac Beag)	896m	C	p240
11.	Meall a' Ghiubhais	887m	C	p245
12.	Beinn a' Chearcaill	725m	G	p245
13.	Baosbheinn	875m	C	p246
14.	Beinn an Eoin	855m	C	p246

Chapter 12

Torridon

Jim Teesdale

The Horns of Alligin from the summit of Sgurr Mhor

To anyone with an interest in the Scottish hills, the name Torridon immediately conjures up images of striking mountains of terraced sandstone capped with quartzite. Writing in his influential *Highland Landscape* W.H.Murray observed that 'Glen Torridon, its lochs and the mountains to either side exhibit more mountain beauty than any other district in Scotland including Skye'. As well as spectacular scenery, the distinctive hills, glens and the adjacent coast in this area also offers some of the best walking and climbing in the British Isles.

The area covered by this chapter lies to the north of Glen Torridon and is almost in the form of a peninsula, bounded by Loch Torridon to the south-west and Loch Maree to the north-east. Four large and complex mountains, Beinn Alligin, Beinn Dearg, Liathach and Beinn Eighe, stand grouped together and occupy the southern part of the area, within easy access of the Glen Torridon road. However, many of the finest features of these highest hills, notably their impressive corries, are hidden from the road and face north towards the lower and less accessible but no less interesting hills of the Flowerdale Forest. From here a number of short rivers flow north-west across the open moorland of the Shieldaig Forest and enter the sea along the shores of Loch Gairloch.

Torridon is usually approached from the east, along the A832 Garve to Gairloch road. Just beyond the south-east end of Loch Maree, at the village of Kinlochewe, directly below Beinn Eighe, the A896 turns off south-west towards Glen Torridon. The atmosphere and scenery has changed little since Queen Victoria passed this way in 1877, on her last Highland tour, when she noted '...mountains towering up, as we advanced, like mighty giants'. Beyond massive Beinn Eighe, the terraced southern flanks of Liathach rise steeply above the road as it follows the River Torridon downstream. Just before the river meets Upper Loch Torridon, the main road swings south then west, towards Shieldaig, while a narrow single-track road branches off north-west to Torridon village. This road continues west and follows a tortuous route along the coast, crossing the Bealach na Gaoithe (*pass of the winds*) and eventually returns to sea level to finish at Diabaig. Just below the pass there is a magnificent view south across Loch Torridon to the Applecross and Coulin hills.

North-west from Kinlochewe, the A832 continues towards Gairloch as a fast road which follows the south-west side of Loch Maree. At Bridge of Grudie look out for a brief tantalising glimpse of Ruadh-stac Mor on the north side of Beinn Eighe. Otherwise the finest views are across Loch Maree to Slioch and the Letterewe Forest. Just before Gairloch, the narrow B8056 branches off west, linking Badachro and the small communities along the coast as far as Redpoint. A footpath continues along the coast to Diabaig, passing the isolated Youth Hostel at Craig.

For a number of years this remote north-west corner of the area has been under threat from controversial proposals for hydro-electric schemes. During the 1980s a planning application for schemes on both the Talladale and Grudie Rivers was successfully opposed by conservation and outdoor organisations, though a small installation was built on the Abhainn Garbhaig, above the Victoria Falls. Vigorous opposition to proposals for damming Loch Gaineamhach, Loch a' Ghobhainn and Loch a' Bhealaich went to a Public Enquiry in 1997 and these plans were withdrawn before any decision was announced. In 2004 another application for an even bigger project involving Loch na h-Oidche was rejected by the Scottish Executive, hopefully preserving one of the most spectacular and truly wild parts of Wester Ross.

Principal Hills

Beinn Alligin (Tom na Gruagaich); 922m; (OS Sheet 19 & 24; NG859601); *mountain of beauty/of the jewel, (hill of the damsel)*

Beinn Alligin (Sgurr Mhor); 986m; (OS Sheet 19 & 24; NG865613); *mountain of beauty/of the jewel, (big peak)*

Much has been written about the magnificent Torridonian triptych of Beinn Alligin, Liathach and Beinn Eighe which dominate the north side of Glen Torridon.

Beinn Alligin lacks the bulk of its easterly neighbours, but lives up to its name when seen from the A896 Shieldaig to Torridon road, particularly on a crisp, clear day in winter or early spring when the snowy tops sparkle above the blue waters of Upper Loch Torridon. Often recommended as an introduction to the hills of this area, Ben Alligin probably has the finest summit views, covering a wonderful combination of islands, coast and mountains and well worth saving for a fine day.

The great sandstone crescent of Beinn Alligin rises from the northern shores of Upper Loch Torridon to form the west side of Coire Mhic Nobuil (*the corrie of Noble's son*), the great rubble filled valley behind Liathach. Curving gracefully inland for some 5km, the summit ridge of Beinn Alligin includes two Munros and a Corbett Top, Na Rathanan, with the conspicuous black cleft of Eag Dhubh na h-Eigheachd (*the black notch of the wailing*) cutting in just below its highest point, Sgurr Mhor.

The south-eastern slopes of the mountain plunge steeply into three deep corries. Coir' nan Laogh lies between Meall an Laoigh (*hill of the calf*) and Tom na Gruagaich at the south end of the ridge. Toll a'Mhadaidh Mor (*big hollow of the wolf*), the wide central corrie below Eag Dhubh, holds a remarkable jumble of enormous boulders which clearly tumbled down from the great rocky gash above. Toll a' Mhadaidh Beag lies between Sgurr Mhor and Na Rathanan, the splendidly named Horns of Alligin.

These three rocky towers are situated on

the final curve of the ridge, whose north-east flanks drop steeply to the Bealach a' Chomhla (*pass of the obstacle*) which separates Beinn Alligin from Beinn Dearg to the east.

In the course of draining these corries, the Abhainn Coire Mhic Nobuil has cut a narrow rocky gorge, crossed by the single-track road which winds its way from Torridon to Diabaig. West of the stone bridge, a large car park is the usual starting point for Beinn Alligin. A stalkers path on this side of the burn rises steadily to join the Altan Glas at the mouth of Coir' nan Laogh. The footbridge which once gave access from the Coire Mhic Nobuil path has been removed because of unsightly erosion caused by parties heading to this point.

The headwall of Coir' nan Laogh gives a straightforward climb to the summit of Tom na Gruagaich. Alternatively, the south-east spur of Na Fasreidhnean gives more of a scramble, exposed in places, up the west edge of Coir' nan Laogh and over Meall an Laoigh to Tom na Gruagaich.

From this summit, cliffs drop steeply north-east into Toll a' Mhadaidh Mor, giving fine views across to Sgur Mhor and the intriguing Eag Dhubh. Continuing north, the main ridge narrows and drops steeply to a bealach at 766m, rising again to the north-east over Point 858m. In contrast with the steep headwalls of Toll a' Mhadaidh Mor to the south-east, open slopes roll away more gently to the north-west.

Another dip in the ridge precedes Sgurr na Tuaigh (*peak of the hatchet*) and the top of Eag Dhubh, a feature to be kept in mind in poor visibility, until finally reaching the

Access and Transport

By road: from Inverness the A9 continues north to the roundabout at Tore, where the A835 leads west to Ullapool. The A832 to Gairloch branches off just beyond Garve and passes through Achnasheen and Kinlochewe. From Kinlochewe the A896 runs through Glen Torridon to Torridon village, continuing past Shieldaig and Kishorn to Lochcarron. From Torridon a single track no-through road links Inveralligin, Alligin Shuas and Diabaig. Just before Gairloch another no-through road, the B8056 leaves the A832 and follows the coast around to Redpoint.

By bus: Inverness to Laide via Achnasheen (Westerbus, tel: 01445-712255); Shieldaig to Kinlochewe (Duncan Maclennan, tel: 01520-755239); Diabaig to Achnasheen (Postbus 91, tel: 08457-740740); Gairloch to Redpoint (Postbus 108, Westerbus).

By rail: Achnasheen is the nearest station on the Inverness to Kyle of Lochalsh line.

Accommodation and Information

Hotels and guest houses: Gairloch, Kinlochewe, Loch Maree, Poolewe, Shieldaig and Torridon.

SYHA hostels: Carn Dearg, Gairloch (tel: 0870 004 1110); Craig (no road access or telephone), Torridon (tel: 0870 004 1154).

Independent hostel: The Kinlochewe Hotel Bunkhouse (tel: 01445-760253)

Club hut: Ling Hut, Glen Torridon (Scottish Mountaineering Club) (NG958562).

Campsites: Torridon (tel: 01349-868486); Gairloch: Strath (tel: 01445-712373) and Sands (tel: 01445-712152).

Tourist Information Centre: Auchtercairn, Gairloch (tel: 01445-712130) (seasonal).

Maps

Ordnance Survey 1:50,000 Landranger sheets 19 (Gairloch and Ullapool), 24 (Raasay and Applecross), 25 (Glen Carron and Glen Affric).
Ordnance Survey 1:25,000 Outdoor Leisure Sheet 8 (The Cuillin and Torridon Hills).
Harveys 1:25,000 Superwalker Waterproof (Torridon) with enlargement of Liathach and visitor guide.

Beinn Alligin and Beinn Dearg from Beinn Bhreac

main summit Sgurr Mhor and its magnificent view. On the north side of Sgurr Mhor steep cliffs drop down to Loch Toll nam Biast (*loch of the beast's hole*). Direct descent into this or the Toll a' Mhadaidh corries is not advised, on account of the steepness of the ground.

The quickest and easiest way down Sgurr Mhor is by reversing the route of ascent. In bad conditions it may be safer to descend west into An Reidh-Choire and then contour back around the base of the mountain.

Most parties will probably want to complete the traverse over Na Rathanan, the three Horns of Alligin. The steep east ridge of Sgurr Mhor drops to a col at 757m then a well marked path follows the sandstone crest giving exposed but easy scrambling.

After the third and lowest Horn, An t-Sail Bheg (816m), the path descends south-east down the crest of the ridge to join a stalkers path which crosses the Allt a' Bhealaich by a wooden bridge. This path joins the popular Coire Mhic Nobuil path just north of another footbridge, returning to the road on the east side of the river. The complete traverse of the mountain can be made in either direction.

Beinn Alligin has some good winter climbs, though being lower down and further west they are less likely to be in condition than other routes in the area.

The north-east face of Tom na Gruagaich above Toll a' Mhadaidh Mor has a number of ice falls. *West Coast Boomer* (300m IV,4 1973) gives a sustained and scenic route up the gully on the left of the face. On the other side of the Horns, on the remote north-west buttress above Toll nam Biast, *Diamond Fire* (225m IV 1985) climbs a huge deep cleft, recommended for an adventure into the unknown.

An Ruadh-mheallan; 672m; (OS Sheet 19 & 24; NG836615); *red hill*

Beinn Bhreac; 624m; (OS Sheet 19 & 24; NG837639); *speckled hill*

Despite its insignificant appearance when seen from Beinn Alligin to the east, An

Beinn Alligin's Legends

The origins of the names of many of the features marked on maps of the Highlands have long since been lost in the mists of time. Fortunately in some areas local legends and folk tales still survive. Torridon is one such area and Beinn Alligin in particular is rich in stories. The distinctive feature on the summit ridge, Eag Dhubh na h-Eigheachd (*the black notch of the wailing*) was named by local shepherds who for many years reported hearing wailing and cries of anguish from the vicinity. One of them tragically fell to his death and the sounds were never heard again. The corrie below, Toll a' Mhadaidh Mor (*big hollow of the wolf*) is reputed to have held the lair of one of the last wolves in Scotland. The unfortunate animal was eventually cornered and slaughtered here along with a litter of cubs. On the other side of the mountain sits Loch Toll nam Biast (*loch of the hollow of the beast*). The beast in question is reputed to have been a legendary water-horse or kelpie whose bellowing was heard under the ice of the frozen loch. Footprints seen on the sand indicated that this particular creature had only three legs.

Ruadh-mheallan has much to recommend it, not least a very fine view. It makes an excellent objective for a short day or when cloud covers the higher tops, and can also be included as part of a longer outing. Beinn Bhreac forms part of a long gentle ridge which runs north-west of Beinn Alligin.

Rising to just over 2000 feet, Beinn Bhreac is not even the highest point on this ridge but features on many older maps and atlases. Ignored by compilers and tickers of lists, it offers an opportunity to venture away from the crowds.

There is parking for a couple of vehicles on the Bealach na Gaoithe, overlooking Loch Diabaigas Airde. This is the highest point on the narrow single-track road

Liathach from Sgurr Dubh

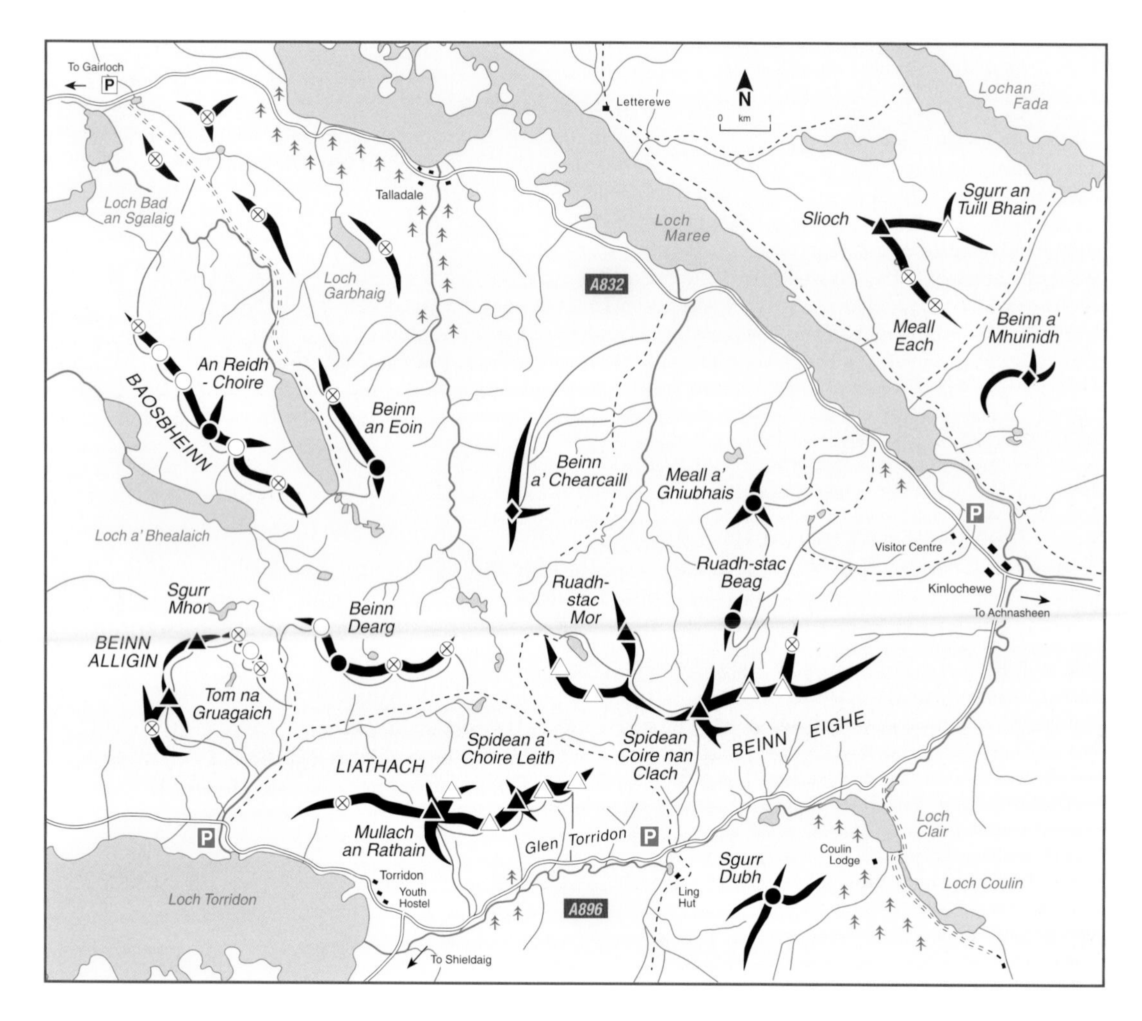

which twists its way from Torridon village to Diabaig. From the pass, An Ruadh-mheallan is clearly visible to the north, separated by some very rugged terrain. Erratic sandstone blocks abound and the approach involves picking a route between rocky knolls and shallow lochans.

As a landmark for the return it is worth trying to identify Loch nan Tri-eileanan with its three distinctive islands. A few stones here mark the remains of a bothy which once housed an illicit still, one of many for which the Alligin area was notorious. This particular establishment was eventually discovered and destroyed by the excisemen, despite the hostility of the local population.

Another lochan sits just below the 500m contour, above which the ground steepens to the summit. The best views are south to the Applecross and Coulin hills and west to the Trotternish hills on Skye, with the featureless back of Beinn Alligin dominating the outlook to the east.

Some awkward crags lie immediately north of the summit and the easiest way to continue to Beinn Bhreac lies to the north-east, towards the grandly named grassy knoll of Meall na h-Odhar-aghaidh, enjoying the views of Baosbheinn beyond. The headwall of the corrie high above Loch Gaineamhach Beag can be contoured without difficulty before gradually traversing up to the summit, an extensive sandstone platform lacking an obvious cairn. The broad ridge which continues south-east has remarkably little vegetation growing in the thin sandy soil.

The top of the next knoll, Creag a' Chirn Duibh (676m) has a spectacular outlook

Spidean a' Choire Leith, Liathach, from the east

with the Toll nam Biast cliffs on the north side of Beinn Alligin and the north end of the Beinn Dearg ridge now in full view. An energetic party could continue onto Beinn Alligin but to return to the starting point drop down towards An Reidh-choire and the Abhainn Alligin. The area around the stream junction due south of An Ruadh-mheallan is known as Braigh an Eireannaich (*high ground of the Irishmen*) and has the remains of a number of old shiel-ings. Keep heading west, looking out for Loch nan Tri-eileanan once again.

Beinn Dearg; 914m; (OS Sheet 24 & 25; NG895608); *red hill*

Denied Munro status by a few centimetres and overshadowed by its taller and more famous neighbours, Beinn Dearg is never-theless a hill of some character. The long narrow ridge which links its summits has some fine situations and great views. Facing the Horns of Alligin across the Bealach a' Chomhla, this ridge curves 1km north from the main summit to Stuc Loch na Cabhaig (888m) (*peak of the loch of haste*). To the east, the ridge winds a further 2km to Carn na Feola (761m) (*hill of flesh*). This section of ridge encloses two north-east facing corries, the extensive An Coire Mor to the west and the smaller Coire Beag to the east.

The shortest and most popular route of ascent uses the Coire Mhic Nobuil footpath, starting from the car park below Beinn Alligin. The path climbs gradually north-east and follows the east side of the river for almost 2km until it crosses by a footbridge. A short distance further on, the path divides and the left branch climbs north towards the Bealach a' Chomhla, giving ample opportunity to study the imposing western flanks of Beinn Dearg.

While it is possible to reach the summit ridge by any of the many gullies which seam the steep terraced sandstone crags, it is easiest to continue almost as far as the bealach and then scramble up the west-ern spur of Stuc Loch na Cabhaig. If approaching from the north, the ridge linking this top with the main summit can be easily reached from An Coire Mor.

Continuing east from the main top, the ridge narrows and offers easy scrambling over a couple of rocky towers which can also be bypassed to the south. Descent to the south is steep and rocky but gets easier further east. From Carn na Feola, a straightforward line of descent meets the Coire Mhic Nobuil path just west of Loch Grobaig.

For an alternative traverse from Coire Dubh Mor, the north ridge of Carn na Feola gives some tricky scrambling. Either way, fine weather will give magnificent views into the spectacular corries of Liathach to the south and the so called 'Empty Quarter' of Flowerdale to the north, while poor conditions would make this a particularly serious outing.

Liathach (Mullach an Rathain);
1023m; (OS Sheet 25; NG912577);
the grey one, (summit of the pulley/row of pinnacles)

Liathach (Spidean a' Choire Leith);
1055m; (OS Sheet 25; NG929579);
the grey one, (peak of the grey corrie)

By any standards, Liathach is one of Scotland's finest mountains. A dramatic ridge of high peaks, it forms a great wall of sandstone terraces which dominates the lower reaches of Glen Torridon. Approached from the east, along the A896 from Kinlochewe, Liathach appears as an impressive monolith rising beyond the sprawling massif of Beinn Eighe, but the true nature and extent of the mountain is better appreciated from the west, driving over from Shieldaig.

A long and relatively gentle western ridge rises from Upper Loch Torridon to Mullach an Rathain, promoted to Munro status in 1981. Continuing east, the ridge narrows and almost half the distance to the other Munro, Spidean a' Choire Leith, is taken up by the pinnacles of Am Fasarinen. Much of Liathach comprises horizontal bands of reddish-coloured sandstone, but the four highest peaks are capped with white quartzite which forms a symmetrical cone on this highest point.

The ridge continues more easily again over Stob a' Coire Liath Mhor and finishes abruptly beyond the final peak, Stuc a'Choire Dhuibh Bhig, whose eastern buttresses drop steeply into Coire Dubh Mor, the glen which separates Liathach from neighbouring Beinn Eighe. A good path through Coire Dubh Mor passes around the north side of Liathach and follows the Abhainn Coire Mhic Nobuil to meet the Inveralligin road at the foot of Beinn Alligin. This gives a popular low-level walk of about 12km with excellent views of the north side of the mountain.

Hidden from any road, the north side of Liathach holds a spectacular series of fine steep-sided corries. The most easterly, Coireag Dubh Beag, lies on the north-west side of Stuc a' Choire Dhuibh Bhig, separated from Coireag Dubh Mor by the broad north ridge of Stob a' Coire Liath Mhor. West of the main summit, Spidean a' Choire Leith, lies the enormous cirque of Coire na Caime (*crooked corrie*). As the name suggests, this is more than just a simple bowl.

Loch Coire na Caime and Loch a' Ghlas-tuill are the largest of the many lochans which dot the floor of the corrie, above

Liathach – 2 Munros, 4 Tops

Mullach an Rathain ; 1023m; (NG912577); *summit of the pulley*
Meall Dearg (Northern Pinnacles); 955m; (NG913579); *red hill*
Am Fasarinen; 927m; (NG923574); *way through difficult ground*
Spidean a' Choire Leith; 1055m; (NG929579); *peak of the grey corrie*
Stob a' Coire Liath Mhor; 983m; (NG932581); *peak of the big grey corrie*
Stuc a' Choire Dhuibh Bhig; 915m; (NG942582); *peak of the little black corrie*

Leaving Mullach an Rathain, Liathach

which the enigmatically named P.C.Buttress divides the upper corrie. Around the eastern headwall a series of gullies and buttresses rise up to the jagged skyline formed by the pinnacles of Am Fasarinen while the west corner of the corrie rises in three steps to Coireag Cham.

This hanging corrie is tucked in below the summit of Mullach an Rathain and enclosed on its north-west side by the splintered Northern Pinnacles and Meall Dearg. Another small corrie, Glas-toll a' Bothain, nestles below the summit on the north-west side of the Northern Pinnacles while the larger Coireag Dhearg lies below the west ridge of Mullach an Rathain.

The foreshortening of the view from the Glen Torridon road gives the southern flanks of Liathach an air of impregnability. From a more comfortable distance, for example from the Coulin hills across the glen to the south, some weaknesses can be picked out on this unique mountain wall. Coire Liath Mhor and Toll a' Mheitheach lie south-east of Spidean a' Choire Leith, while Toll Ban lies south-east of Mullach an Rathain.

'Liathach!' exclaimed the old stalker enthusiastically. 'Man, but there iss no other mountain like her in the whole of Scotland. She iss machestic!' This appraisal, recounted by W.H.Murray in *Undiscovered Scotland* came with a cautionary reminder. 'She iss not to be tampered with!' he warned. 'No indeed, she iss not!'

Depending on transport arrangements the traverse can be tackled in either direction. East to west is possibly more appealing for the views out to the coast, though attention will be focused on the next step for much of the way.

The most straightforward and direct route onto the summit ridge follows the path which leaves the Glen Torridon road east of Glen Cottage, just before the Allt an Doire Ghairbh. The path soon crosses the stream and climbs steeply up its east bank into Toll a' Meitheach. At a fork in the stream bear right into Coire Liath Mhor and continue to a col at 833m on the main ridge south-west of the eastern-most peak, Stuc a'

Leaving Mullach an Rathain on the Liathach ridge in winter

Choire Dhuibh Bhig. This summit gives the closest views of Beinn Eighe to the east and can also be climbed direct from Glen Torridon as follows.

From the car park on the west side of the road bridge over the Allt a' Choire Dhuibh Mhoir an excellent footpath climbs north-west around the base of Stuc a' Choire Dhuibh Bhig. Follow this path for a short distance then break away left to climb the heathery slopes above. As the ground steepens, aim for a gully which gives a short scramble onto the quartzite above, then continue to the top. This route may appeal to purists as a start to a complete traverse of the ridge but is not particularly easy to find in descent.

From the bealach at 833m the main ridge continues north-west to a pair of peaks which have undergone a name change over the years. Older publications refer to Bidean Toll a' Mhuic (960m) (*peak of the pig hole*) which is the lower, eastern summit. More recently this name has been superceded by that of the newer top, Stob a' Choire Liath Mhor, to the west. There have also been reports of problems with compass navigation in this area, caused by magnetic rocks. The next dip in the ridge below the final summit cone of Spidean a' Choire Leith makes a useful route of descent south into Glen Torridon.

A wide gully leads leftwards to a long flat area. From the left (east) end descend a short tier to a wide terrace. Follow this terrace left to an easy break in the crags below, then follow a stream to join the Toll a' Meithach path. This descent requires precise routefinding, with the risk of wandering off along the wrong terrace.

The graceful summit cone of Spidean a' Choire Leith is composed of quartzite blocks, large enough to complicate direction finding in mist. From the summit, care should be taken to avoid accidentally following the short spur which slopes away gently to the south-east, forming a great prow, ringed by steep crags. The main ridge continues south-west, with a spectacular view across the cliffs of Coire na Caime to Mullach an Rathain, the Northern Pinnacles and Meall Dearg.

The pinnacles of Am Fasarinen are of more immediate interest, as this next section of the ridge gives sustained scrambling. Hand and footholds are plentiful, though the exposure is considerable, particularly on the north side. In summer it is possible to follow a series of narrow paths along the southern flanks below the crest of the ridge. These quickly bank out with snow, leaving the route along the crest initially on the south side, then over the summit of An Fasarinen, as the safest alternative in winter.

The difficulties end at Am Fasarinen and the ridge becomes broad and easy again as it continues west to Mullach an Rathain. This newer Munro can be approached or descended from all sides. From the pine wood beside the Glen Torridon road, 1km east of the village junction, a path follows the Allt an Tuill Bhain, crossing sandstone slabs and leading up into Toll Ban. Climb the west side of this corrie to gain the rocky ridge which leads north-west to the summit.

To descend from Mullach an Rathain by this route it is best to go west from the summit for about 100 metres before turning south. Alternatively, the west ridge continues and drops gently to Sgorr a' Chadail (698m) (*peak of sleep*) whose north-western flanks give easy access to the Coire Mhic Nobuil path. The stone chute which drops from a point a few hundred metres west of the summit of Mullach an Rathain directly towards Torridon village has suffered considerable erosion over the years and is not recommended.

The finest feature of Mullach an Rathain is its north-east spur which leads to Meall Dearg and the Northern Pinnacles. Considered as one of the hardest Tops because of the Northern Pinnacles linking it to Mullach an Rathain, Meall Dearg's summit can be gained relatively easily by dropping down a gully well to the east of the summit and traversing the screes before gaining the col between it and the Pinnacles. From here it is a fairly easy scramble, returning by the same route.

The Northern Pinnacles are a series of five shattered pinnacles which rise above Loch Coire na Caime, forming the north-east ridge of Meall Dearg. Covered in loose rocks, this route gives a serious scramble in summer but in winter the complete traverse of Liathach via the Northern Pinnacles gives an outstanding outing at Grade II.

From Coire na Caime, a narrow slanting shelf on the north side of the ridge leads up to the pinnacles. Any difficulties can be turned to the right. Mullach nan Rathain can also be reached by a straightforward climb from Coire na Caime to the col between the summit and the top of Bell's Buttress, the highest and most remote of the buttresses at the back of Coireag Cham.

In summer, the broken vegetatious Torridonian sandstone terraces of Liathach give little worthwhile rock climbing but in winter, low temperatures transform the mountain, giving some of the best ice climbing in Britain. Coireag Dubh Beag has

Shielings

All over the Highlands, in sheltered glens among the hills, the observant walker will notice the occasional green and grassy patch, perhaps with a ring of stones, which marks the site of a shieling. These were temporary summer habitations to which grazing animals were moved in spring to take advantage of rich higher pastures and allow cultivation of the lower ground. The walk to the shielings traditionally began on Beltane, the first day of May, and the women and children usually stayed at the shieling until August, looking after the animals and making cheese and butter.

This way of life died out in Torridon with the end of the Mackenzie lairdship in the early eighteenth century. The new owner wanted the hill pasture for sheep and crofting tenants were only allowed one cow each. The location of a number of shielings in the area can still be identified by the name 'Airigh' such as Loch Airigh Eachainn (*the loch of Hector's shieling*) on the south-west side of An Ruadh-mheallan.

Footless Gully (150m IV,5 1977) which takes the obvious line on the back wall, with *The Headhunter* (200m V,5 1994) to the left and *Headless Gully* (150m V,5 1984) to the right. In Coireag Dubh Mor *Poachers Fall* (160m V,5 1978) is the classic route which follows the right side of the steep wide icefall draining the middle of the back wall, while *The Salmon Leap* (180m VI,6 1986) takes the left side.

Further right, *Foobarbundee* (200m VIII,7 1994) gave the hardest thin ice pitch in Scotland. *George* (200m III,4 1967) and *Sinister Prong* (IV,5 1978) follow the deep gash where the steep back wall of the corrie meets the north ridge of Spidean a' Choire Leith which also gives an interesting Grade I/II scramble. Coire na Caime holds a variety of remote climbs with a mountain atmosphere and an element of exploration. On the south side of Liathach the shapely Pyramid Buttress is located on the short south-east spur of Spidean a' Choire Leith. The icefalls which form here can be seen from the road, glistening in the sun, and give good climbing at Grade V.

Beinn Eighe (Ruadh-stac Mor); 1010m; (OS Sheet 19 & 25; NG951611); *file mountain, (big red stack)*

Beinn Eighe (Spidean Coire nan Clach); 993m; (OS Sheet 19 & 25; NG966597); *file mountain, (peak of the stony corrie)*

Beinn Eighe (Ruadh-stac Beag); 896m; (OS Sheet 19 & 25; NG973614); *file mountain, (little red stack)*

The range of mountains which make up Beinn Eighe form a high ridge which stretches almost 10km west from Kinlochewe and dominates the upper reaches of Glen Torridon. Separated from Liathach by the deep and narrow glen of Coire Dubh Mor, the sandstone strata which forms most of this mountain dips gently to the east and forms only a small section of the Beinn Eighe ridge, on the col between the western tops of Sail Mhor and Coinneach Mhor.

The rest of the ridge has a distinctive pale covering of quartzite and the southern slopes above Glen Torridon are characterised by long unappealing slopes of quartzite screes sweeping down to the road. This south side of the mountain holds a series of steep, open corries which give good access to a number of points on the Beinn Eighe ridge.

In complete contrast, the north side of Beinn Eighe is much more complex and holds many of the range's finest features. To the north-east, a long corrie lies between the main ridge and Ruadh-stac Beag, the Corbett which forms the great north-east spur of Spidean Coire nan Clach.

This corrie appears not to have been distinguished with a name, though high in its south-eastern corner below Sgurr Ban lies a lochan-filled hollow, Toll Ban. As the corrie widens and turns west, it becomes the Toll a' Ghiubhais, separating Ruadh-stac Beag from Meall a' Ghiubhais to the north. West of Ruadh-stac Beag lies the enormous central Coire Ruadh-staca, enclosed on its far side by Ruadh-stac Mor, the other great northern spur of Beinn Eighe which is also its highest summit.

The final north-western corrie, between Ruadh-stac Mor and Sail Mhor, is the spectacular Coire Mhic Fhearchair (*corrie of Farquhar's son*), one of Scotland's best known corries. A large loch fills the mouth of this rocky amphitheatre, dominated by the magnificent Triple Buttresses which rise over 300m from the back wall of the inner recess to the summit of Coinneach Mhor.

Three great conical buttresses of Cambrian quartzite stand side by side on plinths of Torridonian sandstone. Two thirds of the height of the East Buttress is quartzite, reducing to half on the West Buttress. Where the different rocks meet, a distinctive ledge, the Broad Terrace, cuts across the East and Central Buttresses and the upper quartzite tiers are further divided

Beinn Eighe from Meall a' Ghiubhais

into two by another, less pronounced terrace.

This unique spectacle of natural rock architecture makes Coire Mhic Fhearchair a popular approach to Beinn Eighe. From the Coire Dubh Mor car park in Glen Torridon, an excellent path climbs north through the glen. After 3km of steady ascent the path crosses the stream by stepping-stones. Further on, at the watershed, the main path continues westwards towards Coire Mhic Nobuil while the right-hand branch contours around Sail Mhor, rising gradually to gain the lip of Coire Mhic Fhearchair with its spectacular scenery.

The steep broken cliffs of Sail Mhor which form the west wall of the corrie have been described as displaying some of the worst features of Torridonian sandstone, 'all rock from below, all grass from above'. Beyond the loch, wide scree fans can be followed without difficulty to the crest of the ridge, south of the summit of Sail Mhor.

Alternatively, parties heading directly for the Munro Ruadh-stac Mor can reach the col at the south-east corner of the corrie by a straightforward climb. This highest peak stands to the north of the main ridge, rather out on a limb, an easy climb from the col.

Returning to this col, a short arete to the south-west leads to the main ridge at Point 956m. This marks the east end of the mossy Coinneach Mor plateau which makes a pleasant contrast to the hard quartzite elsewhere. The summit at the west end of the plateau is also the best viewpoint. West of this point, the rocks of Ceum Grannda (*the ugly step*) give an exposed but easy scramble down before the ridge continues more gently north-west to the top of Sail Mhor.

From the eastern end of Coinneach Mor the main ridge drops gently south-east for 1km to another col at 821m, beyond which a stony arete turns gradually north-east up to the summit of the second Munro,

Beinn Eighe – 2 Munros, 4 Tops and 1 Corbett

Sail Mhor; 980m; (NG938605); *big heel*

Coinneach Mhor; 976m; (NG944600); *big moss*

Ruadh-stac Mor; 1010m; (NG951611); *big red stack*

Spidean Coire nan Clach; 993m; (NG966597); *peak of the stony corrie*

Ruadh-stac Beag; 896m; (NG973614); *little red stack*

Sgurr Ban; 970m; (NG974600); *ight-coloured peak*

Sgurr nan Fhir Duibhe; 963m; (NG981600); *peak of the dark man*

The main ridge of Beinn Eighe

Spidean Coire nan Clach.

Spidean Coire nan Clach forms a natural mid-point on the main ridge and sends out a short spur, Stuc Coire an Laoigh (866m) (*peak of the corrie of the calf*) south into Glen Torridon. Coire an Laoigh sits tucked in below the summit, to the east of this spur and can be reached by a good stalkers path which climbs up from the road beside a small forestry plantation opposite Loch Bharranch. The path continues up the steep headwall of the corrie to the summit but a more interesting alternative is to scramble to the top of Stuc Coire an Laoigh then follow the crest of the spur.

For many years the height of Spidean Coire nan Clach was seriously underestimated. The trig point is at 972m but the actual summit is 21m higher and located some 200 metres to the north-east. The mountain was promoted to Munro status in 1990. South-west of the summit, the slopes of Coire nan Clach are relatively free of scree and boulders and offer an alternative route to or from the Coire Dubh Mor car park.

Either leave the road by the ruin on the other side of the river from the car park or follow the Coire Dubh Mor path for 1km or so before crossing. Descent by this route will cause less erosion damage than the sandy headwall of Coire an Laoigh.

If transport can be arranged, the traverse of the length of the Beinn Eighe ridge makes a magnificent outing in either direction. From the summit of Spidean Coire nan Clach the ridge continues eastwards, dropping then rising again to the summit of Sgurr Ban. Steep screes fall away to the south and broken crags and gullies to the north, continuing like this to Sgurr nan Fhir Duibhe.

From this summit the main ridge turns north-east towards the final peak, Creag Dhubh (907m) (*black crag*), forming a prominent wide crescent above Coire Domhain. Just beyond the summit of Sgurr nan Fhir Duibhe stand the Bodaich Dubh Beinn Eighe, better known as the Black Carls. Negotiating a way through these shattered rock pinnacles requires some care, particularly in winter. A short section of exposed scrambling can be avoided on the south side of the ridge. If in doubt, this final section of the ridge can be missed out by descending a short distance south-east from the summit of Sgurr nan Fhir Duibhe then follow the broad easy ridge on the south side of Coire Domhain.

Descend to Glen Torridon either by following the east bank of the Allt a' Ghille or by the path on the north side of the Allt a' Chuirn which leaves the road 1km south of Kinlochewe at Carn Shiel. To start the traverse from this point follow this path up the Allt a' Chuirn towards the mouth of Coire Domhain then climb the crest of the ridge ahead to reach the summit of Creag Dubh.

Although very much part of the Beinn Eighe range, Ruadh-stac Beag is often climbed along with its neighbouring Corbett, Meall a' Ghiubhais. However, parties who have already climbed Beinn Eighe from the south may welcome the opportunity to climb it again from the north-east. A good path, known locally as the Pony Track, leaves the A832 Gairloch road about 1km west of Kinlochewe, just before the Scottish Natural Heritage Visitors Centre at Aultroy. As this path gains height, the rugged grandeur of this northern side is gradually revealed, with Creag Dubh dominating the view to the south. Ruadh-stac Beag itself is well defended by crags, screes and large areas of rocky slabs.

From the highest point on the path, the easiest route is to drop down a little then follow the Allt Toll a' Ghiubhais upstream, heading for the col on the south side of the hill which holds Lochan Uaine (*small green loch*). From here it is a straightforward climb over boulders to the summit. The north-east spur of Spidean Coire nan Clach rises immediately above Lochan Uaine and gives an easy scramble onto the main Beinn Eighe ridge.

The enormous corries on the north side

The Triple Buttresses of Coire Mhic Fhearchair

Beinn an Eoin from Beinn a' Chearcaill

of Beinn Eighe all drain into the River Grudie which flows into Loch Maree just below Bridge of Grudie on the A832 Kinlochewe to Gairloch road. An excellent path climbs through Glen Grudie and meets the Allt Coire Mhic Fhearchair at the foot of the north flank of Ruadh-stac Mor. With suitable transport arrangements this makes a spectacular alternative approach to the range.

Beinn Eighe offers a tremendous variety of climbing in summer and winter, particularly in Coire Mhic Fhearchair. The first rock climb on the Triple Buttresses was Gibbs, Backhouse and Mounsey's *East Buttress – Ordinary Route* (210m Difficult 1907) which remains an enjoyable classic. Since then, numerous routes have been recorded and different climbs can be combined on successive tiers. Although very steep in places, the quartzite is well provided with holds and tends to be easier than it looks.

In contrast, the sandstone climbing is more technical and can be deceptively hard. The most popular climb up the Central Buttress is *Pigott's Route* (180m Severe, 4b 1922) although *Hamilton's Route* (Severe 1936) has better rock. Overall, the climbing is very satisfying and the situations are outstanding.

Beyond the Triple Buttresses lie the Eastern Ramparts and the Far East Wall. The latter is in the top left-hand corner of the corrie looking up from the loch. It offers a number of excellent harder routes on sensationally steep quartzite which catch the sun in the afternoon and evening. *Angel Face* (95m E2 1988) climbs above the bulging nose on the left-hand side of the wall while *Seeds of Destruction* (95m E3 1988) gives very sustained climbing from the same start. *Groovin' High* (90m E1 1973) follows the right side of a clean grey pillar. The Eastern Ramparts are the long and complex left flanking wall of the East Buttress, whose central section was first climbed by the devious line of *Boggle* (110m E1 1961).

Robin Smith's route description, recorded in the Ling Hut Climbs Book, is something of a gem. 'Zigzag to reach the left end of the ledge about 12m up. Climb a corner for 6m to a ledge on the left, then pull up into the pale smooth corner on the right. Climb this to below roofs, crawl left over loose blocks and go up and right to reach the Upper Girdle below the pale shallow diedre. Move right and climb up by cracks, grooves, flakes, corners, hand-traverses and mantleshelves away up and right onto the crest of the pillar bounding the diedre. Step left and climb a corridor between roofs to top.' *The Pale Diedre (*105m E2 1980) is considered to be a much better climb, starting from the same point, and taking the corner in the middle of the upper part of the crag.

There is also good rock climbing of a less serious nature on Creag Mhor, a crag on the east flank of Ruadh-stac Mor in Coire Ruadh-staca. The routes here have some intriguing names such as *Thin Man's Ridge* (150m Hard Severe 1971) and The *Independent Pineapple* (120m Severe 1972).

As far back as 1899 Lawson, Ling and Glover climbed the scenic *No. 2 Gully* (300m II) on Sail Mhor, but Coire Mhic Fhearchair is now considered a paradise for modern-style mixed winter climbing which comes into condition very quickly. *East Buttress* (250m IV,4) is the easiest of the Triple Buttresses while *Central Buttress (Piggott's Route)* (250m VI,7 1971) has been described as 'a climb of Alpine stature'. To its right *West Central Gully* (350m VIII,7 1987) is a very hard, serious and spectacular climb. In contrast, *Far West Gully (Fuselage Gully)* (400m I/II) gives the best easy gully in the corrie, with the added interest of the wreckage of a Lancaster bomber which crashed here in 1952. A number of winter climbs have been recorded in other corries and crags on the north side of Beinn Eighe which remains ripe for further exploration.

Meall a' Ghiubhais; 887m; (OS Sheet 19; NG976634); *hill of the pine tree*

Sometimes considered an outlier of Beinn Eighe but seldom climbed as part of a traverse of that range, Meall a' Ghiubhais stands alone, the most accessible of the Torridon hills and a fine viewpoint. Thick woodland still covers its lower north-east slopes, which run into Loch Maree and form one of the most important features of Britain's first National Nature Reserve, declared in 1951. This fragment of native woodland, Coille na Glas-leitre (*wood of the grey slope*) is a remnant of the 'Great Wood of Caledon' which once covered much of the Highlands.

Scottish Natural Heritage maintains a Mountain Trail which climbs through the woods to a height of 550m. Some of the trees here are over 350 years old. From the top of the trail it is straightforward to continue on to the twin summits, the south-west being the higher. An alternative approach along a less artificial path uses the Pony Track described earlier which leads to the bealach between Meall a' Ghiubhais and Ruadh-stac Beag. Both Corbetts can easily be climbed in the same outing from this point.

Beinn a' Chearcaill; 725m; (OS Sheet 19; NG931637); *hill of the girdle*

Beinn a' Chearcaill gives a superb view of the north side of the higher Torridon hills and the chance to cover some relatively unfrequented terrain. The summit stands at the end of a long broad ridge which slopes away to the north. Steep crags on all other sides leaves this northern ridge as the best approach.

A good path leads up Glen Grudie, starting from the house just west of Bridge of Grudie on the A832 Kinlochewe to Gairloch road. There is roadside parking a short distance west of the track up to the house. Avoid the temptation to follow the path for as long as possible. After crossing the Allt a' Choire Bhriste follow the stream up into Coire Briste then climb gentle featureless slopes south-west. Route finding may be

Baosbheinn from Gairloch

difficult in poor visibility. The summit is a large flat area of smooth sandstone, which looks directly into the spectacular Coire Mhic Fhearchair of Beinn Eighe to the south.

For a direct descent to the starting point, walk north along the ridge over A' Choineach Beag (558m) enjoying a fine view of Slioch before dropping down north-east to regain the Glen Grudie path. Alternatively, for a longer outing, descend north-west into Srath Lungard from the col on the northern ridge.

Follow the course of the Allt Strath Lungard as it meanders along the broad strath until it suddenly drops down a spectacular waterfall into the narrow wooded gorge of the River Talladale. Keep above and east of the gorge, traversing the hillside and gradually descend to meet the road a short distance east of the Loch Maree Hotel.

Baosbheinn; 875m; (OS Sheet 19 & 24; NG870654); *wizard's peak/hill of the forehead*

Beinn an Eoin; 855m; (OS Sheet 19; NG905646); *peak of the bird*

Behind the higher Torridon hills, a series of short straths and glens run north through wild and rugged terrain. Bog and bare rock, countless lochs and lochans and short swift-flowing rivers make up the Shieldaig and Flowerdale Forests. Baosbheinn and Beinn an Eoin dominate, forming two almost parallel ridges running south-east to north-west. An approach from the south or east carrying a tent gives a unique wilderness expedition, but both peaks can be climbed in a day from the north, from the A832

Kinlochewe to Gairloch road. From the roadside shed known locally as the Red Barn (painted green at the time of writing) a footbridge crosses the outflow of Am Feur Loch. The surrounding slopes have been fenced as part of a woodland regeneration scheme and an estate track climbs south-east some 10km past Loch na h-Oidhche (*loch of the dark*) and Poca Buidhe cottage almost to the foot of the short steep south ridge of Beinn an Eoin.

For the classic horseshoe traverse, after crossing the Abhainn Loch na h-Oidhche on stepping stones 1km before the loch, climb the north-west spur of Beinn an Eoin and follow the long ridge over three tops to the summit. A steep descent south leads to Gorm-loch na Beinne, to the west of which relatively flat ground gives pleasant easy going across extensive areas of sandstone slabs to reach the south-east end of the fine Baosbheinn ridge. Two minor tops are passed before the main top, Sgorr Dubh.

From here it is possible to descend the north-east spur to An Reidh-choire, though it may be difficult to cross the Abhainn a' Gharbh Choire to regain the estate track, except at the bridge at the outflow of the loch. Continuing north-west along the summit ridge leads eventually to Creag an Fhithich, whose north-west flank drops away very steeply.

Descent of the north-east flank is easier further to the right. Cross the river at a new bridge (NG867694) and follow a new track to rejoin the original track. A number of icefalls have been climbed on the north-west Face of Creag an Fhithich.

Baosbheinn and Beinn Alligin

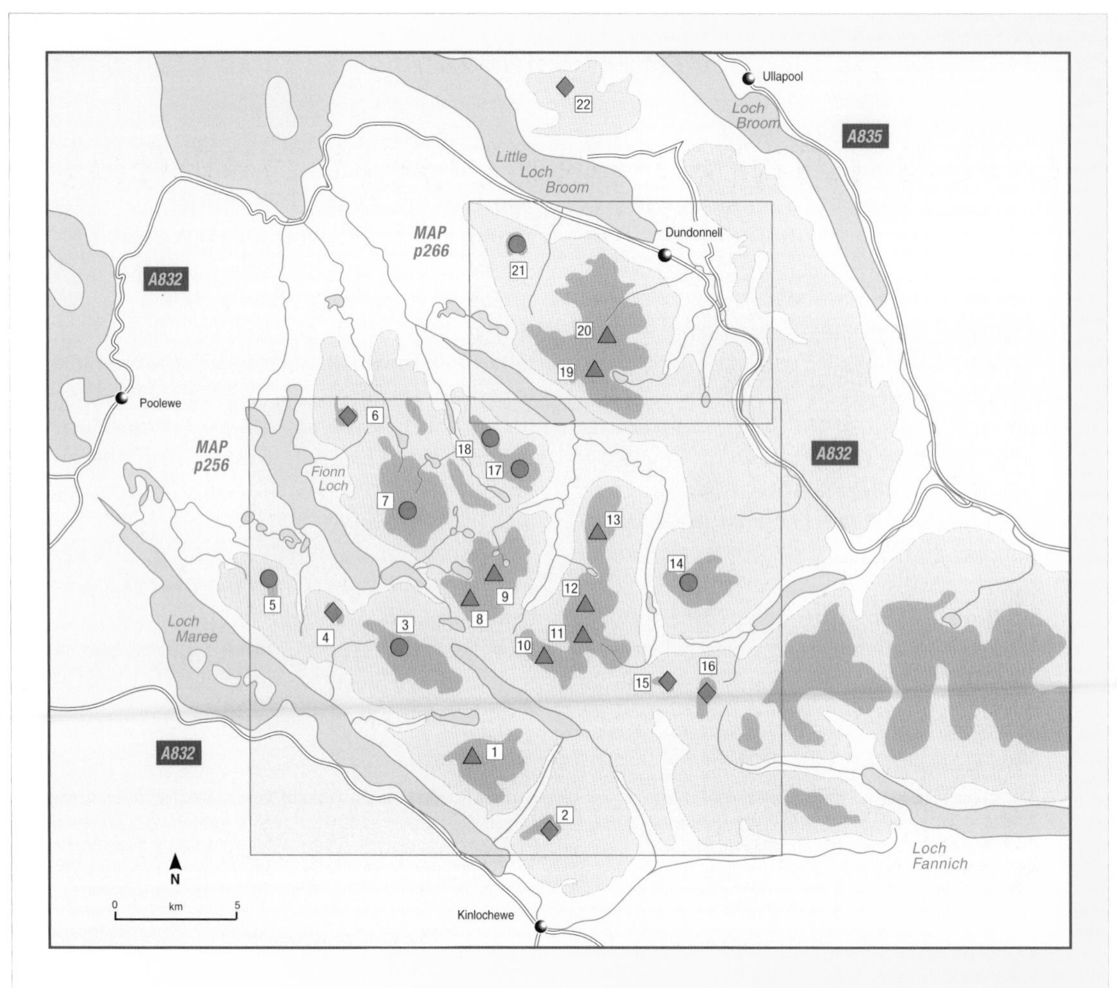

1.	Slioch	981m	M	p251
2.	Beinn a' Mhuinidh	692m	G	p252
3.	Beinn Lair	859m	C	p253
4.	Meall Mheinnidh	722m	G	p255
5.	Beinn Airigh Charr	791m	C	p255
6.	Beinn a' Chaisgein Beag	682m	G	p255
7.	Beinn a' Chaisgein Mor	856m	C	p255
8.	A' Mhaighdean	967m	M	p257
9.	Ruadh Stac Mor	918m	M	p257
10.	Beinn Tarsuinn	937m	M	p259
11.	Mullach Coire Mhic Fhearchair	1018m	M	p259
12.	Sgurr Ban	989m	M	p259
13.	Beinn a' Chlaidheimh	916m	M	p259
14.	Creag Rainich	807m	C	p262
15.	Beinn Bheag	668m	G	p262
16.	Groban	749m	G	p262
17.	Beinn Dearg Mor	910m	C	p262
18.	Beinn Dearg Bheag	820m	C	p262
19.	An Teallach (Sgurr Fiona)	1060m	M	p264
20.	An Teallach (Bidein a' Ghlas Thuill)	1062m	M	p264
21.	Sail Mhor	767m	C	p267
22.	Beinn Ghobhlach	635m	G	p267

Loch Maree to Loch Broom

Jim Teesdale

Sail Liath and Corrag Bhuidhe from Sgurr Fiona, An Teallach

The complex jumble of hills and lochs between Loch Maree and Loch Broom make up one of Scotland's finest mountain wilderness areas. Almost devoid of habitation and roads of any kind, access has traditionally been on foot or by boat, and for the hill-goer the quality of the walking and climbing amply repays the extra effort required. The A832 skirts the perimeter of the area on three sides, serving the communities along the coast. Even from this road, access to the hills is limited by Loch Maree to the south, an extensive area of low-lying bog to the west and the great mass of An Teallach and its outliers to the north, with the mountains continuing eastwards as the Fannaichs.

A series of roughly parallel lochs lie between the hills and divide them into distinctive groups. North-east of Loch Maree, the striking ramparts of Slioch and Beinn a' Mhuinidh overshadow the gentle south-western slopes of Beinn Lair, Meall Mheinnidh and Beinn Airigh Charr. On their north side, this trio in turn form a long escarpment of dramatic crags overlooking the Fionn Loch, the Dubh Loch and Lochan Fada. At the head of the Fionn Loch, the lonely lodge at Carnmore sits in splendid isolation, surrounded by rugged peaks. Successive estate owners have maintained its remoteness, leaving a huge area uniquely free of any sort of road or vehicle tracks.

In the very heart of the mountains, a cluster of Munros, often referred to as the 'Fisherfield Six', are further enhanced by a generous scattering of smaller but no less spectacular lochs and lochans in their many corries. Three rivers, the Gruinard, Inverianvie and Little Gruinard drain north-west into Gruinard Bay, with its magnificent sandy beach. Along the north-eastern edge of this wild vastness, the striking spires of An Teallach and its graceful outlier Sail Mhor stand between Loch na Sealga and Little Loch Broom. Finally, the Scoraig peninsula, a crooked finger of hills, points westwards out into the Minch, sheltering the busy waters of Loch Broom to the north.

Slioch from Loch Maree

Around the edge of the mountains, to the west and north, the coastline is made up of a series of rugged peninsulas, enclosing wide bays and sea-lochs. The largest of these, Loch Ewe was used during World War Two as a gathering point for convoys bound for America and the notorious Murmansk run to Northern Russia. Around the same time, some reckless experimenting with biological warfare saw Gruinard Island infected with deadly anthrax spores. This embarrassment persisted for almost 50 years, until the Ministry of Defence organised a programme of decontamination and the island was finally given the all clear.

The small communities scattered along this coast rely on a mixture of crofting, tourism, fish farming and a variety of economic activities which have been helped by the steady improvement in the road links to Inverness and beyond. The isolation which was a factor in the demise of the original community at Scoraig became an attraction for the new one which has grown up there. Access remains either by footpath from Badrallach or by boat across Little Loch Broom from Badluarach.

Principal Hills

Slioch; 981m; (OS Sheet 19; NH004690); *spear hill*

The sandstone buttresses of Slioch soar up from the surrounding gneiss like the walls of a great castle, dominating the south-east end of Loch Maree. Viewed across the loch from the A832 Kinlochewe to Gairloch road, the mountain offers a magnificent and much photographed profile that more than holds its own against An Teallach and the giants of nearby Torridon.

Steep crags and gullies defend all but its south-eastern flank where two ridges drop down into Gleann Bianasdail, enclosing the broad grassy Coire na Sleaghaich (*corrie of the spear*) which forms a convenient breach for walkers. The usual starting point is a purpose built car park at Incheril, 1km east of Kinlochewe village.

A pleasant track follows the Kinlochewe River north-west through patchy woodland, crossing the Abhainn an Fhasaigh by a footbridge. The historic track to Letterewe and beyond continues in the same direction, traversing the hillside above the north shore of Loch Maree, while a branch turns north-east and enters the narrow defile of Gleann Bianasdail.

Keep an eye open for a herd of wild goats which graze the grassy terraces between the lines of crags on the north-west flanks of Beinn a' Mhuinidh. After 1km, a less distinct path branches north, leading to the col between Sgurr Dubh and Meall Each, and thence into Coire na Sleaghaich. From here, the most popular route to the summit follows the south-east ridge, passing two lochans on the shoulder. There is also a fair hill-walkers path up the corrie all the way to the top.

Older OS maps gave the north and south summits exactly the same height, which caused much confusion over the years about the precise location of the Munro. Slioch was even included in a

Access and Transport

By road: from Inverness the A9 continues north to the roundabout at Tore, where the A835 leads west to Ullapool. The A832 to Gairloch branches off just beyond Garve and passes through Achnasheen and Kinlochewe. This road continues north to Poolewe, Aultbea and Laide, then back east to Dundonnell, rejoining the A835 Ullapool road at Braemore junction.

By bus: Inverness to Gairloch via Dundonnell; Inverness to Laide via Achnasheen; Gairloch to Mellon Charles/Mellon Udrigle; Melvaig to Gairloch. (Westerbus, tel: 01445-712255)

By rail: Achnasheen is the nearest station on the Inverness to Kyle of Lochalsh line.

Accommodation and Information

Hotels and guesthouses: Aultbea, Dundonnell, Gairloch, Kinlochewe, Laide and Poolewe.

SYHA hostel: Carn Dearg, Gairloch (tel: 0870-004-1110).

Independent hostels: Camusnagaul, Dundonnell : Sail Mhor Croft (tel: 01854-633224); Melvaig, Gairloch : Rua Reidh Lighthouse (tel: 01445-771263); Badrallach Bothy (tel: 01854-633281).

Club hut: The Smiddy, Dundonnell (Junior Mountaineering Club of Scotland, Edinburgh Section).

Campsites: near Dundonnell at Ardessie and Badrallach (tel: 01854-633281); near Gairloch at Strath (tel: 01445-712373) and Sands (tel: 01445-731225); Laide (tel: 01445-731225) and Poolewe.

Tourist Information Centre: Auchtercairn, Gairloch (tel: 01445-712130) (seasonal).

Maps

Ordnance Survey 1:50,000 Landranger Sheet 19 (Gairloch and Ullapool).

Munro-ologists list of 'particularly troublesome mountains'. The southern top has the trig point but the northern top has the better view, extending down the length of Loch Maree and across to the northern corries of the Torridon hills, with the many and varied Fisherfield hills stretching away to the north. The currently accepted heights place the southerly top and trig point one metre lower than its more scenic neighbour.

From the summit, it is worth continuing east along the narrow ridge to Sgurr an Tuill Bhain (934m) (*peak of the white hollow*) before descending into Coire na Sleaghaich to rejoin the route of ascent, or continue through Gleann Bianasdail to Lochan Fada. Despite the challenging appearance of Slioch's north-west face, the length of approach and scarcity of information has deterred most climbers, though a number of routes have been recorded in summer and winter on the main gullies and buttresses.

Beinn a' Mhuinidh; 692m; (OS Sheet 19; NH032660); *mountain of the heath*

Beinn a' Mhuinidh forms the east side of Gleann Bianasdail and is distinguished by extensive bands of quartzite cliffs high along its western flanks, culminating in the three tiered nose of the Bonaid Dhonn, the largest exposure of rock above the south-east end of Loch Maree. The normal geological sequence of gneiss, sandstone and quartzite has a final capping of ancient gneiss, marking the line of a thrust zone and the tilted plane of the mountain has left rough featureless slopes dotted with lochans to the north and east. Sharing many similar views with its grander neighbour Slioch, Beinn a' Mhuinidh gives an excellent half days walk. From the car park at Incheril, the most straightforward but least interesting approach is to follow the

Paths in the Loch Maree and Loch Broom Area

A network of excellent paths covers this wild area. Many of them are of historic interest and are still maintained for stalking and fishing. As well as providing good access to otherwise remote hills they also make excellent routes for longer backpacking expeditions. The main through routes are described below, while a number of other paths and tracks which join them are described at appropriate points in the text.

1) Incheril (Kinlochewe) to Poolewe (31km). There is a car park at Incheril, 1km east of Kinlochewe village, from where a footpath leads north-west, following the north side of the Kinlochewe River to the head of Loch Maree. Just beyond the Abhainn an Fhasaigh footbridge, a side branch climbs north-east through Gleann Bianasdail, leading to the east end of Lochan Fada. The main path continues along the hillside above the north side of Loch Maree, climbing 100m above the shore in places, before dropping down to Furnace and Letterewe. Just before the latter, another side branch leads east to the head of Lochan Fada, while the main path turns north and follows the Allt Folais to another path junction. The north-east branch climbs over the Bealach Mheinnidh to the Fionn Loch and Carnmore while the main path crosses the Allt Folais and climbs towards the pass at the head of Srathan Buidhe. Dropping down around the north side of Beinn Airigh Charr, this path follows the Allt na Creige down to Kernsary. From here a private road leads west to the end of Loch Maree at Inveran and follows the River Ewe to Poolewe.

The historic 'postman's route' leaves this path at the head of Srathan Buidhe, heading west then north-west above the steep crags of Creag Tharbh. After about 4km it drops down to the loch-side at Ardlair from where a track leads to Kernsary.

2) Incheril (Kinlochewe) to Corrie Hallie (Dundonnell) (29km). From the car park at Incheril a private road leads north-east, following the north side of the Abhainn Bruachaig to Heights of Kinlochewe. A track branches off and climbs northwards up Gleann na Muice, narrowing to a path which leads to the south-east end of Lochan Fada, where it meets the Gleann Bianasdail path mentioned above. From the end of the loch climb north-east across country to Loch Meallan an Fhudair, then continue in the same direction over the Bealach na Croise. Follow the stream down the other side then cross to join the path on its east side, before it flows into Loch an Nid. This path comes from

Heights of Kinlochewe track along the north side of the Abhainn Bruachaig for a few kilometres, then climb north-west across the steadily rising plateau to the summit. A more sporting alternative from Incheril is to follow the path north-west along the Kinlochewe River for about 3km to below the Waterfall Buttress. A heathery spur to the right of the unmistakable waterfall gives access to the summit plateau.

Climbing interest on Waterfall Buttress goes back as far as 1899 when Glover and Inglis Clark completed *West Climb* (90m Severe) to the left of the waterfall, a route remarkable for its standard and conception at that time. Despite incomplete freezing *The Waterfall* (120m V,5) was first climbed in 1984. Further round on the Bonaid Dhonn, a number of modern rock climbs enjoy magnificent views up Loch Maree and across to Slioch and Beinn Eighe; qualities which help make up for their difficulty of access.

Beinn Lair; 859m; (OS Sheet 19; NG981732); *hill of the mare*

The gentle south-west slopes which rise up from the wooded shores of Loch Maree opposite the A832 Kinlochewe to Gairloch road give no indication of the true nature of Beinn Lair. North-east of the broad summit ridge, a line of cliffs stretches for 5km above Gleann Tulacha and Lochan Fada. Described by Munro in 1905 as 'possibly the grandest inland line of cliffs to be found in Scotland' this hidden face of Beinn Lair is made up of more than twenty buttresses, ridges and ribs, ranging in height from 120m to 420m and separated by deep gullies.

The greatest obstacle to access for climbers or walkers is, of course, Loch Maree, and the summit of Beinn Lair is an equally long way from the road at either Poolewe or Kinlochewe. Neighbouring Meall

Loch a' Bhraoin and continues north, following the Abhainn Loch an Nid until it joins a track 1km before Achneigie. This track climbs uphill across open moorland then drops down through birch woodland to Corrie Hallie on the A832, 4km south-east of Dundonnell.

3) Poolewe to Corrie Hallie (Dundonnell) (36km). As mentioned above, a private road leads from Poolewe to beyond Kernsary, and a path continues along the slope north of the Allt na Creige and past Loch an Doire Crionaich to the end of Srathan Buidhe. A short distance up this narrow glen the path branches. The route continues east to the head of Fionn Loch and crosses the dramatic causeway which separates the Dubh Loch and leads to Carnmore Lodge. From a junction here, the path climbs east then north-east, passing Loch Feith Mhic'-illean before crossing the watershed and continuing down Gleann na Muice Beag and Gleann na Muice to the buildings at Larachantivore. Shenavall bothy stands on the opposite side of Strath na Sealga, but reaching it involves crossing two rivers, the Abhainn Gleann na Muice and the Abhainn Srath na Sealga, which may be impossible during and after wet weather. From Shenevall a path climbs east up a little glen then crosses open moorland towards Loch Coire Chaorachain, and joins the track mentioned above leading down to Corrie Hallie.

4) Loch a' Bhraoin (Braemore) to Gruinard (34km). A private track leaves the A832 Dundonnell road at a gate 6km west of Braemore junction. Following the edge of a forestry plantation, it leads south-west for 1km to a ruined boathouse at the east end of Loch a' Bhraoin. An intermittent path continues west along the north shore of the loch, past Lochivraon cottage, and eventually turns north after crossing the watershed. The route from Kinlochewe joins for a while, passing Loch an Nid, as described above. After a short section of track to Achneigie, the path continues north-west, following the Abhainn Srath na Sealga to Shenavall. In common with the Poolewe path, this river plus the Abhainn Gleann na Muice may prevent further progress in wet weather. On the other side of Strath na Sealga, from the south-east end of Loch na Sealga, an indistinct path follows the south-west shore of the loch to meet the estate track which runs the length of the Gruinard River. 1km below the outflow from Loch na Sealga the confluence of the Allt Loch Ghuibhsachain has to be forded, but otherwise the track leads easily to the A832 Dundonnell to Laide road on the coast, 1km south of Gruinard House.

Looking up the Fionn Loch to Beinn Lair, A' Mhaighdean and Beinn Airigh Charr

Mheinnidh and Beinn Airigh Charr may also be included to make a longer outing. From Kinlochewe, follow the approach already described for Slioch. Beyond the Gleann Bianasdail junction, a delightful path winds up and down above the northern shores of Loch Maree to Furnace and thence Letterewe, through the remaining oak woodland. From Letterewe, an excellent footpath climbs east, following the Abhainn na Fuirneis past Loch Garbhaig. The summit of Beinn Lair can be reached by taking a direct line almost north from the west end of Loch Garbhaig.

A more scenic but slightly longer alternative is to continue along the track to the long, thin lochan (not named on any of the maps) just below the highest point on the track, then make a short steep climb to Point 787m at the south-east end of the long summit ridge. Finally, a straightforward walk north-west leads to the summit, with excellent views across Lochan Fada to A' Mhaighdean, Beinn Tarsuinn and the Fisherfield hills. For a round trip, continue in the same direction and drop down to the Bealach Mheinnidh to meet another excellent path which returns to Letterewe. (This whole route is shown on the north-east corner of the 1:25,000 Cuillin & Torridon Hills Outdoor Leisure OS map.) The Bealach Mheinnidh can also be reached from the north, leaving the Carnmore path near the south end of Fionn Loch.

The north-east cliffs of Beinn Lair form the greatest escarpment of hornblende schist in the country. For rock climbers based at Carnmore, they make an inspiring sight, particularly when the evening sun highlights every rib and buttress. Apart from a flurry of activity one summer, when parties from a number of Scottish and English universities recorded some 21 new routes, rock climbing on Beinn Lair has been eclipsed by harder routes on other crags in the area, with a couple of exceptions.

Wisdom Buttress (220m Very Difficult

1951) has become a classic at its grade, giving exposed, sustained and continuously interesting climbing up a distinctive slender, cigar shaped buttress. The narrow gully immediately to the east is *Bat's Gash* (220m Very Difficult 1951) which has all the traditional ingredients for those who enjoy that sort of thing. In winter, there never seems to be any significant build up of ice, but plenty of challenging mixed climbing awaits those prepared to make the long walk in.

Meall Mheinnidh; 722m; (OS Sheet 19; NG955748); *grassy* or *solitary hill*

Standing between its two more distinguished sisters, remote Meall Mheinnidh is a fine rugged hill whose ascent can be combined with either or both Beinn Lair to the south-east or Beinn Airigh Charr to the north-west. The Carnmore path crosses the foot of the well-defined north-west ridge just after crossing the Srathan Buidhe, route of another path to Letterewe. The south-east slopes are also straightforward from the Bealach Mheinnidh, and the summit is an excellent viewpoint, surrounded by distinctive hills.

Beinn Airigh Charr; 791m; (OS Sheet 10 NG930761); *hill of the bogland shieling*

Most accessible of the Letterewe hills, Beinn Airigh Charr is easily recognised from the coast around Loch Ewe by its distinctive tower shaped northern outlier, Spidean Mairich (*Martha's Peak*) (not named on the OS map). According to legend, the unfortunate Martha, a local shepherdess, made the first traverse of the tower while looking after her flock, only to fall to her death while attempting to retrieve her cromag (*crook*) which she had dropped.

Happier climbers' tales abound of the era of Colonel Whitbread's ownership of Letterewe and Fisherfield, when the estate boat would ferry parties across Loch Maree. In those days it was possible to park at Kernsary farm for the then exorbitant charge of £1, but now the estate favours the principle of the long walk in and cars must be left at Poolewe. This gives a longer but pleasant enough walk along the estate road which follows the east bank of the River Ewe past Inveran. Bicycles are allowed on the tracks, but not the paths, and their use shortens the approach considerably.

Just beyond Loch an Doire Ghairbh, a path (not marked on the OS map) cuts south-east to join the track from Kernsary to Ardlair. Just before descending into the woods beside Loch Maree, an excellent stalkers path climbs east into a shallow corrie, leading eventually to the grassy bealach between Spidean nan Clach (705m) and Meall Chnaimhean (653m). Suddenly the view of the Flowerdale and Torridon hills opens out to the south, and the summit of Beinn Airigh Charr is reached by a short climb across the broad bowl to the east.

Glover and Ling first explored the eastern buttress of Martha's Peak in 1909, returning in 1910 to climb *Face Route* (330m Difficult 1910) on the main tower. Since then there has only been sporadic exploration in summer and winter.

Beinn a' Chaisgein Beag; 682m; (OS Sheet 19; NG965821); *little forbidding hill*

Beinn a' Chaisgein Mor; 856m; (OS Sheet 19; NG982785); *big forbidding hill*

Though not a striking mountain in its own right, two great crags on the south flanks of Beinn a' Chaisgein Mor and its southern outlier Sgurr na Laocainn stand out behind the distinctive white Carnmore Lodge. The barn situated to the west has traditionally offered spartan accomodation for climbers outwith the stalking season. Access from Kernsary follows the right branch of the

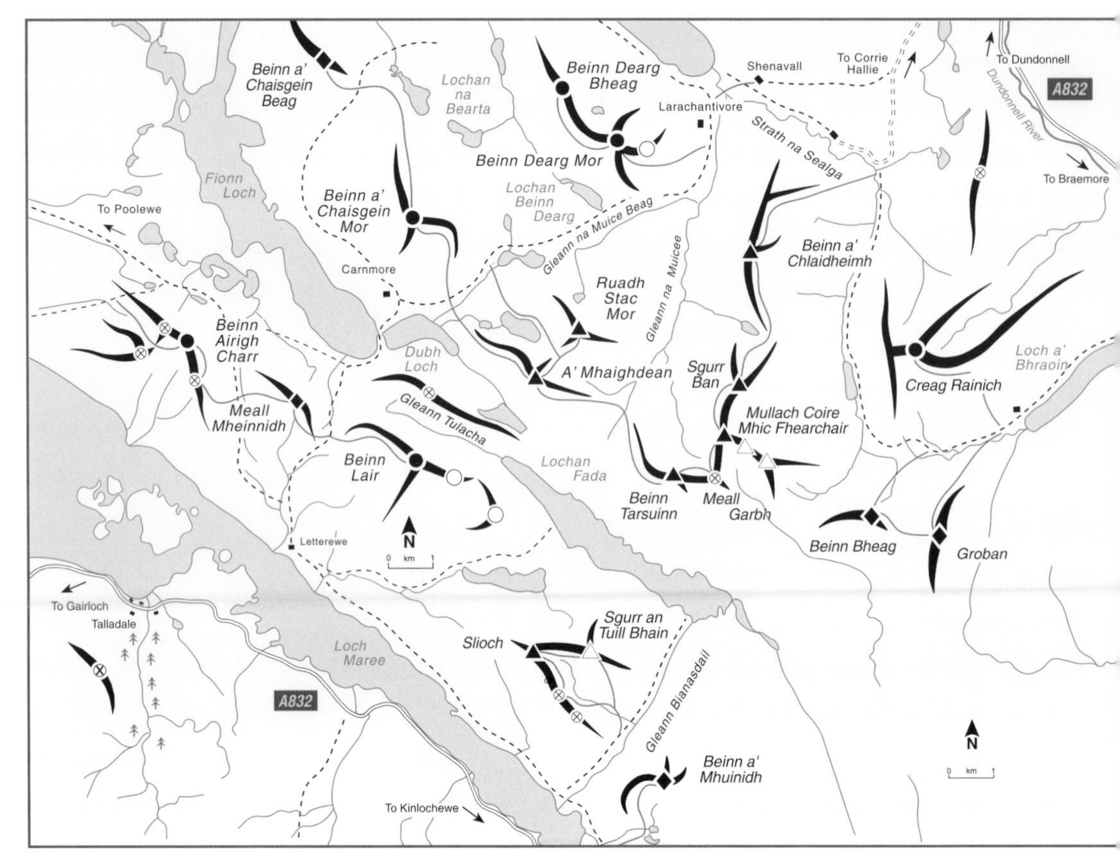

track beyond the farm, through a conifer plantation. Cyclying is permitted to here.

The once notoriously boggy section of path following the Allt na Creige has been re-routed to start further along the estate track and traverse the hillside above the Alt na Creige. The path continues south-east below the cliffs of Beinn Airigh Charr, with a short diversion south to cross the Srathan Buidhe. After passing below the northern cliffs of Meall Mheinnidh, the path finally turns north around the head of the Fionn Loch, crossing a causeway between it and the Dubh Loch.

From a junction just before Carnmore, an excellent stalkers path makes a rising traverse east below the cliffs of Sgurr na Laocainn, then follows the Allt Bruthach an Easain to its source in Lochan Feith Mhic'-illean. Open slopes to the north-west lead to the summit of Beinn a' Chaisgein Mor. A more direct approach from Carnmore involves a steep climb up the gully between Carnmore Crag and Torr na h-Iolaire, described below.

From the summit of Beinn a' Chaisgein Mor a long wide ridge slopes away north, to a broad bealach below Beinn a' Chaisgein Beag. This point can also be reached by taking the other branch of the path which passes Carnmore, skirting the western flanks of Beinn a' Chaisgein Mor parallel with the shores of Fionn Loch then climbing gradually north-east to the bealach. A short climb north-west finally gains the summit of Beinn a' Chaisgein Beag, which has a fine stone-built trig point and extensive views.

To the west and north-west lies an extensive area of unappealing bog dotted with numerous lochans, but there are a couple of reasonable alternative approaches from Gruinard Bay to the north, which make an excellent circuit. A rough vehicle track follows the west bank of the Gruinard River which flows north-west from Loch na Sealga. 1km or so before the loch, follow the tributary Allt Loch Ghiubhsachain by its steep west bank, or if possible to cross the burn, more easily by its east bank. Either way, climb up to meet the end of the stalkers path from Carnmore.

Alternatively, from the car park at Gruinard beach, a footpath follows the east bank of the Inverianvie River, past several impressive waterfalls, to Loch a' Mhadaidh Mor. Skirt the east shore of the loch then follow the Uisge Toll a' Mhadaidh upstream until it is possible either to cross and climb up onto the broad rock strewn north ridge of Beinn a' Chaisgein Beag, or climb higher and approach the summit from the north-east.

Directly above the barn, west of the lodge, Carnmore Crag has some of the finest rock climbing in Britain. One of the few major Scottish crags to catch the sun for most of the day, the pale rough gneiss dries quickly after rain. The classic and very prominent *Fionn Buttress* (240m VS 4c 1957) climbs the left side of the crag. *Balaton* (105m HVS 5b 1966) takes the best line on the Lower Wall, climbing a big corner at the back of the recess. The Upper Wall is very steep, giving sensational exposed climbing. *Dragon* (95m HVS 5a 1957) takes an improbable line between the lower and upper sets of overhangs. *The Sword* (80m E3 5c 1967) takes a big groove line while *Gob* (110m HVS 4c 1960) snakes underneath the main roof before breaking through.

Carnmore Corner (65m E2 5b 1968) is often wet on account of a small spring at the top. *The Orange Bow* (35m E5 6a 1985) climbs the impressive arete to the right. East of Carnmore Crag, Torr na h-Iolaire (not named on the OS map) is the great rocky tower above the Lodge, leading to the summit of Sgurr na Laocainn. The crag is broken by terraces into several tiers and routes can be joined to give longer climbs. *Ipswich Rib* (375m Very Difficult 1956) starts at the lowest rocks of the Lower Wall, with easier ground to the foot of the Upper Summit Buttress, giving the longest route on the crag.

A' Mhaighdean; 967m; (OS Sheet 19; NH007749); *the maiden* or *last sheaf of corn cut in the harvest*

Ruadh Stac Mor; 918m; (OS Sheet 19; NH018756); *big red stack*

Graceful A' Mhaighdean was described by Parker, an early compleater, as 'that most un-get-at-able of all hills' and has always been special to Munro baggers by virtue of its remoteness. It is the only record of a

Loch Maree

Many consider Loch Maree to be the finest of all Highland lochs, with its secluded bays and wooded islands, set among striking hills. It remains the only major loch in the Northern Highlands not to have been altered by hydro-electric schemes. Visitors often wonder why the village at the head of Loch Maree is named Kinlochewe, but it seems likely that at one time the sea did extend this far inland. Timothy Pont, around 1650, wrote of the 'fresch Loch of Ew' as opposed to 'the salt Lochew', noting of the former 'by sum it is called Loch Mulruy'. The loch is named after Saint Maelrubha of Applecross, who, when the area was dominated by the Picts, set up a church on the island of the Holy Well. Prior to this, the island had probably been a centre for pagan worship. Rites involving the sacrifice of bulls continued until the 17th century while other rituals said to cure insanity are reported to have been carried out into the 19th century. Visitors traditionally stuck coins into a tree beside the well, a custom observed by Queen Victoria on her visit in 1877.

The shoreline of Loch Maree was at one time entirely wooded, though now only remnants remain. From 1610 to 1670 one of the earliest blast furnaces in Scotland operated on the east bank of the River Ewe, near Poolewe and there were other ironworks around Loch Maree at Furnace, Talladale, Slattadale and in Glen Docherty. The oak forest which once covered the northern shores of the loch provided the fuel required for the smelting process. Many of the workers were incomers, some of whom still rest in peace at Cladh nan Sasunnach (*burial ground of the southerners*) near the mouth of Gleann Bianasdail.

Looking east to Mullach Coire Mhic Fhearchair from Beinn Lair

Sunday climb in the notebook of the first Munroist, the Reverend A.E.Robertson, who reported 'spending the entire day in heavy rain and seeing nothing' on 29 May 1898. He missed what many consider to be the finest summit view of all the Munros, with a matchless combination of mountain, corrie and loch radiating out in all directions. Neighbouring Ruadh Stac Mor, 1km to the north-east, was elevated to Munro status in 1974, and both hills are usually climbed as part of a greater round, being almost equidistant from Kinlochewe, Poolewe and Dundonnell.

From Carnmore, the north-west ridge of A' Mhaighdean rises gracefully in a series of rocky steps from which the south-west cliffs drop steeply towards the Dubh Loch. This ridge can be reached from the excellent stalkers path which climbs east from the lodge, leaving the path as it climbs the Allt Bruthach an Easain.

Traverse across to the burn which flows from Fuar Loch Beag at the foot of the ridge. Interesting scrambling, with any difficulties easily avoided, leads up to a domed plateau. Perched at the top of the Pillar Buttress, the gneiss summit is the highest outcrop of this ancient rock.

Although surrounded by mountains, the most distinctive landmarks from the summit are the lochs between them. Gorm Loch Mor sits in a rocky hollow directly below the southern cliffs, with Lochan Fada stretching away to the south-east. In the opposite direction, the distinctive white lodge at Carnmore stands out between the Dubh Loch and the Fionn Loch. To the north, secluded Fuar Loch Mor gives an alternative approach from the Shenavall to Carnmore path which climbs up Gleann na Muice Beag.

As the path starts to descend past the west end of Lochan Feith Mhic'-illean follow a branch which crosses the river and climbs south-east. This path continues further than indicated on the OS map, to the broken bealach between the grey gneiss of A' Mhaighdean and the red sandstone of Ruadh Stac Mor. Grassy slopes lead up to the former, while a faint path winds easily through the crags and screes which ring the latter. For an interesting return route to Carnmore from the top of A' Mhaighdean, make a straightforward descent to the south-east then cut back west to Gorm Loch Mor. Follow the north shore of the loch then drop down into the lower corrie, aiming to join the path along the south shore of the Dubh Loch, below the Ghost Slabs. Another alternative, before reaching Gorm Loch Mor, is to traverse the rugged crest of Beinn Tharsuinn Chaol which gives impressive views across to the cliffs of Beinn Lair and the south-west crags of A' Mhaighdean.

On this latter crag, *Pillar Buttress* (150m Very Difficult 1950) gives an enjoyable climb following the crest of the gneiss just below the summit. *Whitbread's Aiguille* (270m Severe 1957) is a good traditional route for climbers who enjoy an exploratory approach. Flanking this south-west side of the north-west ridge, four sandstone buttresses give a number of rock climbs. *Red Slab* (110m Difficult 1957) climbs the third buttress, while the fourth and steepest Gritstone Buttress has a number of shorter climbs on very coarse sandstone.

A number of other crags in the area have climbs recorded, the best of which is probably Maiden Buttress on the south-east side of Carnan Ban, in the small basin of Fuar Loch Beag. *Ecstasy* (115m Severe 1955) follows a rib on the left side of the crag, widening to a V-shaped slab. *Dishonour* (115m Very Difficult 1955) climbs from the left edge of the front face of the buttress.

Beinn Tarsuinn; 937m; (OS Sheet 19; NH039728); *transverse hill*

Mullach Coire Mhic Fhearchair; 1018m; (OS Sheet 19; NH052735); *summit of the corrie of Farquhar's son*

Sgurr Ban; 989m; (OS Sheet 19; NH055745); *light coloured peak*

Beinn a' Chlaidheimh; 916m; (OS Sheet 19; NH061775); *hill of the sword*

These four hills form a continuous ridge almost 9km long which hems in the east side of Gleann na Muice. Along with A' Mhaighdean and Ruadh Stac Mor they make up the 'Fisherfield Six', a popular hill-walkers round. However, there is enough variety of interesting alternative routes to justify return visits to any of these hills.

Roads and Lairds

Until relatively recently, many of the communities along the north-west coast of Scotland were geographically very isolated, and communications with the rest of the country tended to be by sea. Between 1792 and 1797 the British Fisheries Society built a road from Contin to Ullapool, but this was abandoned within 12 years, and there was no reasonable road west of Garve until 1847. Around the same time, the twice weekly mail service established between Dingwall, Poolewe and Stornoway was carried on foot. The route followed the east side of Loch Maree, where the crossing of Creag Tharbh (*bull rock*) presented a major obstacle for the post-runner.

The roads from Loch Maree to Gairloch and Braemore Junction to Dundonnell were initially built to provide employment during the devastating potato famine of 1846 and the latter is still known as 'Destitution Road'. Osgood Mackenzie's classic book *One Hundred Years in the Highlands* outlines the clan history of the area and details many aspects of local life in the 19th century. Born in 1842, a son of the laird of Gairloch, Mackenzie took over the estates of Inverewe and Kernsary in 1862. His gleeful accounts of the unsustainable slaughter of local wildlife make gruesome reading, no doubt reflecting the attitudes of that era. Ironically, his lasting legacy is the magnificent garden he created at Inverewe, on Am Ploc Ard, a barren rocky promontory in Loch Ewe. With the help of carefully planted shelter belts, imported soil and warm sea currents this was gradually transformed into an oasis of colour and fertility with some 2500 species from all over the world. Now in the care of the National Trust for Scotland, it is a popular attraction and well worth a visit.

Distinguished by its terraced sandstone cliffs, Beinn Tarsuinn sits across the head of Gleann na Muice (*valley of pigs*) which drains north into Loch na Sealga. Rather confusingly, another Gleann na Muice to the south-east of the mountain drains away from Lochan Fada. Not in Munro's original list, Beinn Tarsuinn was soon identified as an Ordnance Survey error, and promoted in an early revision of Munro's Tables.

From the summit of A' Mhaighdean, descent south-east leads to a broad bealach (525m) at the head of the northern Gleann na Muice. A series of awkward sandstone ledges can be avoided to the west. This point can also be reached from the direction of Shenavall by taking the path which leads south into Gleann na Muice, and following the Abhainn Gleann na Muice. From the bealach, grassy slopes lead up to the north-west ridge of Beinn Tarsuinn, which narrows as it curves around the small hanging corrie on its north side. From the exposed crest, a series of sandstone crags and screes drop down to the north, while the summit stands on a mossy platform.

Approaching from Kinlochewe, the south-east end of Lochan Fada can be reached from the car park at Incheril either through the narrow defile of Gleann Bianasdail, or along the estate road which passes the Heights of Kinlochewe and finishes part way up the southern Gleann na Muice. In wet weather the latter route avoids having to cross the outflow of Lochan Fada. From the south-east end of the loch climb north, avoiding the crags of Creag Ghlas Mhor, to reach a gently rising ridge which leads to steeper slopes of stepped sandstone and thence the summit.

From the summit of Beinn Tarsuinn the easy south-east shoulder leads down to the narrow Bealach Odhar (*dun coloured pass*) below Meall Garbh (851m). A narrow deer track traverses below the north-west face of this outlier to a second bealach below the summit of Mullach Coire Mhic Fhearchair, which is reached by a steep climb over quartzite blocks.

The highest of these remote hills, the Farquhar in question is thought to have been Farquhar MacIntaggart, who was awarded the Earldom of Ross in the 13th century for his exploits against the Norsemen. Farquhar's son, William, was rewarded with lordship of Skye in 1266. During his pioneering round of all the Munros and Tops, the Reverend A.R.G.Burn, first 'Compleat Munroist', noted in June 1917 that 'this unknown, obscure hill is far finer in outline than the long scree slope Beinn Eighe'.

The west face of Mullach Coire Mhic Fhearchair is craggy sandstone, while the south-east ridge has a fine arete of gneiss with some distinctive pinnacles which are easier to traverse than avoid. Approach from the east via Loch a' Bhraoin (*loch of the showers*) is long and rough but in keeping with the character of the mountain. Leave the A832 Braemore Junction to Dundonnell 'Destitution Road' as it swings round to the north-west.

A locked gate marks a track which skirts a forestry plantation and leads to some ruins at the east end of the loch. This is a particularly impressive spot, gateway to the Fannaichs to the south and Letterewe and Fisherfield to the west. The path leading west literally follows the north shore of the loch to Lochivraon cottage, then continues up the glen, passing the ruin of Feinasheen on the watershed.

Before descending too far, leave the path and cross the glen, skirting around the cliffs of Tom an Fhiodha to gain the east ridge of Sgurr Dubh (918m) (*black peak*). This can also be reached from the south-east end of Lochan Fada, via the Bealach na Croise, an old droving route. From Sgurr Dubh the pinnacled section of ridge gives some scrambling which leads to the eastern top Tom Choinneach (981m) and thence the summit of Mullach Coire Mhic Fhearchair.

To the north, a broad ridge of quartzite scree drops to a bealach, the Cab Coire nan Clach, (not named on the OS 1:50,000 map) south of Sgurr Ban. The quartzite topping of Sgurr Ban makes for particularly rough walking, especially when wet, and the large

Beinn Dearg Mor and Beinn Dearg Bheag

summit cairn stands well to the north-east on the flat summit plateau. A distinctive feature of this hill is the large area of easy angled quartzite slabs on its eastern flanks above Loch an Nid. Straightforward in dry conditions, these are best avoided in the wet. In summer, the green peaklet of Meallan an Laoigh (654m) stands out above the surrounding grey slabs.

Following the north-east spur from Sgurr Ban, two tiny lochans make a useful landmark in poor visibility, marking the bealach south of Beinn a' Chlaidheimh, overlooking Loch a' Bhrisidh nestled in a hanging corrie to the west. Beinn a' Chlaidheimh is distinguished by its long, narrow summit ridge which runs almost north-south, dropping away steeply on the west side. This airy ridge stands in a commanding position above Strath na Sealga to the north and is pleasantly grassy compared to its southern neighbours. Another relatively new Munro, its height was elevated by a couple of metres in the most recent survey.

Approach from the north is usually from Corrie Hallie on the A832 from Braemore Junction, on its final descent to Dundonnell. This is one of the busiest roadside parking spots in the Northern Highlands, particularly in early summer. Shenavall bothy, situated just beyond the south-east end of Loch na Sealga, now attracts visitors from all over the world, and is often crowded. The footpath across the south-east shoulder of Sail Liath has also become badly eroded in recent years. There are, however, plenty of attractive sites for wild camping in Strath na Sealga and Gleann na Muice.

The writer James Hogg, 'The Ettrick Shepherd', journeyed from Letterewe to Dundonnell in 1803 and saw at first hand the effect of the Clearances in this area. In 'Strathinshalloch' (Strath na Sealga) he noted that 'there were considerable crops of corn and potatoes left by the tennants who had removed last term'.

To climb Beinn a' Chlaidheimh from Corrie Hallie, follow the estate track which climbs roughly south-west through wooded Gleann Chaorachain, crossing a featureless ridge then dropping down to meet the Abhainn Loch an Nid. This river becomes the Abhainn Strath na Sealga lower down, and may be impossible to cross during or just after wet weather. The typical sandstone terracing on the north-east slopes of Beinn a' Chlaidheimh gives a rough but straightforward climb, which is also the best line of descent, avoiding the crags at the north end of the ridge. An alternative approach from Strath na Sealga climbs the steeper north-west shoulder.

Creag Rainich; 807m; (OS Sheet 19; NH096751); *bracken crag*

Inconspicuous Creag Rainich stands isolated in a corner of the Dundonnell Forest between Loch a' Bhraoin and Loch an Nid. Usually bypassed by climbers on their way to greater things, it gives excellent views of its grander neighbours.

The easiest route to the top climbs grassy slopes north-west from the west end of Loch a' Bhraoin, crossing a knoll at 749m. The boggy northern slopes of Creag Rainich drain into a fine waterfall, the Eas Ban, which drops into a wooded gorge above Strath na Sealga. The steeper west side is lined with grassy terraces between sandstone crags, but can be climbed without difficulty above Loch an Nid. Descent to the north-east along a long heathery ridge provides an alternative to the rough Loch a' Bhraoin path.

Beinn Bheag; 668m; (OS Sheet 19; NH086714); *little hill*

Groban; 749m; (OS Sheet 19; NH099709); *point of rock*

Groban and Beinn Bheag are two neighbouring rounded hills, separated by the Bealach Gorm. Their location, between the Letterewe and Fisherfield hills to the west and the Fannaichs to the east, makes them fine viewpoints. Ascent from the north is straightforward, leaving the path which continues west beyond Loch a' Bhraoin. The flat summit of Beinn Bheag has two cairns. The eastern cairn is higher but the western cairn gives the better views, particularly looking south-west over Lochan Fada to Slioch and the Beinn Eighe range beyond. The views from Groban are not quite so spectacular but most parties will probably wish to climb both peaks. It is also feasible to include Creag Rainich in a longer round.

Approach from the south is longer and even more scenic. From the car park at Incheril, just east of Kinlochewe, a private road follows the pleasant Abhainn Bruachaig to Heights of Kinlochewe, where a track branches off left and climbs north up the bleak Gleann na Muice. Where the track finally ends, two narrow diverging paths continue.

The eastern fork climbs over the shoulder of Meallan Odhar into the head of Gleann Tanagaidh. This has a particularly wild and remote atmosphere, with a broad river gently meandering between wide grassy flats. A short straightforward climb north-east leads to the Bealach Gorm. The other branch of the path continues to the head of Gleann na Muice and the east end of Lochan Fada.

The last few kilometres across moorland to the Bealach na Croise at the west end of Beinn Bheag are rougher going underfoot, but make a logical round trip. In March 1746, Lord Louden and Principal Forbes of Culloden escaped south over the Bealach na Croise with about eight hundred men on their epic retreat from Dornoch to Skye to avoid capture by Prince Charlie's Jacobite troops.

Beinn Dearg Mor; 910m; (OS Sheet 19; NH032799); *big red hill*

Beinn Dearg Bheag; 820m; (OS Sheet 19; NH020811); *little red hill*

The magnificent sandstone twins, Beinn Dearg Mor and Beinn Dearg Bheag, stand shoulder to shoulder, in splendid isolation, in the heart of the Fisherfield Forest. The outline of their rugged ridges and corries tantalises the approaching climber and draws the eye from the surrounding Munros. Sir Hugh himself described them as

An Teallach from the road just south of Dundonnell

being 'a long way from anywhere' while Hamish Brown suspected that 'they are more often admired than climbed'.

From the summit of Beinn Dearg Mor two wing-like ridges curve out to the north-east, enclosing the rugged Coire nan Clach as they drop steeply into Strath na Sealga. Photographs of this side of the mountain from Shenavall are often mistaken for its grander neighbour, An Teallach. To the north-west, Loch Toll an Lochain sits in a broad, shallow corrie below the bealach joining Beinn Dearg Bheag. On the other side of the ridge linking the two summits, uniform slopes drop steeply south-west into Srath Beinn Dearg, sometimes referred to as the 'Lost Valley'.

The most popular approach to these hills is from Shenavall, enjoying the spectacular views into Coire nan Clach. The path to Shenavall and the possible difficulties in crossing the two rivers in Strath na Sealga in wet weather have been mentioned earlier. From the buildings at Larachantivore, the easiest way to the top of Beinn Dearg Mor is via the small hanging corrie south-east of the summit. Slightly longer, but more interesting, the narrow rocky ridge which encloses the south-west side of this corrie is also a straightforward climb.

The large summit cairn is spectacularly situated on a narrow and exposed rocky platform, jutting out above the cliffs of Coire nan Clach. In clear weather there are magnificent views all around, while cloud and mist makes this a very dramatic spot, peering over the edge into a deep abyss.

There are no difficulties on the ridge which runs north-west to Beinn Dearg Bheag. In descent, Loch Toll an Lochain can be reached down the steep headwall from the bealach between the peaks and straightforward slopes lead down to Loch na Sealga. A more interesting approach to the lower peak comes up from the coast along the estate track which follows the west bank of the Gruinard River to the north-west end of Loch na Sealga. This is a quicker approach if a bicycle is used.

The summit can be seen to the south from the start, where the track leaves the A832 Dundonnell to Laide road. Avoid the wooded crags directly above the loch and

Corrag Bhuidhe and Sgurr Fiona, An Teallach

gain the rough undulating spur of Carn Airigh an Easain (348m) which leads to the north-west ridge proper. This gradually narrows and gives enjoyable scrambling over several rocky towers.

The climbing potential of Beinn Dearg Mor was first investigated by Sang and Morrison in 1899. The crags are disappointing for summer climbing but give a number of worthwhile routes in winter.

An Teallach (Sgurr Fiona); 1060m; (OS Sheet 19; NH064837); *the forge, (white* or *wine peak)*

An Teallach (Bidean a' Ghlas Thuill); 1062m; (OS Sheet 19; NH068843); the forge, *(pinnacle of the grey-green hollow)*

The unmistakable sandstone spires of An Teallach stand out from many points in the Northern Highlands. Without doubt one of Scotland's finest mountains, it is best seen from the A832 'Destitution Road' travelling north-west from Braemore Junction towards Dundonnell. The spectacular cliff scenery of its enormous eastern corries can be appreciated even from the roadside, while the traverse of its many tops gives a magnificent outing, involving some serious scrambling.

The backbone of the mountain rises from the head of Little Loch Broom and runs roughly north to south. Steep, open slopes drop away to the west, forming a long spur which stretches out above Loch na Sealga to Sgurr Ruadh (761m). A sharply pinnacled twisting ridge links the main tops, with three great spurs projecting eastwards. Glas Mheall Mor, Glas Mheall Liath and Sail Liath enclose two enormous corries, Glas Tholl and Toll an Lochain.

The latter is particularly impressive, and it is well worth visiting Loch Toll an Lochain, at the foot of the surrounding cliffs and screes, to take in some of the unique atmosphere of the place. Much of the rock is dark red Torridonian sandstone, but the eastern spurs are capped with Cambrian quartzite which has formed distinctive pale grey screes.

The traverse of An Teallach is a serious undertaking, particularly in winter conditions. The route chosen should take into account weather, snow conditions and day length, as well as the fitness and experience of the party. Sadly, the mountain has claimed a number of lives. The shorter of the two most popular ascent routes approaches from Dundonnell and avoids the main difficulties. However, many would consider that simply going up and down by this route misses much of the interest and character of the traverse.

As the A832 from Braemore junction enters Dundonnell, a few hundred metres east of the hotel, a rough path winds steeply up over the shoulder of Meall Garbh. Either follow the broad ridge which turns south, rising over a couple of knolls, or follow the path into the corrie to the south. Both routes lead to an unnamed top (919m) on the main ridge which overlooks Glas Tholl.

A short diversion from here gives a gentle climb to the quartzite-capped summit of the north-eastern spur, Glas Mheall Mor. The steep eastern slopes of this spur can be descended to reach the burn which drains Glas Tholl, meeting a path further downstream which returns to the A832 opposite Dundonnell House. The final few hundred metres of this path are rather overgrown with rhododendron thickets.

From the unnamed top, an easy climb leads on to Bidein a' Ghlas Thuill, the highest point on An Teallach. Running east from this summit, the spur of Glas Mheall Liath separates the deep corries of Glas Tholl to the north-east from Toll an Lochain to the south-west. Walking out to this top gives a straightforward diversion to admire the scenery, but not a useful descent route. A line of awkward crags bars access to Coir' a' Ghiubhsachain. The steep corrie headwall of Glas Tholl can, however, be descended from the col north of Bidean a' Ghlas Thuill.

To continue to Sgurr Fiona, 1km to the south-west, a steep but easy descent is followed by re-ascent of the steep and in places rocky connecting ridge. The second highest point on the mountain, Sgurr Fiona

An Teallach – Names and Tops

There are a number of interesting suggestions to explain the derivation of the Gaelic 'teallach' (*blacksmith's forge*). Depending on cloud conditions, the sandstone buttresses can take on a warm red glow at sunrise and sunset, while at other times the mist drifts like smoke through the pinnacles. In earlier times, tinkers, the traditional travelling people, are reputed to have set up their forges in one of the corries. Lord Berkeley's Seat, the spectacular pinnacle which overhangs Coire Toll an Lochain, is said to be named after the eponymous gentleman who sat with his feet dangling over the edge for a bet. More recently, the old smiddy in Dundonnell has been converted into a climbing club hut, retaining the bellows and forge. From north to south, the following 2 Munros and 7 Tops make up the An Teallach ridge:

Glas Mheall Mor; 979m; (NH076853); *big greenish-grey hill,*
Bidein a' Ghlas Thuill; 1062m; (NH068843); *pinnacle of the grey-green hollow,*
Glas Mheall Liath; 960m; (NH077840); *greenish-grey hill,*
Sgurr Creag an Eich; 1017m; (NH055838); *peak of the rock of the horse,*
Sgurr Fiona; 1060m; (NH064837); *white* or *wine peak,*
Lord Berkeley's Seat; c1030m; (NH064835),
Corrag Bhuidhe; 1047m; (NH064834); *yellow finger,*
Stob Cadha Gobhlach; 960m; (NH068825); *peak of the forked pass,*
Sail Liath; 954m; (NH071824); *grey heel.*

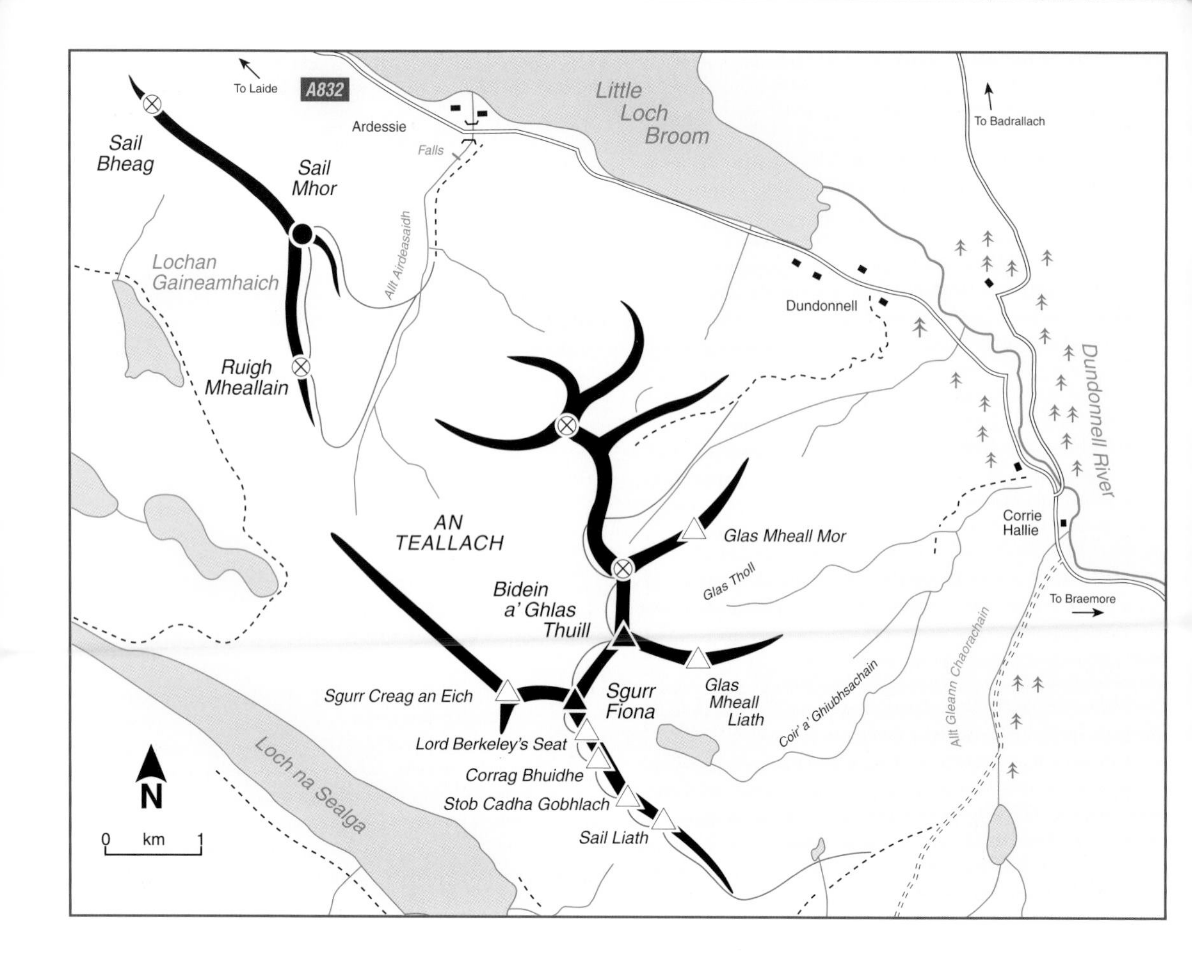

was promoted to Munro status in 1981. A narrow ridge to the west leads to Sgurr Creag an Eich. Coir a' Ghamhna to the south gives a possible way down into Strath na Sealga and Shenavall, though there is much unpleasant scree, and the burn which eventually drains into Loch na Sealga should be crossed high up, before it tumbles over waterfalls and enters a small gorge.

North-west from Sgurr Creag an Eich, a long rocky spur leads down to Sgurr Ruadh and gives an alternative approch to An Teallach. From the A832 Dundonnell to Laide road at Ardessie, Sgurr Ruadh can be climbed directly by following the Allt Airdeasaidh past the Ardessie Falls. For a longer day, Sail Mhor (767m) can be climbed first.

The other popular starting point to traverse An Teallach is Corrie Hallie, 3km south-east of Dundonnell on the A832, which gives at least two options. Either follow the route for Shenavall described earlier, but instead of descending into Strath na Sealga, continue up the broad south-east shoulder of Sail Liath. Alternatively, leave the track much earlier and cross the Allt Gleann Chaorachain to reach the crest of the long quartzite escarpment which meets the eastern flank of Sail Liath at Lochan na Bradhan.

This escarpment can also be reached from the other side by leaving the A832 nearer Dundonnell and following the path opposite Dundonnell House along the north side of the Coir' a' Ghiubhsachain burn as mentioned above. When the path peters out, continue following the burn, until it is possible to cross and pick a way up through the crags and onto the escarpment. From Lochan na Bradhan a straightforward climb west leads up to the flat summit of Sail Liath, at the south end of the An Teallach ridge.

To start the traverse from Sail Liath, descend west to the Cadha Gobhlach (*forked pass*). A small rocky pinnacle stands between the two branches of the gully which leads up to the pass, and provides a fine viewpoint. A gentle rise leads over Stob Cadha Gobhlach, then easy rocks lead to Corrag Bhuidhe Buttress, a short level rocky ridge. The next section of the ridge, the narrow crest of Corrag Bhuidhe, comprises four airy rock towers, followed by the leaning spire of Lord Berkeley's Seat jutting out over Toll an Lochain.

A direct line, following the crest of the ridge, gives excellent but very exposed scrambling. The so-called 'bad step' is a short steep pitch on the first tower, where a slip could be disastrous unless roped. This is particularly difficult in winter and should be considered climbing. All the difficulties can be avoided by narrow paths which traverse the south-west side of the ridge below the crest, leading to the shapely summit of Sgurr Fiona.

The wonderful Torridonian sandstone architecture of An Teallach is too broken and vegetated to provide good rock climbing. However, a number of worthwhile winter routes have been climbed, following long couloirs, chimneys and terraced buttresses. Despite spectacular scenery they do not equal their Torridon rivals for quality.

Sail Mhor; 767m; (OS Sheet 19; NH033887); *big heel*

The graceful profile of Sail Mhor contrasts with the pinnacled ramparts of its distinguished neighbour, An Teallach. Both rise up from a great sandstone plateau to tower above the southern shores of Little Loch Broom and like many summits close to the coast, Sail Mhor is a particularly fine viewpoint.

From the scattering of houses at Ardessie, on the A832 Dundonnell to Aultbea road, a path follows the east bank of the Allt Airdeasaidh, past the Ardessie Falls. The burn should be crossed eventually, to follow a tributary into the southern corrie, then climb up the south-east spur to the broken summit. Return the same way or extend the traverse by continuing south over Ruigh Mheallain (594m) before descending to rejoin the Allt Airdeasaidh.

For a longer outing, if transport can be arranged, there are several possibilities. Continuing south-east gives an alternative approach to An Teallach. Heading north-west over Sail Bheag (409m) and down to the road gives more opportunity to enjoy the views of the coast. Dropping down south-west to Lochan Gaineamhaich to join the stalkers path which leads out to Gruinard crosses some rugged and seldom frequented country.

Beinn Ghobhlach; 635m; (OS Sheet 19; NH055943); *forked hill*

The conspicuous twin tops of Beinn Ghobhlach dominate the Scoraig peninsula, the rugged narrow finger of land which separates Little Loch Broom from Loch Broom. A distinctive landmark from both the north and south, the hill looks deceptively high, with superb views in all directions.

A narrow road leaves the A832 Braemore Junction road about 3km south-east of Dundonnell, skirting the line of west facing cliffs at the base of the peninsula, then dropping down to the houses at Badrallach. Parking is rather limited at the road end. A fine footpath continues west along the coast, serving the isolated community at Scoraig.

After about 1km, leave the path to make a rising traverse up and over the ridge to the north, above two lochans. From this point, it is possible to cross between the lochans and climb the south-west flanks, heading just west of the summit. Alternatively, cross around the west end of Loch na h-Uidhe, above a spectacular waterfall, to reach the west ridge.

From the top, it is worth following the horseshoe ridge around to the other top, before descending into the intervening west facing corrie. Regain the Scoraig path just north of the Creag a' Chadha headland.

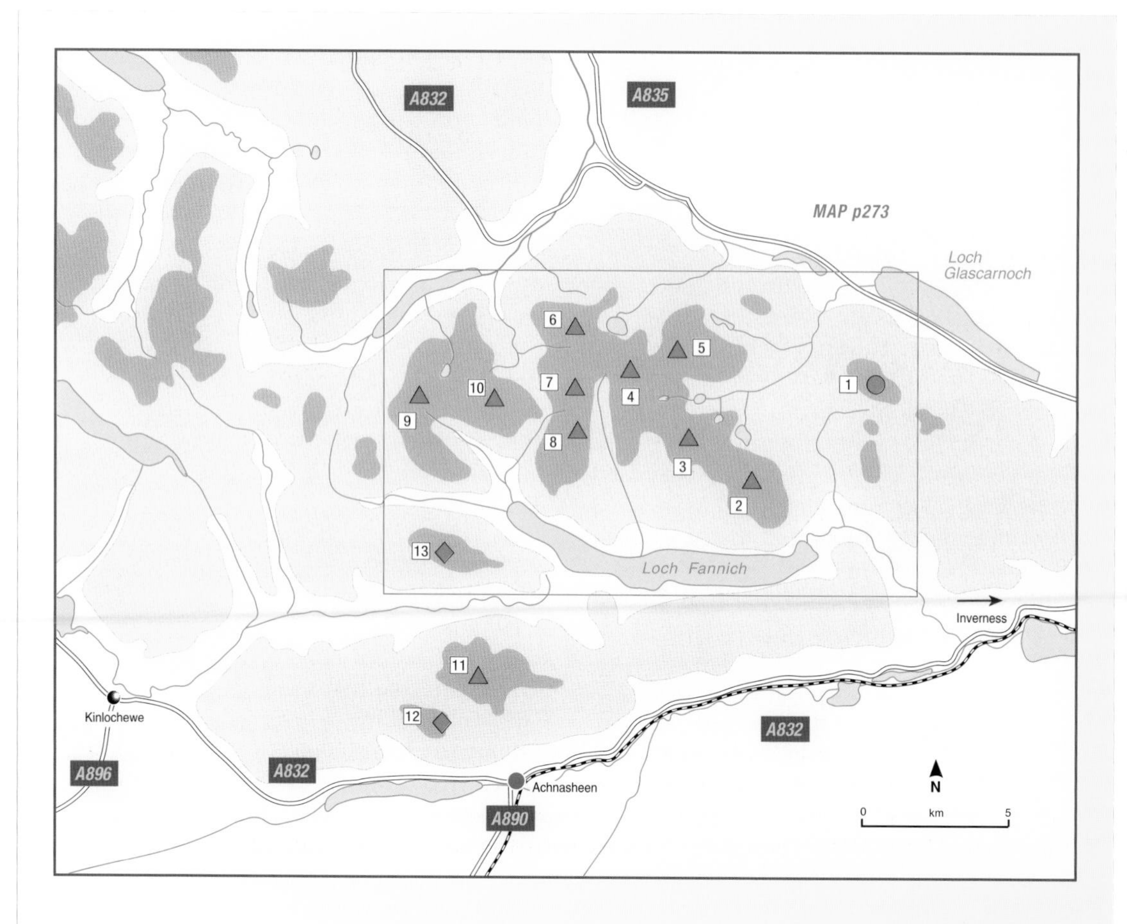

1.	Beinn Liath Mhor a' Ghiubhais Li	766m	C	p270
2.	An Coileachan	923m	M	p270
3.	Meall Gorm	949m	M	p270
4.	Sgurr Mor	1110m	M	p272
5.	Beinn Liath Mhor Fannaich	954m	M	p272
6.	Meall a' Chrasgaidh	934m	M	p274
7.	Sgurr nan Clach Geala	1093m	M	p274
8.	Sgurr nan Each	923m	M	p274
9.	A' Chailleach	997m	M	p275
10.	Sgurr Breac	999m	M	p275
11.	Fionn Bheinn	933m	M	p276
12.	Meall a' Chaorainn	705m	G	p276
13.	Beinn nan Ramh	711m	G	p277

The Fannaichs

Alec Keith

Approaching An Coileachan from the south-east

The Fannaichs are a compact group of high mountains located at the thin eastern end of the great wedge of wild land which stretches north-west from the village of Garve all the way to the coast. For hillwalkers and climbers the easily accessible corries and long high ridges of the Fannaichs contrast with the wilder and more remote hills of the adjoining Loch Maree to Loch Broom area. Longer expeditions are also possible, taking in parts of both areas. The Bealach na h-Imrich (c550m) (NH108705) forms the logical boundary between the two, on the western march of the Fannich Forest, where the ever twisting Highland watershed takes a determined swing to the east. Apart from a few isolated outliers to the south, most of the hills lie on or close to this watershed, to the north of Loch Fannich.

The origin of the name is obscure, but Loch Fannich is the most significant natural feature of the area. Deepened by the dam at its eastern end, water collecting in this crescent shaped loch is piped down to the hydro-electric power station at Grudie Bridge in Strath Bran. From here the water enters Loch Luichart which supplies another power station in Strath Conon. Loch Fannich remains one of the least frequented of Scotland's great freshwater lochs. Some of the finest views of the higher Fannaichs and their secluded corries are seen looking north across the loch from the lower Strath Bran hills.

Unfortunately bulldozed tracks have been extended on both sides of the loch in recent years. Not shown on the OS map, a track now contours the north side of Beinn nan Ramh and continues a considerable distance west up the Abhainn a' Chadh' Bhuidhe, while on the other side of Loch Fannich another track climbs some distance north into Coire Mor.

The A832 Gairloch road forms the southern boundary of the Fannaichs, branching off the A835 Ullapool road just west of Garve and following the railway through Strath Bran to Achnasheen. A low ridge of hills separates Loch Fannich from Strath Bran, culminating in the isolated Munro Fionn Bheinn. Apart from a fleeting glimpse into Garbh Choire Mor of An Coileachan, little can be seen of the south side of the higher Fannaich hills from this road. It is no longer possible to obtain permission to drive up the private road from Grudie Bridge to Fannich Lodge and approach from this side is longer and less popular than from the north.

The Ullapool road forms the northern boundary, turning north-west soon after leaving Garve, and passing Inchbae Lodge and the Aultguish Inn as it gradually crosses the Dirrie More (*great climb*). Just west of Aultguish another hydro dam holds back the extensive waters of Loch Glascarnoch and the next section of road can be difficult in snowy conditions. Rising gradually from the roadside, the Fannaichs form a line of rounded tops to the south-west, culminating in the distinctive summit cone of Sgurr Mor. The highest peak north of Carn Eighe in Glen Affric, Sgurr Mor stands above Braemore Junction where the A832 branches off south-west and follows the Abhainn Cuileig upstream before turning north-west towards Dundonnell.

The long smooth ridges which link the Fannaich summits give excellent walking and are ideally suited to long traverses. Apart from isolated Fionn Bheinn, it is possible to climb the other nine Munros in the area in one outing, though few parties will have the energy or the inclination for such a long day. Depending on transport arrangements and the use of cycles, the hills can be climbed in a variety of interesting combinations and offer good ski-touring when conditions are suitable. There is also excellent winter climbing at all grades.

Principal Hills

Beinn Liath Mhor a' Ghiubhais Li; 766m; (OS Sheet 20; NH281713); *big grey hill of the colourful pine*

Close to the road and easily accessible, Beinn Liath Mhor a' Ghuibhais Li is suitable for a short outing. Standing above Loch Glascarnoch, this isolated and rather featureless dome has a fine view to match its grand name.

The northern ridges and corries of the main Fannaich massif stretch away immediately to the west while across the Dirrie More to the north stands Beinn Dearg and its neighbours. Much of the northern and eastern flanks of the hill above the A835 have been planted with conifers in the 1990s but the most direct route to the summit remains clear of trees. From the road follow the line of the stream which flows north-east down the hill into Loch Glascarnoch.

A slightly longer alternative route starts at the car park west of the bridge over the Abhainn an Torrain Duibh just beyond the end of Loch Glascarnoch. A bulldozed track climbs through the forestry plantation, following the line of the river. From the gate at the end of this track, climb the broad north-west ridge to the flat stony summit. This has some of the finest examples of solifluction boulder ramparts in Scotland, distinctive stripes caused by freeze-thaw processes.

An Coileachan; 923m; (OS Sheet 20; NH241680); *the little cock*

Meall Gorm; 949m; (OS Sheet 20; NH221696); *blue hill*

An Coileachan and Meall Gorm stand side by side at the south-east end of the main Fannaich ridge. Rounded in outline, their distinguishing features are a series of corries on their north-eastern flanks. Garbh Choire Mor on the south-east spur of An Coileachan, above the Loch Fannich dam, is particularly impressive, especially in winter. Despite its relatively low altitude, it has a number of good winter climbs. The corrie and the climbing conditions can be seen clearly from a point on the A832 Achnasheen road just west of Garve. None of the other corries have such spectacular cliffs, but they hold some lovely lochans instead.

All the approaches to this pair of hills are long. From the south-east, parties prepared to walk or cycle up the private road which follows the River Grudie will have the bonus of views into Garbh Choire Mor, whose southern rim can be followed to gain the south-east spur of An Coileachan.

Alternatively, the south and south-eastern slopes of this hill give easier climbing from further along the road towards Fannich Lodge.

From the summit of An Coileachan, a broad ridge leads north-west, down to the Bealach Ban (775m), continuing over an unamed intermediate top (922m) to Meall Gorm, which has a windbreak shelter near its summit cairn. The south ridge of Meall Gorm can also be climbed using an excellent stalkers path which starts in the trees beside Fannich Lodge and passes just west of the outlier Creag a' Choire Riabhaich (599m).

From the summit of Meall Gorm, the broad Fannaich ridge continues north-west to Meall nam Peithirean (974m). This has a long southern spur, Druim Reidh (*level ridge*), with a long line of crags on its eastern flank, overlooking Coire Beag. Like neighbouring Coire Mor, the lower ground coming up from Loch Fannich is rough and peaty. Beyond Meall nam Peithirean the ridge turns almost north, climbing to the summit of Sgurr Mor.

From the north, all the approaches to An Coileachan and Meall Gorm are long and rugged. There is ample parking near the west end of Loch Glascarnoch, where the the A835 Garve to Braemore Junction road crosses the Abhainn an Torrain Duibh. A narrow path follows the west bank of the river upstream, to the junction of the Allt an Loch Sgeirich and the Abhainn a' Ghiubhais Li. In dry conditions, cross the former and follow the latter to a footbridge (NH254713) which is not marked on the OS map. In wet weather, the Allt an Loch Sgeirich may be impassable, but this point can also be reached from the road by following the bulldozed track (not marked on the OS map) south-west through the forestry plantation on the northern slopes of Beinn Liath Mhor a' Ghiubhais Li. From the end of this track follow the south side of the Abhainn a' Ghiubhais Li.

A variety of possible routes continue from the south side of the footbridge. The broad ridge of Meallan Buidhe (633m) lies

Access and Transport

By road: from Inverness the A9 continues north to the roundabout at Tore, where the A835 leads west to Ullapool. The A832 to Gairloch branches off just beyond Garve, leading through Achnasheen and Kinlochewe, with the A832 to Dundonnell branching off at Braemore junction.

By bus: Inverness to Ullapool (Scottish Citylink Service 961, tel: 08705-505050); Inverness to Gairloch via Dundonnell; Inverness to Laide via Achnasheen (Westerbus, tel: 01445-712255).

By rail: the Inverness to Kyle of Lochalsh line runs south of the area with stations at Garve, Lochluichart, Achanalt and Achnasheen.

Accommodation and Information

Hotels and guesthouses: Achnasheen, Dundonnell, Garve, Kinlochewe, Ullapool.

SYHA hostel: Ullapool (tel: 0870-004-1156)

Independent hostels: Aultguish Inn Bunkhouse (tel: 01997-455254); Kinlochewe Hotel Bunkhouse (tel: 01445-760253); Ullapool: West House (tel: 01854-613126)

Club huts: Inver Croft near Achnasheen (Jacobites Mountaineering Club); Dundonnell: The Smiddy, Dundonnel (JMCS, Edinburgh Section)

Campsites: Dundonnell: Ardessie and Badrallach (tel: 01854-633281); Ullapool

Tourist Information Centre: Argyll Street, Ullapool (tel: 01854-612135) (limited winter hours)

Maps

Ordnance Survey 1:50,000 Landranger sheets 19 (Gairloch and Ullapool), 20 (Beinn Dearg and Loch Broom), 25 (Glen Carron and Glen Affric).

Descending south from Sgurr Mor towards Meall Gorm

directly above. Either cross this rounded hill or skirt round it to the west, above Loch Gorm, heading for the col on the other side, between Loch Gorm and Loch nan Eun, then climb due south to the summit of An Coileachan.

Alternatively, continue up the south side of the Abhainn a' Ghiubhais Li, following an ill-defined path which crosses the outflow of Loch Gorm, then climbs in zigzags past Loch an Eilein to reach the flat top of Meall Gorm about 200 metres east of the summit. The Abhainn a' Ghiubhais Li can also be followed past Loch Li to its source, Loch an Fhuar Thuill Mhoir. From the lip of this corrie a short climb south-west leads to the col west of Creachan Rairigidh. From here a stalkers path leads south-east to the next col (836m) and continues to the summit of Meall Gorm.

For a slightly longer outing taking in Beinn Liath Mhor Fannaich and Sgurr Mor first, follow the narrow path up the north side of the Allt an Loch Sgeirich from the junction mentioned above. After about 2km cross the burn. Even in spate conditions this should be possible at the small island (NH247726). Climb the broad north-east flank of Creag Dubh Fannaich (757m) and continue over this outlier to gain the easy south-east shoulder of Beinn Liath Mhor Fannaich.

Sgurr Mor; 1110m; (OS Sheet 20; NH203718); *big peak*

Beinn Liath Mhor Fannaich; 954m; (OS Sheet 20; NH219724); *big grey hill of Fannaich*

The shapely summit of Sgurr Mor is the highest point in the Northern Highlands and forms the central hub of the main Fannaich ridges. Beinn Liath Mhor Fannaich, its neighbour to the north-east, is rather isolated from the rest of the range, but is easily accessible from the road. There is ample parking by the dam at the west end of Loch Droma, opposite Lochdrum, where the A835 from Garve starts dropping down towards Braemore Junction.

From the south side of the dam, a rough track follows a hydro pipeline west to the Allt a' Mhadaidh, which is crossed at a small dam. A path continues upstream to Loch a' Mhadaidh. This is a particularly impressive spot, with an extensive steep dark crag rising directly above the far shore of the loch. Skirt these to the west and climb the headwall to the col between Carn na Criche (961m) (*boundary cairn*) and the next Munro, Meall a' Chrasgaidh. A short detour to the north-west will allow the latter to be included before continuing east to Carn na Criche.

A short descent south-east from this Top leads to the foot of the summit cone of Sgurr Mor whose summit cairn is perched close to the edge above the north-east cliffs. On a clear day there are extensive views to enjoy in all directions.

To continue towards Beinn Liath Mhor Fannaich, descend south-east for a short distance then turn north-east. In poor visibility this will require careful navigation. The ridge to follow drops away steeply on its north-west side but there is a stalkers path just below the crest on the opposite side. To return to the Loch Droma car park from the summit of Beinn Liath Mhor Fannaich, the best way down is to descend into the north-east corrie then skirt the west end of Loch Sgeireach and continue down to join the Allt a' Mhadaidh path. The route down the easy south-east shoulder and over Creag Dhubh Fannaich (757m) to the Abhainn an Torrain Duibh car park has already been described.

A number of winter climbs have been recorded on the north sides of these hills. On Sgurr Mor *The Resurrection* (320m III 1980) gives a serious climb with a great alpine atmosphere which finishes at the summit cairn. On Carn na Criche the first route on the impressive crag above Loch a'

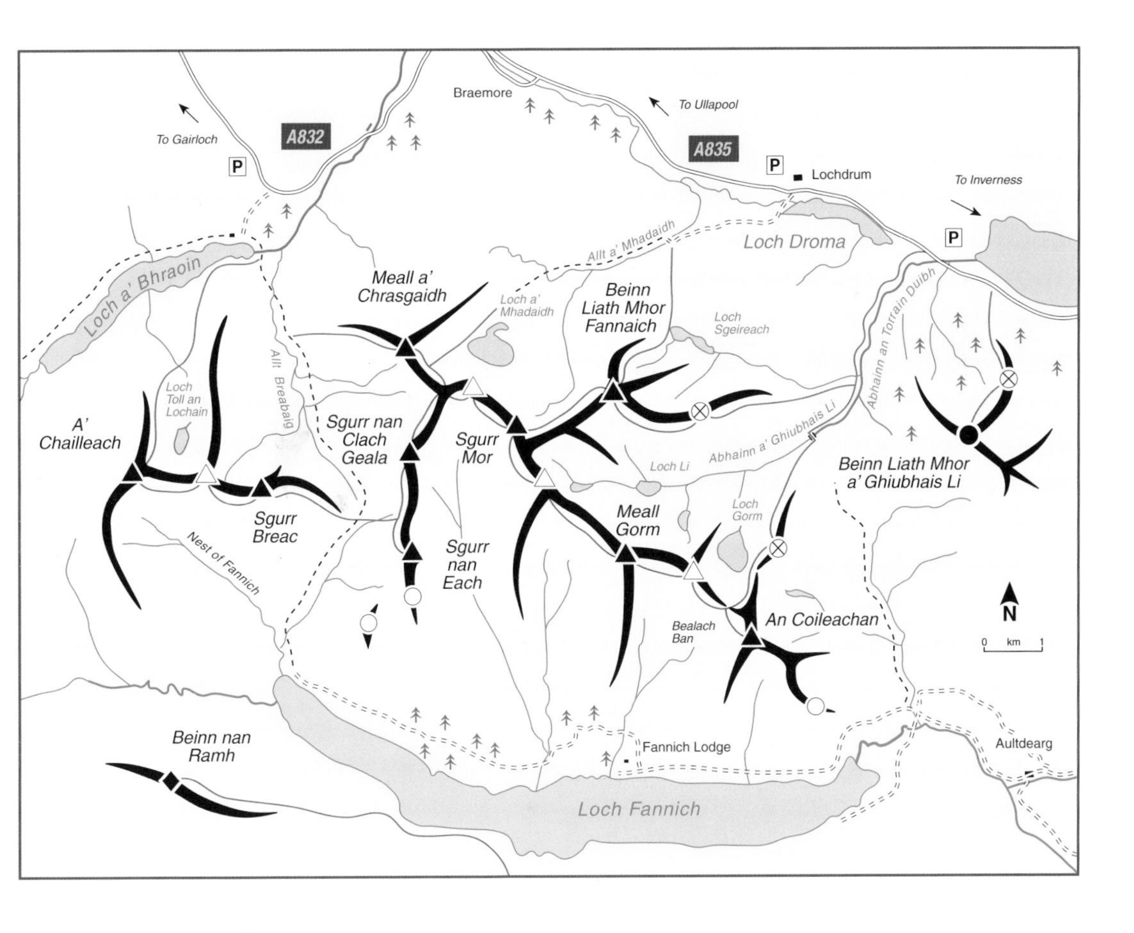

Sgurr nan Each

Mhadaidh was *The Boundary* (275m IV,5 1983) which climbs the prominent icefall visible from the road.

Meall a' Chrasgaidh; 934m; (OS Sheet 20; NH184733); *hill of the crossing*

Sgurr nan Clach Geala; 1093m; (OS Sheet 20; NH184715); *peak of the white stones*

Sgurr nan Each; 923m; (OS Sheet 20; NH184697); *peak of the horses*

Sgurr nan Clach Geala is the most impressive of the Fannaich hills, with a distinctive hanging corrie and steep buttresses high on its north-east side. Along with its neighbours, Meall a' Chrasgaidh and Sgurr nan Each to the north and south respectively, these three hills form a high ridge east of the path which links the east end of Loch a' Bhraoin and the west end of Loch Fannich.

A number of approaches to this ridge are possible but the route from Loch a' Bhraoin on the north-west side is the most direct and offers the best round trip. This can also be linked with the two Munros of the Western Fannaichs to give an excellent longer outing.

At the east end of the loch, a wooden bridge crosses the outflow and a path leads south-east to meet and ford the Allt Breabaig. There is a bridge at NH163747 if the river is high, but usually it is a boulder hop or shallow wade. A short distance beyond, leave this path and climb the north-west ridge of Meall a' Chrasgaidh which leads easily to the summit. Two other stalkers paths approach the north side of the hill, but both start further away and lower down the A832, closer to Braemore Junction.

The other popular approach is from the north-east, from the A835 Dirrie More road at the west end of Loch Droma, as described for Sgurr Mor. From the col north-west of Carn na Criche a short climb leads to the summit of Meall a' Chrasgaidh.

South of this col and slightly higher, Am Biachdaich (*place of the fattening*) is a wide hollow with a tiny lochan. As the name suggests, rich grazing on these high cols attracts large numbers of deer in the summer. A broad ridge rises south from here, above the east facing cliffs of Sgurr nan Clach Geala, narrowing towards the summit and giving easy but exhilarating walking and fine views. From Sgurr nan Clach Geala, an easy descent south leads to another col, the Cadha na Guite (not named on the OS map).

West of here, a few hundred metres lower, the path from Loch a' Bhraoin reaches its highest point before dropping down to Loch Fannich. Continuing south from the Cadha na Guite, the crest of the ridge curves gracefully up to the summit of Sgurr nan Each, above a line of crags facing east into Coire Mor. The easiest way down is to return to the Cadha na Guite then descend west to meet the Loch a'Bhraoin path. If considering an approach from Loch Fannich to the south, bear in mind that these southern corries are rough and boggy and the southern slopes of Sgurr nan Each give much easier walking.

The crags on the east side of Sgurr nan Clach Geala give some magnificent winter climbing. Six narrow buttresses and the gullies between them have been climbed by routes of all grades. *Gamma Gully* (210m V,5 1965) is probably the best of the gullies. *Skyscraper Buttress Direct* (240m VI, 6 1978/1986) gives a sustained mixed climb which has been described as 'one of the finest expeditions in the Northern Highlands'. The mica-schist rock does not give very good summer rock climbing.

A' Chailleach; 997m; (OS Sheet 19; NH136714); *the old woman*

Sgurr Breac; 999m; (OS Sheet 20; NH158711); *speckled peak*

A' Chaileach and Sgurr Breac stand due south of Loch a' Bhraoin and are sometimes refered to as the Western Fannaichs. Along with Tomain Coinich (935m) (*little mossy hill*), the Top which separates them, they form part of a long ridge which curves around the head of the evocatively named Nest of Fannich to the south. This long U-shaped corrie opens out onto the west end of Loch Fannich.

Of more practical interest to walkers, two long spurs run north, enclosing the rugged corrie of Loch Toll an Lochain. Druim Reidh (*level ridge*) is the north ridge of Toman Coinich, while further west Sron na Goibhre forms the north ridge of A' Chailleach. The east ridge of Sgurr Breac drops to a bealach at about 550m, beyond which rise the south-west slopes of Sgurr nan Clach Geala on the main Fannaich ridge. The usual approach follows the path which crosses this bealach, described above,

Loch A' Bhraoin

Loch a' Bhraoin (*loch of the showers*) lies on the north-west side of the Fannaichs, 1km south-west of the A832, 6km from Braemore Junction. A private track leaves the road as it follows a broad curve north-west towards Dundonnell. The approach from here to the Fisherfield and Letterewe hills further west has already been described, and this is also an important gateway to the Fannaichs. The east end of the loch is particularly atmospheric with the substantial ruins of a cottage and boathouse and the hills rising beyond. According to a grisly legend, there are a number of graves hereabouts, the last resting place of a gang of Lochaber men who had been cattle raiding in Strath More. As they made their way homeward with their booty, an Ullapool man followed, disguised as a beggar. Waiting until darkness, he wreaked a terrible vengeance, killing them as they slept. One man was deliberately spared to tell a cautionary tale when he got home.

More recently, in the 1990s, Loch a' Bhraoin was threatened with enlargement by a hydro-electric scheme. After considerable opposition from hill-goers, a less obtrusive alternative was built on the Abhainn Cuileig in Gleann Mor, below the Corrieshalloch Gorge.

Sgurr Breac and A' Chailleach from Carn na Criche

linking the east end of Loch a' Bhraoin, with the west end of Loch Fannich. From the bealach, pick a way throught some rocky outcrops onto the east ridge of Sgurr Breac, then climb more easily to the summit. A broad ridge continues west, offering extensive views in that direction towards the Letterewe and Fisherfield hills and An Teallach. Either cross the rounded summit of Toman Coinich or skirt it to the south, to reach the rim of the Toll an Lochain corrie. Follow this until it joins the Sron na Goibhre ridge, then climb south-west to the summit of A' Chailleach.

The northern spur, Sron na Goibhre is well marked by fence posts which can be followed in descent. Avoid the crags at its northern end by dropping down into the mouth of the corrie to the east. The Druim Reidh spur of Tomain Coinich can also be used for ascent or descent from the Loch a' Bhraoin path, but the popularity of this route has caused some erosion.

Fionn Bheinn; 933m; (OS Sheet 20; NH147621); *white hill*

Meall a' Chaorainn; 705m; (OS Sheet 19; NH136604); *hill of the rowan tree*

Fionn Bheinn and Meall a' Chaorainn are the highest points on the long ridge of rounded hills which runs in an east-west direction, to the south of Loch Fannich. South again, the A832 Garve to Achnasheen road and the adjacent railway line both run parallel with this ridge as they climb west through Strath Bran. Forestry plantations cover the lower slopes for much of the way. Both summits make fine viewpoints from which to admire the many surrounding hills but the walker will find them inconveniently located in the corners of three OS map sheets 19, 20 and 25.

Fionn Bheinn gives a short day, and is usually climbed from Achnasheen. It is often fitted in 'en route' to elsewhere, or even between trains. In suitable conditions, it gives a popular ski tour. The gentle southern slopes can be climbed almost anywhere, but the line of the Allt Achadh na Sine is usually followed. The most interesting route gains the grassy spur of Creagan nan Laogh, continuing north-west to the summit. Two corries, Toll Mor and Toll Beag, give Fionn Bheinn a bit more character on its north-eastern side and offer some winter climbing.

Parties content with the Munro can continue east, descending the ridge which skirts above the two corries to Sail an Tuim Bhain. A footpath crosses this ridge, leading south and back to the road just east of Achnasheen. Alternatively, continue to the Graham by dropping south from the summit to the bealach at the head of the unpleasant sounding Coire Bog, then climb south-west to the summit. Meall a' Chaorainn can also be climbed from the A832 a few kilometres west of Achnasheen. A forestry track climbs north from Loch a' Chroisg, following the Allt Duchairidh. On leaving the trees, the track becomes a stalkers path which climbs out of the narrow glen and crosses the north-west ridge of the hill. This ridge can be followed to the summit. If tempted to take a more direct line back down to the path, beware of the numerous crags on this south-west slope.

Beinn nan Ramh; 711m; (OS Sheet 19; NH139662); *hill of the oar*

The great whale-back ridge of Beinn nan Ramh stands alone, to the north of Fionn Bheinn, overlooking the west end of Loch Fannich. The effort of reaching this remote summit is rewarded by superb views north-east across the loch into the southern corries of the higher Fannaichs and tantalising glimpses of the Fisherfield and Letterewe hills to the north-west.

The various possible approaches from the south and west are all long. On the A832 some 4km east of Achnasheen, at a gap between two of the many forestry plantations strung along the north side of Strath Bran, a very high locked gate gives access to a rough estate track (NH199599). This climbs north over the long eastern shoulder of Fionn Bheinn then drops down to the south shore of Loch Fannich.

An old rusty iron signpost for Cabuie Lodge is a reminder of the original purpose of this track. Named after the Cadha Buidhe (*yellow pass*) to the west, Cabuie Lodge was situated at the west end of Loch Fannich, but was demolished when the hydro dam was built. Although the final section of track was inundated by the rising water, the site of the lodge remains high and dry. Directly across Loch Fannich lie the ruins of Nest of Fannich, one of the most magnificently situated bothies in the Highlands, sadly destroyed by fire in the 1980s.

Turning west, the track follows a concrete hydro pipeline into Srath Chrombuill. Leaving this hydro track, a newly bulldozed estate track (not marked on the OS map) branches north, contouring the north-eastern flank of Beinn nan Ramh and extending some distance up the Abhainn a' Chadh' Bhuidhe. From this track, a short climb gains the gentle grassy east ridge of Beinn nan Ramh which gradually widens near the summit. From Loch a' Chroisg, west of Achnasheen, the stalkers path already described which leads onto the north-west ridge of Meall a' Chaorainn continues north-east and drops down into Srath Chrombuill, due south of the summit of Beinn nan Ramh. This would give a more direct but slightly rougher approach on foot. Srath Chrombuill and the west end of the hill can also be approached from Incheril, just east of Kinlochewe, by following the private estate road east past Heights of Kinlochewe. Parties undertaking a longer expedition linking the Fannaich and the Kinlochewe hills may consider taking in Beinn nan Ramh as an alternative to the tedious trackless middle section of Srath Chrombuill.

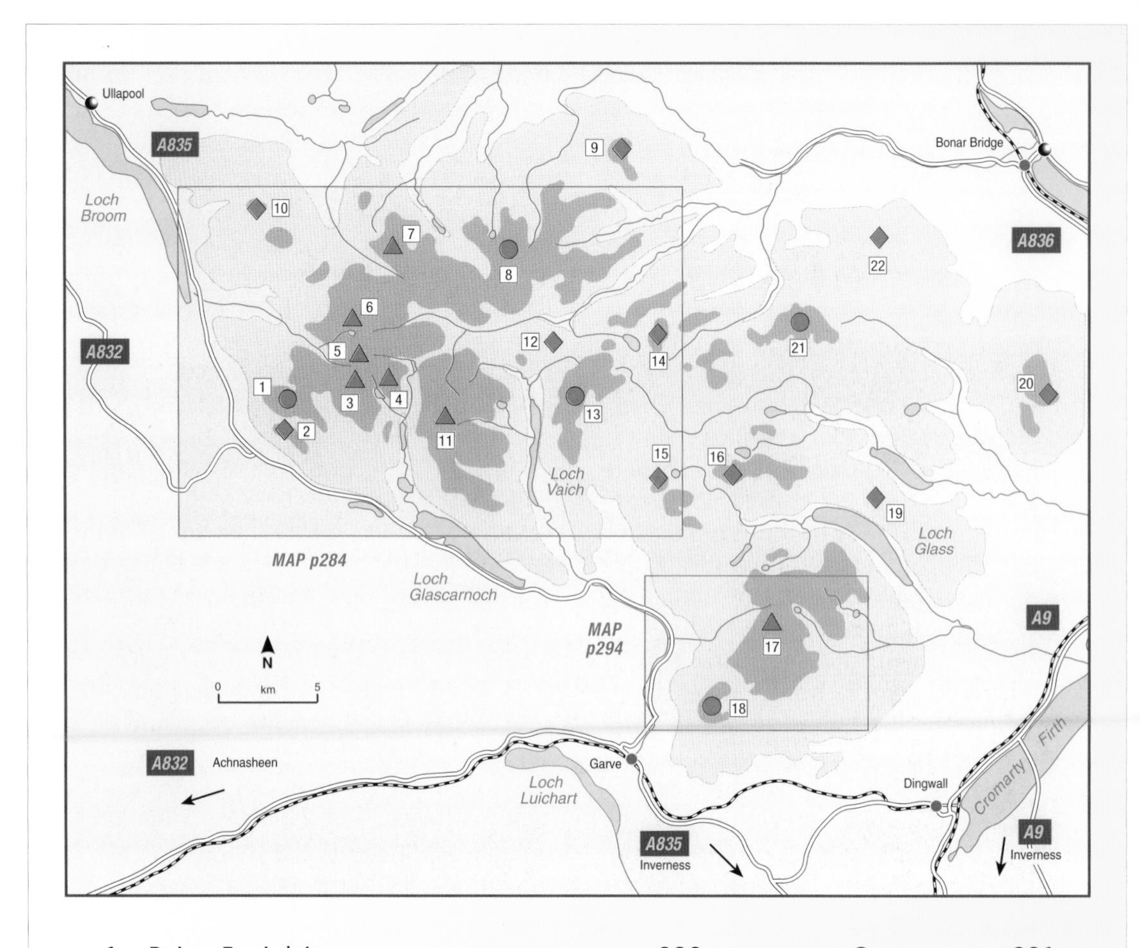

1.	Beinn Enaiglair	889m	C	p281
2.	Meall Doire Faid	730m	G	p281
3.	Beinn Dearg	1084m	M	p282
4.	Cona' Mheall	978m	M	p282
5.	Meall nan Ceapraichean	977m	M	p286
6.	Eididh nan Clach Geala	927m	M	p286
7.	Seana Bhraigh	926m	M	p286
8.	Carn Ban	845m	C	p289
9.	Carn a' Choin Deirg	701m	G	p289
10.	Meall Dubh	667m	G	p290
11.	Am Faochagach	953m	M	p290
12.	Meall a' Chaorainn	632m	G	p290
13.	Beinn a' Chaisteil	787m	C	p291
14.	Beinn Tharsuinn	710m	G	p292
15.	Carn Loch nan Amhaichean	697m	G	p293
16.	Beinn Nan Eun	743m	G	p293
17.	Ben Wyvis	1046m	M	p293
18.	Little Wyvis	764m	C	p295
19.	Meall Mor	738m	G	p295
20.	Beinn Tharsuinn	692m	G	p297
21.	Carn Chuinneag	838m	C	p297
22.	Carn Salachaidh	647m	G	p297

Chapter 15

Beinn Dearg and Easter Ross

Jim Renny

Beinn Dearg and Cona' Mheall from the slopes of Am Faochagach

The mountains of Beinn Dearg and Easter Ross stretch from coast to coast, with a mere 43km separating Loch Broom in the west from the Kyle of Sutherland in the east. This is the narrowest part of the Highlands and the roads north literally squeeze past at sea level. As elsewhere, climate and many local characteristics are quite different on each side of the country, adding to the interest and variety of this extensive area. Scotland's amazing topographic asymmetry means that the watershed here runs very close to the west coast. In consequence, most of the Easter Ross hills rise out of a network of eastward draining glens, some of them of great length.

On the western edge of the area, Beinn Dearg and its close neighbours dominate Loch Broom and the ridges linking these craggy summits give exhilarating walking and satisfying rounds with extensive views. In contrast, the rest of the hills are much more rounded in shape and spread out, forming extensive plateaux, culminating in the great massif of Ben Wyvis to the south-east. The proximity of the higher hills to the main roads around the southern boundaries of the area belies the great tracts of remote high ground which lie beyond. No public roads cross or even penetrate any great distance into the hills, though there are a number of private estate roads and tracks on which a cycle can be very useful. For those with the time and the inclination, the diverse character of the Easter Ross hills is best appreciated by undertaking a longer backpacking trip, for which there are a number of possible routes.

Much of the Highland population lives and works around the edge of these hills, particularly to the south and east, in the city of Inverness and in Dingwall and the smaller Easter Ross towns and villages. Fortunately this has had little impact on the hills which are no more popular or busier than any others in the Highlands, with the possible exception of Ben Wyvis.

The A835 Dingwall to Ullapool road is a vital artery for much of the North-west Highlands and beyond and also marks the boundary separating Easter Ross from the Fannaichs and Wester Ross. The drive is usually pleasant and relatively fast, even with the caravans and coaches of summer, but the higher sections of the Dirrie More (*great climb*) can be snow-bound in winter. The road skirts the west side of the Ben Wyvis massif which dominates the south-eastern corner of Easter Ross and the shortest approach to this popular mountain starts here. As the road gradually climbs the Dirrie More it passes the foot of Strath Rannoch and Strath Vaich, which give access to a number of hills to the north. Beyond Loch Glascarnoch, the road passes Beinn Dearg and its neighbours, giving access to either end of their inter-linked ridges. North of Braemore Junction, the road descends past the spectacular Corrieshalloch Gorge into wooded Strath More and follows the shores of Loch Broom to Ullapool.

Some complex geography adds to the interest of the north-west side of the higher hills. The short Ullapool River has its source in Loch Achall, fed through Glen Achall by the Rhidorroch River whose main tributary, the River Douchary, has its source high on Seana Bhraigh. To the north of Ullapool, Strath Kanaird, the Cromalt Hills and the Rhidorroch Forest form a quiet corner of low hills and empty glens, bounded to the west by the A835 which continues to Ledmore Junction, with the dramatic Coigach and Assynt hills beyond.

The head of the Cromarty Firth marks the eastern boundary of the Easter Ross hills. Continuing north, this boundary follows the A836 which leaves the A9 just beyond Evanton and climbs over the Struie (215m) to Ardgay and Bonar Bridge at the head of the Dornoch Firth. As the road drops steeply towards the sea, the panorama north-west across the Kyle of Sutherland is known locally as 'the Million Dollar View'. The origins of this name are uncertain, but the sight has gladdened the heart of many a returning native of the far north. South of the Struie, Glen Glass and Strath Rusdale both carry public roads a short distance west and give limited access to a few hills, but the most useful approach is from Ardgay. Two minor roads extend part way up Strathcarron, on both sides of the River Carron, and join at a bridge just east of The Craigs. A number of glens converge hereabouts, Strath Cuileannach from the north-west, Glen Alladale and Gleann Mor from the west and Glen Calvie from the south.

North of Bonar Bridge, the splendid Gothic pile of Carbisdale Castle, Scotland's grandest youth hostel, sits at the junction of Strath Oykel and Achany Glen, overlooking the Kyle of Sutherland. Sometimes known as 'the Castle of Spite', it was built early in the 20th century by the dowager Duchess of Sutherland after she had fallen out with the family of her late husband. The River Oykel forms a natural boundary with the Sutherland hills to the north and was once the route of an important drove road from the north-west.

During the Civil War, James Graham, the ill-fated Marquis of Montrose, fled this way in April 1650 after his defeat at Carbisdale. Seeking refuge with Macleod of Assynt at Ardvreck Castle, he was betrayed for the huge sum of £25,000 and taken to Edinburgh, where he was executed without a trial, by order of the Scottish Parliament. According to legend his jewelled orders of chivalry still lie buried on a ridge above the River Oykel. From Oykel Bridge, Glen Einig leads south-west to Strath Mulzie and the north side of Seana Bhraigh, while the A837 continues north-west across to Ledmore Junction in Assynt.

Principal Hills

Beinn Enaiglair; 889m; (OS Sheet 20; NH225805); *hill of the timid birds or brow cliff*

Meall Doire Faid; 730m; (OS Sheet 20; NH221792); *hill of the lumpy thicket*

A delightful pair of hills, Beinn Enaiglair and Meall Doire Faid stand side by side, close to the road. They offer a number of possibilities for short or longer outings, the highlight of which will be the extensive views of their higher neighbours.

There is ample parking at Braemore Junction, where the A832 Dundonnell road leaves the A835 Garve to Ullapool road. Unfortunately, following construction of a new lodge, the estate is very hostile to walkers using the private track through the forest. The signposted alternative following the forest fence is rather rough and boggy, so a more direct route up Meall Doire Faid may be preferred. The stalkers path which leaves the forest and passes north of the Home Loch completely encircles Beinn Enaiglair, and either summit can easily be reached from the bealach between them. In the eastern corrie of Beinn Enaiglair a path (not shown on the OS map) climbs almost to the summit.

From the bealach north-east of Beinn Enaiglair, a short climb leads to Iorguill (872m) (*hill of the battle*), which gives an alternative approach to Beinn Dearg. To the south-east of Beinn Enaiglair, a stalkers path

Access and Transport

By road: from Inverness the A9 continues north to the roundabout at Tore. The A835 Ullapool road gives access to the the western hills, while continuing north on the A9 over the Cromarty Bridge gives access from the east. Beyond Evanton the A836 continues north through Ardgay and Bonar Bridge to Lairg. Beyond Bonar Bridge the A837 runs west to Ledmore junction in Assynt.

By bus: Inverness to Ullapool (Scottish Citylink Service 961, tel: 08705-505050); Gairloch to Ullapool (Westerbus, tel: 01445-712255); Inverness to Dingwall to Contin (Spa Coaches, tel: 01997-421311); Tain to Bonar Bridge to Lairg (Macleod's Coaches, tel: 01408-641354); Dingwall to Heights of Fodderty; Ardgay to The Craigs; Ardgay to Easter Fearn to Strathoykel; Drumbeg to Lochinver to Lairg (Postbus, tel: 08457-740740).

By rail: the Inverness to Kyle of Lochalsh line runs south of Ben Wyvis, with stations at Dingwall and Garve. The Inverness to Wick - Thurso line skirts the east of the area with stations at Dingwall, Alness, Tain, Ardgay, Culrain, Invershin and Lairg.

Accommodation and Information

Hotels and guesthouses: found in most of the Mid and Easter Ross towns and villages plus Ardgay, Aultguish, Bonar Bridge, Inchbae, Laide, Ullapool.

SYHA hostels: Carbisdale Castle, Culrain (tel: 0870-004-1109); Ullapool (tel: 0870-004-1156)

Independent hostels: Aultguish Inn Bunkhouse (tel: 01997-455254); Evanton : Black Rock Bunkhouse (tel: 01349-830917); Ullapool : West House (tel: 01854-613126)

Campsites: Evanton (tel: 01349-830917); Lairg (tel: 01549-402447); Ullapool

Tourist Information Centres: Strathpeffer, The Square (tel: 01997-421415) (seasonal); Lairg, Ferrycroft Countryside Centre (tel: 01549-402160) (seasonal); Ullapool, Argyle Street (tel: 01854-612135) (limited winter hours)

Maps

Ordnance Survey 1:50,000 Landranger sheets 20 (Beinn Dearg & Loch Broom) and 21 (Dornoch & Alness).

Beinn Dearg and Cona' Mheall from the Fannaichs

continues along an undulating ridge before dropping to the road at Lochdrum cottage, opposite Loch Droma dam.

Beinn Dearg; 1084m; (OS Sheet 20; NH259811); *red hill*

Cona' Mheall; 978m; (OS Sheet 20; NH274816); *adjoining hill*

Looking south-east from the harbour at Ullapool, Beinn Dearg and its neighbours dominate the head of Loch Broom. The summit of Beinn Dearg is the highest point north of the Inverness to Ullapool road, with Cona' Mheall, as its name suggests, standing close by to the east, linked by a broad high saddle. Steep and extensive cliffs line much of the northern and eastern flanks of Beinn Dearg while gentler slopes fall away to the south and west.

Cona' Mheall is a fine hill in its own right, with a long narrow summit ridge curving up from the south-east. Enclosed between this ridge and the south-east ridge of Beinn Dearg is the deep rocky bowl of Coire Ghranda (*gloomy corrie*). This distinctive feature stands out from as far east as the Black Isle and is well seen from the A835 Garve to Ullapool road as it crosses the Dirrie More.

Both hills are usually climbed together, with the approach from the north offering the easiest walking underfoot, despite starting at sea level. Leave the A835 at Inverlael, at the head of Loch Broom, where parking at the gate beside the phone box is often crowded. The first 3km climbs gently up through the Lael Forest. Some of the network of tracks here are signposted as cycle routes and careful navigation is required at various junctions, to ensure finally leaving the forest on the path which climbs up Gleann na Sguaib.

This path follows the north side of the River Lael past a series of attractive pools and waterfalls. In snowy conditions this route can become very strenuous. A group of tiny lochans mark the Bealach a' Choire Ghranda at about 850m. From here contour east around the south side of Point 886m to reach the final boulder strewn north-west slopes of Cona' Mheall, which give an easy climb to the summit. Older hill-goers may remember when this had the distinction of being one of the few Munros without a summit cairn but one has now appeared at the north-east end of its flat top. Continue a short distance further in the same direction to enjoy the best of the magnificent view. From the Bealach a' Choire Ghranda, the final climb to the summit of Beinn Dearg follows a substantial drystane dyke directly up the broad north-east ridge. The highest point lies about 300 metres south of a sharp bend in the wall, which continues down the long north-west shoulder of Diollaid a' Mhill Bhric, following the edge of the line of cliffs above Gleann na Sguaib. After about 2km the wall finishes suddenly at a big boulder, from which it is a steep but relatively straightforward descent into the glen to rejoin the path. This gives a useful way down which is easy to follow in bad visibility.

Various approaches from the south are also possible. The round of Coire Ghranda and the traverse of the four Munros of the Beinn Dearg group both give memorable outings. From Braemore Junction it is feasible to take in Beinn Enaiglair then continue north-east over Iorguill (872m) and join the north-west spur of Beinn Dearg at Point 836m. Routes from higher up the Dirrie More tend to be wetter underfoot and involve serious river crossings, with the bonus of dramatic views into Coire Ghranda.

A good track (not marked on the OS map) leads east from Lochdrum cottage, at the west end of Loch Droma. This track branches near the other end of the loch (NH268752) with one branch climbing north across a low ridge and finishing at some ruined shielings on the north-west side of Loch a' Gharbhrain. This path can be joined by parking a short distance east of Loch Droma in an old quarry (NH272747) and cutting north across the moor.

The south ridge of Cona' Mheall is best taken in ascent, which involves crossing the Allt a' Gharbhrain. This may be awkward in normal conditions and impossible in spate. The ground north to Loch Coire Lair is notoriously rough and boggy underfoot so traverse the slopes of Leac an Tuadh above the loch and climb up to the lip of Coire Ghranda. From here, a route up through rocky outcrops to the crest of the south ridge is easy to pick out in ascent but may not be obvious in descent.

The ridge itself is narrow and involves some easy scrambling, becoming broader as it approaches the flat, bouldery summit. A couple of short rock steps can either be turned or climbed direct. The broad east ridge of Cona' Mheall gives a straightforward link with the north-west side of Am Faochagach. Make for the outflow of Loch Prille then climb the outlier Meallan Dubh (882m).

To climb Beinn Dearg from Loch a' Gharbhrain, follow the Allt a' Gharbhrain upstream, crossing when and where possible, then climb north out of this glen, aiming for the south ridge of Point 885m, avoiding the many slabby outcrops flanking these heavily glaciated corries. Continue north, following the top of the Coire Ghranda cliffs, until a broad spur leads west to the summit of Beinn Dearg.

If following this route in descent in winter or early spring, it is essential to take the correct line from the summit and avoid the cornices and steep exposed slopes on either side of this spur. A less serious alternative may be to descend the broader south spur which flanks the upper un-named south-east corrie, whose outflow joins the upper reaches of the Allt a' Gharbhrain.

Beinn Dearg also offers some excellent winter climbing. The craggy northern side of Diollaid a' Mhill Bhric, the long sloping north-west shoulder of the mountain, is lined with well defined gullies and ribs above Gleann na Squaib. The most famous of these is *Emerald Gully* (150m IV,4 1970) which usually has at least two big ice pitches. These cliffs finish at a broad gully, the Cadha Amadan (*fools pass*). Beyond here, the so called West Buttress is in fact a complex cliff, which curves away out of sight.

Hidden from view during the approach up the glen, the classic *Penguin Gully* (350m III, 4 1964) was first climbed by Tom Patey, Bill Murray and Norman Tennant, a rare combination of some of the greatest Scottish winter climbing talents of the pre- and post war eras. On the other side of Bealach a' Choire Ghranda, Coire Ghranda

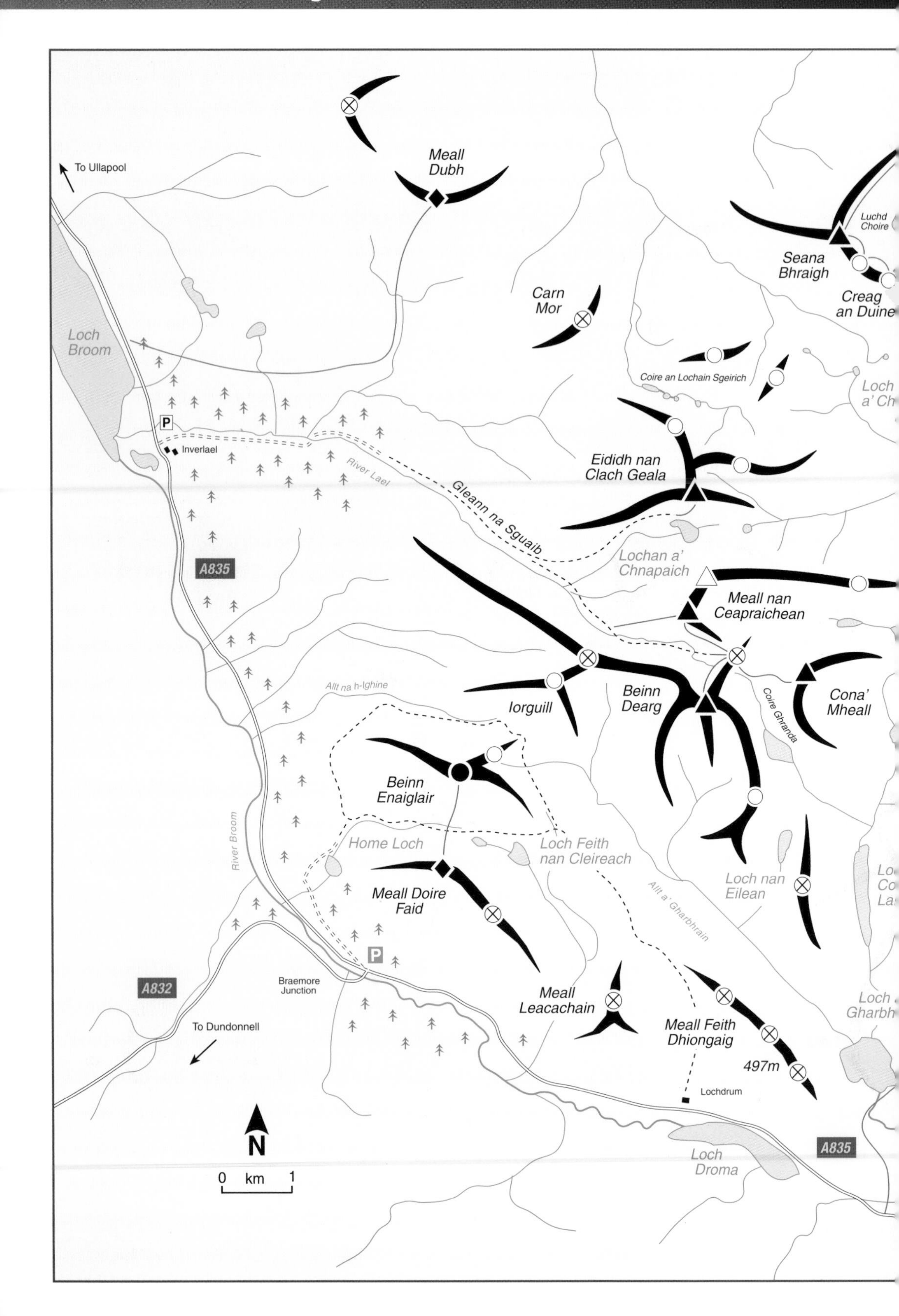

Meall Dubh
To Ullapool
Luchd Choire
Seana Bhraigh
Creag an Duine
Carn Mor
Loch Broom
Coire an Lochain Sgeirich
Loch a' Ch
P
Inverlael
Eididh nan Clach Geala
River Lael
Gleann na Sguaib
Lochan a' Chnapaich
A835
Meall nan Ceapraichean
Cona' Mheall
Beinn Dearg
Iorguill
Allt na h-Ighine
Coire Ghranda
Beinn Enaiglair
River Broom
Home Loch
Loch Feith nan Cleireach
Meall Doire Faid
Loch nan Eilean
Allt a' Gharbhrain
A832
Braemore Junction
Meall Leacachain
Meall Feith Dhiongaig
To Dundonnell
497m
Lochdrum
N
0 km 1
Loch Droma

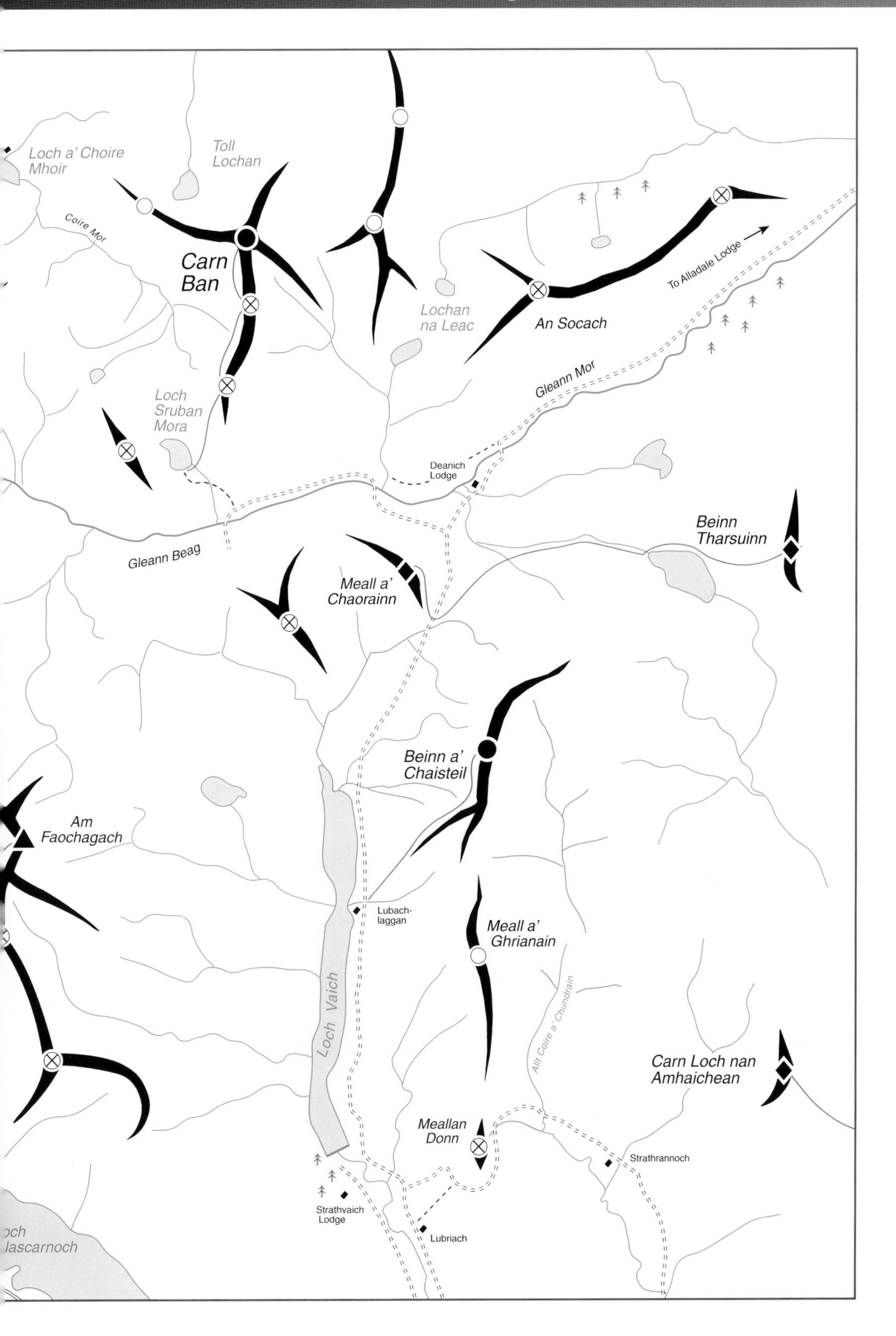
Loch a' Choire
Mhoir
Toll
Lochan
Coire Mor
Carn
Ban
Lochan
na Leac
An Socach
To Alladale Lodge
Gleann Mor
Loch
Sruban
Mora
Deanich
Lodge
Gleann Beag
Beinn
Tharsuinn
Meall a'
Chaorainn
Beinn a'
Chaisteil
Am
Faochagach
Lubach-
laggan
Meall a'
Ghrianain
Loch Vaich
Allt Coire a' Chundrain
Carn Loch nan
Amhaichean
Meallan
Donn
Strathrannoch
Strathvaich
Lodge
Lubriach
lascarnoch

itsef has a wonderful wild atmosphere, with huge vegetated cliffs and a dark lochan. The lower crag was first explored by the ubiquitous J.H.B.Bell in June 1946, though its winter potential was only realised relatively recently. Mick Fowler's audacious *Ice Bomb* (115m VII,7 1988) climbs the impressive fault in the centre of the upper crag. On the opposite side of the corrie, the western cliffs of Cona' Mheall give pleasant scrambling and a few summer and winter climbs have been recorded.

Meall nan Ceapraichean; 977m; (OS Sheet 20; NH257825); *hill of the stubby hillocks*

Eididh nan Clach Geala; 927m; (OS Sheet 20; NH257842); *web of the white stones*

Meall nan Ceapraichean and Eididh nan Clach Geala lack some of the character of their taller neighbours, and are usually climbed as part of a longer round. If transport can be arranged, the traverse of the whole Beinn Dearg range from Loch Droma to Loch Broom is a magnificent outing in either direction.

Steep and craggy to the west and south, Meall nan Ceapraichean is a short easy climb by its south-east shoulder, from the Bealach a'Choire Ghranda below the summit of Beinn Dearg. North-east of Meall nan Ceapraichean, a subsidiary top Ceann Garbh (967m) (not named on the OS map) overlooks Lochan a' Chnapaich. To the east of this top, a long spur descends gradually over Cnap Coire Loch Tuath, into the peat hags of Gleann Beag. This gives the best access to the Beinn Dearg range from the east. To the south of this spur, Loch Tuath is the highest in a chain of six lochs descending through Coire Lair to Loch Glascarnoch, though the wet and boggy nature of this glen has already been mentioned. The route to Eididh nan Clach Geala continues north-east over Ceann Garbh, bypassing some lines of crags and descending to a bealach between two tiny lochans. From here, a short climb north-west up an easy grass slope leads to the summit which is marked by two cairns, the north-west being the higher. To climb the mountain from Inverlael, follow the Gleann na Sguaib path to a fork at the Eas Fionn waterfall. Take the left branch which climbs up towards Lochan a' Chnapaich and cut up onto the broad west ridge of Eididh nan Clach Geala with its tiny lochan and the quartzite boulders which give the hill its name. To continue to Seana Bhraigh from the summit of Eididh nan Clach Geala, drop down to the col to the north then head eastwards along the shoulder, aiming directly for Loch a' Chadha Dheirg, to join the route described below.

Seana Bhraigh; 926m; (OS Sheet 20; NH281878); *old height*

Seana Bhraigh is the summit of an extensive plateau at the head of Strath Mulzie which forms the watershed at the narrowest point on the Scottish mainland. Its extensive western flanks above Cadha Dearg (*red pass*) drain north then west into Glen Douchary and the short Ullapool River, while to the south, rough boggy ground dotted with rocky outcrops leads east into Gleann Beag, Gleann Mor and Strathcarron. However, Seana Bhraigh's most impressive features are its three enormous northern corries. From the summit, steep vegetated cliffs fall some 400m to Loch Luchd Choire, bounded to the north-west by broad heathery slopes which drop gently north into Strath Mulzie.

To the north-east, the narrow rocky spur of Creag an Duine rears up to the distinctively pointed peak of An Sgurr, east of which easier slopes drop into Feich Coire. Neither of these features is named on the OS map. Further east, Coire Mor cuts deep into the rounded dome of Carn Ban (845m). All three corries drain into Loch a' Choire Mhoir, beyond which desolate Strath Mulzie widens out and curves around to the north-east. Remote from any direction, an

Eididh nan Clach Geala and Beinn Dearg from Beinn Enaiglair

ascent of Seana Bhraigh can be treated as a challenging day from the nearest public road or an opportunity for more extensive exploration of the surrounding hills and glens which make up this wild heart of Easter Ross.

Many Munro baggers follow in the footsteps of first Munroist, the Reverend A.E.Robertson, who combined Seana Bhraigh with Eididh nan Clach Geala from his base at Inverlael in May 1899. A more direct route, missing out the latter, starts from the same place, at the head of Loch Broom on the A835 Braemore Junction to Ullapool road.

Leaving the Lael Forest, a stalkers path from the ruin at Glensguaib climbs the Druim na Saobhaidhe ridge to a height of about 450m. The path then crosses the Allt Gleann a' Mhadaidh and continues climbing to Coire an Lochain Sgeirich, with its string of five lochans. The path finishes a short distance beyond, on a flat saddle at just over 800m, where the route from Eididh nan Clach Geala joins. In poor visibility, careful navigation will be required from here. Aim to find Loch a' Chadha Dheirg before skirting the steep slopes which drop into Cadha Dearg, climbing north up easier slopes to point 906m above the cliffs of Luchd Choire. From here follow the cliff edge north-west to the summit cairn.

The north facing crags above Cadha Dearg can give some good winter climbing such as *Geddes's Gully* (250m V,5 1986) which follows the gully splitting the highest part of the crag. The youngest Munroist of his time, Mike Geddes went on to become an outstanding climber with an unrivalled knowledge of remote corners of the North-west Highlands. He had been aware of the potential of this cliff for many years, waiting for the opportunity and the right conditions. Shortly before his untimely death from cancer, he mentioned it to his long time climbing partner, Alan Rouse. Ironically, Rouse finally climbed the

Seana Bhraigh and the Coigach peaks

route just before his own tragic death, trapped in a storm near the summit of K2, after making the first British ascent of the world's second highest peak.

An alternative approach from Ullapool uses the private estate road which follows the Ullapool River past Loch Achall to East Rhidorroch Lodge in Glen Achall. This can also be reached from Leckmelm by the rough track through Srath Nimhe. The Glen Douchary path passes a series of fine waterfalls on the north-west side of Meall nam Bradhan (677m) while to the north-east, an alternative path follows the Allt nan Caorach through an impressive narrow ravine. Either route gives access to the straightforward north-west shoulder of Seana Bhraigh.

Strath Mulzie gives the longest but most satisfying approach with views of the great north-eastern corries and An Sgurr. This can be reached either from Glen Achall to the west, through the Allt nan Caorach ravine, or by the private estate road to Corriemulzie Lodge from Oykell Bridge on the A837 Bonar Bridge to Ledmore Junction road. From the lodge, a rough estate track continues all the way to Loch a' Choire Mhoir.

The finest ascent is a scramble up the steep, narrow Creag an Duine ridge on the east side of Luchd Choire, which is much easier than it appears from below. From the top of An Sgurr, a short scramble down and up again leads to the summit plateau. Follow the rim of the Luchd Choire over the rounded dome of Point 906m to reach the summit. The ridge on the west side of Luchd Choire gives a straightforward descent. Seana Bhraigh holds snow well and a ski approach is often feasible. The winter climbing potential of the Luchd Choire was first discovered by the Corriemulzie Club, a keen group of mainly ex-St Andrews University climbers with a penchant for exploration, who produced a *'Rock and Ice Guide to Easter Ross'* in 1966. Long approaches have ensured that this area remains the preserve of enthusiasts.

Carn Ban; 845m; (OS Sheet 20; NH338875); *white peak*

A great dome shaped hill, flecked with the white quartzite which gives it its name, Carn Ban stands in the remote heart of the Freevater Forest. This wild uninhabited expanse of rolling hills, deep corries and long glens is best appreciated on an extended visit. Text book U-shaped valleys give the impression that the glaciers have not long since retreated, leaving a generous scattering of broken crags and lonely lochs. While it is possible to combine an ascent with its Munro neighbour, Seana Bhraigh, to the west, Carn Ban is a worthwhile objective in its own right and perhaps an opportunity to approach from a different direction.

From the north, the most rewarding approach to Seana Bhraigh, up Strath Mulzie to Coire Mor, also gives a straightforward but long approach to Carn Ban. An excellent alternative, especially with the help of two wheels, is to come from the south or east. Even these remote glens have been harnessed for hydro electricity, and, thanks to the Hydro-Board, an estate track comes up from the south through Strath Vaich, from the A835 Garve to Ullapool road. The track divides as it drops down into Gleann Beag, just before Deanich Lodge, south-east of Carn Ban. The right branch continues north-east through Gleann Mor and rejoins the public road 2km south of The Craigs in Strathcarron, just before Glencalvie Lodge.

For Carn Ban, take the left branch which crosses the river and continues upstream for another 1km or so. Just before another bridge near the end of the track, a path climbs the steep northern flank of the glen, passing a couple of impressive cascades and leads to Loch Sruban Mora. Continue climbing gradually north, over a couple of subsidiary bumps, enjoying the view which gradually opens out towards the summit.

To the north-west the distinctive profiles of the Coigach and Assynt hills seem deceptively far below, in contrast with neighbouring Bodach Mor (822m) and Bodach Beag (837m) to the north-east which appear higher than they actually are. Beyond them, in the far distance, only the outlines of Ben Klibreck and Beinn Armine break up the emptiness of that corner of Sutherland. To the south-west, Beinn Dearg and the Fannaichs beyond bristle with peaks, in contrast with broad rolling Ben Wyvis and its satellites to the south-east.

There are also opportunities for adventurous climbers. Rock climbs have been recorded in Gleann Beag and there are winter climbs on the cliffs of Coire Toll Lochan and the un-named corrie to the east, which stretch between Carn Ban, Bodach Beag and Bodach Mor. There are three winter climbs on the north-east face of Meall nam Fuaran (674m) and at the head of Glen Alladale, the 240m high Alladale Wall on the north-east face of An Socach (745m) has a number of rock climbs. The rock is an extraordinary form of glaciated quartzite with no scree and little loose rock, giving delicate climbing on small wrinkles with little protection and poor belays.

Carn a' Choin Deirg; 701m; (OS Sheet 20; NH397923); *hill of the red dog*

Carn a' Choin Deirg is the highest top in a fine, remote horseshoe of hills wedged between Strath Cuileannach and Alladale, whose rivers converge in Strathcarron. The best approach, with the most appealing views and the fewest peat hags, is by way of Alladale Lodge. From the end of the public road at the bridge near the entrance to Glencalvie Lodge, follow the estate track west alongside the river, past Alladale Lodge, then climb the eastern spur of Carn Alladale (636m).

From the top of Carn Alladale, head north-west along a broad ridge, passing a couple of lochans and over three smaller tops to the summit of Carn a' Choin Deirg.

Coire Mor of Seanna Bhraigh from Carn Ban

On a clear day there are unusual views of Beinn Dearg and the Coigach and Assynt hills. It is a straightforward descent into the U-shaped valley of the Allt a' Chlaiginn to join the stalkers path which leads back to Alladale.

Meall Dubh; 667m; (OS Sheet 20; NH225886); *black hill*

The hill named as Meall Dubh on the map is actually the rockier Point 642m situated a couple of kilometres to the north-west of the highest point. Rounded and devoid of any distinctive features, Meall Dubh itself offers an excellent short outing with a magnificent view.

To the south-west the network of tracks through the Lael Forest are signposted as cycle routes from two car parks north (NH177868) and south (NH185845) of Inverlael on the A835 Braemore Junction to Ullapool road. Using a cycle, these tracks give a zigzag climb up to the start of a new track following the line of a stalkers path at NH206857, with the prospect of a speedy descent by the same route.

Alternatively, from Leckmelm on the north-west side of the hill, a slightly overgrown forestry track leaves the road and climbs up through a narrow steep sided glen into Strath Nimhe. As the track leaves the trees, nearby An Teallach dominates the view behind and as the climb continues, the Fisherfield and Fannaich hills come into view further south, along with the Coigach hills to the north. Leave the track and cross the Allt Raon a' Chroisg below a distinctive rocky cascade on the opposite hillside, picking a way through peat hags to reach Point 642m, then continue to the summit. This is good terrain for a short ski tour in suitable conditions.

Am Faochagach; 953m; (OS Sheet 20; NH303793); *heathery place*

Meall a' Chaorainn; 632m; (OS Sheet 20; NH360827); *hill of the rowan tree*

Am Faochagach is the highest point on the crescent shaped range of great rounded hills which curves north for some 18km, between Strath Vaich and Loch Glascarnoch, enclosing a line of corries which drain east into Loch Vaich. At the northern end, Meall a' Chaorainn terminates the range, somewhat isolated from its neighbours, overlooking the pass where the Strath Vaich track crosses to join Gleann Beag and Gleann Mor. With good snow cover this is excellent ski-touring terrain.

Sir Hugh Munro himself had something of an epic on Am Faochagach in March 1901. According to H.G.S.Lawson, who joined him at the Aultguish Inn the following day, '...coming down by Strath Vaich, he had difficulty in crossing a stream in the dark...eventually he returned to a keepers house, the occupier of which mounted him on a steed and sent him down the glen in great style. He ultimately arrived at the inn well after midnight'. Am Faochagach remains a hill that most climb out of duty rather than desire, though there is a choice of worthwhile routes and some fine views, particularly west into Coire Ghranda of Beinn Dearg. A round of Coire Lair, taking in Cona' Mheall, makes an excellent outing.

The shortest of several possible approaches to Am Faochagach from the A835 Garve to Ullapool road starts from the bridge over the Abhainn an Torrain Duibh at the west end of Loch Glascarnoch. This involves crossing the Abhainn a' Gharbhrain, which can be impossible in all but dry or frosty conditions. Once across, straightforward slopes to the north-east lead up to Sron Liath, some 3km south of the summit along a broad ridge. From slightly further west along the road, the first section of the popular approach to Cona' Mheall can be followed from the east end of Loch Droma, before crossing the outflow from Loch Coire Lair to gain the easy south-western slopes of the mountain. With two rivers to cross, this can also be a wet route. The driest but longest alternative comes up Strath Vaich to the south-east.

There is ample parking beside the A835, east of Black Bridge, from which an excellent private road leads past Strathvaich Lodge to the Loch Vaich dam. Follow the west shore of the loch to the Allt Glas Toll Mor, then climb the long south-east spur over Meall Gorm (885m) to the summit. The continuation to Cona' Mheall descends north-west over Meallan Ban (882m) to the outflow of Loch Prille and then up the east ridge of Cona' Mheall.

Standing just over 1km south-west of Deanich Lodge in Gleann Mor, Meall a' Chaorainn is a long way from any public road. Its summit is only a short stiff climb of 300m up steep heathery slopes from the highest point on the track which crosses its eastern flanks, linking Strath Vaich, Gleann Beag and Gleann Mor.

Beinn a' Chaisteil; 787m; (OS Sheet 20; NH370801); *hill of the castle*

Beinn a' Chaisteil tops the long gentle ridge which forms the east side of Strath Vaich. It can be climbed either as an excellent short outing or as the start (or finish) to a longer expedition into the wild and remote hills and glens to the north. Approaching along the private road to Strathvaich Lodge from the A835 Garve to Ullapool road, just before the bridge above the weir near Lubriach cottage, a gravel track continues up the east side of the glen, climbing steeply over a small knoll. From the crest of the rise, the view north along Loch Vaich to the hills and corries beyond has a real feeling of wilderness. The most direct way to the top follows the track along the lochside as far as the abandoned keepers cottage at Lubachlag-gan. From here, an indistinct path climbs up the north side of the burn and leads onto the ridge a short distance south of the summit.

A more interesting alternative is to take a right turn before the climb up to Loch Vaich, following a rough track which leads over into neighbouring Strath Rannoch. Well before the watershed, make a rising heathery traverse towards the skyline ridge. Extensive views gradually open out as this leads in due course to the summit of Meall a' Ghrianain (772m) (*sunny hill*).

The vast area of peat hags to the east must rank as one of the least appealing

Loch Vaich and Beinn a' Chaisteil

mountain areas in Scotland, at least to two legged hill-goers. Continue north along the broad ridge to the summit of Beinn a' Chaisteil, looking out for an unexpected view of Suilven over the shoulder of Seana Bhraigh to the north-west.

Beinn Tharsuinn; 710m; (OS Sheet 20; NH412829); *transverse hill*

Isolated Beinn Tharsuinn can be combined with one of its distant neighbours as a challenging outing, or used as an opportunity to visit a remote corner of the map. Much of the distance can be covered on two wheels, using the estate track which runs up Strath Vaich.

From the highest point on this track, on the south-east shoulder of Meall a' Chaorainn, contour along a gravel track which branches off north-east, leading to a small dam. Follow the feeder stream up to the Crom Loch, which sits at the foot of the easy western slopes of Beinn Tharsuinn.

The alternative approach from the north-east, through Glen Calvie, gives a more interesting walk. From Ardgay, the public road up Strathcarron leads as far as the bridge just before Glencalvie Lodge. An estate track continues south, past the lodge, leading up Glen Calvie. From the bridge where the track crosses the Water of Glencalvie, a stalkers path climbs up through the trees.

Leave this track to gain the Leac Ghorm ridge over Dunach Liath (551m) and continue south to Dunan Liath (691m). Beinn Tharsuinn lies 2km due south via a short descent to a broad shoulder. The Diebidale Ridge runs north-east from the summit, rising over Point 691m after a short steep descent. From Mullach Creag Riaraidh near the end of this long ridge, either drop down steeply into Glen Diebidale to meet the end of the track back through Glen Calvie or continue along the ridge to meet a stalkers path leading to Diebidale,then follow this down the west side of the glen to rejoin the Glen Calvie track at the bridge over the Water of Calvie.

Carn Loch nan Amhaichean; 697m; (OS Sheet 20; NH411757); *hill of the neck-shaped loch*

Beinn nan Eun; 743m; (OS Sheet 20; NH448759); *hill of the bird*

Carn Loch nan Amhaichean gives magnificent views over a wide area. From the A835 Garve to Ullapool road, almost opposite the Inchbae Lodge Hotel, a farm track follows the river north up Strath Rannoch, at first through forestry plantations, then open moorland. Just beyond Strathrannoch Farm, a faint track follows the north side of the Allt a' Choire-rainich above an unexpected rocky defile, beyond which the burn can be crossed by boulder hopping.

Climb the heathery hillside above in a north-easterly direction, towards a huge distinctive boulder on the skyline. The summit lies just beyond. To the east, the wind turbines on Meall an Tuirc catch the eye immediately, with the great rounded haunches of Ben Wyvis rising to the south-east. Looking in the opposite direction, the twin summits of Carn Chuinneag stand out above a vast area of peat hags while round to the west the entire skyline is crowded with peaks.

The view from Beinn nan Eun, its more remote and less shapely eastern neighbour, is even more extensive. Ben Rinnes stands out, alone above Strath Spey, 90km to the south-east, while Morven and the Caithness hills can be seen 76km to the north-east.

For a longer outing to take in this second Graham, descend the north ridge of Carn Loch nan Amhaichean, then drop down to the north shore of Loch nan Amhaichean. Follow the eastern outflow, then contour south until it is possible to cross the Abhainn Beinn nan Eun to reach the easy western spur of Beinn nan Eun. The river may be difficult to cross in spate. An alternative approach from the east, from Loch Glass, also involves this river crossing. A vehicle track now follows the river about 4km beyond Wyvis Lodge, to the impressive waterfall shown on the OS map.

Ben Wyvis; 1046m; (OS Sheet 20; NH463683); *majestic hill*

On the drive north up the A9, as the Cairngorms are left behind, the great massif of Ben Wyvis appears on the northern skyline, dominating the Beauly Firth. Over in Ross-shire, 'the Ben' as it is referred to locally, has always occupied a special place in the hearts of the people of the Black Isle and Easter Ross, forming a magnificent backdrop to their daily activities. It used to be said that passengers on the train from Inverness to Wick had Ben Wyvis in sight for half their journey.

Historical records indicate that local lairds, notably the Munros and Mackenzies, once held land from the Crown on condition that they could produce a snowball on demand any day of the year. Unfortunately for walkers and climbers, the mountain seems to attract more than its share of bad weather. The first documented ascent of 'Ben-we-vis' by James Robertson in June 1767 noted that 'on the summit I was whitened by a fall of snow'. More recently, during the first continuous winter round of the Munros, Martin Moran almost came to grief here in January 1985, caught in a slab avalanche.

Often capped with cloud, the uniform green southern and western slopes of Ben Wyvis are skirted with forestry plantations which hide two impressive eastern corries and the long smooth ridges linking the summit, Glas Leathad Mor (*big green grassy slope*) with its three tops and various outliers. The normal route of ascent for an estimated 8,000 walkers per year is from the west. An excellent new path follows the north side of the Allt a' Bhealaich Mhoir, starting some 500 metres south of Garbat on the A835 Garve to Ullapool road. If the small car park on the east side of the road is full, there is more space further on, opposite Garbat.

The path climbs up the west ridge of the first top, An Cabar (946m) (*the antler*). From here the wide ridge leading north-east to the summit and beyond is covered by the largest continuous area of moss heath in Scotland, a particularly fragile habitat. This can be a particularly testing place in bad weather. If approaching on a compass bearing, note that there is a very slight change in direction for the final 300 metres to the summit cairn, to avoid walking over the edge into Coire na Feola.

On a clear day the extensive panorama of mountains stretching across the west contrasts with more unusual views to the east. The wind turbines on Meall an Tuirc look remarkably close and there are usually a number of oil rigs moored in the shelter of the Cromarty Firth. For an even better view it is worth walking out onto the spur of An t-Socach (1006m) (*the beak*) which separates Coire na Feola and Coire Mor. Both corries have impressive crags of folded Moine schists along their south sides which offer some remote winter climbs.

To traverse the mountain, continue north along the summit ridge to Tom a' Choinnich (953m) (*mossy hillock*) then descend its grassy south-west ridge. Follow the Allt a' Gharbh Bhaid into the Garbat Forest, much of which has been clear felled. A forest track cuts back to join the ascent path. Alternatively, if transport has been arranged, from Tom a' Choinnich follow the undulating ridge east over Glas Leathad Beag (928m) (*small green grassy slope*) (not named on the OS map). This Top has been strongly tipped for elevation to full Munro status in the next revision of the Tables.

Descend over Fiaclach and pick up an unmarked stalkers path down to the private estate road which follows the south-west shore of Loch Glass to join the public road from Evanton at Eileanach Lodge.

A route from Dingwall, something of a local tradition at mid-summer, goes from Achterneed, above the A834 Dingwall to Strathpeffer road. The first part of this lengthy approach follows a forestry track which is closed to vehicles by a barrier of large boulders. If using a cycle to reach the end of the track, be very careful to note where it is left parked, since the blocks of young trees thereabouts are particularly featureless.

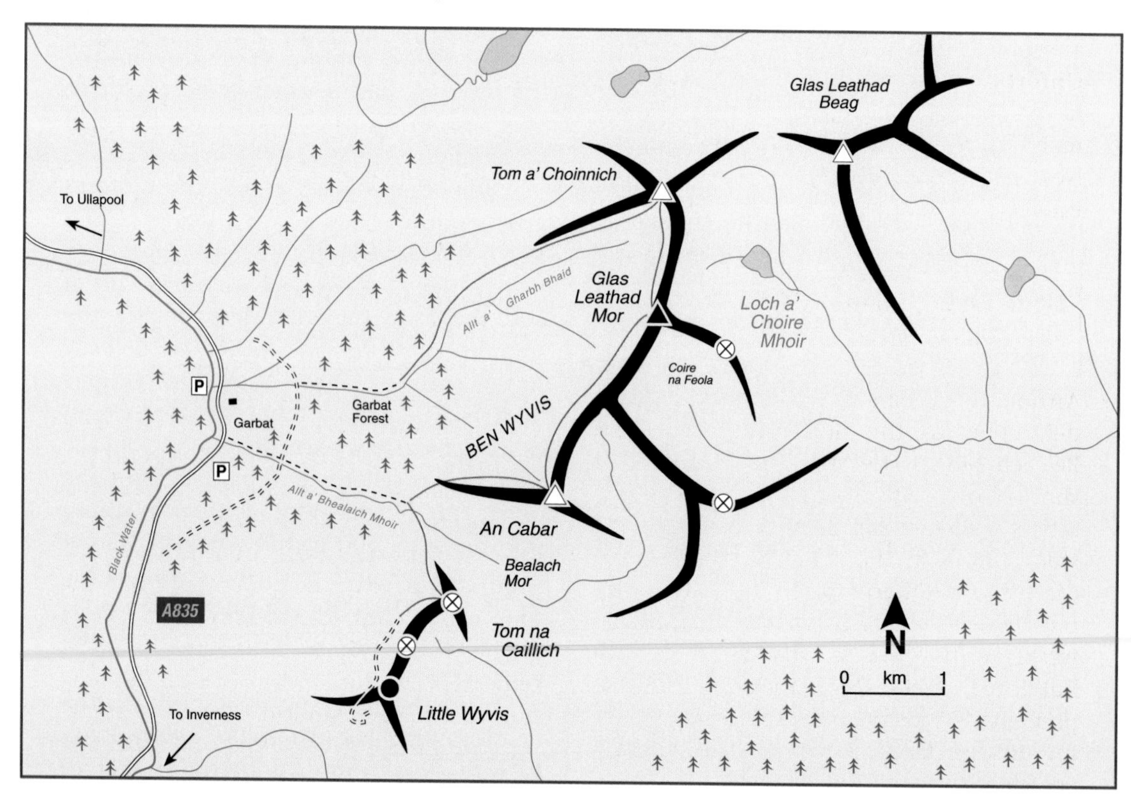

Ben Wyvis from the west

Ben Wyvis has long been popular for ski-touring. Coire na Feithe Riabhaich, east of An Cabar, has a reputation for good ski runs and holds snow until well into the spring. Unfortunately, downhill ski developers have also had their eyes on this corrie for many years. The most recent proposal, the New Highland Railway, was launched by interests in Strathpeffer in 1999.

However the new Ben Wyvis path up the Allt a' Bhealaich Mhoir makes the northern approach more appealing. Beyond the forestry gate, cross the river and make a short steep heathery climb south up to the col between Tom na Caillich (706m) and Little Wyvis. A pleasant undulating ridge with ever-widening views continues to the top.

Little Wyvis; 764m; (OS Sheet 20; NH429644); *little majestic hill*

Although overshadowed by its massive neighbour to the north-east across the Bealach Mor, Little Wyvis gives a popular short outing with a fine view, particularly satisfying when big brother has his head stuck firmly in the cloud, as is often the case. The southern flanks are extensively planted with young conifers and the south-west side above Garve is badly scarred with bulldozed tracks. The landowner here is particularly sensitive about walkers disturbing his deer farming activities and discourages access at any time of year.

Meall Mor; 738m; (OS Sheet 20; NH515745); *big hill*

Meall Mor forms a broad ridge between Loch Glass and Loch Morie, giving fine views of the east side of Ben Wyvis, in the heart of an interesting corner of Easter Ross. The distinctive wind turbines spread across the crest of Meall an Tuirc (625m) to the south-east have to some extent eclipsed the 18th century folly on nearby Cnoc Fyrish (452m) as a landmark. The latter, built by General Sir Hector Munro of Novar (no relation to Sir Hugh Munro) are said to represent the gates of Negapatnam, scene of one of the General's military victories in India.

Bill Morrison

Carn Chuinneag from Bonar Bridge

The short climb up Cnoc Fyrish gives a fine view. A signposted path follows the north-east shoulder from a car park (NH627715) in the forest less than 2km along the road to Boath after the turn off from the B9176 Struie road.

Approaching Meall Mor from the south gives the best views of Ben Wyvis and Loch Glass. Leave the A9 Inverness to Tain road after the Cromarty Firth bridge, following signposts to Evanton. Beyond the village, just north of the bridge over the River Glass, a narrower road climbs up Glen Glass. After about 7km the public road finishes at a bridge just before Eileanach Lodge, where it is possible to park. A forestry track on the east side of the river and the estate road on the west both lead in the same direction. The latter gives better views of Meall Mor and the windmills, but be sure to cross the river by the bridge above the weir, at the outflow from Loch Glass.

Continue along the forestry track to another junction, and another choice of routes. The right branch is shorter and gains height steadily, while the alternative follows the eastern shores of Loch Glass and offers better views, particularly when the track leaves the trees and swings east to climb steeply to rejoin the other branch.

From the top corner of the forest, the swish of the giant white propellers can now be heard, and the track continues further than indicated on the map, almost to the bealach between Meall Mor and Meall an Tuirc. A tussocky ridge continues north-west to the summit, with its extensive views. An access road for the wind farm comes up from Strath Rusdale, to the north-east, but note that the Meall an Tuirc on the east edge of OS Sheet 20 is not the same as the Meall an Tuirc on the west edge of OS Sheet 21. Lower down Glen Glass, below Assynt House, the Black Rock Gorge is a very impressive feature. This deep narrow chasm cuts through the Old Red Sandstone for almost 2km, its walls dropping vertically 40m in places. Also known as 'the Black Rock of Novar', it is associated with a number of local legends, including one concerning the lovely Lady of Balconie, who disappeared in tragic circumstances after making a pact with the Devil. There are also various reports of bold people having jumped across and more recently at least one party has traversed the length of the gorge at water level.

Beinn Tharsuinn; 692m; (OS Sheet 21; NH606792); *transverse mountain*

Surrounded by a miniature range of lower tops, Beinn Tharsuinn has the distinction of being the highest point on OS Sheet 21. It gives magnificent views of the Black Isle and the eastern seaboard of Ross and Cromarty and a surprising glimpse along Strath Oykel to the more distant hills of Coigach and Assynt to the north-west.

Approach is possible from the east, from a large car parking area where the A836 Evanton to Ardgay road crosses the Strathrory River on the climb up Struie hill. This side is also being considered for another wind farm. A more pleasant and varied approach comes up from the lush green fields and forests of Strath Rusdale to the south. Leave the road at Ardross Mains, and follow a forestry track past Loch Dubh, climbing up through maturing plantations to reach the heathery slopes of Tom Leathann, with its distinctive 'stone man' summit cairn.

For the final climb to the top of Beinn Tharsuinn, trend slightly west to avoid an extensive area of peat hags. On reaching the summit, the view north-west up Strath Oykel is suddenly revealed, with the distinctive outlines of Cul Mor, Suilven and Canisp towering in the distance, contrasting with the gentle curves of the surrounding Easter Ross hills. Avoiding more peat hags, it is worth returning over the whaleback of Cnoc an t-Sidhean Mor, resting place of a number of large glacial erratic boulders.

Carn Chuinneag; 838m; (OS Sheet 20; NH483833); *peak of the milk pail*

The distinctive twin tops of Carn Chuinneag stand out among the rolling hills of Easter Ross, easily recognised from many northern summits. The easiest approach comes from the north, up Glen Calvie. From Ardgay, at the head of the Dornoch Firth, the public road up Strathcarron turns south at The Craigs and ends just before the bridge leading to Glencalvie Lodge.

A private estate track continues south through Glen Calvie. When this track reaches the mouth of Glen Diebidale it suddenly turns east and climbs across the north side of Carn Chuinneag to a height of 437m. Further on, the track descends a little then turns south-east, dropping gradually into extensive forestry plantations in Strath Rusdale. The public road resumes again at Braeantra (NH567781) 7km north-west of Ardross, giving a longer approach from this side.

From the sudden bend in the track at the Glen Diebidale junction, a stalkers path climbs the north spur of the lower top (830m) and meets another path not far below the summit. This path climbs the north-east side of the hill from the Glen Calvie-Strath Rusdale track just east of the bridge over the Salachie Burn and can be used to make a short traverse of the hill. The mountain holds snow well and the two north-west corries overlooking Glen Diebidale give pleasant short ski runs.

Carn Salachaidh; 647m; (OS Sheet 20; NH518874); *dirty hill*

Carn Salachaidh is a rather isolated outlier, worth climbing on a clear day for the extensive views, particularly of the Coigach and Assynt hills to the north-west.

The shortest approach is from the north, from the Strathcarron road which comes west from Ardgay, following the south side of the river. Just south of Gruinards Lodge, a stalkers path climbs up through trees to the open moor, crossing the eastern shoulder of Carn Mor (279m) then descending to the Allt a' Ghlinne.

This path continues part way up the northern slopes of Carn Salachaidh, whose summit is a jumble of huge granite blocks. An alternative approach is from the Glen Calvie-Strath Rusdale track which crosses the foot of the hill to the south-west.

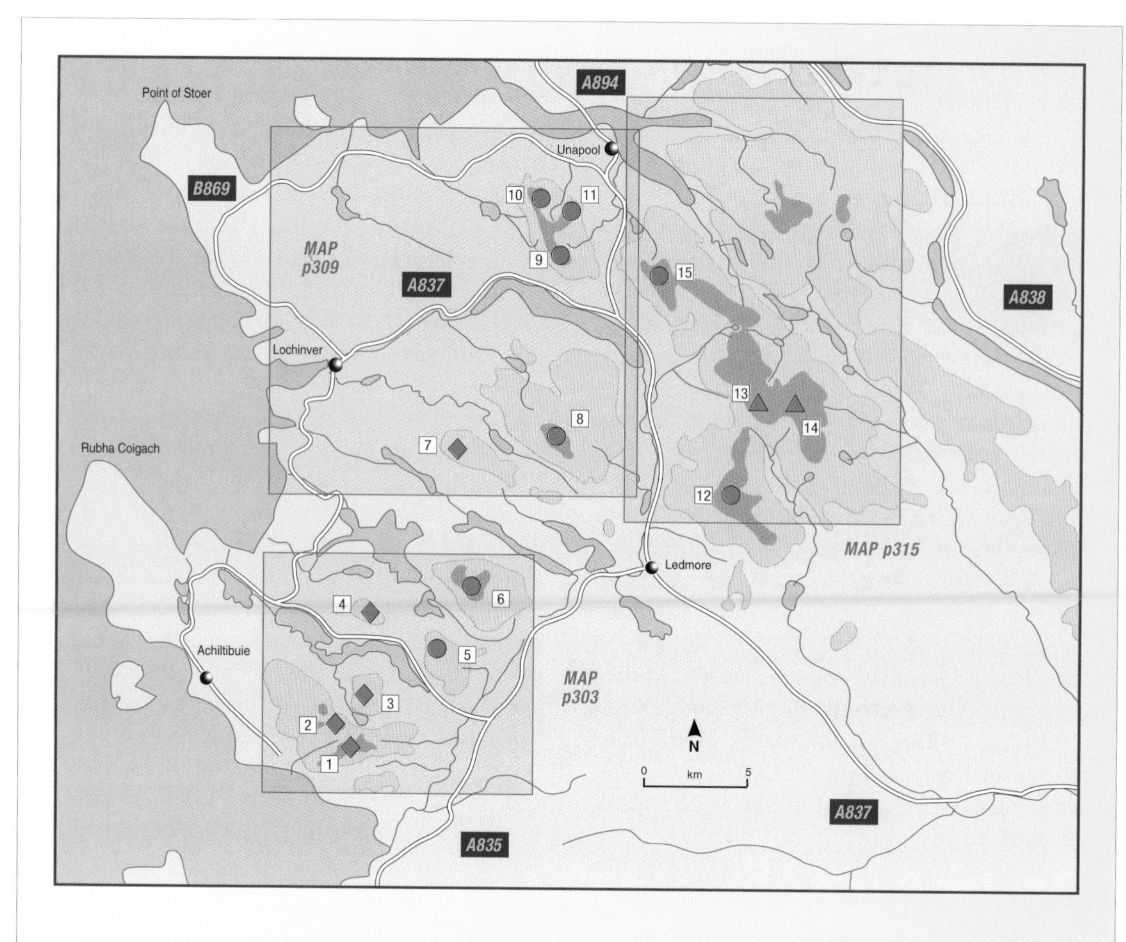

1.	Ben Mor Coigach	743m	G	p302
2.	Sgurr an Fhidhleir	705m	G	p302
3.	Beinn an Eoin	619m	G	p305
4.	Stac Pollaidh	612m	G	p305
5.	Cul Beag	769m	C	p306
6.	Cul Mor	849m	C	p307
7.	Suilven	731m	G	p308
8.	Canisp	847m	C	p311
9.	Quinag (Spidean Coinich)	764m	C	p311
10.	Quinag (Sail Gorm)	776m	C	p311
11.	Quinag (Sail Gharbh)	808m	C	p311
12.	Breabag	815m	C	p313
13.	Conival	987m	M	p314
14.	Ben More Assynt	998m	M	p314
15.	Glas Bheinn	776m	C	p316

Chapter 16

Coigach and Assynt

Jim Teesdale

Stac Pollaidh from Cul Mor

Coigach and Assynt have some of the most dramatic and interesting mountains in Britain. For the hillwalker, each one is a gem, offering short outings or longer traverses and rounds. Climbers are spoilt for choice with a tremendous variety of possibilities, from routes of all grades on the popular coastal crags at Reiff to challenging mixed winter climbs of the highest standard.

The mountains are divided into two distinct groups by the line of the Moine Thrust, a remarkable geological feature which is also followed by the main road north. West of the road, Torridonian sandstone has been eroded into fantastic cones and pyramids, many with protective caps of quartzite. Rugged in character and modest in height, the isolated hills of Coigach and west Assynt rise up with distinctive individual profiles to form a unique landscape.

Grey Lewisian gneiss underlies much of the lower ground, eroded into a myriad of hillocks and lochan-filled hollows, and this hard, ancient rock has weathered to produce meagre, infertile soil. The gneiss rises much higher to the east of the road, where the hills of east Assynt form a long high range stretching roughly northwards from Ledmore. On their western slopes, a belt of Cambrian limestone has formed a line of bright green swards and limestone pavements running from Elphin to Inchnadamph, with characteristic caves, sink holes and even a marble quarry.

Together, the whole area forms a broad peninsula, with two long flat headlands, the Rubha Mor and the Rubha Stoer, enclosing the great sweep of Enard Bay. Fringed by islands, with many smaller headlands and bays, the mountains inland are never far from the sea. Ben More Assynt, the highest point in Coigach and Assynt, is also the most easterly of the hills.

Jim Teesdale

The impressive prow of Sgurr an Fhidhleir

Glen Cassley, running south-east to join Strath Oykel at Rosehall, and the Abhainn an Loch Bhig, flowing north-west into Loch Beag at the head of Loch Glencoul, effectively form the eastern boundary of the area.

Historically, Coigach formed the north-west tip of the old county of Ross and Cromarty and the name means 'fifth part', from the old Celtic custom of dividing land into five parts. Coigach was under the sway of the MacNicols until about the 14th century, when the Macleods of Lewis gradually took control. The line of the River Kirkaig, the Fionn Loch and Loch Veyatie was the county march with the south-west corner of Sutherland and the neighbouring parish of Assynt. The origins of the name Assynt are less clear, coming either from the Norse 'ass' (*ridge*) and 'endi' (*end*) or the Gaelic 'as-sint' (*in and out*). The Vikings certainly used the distinctive pillar of Suilven as a landmark and left plenty of evidence of their passing in their place names.

Assynt was the legendary hunting ground of the Thanes of Sutherland and the ruins of Ardvreck Castle, the family stronghold, can still be seen on the narrow peninsula overlooking Loch Assynt just south of Skiag Bridge. Built in 1597, the Seaforth Mackenzies took possession of the castle in 1691 as settlement of a debt, and the new owners built nearby Calda House in 1695. The house burned down in mysterious circumstances in 1737 and in 1760 Assynt was bought back by the original Sutherland family.

As elsewhere in the North-west Highlands, most of the human population is scattered along the coast and served by a network of narrow twisty roads. A single-track road turns off north-west from the main A835 Ullapool to Elphin road at Drumrunie, and follows the northern shores of Loch Lurgainn, Loch Bad a' Ghaill and Loch Osgaig towards the coast. With Cul Beag and Stac Pollaidh rising directly from the roadside to the north, and Ben Mor Coigach and its extensive outliers to the south, this is a spectacular drive.

Beyond the Aird of Coigach, the road divides at the head of Achnahaird Bay. The campsite here is popular with walkers and climbers, with the added attraction for families of a sheltered sandy beach. From Achnahaird, one road continues north-west across the Rubha Mor and finishes at Reiff, giving access to the rock climbing on the extensive coastal cliffs. The other road continues south through the village of Achiltibuie and several smaller townships, finishing at Culnacraig. The clusters of houses strung out along the coast of the peninsula look south-west across to the Summer Isles.

Around 1810 the first tenants were moved to the shore near Achiltibuie and Badenscallie to create a sheep farm at Inverpolly and between 1812 and 1820 large areas of Coigach were cleared of people to make way for sheep. Attempts to clear the same families again in 1852-53 met with resistance, largely from the women. Wide coverage by national newspapers led to the estate abandoning its plans, marking a turning point in the sad history of the Highland clearances. As elsewhere, tourism and fish farming now help sustain the crofting communities scattered around the periphery.

Crofters at Achiltibuie and Strathcanaird have enclosed an area of 3500 acres with a 20km deer fence, aiming to recreate some of the mixed woodland that once covered the area. A grant of almost £1million under the Woodland Grant Scheme made this project the largest ever undertaken on crofting land. Ben Mor Coigach is managed by the Scottish Wildlife Trust as a nature reserve. Coigach also became the home of Dr Tom Longstaff, one of the greatest of the early Himalayan climbers and explorers. After a long and illustrious career he retired to Badentarbat and wrote his fascinating autobiography *This My Voyage*, published in 1950.

Access and Transport

By road: from Inverness the A9 continues north to the roundabout at Tore, from which the A835 leads west to Ullapool, then continues north through Elphin to join the A837 from Lairg and Bonar Bridge at Ledmore junction. From Drumrunie, a single track road leads to Achiltiebuie and the Rubha Mor peninsula, with a branch following the coast to Lochinver. From Ledmore junction the A837 continues to Lochinver, with the A894 branching off at Skiag bridge to Unapool and Scourie. Just before Unapool the single track B869 follows the coast around to Lochinver.

By bus: Achiltiebuie to Ullapool (Spa Coaches, tel: 01997-421311); Drumbeg to Lochinver to Lairg ; Scourie to Elphin (Postbus, tel: 08457-740740); Drumbeg to Lochinver to Ullapool (KSM Motors).

By rail: Lairg is the nearest station on the Inverness to Wick/Thurso line.

Accommodation and Information

Hotels and guesthouses: Achiltiebuie, Altnacealgach, Elphin, Inchnadamph, Kylesku, Lochinver, Stoer, Ullapool.

SYHA hostels: Achininver, Achiltiebuie (tel: 0870-004-1101); Achmelvich Beach (tel: 0870-004-1102); Ullapool (tel: 0870-004-1156).

Independent hostels: Inchnadamph Lodge (tel: 01571-822218); Kylesku Lodges (tel: 01971-502003); West House, Ullapool (tel: 01854-613126)

Club hut: Elphin: Naismith Hut (Scottish Mountaineering Club)

Campsites: Achmelvich (tel: 01571-844393); Achnahaird (tel: 01854 612135); Ardmair (tel: 01854-612054)

Tourist Information Centres: Lochinver (tel: 01571-844330) (seasonal); Ullapool, Argyle Street (tel: 01854-612135) (limited winter hours)

Maps

Ordnance Survey 1:50,000 Landranger Sheet 15 (Loch Assynt).

An even narrower road leaves the Achiltibuie road 4km east of Achnahaird and climbs north over the long western shoulder of Stac Pollaidh. Ominously sign-posted as unsuitable for caravans, it follows a particularly tortuous route, occasionally touching the coast then cutting inland, until it eventually reaches Lochinver via Inverkirkaig. A short distance east of this road lies Loch Sionascaig, in the heart of the Inverpolly National Nature Reserve. This is the second largest such area in the country after the Cairngorms, protecting a variety of interesting habitats.

Loch Sionascaig itself is dotted with islands and ringed by numerous bays and inlets, best appreciated either from the surrounding summits of Stac Pollaidh, Cul Mor and Suilven, or with the help of a canoe. Lochinver was described in 1840 as 'the only place deserving the name of village in Assynt' and is now an important fishing harbour with good road access along the A837 road from Skiag Bridge. The late Norman MacCaig, widely regarded as one of Scotland's greatest modern poets, spent his summer holidays in a cottage at nearby Achmelvich for some thirty years. Applying the clarity, sharp insight and wit for which his poetry is noted, MacCaig celebrated the delights of the landscape, wildlife and way of life of the North-west Highlands in many of his poems. Achmelvich also has a campsite and a sandy beach.

From Lochinver, the coast road continues north-west as the B869, serving the communities of Achmelvich, Clachtoll and Stoer before turning east past Drumbeg and Nedd to rejoin the main A894 Skiag Bridge to Kylesku road at Unapool. A glance at the map reveals a lot of fresh water in this corner of Assynt. It was here in 1992 that the local crofters got together and formed the Assynt Crofters' Trust which succeeded in buying the land they had rented for generations. This historic achievement was supported and applauded throughout Scotland, opening up the possibility of 'community buy-outs' in other crofting areas.

This northern corner of Assynt is dominated by the crags and corries of Quinag and separated from the hills to the south by the waters of Loch Assynt. To the north, a narrow finger of sea points east from the corner of Eddrachillis Bay. Loch a' Chairn Bhain narrows dramatically at Kylesku, then continues deep inland as Loch Glendhu and Loch Glencoul. The latter narrows further as Loch Beag, finishing almost at the foot of the spectacular Eas a' Chual Aluinn waterfall.

Principal Hills

Ben Mor Coigach; 743m; (OS Sheet 15; NC094042); *big hill of Coigach*

Sgurr an Fhidhleir; 705m; (OS Sheet 15; NC094054); *peak of the fiddler*

Conspicuous from many hills south of Ullapool, the massive south-west ridge of Ben Mor Coigach dominates the view to the north. This continuous line of steep sandstone, seamed with gullies, is particularly impressive when seen from the A835 Ullapool to Elphin road as it returns to sea level at Ardmair.

Writing in the 1930s, F.Reid Corson described this ridge as 'hanging like a gigantic curtain across the northern sky', running almost horizontally some 3km. Garbh Choireachan (733m) is the blunt western spur which rises abruptly from the sea and Speicin Coinnich (717m) forms the shapely rocky point at the eastern end from which long heathery slopes drop gently eastwards. Continuing north, as the road approaches the junction at Drumrunie the complex topography of the north side of the mountain is revealed, with its steep cliffs and deep corries, narrow ridges and shapely summits, dominated by neighbouring Sgurr an Fhidhleir with its great rocky 'Nose'.

There are several possible starting points to climb Ben Mor Coigach. The shortest and most direct route starts from Culnacraig,

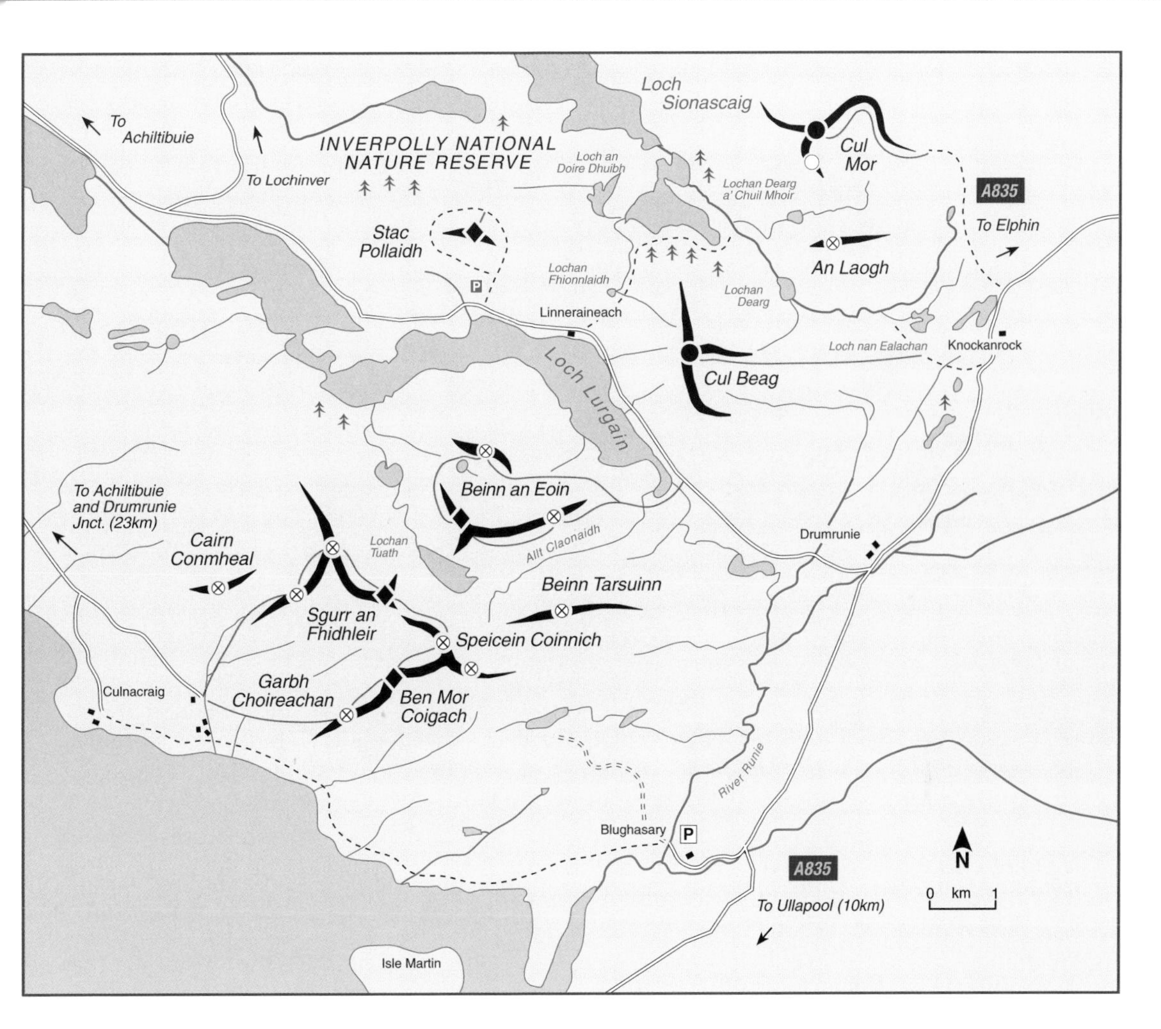

beyond Achiltibuie, parking at the end of the public road, where it crosses the Allt a' Choire Reidh. Make a rising traverse, aiming to meet the Allt nan Coisiche above its ravine, then scramble up weathered sandstone onto Garbh Choireachan.

A long ridge continues north-east to Ben Mor Coigach. Several sandstone towers along its narrow crest are all easily avoided or tackled direct. The main summit has a large sheltered cairn built on a small open plateau which stands out north from the main ridge. On a clear day the views are magnificent. A number of parties who have been unfortunate enough to encounter poor visibility have reported problems with compass needle deflection.

Most parties will want to continue to Sgurr an Fhidhleir. Follow the ridge north-east to the rim of the corries below, then turn north and follow the edge round, dropping steeply to the broad col between the two peaks, before the final climb to the airy summit. This col can also be reached from the north-east side, approaching via the Allt Claonaidh and Lochan Tuath, either using the stepping stones at the east end of Loch Lurgainn, or by crossing the moorland from further east. From the south end of Lochan Tuath, a prominent earthy gully to the south of the peak gives a straightforward approach to the col.

To descent to Culnacraig, either drop directly south-west down into Choire Reidh or continue the traverse of the ridge. Follow the north-west shoulder of Sgurr an Fhidhleir to Point 648m then turn south-west over Beinn nan Caorach (649m) and Cairn Conmheall (541m). The latter has a few rock climbs on its western cliff. *Acheninver*

Ben Mor Coigach and the Summer Isles

Pinnacle (150m Very Difficult 1955) climbs the right edge of a prominent pinnacle. Descending north-west from Point 648m leads down to the west end of Loch Lurgainn which can be crossed to reach the road below Stac Pollaidh.

The approaches to Ben Mor Coigach from the east give longer walks but saves the drive through the heart of Coigach to reach Culnacraig. From the end of the road at Blughasary in Strath Canaird there are two possible routes. Reports that the local postman used to deliver mail to Achiltibuie along the coastal path will surprise anyone following this route which is muddy at the east end, indistinct at the west end and very rough and exposed in places in between. However, it does give access to the north-west side of Garbh Choireachan, and joins the route from Culnacraig.

A less strenuous route from Blughasary follows a bulldozed estate track, shown as a path on the OS map, which leads north then west to Loch Eadar dha Bheinn. From the east end of the loch make a short steep climb onto the east shoulder of Speicin Coinnich. This top lies at the eastern end of Ben Mor Coigach's summit ridge which can also be approached from the highest point on the A835 Ullapool to Ledmore Junction road as it climbs out of Strath Canaird, using a footbridge across the River Runie. A direct line from the bridge gives interesting scrambling on the rocky upper steps, while an easier alternative follows the line of the Allt a' Phollain Riabhaich towards Beinn Tarsuinn (544m), whose broken heathery north-east ridge can also be reached from the Achiltibuie road just west of Drumrunie.

Rock climbing on the North Buttress of Sgurr an Fhidhleir, the distinctive *'Fiddler's Nose'*, has a long history. Ling and Sang made a brave attempt as far back as 1907, reaching high on the buttress only to be repulsed by exposed sandstone slabs. The same outcome awaited a number of other strong parties over the years until Drasdo and Dixon finally succeeded in 1962. *Direct Nose Route* (245m Hard Very Severe 5a) follows an obvious grassy groove twisting up the centre of the buttress to the three Pale Slabs then finishes directly up the spur. In rare winter conditions this becomes a superb climb of alpine stature graded VII, 8, giving strenuous climbing using frozen turf and torqued picks with excellent protection. A number of other lines have been climbed in summer and winter.

Beinn an Eoin; 619m; (OS Sheet 15; NC105064); *hill of the bird*

The twin peaks of Beinn an Eoin form a delightful little horseshoe in the heart of Coigach, giving an excellent short and easily accessible traverse. From the east end of Loch Lurgainn there are stepping stones across the inflowing burn adjacent to a gate through the new deer fence. Park with care on the single track road above. The long heathery spur of Cioch Beinn an Eoin (380m) ends abruptly in a prow of loose sandstone blocks. These are best avoided on the south side to gain the slabby ridge which curves around to the main summit, Sgorr Deas (*south peak*).

The west side is craggy but vegetated, with fine views across Lochan Tuath to the north-eastern cliffs of Sgurr an Fhidhleir with its distinctive nose. There are more steep crags on the north side so do not leave it until too late before descending to the lochan nestling in the hanging corrie below Sgorr Tuath (589m) (*north peak*). A short scramble leads to the summit which features a dramatic narrow rock cleft and fine views to the north. Broken rocky ribs fall steeply down towards Loch Lurgainn, and beyond the summit there are some fine sandstone pinnacles, after which easy heathery slopes lead south-east into the corrie and a straightforward traverse back through newly planted trees.

Stac Pollaidh; 612m; (OS Sheet 15; NC107106); *steep rock at the pool*

Few hills in Scotland are as striking or as popular as Stac Pollaidh, a mountain in the final stages of erosion. Unprotected by a quartzite cap, its summit crest of highly weathered sandstone towers and pinnacles extends for almost 1km, rising from steep heather-covered screes.

From a distance its distinctive profile is instantly recognisable but the anglicised version of its name has nothing to do with any resemblance to cockatoos, as suggested by the distinguished author of a previous edition of this guide. Others have visualised fossilised stegosaurs, irascible porcupines, saw blades or even fairytale castles. Be prepared to let your imagination run wild!

Stac Pollaidh is very accessible, rising directly above the Achiltibuie road as it skirts the north side of Loch Lurgainn. A purpose built car park situated between the road and the loch due south of the summit makes a convenient starting point for most walkers. Unfortunately, the passage of an estimated 30,000 pairs of feet climbing direct to the eastern end of the summit ridge each year has caused terrible erosion. This route has been condemned as dangerous by Scottish Natural Heritage which has funded improvements to an alternative path. This crosses the eastern shoulder and leads around to the north side of the hill before it zigzags up to a saddle on the summit crest.

Numerous paths thread between the pinnacles and around the steep rocky corners which make up this remarkable feature. There are no serious difficulties until a small tower blocks the way just below the highest point at the top of the West Buttress. This tower can be climbed direct, or avoided by dropping into a gully on the south side for a few metres then scrambling up a steep slab. Either way should be tackled with care.

Magnificent panoramas can be enjoyed from all along the summit crest, with the view north-east across Loch Sionascaig giving a particularly fine profile of Suilven. Most of the gullies on either side of the summit crest can be descended. On the south side, a large gully east of the summit

Jim Renny

Stac Pollaidh from the south-west

leads into Pinnacle Basin where *'The Sphinx'*, *'Tam O'Shanter'* and the *'Virgin and Child'* are some of the mountain's finest sandstone sculptures. The much photographed *'Lobster Claw'* collapsed some years ago as a result of continuing natural erosion.

A more gentle approach to the foot of the East Buttress can be made from Linneraineach, offering finer views and an easier gradient. Scrambling up the East Buttress requires careful route finding, with horizontal ledges offering frequent lines of escape to the northern side. The south-west corner of the West Buttress offers more serious climbing at about Difficult standard, starting at the prominent *Baird's Pinnacle* (also called *The Forefinger*) and first climbed in 1906 by Charles Walker, Dr William, Mrs Jane and Miss Mabel Inglis Clark. Mother and daughter were competent climbers who founded The Ladies' Scottish Climbing Club two years later.

Writing about their climb, Dr Inglis Clark enthused about 'great slabs of rough sandstone, set almost vertically, affording excellent friction grips but refusing hitches when they would be most desirable.' With a sunny aspect, quick drying rock and a stupendous outlook, rock climbing on Stac Pollaidh continues to be popular. On the harder modern routes, camming devices such as 'Friends' are particularly useful for protection.

Cul Beag; 769m; (OS Sheet 15; NC140088); *little back*

Similar in many ways to its larger northern neighbour Cul Mor, with gentle slopes to the east and crags to the north and west, Cul Beag can be climbed from just about anywhere on the road between Drumrunie and Linneraineach. The easiest but longest route leaves the road soon after crossing the bridge over the Allt Liathdoire and makes a rising traverse into the broad south-east corrie, continuing to the lochan on the bealach between the summit and Meall

Dearg, its craggy eastern outlier.

Another long approach offering closer views of the south-west cliffs of Cul Mor leaves the road at the plantation just east of Linneraineach and follows the path across the western shoulder of the hill to Loch an Doire Dhuibh. From the east end of the loch climb up to Lochan Dearg and continue east, avoiding the northern cliffs of Cul Beag and Meall Dearg to join the route crossing from Cul Mor which climbs the eastern slopes of Meall Dearg and on to the top. A much more direct alternative leaves the path just beyond Lochan Fhionnlaidh and climbs to the shoulder between Cul Beag and its northern spur.

Descent to the east over Meall Dearg follows the ridge above Creag Dhubh and eventually meets a stalkers path from Knockanrock. It is also feasible to descend to the road at the east end of Loch Lurgainn using the steep shallow corrie west of the southern Creag Dhubh.

Overlooking Loch Lurgainn, the western crags of Cul Beag offer lots of potential for scrambling over short rocky steps and grassy terraces. *Lurgainn Edge* (75m Very Difficult 1958) has become a popular route, following the right hand edge of the distinctive Y-shaped gully south-west of the summit. A few other rock climbs have also been recorded in this vicinity and some winter routes have been climbed in the corries to the north.

Cul Mor; 849m; (OS Sheet 15; NC162119); *big back*

Highest of the Coigach hills, the gentle eastern slopes of Cul Mor rise up from the green fields of Elphin, its distinctive twin quartzite capped summits connected by a graceful curving saddle. To the south and west, bands of sandstone cliffs rise up from Gleann Laoigh (*valley of the calf*) and the chain of lochs leading to Loch Sionascaig in the remote heart of the Inverpolly National Nature Reserve. North of the summit and hidden from the road, the wide and deep Coire Gorm (*blue corrie*) is circled by crags which face towards Suilven. In the foreground, Loch Veyatie and the Fionn Loch form a long moat which separates the two mountains.

Cul Mor is usually climbed from the A835 Ullapool to Elphin road just north of the Knockan Crag visitors centre. A gate marks the start of a well made stalkers path which leads onto Meallan Diomhain, the mountain's broad eastern shoulder. When the path ends, a line of cairns continues onto an open plateau. To reach the summit either follow the north-east ridge overlooking Coire Gorm or contour to the hanging corrie between the summit and Creag nan Calman (828m) (*crag of the dove*). From the summit, the broad north-west ridge Sron Gharbh (*rough nose*) gives pleasant walking on rough flat sandstone and a magnificent view.

It is possible to descend into Coire Gorm from the col below the north-west top and contour the northern flanks of the mountain back to the stalkers path. Beyond Coire Gorm on the north-west shoulder there is a distinctive rock pinnacle, Bod a' Mhiotailt (*old man*). Another possible descent from the bare gravel col below Creag nan Calman trends east then curves below steep sandstone cliffs to the sandy shore of Lochan Dearg a' Chuil Mhoir, a strange and beautiful 'hidden valley' tucked in between Cul Mor and its rocky satellite An Laogh (546m) (*the calf*). Avoid the precipitous waterslide at its outflow by making a descending traverse south into Gleann Laoigh, then either continue to Cul Beag or return to Knockanrock.

A more challenging ascent of Cul Mor can be made from the Achiltibuie road, following the stalkers path which starts just east of Linneraineach. The bridge over the channel between Lochan Gainmheich (*sandy loch*) and Loch Sionascaig disappeared many years ago, so the right-hand path to the head of Loch an Doire Dhuibh (*loch of the dark wood*) is likely to be a drier option. Above the floor of Gleann Laoigh a broad terrace runs the length of the south-western cliffs. A rocky ridge, bounded on its

Cul Mor from Stac Pollaidh

left by a gully draining into a deep-cut burn gives a pleasant scramble onto Creag nan Calman.

A number of winter routes have been recorded in Coire Gorm since the mid-'90s. Its very steep vegetated walls will continue to attract the modern winter climber. *The Cul* (165m V,6 1991) follows a steep chimney which provides much more than meets the eye. There are a few rock climbs on the south face of An Laogh.

Suilven; 731m; (OS Sheet 15; NC153183); *the pillar*

A favourite of photographers and poets, the distinctive profile of Suilven makes it one of the most instantly recognisable mountains in Britain. Most westerly of the Assynt hills, the Norse 'sul-r' (*pillar*) of the Viking invaders has been a prominent and reassuring landmark to sailors and fishermen ever since. Approaching from the opposite direction, along the A837 from Bonar Bridge to Ledmore Junction, every hill lover will feel a sudden surge of excitement when 'the Matterhorn of the north' suddenly comes into view. Eighteenth century traveller Thomas Pennant called it *'Sugar Loaf Mountain'*, an apt description of the symmetrical cone seen from Lochinver.

However, the true nature of Suilven's triple-peaked ridge is best seen from its neighbours to the north or south, revealing a narrow 2.5 km long sandstone ridge which drops away steeply on both sides, sitting high and dry above the surrounding lochs and moorland like a great stranded ship. Caisteal Liath (731m) (*grey castle*), a rounded red flanked tower, forms the highest point at the north-west end of the ridge, separated from the sharp central peak, Meall Mheadhonach (723m) by a prominent col, the Bealach Mor. South-east of this peak, a steep sided notch isolates Meall Bheag (610m) (not named on the OS map) from the rest of the ridge.

Despite its forbidding appearance, the ascent of Suilven via the Bealach Mor is relatively straightforward, though the approach from any direction is long, with good paths at least part of the way. The narrow ridge gives a memorable traverse if suitable transport arrangements can be made. From the north, a path leaves the A837 Skiag Bridge to Lochinver road at the west end of Loch Assynt, a few hundred metres east of Little Assynt. Fording the Allt an Tiaghaich can be a problem in wet weather, after which a path winds across the grain of the country to Suileag bothy.

This point can also be reached from Lochinver by taking the single track road east towards Glencanisp Lodge, with ample parking at the end of the public road, 800 metres before the lodge. A footpath leads east to join the Little Assynt path just south-west of Suileag, and continues south-east to a bridge at the outflow of Loch na Gainimh. This path leads eventually through to Elphin by way of Lochan Fada and Cam Loch, but for Suilven a rough path climbs south-west from the bridge, boggy in places, to the steep but straightforward gully leading to the Bealach Mor. A gap in the remarkable dry stone dyke which crosses the ridge above gives easy access to the broad summit of Caisteal Liath.

An alternative and more varied route from the west follows the old county boundary up the beautiful wooded gorge of the River Kirkaig, past the magnificent Falls of Kirkaig. There is a car park 5km south of

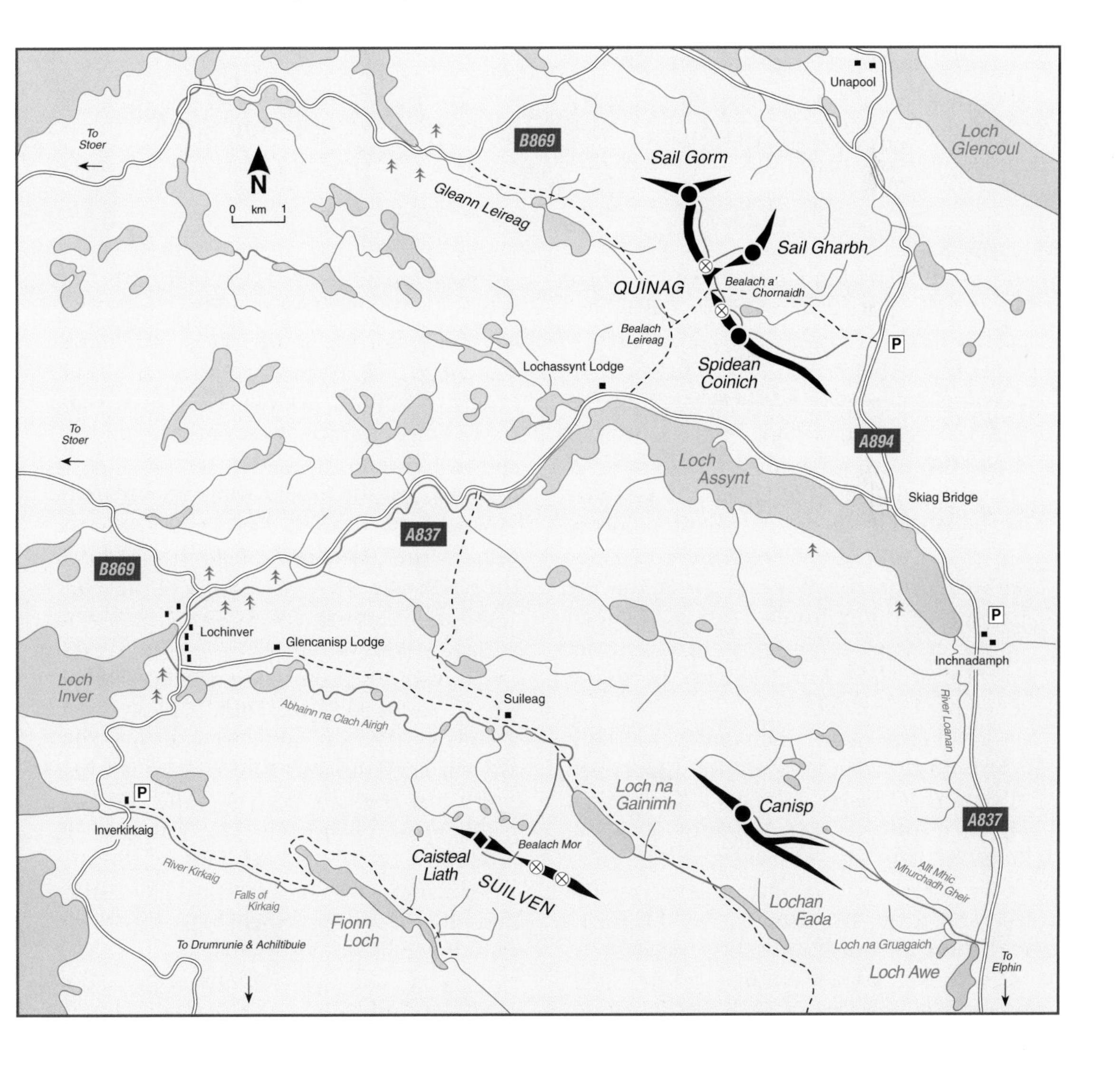

Suilven from Fionn Loch

Lochinver, just past Inverkirkaig, and the path is well signposted. Suilven itself is hidden from view until above the falls. As the path winds around the north-west end of the Fionn Loch the mountain suddenly appears in all its glory. Look out for a boggy shortcut before the river outflow. Follow the path along the north-east side of the loch until it crosses the burn flowing down from the Bealach Mor which is reached by way of a heathery scree chute.

From the east, the long moorland approach starts on the path from Elphin to Glencanisp Lodge already mentioned, which meets the A835 Elphin to Ledmore Junction road just north-east of Elphin, a short distance east of the bridge across the Ledmore River. The path follows the northern shore of the Cam Loch, then climbs north towards Lochan Fada. Before reaching the lochan, strike off west along the broad shoulder of Meall na Braclaich (375m) and climb gradually to Meall Bheag, the eastern top. Beyond here the ridge is exposed and requires care. A steep gap separates the central peak Meall Mheadhonach, and difficulties are best avoided on the north side. The final section to the main summit of Caisteal Liath is a fine ridge walk with easy scrambling.

Suilven can also be approached from the east by canoe or kayak. From the Cam Loch a short portage is required to pass the waterfall on the Abhainn Mor and reach the south-east end of Loch Veyatie. A 7km paddle leads almost to the foot of the mountain, below the Bealach Mor.

A handful of rock climbs have been described on the north-west cliffs of Caisteal Liath. Charles Pilkington and Horace Walker, two of the most active British climbers of the Victorian era, climbed a vegetated gully near the right end of the buttress in 1892, during the latter's presidency of the Alpine Club. This route was repeated in winter one hundred years later (140m II) as a fine prelude to a traverse of the ridge. The cliff to the left has some clean rock and three Hard Severe rock climbs, any of which would give a memorable traditional mountain day. Be prepared for some vegetation and greasy rock in the wet, with a splendid feeling of openness.

Canisp; 847m; (OS Sheet 15; NC203187); *white hill* or *can-shaped roof*

Canisp takes the form of a steep sided ridge running south-east to north-west, with the A837 Ledmore Junction to Inchnadamph road skirting its eastern flank. Despite its lack of distinctive features, the mountain has the advantages of location, accessibility and altitude which make it a superb vantage point from which to appreciate its more shapely neighbours and the rugged terrain from which they rise.

The shortest approach leaves the road at the north end of Loch Awe, 4km north of Ledmore Junction, with plenty of roadside parking. The River Loanan can be crossed by stepping stones or a footbridge (not marked on the OS map) then boggy ground leads to the broad south-east ridge. Follow this easily to the summit, past outcrops of the pale quartzite which may have given the mountain its name.

An alternative route follows the line of the Allt Mhic Mhurchaidh Gheir which drops in a series of small waterfalls and pools, inviting for a dip on a hot summer's day.

A traverse is the ideal way to appreciate Canisp and its surroundings and the easy north-west ridge is served by a stalkers path which joins the Glencanisp Lodge to Elphin path on the north side of Loch na Gainimh. The south-east slopes of Canisp are reported to hold snow well and offer a rare opportunity for ski-touring in these hills.

Quinag (Spidean Coinich); 764m; (OS Sheet 15; NC206277); *milk pail (peak of the moss)*

Quinag (Sail Gorm); 776m; (OS Sheet 15; NC198304); *milk pail (blue heel)*

Quinag (Sail Gharbh); 808m; (OS Sheet 15; NC209292); *milk pail (rough heel)*

Pronounced 'koonyak' from the Gaelic '*cuinneag*', Quinag is last in the great chain of hills formed from the Torridonian sandstone which stretches from Applecross to Cape Wrath. More a massif than a single mountain, its towering crags, deep corries and high ridges draw the eye from all directions. Almost encircled by public roads, a straightforward climb gives the rare opportunity to collect three Corbetts in one outing. Its many summits are arranged along a sort of twisted Y shape, the largest arm of which rises in a long gentle slope from Skiag Bridge on the north-east shore of Loch Assynt, over a rocky hump to Spidean Coinich. This south-east slope has a widely exposed cover of white quartzite, scattered with boulders, giving pleasant walking when dry but slippery when wet. A line of crags drops steeply into the eastern corrie and Bucket Buttress, a small quartzite cliff directly below the summit, has a number of short, sustained winter cragging routes.

One popular route of ascent starts 1km south of the watershed on the A894 between Skiag Bridge and Kylesku where an old quarry provides a large parking area east of the road. A stalkers path leads north-west and after a short distance, a cairn marks a parting of the ways. The main path continues up to Lochan Bealach Cornaidh, skirting the north shore of the loch then climbing steeply to the Bealach a' Chornaidh, while the route to Spidean Coinich follows the south-east spur above the quartzite crags. North from Spidean Coinich, a narrow ridge leads over Creag na h-Iolaire Ard (713m) (*high crag of the eagle*)

Spidean Coinich, Quinag

(not named on the OS map).

Ahead, the tops look surprisingly green, but first the ridge drops steeply to the broad Bealach a' Chornaidh which is easily accessible from the east, as just described, or from the west, as follows. From further west along the A837 Skiag Bridge to Lochinver road at Tumore, on the northern tip of Loch Assynt, a sign-posted right of way starts just west of the house and crosses the Bealach-Leireag through Gleann Leireag to the coastal township of Nedd. Leave this path at its highest point and make a rising traverse north-east up heathery slopes to gain the Bealach a' Chornaidh. This western flank of Quinag forms an impressive 3km long wall of crags cut with gullies, rising 200m in height in places. A number of climbs have been recorded in summer and winter, including Tom Patey's *The Water Pipe* (150m II 1965), one of the finest deep gullies in Scotland.

From the Bealach a' Chornaich, a steep climb north gains the flat unnamed Point 745m. Two great spurs branch out from here, enclosing a deep, steep sided north-east corrie drained by the Allt a' Bhathaich (*burn of the byre*). Continuing along the line of the main ridge northwards, a small, truncated top can be climbed direct or contoured on its eastern side, followed by another rounded top before the long final slope to the summit of Sail Gorm. A steep rocky buttress drops away to the north, with easier slopes leading off either flank. The underlying gneiss rises to a height of 600m on this north face.

East of the junction top, a short steep drop leads to an open level saddle from which the north-east spur rises gradually to the broad quartzite summit of Sail Gharbh, highest point on Quinag. This spur continues for almost 1km to the top of the magnificent Barrel Buttress, Quinag's most impressive feature, comprising huge vertical steps of sandstone, seamed with deep gullies and crossed by occasional narrow terraces.

First climbed in summer 1907, Raeburn, Mackay and Ling's vegetated *Original Route*

(270m Very Difficult 1907) was repeated in winter 88 years later by Simon Richardson and Roger Webb, giving a formidable route graded VI,7. These northern buttresses of Sail Gharbh and Sail Gorm make a magnificent sight driving south over the graceful curve of the Kylesku Bridge.

Breabag; 815m; (OS Sheet 15; NC287157); *little height*

Breabag is the broad whale-back ridge which separates the upper reaches of Glen Oykel from the line of the Moine Thrust and the main A837 north from Ledmore Junction. The hill is an offshoot of the main Ben More Assynt ridge and Gaelic authority Professor W.J.Watson speculated that the name derived from 'breab beag' (*little kick*) as though separated from its neighbours by the swing of a mighty foot. A fine line of crags and corries on the eastern side are hidden from view from the road and this has tended to be a neglected hill, overshadowed by its grander neighbours. The highest point is not even named on the OS map, though it is sometimes called after nearby Creag Liath to the south-west.

The most direct and popular approach follows the Allt nan Uamh (*burn of the caves*) with its famous Bone Caves and various other limestone features. Excavations of these caves have unearthed the remains of animals dating back to the last Ice Age and evidence of habitation by Upper Paeleolithic Man. There is a car park in front of the fish hatchery beside the A837, some 6km north of Ledmore Junction.

The path to the Bone Caves has been much improved, but rather than climbing up to the caves, continue following the burn either all the way up to a tiny lochan on the shoulder north of the summit, or take a more direct line to the top from beyond the caves. For a more interesting descent, continue north over Point 718m and Breabag Tarsuinn (649m) before dropping down to the north-east into the narrow defile below Conival. Descend the south bank of the Allt a' Bhealaich to join the Traligill Caves path leading down to

Eas a' Chual Aluinn

Some 200m in height, the Eas a' Chual Aluinn (*splendid waterfall of Coul*) is the highest waterfall in Britain. Anglicised to Eas Coul Aulinn or even Eas Coulin, locally the fall is known as 'The Maiden's Tresses'. According to legend, a local girl betrothed to a man she did not love went into hiding on the cliffs of Leitir Dubh. When a search party came looking for her, she threw herself off the cliff in despair and her tresses spread out to form the waterfall.

During the summer tourist season, a cruise boat sails from Kylesku up Loch Glencoul to view the falls and the south shore of the loch can also be followed on foot. Leave the A894 Skiag Bridge to Kylesku road at the bridge over the Unapool Burn and avoid the steep cliffs at Eilean an Tuim and Loch Beag by traversing the hillside above. This route is not recommended in bad weather. Alternatively, a good stalkers path approaches the fall from above, leaving the A894 at either end of Loch na Gainmhich (*sandy loch*). At the north end of the loch, a deep quartzite gorge holds the 'Wailing Widow Fall', another impressive feature associated with more tragic legends. The path climbs south-east over the Bealach a' Bhuirich (*pass of the roaring*) and the stream feeding the fall is marked with a cairn. If the stream is crossed just before it tumbles over the cliff edge, grassy terraces to the east give a good view of the fall and descent to the floor of the glen is possible with care. During a hard freeze in February 1986, Andy Cunningham and Andy Nisbet managed a winter ascent of the frozen fall, graded V,5 despite water still flowing down the centre.

Inevitably comparisons have been made between Eas a' Chual Aluinn and the Falls of Glomach in Kintail. Draining a much larger area, the latter discharge a much greater volume of water. In average conditions this has been estimated at about 250 litres per second compared with about 1600 litres per second respectively. The nearby Falls of Kirkaig south-west of Suilven discharge some 7000 litres per second.

Sail Garbh, Quinag

Inchnadamph. The entrances to these caves are worth exploring with a torch.

Conival; 987m; (OS Sheet 15; NC303199); *adjoining hill*

Ben More Assynt; 998m; (OS Sheet 15; NC318201); *big hill of Assynt*

Close neighbours Conival and Ben More Assynt are the highest summits in Sutherland and form part of a 17km long continuous range of hills which stretches north from the upper reaches of Glen Oykel. The high ground seldom drops below a height of 600m, but the summits are relatively inconspicuous from the A837 Ledmore Junction to Kylesku road which skirts the range to the west.

These two Munros are best viewed from a distance. Lewisian gneiss, one of the oldest rocks in Europe, reaches its greatest height in Scotland on Ben More Assynt, capped with quartzite on the summit. Cambrian limestone on the lower western slopes gives lush green vegetation with a rich variety of plant-life above ground and extensive systems of caves and watercourses below.

Near the east end of Loch Assynt, the Inchnadamph Hotel is a popular haunt of walkers, cavers, fishermen, botanists and geologists and is the usual starting point to climb both hills. The first recorded ascent of Ben More Assynt was by William, Charles and Robert Inglis in 1863. Sons of a Borders' minister who introduced them to hillwalking in the 1840s, the brothers had previously made the first Scottish ascent of Monte Rosa in 1857, only the sixth ascent of Switzerland's highest peak.

There is ample parking at the turn-off to the hotel. On the far side of the bridge over the River Traligill (*ravine of the Trolls*) a farm track leaves the A837 and leads past Glenbain cottage to a small plantation. Two footpaths continue beyond here. One path leads south-east, crossing the river by a wooden bridge and climbs up to Loch Mhaolach-coire. Known locally as Loch

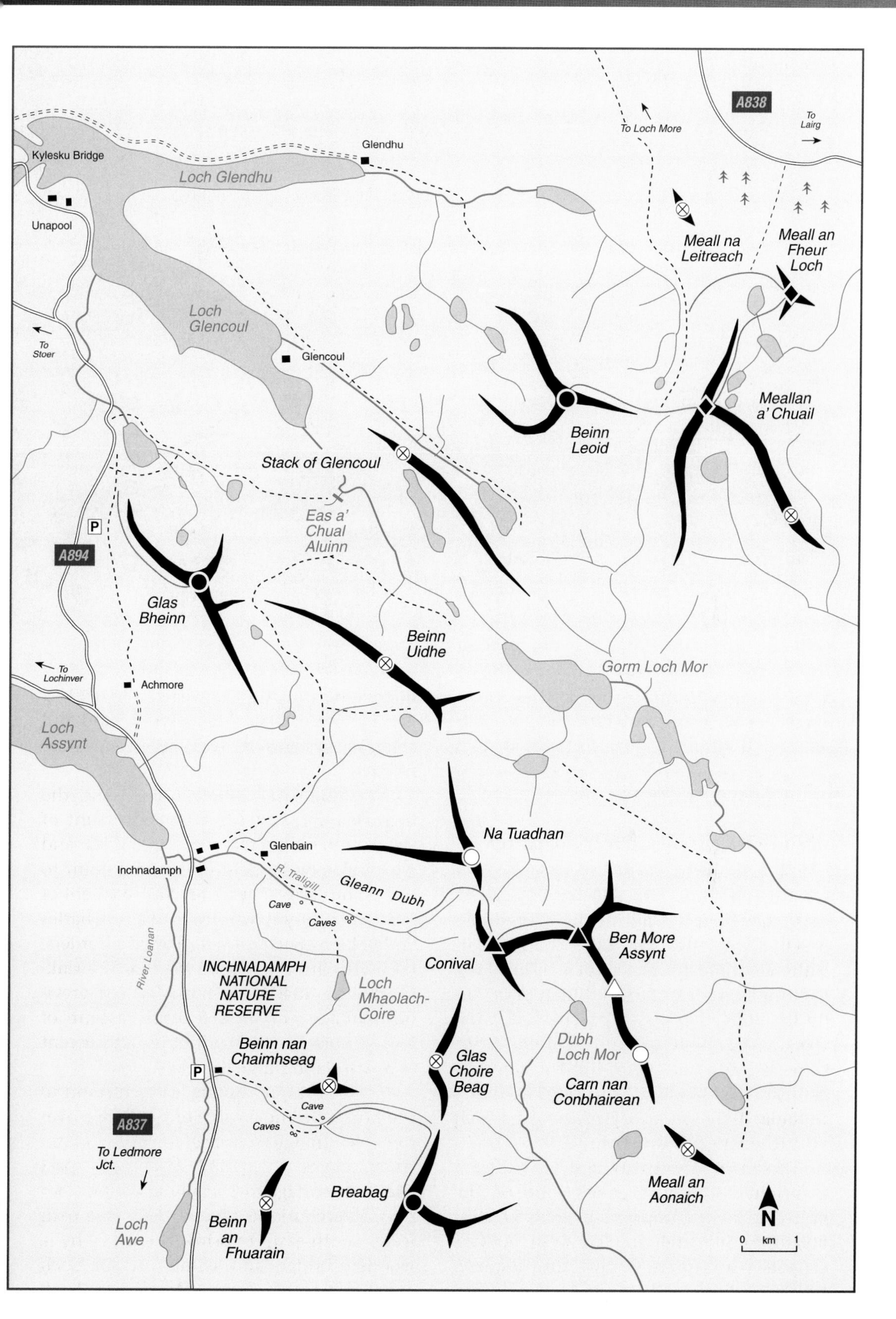

A838
To Loch More
To Lairg
Kylesku Bridge
Glendhu
Loch Glendhu
Unapool
Meall na Leitreach
Meall an Fheur Loch
Loch Glencoul
To Stoer
Glencoul
Meallan a' Chuail
Beinn Leoid
Stack of Glencoul
Eas a' Chual Aluinn
A894
Glas Bheinn
Beinn Uidhe
To Lochinver
Achmore
Gorm Loch Mor
Loch Assynt
Na Tuadhan
Glenbain
Inchnadamph
R. Traligill
Gleann Dubh
Cave
Caves
Ben More Assynt
River Loanan
Conival
INCHNADAMPH NATIONAL NATURE RESERVE
Loch Mhaolach-Coire
Dubh Loch Mor
Beinn nan Chaimhseag
Glas Choire Beag
Carn nan Conbhairean
Cave
Caves
A837
To Ledmore Jct.
Breabag
Meall an Aonaich
Loch Awe
Beinn an Fhuarain
N
0 km 1

Ben More Assynt from Breabag

Gillieroo, this is the home of a rare breed of red-speckled trout. This path also passes several cave entrances which give access to an extensive system of underground passages. These have been explored and mapped over a number of years by members of the Grampian Caving Club.

The route to Conival keeps to the north side of Gleann Dubh, but the path beyond has become badly eroded as it crosses an area of soft peat. This can be avoided by making a rising traverse soon after the path junction, crossing the south-west face of Beinn an Fhurain to the bealach on the north side of Conival. The summit lies 1km further up the rough screes of the broad north ridge, climbed by picking a way through shattered quartzite outcrops. Hidden from view during the approach, the summit of Ben More Assynt lies 1.5 km to the east, a rough walk over quartzite blocks, which can be slippery in the wet. The slopes to the south drop steeply into Garbh Choire at the head of Glen Oykel, while the northern slopes drop more gently into Coire a' Mhadaidh and the wild watery head of Glen Cassley. On the return, it is possible to descend into Garbh Choire from the bealach between the two summits. However, a fine ridge continues south-east from Ben More Assynt, narrowing and crossing a few steps of exposed slabs to give an interesting traverse for 1km to the South Top (960m).

Descent into Garbh Choire is possible from the cols on either side of this Top but the south-west slopes below are seamed with steep gullies. These are best avoided in wet or wintry conditions by continuing south-east over Carn nan Conbhairean (868m) before descending easier slopes to the south-west. Contour back to Dubh Loch Mor then make a rising traverse west through the narrow gap between Conival and Breabag Tarsuinn. From the north-west side of the gap, follow the south bank of the Allt a' Bhealaich to join the Loch Mhaolach-coire path described above.

Glas Bheinn; 776m; (OS Sheet 15; NC254264); *grey green hill*

From the summits of Ben More Assynt and Conival, a chain of rounded hills stretches north-west for a further 9km, and the ground continues above a height of 600m until it finally drops to sea level beyond Glas Bheinn. Often neglected, like Breabag, in favour of its taller and more distinctive neighbours, Glas Bheinn makes a fine viewpoint, suitable for a short day or as part of one of the finest high level walks in the Northern Highlands.

Starting just north of the highest point on the A894 Skiag Bridge to Kylesku road (261m), a stalkers path leads east, towards the southern end of Loch na Gainmhich. Soon after leaving the road, this path crosses a broad stony cart track. This is the old 'Marble Road', built in the late 18th century to transport marble from a quarry at Ledmore to the harbour at Kylesku. Follow this track south for a short distance then make for the north-west ridge of Glas Bheinn, which gives a straightforward climb to the summit. It is worth continuing to the rim of the northern corrie to view the short but spectacular cliffs, bristling with ribs and pinnacles, which overlook Loch a' Choire Dheirg.

For a longer outing, continue south-east from the summit. The main ridge gradually narrows and curves to the east, forming a narrow rocky rib which descends to a saddle. From this point a stalkers path winds its way eventually down to Inchnadamph, while the high ground rises again to the south-east. A long boulder strewn slope climbs gradually to the summit of Beinn Uidhe (740m) (*hill of the ford*) and continues south-east over Mullach an Leathaid Riabhaich before dropping a little to skirt around Loch nan Cuaran.

The terrain here is particularly rough, scattered with boulders and outcrops of quartzite. Picking a way through could be difficult in poor visibility. In such conditions the path to Inchnadamph from the west end of the loch might provide a welcome escape. The terrain soon gets much easier continuing almost due south, across a couple of broad mossy basins towards Beinn an Fhurain (806m) (*hill of the spring*).

Bits of aircraft wreckage scattered around a simple tubular metal cross form a poignant memorial to the four crew of an Avro Anson which crashed here on 14 April 1941. In an era before any mountain rescue service the wreck was not discovered until twelve days later by a local shepherd. The remains of the unfortunate airmen were buried on the site, one of only two such high ground burials in Britain.

Collectors of Corbett Tops will want to make a slight east detour across to the rugged summit of Na Tuadhan (860m) (*the hatchet*) (not named on the OS map). This is worth visiting to look down its broken rocky buttresses into remote Coire a' Mhadaidh on its south-east side. Beyond the tiny lochan to the south-west lies the bealach above Gleann Dubh and the popular route up Conival and Ben More Assynt from Inchnadamph. A fit party with suitable transport arrangements could continue for an even longer traverse.

The Moine Thrust and Knockan Crag

According to legend, the old Norse gods came here when the world was still young and malleable so that they could practise mountain building before returning across the North Sea to model Norway with more experienced hands. Coigach and Assynt have long been a classic study area for geologists from all over the world. Early geologists were puzzled by the unusual sequence of rocks of different ages in the area until a pair of eminent Victorians, Peach and Horne, came up with an explanation. They found evidence which showed that 430 million years ago, during the Caledonian mountain building period, the Moine Thrust pushed older rocks over younger rocks.

Their work is commemorated by a memorial at the east end of Loch Assynt inscribed 'To Ben N.Peach and John Horne who played the foremost part in unravelling the geological structure of the North-west Highlands. 1883-1897. An international tribute erected 1930'. Further details of the fascinating geology of the North-west Highlands are explained at Scottish Natural Heritage's interpretative facility at Knockan Crag just south of Elphin which was given a major upgrade in 2001.

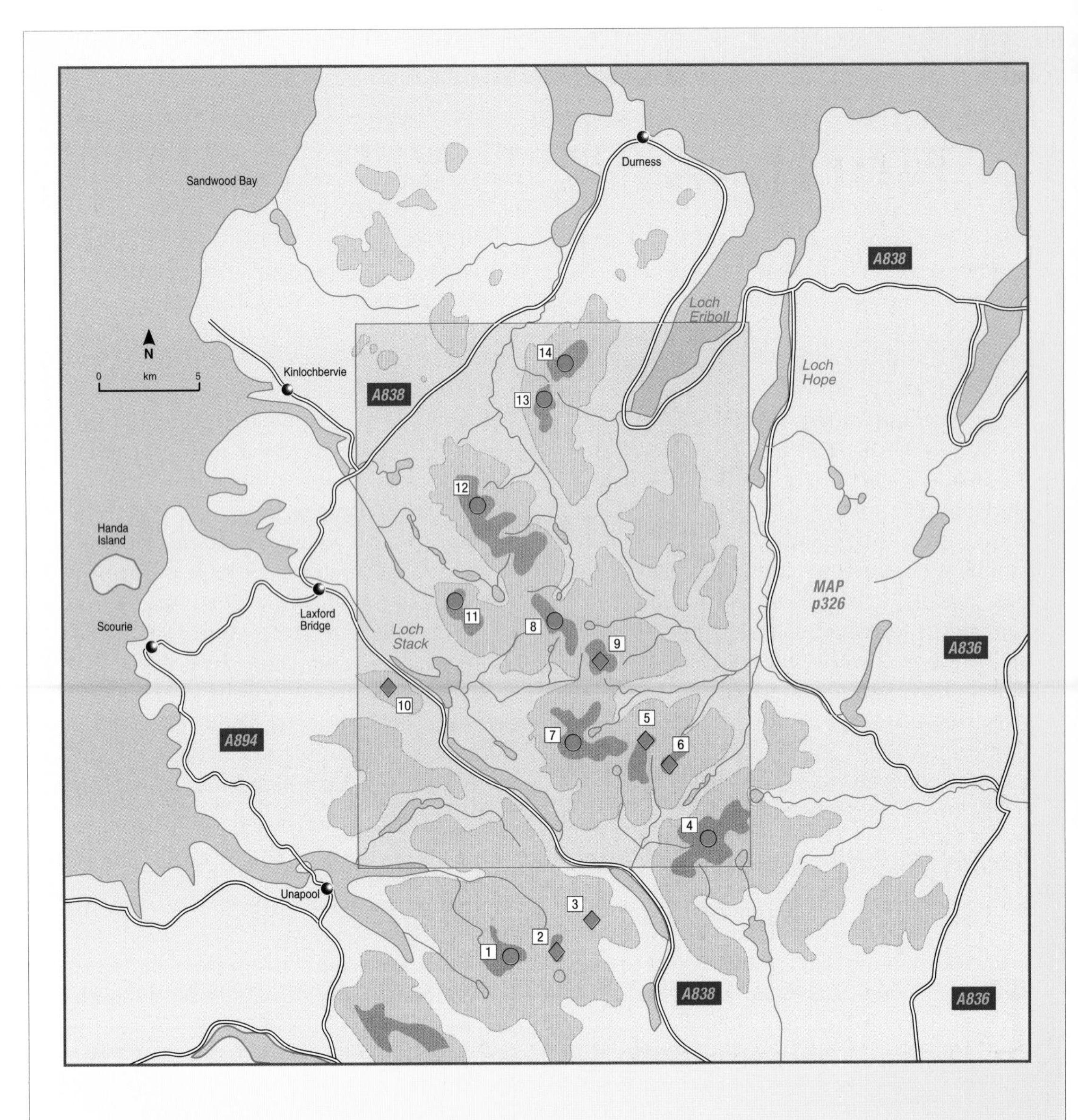

1. Beinn Leoid	792m	C	p321
2. Meallan a' Chuail	750m	G	p321
3. Meall an Fheur Loch	613m	G	p321
4. Ben Hee	873m	C	p322
5. Carn an Tionail	759m	G	p323
6. Beinn Direach	688m	G	p323
7. Meallan Liath Coire Mhic Dhughaill	801m	C	p324
8. Meall Horn	777m	C	p325
9. Sabhal Beag	732m	G	p325
10. Ben Stack	721m	G	p325
11. Arkle	787m	C	p325
12. Foinaven (Ganu Mor)	914m	C	p327
13. Cranstackie	800m	C	p330
14. Beinn Spionnaidh	772m	C	p330

North-west Sutherland

Alec Keith

Foinaven and Arkle from above Loch Inchard

Bounded on two sides by the Atlantic Ocean, north-west Sutherland is the most remote and sparsely populated corner of the Scottish mainland. Despite the absence of Munros, its hills offer an excellent variety of walking and climbing with extensive views. The only public road through these hills follows the long narrow depression which holds Loch Shin and a chain of smaller lochs; A' Ghriama, Merkland, More and Stack. Running north-west from coast to coast alongside these lochs, this road starts as the A836 at Bonar Bridge at the head of the Dornoch Firth and becomes the A838 just beyond Lairg. Touching the west coast at the head of Loch Laxford, it joins the A894 at Laxford Bridge and turns north-east, finally reaching the north coast at Durness.

The village of Lairg at the south-east end of Loch Shin serves as the hub of central Sutherland, with a railway station and a network of roads radiating out in all directions. The Lairg sheep sales are still the biggest in Europe, though a series of agricultural crises have cast a shadow over this mainstay of the local economy. Loch Shin became Scotland's fourth biggest freshwater loch following hydro-electrification but is rather bleak for much of its 28km length. The scenery improves further west, with hills rising up on either side of the smaller lochs. A small group of rounded, grassy hills to the south of the road separates the Assynt peaks from the rugged hills of the Reay Forest to the north. Although easily accessible from the road, these southern hills have a much wilder and remoter feel when approached from the west. Beinn Leoid, the highest of this group, may have been named after one of the Macleods of Assynt who hunted deer there centuries ago. In late summer, after the harvest was over, all the clansmen took part in a great deer drive, driving their prey to a deer trap on Ben More Assynt.

North of the road, in contrast, the Reay hills are much more rugged, with broad rock

Access and Transport

By road: from Inverness the A9 continues north to the roundabout at Tore, where the A835 leads west to Ullapool, continuing north to join the A837 at Ledmore junction. At Skiag Bridge, the A894 continues north over the Kylesku Bridge and through Scourie to Laxford Bridge, where it joins the A838 from Lairg. The single-track B801 leaves this road at Rhiconich, leading to Kinlochbervie and Oldshoremore. The A838 reaches the north coast at Durness and continues east to Tongue.
From Tore roundabout, the A9 continues north over the Cromarty Bridge. Beyond Evanton the A836 leads through Ardgay and Bonar Bridge to Lairg, continuing north through Altnaharra to Tongue. From Altnaharra a narrow single-track road leads north-west to join the A838 at Hope, between Durness and Tongue.

By bus: Thurso to Tongue; Durness to Lairg (via Altnaharra); Talmine to Tongue to Lairg; Durness to Lairg (via Kinlochbervie & Scourie) (Postbus tel: 08457-740740); Inverness to Durness (via Lairg and Ardross) (Mrs I.P.MacKay tel: 01971-511343 or 511287).

By train: Lairg and Thurso are the nearest stations on the Inverness to Thurso line.

Accommodation and Information

Hotels & guesthouses: Altnaharra, Durness, Kinlochbervie, Lairg, Rhiconich, Scourie, Talmine, Tongue.

SYHA hostels: Durness (tel: 0870-004-1113); Tongue (tel: 0870-004-1153)

Independent hostels: Lazy Crofter Bunkhouse, Durness (tel: 01971-511209/511366)

Camp sites: Durness, Lairg (tel: 01549-402447), Scourie; (tel: 01971-502060), Talmine.

Tourist Information Centres: Durness (tel: 01971-511259) (limited winter service);
Lairg (01549-402160)

Maps

Ordnance Survey 1:50,000 Landranger sheets 9 (Cape Wrath), 15 (Loch Assynt),
16 (Lairg and Loch Shin).

strewn ridges and deep corries, culminating in the magnificent quartzite massif of Foinaven. West of the road, the isolated cone of Ben Stack forms a prominent landmark.

Many of the roads in central Sutherland still have sections of single track, so the fastest approach to the hills from the south is via Ullapool and Assynt, over the graceful curve of the Kylesku Bridge. From Eddrachillis Bay to Loch Laxford the harsh rocky landscape of hillocks and lochan-filled hollows is known in Gaelic as Ceathramh Garbh (*rough quarter*). Apart from the village of Scourie, houses are few and far between. The road from Kylesku to Durness was built in the early 19th century thanks to the Marquess of Stafford. As first Duke of Sutherland he went on to become the most hated man in the Highlands, responsible for the infamous Sutherland Clearances. The most recent improvements to the road allow the swift passage of the enormous refrigerated lorries which transport the landings of fish from the busy harbour at Kinlochbervie. Fortunately traffic is relatively light most of the time and it is still possible for even the motorist to appreciate what Tom Weir described as 'the epitome of wildest Sutherland – a mixture of savagery and charm'.

The tortuous coastline of north-west Sutherland twists in every direction, forming wide bays dotted with islands and skerries, and four great sea lochs, Inchard, Laxford, Durness and Eriboll reach deep inland. Lewisian gneiss, the underlying rock, gives the coastline its complexity, rising at Cape Wrath to form great multi-coloured cliffs veined with pegmatite, reaching a height of over 120m. From the top, on a clear day it is possible to see the island of North Rona, some 70km to the north-west, the only landfall before the North Pole. These dramatic cliffs continue eastwards, dropping to the gem of sandy beach at Kearvaig, beyond which the Torridonian sandstone cliffs of Clo Mor rise to a height of 291m at their eastern end, forming the highest sea cliffs on the British mainland at Cleit Dubh. South of Cape Wrath, sandstone cliffs with sections of gneiss stretch most of the way to the mouth of Loch Inchard.

Inland from Cape Wrath, low rolling hills make up the empty wilderness of the Parph Moor, a rich source of legends. This was said to be the haunt of the Cu-Saeng, a terrible creature which would allow no one who had seen it to live to tell the tale. Reports of its shadow cast on a hillside indicated that it had two heads. A more tangible hazard is still found east of Kearvaig in the form of the United Kingdom's only ship-to-shore firing range. At present it is only used for a few weeks of the year and is clearly sign-posted. Remote Creag Riabhach (485m) is the highest of the lonely Parph hills which give rugged walking and excellent views. A few rock climbs have been recorded on the steep and extensive sandstone cliffs on the north-east side of Creag Riabhach. Despite much speculation about its potential for new routes, this remains one of the least visited of the big crags in Scotland.

The village of Durness lies between the Kyle of Durness and Faraid Head and an abandoned military installation nearby has been transformed into the flourishing Balnakeil Craft Village. East of Durness the coastline continues with a mixture of limestone, Moinian rocks and quartzite to the mouth of Loch Eriboll. Just beyond the village, at the head of a narrow inlet close to the road, the Allt Smoo plunges into the limestone Smoo Cave, popularised by Sir Walter Scott, following his visit in 1814.

From the road a path leads down to the mouth of the first and most accessible of three great caverns. In the tourist season boat trips sail right inside. Back in the 17th century, Sir Donald Mackay, first Lord Reay, was reputed to have dabbled in the black arts and had several tussles with the Devil himself. Legend has it that on one occasion, Lord Reay managed to trap the Devil and three attendant witches deep inside Smoo Cave, but they escaped by blowing holes in the roof, allowing the Allt Smoo to flow in.

Principal Hills

Beinn Leoid; 792m; (OS Sheet 15; NC320294); *hill of the slope*

Meallan a' Chuail; 750m; (OS Sheet 15; NC344292); *hill of the cudgel*

Meall an Fheur Loch; 613m; (OS Sheet 16; NC361310); *grassy hill of the loch*

This little group of rounded hills stands between the Assynt peaks to the south-west and the Reay Forest to the north. Long and challenging approaches from the west give them a feeling of remoteness and inaccessibility. Alternatively, they can be climbed easily in a day from the east, as follows.

From the A838 Lairg to Laxford Bridge road, midway between Loch Merkland and Loch More, a well marked stalkers path climbs steeply due south between two forestry plantations. When the path begins to level out strike roughly south-east to reach the extensive flat summit area of Meall an Fheur Loch, east of Loch Cul a' Mhill. (The actual summit is about 200 metres off the edge of OS Sheet 15). Cross the burn which flows from Loch Cul a' Mhill into Loch Iol-ghaoith, then climb the broad shoulder leading on to the elegant curving summit ridge of Meallan a' Chuail. To continue to Beinn Leoid, descend the western spur to the broad saddle above Loch Dubh. A stalkers path from Lochmore Side to the north also finishes here. Follow the east ridge of Beinn Leoid above broken crags to the summit.

The western side of Beinn Leoid is much more interesting, with a variety of possible

Arkle and Loch na Faoleige

approaches. From the narrows at Kylesku the tidal waters of Lochs Glendhu and Glencoul stretch deep into their rugged glens, offering the most direct access. The old ferry slip is ideal for launching canoes or it may be possible to arrange to be put ashore by the boat which carries sightseers up into Loch Beag for a closer look at the Eas a' Chual Aluinn waterfall. From the lodge at Glencoul an excellent path climbs south-east through Glen Coul, passing beneath the Stack of Glencoul (494m) to the south and an impressive line of crags to the north. The Stack of Glencoul is the north-west end of a long ridge and forms a great prow towering over Loch Dubh, most impressive when seen from the west and a worthwhile objective in its own right. When the Glen Coul path reaches the north-west end of Loch an Eircill climb north-east, picking a way up grassy slopes between the occasional peat hags to the summit of Beinn Leoid.

Loch Beag can also be reached on foot across the rough tussocky ground above the south-west shores of Loch Glencoul. Leave the A834 Skiag Bridge to Scourie road where it crosses the Unapool Burn. The traverse of steep ground west of Eilean an Tuim requires some care. Finally, from Kylestrome, an estate track runs along the north side of Loch Glendhu to Glendhu Lodge, continuing up Gleann Dubh to the north-eastern slopes of Beinn Leoid.

Ben Hee; 873m; (OS Sheet 16; NC426339); *fairy hill*

Situated just east of the rugged Atlantic-North Sea watershed, the rounded tops of Ben Hee rise from the western edge of an extensive tract of bleak moorland and forestry plantations north-west of Lairg, between Loch Shin and Loch Naver. An old drove road once skirted its northern and western flanks, crossing the Bealach nam Meirleach (*robbers pass*). This is now an estate track linking the A838 Lairg to Laxford Bridge road at Loch Merkland with Strath More, via Gobernuigach Lodge.

The quickest and most direct approach to Ben Hee leaves the A838 at West Merkland. Follow this track for just over 1km then branch off east along a stalkers path. This follows the Allt Coir a' Chruiteir and eventually peters out below the broad south-west shoulder of the hill. From the summit there is a fine view of Ben Hope to the north while the full length of Loch Shin stretches out to the south. A direct return to the start can be made along the rough north-west spur Sail Garbh, though a longer and more scenic alternative is to traverse the unnamed north-east top (851m). The broad grassy ridge curving down from the summit has some unusual hollows caused by landslips. From this top either contour back, or descend the rock strewn north-west flank with its hidden lochan, aiming to join the short stalkers path which crosses the narrow neck of ground between Loch an Aslaird and Loch an t-Seilg before meeting the main track.

The eastern flanks of Ben Hee are much steeper, with an impressive line of crags, corries and three high lochs best appreciated by a longer approach from the east. A path leaves the Altnaharra to Hope road some 7km west of the Strathnaver crossroads, leading to Loch Coire na Saidhe Duibhe, beyond which it is possible to pick a way up through the crags to reach the north-east top.

Carn an Tionail; 759m; (OS Sheet 16; NC392390); *cairn of the gathering place*

Beinn Direach; 688m; (OS Sheet 16; NC406380); *straight hill*

Tucked in between higher neighbours, Carn an Tionail and Beinn Direach give a fine horseshoe traverse north of Loch Merkland, with extensive views of the northern hills. Start as for Ben Hee at West Merkland and follow the estate track east towards the Bealach nam Meirleach. Cross the Allt na Glaise to gain the long south ridge of Carn an Tionail. There is a tiny stone shelter on the col between the south top A' Ghlaise

Historic Sutherland

Sutherland was literally the 'South Land' of the Viking jarls of Orkney who displaced the native Picts late in the 9th century, bringing with them the roots of many familiar place names. Laxford from Lax Fjord (*salmon loch*), the distinctive cliffs around Cape Wrath from Hvarf (*turning point*) which became Parph in Gaelic, and Arkle possibly from Ark-fjall (*ark mountain*). Loch Eriboll, from Eyrr-bol (*beach town*), was used as an anchorage by King Haakon in 1263, prior to his defeat in the Battle of Largs which marked the end of Norse domination of northern Scotland. Known to many servicemen as 'Lock 'Orrible' during World War Two, it was used as an assembly point for Atlantic convoys. Loch Eriboll's potential as a sheltered deepwater haven was never developed during the North Sea oil boom, but it has been identified as a possible site for another 'superquarry'.

With the decline of Norse power, Gaelic settlers of the Clan Morgan moved north into Strath Naver, becoming Clan Mackay and spreading over the north. After several centuries of clan battles with the Murrays, Sinclairs and Macleods, things had settled down by the 17th century and the hills of north-west Sutherland became the cherished hunting grounds of the Lords of Reay. Towards the end of the 18th century the Countess Elizabeth of Sutherland married George Granville Leveson-Gower, the wealthy Marquess of Stafford and by the time the 7th Lord Reay sold up in 1839 they had acquired almost the entire county of Sutherland, the largest private landholding in Scotland. This estate has since been broken up but much of the area is still managed as sporting estates, with the Westminster family now the largest landowners. In the 1960s the Duke of Westminster's famous racehorses Foinaven and Arkle made these two remote mountains household names.

Meallan Liath Coire Mhic Dhughaill looking towards Ben Hope

and the summit. To continue to Beinn Direach, descend north-eastwards initially and gradually curve back to the rough bealach with its huge boiler plate slabs. A short climb of 150m leads to the summit which thereby just qualifies as a Graham.

Meallan Liath Coire Mhic Dhughaill;
801m; (OS Sheet 15; NC357391);
little grey hill of the corrie of Dougall's son

As well as its distinctive name and a complex and convoluted series of radiating spurs and ridges extending onto all three OS Sheets of the area, Meallan Liath Coire Mhic Dhughaill offers a choice of interesting approaches and a magnificent panorama of the Sutherland and Caithness hills. From the south, leave the A838 Lairg to Laxford Bridge road just south of Kinloch. A private road leads to Aultanrynie but just before the house take a stalkers path on the right.

Ignoring a left branch, climb steadily up a series of easy zigzags onto the broad undulating ridge of Meallan Liath Beag. It is worth making a short detour to take in the Corbett Top Carn Dearg (796m) before continuing west towards the summit with its fine views. To return to Aultanrynie, descend due south, keeping slightly left to avoid crags and screes, heading east of the flat peaty knoll of Meall Reinidh.

To the north-west of the mountain, on the east side of Loch Stack, an estate cottage and a more modern cattle shelter at Lone mark the start of two excellent stalkers paths which give good access to the surrounding hills. Lone is reached by a private estate road which leaves the A838 1km north of the small settlement of Achfary, crossing a bridge at the south end of Loch Stack. From Lone, follow the path which climbs east for 7km to the Bealach na Feithe. Before the highest point, leave the path and climb south over Meall Garbh (754m) and continue along the pleasant ridge which twists south-west to the summit of Meallan Liath Coire Mhic Dhughaill.

The most direct descent back to Lone follows the north-west spur Sail Rac but a longer and more interesting alternative is to follow the ridge east to Carn Dearg (797m) and enjoy the spectacular views down to Coire Loch some 300m below. The floor of the corrie can be reached directly from Carn Dearg either by picking a descent between small crags or more easily by following the ridge north-east down to Lochan a' Bhealaich below Carn an Tionail. From the eastern end of Coire Loch a gradual climb north over the eastern shoulder of Meall Garbh leads back to the Bealach na Feithe to rejoin the path to Lone.

Meall Horn; 777m; (OS Sheet 9; NC352449); *hill of the eagle*

Sabhal Beag; 732m; (OS Sheet 9; NC373429); *little barn*

Inconspicuous from the west, Meall Horn and Sabhal Beag stand side by side, holding some fine corries on their north-east sides. Both hills are usually climbed together either as a short day or as part of a longer traverse. The stalkers path which climbs north-east from Lone follows the Allt Horn and crosses the Bealach Horn (c510m) at the southern end of the Foinaven ridge. This bealach can also be reached from Arkle, by continuing north-east after descending from Meall Aonghais. A short climb south-east from the bealach leads to the top of Creagan Meall Horn (731m) and the start of a pleasant ridge which continues south-east to the summit of Meall Horn. Steep craggy slopes drop away to the north-east into the corries of An Dubh Loch and Lochan Ulbha.

The summit can be reached slightly more directly by leaving the Lone path at a height of about 400m and climbing east to reach the broad col on the ridge. Another direct line from Lone follows the south-west spur over Creachan Thormaid (608m). The ridge winds easily onwards for another 3km over Sabhal Mor (703m) (*big barn*) to the higher Sabhal Beag. Due south of the summit lies the Bealach na Feithe (c450m), the mid-point on the other excellent stalkers path linking Lone and Gobernuisgach Lodge. From here either continue on to Meallan Liath Coire Mhic Dhughaill or return to the start.

Ben Stack; 721m; (OS Sheet 9; NC269423); *steep hill*

The shapely cone of Ben Stack catches the eye from many distant points. Situated just north of Achfary, this attractive hill is the most prominent feature on the west side of the A838 Lairg to Laxford Bridge road and makes a particularly fine viewpoint, easily climbed from either end of Loch Stack. At the southern end start climbing north-west from anywhere on the A838, rather boggy at first, giving way to tussocky heather and rocky outcrops.

Keep above a dyke of outcropping gneiss and cross a small top before the final grassy summit, which is also the most northerly Graham. From just beyond the north-west end of Loch Stack a stalkers path leaves the road, climbing due west. Follow this to just above Loch na Seilge then climb steeply but easily south-east through a rocky band to the summit. Some short rock climbs have been recorded on the two bands of cliffs on the north-east side.

Arkle; 787m; (OS Sheet 9; NC302461); *ark hill*

Arkle is a very distinctive mountain which stands on the north-east side of Loch Stack. An impressive sight from the A838 Achfary to Laxford Bridge road, its south-west flanks form a uniform slope split by prominent gullies and finely banded by gleaming quartzite screes. A broad ridge links with the south-east end of the Foinaven massif to form a fine ring of corries and stepped lochans which opens out to the north-west.

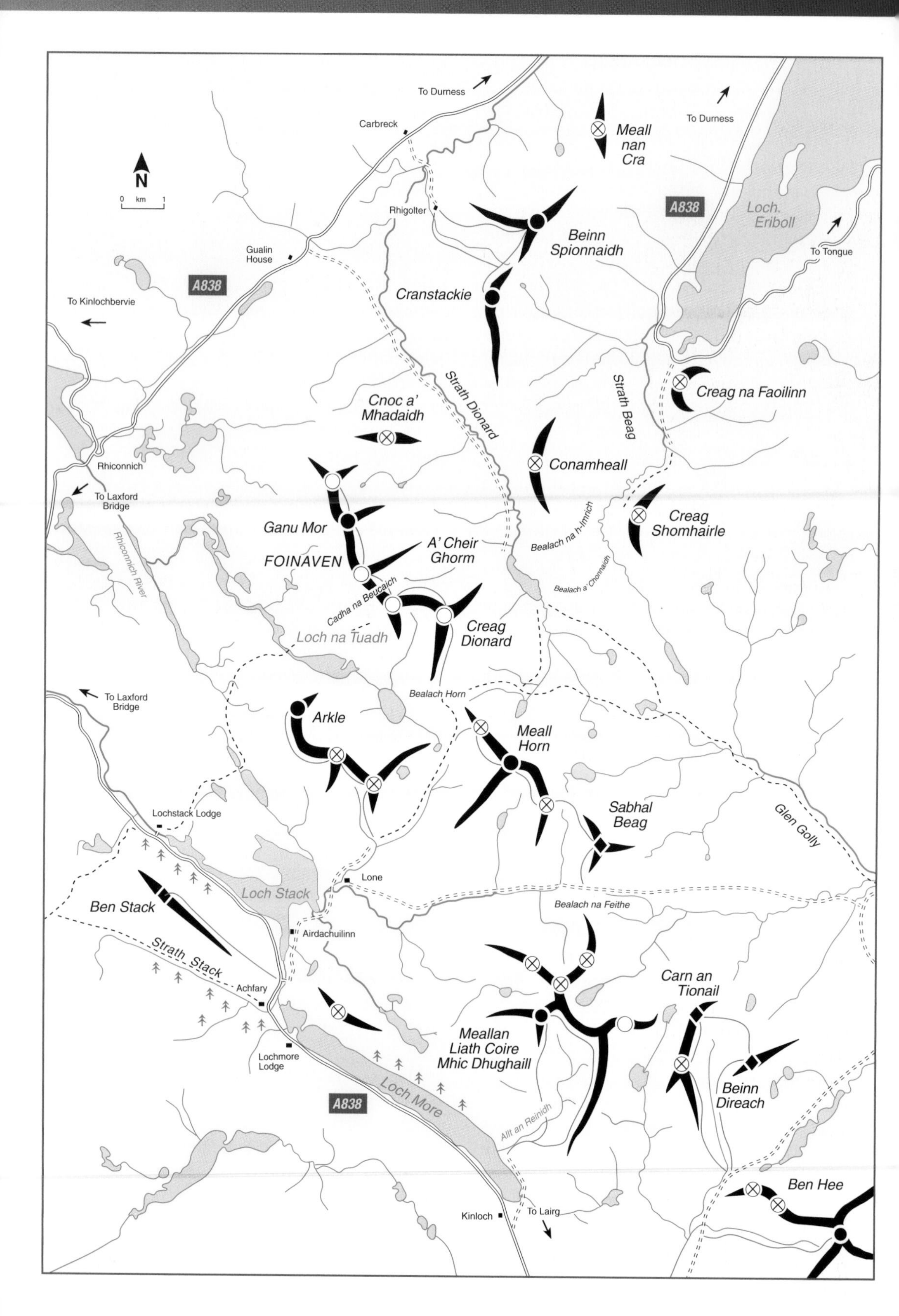
To Durness
Carbreck
Meall nan Cra
To Durness
N
0 km 1
Rhigolter
A838
Loch. Eriboll
To Tongue
Beinn Spionnaidh
Gualin House
A838
Cranstackie
To Kinlochbervie
Strath Dionard
Strath Beag
Creag na Faoilinn
Cnoc a' Mhadaidh
Conamheall
Rhiconnich
To Laxford Bridge
Creag Shomhairle
Ganu Mor
A' Cheir Ghorm
Bealach na h-Imrich
FOINAVEN
Rhiconnich River
Bealach a' Chonnaidh
Cadha na Beucaich
Creag Dionard
Loch na Tuadh
Bealach Horn
To Laxford Bridge
Arkle
Meall Horn
Sabhal Beag
Glen Golly
Lochstack Lodge
Lone
Loch Stack
Ben Stack
Bealach na Feithe
Airdachuilinn
Strath Stack
Carn an Tionail
Achfary
Meallan Liath Coire Mhic Dhughaill
Lochmore Lodge
Beinn Direach
A838
Loch More
Allt an Reinidh
Ben Hee
Kinloch
To Lairg

Loch More and Ben Stack

The summit ridge of Arkle curves north-east, in the shape of a sickle, narrowing to give steep drops to the east and more gentle slopes to the west. The easiest approach is from Lone, on the east side of Loch Stack. Follow the stalkers path which climbs north-east up the Allt Horn through a small plantation before striking up to the southern top (758m). A short descent west down bouldery slopes leads to the head of a wide heathery gully. This gully gives another straightforward approach to the summit, reached by leaving the Allt Horn path just before the small plantation and following a slanting rake below the south-west screes. From the top of the heathery gully the summit ridge narrows and rises more steeply, following a natural pavement of quartzite eroded with deep fissures, which leads to the top.

To the north and west of Arkle a myriad of lochans lie scattered over the lower ground. From Lochstack Lodge, at the north-west end of Loch Stack, a well marked stalkers path winds almost 8km around the north-west flanks of the mountain to finish on the south-west slopes of Foinaven. This path can be reached from the summit of Arkle either by descending the ridge as it drops to the north-east, past Loch an Tuath or more easily by way of the north-west slopes of Sail Mhor.

The terrain here is rather bouldery but the 5km along the road from Lochstack Lodge back to Achfary gives superb views across Loch Stack to Arkle. The quickest and most direct descent to Lone is to trend south-east from the summit along the ridge, continuing down over Meall Aonghais (581m) to rejoin the Allt Horn path.

Foinaven (Ganu Mor); 914m; (OS Sheet 9; NC315507); *hill of the warts (big head)*

Finest of the north-west Sutherland hills, Foinaven is almost a range of mountains in miniature, comprising the highest Corbett, Ganu Mor (*big head*) plus four tops. Often mis-spelt, the name Foinaven derives from an older form Foinne-bheinn, which has nothing to do with the colour of its massive screes which would be Fionn-bheinn (*white mountain*).

Viewed from the road which skirts the west side of this sprawling massif, these continuously steep slopes of quartzite scree look most uninviting but around on the east side of the mountain four great spurs stretch out into Strath Dionard, enclosing deep corries. Predominantly sharp angular quartzite, the Foinaven ridge extends some 5km in a roughly north-south direction. The traverse is a highly recommended and challenging walk and its many crags and corries offer a wide variety of climbing in summer and winter.

The quickest way up Ganu Mor starts from the A838 Rhiconich to Durness road, either at Gualin House, close to the highest point on the road, or further west, where the going can be drier underfoot. Cross the moorland and climb over the northern top Ceann Garbh (902m) (*rough head*). In winter, when the ground is frozen, this can give a very fast approach, but scenically this route has little to recommend it. If followed in reverse, when descending to the road from Ceann Garbh be wary of a lower band of short cliffs which can be difficult to see from above.

The magnificent traverse of the full length of the Foinaven ridge is more often started from Lone, on the east side of Loch Stack. Follow the stalkers path up the Allt Horn to the Bealach Horn (c510m). Leave the path and continue climbing north up grass, boulders and bare rock to the featureless south top, An t-Sail Mhor (778m) (called Creag Dionard in some guidebooks). A broad stony ridge continues to the next top, Stob Cadha na Beucaich (808m) (not named on the OS map) then a steep drop leads down to the Cadha na Beucaich (*pass of the bellowing*). The corrie to the east is

Rats, Puffins, and Tyrolean Rope Tricks

The extensive coastal cliffs and offshore sea stacks offer some challenging and enjoyable rock climbing. Handa Island, now a Scottish Wildlife Trust reserve accessible from Tarbet, was the scene of a famous early climbing feat in 1876. On the north-west corner of the island, the impressive 100m sandstone Great Stack is almost enclosed within a deep geo. Visiting to cull sea birds, an adventurous party of Lewis men stretched a long rope across the top of the stack from the cliff tops on either side and 26 year old Donald MacDonald boldly climbed across hand over hand.

This feat was subsequently repeated in 1967 by Tom Patey using modern climbing hardware, and an ascent from sea level followed two years later. This tyrolean rope is no longer allowed since 500 pairs of puffins nest in burrows on the flat top of the Great Stack. Rats on the main island have driven the puffins on to the stack. The rats were killed in 2002 but puffins had not established many nest sites off the stack by 2003.

Patey also made the first ascent of the spectacular *Am Buachaille* (55m HVS 5b 1967) which stands off the south end of magnificent Sandwood Bay. An easier line was climbed by a party of 14 one week later. Poor quality rock makes this one of the less popular of the classic sea stack climbs and at least one subsequent party has been forced to bivouac on top after missing low tide.

Near the crofting township of Sheigra a headland of gneiss interrupts the sandstone. Easy access to steep walls of fast drying immaculate rock with incut holds and good protection has made this an increasingly popular location. At least 50 other crags in the area have been developed at the end of the '90s.

The stacks around Cape Wrath, A' Chailleach, Am Bodach and nearby Stack Clo Kearvaig were all climbed in 1989. In a flurry of activity along the north coast that year, Mick Fowler and friends used an aptly named inflatable boat 'Deflowerer' for access. They also finally climbed the great sandstone cliffs of Clo Mor. A previous unsuccessful attempt by a strong party in the 1970s had involved 10 days of hanging belays and bivouacs.

Foinaven from Conamheall

now called Coire na Lurgainn on the OS map but previous guides have called it Coire na Lice. Continuing north, the ridge is dominated by Lord Reay's Seat, a small rocky peak easily bypassed on its west side.

A' Ch'eir Ghorm (869m) is the next top which sends out a narrow spur to the north-east. This spur offers interesting scrambling if taken direct, and makes a worthwhile diversion to appreciate its unique situation with screes and cliffs falling away on each side.

W.A.Poucher described Foinaven as 'one of the most remarkable peaks in Scotland' on account of 'its bewildering erosion'. He was particularly taken with A' Ch'eir Ghorm and wrote that 'to sit alone on its crest and listen to the falling of its disintegrated quartzite blocks is one of the most eerie experiences in Britain'.

It is possible to descend north-east into Strath Dionard from the start of this spur. First drop down into Choire Leachaich then follow a more or less direct route down into Coire Duail by way of the stream which cuts through the crags between Ganu Mor and Cnoc Duail.

To continue along the main ridge from A' Ch'eir Gorm to Ganu Mor, descend north-west for a short distance then climb north over a minor top. Beyond here the ridge broadens before reaching its highest point, which has two cairns, about 100 metres apart. The larger eastern cairn is the summit. If transport has been arranged, continue north over Ceann Garbh to reach the A835 as already described. Otherwise, the most direct route back to Lone is to reverse the ridge.

Much of the interest on Foinaven, particularly for the climber, is located on the impressive crags and corries on its eastern side. These are best appreciated by approaching from Gualin House up the private Strath Dionard estate track. This controversial feature was built to improve access to the fishing on Loch Dionard and solve the worsening problem of the muddy

Beinn Spionnaidh and Cranstackie

mess caused by the frequent passage of all-terrain vehicles. Unfortunately a large sign on the gate at Gualin House indicates the hostility of the estate to mountain bikes (although with no legal basis) and the track starts with a considerable drop to meet the River Dionard. A shorter alternative approach to Loch Dionard starts from the head of Loch Eriboll. This follows the approach to Cranstackie through Strath Beag, then crosses the Bealach na h-Imrich (c 230m) on the south shoulder of Conamheall (482m). From the north end of Loch Dionard, the steep screes of A' Ch'eir Ghorm can be climbed south of the crags. From the south end of the loch, following the west bank of the Allt an Easain Ghil upstream will eventually join the stalkers path already described which crosses the Bealach Horn at the southern end of the main ridge. This gives a useful approach to some of the climbs, but makes a very round-about route to the summit.

Cranstackie; 800m; (OS Sheet 9; NC350556); *rocky peak*

Beinn Spionnaidh; 772m; (OS Sheet 9; NC362573); *hill of strength*

In contrast with the rugged crags and corries of Foinaven on the opposite side of Strath Dionard, Cranstackie and Beinn Spionnaidh form a long grassy ridge which stretches down to the coast between Loch Eriboll and the Kyle of Durness.

They offer pleasant hillwalking with magnificent views on the most northerly high ground in mainland Britain. Lacking any prominent crags, a rough band of gneiss and quartzite skirts the long south-west flank of Cranstackie which overlooks Strath Dionard. These western slopes are uniformly steep grass and boulders while the eastern side falls away more gradually towards Loch Eriboll.

The most direct approach from the A838 Rhiconich to Durness road starts from Carbreck, 10km north-east of Rhiconich. A private vehicle track crosses the River Dionard and leads to the cottage at Rhigolter. From here either climb into the high corrie and then onto the saddle between the two tops or alternatively take the steeper north-west shoulder of either peak.

For a longer day with closer views across to Foinaven, the long gentle whaleback ridge stretching north from Conamheall (482m) can be reached from the head of Loch Eriboll. The main problem with this route is crossing the river in Strath Beag. A boggy track leaves the A838 Durness to Hope road below Creag na Faolinn, and leads to the cottage at Strabeg.

The bridge marked on the map has been reduced to a single girder and it may be more prudent to continue past Creag Shomhairle and try to cross further upstream.

The excellent west facing gneiss of this extensive crag has some good rock climbing at the southern end. The remaining natural woodland here has been fenced to keep out grazing animals and is alive with birdsong in spring. The south-east flanks of Beinn Spionnaidh give a straightforward descent to the road and the forestry plantations on the lower slopes are easy to avoid.

From the summit, the main ridge continues north-east over Carn an Righ. According to legend, Robb Donn, the great Gaelic bard, having given up poaching, filled his beloved gun with tallow and buried it deep in the rocks there. He was finally laid to rest in 1777 by the now ruined church at Balnakeil but his weapon has never been found.

Cape Wrath Coastal Walk

Extremities hold a fascination for most people, and this furthest north-west corner of mainland Britain remains the most difficult of access. In the summer season there are enough adventurous tourists to sustain a tiny passenger ferry from the Cape Wrath Hotel at Keoldale across the Kyle of Durness. A mini-bus then bumps along the rough road which twists and turns its way some 16km around the northern edge of the wild Parph Moor to the now automated lighthouse built in 1828 above the dramatic cliffs which form Cape Wrath.

An approach by foot is much more satisfying and the route from the south, via Sandwood Bay, gives one of the most exhilarating coastal walks in the British Isles. Since their acquisition of Sandwood Estate in 1993, the John Muir Trust has established a car park at Blairmore and volunteers have been working to restore the 5km of badly eroded path which leads to Sandwood Bay. It is also possible to follow the coast from Sheigra, which allows a closer look at the impressive offshore stack Am Buachaille (*the herdsman*). Seton Gordon described Sandwood Bay as 'the most beautiful place on all the west coast of the Scottish mainland' and many walkers now come to enjoy this magnificent sweep of sand with its crashing surf and rolling marram dunes. Swimming is not advised because of currents and a very strong undertow. Before the Cape Wrath lighthouse was built, the beach received the wrecks of many of the ships which foundered along this treacherous coast.

The outflow from the large freshwater Sandwood Loch is an easy ford and the next 12km follow the continuous line of cliffs past numerous headlands and rocky inlets. Apart from sheep tracks there is no path, but the going underfoot is good. Two river crossings may cause problems in spate. In Strath Cailleach a series of rocky falls where the river drops into the sea usually gives a crossing, the only alternative being a long detour inland. 3km further north, the Keisgaig River can usually be crossed where it tumbles into a rocky bay below a ruined shelter. Two fine sea stacks, A' Chailleach (*the old woman*) and Am Bodach (*the old man*) stand offshore, 1km south of the lighthouse. If planning to continue walking east along the north coast, please remember that the area beyond Kearvaig Bay is used as a military firing range, well sign-posted with warnings. The Tourist Information Centre in Durness has details of range use but there are unexploded shells lying around, so walk with extra care in this area! Sgribhis-bheinn (371m) has a fine view south across the Parph Moor to the higher hills beyond.

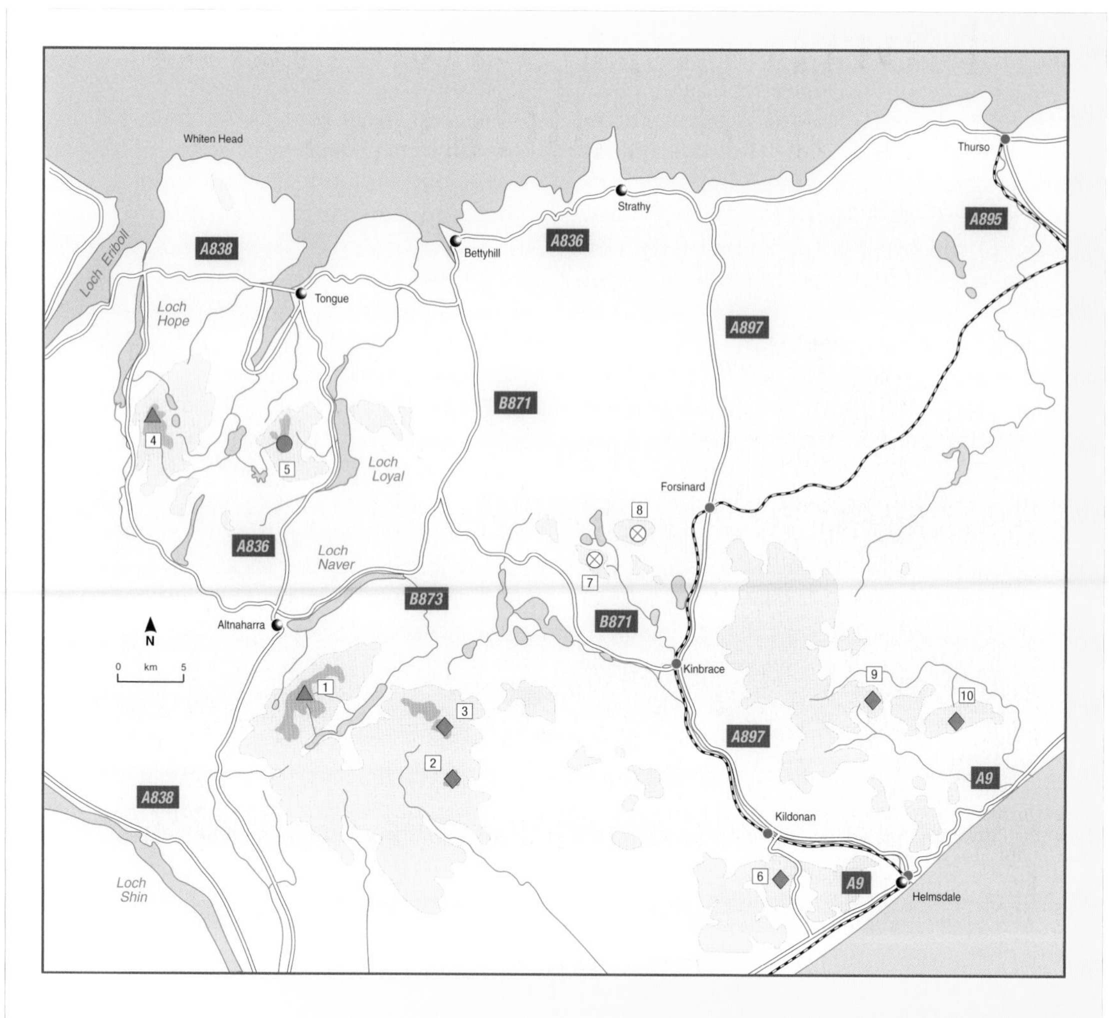

1.	Ben Klibreck	962m	M	p336
2.	Creag Mhor	713m	G	p336
3.	Ben Armine	705m	G	p336
4.	Ben Hope	927m	M	p337
5.	Ben Loyal	764m	C	p339
6.	Beinn Dhorain	628m	G	p340
7.	Ben Griam Mor	592m	O	p341
8.	Ben Griam Beg	580m	O	p341
9.	Morven	706m	G	p341
10.	Scaraben	626m	G	p341

Chapter 18

North-east Sutherland and Caithness

Hamish Brown

Ben Klibreck from Vagastie

Approaching the north-eastern extremity of mainland Britain, the final isolated mountains of Sutherland give way to the lower, flatter landscape of Caithness with its coastal cliffs and sea stacks.

Although there are no long rounds of tops and few spectacular corries, the area still has plenty to offer climbers and hill walkers. Individually or in small groups, the rolling heathery hills have their own unique character, enhanced by sweeping views across the vastness of the far north. Their open corries, lochs and bogs drain into long wide straths whose rivers offer some of the country's most exclusive game fishing.

Strath More, Strath Naver and Strath Halladale flow north into the Pentland Firth while Strath Kildonan, Strath Brora and Strath Fleet drain east into the North Sea. Following the Clearances of the 19th century these straths remain sparsely populated, largely the preserve of sporting estates and some forestry. Crofting, fishing and increasingly tourism sustains the small communities along the Sutherland coast.

Farming and fishing remain the mainstay of Caithness whose remoteness and sparse population made an ideal location for the post-war nuclear industry which set up at Dounreay. Some of the incoming 'atomics' have been active on the local hills and crags but these remain relatively unfrequented compared with further south. A famous eight iron golf club still sits beside one summit cairn ready for the occasional visitor prepared to search around for the hidden balls to play a few shots.

Leaving Easter Ross just north of the historic town of Tain, the A9 crosses the Dornoch Firth and continues north-east along the Sutherland coast through the villages of Golspie, Brora and Helmsdale. Beinn Dhorain is the highest of the small group of hills south of the Strath of Kildonan (Strath Ullie) which runs north-west from Helmsdale to Kinbrace, near the head of Strath Halladale. To the north, Morven and Scaraben rise beyond the Ord of Caithness, while the main road continues along the coast to the town of Wick and finally John O'Groats.

The other hills in the area are usually approached from further west, through the village of Lairg, at the south-east end of Loch Shin. Continuing north on the A836, the loch is quickly left behind as the road gradually climbs through Strath Tirry. Featureless moorland and conifer plantations stretch into the distance in all directions, and the hills seem a long way off, until the road drops into Strath Vagastie, below Ben Klibreck.

Just south of the watershed, the lonely Crask Inn has long provided travellers with the opportunity for a welcome refreshment on one of the bleakest and most desolate sections of road in Britain, particularly in the depths of winter when it is easily blocked by snow. Such conditions can give fine ski-touring but the weather in this area should not be underestimated. Nearby Altnaharra shares the record with Braemar in Aberdeenshire for the lowest recorded UK temperature of the 20th century with minus 27.2 degrees Celsius (minus 17.0 degrees Fahrenheit) on 29 December 1995. In the Great Storm of January 1978 a train from Inverness to Wick was lost for a number of hours in the blizzard and three unfortunate motorists died, trapped in their vehicles near the Sutherland-Caithness boundary. One very lucky drapery salesman was rescued four days later, having kept warm by wrapping himself in samples of ladies tights.

Altnaharra is little more than a hotel and a few houses situated at the foot of Strath Vagastie, at the west end of Loch Naver. Three roads lead to the north coast from the cross-roads just beyond the village. To the east, the B871 follows the north side of Loch Naver then continues north to Syre and down Strath Naver to the villages of Bettyhill and Farr on the coast. To the west, another narrow single track road skirts Ben Hee and the North-west Sutherland hills before dropping north into Strath More. This road passes Ben Hope and Loch Hope before reaching the coast near the mouth of Loch Eriboll. Finally, the A836 continues north between Ben Loyal and Loch Loyal, then drops down to the village of Tongue.

As ever, the contrasts apparent in the landscape are explained by the underlying geology. The fertile farmland of lowland Caithness sits on flagstones and conglomerates of Old Red Sandstone which rises to its maximum height on the summit of Morven and forms much of the coastal strip down through Easter Ross and the Black Isle to the Moray Coast. Inland, Sutherland is largely formed from the Moine series of rocks, mainly schists, named from the lonely peninsula, A' Mhoine, which stretches out between Loch Eriboll and the Kyle of Tongue, culminating in the cliffs of Whiten Head. The uniform nature of these Moine rocks has led to relatively even erosion resulting in the great stretches of low lying moorland characteristic of central and north-east Sutherland.

As well as reduced scenic appeal this has also limited climbing possibilities, with the exception of the eastern sides of Strath More and Strath Vagastie where the Moine rises high enough to form Munros. At Strath More, the schists are exposed as a line of cliffs forming the west flank of Ben Hope, rising to the summit ridge in two great steps. This Moine schist contains many intrusions but Ben Loyal stands out as the only igneous mountain in the area, weathered into characteristic crags and tors.

As the earliest inhabitants of Scotland gradually spread north along the coast, Caithness and east Sutherland was clearly to their liking and prehistoric remains abound in the form of chambered cairns, burial mounds, hut circles, hill forts and brochs. As elsewhere the

Vikings left their mark with many place-names. An Ceann Geal (*headland of the stranger*) of the native Gael was the landmark Hvitir (*white headland*) of the Norsemen who sailed past the pale quartzite stacks of The Maiden offshore of Whiten Head.

A short distance inland, the magnificent views from the summit of Ben Hutig (408m) can have changed little since those turbulant times. This fine little hill gives a short outing from West Strathan, near the end of the road through Melness. One of the earliest recorded travellers in the Highlands, the cartographer Timothy Pont, was minister in Dunnet, Caithness, around the turn of the 16th century. Of Loch Shin he noted 'the mightiest and longest salmond in all Scotland are in this loch', and he designated the country east of the loch 'extreem wilderness'.

Some of the earliest documented hill climbs in Scotland were made in this area by James Robertson. A botanist by training, he was appointed by the Commissioners of the Forfeit Estates to investigate the economic potential of the Highlands and particularly the Jacobite estates. In the course of a journey in 1767 he climbed Morven and Scaraben in Caithness and Ben Klibreck and Ben Hope in Sutherland.

Access and Transport

By road: from Inverness the A9 continues north past the roundabout at Tore and over the Cromarty Bridge. Just beyond Evanton the A836 branches off, leading north through Lairg and Altnaharra to reach the north coast at Tongue. This road follows the coast east through Bettyhill, Strathy, Melvich, Reay, Thurso and Dunnet to John O' Groats. From Altnaharra the B873 cuts north-east to join the A836 near Bettyhill.

From the Cromarty Bridge the A9 continues north-east past Alness, Invergordon and Tain, across the Dornoch Bridge and past Dornoch to Golspie. The road then follows the coast through Brora, Helmsdale, Dunbeath, Latheronwheel, Lybster and Wick before reaching John O' Groats. From Helmsdale the A897 leads north to join the A836 near Melvich. The B871 links Kinbrace on the A897 with Syre on the B873.

By bus: there are a number of services along the coast and across north-east Caithness.

By rail: the Inverness to Wick/Thurso line goes inland to Lairg, then along the coast through Golspie, Brora and Helmsdale before turning inland again to Kildonan, Kinbrace and Forsinard.

Accommodation and Information

Hotels & guesthouses: many can be found in the towns and villages along the Caithness and Sutherland coast and inland at Altnaharra, Forsinard, Garvault, Lairg and Rogart.

SYHA hostels: Helmsdale (tel: 0870-004-1124); John O' Groats (tel: 0870-004-1129); Tongue (tel: 0870-004-1153)

Independent hostels: Railway Carriages, Rogart (tel: 01408-641343); Sandra's Backpackers, Thurso (tel: 01847-894575/890111); Thurso Youth Club Hostel (tel: 01847-892964)

Campsites: Bettyhill (tel: 01641-521273), Brora, Dunnet (tel: 01847-821319), Helmsdale, Lairg (tel: 01549-402447), Lothbeg, Reay, Thurso, Wick (tel: 01955-605429).

Tourist Information Centres: Dornoch (tel:01862-810400) (open all year); John O' Groats (tel: 01955-611373) (seasonal); Thurso (tel: 01847-892371) (seasonal); Wick (tel: 01955-602596) (limited winter hours)

Maps

Ordnance Survey 1:50,000 Landranger sheets 9 (Cape Wrath), 10 (Strathnaver), 11 (Thurso and Dunbeath), 12 (Thurso and Wick), 16 (Lairg and Loch Shin) and 17 (Helmsdale).

Principal Hills

Ben Klibreck; 962m; (OS Sheet 16; NC585299); *hill of the cliff slope*

Central and eastern Sutherland is dominated by the great sprawling mass of Ben Klibreck which rises in splendid isolation above a vast area of featureless moorland. The main backbone of the mountain is a long curving ridge running roughly south-west to north-east. Steep heathery slopes fall away to the north-west into Strath Vagastie and Loch Naver while great spurs extend south-east, enclosing a series of wide grassy corries. These drain into Loch Choire and its western extension Loch a' Bhealaich, beyond which rise the lower neighbouring tops of Ben Armine.

Ben Klibreck is usually climbed from the A836 Lairg to Altnaharra road which runs below the north-west flank of the mountain, through Strath Vagastie. Various possible routes start at different points along the road, but all converge on a saddle (688m) on the main ridge above Loch nan Uan. For a longer outing, traversing the mountain, start at the lonely Crask Inn, from where a gentle climb over moorland and heather leads onto Cnoc Sgriodain (544m), the most westerly outlier of the main ridge.

This point can also be reached more directly by leaving the A836 further north, where it crosses the Allt a' Chraisg. Follow the broad ridge east to Carn an Fheidh (808m) then descend north to the saddle at 688m. The quickest and most direct routes to this point start either from roadside parking west of the south end of Loch na Glas-choille, or alternatively, if the river is in spate, cross the footbridge further upstream, just north of Vagastie. From the saddle follow the ridge north to A' Chioch (747m) then east to reach the main summit Meall na Con (*hill of the dog*).

For a round trip, returning to Crask Inn, make a straightforward descent south-east over the spur of Meall an Eoin (774m) to meet the path which follows the north-west shores of Loch Choire and Loch a' Bhealaich, crossing the picturesque Bealach Easach into Srath a' Chraisg. For a longer traverse, continue north-east along the ridge to Meall Ailein (721m). This top can also be reached from the southern shores of Loch Naver by a path from Klibreck (Clebrig) Farm, reached by a track which leaves the main road just south of Altnaharra.

Descend the south-east spur of Meall Ailein to Loch Choire to join the Bealach Easach path. A monument on this spur commemorates the two unfortunate crew of a Sea Vampire jet which crashed here in 1955.

Some rock climbs have been described on the broken crags which rise up to the ridge west of the main summit and there are some winter routes on the north-east face of Creag an Lochain.

Creag Mhor; 713m; (OS Sheet 16; NC698240); *big rock*

Ben Armine; 705m; (OS Sheet 16; NC695273); *hill of the warrior or hero*

A range of low, rounded hills stand south-east of Ben Klibreck. Meall Ard (634m), Creag na h-Iolaire (694m), Meall nan Aighean (695m) and Creag a' Choire Ghlais (705m) rise one behind the other from Loch Choire Lodge at the north-east end of Loch Choire to form the broad ridge of Ben Armine.

This high ground continues south-east then turns south over Creag Mhor, finally dropping down after some 14km to Ben Armine Lodge beside the Black Water River. The gentle western slopes of the range drain into this tributary of the River Brora which flows south-east into the North Sea. Ben Armine Lodge can be reached by a private estate road which comes up from Sciberscross in Strath Brora, 16km inland of

Ben Hope and Loch Hope

Brora. The easy-angled northern slopes of Ben Armine feed the Mallart River, and thence the River Naver which flows north into the Pentland Firth. In contrast, the eastern flanks of Creag Mhor and Creag a' Choire Ghlais fall away steeply, forming a line of five impressive grassy corries.

Very much stalking and fishing country, these are remote hills, but a network of private estate roads and tracks gives good cycle access and a number of possibilities for long distance through routes. The easiest approach, with the help of two wheels, is from the B871 Kinbrace to Syre road 6km west of Kinbrace. Just before Badanloch Lodge a sand and gravel estate road skirts the south-east end of Loch Badanloch, continuing west towards Loch Choire Lodge. Some 4km before the lodge, a stalkers path branches off south-east, below the eastern corries. This provides a good route of return from a north-south traverse. From the start of the path an easy climb gains the ridge, which then gives a pleasant walk despite occasional peat hags. Creag Mhor offers the best view.

To the south-west the tops of Cul Mor and Cul Beag in Coigach just peek out from behind Ben More Assynt, while further south the distinctive twin tops of Carn Chuinneag stand out. On a clear day, to the south-east, the huge statue of the Duke of Sutherland looking out from the top of Beinn a'Bhragaidh above Golspie is a grim reminder of the sad history of the desolate glens all around.

Ben Hope; 927m; (OS Sheet 9; NC477501); *hill of the bay*

The great craggy wedge of Ben Hope stands alone at the southern end of Loch Hope. Worthy of its distinction as the most northerly Munro, its steep western flanks drop almost to sea level in two huge rocky tiers to meet the narrow road through Strath More. The lower tier reaches a height of 300m, cloaked along the bottom with a fine birch wood and enclosing a long shallow south draining corrie and the Dubh-loch na Beinne. Above this the upper tier rises another 600m in a series of crags, rocky ribs and shallow gullies. A narrow rocky ridge rises up from the north-east, while a series of east facing corries hold a handful of attractive hill lochs. Gentler slopes drop away to the south and south-east.

The single-track road through Strath More from Altnaharra to Hope is one of the narrowest in the Highlands and should be driven with particular care. While baggers and record breakers may wish to hurry on and climb Ben Klibreck in the same day, Ben Hope is well worth savouring.

Approaching from the south, most parties will want to stop and take a closer look at the impressive remains of the road-side broch Dun Dornaigil. Also known as Dun Dornadilla, this is one of the best examples in Sutherland of this pre-Pictish style of fortification unique to the north of Scotland, built about 2000 years ago, and shaped like a miniature cooling tower. Above the distinctive triangular lintel of the doorway the walls still stand over 6m high.

Less than 1km north of the broch, the long south ridge of Ben Hope, Leiter Mhuiseil, can be reached by a steep climb up the well marked path from the house at Alltnacaillich. This path passes a fine water-fall where the Allt na Caillich (*burn of the old woman*) drops into Strath More but a shorter and more popular route starts 2km further north where the road crosses another unnamed burn.

A signpost marks the start of this route which climbs up to the south end of the shallow corrie between the rocky tiers, continuing up through a break in the upper crags to reach the broad grassy summit ridge. A line of cairns marks the top of the western cliffs and the route to the summit plateau with the trig point located near the north-east edge.

For a more challenging ascent, the north ridge of the mountain rises above the Dubh-loch na Beinne. This can be reached either by a rising traverse from the shallow corrie previously mentioned or alternatively from the Moine Path. This broad grassy track is a right of way to the Kyle of Tongue which leaves the road opposite the southern end of Loch Hope. Follow the track for a short distance beyond the deer fence enclosing the lower woodland, then climb steep heather up the lower tier to reach the Dubh-loch. Gain the north ridge by cutting up through the crags above. These gradually peter out as the foot of the ridge curves north-east towards Loch na Seilg.

The route is straightforward until a short dip below the final section where the true ridge rears up to give some 10m of very exposed scrambling up steep rock. Most parties will prefer the obvious easier alter-native, 30 metres to the left across the head of the corrie where a shallow gully avoids the difficult section to rejoin the ridge as it broadens towards the summit.

An alternative descent, giving closer views of the north-eastern corries and a fine view of Ben Loyal, follows the edge of these corries south-east to Sail Romascaig (718m) before descending east to An Gorm-loch, avoiding the steep bands of crags above the loch. The Moine Path can be rejoined either by keeping low and skirting Loch a' Ghobha-Dhuibh and Loch na Seilg, or by traversing Meallan Liath and Creag Riabhach Mhor with their many rocky knolls.

A number of climbs have been recorded on the north-west cliffs overlooking Loch Hope. None stand out, though the ridge to the south of the distinctive wide gully, origi-nally climbed by J.H.B.Bell in 1933, gave an excellent winter climb *Bell's Ridge* (240m III 1985). Ben Hope has the distinction of being the source of the only recorded diamond discovered in Scotland, in the 19th century.

The granulite and horneblende schists which make up the mountain are also reported to throw compasses haywire. This was one of many explanations put forward to explain the mysterious loss in 1942 of a Short Sunderland flying boat carrying the Duke of Kent which crashed in the nearby Berriedale hills.

Ben Loyal across Lochan Hakel

Ben Loyal; 764m; (OS Sheet 10; NC578488); *law hill*

With its instantly recognisable and much photographed north-west profile overlooking the Kyle of Tongue, Ben Loyal was acclaimed 'queen of Highland mountains' as far back as the New Statistical Account of 1840. From the shores of Lochan Hakel, with its legend of lost Jacobite gold, the combination of loch and moorland beneath towering crags and corries still gives one of the finest mountain views in Britain.

Isolated from its neighbours, Ben Loyal is the only igneous mountain in the north, composed of syenite, a form of granite with little or no quartz which has weathered into rugged tors similar to those found in the Cairngorms. This rock is also reported to be magnetic and to affect compasses.

Four castellated tops help make Ben Loyal a hill of great character, giving an interesting but straightforward traverse. From the village of Tongue the A838 north coast road continues west towards Durness along the relatively modern causeway crossing the Kyle of Tongue, while the old road still winds its way around the head of the Kyle, an area dotted with prehistoric remains.

Leaving this road some 2km south of Tongue, a private road leads to Ribigill farm but cars are allowed to drive to here. From here a track continues south past the abandoned cottage at Cunside and follows a burn up steep grass and heather onto Sgor Chaonasaid (708m) at the north end of the ridge. Continue south past the twin tors of Sgor a' Bhatain (700m) (*the boats*) which lie slightly to the west, to reach the highest top, An Caisteal (764m) (*the castle*), with its extensive views. There are steep drops on the south and east sides of the summit tor, which requires care in mist.

The next top to the south is sometimes known as Heddles Top (741m) from which a subsidiary ridge curves away north-west to Sgor a' Chleirich (642m) (*cleric's peak*), a sharply cut peak which drops away steeply on its west side. Descent into the dramatic un-named north-west corrie is easiest from the lowest point between these two tops. Steep broken grassy slopes lead from the

Jim Teesdale

Following the track from Braemore Lodge towards Maiden Pap and Morven

corrie to the woods of Coille na Cuile, rejoining the path near Cunside. Alternatively continue south along the main ridge over the featureless southern top of Carn an Tionail (714m) (*cairn of the gathering*), then descend west around the flanks of the distinctive conical Point 568m to Coille na Cuile.

The A836 from Altnaharra to Tongue skirts the eastern flanks of the mountain, following the western shores of Loch Loyal. Ascent from here is straightforward but can be very wet and boggy underfoot, and lacks the scenic quality of the north-west side.

Some impressive rock climbs have been recorded on the south-west face of Sgor a' Chleirich, overlooking Loch Fhionnaich. Steep vegetation, loose rock and a distinct lack of protection offer a considerable challenge. *Gog* (280m E3 1970s) featured as one of Himalayan veteran Martin Boysen's 'desert island climbs' though its description is a little imprecise and the grade speculative, and it is still awaiting a second ascent.

Beinn Dhorain; 628m; (OS Sheet 17; NC925156); *hill of the otter*

Highest of the small range of rounded hills west of Helmsdale, the east flank of Beinn Dhorain rises steeply from the narrow road through lonely Glen Loth. This leaves the A9 just south of Lothbeg, where an ominous sign warns motorists that snow is not cleared in winter. Lacking even passing places, the road is little better than a farm track, but there is ample parking by a gate due east of the summit of the hill.

Close by, the impressive standing stone Clach Mhic Mhios is one of many prehistoric remains in this once populous glen. One of the last wolves in Scotland is reputed to have been killed in nearby Glen Sletdale in about 1700. A century or so later the human population was cleared to make way for sheep and ironically the controversial statue of the Duke of Sutherland can be seen from the summit.

For a good view of the Caithness hills continue north a short distance to the trig point on Ben Uarie (623m). The cone of Morven and the three gentle bumps of Scaraben stretch across the skyline to the north-east with the twin humps of Ben Griam Mor and Ben Griam Beg to the north-west.

Immediately below, the Strath of Kildonan was the scene of a Highland gold rush in 1869 when the Kildonan and Suisgill Burns attracted gold panners. Few fortunes were made, but licences can still be obtained from Suisgill Estate for anyone who wants to try their luck.

Ben Griam Mor; 592m; (OS Sheet 17; NC806389); *big dark hill*

Ben Griam Beg; 580m; (OS Sheet 10; NC832412); *little dark hill*

Despite their modest height, the twin sandstone cones of Ben Griam Mor and Ben Griam Beg stand out above the flatness of the surrounding Flow Country. Ben Griam Beg is well seen from the A897 Kinbrace to Melvich road and has the distinction of having the remains of the highest hill fort in Scotland on its summit. Thick stone walls enclose an area some 150 metres by 60 metres with an entrance to the north. On the south side of the hill the remains of other walls and enclosures suggest a much larger defended and occupied area.

From the east Ben Griam Beg can be approached via the private track to Greamachary which leaves the A897 at a railway crossing. The nearby Balloch cottage marked on older maps no longer exists. An alternative route approaches from the west, following an anglers path to Loch Coire nam Mang which leaves the B871 Syre to Kinbrace road just south of the Garvault Hotel junction and crosses the west flank of Ben Griam Mor. From Forsinard it is apparently possible most years to enjoy some skiing on the surrounding slopes.

Morven; 706m; (OS Sheet 17; ND004285); *big hill*

Scaraben; 626m; (OS Sheet 17; ND066268); *divided hill*

The distinctive Old Red Sandstone cone of Morven forms the highest point in Caithness, contrasting with the three rounded tops of white Moine quartzite which make up nearby Scaraben. In between stand Maiden Pap (484m), the most realistic of Scotland's many breast-like hills and the unusual conglomerate tors on Smean (509m) which make up this unique group of attractive little hills.

The easiest approach is from Braemore, along a single track road sign-posted from the A9 Brora to Wick road just south-west of Dunbeath. The public road ends at the bridge over the Berriedale Water and a good track continues west past the estate cottages at Braeval. South of this track, Maiden Pap gives delightful scrambling to its summit, on rough sandstone conglomerate. The track finishes at the derelict farm at Corrichoich, beyond which a scattering of stones on a knoll beside the river mark the remains of a prehistoric wheelhouse.

The summit of Morven lies further west across flat moorland, reached by a straightforward climb almost anywhere up uniformly steep heather and sandstone boulders.

On a clear day the view north extends to Orkney and the Old Man of Hoy. After contemplating the flatness of the rest of Caithness it is an easy descent east to a broad saddle, then across the shoulder of Carn Mor (477m) to the distinctive tors of Smean. Continuing south-east to another broad saddle, a gentle climb leads onto Sron Gharbh (608m), the westernmost of the three tops of Scaraben.

A wide ridge stretches east over the main top (626m) to East Scaraben (591m). Descend to the north to reach a track on the south-west side of the river, which leads back to the bridge.

Further Reading

The books listed below have all been published or reprinted recently. Locally written and produced information on short walks, sites of historic and wildlife interest etc is available in local shops and tourist information centres.

The principal walking and climbing guides for the North-West Highlands are published by the Scottish Mountaineering Trust and Scottish Mountaineering Club. See the publications list at the rear endpaper of this book.

Beinn Eighe The Mountain Above the Wood J. Laughton Johnston & Dick Balharry 2001 Birlinn
Story of the first 50 years of Britain's first National Nature Reserve.

Burn on the Hill Elizabeth Allan 1995 Bidean Books
Diary extracts from Father Ronnie Burn, first 'Compleat Munroist'.

Cape Wrath Trail, The David Paterson 1996 Peak Publishing
Stirring words and photographs.

Collected Poems, A New Edition Norman MacCaig 1990 Chatto and Windus
Poet celebrates the delights of the North-west Highlands.

Collins Encyclopaedia of Scotland John & Julia Keay (Editors) 1994 Harper Collins
Essential reference for places and people.

Dam Builders, The James Miller 2002 Birlinn
Impressively illustrated account of the hydro developments.

Exploring the Far North West of Scotland Richard Gilbert 1994 Cordee
Walker's guide to hills, glens and coastline of Wester Ross and Sutherland.

First Munroist, The Peter Drummond & Ian Mitchell 1993 Ernest Press
Life, Munros and photographs of Reverend AE Robertson.

Glens of Ross-shire, The Peter D.Koch-Osborne 2000 Cicerone Press
Personal survey for mountain bikers and walkers – handwritten work of art.

Grahams, The Andrew Dempster 2003 Mainstream
A hill-walkers guide to Scotland's 2,000ft peaks. Paperback reprint.

Great British Ridge Walks Bill Birkett 1999 David & Charles
11 out of the 50 located in the North-west Highland area.

Hamish's Mountain Walk/Climbing the Corbetts Hamish Brown 1997 Baton Wicks
Omnibus reprint. Few authors know these hills better.

High Ground Wrecks and Relics David J.Smith 1997 Midland
Locations and details of aircraft hulks.

Highland Bridges Gillian Nelson 1990 Aberdeen University Press
Illustrations and points of special interest.

Highlands, The Joanna Close-Brooks 1995 HMSO
Introduction to the rich archaeological heritage of the area.

Highways & Byways In The West Highlands Seton Gordon 1995 Birlinn
Paperback reprint of indispensable 1935 classic.

History of Knoydart Denis Rixon 2000 Birlinn
In depth treatment of the area's past.

Hydro Boys, The Emma Wood 2002 Luath Press
History of hydro power and the people who made it happen.

Isolation Shepherd Iain R.Thomson 1983 Bidean Books
Four years of family living near remote Loch Monar, before hydro electrification.

Last Hundred, The Hamish Brown 1994 Mainstream
Lively reminiscences including Hamish's Top 20 Scottish hills.

Last Of The Free James Hunter 1999 Mainstream
A millennial history of the Highlands and Islands.

Lonely Hills & Wilderness Trails Richard Gilbert 2000 David & Charles
Includes accounts of many North-West Highland outings.

Long Horizon, The Iain R.Thomson 1999 Strathglass Books
Vivid picture of Highland life and values.

Magic Mountains Rennie McOwan 1996 Mainstream
Analysis of Scottish hill tales of ghosts, faeries, witches and other supernatural things.

Munro Phenomenon, The Andrew Dempster 1995 Mainstream
Exploration of many aspects of this cult pursuit.

Nature of Scotland, The Magnus Magnusson & Graham White (Editors) 1991 Canongate
Landscape, wildlife and people – large format.

Norman MacCaig Marjory McNeil 1996 Mercat Press
A study of the life and work of this great Scottish poet.

North To The Cape Denis Brook & Phil Hinchliffe 1999 Cicerone Press
A trek from Fort William to Cape Wrath – packed with information.

North West Highlands, The Tom Atkinson 1999 Luath Press
Interesting mix of history, folklore and visitor information.

On The Other Side Of Sorrow James Hunter 1995 Mainstream
Nature and people in the Scottish Highlands.

One Man's Mountains Tom Patey 1997 Canongate
Paperback reprint of posthumously published collection of essays and songs.

Relative Hills of Britain, The Alan Dawson 1992 Cicerone Press
Facts and figures about Marilyns (hills at least 500 feet higher than their surroundings.)

Ross & Cromarty Elizabeth Beaton 1992 Royal Incorporation of Architects in Scotland
An illustrated architectural guide.

Ross and Cromarty A Historical Guide David Alston 1999 Birlinn
Combination of illustrated guidebook and narrative.

Scotland Land of Mountains Colin Baxter & Des Thompson 1995 Colin Baxter
Ecologist and photographer explore fragile montane habitat.

Scotland's Mountains Before The Mountaineers Ian Mitchell 1998 Luath Press
Explorations and ascents before mountaineering became a popular sport.

Scottish Hill Tracks DJ Bennet & C Stone (Editors) 2004 Scottish Rights of Way Society
Guide to hill paths, old roads and rights of way.

Scottish Islands, The Hamish Haswell-Smith 1996 Canongate
Comprehensive guide to every Scottish island, including Handa.

Scottish Lochs, The Tom Weir 1985 Constable
A mine of information.

Touring Scotland-Wester Ross Ross Finlay 1971 Foulis
Lots of local history.

Walking the Watershed Dave Hewitt 1994 TACit Press
Interesting variation on the theme of a long challenging Scottish hillwalk.

Waterfalls of Scotland, The Louis Stott 1987 Aberdeen University Press
More than 750 picturesque Scottish locations, that are even better in the rain.

Who Owns Scotland Andy Wightman 1996 Canongate
Comprehensive listings and analysis of current pattern of land ownership.

Who Owns Scotland Now? Auslan Cramb 1996 Mainstream
Use and abuse of private land; chapters on Assynt, Letterewe, Lochiel and Sutherland Estates.

Wild Scotland James McCarthy 1998 Luath Press
Site by site guide.

Glossary of Common Gaelic Words

A

abar, aber	*river mouth, confluence*
abhainn, amhainn	*stream, river*
achadh	*field plain, meadow, homestead*
aird, ard	*high point, promontory*
àiridh, àirigh	*shieling*
allt, ault	*burn, stream*
an	*the*
aonach	*ridge, height, solitary*
ath	*ford*

B

bà	*cattle*
bac	*bank, bend*
bàn, bhàn	*white*
baile, bhaile	*town, township*
bàrr	*top, summit, crop*
bealach, bhealach	*pass, col*
beag, bheag	*small*
beith, beithe	*birch tree*
beinn, bheinn	*hill, mountain, peak*
breac, bhreac	*speckled*
bidean, bidein	*peak*
binnean, binnein	*peak*
bò	*cow*
bodach	*old man*
bothan	*hut, bothy*
braigh, bhraigh	*brae, high place*
buachaille	*herdsman*
buidhe, bhuidhe	*yellow*
buiridh, bhuiridh	*bellowing (of stags)*

C

cailleach	*old woman*
caisteal	*castle*
camas, camus	*bay, channel, creek*
caol, caolas	*narrows, strait*
caor (pl. caorann)	*rowan*
caora (pl. caorach)	*sheep*
capull	*horse (a mare)*
càrn	*cairn, hill, pile of stones*
ceann	*head*
cioch (gen. ciche)	*breast, pap*
ciste	*chest, coffin*
clach	*stone, stony*
clachan	*village, stepping stones*
cleit	*cliff crag, reef*
cnap, cnoc	*hillock, lump*
coille	*wood, forest*
coinneach	*mossy place*
coire	*corrie, high mountain valley*
corran	*low pointed promontory, sickle*
creachan	*clam*
creachann	*bare summit*
creag	*cliff, crag*
crois	*cross*
croit	*croft*
cruach	*hill, heap, stack*
cùl	*back*

D

da	*two*
dail	*dale, field, plain*
damh	*stag*
darach	*oak, oakwood*
dearg	*red*
deas	*south*
diollaid	*saddle*
donn	*brown*
dorus	*door, gate, strait*
drochaid	*bridge*
drum, druim	*ridge*
dubh, duibh	*black*
dùn	*fort*

E

each	*horse*
eag (eagach)	*notch (notched place)*
ear	*east*
eas	*waterfall*
eighe	*file, notched*
eilean	*island*
eun (gen. eoin)	*bird*

F

fada (gen. fhada)	*long*
faochag	*whelk*
fearn	*alder tree*
fiadh	*deer*
fionn	*white*
fraoch	*heather*
frìth (gen. frithe)	*deer forest*
fuar	*cold*
fuaran	*well*

G

gabhar	*goat*
gaoth	*wind*
garbh	*rough*

geal	*white*
gèarr	*short, a leap, hare*
gille	*young man, boy*
glac, glaic	*hollow, trough, bell*
glas, ghlas	*green, grey*
gleann	*glen*
gorm	*blue, also green*

I

iar	*west*
iasgair	*fisherman*
inbhir, inver	*rivermouth, confluence*
inch, innis	*island, meadow*
iolaire	*eagle*

K

ken, kin (from ceann)	*head*
knock (from cnoc)	*hillock*
kyle (from caol)	*narrows, strait*

L

ladhar	*hoof, fork*
lag, lagan	*hollow*
lairig	*pass*
laogh	*calf*
làrach	*dwelling place*
leac	*slab, stone, grave, gravestone*
leathad	*slope*
leitir	*slope*
liath	*grey, blue*
lochan	*small loch*

M

maighdeann (mhaighdean)	*maiden*
meirg	*rust-coloured*
mam	*rounded hill*
maol	*headland, bare hill, bald*
meadhon	*middle*
meall	*hill*
moin	*bog, moss*
monadh	*moor, countryside*
mòr, mhòr	*big*
muc (gen. muic)	*pig*
muileann (gen. mhuilinn)	*mill*
mullach	*top, summit*

N

na, nan	*of, of the*

O

odhar	*dun-coloured, smooth*

P

poit	*pot*

R

ràth	*fort*
righ	*king*
ròn	*seal*
ruadh	*red*
rubha, rudha	*point, promontory*
ruighe	*shieling*

S

sàil	*heel, brine, seawater*
sgurr	*rocky peak*
seann	*old*
sgeir	*reef, rock*
sgiath	*wing*
sgor, sgorr, sgurr	*rocky peak*
sìth (sìthean)	*fairy (fairy hill), also peace*
slochd	*deep hollow, pit*
sneachd	*snow*
spidean	*peak*
srath	*strath, wide level glen*
sròn	*nose*
stac	*steep rock, sea-stack*
stob	*peak*
stuc	*peak, steep rock*
suidhe	*seat*

T

teallach	*forge, hearth*
tigh	*house*
tioram	*island; dry at low tide*
tìr	*land*
tobar	*well*
toll, tholl	*hole*
tom	*hill*
tòrr	*small hill*
tuath	*north*

U

uaine	*green*
uamh	*cave*
uig	*bay*
uisge	*water*

A

B

C

M

Durness
North-West
Sutherland
Laxford
Bridge
Altnaharra
Unapool
Lochinver
Assynt
Ledmore
Coigach
Ullapool
Loch
Broom
Beinn Dearg
Poolewe
Gairloch
Loch
Maree
The Fannaichs
Easter Ross
Garve
Kinlochewe
Torridon
Achnasheen
Strathconon
Torridon